DATE DUE

FE 17 '95	AG 9 '01	
MR 31 '95	AP 8 '05	
JE 4 '95	JE 9 '05	
	AF 20 '05	
NO 27 '95		
DE 22 '95	JE 6 '05	
MR 22 '96	MY 11 '09	
MR 1 '97	JE - 6 '09	
MY 29 '97		
JE 9 '97		
AG 4 '97		
MR 3 '98		
MY 11 '99		
MY 27 '99		
00.62 HR		
JE 5 '00		
AP 16 '01		

FIFTH EDITION

MICROECONOMICS

PRIVATE AND PUBLIC CHOICE

FIFTH EDITION

MICROECONOMICS

PRIVATE AND PUBLIC CHOICE

JAMES D. GWARTNEY

Florida State University

RICHARD L. STROUP

Montana State University

with the assistance of
A. H. STUDENMUND

Occidental College

HARCOURT BRACE JOVANOVICH, PUBLISHERS
and its subsidiary, Academic Press

San Diego   New York   Chicago   Austin   Washington, D.C.
London   Sydney   Tokyo   Toronto

Requests for permission to make copies of any part of the work should be mailed to: Copyrights and Permissions Department, Harcourt Brace Jovanovich, Publishers, Orlando, Florida 32887.

ISBN: 0-15-518889-5
Printed in the United States of America

Photo credits: p. 16, Bettmann Archive; p. 63, Historical Picture Service, Chicago.

PREFACE

This is an exciting time to teach and study economics. Knowledge of economics enhances our understanding of the changing world in which we live. Economic factors underlie seemingly disconnected events—from the outcome of presidential elections in the United States to political changes in the Soviet Union, China, and Eastern Europe. Why, in some countries, are many people rich, while in other countries the majority lives on the edge of starvation? What forces lead to economic prosperity? What can governments do to promote prosperity? Is there a danger that we will soon run out of key economic resources? Throughout this textbook, we will use the tools of economics to address these and other crucial questions.

FIFTH EDITION

As in previous editions, our approach emphasizes the importance of the economic way of thinking. We want to stimulate students, challenge their reasoning ability, and teach them to *think* like economists. To meet these objectives, we expanded the use of examples; drew from real-world data more freely as a means of enriching the theory; and doubled the number of critical analysis questions at the end of each chapter. In addition, we integrated a "Great Debates" series—short readings that provide contrasting views on major issues of our day—into the accompanying *Coursebook*. We think these features will make the study of economics more relevant for both student and teacher.

CHANGES IN THE CORE MICROECONOMICS

As in previous editions, we use applications and case studies to buttress the core microeconomic theory. The structure of the core microeconomics is quite similar to that of the previous edition. However, we have included several new features that broaden coverage and reflect recent developments. The following brief list indicates the major areas in which our coverage of microeconomic topics is either expanded or substantially revised in this edition.

- Principal-agent theory enriches our analysis of business organization and the theory of the firm (Chapter 7) as well as the operation of the political process (Chapter 19).
- The role of entrepreneurship is stressed throughout our analysis of supply and demand, theory of the firm, and market allocation.

- The impact of corporate takeovers on organizational efficiency and market allocation is analyzed (Chapter 7).
- The impact of fringe and mandated benefits on labor market outcomes is explored (Chapter 13).
- Our coverage of the "Great Productivity Slowdown" and its importance is expanded (Chapter 13).
- Overlapping material in the public choice chapters (Chapters 4 and 19) is consolidated and improved.
- Recent data in international income comparisons based on the purchasing power parity method are incorporated into our analysis of both economic development and comparative systems (Chapters 22 and 23).
- Recent economic developments in both the Soviet Union and China are integrated into our coverage of comparative economic systems (Chapter 23).

DISTINGUISHING FEATURES OF OUR APPROACH

As we stated previously, our primary goal is to challenge students to think like economists. The following points are of specific interest in this regard:

1. *Economic Principles Are Presented in a Highly Readable Fashion.* Difficult language and terminology can often hinder successful learning, particularly of economic concepts. Without sacrificing accuracy, we have sought to employ simple language. Simplicity, however, has not been substituted for depth. Rather, our aim is to highlight the power and accessibility of economic concepts. Where complex ideas are essential to our analysis, they are developed fully. We believe that the economics required for the 1990s can be comprehensible to the student as well as challenging and applicable to the real world.

2. *Economic Reasoning and Its Applications Are Emphasized.* Although models, theories, and exercises are important, they are only tools with which to develop the economic way of thinking. Abstractions and mechanics are not stressed in such a way as to obscure major concepts. We consistently emphasize the basics and their real-world applications.

3. *Economic Tools Are Applied to Both the Market and the Political Process.* Most textbooks tell students how an *ideal* market economy would operate, how real-world markets differ from the hypothetical ideal, and how ideal public policy can correct the shortcomings of the market. In addition to discussing these three basic issues, we analyze what real-world public policy is *likely to do*. Building on recent developments in the area of public choice, we apply the tools of economics to the political process as well as to market allocation. We think this approach emphasizes both the power and relevance of economics.

4. *The Role of the Individual Decision-Maker Is Stressed.* Students often feel that economists exclude human beings from the economic process. In most economics textbooks, business decision-makers are depicted as having perfect knowledge of demand and cost. Like computers, they always arrive at the maximum-profit solution. Likewise, government planners, knowing precisely the deficiency in aggregate demand and the size of the multiplier, simply increase government spending by the right amount to restore full employment.

The employer, knowing the marginal productivity of each resource, utilizes each in exactly the proper proportion. Decision-making is treated as a mechanical exercise, removed from the real world. Throughout this book, we stress the importance of information, uncertainty, trial-and-error decision-making, expectations, and other factors that influence real-world choices. Economics is more than a set of guidelines. If students are to be convinced of its applicability, we must delineate the dynamic factors that influence and motivate human beings.

ORGANIZATIONAL FEATURES

We have employed several organizational features designed to make the presentation more understandable and interesting.

1. *Myths of Economics*   In a series of boxed articles, commonly held fallacies of economic reasoning are dispelled. Each myth is followed by a concise explanation of why it is incorrect and is presented within a chapter containing closely related material.
2. *Applications in Economics*   These boxed features apply economic theory to real-world issues and controversies. They add breadth on topics of special interest and illustrate the relevance of basic principles to the world in which we live.
3. *Measures of Economic Activity*   Measurement is an important element of economics. These features explain how important economic indicators such as the Consumer Price Index, unemployment rate, and index of leading indicators are assembled.
4. *Outstanding Economists*   These brief profiles stress the contributions of several economists, both current and historical, whose work has been important in the development of the field. This series is designed both to enhance the student's appreciation of economic history and to provide depth on the contributions of several present-day economists.
5. *Chapter Focus Questions and Closing Summaries*   Each chapter begins with several questions that summarize the focus of the chapter. A summary, which provides the student with a concise statement of the material (chapter learning objectives), appears at the end of each chapter. Reviewing the focus questions and chapter summaries will help the student better understand the material and integrate it into the broader economic picture.
6. *Key Terms*   The terminology of economics is often confusing to introductory students. Key terms are introduced in the text in color type; simultaneously, each term is defined in the margin opposite the first reference to the term. A glossary containing the key terms also appears at the end of the book.
7. *Critical Analysis Questions.*   Each chapter concludes with a set of discussion questions designed to test the student's ability to analyze an economic problem and to apply economic theory to real-world events. Appendix B at the end of the text contains suggested answers for approximately half of the critical analysis questions. We think these answers, illustrating the power of economics, will interest students and will help them develop the economic way of thinking.

SUPPLEMENTARY MATERIALS

A complete set of support materials accompanies this textbook and includes:

Coursebook. We call the student handbook accompanying the textbook a *Coursebook,* since it is more than a study guide. Of course, it contains numerous multiple choice, true-false, and discussion questions permitting students to self-test their knowledge of each chapter. Answers and short explanations for most questions are provided in the back of the *Coursebook.* Each chapter also contains problem and project exercises designed to improve the student's knowledge of the mechanics. A set of short readings chosen to supplement the classroom teaching of important topics is also included in the *Coursebook.* Several of the readings are arranged in a debate format and cover areas of controversy in economics. Discussion questions follow each article, challenging students to demonstrate their understanding of the material and their ability to distinguish a sound argument from economic nonsense. Like the textbook, the *Coursebook* is designed to help students develop the economic way of thinking.

Testbanks. Two testbanks accompany the Fifth Edition. Testbank I contains over 2,900 multiple-choice questions, most of which have been extensively tested in the classroom. Within each chapter, the questions correspond to the major subheadings of the text. Testbank II, prepared by J. J. Bethune of Bellarmine College, provides approximately 1,800 new multiple-choice questions. This expanded stock of questions should be of particular interest to our past users. Both testbanks are available on computer diskette.

Instructor's Manual. The *Instructor's Manual* is divided into two parts. The first part, which is also available on computer diskette, is a detailed outline of each chapter in lecture-note form. It is designed to help instructors organize and structure their current lecture notes according to the format of the Fifth Edition of *Economics: Private and Public Choice.* Instructors can easily prepare a detailed, personalized set of notes by revising the computerized form of the notes. The second part of the *Instructor's Manual* contains teaching tips, sources of supplementary materials, and other helpful information. Part 3 provides instructors with several games designed to illustrate and enliven important economic concepts. Suggested answers to most of the critical analysis questions that were not answered in Appendix B of the text are also provided in the *Instructor's Manual.*

Color Transparencies. Color transparencies of the major exhibits of the Fifth Edition have been especially prepared for overhead projectors. They are available to adopters upon request.

Computer Simulation Package. *ECO Talk,* a computer simulation package, is available free to adopters (and to their students for a nominal fee). *ECO Talk* consists of ten microeconomic and ten macroeconomic models designed to help users master important concepts through simulations, practice with graphics, and quizzes on the models. *ECO Talk* was developed by Michael Claudon of Middlebury College and Kipley Olson of Apple Computer. While it is not tied to a specific textbook, it contains the primary models presented in this textbook.

ACKNOWLEDGMENTS

A project of this type is a team effort. Several people contributed substantially to the development of this edition. Once again, Woody Studenmund provided valuable direction and insightful comments. He also helped us get some bugs out of the macroeconomic material. Several of his associates at Occidental College, including Robby Moore, Jim Whitney, and Jim Halstead also contributed helpful suggestions.

Ron Brandolini (Valencia College) provided pertinent suggestions for new material as well as thoughtful comments regarding this revision. In addition, he reviewed every chapter of the new edition.

As always, we have benefitted from the reviews and comments of many people. We have revised material in light of suggestions made by reviewers, users, friends, and even a few competitors. The text continues to be strengthened as the result of their contributions and we appreciate them. In particular, we would like to thank: Paul Azrak (Queensborough Community College); Norlin Masih (St. Cloud State University); and Richard Torz (SUNY-Queens College) for their contributions to this edition. We would also like to thank David Sollars, Robert Lawson, Michael Patrono, and Scott Wood for research assistance in the preparation of this edition.

We would like to express our appreciation to the following for their helpful suggestions on the Fifth Edition: Lucinda Coulter-Burbach, Seminole Community College; Sue Hayes, Sonoma State; Fred Goddard, University of Florida; Larry Lichtenstein, Canisius College; Jeffrey Herbener, Washington and Jefferson College; Lawrence Martin, Michigan State University; J. P. Egan, University of Wisconsin, Eau Claire; Michael White, St. Cloud State University; Dona A. Derr, Rutgers College; Don Millman, Itasca Community College; Nathan Eric Hampton, St. Cloud State University; D. E. Morris, University of New Hampshire; James T. Bennett, George Mason University; Jeffrey Young, St. Lawrence University; Robert Puth, University of New Hampshire; Sam Osemene, Prairie View A & M University; Harold Katz, U.S. Merchant Marine Academy; James Wible, University of New Hampshire; Frank Scott, University of Kentucky; John Neal, Lake Sumter Community College; Wilson Mixon, Berry College; James Long, Auburn University; Denise Rogers, Arizona Western College; Patrick McMurry, Missouri Western State College; William Jahn, American Institute of Business; David Emery, St. Olaf College; Joseph M. Lammert, Raymond Walters College; Abdalla Gergis, Framingham State College; Darrell Irvin, Spokane Community College; Ken Somppi, Auburn University; Seren Burg, Eastern Michigan University; James A. Dunlevy, Miami University; Michael Loewy, George Washington University; John C. McCarthy, Armstrong State College; Eric N. Baklanoff, University of Alabama; William Steiden, Bellarmine College; Julia Lee, University of Louisville; Marshall Edwards, Armstrong State College; John Leevries, Brainerd Community College; John Bethune, Bellarmine College; Pati Crabb, Bellarmine College; Terry R. Ridgway, University of Nevada, Las Vegas; Dale Bails, Memphis State; Luther D. Lawson, University of North Carolina–Wilmington; Jack Morgan, University of North Carolina–Wilmington; William Sher, Duquesne University; Donald L. Alexander, Pennsylvania State University; Kevin C. Sontheimer, University of Pittsburgh; Kurt Rethwisch, Duquesne University; Marsha Goldfarb, University of Maryland–Baltimore County; Arthur Janssa, Emporia

State University; Chas C. Milliken, Siena Heights College; Thomas Wyrick, Southwest Missouri State University; Jim Scheib, Red Rocks Community College; Alan Sleeman, Western Washington University; Robert E. Williams, The School of the Ozarks; Anthony Yezer, George Washington University; L. Aubrey Drewery, Birmingham Southern College; Ernest M. Buchholz, Santa Monica College; Shirley Svorny, California State University–Northridge; Henry Demmert, Santa Clara University; C. Fred DeKay, Seattle University; David O. Whitten, Auburn University–Main Campus; Randall G. Holcombe, Florida State University; Ralph Bristol, University of New Hampshire–Durham.

We are also indebted to the excellent team of professionals at Harcourt Brace Jovanovich. John Carey and Rick Hammonds (acquisitions editors), Margie Rogers (manuscript editor), and Paula Bryant (production editor) provided us with guidance, editorial assistance, and encouragement. We would also like to thank Susan Holtz (art editor), Lesley Lenox (production manager) and Cathy Reynolds (designer) for their contributions.

Finally, we would like to acknowledge the assistance of Amy Gwartney and Jane Stroup, both of whom contributed in numerous ways to the success of this project. Without their assistance and encouragement, we would have been unable to meet the demands and deadlines of this project. We dedicate this edition to them.

A NOTE TO STUDENTS

This text contains several features that we think will help you maximize (a good economics term) the returns derived from your study effort. Our past experience indicates that awareness of the following points will help you to use the book more effectively.

- Each chapter begins with a series of focus questions which communicate the central issues of the chapter. Before you read the chapter, briefly think about the focus questions, why they are important, and how they relate to the material of prior chapters.
- The textbook is organized in the form of an outline. The headings within the text are the major points of the outline. Minor headings (contained in the margins) are subpoints under the major headings. In addition, important subpoints within sections are often set off and numbered. Sometimes thumbnail sketches are used to help the reader better organize important points. Careful use of the headings and thumbnail sketches will help you better visualize the organization of the material.
- A summary appears at the end of each chapter. Use the summary as a checklist to determine whether or not you understand the major points of the chapter.
- Review of the exhibits will also provide you with a summary of each chapter. The accompanying legend briefly describes the content and analysis of each exhibit. After studying the chapter, briefly review the exhibits to ensure that you have mastered the central points.
- The key terms introduced in each chapter are defined in the margins. As you study the chapter, go over the marginal definition of each key term as it is introduced. Later, you may also find it useful to review the marginal definitions. If you have forgotten the meaning of a term introduced earlier, consult the glossary at the end of the book.
- The boxed features provide additional depth on various topics without disrupting the flow of the text. In general, the topics of the boxed features have been chosen because of their relevance as an application of the theory or because of past student interest in the topic. Reading the boxed features will supplement the text and enhance your understanding of important economic concepts.
- The Critical Analysis Questions at the end of each chapter are intended to test your understanding of the economic way of thinking. They provide you with another opportunity to review each chapter. Answers to approximately 40 percent of these questions are provided in Appendix B.

■ If you are having trouble, be sure to obtain a *Coursebook* and work the questions and problems for each chapter. The *Coursebook* also contains the answers to the multiple-choice questions and a brief explanation of why an answer is correct (and other choices incorrect). In most cases, if you master the concepts of the test items in the *Coursebook,* you will do well on the quizzes and examinations of your instructor.

CONTENTS

PART ONE | **THE ECONOMIC WAY OF THINKING—AN INTRODUCTION** | **1**

1 The Economic Approach   3

2 Some Tools of the Economist   29

| PART TWO | MICROECONOMICS | 129 |

MEASURES OF ECONOMIC ACTIVITY

MYTHS OF ECONOMICS

APPLICATIONS IN ECONOMICS

FIFTH EDITION

MICROECONOMICS

PRIVATE AND PUBLIC CHOICE

ONE

THE ECONOMIC WAY OF THINKING— AN INTRODUCTION

1

THE ECONOMIC APPROACH

The ideas of economists and political philosophers, both when they are right and when they are wrong, are more powerful than is commonly understood. Indeed, the world is ruled by little else. Practical men, who believe themselves to be quite exempt from any intellectual influences, are usually slaves of some defunct economist.[1]

John Maynard Keynes

CHAPTER FOCUS

■ Why is scarcity a key economic concept, even in an affluent economy?

■ How does scarcity differ from poverty?

■ What are the basics underlying the economic way of thinking? What is different about the way economists look at choices and human decision-making?

■ What is the difference between positive and normative economics?

As the strong influence of Professor Keynes's own work has since proved, ideas have consequences. They influence events in the real world. In turn, ideas are influenced by real-world experience. Economic ideas are no exception. The events and patterns of the last 20 years—inflation rates that soared and declined, high unemployment, recession and recovery—have made a dramatic impact on the economics profession. They have also generated additional interest in the subject matter of economics. People are now trying to more fully understand these continually unfolding economic events.

This book will help you understand the recent upheavals in economic thinking and the policies suggested by various theories. Your ability to analyze new policy directions will be increased. This is not to imply that economics provides the answers to the problems of the world. Economics is not an answer, but rather a way of thinking. In fact, economics is more likely to provide an appreciation of the limitations of ''grand design'' proposals than it is to offer utopian solutions. Nevertheless, we believe that ''economic thinking'' is a powerful tool capable of illuminating a broad range of real-world events. Our goals are to communicate the basics of economics and to illustrate their power.

WHAT IS ECONOMICS ABOUT?

Economics is about people and the choices they make. The unit of analysis in economics is the individual. Of course, individuals group together to form collective organizations such as corporations, labor unions, and governments. Individual choices, however, still underlie and direct these organizations. Thus, even when we study collective organizations, we will focus on the ways in which their operation is affected by the choices of individuals.

SCARCITY AND CHOICE

Scarcity: Fundamental concept of economics which indicates that less of a good is freely available than consumers would like.

Economic Good: A good that is scarce. The desire for economic goods exceeds the amount that is freely available from Nature.

Economic theory evolves from fundamental postulates about how individual human beings behave, struggle with the problem of scarcity, and respond to change. The reality of life on our planet is that productive resources—resources used to produce goods—are limited. Therefore, goods and services are also limited. In contrast, the desires of human beings are virtually unlimited. These facts confront us with the two basic ingredients of an economic topic—scarcity and choice. **Scarcity** is the term used by economists to indicate that people's desire for a ''thing'' exceeds the amount of it that is freely available from Nature. Nature has always dealt grudgingly with us; the Garden of Eden has continually eluded our grasp.

A good that is scarce is an **economic good**. The first column of Exhibit 1 contains a partial listing of scarce or economic goods. The list includes food, clothing, and many of the items that all of us commonly recognize as material goods. It also includes some items, however, that may surprise you. Is leisure a good? Would you like to have more leisure time than is currently available to you? Most of us would. Therefore, leisure time is a scarce good. What about clean air? A few years ago many economics texts classified clean air as a free

---

[1]John Maynard Keynes (1883–1946) was an English economist whose writings during the 1920s and 1930s exerted an enormous impact on both economic theory and policy. Keynes established the terminology and the economic framework that are still widely used today when economists study problems of unemployment and inflation.

EXHIBIT 1 ■ A General Listing of Desired Economic Goods and Limited Resources	
Economic Goods	Limited Resources
Food (bread, milk, meat, eggs, vegetables, coffee, etc.)	Land (various degrees of fertility)
Clothing (shirts, pants, blouses, shoes, socks, coats, sweaters, etc.)	Natural resources (rivers, trees, minerals, oceans, etc.)
Household goods (tables, chairs, rugs, beds, dressers, television sets, etc.)	Machines and other man-made physical resources
Space exploration	Nonhuman animal resources
Education	Technology (physical and scientific "recipes" of history)
National defense	Human resources (the knowledge, skill, and talent of individual human beings)
Recreation	
Leisure time	
Entertainment	
Clean air	
Pleasant environment (trees, lakes, rivers, open spaces, etc.)	
Pleasant working conditions	
More productive resources	

Our history is a record of our struggle to transform available, but limited, resources into things that we would like to have—economic goods.

good, made available by Nature in such abundant supply that everyone could have all of it they wanted. This is no longer the case. Our utilization of air to dispose of wastes has created a scarcity of clean air. Many of the residents of Los Angeles, New York, and other large cities would like to have more clean air.

Few of us usually think of environmental conditions as economic goods. However, if you would like to have more open spaces, green areas, or dogwood trees, you will recognize that these things are scarce. They, too, are economic goods.

Choice: The act of selecting among alternatives.

Since scarcity of productive resources, time, and income limit the alternatives available to us, we must make choices. **Choice** is the act of selecting among restricted alternatives. A major focus of economics concerns how people choose when the alternatives open to them are restricted. The choices of the family shopper are restricted by the household budget, market prices, and the shopper's own imagination about ways to satisfy wants. The choices of business decision-makers are restricted by competition from other firms, the cost of productive resources, technology, and their own entrepreneurial ability to open new markets or use new techniques to satisfy customers' wants. The spending choices of political decision-makers are restricted by the taxable income of the citizenry and voter opposition to taxes. The selection of one alternative generally necessitates doing without others. If you choose to spend $10 going to a football game, you will have $10 less to spend on other things. Similarly, if you choose to spend an evening watching a movie, you must forgo spending the evening playing Ping-Pong (or participating in some other activity). You cannot have your cake and eat it, too.

Each day, we all make hundreds of economic choices, even though we are not normally aware of doing so. Choosing when to get up in the morning, what to eat for breakfast, how to travel to work, what television program to watch—all of these are economic decisions. They are economic decisions because they involve the utilization of scarce resources (for example, time and income). We all are constantly involved in making choices that relate to economics.

OUR CONSTANT STRUGGLE WITH SCARCITY

Resource: An input used to produce economic goods. Land, labor, skills, natural resources, and capital are examples.

Scarcity restricts us. How can we overcome it? **Resources,** including our own skills, can be used to produce economic goods. Human effort and ingenuity can be combined with machines, land, natural resources, and other productive factors (see the second column of Exhibit 1) to increase the availability of economic goods. These are "tools" in our struggle with scarcity. It is important to note that most economic goods are not like manna from heaven. Human energy is nearly always an ingredient in the production of economic goods.

The lessons of history confirm that our desire for economic goods far outstrips our resources to produce them. Are we destined to lead hopeless lives of misery and drudgery because we are involved in a losing battle with scarcity? Some might answer "Yes," pointing out that a substantial proportion of the world's population go to bed hungry each night. The annual income of a typical person in countries such as Pakistan and India is less than $400. Moreover, the population in these and other areas is increasing almost as rapidly as their output of material goods.

At the same time, the grip of scarcity has been loosened in most of North America, Western Europe, Japan, and the Soviet Union. Most Americans, Japanese, and Europeans have an adequate caloric intake and sufficient housing and clothing. Many own luxuries such as dishwashers, video cassette recorders, microwave ovens, and swimming pools. Over the last century, the average number of hours worked per week has fallen from 60 to about 40 in most Western nations. From a material viewpoint, life is certainly more pleasant for these people than it was for their ancestors 250 years ago. Despite this progress, though, scarcity is still a fact of life, even in relatively affluent countries. Most of us have substantially fewer goods and resources and less time than we would like to have.

It is important to note that scarcity and poverty are not the same thing. Poverty implies some basic level of need, either in absolute or relative terms. Absence of poverty means that the basic level has been attained. In contrast, the absence of scarcity means that we have not merely attained some basic level, but have acquired as much of all goods as we desire. Poverty is at least partially subjective, but there is an objective test for scarcity. If people are willing to pay—give up something—for a good, that good is scarce. Even though the battle against poverty may ultimately be won, the outcome of the battle against scarcity is already painfully obvious. Our productive capabilities and material desires are such that goods and services will always be scarce.

THE ECONOMIC WAY OF THINKING

It [economics] is a method rather than a doctrine, an apparatus of the mind, a technique of thinking which helps its possessor to draw correct conclusions. [J. M. Keynes]

Reflecting on a television appearance with economist Paul Samuelson and other social scientists (noneconomists), Milton Friedman stated that he was amazed to find that economists, although differing in their ideological viewpoints, usually find themselves to be allies in discussions with other social scientists.[2] One does not have to spend much time around economists to recognize that there is an "economic way of thinking." Admittedly, economists, like others, differ widely in their ideological views. A news commentator once remarked that "any half-dozen economists will normally come up with about six different policy prescriptions." Yet, in spite of their philosophical differences, there is a common ground to the approach of economists.

Economic Theory: A set of definitions, postulates, and principles assembled in a manner that makes clear the "cause-and-effect" relationships of economic data.

That common ground is **economic theory,** developed from basic postulates of human behavior. Theory has a reputation for being abstract and difficult, but this need not be the case. Economic theory, like a road map or a guidebook, establishes reference points indicating what to look for, and how economic issues are interrelated. It helps us understand the relationships among complex and often seemingly unrelated events in the real world. A better understanding of cause-and-effect relationships will enhance our ability to accurately predict the likely consequences of alternative policy choices. Economics has sometimes been called the "science of common sense." This is as it should be. After all, common sense is nothing more than a set of beliefs based on sound theories that have been tested over a long period of time and found to be accurate.

This is not to say, however, that the person who has not studied economics will come to the same conclusions on an economic question as the serious student would. Each component of the theory may be common sense, but putting the components together can lead us to conclusions very different from those of the person thinking about the same problem without the apparatus of economics.

EIGHT GUIDEPOSTS TO ECONOMIC THINKING

The economic way of thinking involves the incorporation of certain guidelines— some would say the building blocks of basic economic theory—into one's thought process. Once these guidelines are incorporated, we believe that economics can be a relatively easy subject to master.

Students who have difficulty with economics almost always do so because they fail to develop the economic way of thinking. Their thought processes are not consistently directed by a few simple economic concepts or guideposts. Students who do well in economics learn to use these basic concepts and allow their thought processes to reflect them. We will outline and discuss eight principles that characterize economic thinking and that are essential to the understanding of the economic approach.

1. Scarce Goods Have a Cost—There Are No Free Lunches. The benefits of scarce goods can be obtained only if someone is willing to exert personal effort or give up something. The use of scarce goods to meet one "need" means less resources (time, energy, tools, and so on) to meet "needs" in other areas. When it comes to the use of scarce resources to produce valued products, there is not such a thing as a free lunch.

The cost of many scarce goods is obvious. The purchaser of a new car must give up $11,000 of purchasing power over other goods to own the car. Similarly, the cost to the purchaser of a delightful meal, new clothes, or a Las Vegas week-

---

[2]The philosophical views of Professor Friedman and Professor Samuelson differ considerably. They are often on opposite sides of economic policy issues.

end is obvious. But, what about a good such as public elementary education? The ''scarce goods have a cost'' concept is just as true for goods provided through government as for goods provided by private producers. Even though the education is usually free to students, it is not free to the community. Buildings, books, and teachers' salaries must be paid for from tax revenues. The taxpayer incurs the cost. If these scarce resources were not used to produce elementary education, they could be used to produce more recreation, entertainment, housing, and other goods. Providing for public education means that some of these other scarce goods must be forgone.

Similarly, provision of free medical service, recreation areas, tennis courts, and parking lots involves the use of scarce resources. Again, something must be given up if we are to produce these goods. Taxpayers usually bear the cost of ''free'' medical services and tennis courts. Consumers often bear the cost of ''free'' parking lots in the form of higher prices in areas where this service is provided.

By now the central point should be obvious. Economic thinking recognizes that the provision of a scarce good, any scarce good, involves a cost. We must give up other things if we are to have more of a scarce good. Economic goods are not free.

2. Decision-Makers Choose Purposefully. Therefore, They Will Economize. Since resources are scarce, it is all the more important that decisions be made in a purposeful manner. Decision-makers do not deliberately make choices in a manner that wastes valuable resources. Recognizing the restrictions imposed by their limited resources (income, time, talent, and so on), they seek to choose wisely; they try to select the options that best advance their own personal objectives. In turn, the objectives or preferences of individuals are revealed by the choices they make. **Economizing behavior** results directly from purposeful decision-making. Economizing individuals will seek to accomplish an objective at the least possible cost. When choosing among things that yield equal benefit, an economizer will select the cheapest option. For example, if a hamburger, a fish dinner, and a New York sirloin steak are expected to yield identical benefits, economizing behavior implies that the cheapest of the three alternatives, probably the hamburger, will be chosen. Correspondingly, when choosing among alternatives of equal cost, economizing decision-makers will select the option that yields the greatest benefit. Purposeful decision-makers will not deliberately pay more for something than is necessary.

Purposeful choosing implies that decision-makers have some basis for their evaluation of alternatives. Economists refer to this evaluation as utility. **Utility** is the benefit or satisfaction that an individual expects from the choice of a specific alternative. The utility of an alternative is highly subjective, often differing widely from person to person.

3. Incentives Matter—Human Choice Is Influenced in a Predictable Way by Changes in Economic Incentives. This guidepost to clear economic thinking might be called the basic postulate of all economics. As the personal benefits from choosing an option increase, other things constant, a person will be more likely to choose that option. In contrast, as the costs associated with the choice of an item increase, the person will be less likely to choose that option. For a group, this basic economic postulate suggests that making an option more attractive will influence

Economizing Behavior: Choosing the objective of gaining a specific benefit at the least possible cost. A corollary of economizing behavior implies that when choosing among items of equal cost, individuals will choose the option that yields the greatest benefit.

Utility: The benefit or satisfaction expected from a choice or course of action.

more people to choose it. In contrast, as the cost of a selection to the members of a group increases, fewer of them will make this selection.

This basic postulate of economics is a powerful tool because its application is so widespread. Incentives affect behavior in virtually all aspects of our lives, ranging from household decision-making to political choices. Incentives matter in both capitalist and socialist countries. They may be either monetary or nonmonetary.

According to this basic postulate, what would happen to the birthrate if the U.S. government (a) removed the income tax deduction for dependents, (b) imposed a $1,500 "birth tax" on parents, and (c) made birth-control pills available, free of charge, to all? The birthrate would fall—that's what. In fact, several governments around the world recognize this, and provide economic inducements to increase or decrease birthrates. Canada, for example, provides payments to couples with larger families to encourage population growth, while China penalizes couples who have more than one child.

What would happen if the government imposed a $5,000 tax on smokestacks, required automobile owners to pay a larger license fee for cars with higher exhaust levels, and gave a 10 percent tax reduction to all corporations that did not use the air for waste disposal purposes? Answer: There would be a decline in air pollution levels. Economics suggests that any policy shift that increases the cost and/or reduces the benefits of a specific activity will reduce the frequency of that activity.

Our analysis indicates that an instructor could influence the incidence of cheating on an examination simply by changing the payoffs to students. There

MYTHS OF ECONOMICS

"Economic analysis assumes people act only out of selfish motives. It rejects the humanitarian side of humankind."

Probably because economics focuses on the efforts of individuals to satisfy material desires, many casual observers of the subject argue that its relevance hinges on the selfish nature of humankind. Some have even charged that economists, and the study of economics, encourage people to be materialistic rather than humanitarian.

This point of view stems from a fundamental misunderstanding of personal decision-making. Obviously, people act for a variety of reasons, some selfish and some humanitarian. The economist merely assumes that actions will be influenced by costs and benefits, as viewed by the decision-maker. As an activity becomes more costly, it is less likely that a decision-maker will choose it. As the activity becomes more attractive, it is more likely that it will be chosen.

The choices of both the humanitarian and the egocentric individual will be influenced by changes in personal costs and benefits. For example, both will be more likely to try to save the life of a small child in a three-foot swimming pool than in the rapid currents approaching Niagara Falls. Both will be more likely to give a needy person their hand-me-downs rather than their best clothes. Why? Because in both cases, the latter alternative is more costly than the former.

Observation would suggest that the right to control one's destiny is an "economic" good for most persons. Most of us would prefer to make our own choices rather than have someone else decide for us. But, is this always greedy and selfish? If so, why do people often make choices in a way that is charitable toward others? After all, many people freely choose to give a portion of their wealth to the sick, the needy, the less fortunate, religious organizations, and charitable institutions. Economics does not imply that these choices are irrational. It does imply that if you make it more (less) costly to act charitably, fewer (more) persons will do so.

Economics deals with people as they are—not as we would like to remake them. Should people act more charitably? Perhaps so. But this is not the subject matter of economics.

would be little cheating on a closely monitored, individualized, essay examination. Why? Because it would be difficult (that is, costly) to cheat on such an exam. Suppose, however, that an instructor gave an objective "take-home" exam, basing students' course grades entirely on the results. More students would be likely to cheat because the benefits of doing so would be great and the risk (cost) minimal.

Economic reasoning recognizes that many factors help determine how people make decisions. Morality, for example, might be a strong factor in the situations discussed above. Incentives, though, will also be important. The economic way of thinking never loses sight of the fact that changes in incentives exert a powerful and predictable influence on human decisions. (The boxed feature "Do Incentives Matter?" gives yet another application of this principle.)

4. Economic Thinking Is Marginal Thinking. Fundamental to economic reasoning and economizing behavior are the effects of decisions made to change the status quo. Economists refer to such decisions as **marginal.** Marginal choices always involve the effects of net additions to or subtractions *from the current conditions*. In fact, the word "additional" is often used as a substitute for marginal. For example, we might ask, "What is the marginal (or additional) cost of producing one more automobile?" Or, "What is the marginal (or additional) benefit derived from one more glass of water?"

Marginal decisions need not always involve small changes. The "one more unit" can be large or small. For example, the decision to build a new plant is a marginal decision. It is marginal because it involves additional costs and additional benefits. *Given the current situation,* what marginal benefits (additional sales revenues, for example) can be expected from the plant, and what will be the marginal cost of constructing the facility? The answers to these questions will determine whether or not building the new plant is a good decision.

It is important to distinguish between "average" and "marginal." Even

> **Marginal:** Term used to describe the effects of a change, given the current situation. For example, the marginal cost is the cost of producing an additional unit of a product, given the producer's current facility and production rate.

APPLICATIONS IN ECONOMICS

Do Incentives Matter?

How generally can we apply the "incentives matter" principle? Does it apply, for example, to drinking and driving? Will changing the incentives with regard to drinking and driving change behavior? Consider the case of Norway, the country that has the toughest drunk-driving laws in the Western world.[3] Drinking a single can of beer before driving can put a first offender in jail for a minimum sentence of three weeks. These drivers generally lose their licenses for up to two years and often get stiff fines as well. Repeat offenders are treated even more harshly.

These laws are far more Draconian than those of the United States. And the results?

1. One out of three Norwegians arrives at parties in a taxi, while nearly all Americans drive their own cars.
2. One out of ten Norwegian partygoers spends the night at the host's home; Americans seldom do.
3. In Norway, 78 percent of drivers totally avoid drinking at parties, compared to only 17 percent of American drivers.

Norwegians do like to drink, though they consume only half as much alcohol as Americans. The strong incentives built into Norwegian law, however, clearly make a difference in the incidence of drunken driving in that country. Once again, incentives do matter, and matter in a big way.

---

[3]The information in this feature is taken from L. Erik Calonius, "Just a Bottle of Beer Can Land A Motorist in Prison in Norway," *Wall Street Journal,* August 16, 1985, p. 1.

though a manufacturer's current average cost (total cost divided by total number of cars produced) of producing automobiles may be $10,000, for example, the marginal cost of producing an additional automobile (or an additional 1,000 automobiles) might be much lower; say, $5,000 per car. Costs associated with research, testing, design, molds, heavy equipment, and similar factors of production must be incurred whether the manufacturer is going to produce 1,000 units, 10,000 units, or 100,000 units. Such costs will clearly contribute to the average cost of an automobile. However, since these activities have already been undertaken to produce the manufacturer's current output level, they may *add little* to the cost of producing *additional* units. Thus, the manufacturer's marginal cost may be substantially less than the average cost. When determining whether to expand or reduce the production of a good, the choice should be based on marginal costs, not the current average cost.

We often confront decisions involving a possible change from the current situation. The marginal benefits and marginal costs associated with the choice will determine the wisdom of our decisions. What happens at the margin is therefore an important part of economic analysis.

5. Information, like Other Resources, Is Scarce. Therefore, Knowledge About the Future Is Scarce. It is difficult, if not impossible, to anticipate the results of many decisions. Would a different car be better than the one you now use? Would a vacation in the mountains be better than one at the seashore? Are political candidate A's positions better than those of candidate B? It is difficult to recognize what all of the options are, and to know how important each of the differences among them will be. Rational decision-makers recognize that it is costly to obtain information and make complex calculations. Although additional information and techniques that improve one's decision-making capabilities are valuable, often the potential benefit is less than its expected cost. Sensible consumers will conserve on these limited resources, therefore, just as they conserve on other scarce resources.

6. Remember the Secondary Effects—Economic Actions Often Generate Secondary Effects in Addition to Their Immediate Effects. Frederic Bastiat, a nineteenth-century French economist, stated that the difference between a good and a bad economist is that the bad economist considers only the immediate, visible effects, whereas the good economist is also aware of the **secondary effects,** effects that are indirectly related to the initial policy and whose influence might only be seen or felt with the passage of time.

Secondary effects are important in areas outside of economics. The immediate effect of an aspirin is a bitter taste in one's mouth. The indirect effect, which is not immediately observable, is relief from a headache. The immediate effect of drinking six quarts of beer might be a warm, jolly feeling. The indirect effect, for many, would be a pounding headache the next morning. In economics, too, the secondary effects of an action may be quite different from the initial impact. According to the economic way of thinking, the significant questions are: In addition to the initial result of this policy, what other factors will be affected? How will future actions be influenced by the changes in economic incentives that have resulted from policy A?

An economic system is much like an ecological system. An ecological action sometimes generates indirect and perhaps unintended secondary effects. For ex-

Secondary Effects: Economic consequences of an initial economic change, even though they are not immediately identifiable. Secondary effects will be felt only with the passage of time.

ample, the heavy use of a pesticide on a field to kill a specific population of insects may have an undesirable effect on other creatures. Economic actions can generate similar results. For example, price controls on natural gas have the desired effect of reducing heating expenditures for some consumers, but they also reduce both conservation of gas by those consumers and the incentive of producers to bring more natural gas to the market. Other consumers will therefore be forced to rely more heavily on other, more expensive energy sources, pushing the prices of these energy sources upward. Thus, the controls also generate an unintended result: an increase in the energy costs for some consumers. Good economic thinking demands that we recognize the secondary effects, which will often be observed only with the passage of time.

7. The Value of a Good or a Service Is Subjective. Preferences differ, sometimes dramatically, between individuals. How much is a ticket to see tonight's performance of the Bolshoi Ballet worth? *Different people will have very different answers!* Some would be willing to pay a high price indeed, while others might even be willing to pay to avoid the ballet if attendance were mandatory. Even for a given individual, circumstances can change from day to day. Alice, who usually would value the ballet ticket at $20, is invited to a party, and suddenly becomes uninterested in the ballet tonight. Now what is the ticket worth? If she knows a friend who would give her $5 for the ticket, it is worth at least that much. If she advertises on a bulletin board and gets $10 for it, a higher value is created. *One thing is certain: the value of the ticket depends on many things, among them who uses it and when.*

Seldom will one individual know how others value an item. Consider how difficult it often is to know what would make a good gift, even for a close friend or family member! So, arranging trades or otherwise moving items to higher-valued users and uses can be very valuable, but is not a simple task. In fact, how society promotes such coordination in the behavior of individuals is a key subject in many of the chapters that follow.

Scientific Thinking:
Development of theory from basic postulates and the testing of the implications of that theory as to their consistency with events in the real world. Good theories are consistent with and help explain real-world events. Theories that are inconsistent with the real world are invalid and must be rejected.

8. The Test of a Theory Is Its Ability to Predict. Economic Thinking Is *Scientific Thinking.* The proof of the pudding is in the eating. The usefulness of an economic theory is revealed by its ability to predict the future consequences of economic action. Economists develop economic theory from an analysis of how incentives will affect decision-makers. The theory is then tested against events in the real world. Through testing, we either confirm the theory or recognize the need for amending or rejecting it. If the events in the real world are consistent with a theory, we say that the theory has predictive value. In contrast, theories that are inconsistent with real-world data must be rejected.

If it is impossible to test the theoretical relationships of a discipline, the discipline does not qualify as a science. Since economics deals with human beings, who can think and respond in a variety of ways, can economic theories really be tested? The answer to this question is yes, if, *on average,* human beings respond in predictable and consistent ways to changes in economic conditions. The economist believes that this is the case. Note that this does not necessarily imply that *all* individuals will respond in a specified manner. Economics usually does not seek to predict the behavior of a specific individual; instead, it focuses on the general behavior of a large number of individuals.

How can we test economic theory when controlled experiments with all the interactions of real life are not feasible? This is a problem, but economics is no different from astronomy in this respect. Astronomers must also deal with the world as it is. They cannot change the course of the stars or planets to see what impact the change would have on the gravitational pull of the earth.

So it is with economists. Limited experiments are sometimes possible. For example, experiments comparing the reaction of competing individuals to different forms of an auction might be conducted with actual money payoffs at stake. But economists cannot perform full-scale tests under real-world conditions. They cannot arbitrarily change the price of cars or unskilled labor services just to observe the effect on quantity purchased or level of employment.

Still, economic theory can be tested in real-world situations. Economic conditions (for example, prices, production costs, technology, transportation cost, and so on), like the location of the planets, do change from time to time. As actual conditions change, economic theory can be tested by comparing its predictions with real-world outcomes. Just as the universe is the laboratory of the astronomer, the real world is the laboratory of the economist.

In some cases, observations of the real world may be consistent with two (or more) economic theories. Given the current state of our knowledge, we will sometimes be unable to distinguish between competitive theories. Much of the work of economists remains to be done, but in many areas substantial empirical work has been completed. Throughout this book, we will refer to this evidence in an effort to provide information with which we can judge the validity of various economic theories. We must not lose sight of the scientific method of thinking, because it is a requisite for sound economic thinking.

POSITIVE AND NORMATIVE ECONOMICS

Positive Economics: The scientific study of ''what is'' among economic relationships.

Economics as a social science is concerned with predicting or determining the impact of changes in economic variables on the actions of human beings. Scientific economics, commonly referred to as **positive economics,** attempts to determine ''what is.'' Positive economic statements postulate a relationship that is potentially verifiable or refutable. For example: ''If the price of butter were higher, people would buy less.'' Or, ''As the money supply increases, the price level will go up.'' We can statistically investigate (and estimate) the relationship between butter prices and sales, or between the supply of money and the general price level. We can analyze the facts to determine the correctness of a statement about positive economics.

Normative Economics: Judgments about ''what ought to be'' in economic matters. Normative economic views cannot be proved false, because they are based on value judgments.

Normative economics involves the advocacy of specific policy alternatives, because it uses ethical judgments as well as knowledge of positive economics. Normative economic statements concern ''what ought to be,'' given the philosophical views of the advocate. Value judgments may be the source of disagreement about normative economic matters. Two persons may differ on a policy matter because one is a socialist and the other a libertarian, one a liberal and the other a conservative, or one a traditionalist and the other a radical. They may agree as to the expected outcome of altering an economic variable (that is, the positive economics of an issue), but disagree as to whether that outcome is ''good'' or ''bad.''

In contrast with positive economic statements, normative economic statements cannot be tested and proved false (or confirmed to be correct). "The government *should* increase defense expenditures." "Business firms *should not* maximize profits." "Unions *should not* increase wages more rapidly than the cost of living." These normative statements cannot be scientifically tested, since their validity rests on value judgments.

Positive economics does not tell us which policy is best. The purpose of positive economics is to increase our knowledge of all policy alternatives, thereby eliminating one source of disagreement about policy matters. The knowledge that we gain from positive economics also serves to reduce a potential source of disappointment with policy. Those who do not understand how the economy operates may advocate policies that are actually inconsistent with their philosophical views. Sometimes what one thinks will happen if a policy is instituted may be a very unlikely result in the real world.

Our normative economic views can sometimes influence our attitude toward positive economic analysis. When we agree with the objectives of a policy, it is easy to overlook its potential liabilities. Desired objectives, though, are not the same as workable solutions. The actual effects of policy alternatives often differ dramatically from the objectives of their proponents. A new law forcing employers to double all wage rates might be intended to help workers, but the resulting drop in the number of workers employed would be disastrous despite the good intentions. Proponents of such a law, of course, would not want to believe the economic analysis that predicted the unfortunate outcome.

Sound positive economics will help us evaluate more accurately whether or not a policy alternative will, in fact, accomplish a desired objective. The task of the professional economist is to expand our knowledge of how the real world operates. If we do not fully understand the implications, including the secondary effects, of alternative policies, we will not be able to choose intelligently among the alternatives. It is not always easy to isolate the impact of a change in an economic variable or policy. Let us consider some of the potential pitfalls that retard the growth of economic knowledge.

PITFALLS TO AVOID IN ECONOMIC THINKING

VIOLATION OF THE *CETERIS PARIBUS* CONDITION

Economists often preface their statements with the words *ceteris paribus,* meaning "other things constant." "Other things constant, an increase in the price of housing will cause buyers to reduce their purchases." Unfortunately for the economic researcher, we live in a dynamic world. Other things seldom remain constant. For example, as the price of housing rises, the income of consumers may simultaneously be increasing. Both of these factors, higher housing prices and an expansion in consumer income, will have an impact on housing purchases. In fact, we would generally expect them to exert opposite effects—higher prices retarding housing purchases but the rise in consumer income stimulating the demand for housing. The task of sorting out the specific effects of interrelated variables thus becomes more complex when several changes take place simultaneously.

Economic theory acts as a guide, suggesting the probable linkages among economic variables. However, the relationships suggested by economic theory must be tested for consistency with events in the real world. Statistical procedures are often used by economists to correctly identify and more accurately measure relationships among economic variables. In fact, the major portion of the day-to-day work of many professional economists consists of statistical research.

ASSOCIATION IS NOT CAUSATION

In economics, causation is very important. The incorrect identification of causation is a potential source of error. Statistical association alone, though, does not establish causation. Perhaps an extreme example will illustrate the point. Suppose that each November a witch doctor performs a voodoo dance designed to arouse the cold-weather gods of winter and that soon after the dance is performed, the weather in fact begins to turn cold. The witch doctor's dance is *associated with* the arrival of winter, but does it cause the arrival of winter? Most of us would answer in the negative, even though the two are linked statistically.

Unfortunately, cause-and-effect relationships in economics are not always self-evident. For example, it is sometimes difficult to know whether a rise in income has caused people to buy more or, conversely, whether an increase in people's willingness to buy more has created more business and caused incomes to rise. Similarly, economists sometimes argue whether rising money wages are a cause or an effect of inflation. Economic theory, if rooted to the basic postulates, can often help to determine the source of causation, even though competitive theories may sometimes suggest differing directions of causation.

THE FALLACY OF COMPOSITION

What is true for the individual (or subcomponent) may not be true for the group (or the whole). If you stand up for an exciting play during a football game, you will be better able to see. But, what happens if everyone stands up at the same time? What benefits the individual does not benefit the group as a whole. When everyone stands up, the view for individual spectators fails to improve; in fact, it probably becomes even worse.

Fallacy of Composition: Erroneous view that what is true for the individual (or the part) will also be true for the group (or the whole).

People who argue that what is true for the part is also true for the whole may err because of the **fallacy of composition.** Consider an example from economics. If you have an extra $10,000 in your bank account, you will be better off. But, what if everyone suddenly has an additional $10,000? This increase in the money supply will result in higher prices, as people with more money bid against each other for the existing supply of goods. Without an increase in the availability (or production) of scarce economic goods, the additional money will not make everyone better off. What is true for the individual is misleading and often fallacious when applied to the entire economy.

Microeconomics: The branch of economics that focuses on how human behavior affects the conduct of affairs within narrowly defined units, such as individual households or business firms.

Potential error associated with the fallacy of composition highlights the importance of considering both a micro- and a macroview in the study of economics. Since individual human decision-makers are the moving force behind all economic action, the foundations of economics are clearly rooted in a microview. Analysis that focuses on a single consumer, producer, product, or productive resource is referred to as **microeconomics.** As Professor Abba Lerner put it, "Microeconomics consists of looking at the economy through a microscope, as it were, to see how the millions of cells in the body economic—the individuals or households as consumers, and the individuals or firms as producers—play their part in the working of the whole organisms."[4]

[4]Abba, P. Lerner, "Microeconomy Theory," in *Perspectives in Economics,* ed. A. A. Brown, E. Neuberger, and M. Palmatier (New York: McGraw-Hill, 1968), p. 29.

Macroeconomics: The branch of economics that focuses on how human behavior affects outcomes in highly aggregated markets, such as the markets for labor or consumer products.

As we have seen, however, what is true for a small unit may not be true in the aggregate. Macroeconomics focuses on how the aggregation of individual microunits affects our analysis. Macroeconomics, like microeconomics, is concerned with incentives, prices, and output. In macroeconomics, however, the markets are highly aggregated. In our study of macroeconomics, the 90 million households in this country will be lumped together when we consider such topics as the importance of consumption spending, saving, and employment. Similarly, the nation's 18 million firms will be lumped together into something we call "the business sector."

What factors determine the level of aggregate output, the rate of inflation, the amount of unemployment, and interest rates? These are macroeconomic questions. In short, macroeconomics examines the forest rather than the individual trees. As we move from the microcomponents to a macroview of the whole, it is important that we bear in mind the potential pitfalls of the fallacy of composition.

WHAT DO ECONOMISTS DO?

The primary functions of economists are to teach, conduct research, and formulate policies. Approximately one half of all professional economists are affiliated with academic institutions. Many of these academicians are involved both in teaching and in scientific research.

OUTSTANDING ECONOMIST

Adam Smith (1723–1790) and the Historical Roots of Economics

The foundation of economics as a systematic area of study was laid in 1776, when Adam Smith published his monumental work, *An Inquiry Into the Nature and Causes of the Wealth of Nations*. Perhaps the most influential book since the Bible, *The Wealth of Nations* was nothing less than a revolutionary attack on the existing orthodoxy. Smith declared that the wealth of a nation did not lie in gold and silver, but rather was determined by the goods and services— whether produced at home or abroad—available to the people.

To increase the nation's hoard of gold and silver, the political and intellectual leaders of Smith's time placed numerous constraints on economic freedoms. Political institutions encouraged citizens to sell their produce abroad in exchange for gold and

silver, and discouraged or restrained the purchase of foreign-made goods. Monopolies and guild associations were protected from competition. People thought then that economic activities motivated by private gain were antisocial.

In contrast, Smith argued that a free exchange market economy would harness self-interest as a creative force. Since one gets ahead in a market economy by helping others in exchange for income, people seeking their own gain will provide valuable goods and services to others. As Smith put it:

> Man has almost constant occasion for the help of his brethren, and it is in vain for him to expect it from his benevolence *only* [emphasis added]. . . . Whoever offers another a bar-

The job of the research economist is to increase our understanding of economic matters. The tools of statistics and mathematics help the researcher carry out this task. Government agencies and private business firms generate a vast array of economic statistics on such matters as income, employment, prices, and expenditure patterns. A two-way street exists between statistical data and economic theory. Statistics can be used to test the consistency of economic theory and measure the responsiveness of economic variables to changes in policy. At the same time, economic theory helps to explain *which* economic variables are likely to be related and *why* they are linked. Statistics do not tell their own story. We must utilize economic theory to properly interpret and better understand the actual statistical relationships among economic variables.

Economics is a social science. The fields of political science, sociology, psychology, and economics often overlap. Because of the abundance of economic data and the ample opportunity for scientific research in the real world, economics has sometimes been called the "queen of the social sciences." Reflecting the scientific nature of economics, the Swedish Academy of Science in 1969 instituted the Nobel Prize in Economic Science. The men and women of genius in economics now take their place alongside those in physics, chemistry, physiology and medicine, peace, and literature.

A knowledge of economics is essential for wise policy-making. Policy-makers who do not understand the consequences of their actions will not likely reach their goals. Recognizing the link between economic analysis and policy, Congress in 1946 established the Council of Economic Advisers. The purpose of the council

gain of any kind, proposes to do this: Give me that which I want, and you shall have this which you want; it is in this manner that we obtain from one another the far greater part of those good offices which we stand in need of. It is not from the benevolence of the butcher, the brewer, or the baker, that we expect our dinner, but from their regard to their own interest.

Furthermore, Smith argued that if kings and politicians would remove legal restrictions that retard productive activity and exchange, the "invisible hand" of market prices would direct individuals and resources into those areas of their greatest productivity. Coordination, order, and efficiency would result, despite the absence of a central authority that planned and directed the economy. Smith believed that this process provided the key to production and the wealth of nations.

As Keynes noted 160 years later, the world is ruled by ideas. Even though Smith's thinking conflicted with the social environment of his time, his idea that self-interest, economic freedom, and national wealth were all in harmony eventually changed the world. English historian Henry Thomas Buckle declared that *The Wealth of Nations* represented "the most valuable contribution ever made by a single man towards establishing the principles on which government should be based."

Smith's ideas greatly influenced those who mapped out the structure of the U.S. government. By the end of the eighteenth century, institutional reform had lifted the hand of government from many areas of economic activity in England and throughout Europe. The nineteenth century, the "era of economic freedom," was one of industrialization and growing prosperity in the Western world. Adam Smith, more than anyone else, established the intellectual climate in which this could happen.

By the time of Smith's death in 1790, five editions of *The Wealth of Nations* had been published, and it had been translated into several foreign languages. The study of the relationship between production, exchange, and wealth began to occupy the time of an increasing number of intellectuals. Political economy—later divided into economics and political science—became a new and widely accepted field of study in major universities throughout the world.

is to provide the president with analyses of how the activities of the federal government influence the economy. The chairmanship of the Council of Economic Advisers is a cabinet-level position.

FINAL WORD

The primary purpose of this book is to encourage you to develop the economic way of thinking so that you can differentiate sound reasoning from economic nonsense. Once you have developed the economic way of thinking, economics will be relatively easy. Using the economic way of thinking can also be fun. Moreover, it will help you become a better citizen. It will give you a different and fascinating perspective on what motivates people, why they act the way they do, and why their actions are sometimes in conflict with the best interest of the community or nation. It will also give you some valuable insight into how people's actions can be rechanneled for the benefit of the community at large.

Economics is a relatively young science. Current-day economists owe an enormous debt to their predecessors. The Outstanding Economist feature analyzes the contribution of Adam Smith, the father of economics.

CHAPTER SUMMARY

1. Scarcity and choice are the two essential ingredients of an economic topic. Goods are scarce because desire for them far outstrips their availability from Nature. Since scarcity prevents us from having as much of everything as we would like, we must choose among the alternatives available to us. Any choice involving the use of scarce resources requires an economic decision.
2. Scarcity and poverty are not the same thing. Absence of poverty implies that some basic level of need has been met. Absence of scarcity would mean that all of our desires for goods have been met. We may someday be able to eliminate poverty, but scarcity will always be with us.
3. Economics is a method of approach, a way of thinking. The economic way of thinking emphasizes the following:
   a. Among economic goods, there are no free lunches. Someone must give up something if we are to have more scarce goods.
   b. Individuals make decisions purposefully, always seeking to choose the option they expect to be most consistent with their personal goals. Purposeful decision-making leads to economizing behavior.
   c. Incentives matter. People will be more likely to choose an option as the benefits expected from that option increase. In contrast, higher costs will make an alternative less attractive, reducing the likelihood that it will be chosen.
   d. Marginal costs and marginal benefits (utility) are fundamental to economizing behavior. Economic reasoning focuses on the impact of marginal changes.
   e. Since information is scarce, uncertainty will be present when decisions are made.
   f. In addition to their initial impact, economic events often alter personal incentives in a manner that leads to important secondary effects that may be felt only with the passage of time.
   g. The value of a good or service is subjective, and will differ among individuals.
   h. The test of an economic theory is its ability to predict and to explain events in the real world.
4. Economic science is positive. It attempts to explain the actual consequences of economic actions and alternative policies. Positive economics alone does not state that one policy is superior to another. Normative economics is advocative; using value judgments, it makes suggestions about ''what ought to be.''
5. Testing economic theory is not an easy task. When several economic variables change simultaneously, it is often difficult to determine the relative importance of each. The

direction of economic causation is sometimes difficult to ascertain. Economists consult economic theory as a guide and use statistical techniques as tools to improve our knowledge of positive economics.

6. Microeconomics focuses on narrowly defined units, such as individual consumers or business firms. Macroeconomics is concerned with highly aggregated units, such as the markets for labor or goods and services. When shifting focus from micro- to macrounits, one must be careful not to commit the fallacy of composition. Both micro- and macroeconomics use the same postulates and tools. The level of aggregation is the distinction between the two.

7. The origin of economics as a systematic method of analysis dates back to the publication of *The Wealth of Nations* by Adam Smith in 1776. Even though legal restraints on economic activity abounded at the time, Smith argued that production and wealth would increase if individuals were left free to work, produce, and exchange goods and services. Smith believed that individuals pursuing their own interests would be led by the "invisible hand" of market incentives (prices) to employ their productive talents in a manner "most advantageous to the society." Smith's central message is that when markets are free—when there are no legal restraints limiting the entry of producer-sellers—individual self-interest and the public interest are brought into harmony.

CRITICAL ANALYSIS QUESTIONS

1. Indicate how each of the following changes would influence the incentive of a decision-maker to undertake the action described.
   (a) A reduction in the temperature from 80° to 50° on one's decision to go swimming.
   (b) A change in the meeting time of the introductory economics course from 11:00 A.M. to 7:30 A.M. on one's decision to attend the lectures.
   (c) A reduction in the number of exam questions that relate to the text on the student's decision to read the text.
   (d) An increase in the price of beef on one's decision to have steak every night this week.
   (e) An increase in the rental price of apartments on one's decision to build additional housing units.

*2. "The government should provide goods such as health care, education, and highways because it can provide them free." (True or false; explain)

3. **What's Wrong with this Economic Experiment?**
   A researcher hypothesizes that the medical attention received by U.S. citizens is inadequate because many people cannot afford medical care. The researcher interviews 100 randomly selected individuals and asks them, "Would you use physician services or hospital and nursing-home medical facilities more if they were not so expensive?" Ninety-six of the 100 answer in the affirmative. The researcher concludes that there is a critical need to allocate more resources to the provision of free medical care for all citizens.

4. "Reasonable rental housing could be brought within the economic means of all if the government would prevent landlords from charging more than $200 per month rent for a quality three-bedroom house." Use the economic way of thinking to evaluate this view.

5. SENATOR DOGOODER: I favor an increase in the minimum wage because it would help the unskilled worker.
   SENATOR DONOTHING: I oppose an increase in the minimum wage because it would cause the unemployment rate among the young and unskilled to rise.

*Asterisk denotes questions for which answers are given in Appendix C, Selected Answers.

Is the disagreement between Senator Dogooder and Senator Donothing positive or normative? Explain.

*6. The United States recently raised the personal exemption from $1,080 to $2,000 and thereby increased the tax-saving provided to parents of children. According to the basic postulate of economics, how will this change affect the birth rate?

*7. The economic way of thinking stresses that good intentions lead to sound policy. (True or false; explain)

8. Economic theory postulates that self-interest is a powerful motivation for action. Does this imply that people are selfish and greedy? Do self-interest and selfishness mean the same thing?

*9. Congress and government agencies often make laws to help protect the safety of product consumers. New cars, for example, are required to have many safety features before they can be sold in the United States. These rules do indeed provide added safety for buyers, although they also add to the cost and price of the new vehicles. But can you think of secondary effects of the laws which tend to undercut or reduce the intended effect of increasing auto safety?

*10. "Individuals who economize are missing the point of life. Money is not so important that it should rule the way we live." Evaluate.

11. "Positive economics cannot tell us which agricultural policy is better, so it is useless to policymakers." Evaluate.

12. "I examined the statistics for our basketball team's wins last year, and found that when the third team played more, the winning margin increased. If the coach played the third team more, we would win by a bigger margin." Evaluate.

ADDENDUM

UNDERSTANDING GRAPHS

Economists often use graphs to illustrate economic relations. Graphs are like pictures. They are visual aids that can communicate valuable information in a small amount of space. It has been said that a good picture is worth a thousand words. But, one must understand the picture (and the graph) if it is to be enlightening.

This addendum is designed to illustrate the use of simple graphs as an instrument of communication. Many students, particularly those with an elementary mathematics background, are already familiar with this material, and they may safely ignore it. This addendum is for those who need to be assured that they have the ability to understand graphic economic illustrations.

THE SIMPLE BAR GRAPH

A simple bar graph can often help one better visualize comparative relationships. It can be used to illustrate how an economic indicator varies among countries, time periods, or under alternative economic conditions. A bar graph is nothing more than a visual aid. Nevertheless, it is sometimes a valuable illustrative tool.

Exhibit A-1 shows how a bar graph can be used to illustrate economic data. Exhibit A-1a presents tabular data on the income per person in 1986 for several countries. Exhibit A-1b (next page) uses a bar graph to illustrate the same data. The horizontal scale of the graph indicates the total income per person in 1986. A bar is constructed indicating the income level of each country. The length of each bar is in proportion to the per person income of the country. Thus, the length of the bars makes it easy to see how the per capita income varies across the

EXHIBIT A–1

International Comparison
of Income per Person

(a) Chart Presentation

Country	Total Income Per Person, 1986
Switzerland	17,680
United States	17,480
Canada	14,120
Sweden	13,160
Japan	12,840
France	10,720
United Kingdom	8,870
Hong Kong	6,910
Mexico	1,860
Egypt	760
India	290

Source: *World Development Report, 1988.*

(b) Bar Graph Presentation

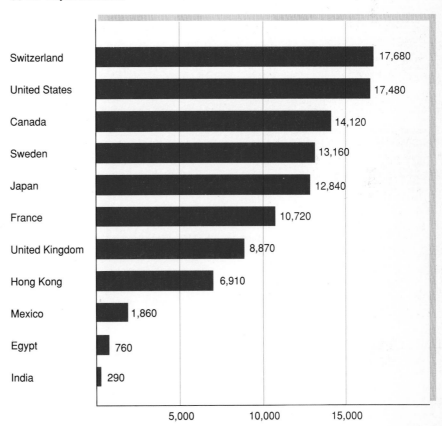

Total income per person, 1986

countries. For example, the extremely short bar for India makes it easy to visualize that income per person in India is only a small fraction of the comparable figure for Switzerland, the United States, and several other countries.

LINEAR GRAPHIC PRESENTATION

Economists are often interested in illustrating variations in economic variables with the passage of time. A linear graph with time on the horizontal axis and an economic variable on the vertical axis is a useful tool to indicate variations over time. Exhibit A-2 illustrates a simple linear graph of changes in consumer prices (the inflation rate) in the United States between 1960 and 1987. The table of the exhibit presents data on the percent change in consumer prices for each year. Beginning with 1960, the horizontal axis indicates the time period (year). The inflation rate for a country is plotted vertically above each year. Of course, the height of the plot (line) indicates the inflation rate during that year. For example, in 1975, the inflation rate was 7.0 percent. This point is plotted at the 7.0 percent vertical distance directly above the year 1975. In 1976, the inflation rate fell to 4.8 percent. Thus, the vertical plot of the 1976 inflation rate is lower than for 1975. The inflation rate for each year (frame a) is plotted at the corresponding height directly above the year. The linear graph is simply a line connecting the points plotted for each of the years 1960 through 1987.

The linear graph makes it easy to visualize what happens to the inflation rate during the period. As the graph shows, the inflation rate rose sharply between 1965 and 1969, in 1973–1974 and again in 1977–1979. It was substantially higher during the 1970s than it was in the early 1960s or the mid-1980s. While the linear

---

EXHIBIT A–2

EXHIBIT A–2

Changes in the Level of Prices in the United States, 1960–1987

The tabular data (a) of the inflation rate is presented in graphic form in (b).

(a) Chart Presentation

Year	Percent Change in Consumer Prices	Year	Percent Change in Consumer Prices
1960	1.5	1975	7.0
1961	0.7	1976	4.8
1962	1.2	1977	6.8
1963	1.6	1978	9.0
1964	1.2	1979	13.3
1965	1.9	1980	12.4
1966	3.4	1981	8.9
1967	3.0	1982	3.9
1968	4.7	1983	3.8
1969	6.1	1984	4.0
1970	5.5	1985	3.8
1971	3.4	1986	1.1
1972	3.4	1987	4.4
1973	8.8		
1974	12.2		

Source: *Economic Report of the President, 1988*, Table B–61.

(b) Running Linear Graph

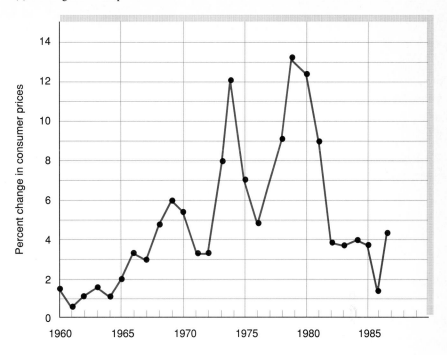

graph does not communicate any information not in the table, it does make it easier to see the pattern of the data. Thus, economists often use simple graphics rather than tables to communicate information.

DIRECT AND INVERSE RELATIONSHIPS

Economic logic often suggests that two variables are linked in a specific way. Suppose an investigation reveals that, other things constant, farmers supply more wheat as the price of wheat increases. Exhibit A-3a presents hypothetical data indicating the relationship between the price of wheat and the quantity supplied by farmers.

The information contained in Exhibit A-3a can also be illustrated with a simple two-dimensional graph. Suppose we measure the quantity of wheat supplied by farmers on the *x*-axis (the horizontal axis) and the price of wheat on the *y*-axis (the vertical axis). Points indicating the value of *x* (quantity supplied) at alternative values of *y* (price of wheat) can then be plotted. The line (or curve) linking the points together illustrates the relationship between the price of wheat and amount supplied by farmers.

In the case of price and quantity supplied of wheat, the two variables are *directly related*. When the *y*-variable increases, so does the *x*-variable. When two variables are directly related, the graph illustrating the linkage between the two will slope upward to the right (as in the case of *SS* of Exhibit A-3b).

Sometimes the *x*-variable and the *y*-variable are *inversely related*. A decline in the *y*-variable is associated with an increase in the *x*-variable. Therefore, a

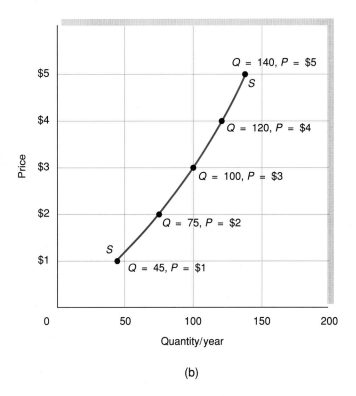

EXHIBIT A–3

A Direct Relationship Between Variables (hypothetical data)

As the table (a) indicates, farmers are willing to supply more wheat at a higher price. Thus, there is a direct relation between the price of wheat and the quantity supplied. When the x- and y-variables are directly related, a curve mapping the relationship between the two will slope upward to the right like SS.

Price	Amount of Wheat Supplied by Farmers Per Year (millions of bushels)
$1	45
2	75
3	100
4	120
5	140

(a)

(b)

curve picturing the inverse relationship between x and y slopes downward to the right.

Exhibit A-4 illustrates this case. As the data of the table indicate, consumers purchase *less* as the price of wheat increases. Measuring the price of wheat on the y-axis (by convention, economists always place price on the y-axis) and the quantity of wheat purchased on the x-axis, the relationship between these two variables can also be illustrated graphically. If the price of wheat was $5 per bushel, only 60 million bushels would be purchased by consumers. As the price declines to $4 per bushel, annual consumption increases to 75 million bushels. At still lower prices, the quantity purchased by consumers will expand to larger and larger amounts. As Exhibit A-4b illustrates, the inverse relationship between price and quantity of wheat purchased generates a curve that slopes downward to the right.

EXHIBIT A–4

An Inverse Relationship Between Variables (hypothetical data)

As the table (a) shows, consumers will demand (purchase) more wheat as the price declines. Thus, there is an inverse relationship between the price of wheat and the quantity demanded. When the x- and y-variables are inversely related, a curve showing the relationship between the two will slope downward to the right like DD.

Price	Amount of Wheat Demanded by Consumers Per Year (millions of bushels)
$1	170
2	130
3	100
4	75
5	60

(a)

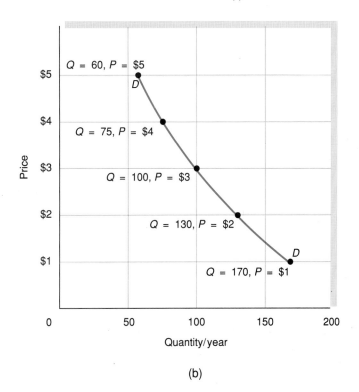

(b)

COMPLEX RELATIONSHIPS

Sometimes the initial relationship between the x- and y-variables will change. Exhibit A-5 illustrates more complex relations of this type. Frame A-5a shows the typical relationship between annual earnings and age. As a young person acquires work experience and develops skills, earnings usually expand. Thus, *initially*, age and annual earnings are directly related; annual earnings increase with age. However, beyond a certain age (approximately age 55), annual earnings generally decline as workers approach retirement. As a result, the initial direct relationship between age and earnings changes to an inverse relation. When this is the case, annual income expands to a maximum (at age 55) and then begins to decline with years of age.

Exhibit A-5b illustrates an initial inverse relation that later changes to a direct relationship. Consider the impact of travel speed on gasoline consumption per mile. At low speeds, the automobile engine will not be used efficiently. As speed

EXHIBIT A–5
Complex Relationships

At first, an increase in age (and work experience) leads to a higher income but later earnings decline as the worker approaches retirement (a). Thus, age and annual income are initially directly related but at approximately age 55 an inverse relation emerges. Frame (b) illustrates the relationship between travel speed and gasoline consumption per mile. Initially, gasoline consumption per mile declines as speed increases (an inverse relation), but as speed increases above 40 miles per hour, gasoline consumption per mile increases with the speed of travel (direct relation).

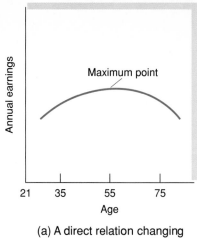

(a) A direct relation changing to inverse

(b) An inverse relation changing to direct

increases from 5 mph to 10 mph and on to a speed of 40 mph, gasoline consumption *per mile* declines. In this range, there is an inverse relationship between speed of travel (*x*) and gasoline consumption per mile (*y*). However, as speed increases beyond 40 mph, more gasoline per mile is required to achieve the additional acceleration. At very high speeds, gasoline consumption per mile increases substantially with speed of travel. Thus, gasoline consumption per mile reaches a minimum and a direct relationship between the *x*- and *y*-variables emerges beyond the minimum point (40 mph).

SLOPE OF A STRAIGHT LINE

In economics, we are often interested in how much the *y*-variable changes in response to a change in the *x*-variable. The slope of the line or curve reveals this information. Mathematically, the slope of a line or curve is equal to the change in the *y*-variable divided by the change in the *x*-variable.

Exhibit A-6 illustrates the calculation of the slope for a straight line. The exhibit shows how the daily earnings (*y*-variable) of a worker change with hours worked (the *x*-variable). The wage rate of the worker is $5 per hour. Thus, when 1 hour is worked earnings are equal to $5; for 2 hours of work, earnings jump to $10, and so on. A one-hour change in hours worked leads to a $5 change in earnings. Thus, the slope of the line ($\Delta Y / \Delta X$) is equal to 5. (The symbol Δ means "change in.") In the case of a straight line, the change in *y* per unit change in *x* is equal for all points on the line. Thus, the slope of a straight line is constant for all points along the line.

Exhibit A-6 illustrates a case in which there is a direct relation between the *x*- and *y*-variable. For an inverse relation, the *y*-variable decreases as the *x*-variable increases. So, when *x* and *y* are inversely related, the slope of the line will be negative.

SLOPE OF A CURVE

In contrast with a straight line, the slope of a curve is different at each point along the curve. The slope of a curve at a specific point is equal to the slope of a line tangent to the curve at the point. (A tangent is a line that just touches the curve.) Exhibit A-7 illustrates how the slope of a curve at a specific point is determined.

EXHIBIT A–6

The Slope of a Straight Line

The slope of a line is equal to change in y divided by the change in x. The line above illustrates the case in which daily earnings increase by $5 per hour worked. Thus, the slope of the earnings function is 5 ($5 ÷ 1 hr). For a straight line, the slope is constant at each point on the line.

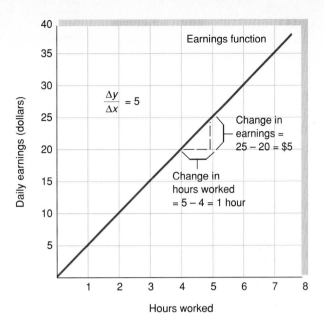

First, let us consider the slope of the curve at point A. A line tangent to the curve at point A indicates that y changes by 1 unit when x changes by 2 units at point A. Thus, the slope ($\Delta Y/\Delta X$) of the curve at A is equal to 1/2.

Now, consider the slope of the curve at point B. The line tangent to the curve at B indicates that y changes by 2 units for each one unit change in x at point B. Thus, at B the slope ($\Delta Y/\Delta X$) is equal to 2. At point B, a change in the x-variable

EXHIBIT A–7

The Slope of a Nonlinear Curve

The slope of a curve at any point is equal to the slope of the straight line tangent to the curve at the point. As the lines tangent to the above curve at point A and B illustrate, the slope of a curve will change from point to point along the curve.

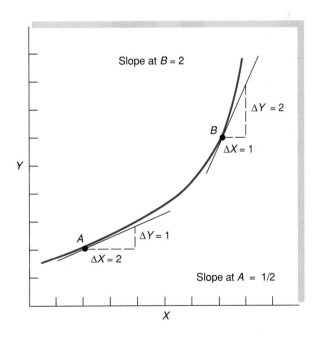

leads to a much larger change in y than was true at point A. The greater slope of the curve at B reflects this greater change in y per unit change in x at B relative to A.

GRAPHS ARE NOT A SUBSTITUTE FOR ECONOMIC THINKING

By now you should have a fairly good understanding of how to read a graph. If you still feel uncomfortable with graphs, try drawing (graphing) the relationship between several things with which you are familiar. If you work, try graphing the relationship between *your* hours worked (x-axis) and *your* weekly earnings (y-axis). If need be, refer to Exhibit A-6 to help guide you with this exercise. Can you graph the relationship between the price of gasoline and your expenditures on gasoline? Graphing these simple relationships will give you greater confidence in your ability to grasp more complex economic relationships presented in graphs.

This text uses only simple graphs. Thus, there is no reason for you to be intimidated. Graphs look much more complex than they really are. In fact, they are nothing more than a simple device to communicate information quickly and concisely. One cannot communicate anything with a graph that cannot be communicated verbally.

Most important, graphs are not a substitute for economic thinking. While a graph may illustrate that two variables are related, it tells us nothing about the cause-and-effect relationship between the variables. To determine probable cause and effect, we must rely on economic theory. Thus, the economic way of thinking, not graphs, is the power station of economic analysis.

2

SOME TOOLS OF THE ECONOMIST

The goods people sell usually are made by processes using a high proportion of the skills they are gifted in, whereas the goods people buy usually are made by processes they are comparatively ungifted in.[1]

Robert A. Mundell

CHAPTER FOCUS

■ What is an "opportunity cost"? Why do economists place so much emphasis on opportunity cost?

■ What does a production possibilities frontier demonstrate?

■ How do specialization and exchange create value?

■ What three economizing decisions are faced by every economy?

■ How do the two major methods of economic decision-making—the market and government planning—compare?

In the last chapter, you were introduced to the economic approach. In this chapter, we discuss a few important tools that will help you develop the economic way of thinking.

WHAT SHALL WE GIVE UP?

Scarcity calls the tune in economics. We cannot have as much of everything as we would like. Most of us would like to have more time for leisure, recreation, vacations, hobbies, education, and skill development. We would also like to have more wealth, a larger savings account, and more consumable goods. However, all of these things either are scarce or require the use of scarce resources. They are in conflict with one another. We can have more leisure time if we sacrifice some wealth. We can increase our current consumption if we reduce our rate of saving. Choosing one requires us to give up something of the other.

OPPORTUNITY COST IS THE HIGHEST VALUED OPPORTUNITY LOST

An unpleasant fact of economics is that the choice to do one thing is, at the same time, a choice not to do something else. Your choice to spend time reading this book is a choice not to play tennis, go out on a date, listen to a math lecture, or attend a party. These things must be given up because of your decision to read. The highest valued alternative that must be sacrificed because one chooses an option is the **opportunity cost** of the choice.

Opportunity Cost: The highest valued benefit that must be sacrificed (forgone) as the result of choosing an alternative.

Note that the cost of an event is not the drudgery and undesirable aspects that may be associated with that event. The distinction between (a) the undesirable attributes of option A and (b) the highest valued opportunity forgone (option B) in order to realize option A, is fundamental because only option B is considered a cost by the economist.[2] Of course if option B is more pleasant, the opportunity cost of A is larger. Cost, in economics, has to do with comparing options, not with evaluating a single option by itself.

Costs are subjective. (So are benefits. After all, a cost is a sacrificed benefit!) A cost exists in the mind of the decision-maker. It is based on expectation—the expected value of the forgone alternative. Cost can never be directly measured by someone other than the decision-maker because only the decision-maker can place a value on what is given up.[3] In fact, this is one reason that voluntary trade is so critical in the creation of value, as we discussed in the last chapter. Only individuals are in a position to evaluate options for themselves, and to decide whether a possible trade is personally a good thing.

Cost, however, often has a monetary component that enables us to approximate its value. For example, the cost of attending a ballet is the highest valued opportunity lost due to: (a) the time necessary to attend and (b) the purchasing

[1]Robert A. Mundell, *Man and Economics: The Science of Choice* (New York: McGraw-Hill, 1968), p. 19.
[2]For an excellent in-depth discussion of this subject, see A. A. Alchian, "Cost," in *International Encyclopedia of the Social Sciences* (New York: Macmillan, 1969), 3:404–415.
[3]See James M. Buchanan, *Cost and Choice* (Chicago: Markham, 1969), for an analysis of the relationship between cost and choice.

power (that is, money) necessary to obtain a ticket. The monetary component is, of course, objective and can be measured. When nonmonetary considerations are relatively unimportant, the monetary component will approximate the total cost of an option.

OPPORTUNITY COST AND THE REAL WORLD

Is real-world decision-making influenced by opportunity cost? Remember, the basic economic postulate states that an option is more likely to be chosen when its cost to the decision-maker is less. So, economic theory does imply that differences (or changes) in opportunity cost will influence how decisions are made.

Some examples will demonstrate the real-world application of the opportunity cost concept. Poor people are more likely to travel long distances by bus, whereas the wealthy are more likely to travel by airplane. Why? A simple answer would be that the bus is cheaper; therefore, the poor will be more likely to purchase the cheaper good. But, is the bus cheaper for a relatively well-off individual whose opportunity cost of travel time is high? Suppose that a round-trip airline ticket from Kansas City to Denver costs $150, whereas a bus ticket costs only $110. The bus requires ten hours of travel time, however, and the airplane only two hours. Which would be cheaper? It depends on one's opportunity cost of time. If one's opportunity cost is evaluated at less than $5 per hour, the bus is cheaper, but if one's time is valued at more than $5 per hour, the airplane is clearly the cheaper option. Since the opportunity cost of the travel time will usually be greater for the wealthy than for the poor, the airplane is likely to be much cheaper for those with high incomes.

The concept of opportunity cost also helps us understand labor allocation and wage differences. Setting aside the nonmonetary aspects of a job for the moment, workers whose skills make them valuable to other employers will have to be paid enough to compensate them for what they could be making elsewhere—their highest valued employment alternatives. Thus, a filling station owner is unlikely to hire a physician to pump gas because the physician would have to be paid at least his or her opportunity cost—perhaps $100 per hour or more for delivering babies or performing surgery. Similarly, since the job opportunities forgone on other jobs will be greater for a skilled carpenter than for an unskilled worker, an employer must pay the skilled carpenter a higher wage. Skills and abilities, if they create more valuable alternatives, increase one's earning capability.

Elderly retirees watch considerably more television than high-income lawyers, accountants, and other professionals. Why? Is it because the elderly can better afford the money cost of a TV? Clearly, this is not the case. The time cost, though, is another matter. Consider the difference in the opportunity cost of time between the retirees and the professionals. In terms of lost earnings, watching television costs the professional a lot more than it costs the elderly. The professional watches less TV because it is an expensive good in terms of time.

Why do students watch less television and spend less time at the movies or on the beach during final exam week? Recreation is more costly then, that's why. Using valuable study time to go to the beach might well mean lower grades in several classes, although a student's grade in economics might be unaffected if he or she kept up during the semester and developed the economic way of thinking!

By now you should have the idea. Choosing one thing means giving up others that might have been chosen. Opportunity cost is the highest valued option sacrificed as the result of choosing an alternative.

TRADE CREATES VALUE

We learned in the last chapter that preferences are subjective, are known only to the individual, and differ among individuals. This means that merely trading— rearranging goods and services among people—can create value. In our Chapter 1 example, the value to Alice of a ticket to attend the Bolshoi ballet performance was zero once she received the party invitation, but the value to other individuals was greater. Suppose the value of the ticket to Jim, who bought it at the advertised price of $10, was $11. An unforeseen change in Alice's schedule had destroyed the value of the performance that evening for her, but trading (selling) the ticket to Jim created $10 in value for her, and it netted $1 in value for Jim—the $11 value he placed on the performance minus the $10 he gave to Alice. The performance remained the same, and the seats available remained the same, but value had been created just as surely as if an additional seat had been made available. *It is wrong to assume that a particular good or service has value just because it exists, independently of the circumstances and who uses it.*[4] As the example of the ballet ticket illustrates, the value of goods and services depends on who uses them, when they are used, and where they are used, as well as on their own physical characteristics.

TRANSACTION COSTS— A BARRIER TO TRADE

Unfortunately, Alice did not know about Andrew, another ballet fan, who would have been willing to pay $15 for the ticket. Andrew lives off campus and failed to see the bulletin board ad, so the potential for another $4 increase in value failed to materialize. A trade to achieve the additional value by putting the ticket into Andrew's hands was overlooked. Still, if Jim and Andrew happen to meet and talk about the ballet before the show, the additional $4 in value for the ticket could be created by another transaction: Jim trading the ticket to Andrew. Such a transaction is unlikely, though, because it would be costly to arrange by other than pure chance. Andrew would have to learn that Jim has the ticket, which seat and what performance the ticket is for, and finally, a price would have to be agreed on. Given the cost of acquiring the necessary information and conducting the trade, the potential exchange between Andrew and Jim will probably not take place.

While exchange creates value, it is also costly. The costs of the time, effort, and other resources necessary to search out, negotiate, and conclude an exchange are called **transaction costs.** Transaction costs reduce our ability to gain from mutually advantageous potential trades.

Transaction Costs: The time, effort, and other resources needed to search out, negotiate, and consummate an exchange.

Since exchange is costly, we should not expect all potentially valuable trades to take place, any more than we expect all useful knowledge to be learned, all safety measures to be taken, or all potential ''A'' grades to be earned. Frequent fliers know that if they never miss a flight, they are probably spending too much time waiting in airports. Similarly, the seller of a car, a house, or a ballet ticket

---

[4]An illuminating discussion of this, the ''physical fallacy,'' is found in Thomas Sowell, *Knowledge and Decisions* (New York: Basic Books, 1980), pp. 67–72.

OUTSTANDING ECONOMIST

**Thomas Sowell
(1930–   )**

Adam Smith and his colleagues called themselves political economists because they recognized that 'the wealth of nations," the prosperity of any economy, depends upon what happens in both the political and economic realms. But over the years, economics came to be separated from the study of political institutions. It also became concerned more with abstract logic, mathematics, and mechanical laws of behavior, and less with the principles underlying human interactions.

Thomas Sowell is one of the foremost economists who has revived the tradition of ''political economy.'' Like Smith before him, he recognizes the critical importance of the institutions—the ''rules of the game''—which shape human interactions. His book, *Knowledge and Decisions,* stresses the difficulty of obtaining knowledge, and the way different institutional arrangements provide different kinds and amounts of scarce information.

Knowledge and Decisions also introduces the concept of the ''physical fallacy''—the error that many people make when they assume that two physically identical objects must have the same value. People value things differently. An opera ticket may be worth $25 to one person, and nothing to another. Two physically identical items may differ in value for other reasons, too. The items may be in different locations in time or space. The Cuisinart on the department store shelf is worth more than one in a warehouse on the boat dock. By getting it to a place where the customer can easily see it and buy it, the distributor has added value to the product, even though the physical object itself is not changed.

Sowell points out that failure to understand the physical fallacy has been the cause of much misery. It has led people to be hostile toward ''middlemen''—people who add value by bringing goods (and knowledge) from the producer to the customer—largely because their contribution to the goods' value is not physical, and thus not easily seen.

Sowell's willingness to apply economic thinking to a wide array of human activities beyond traditional markets reflects the tradition at the University of Chicago, where he earned his Ph.D. in economics after receiving earlier degrees from Columbia and Harvard Universities. In 1980 he became a Senior Fellow at the Hoover Institution. In addition to a number of books on economics, he has published extensive studies of the effects of ethnic and racial discrimination in both the United States and other countries.

knows that to find that single person in the world who would be willing to pay the most money is not worth the enormous effort required to locate that buyer. The cost of perfection in exchange, as in other endeavors, is just too high.

THE MIDDLEMAN AS A COST REDUCER

Middleman: A person who buys and sells, or who arranges trades. A middleman reduces transaction costs, usually for a fee or a markup in price.

Since there are gains from exchange, some people specialize in providing information and arranging trades. Such a specialist is commonly called a **middleman.** Often, people believe that middlemen are unnecessary; that they simply add to the buyer's expense without benefitting the seller. Now that we recognize transactions costs, however, we can see the fallacy of this view. The auto dealer, for example, can help both the makers and the buyers of cars. By keeping an inventory of autos, and by hiring knowledgeable sales people, the dealer helps the car shopper learn about the many cars offered, and how each car looks, performs, and ''feels.'' (Don't forget that preferences are subjective; they are not objectively known to others.) Car buyers also like to know that the local dealer will honor the warranty, and provide parts and service for the car when they are needed. The car marker, by using the dealer as a middleman, is able to concentrate on designing and making cars, leaving to middlemen—dealers—the task of marketing and servicing them in each community.

Grocers are another provider of middleman services. Each of us could deal with food producers directly, buying in large quantities, perhaps shopping through catalogues to choose what we want. If we did, though, we wouldn't be able to squeeze the tomatoes! Besides, we would each need giant refrigerators, freezers, and storerooms at home to hold huge quantities of food. Or, perhaps we could form consumer cooperatives, banding together to eliminate the middleman, using our own warehouses and our own volunteer labor to order, receive, display, redistribute, and collect payment for the food. In fact, some cooperatives like this do exist, but most people prefer instead to hire the space, and do the planning, record keeping, and labor through the grocer, paying the usual markup for middleman services.

Stockbrokers, publishers of the yellow pages, and merchants of all sorts are middlemen—specialists in selling, guaranteeing, and servicing the items traded. For a fee, they reduce transaction costs both for the shopper and for the seller.

Transaction costs hinder the gain realized from trade; middlemen reduce transaction costs. Simply by making exchange cheaper and more convenient, middlemen cause more efficient trades to happen. In so doing, they themselves create value.

WHAT IS TRADED—PROPERTY RIGHTS

The buyer of an automobile or an apple may take the item home. The buyer of a steamship or an office building, though, might never touch it. When exchange occurs, it is really the rights—the **property rights**—to the item that change hands. It is ownership and control that count, rather than physical possession.

Property Rights: The right to use, control, and obtain the benefits from a good or service.

Private Property Rights: Property rights that are exclusively held by an owner, and that can be transferred to others at the owner's discretion.

Private property rights exist when property rights are (a) exclusively controlled by one owner and (b) transferable to others. Private ownership of property rights gives owners a chance to act selfishly. However, since they link responsibility to authority, they also make owners accountable for their actions.

1. *Private owners can gain by employing their resources in ways that are beneficial to others. On the other hand, owners bear the opportunity cost of ignoring the wishes of others.* If someone values an asset more than its current owner, the current owner can gain by paying heed to the wishes of others. For example, suppose Ed owns a car that others would also like to have. What incentive is there for Ed to pay attention to the desires of the others? If someone else values the car at $1,000, while Ed values it at only $800, then Ed can gain by selling the car at any price higher than $800. To turn down the offer of $1,000 costs Ed $200 more than the $800 the car is worth to him. In fact, if transaction costs are low (if search is cheap and easy), Ed might gain by searching for people (potential buyers) who want the car more than he does. If he fails to yield to the desires of others, Ed "pays" the opportunity cost for continued ownership of the

car by not receiving the $1,000. Failing to consider the wishes of others may penalize the potential buyer, but it would also hurt Ed. When potential buyers and sellers know that cars are privately owned and thus easily transferable, each has every incentive to search out mutually advantageous trades. After all, if they find such a trade, only the buyer and seller have to approve the deal, and both will gain.

As a second example, suppose Ed owns a house and will be out of town all summer. Will the house stay vacant, or will Ed let someone else use it during those months? We don't know, but we do know that Ed can rent the house to someone else if he chooses, and that if he does not, he will pay the opportunity cost—the rental payments he could get, minus any damages, added upkeep, and transaction costs. Ownership of the private property rights has again faced Ed with the opportunity costs of his actions, making him responsible for whether or not he grants the wishes of others regarding the use of his property.

2. *The private owner has a strong incentive to properly care for the item he or she owns.* Will Ed change the oil in his car? Will he take care to see that the seats do not get torn? Probably so, since not being careful about these things would reduce the car's value, both to him and to any future owner. The car and its value—the sale price if he sells it—belong just to Ed, so he would bear the burden of a fall in the car's value if the oil ran low and ruined the engine, or if the seats were torn. As the owner, Ed has both the authority and the incentive to protect the car against harm or neglect. Private property rights give the owner a strong incentive for good stewardship.

3. *The private owner has an incentive to conserve for the future, if the item is expected to be worth more then.* Suppose our man Ed owns a case of very good red wine, which is only two years old. Age will improve it substantially if he puts it in his cellar for another five years. Will he do so? Well, if he does not, he will personally bear the consequences. He (and presumably his friends) will drink wine sooner, but they will sacrifice quality. Also, Ed will forgo the chance to sell the wine later for much more than its current worth. The opportunity cost of drinking the wine now is its unavailability later. Ed bears that cost. Private property rights assure that Ed has the authority to preserve the wine, and that he gains the benefits if he does so. If the greater quality is expected to be worth the wait, then Ed can capture the benefits of not serving the wine "before its time."

In a similar way, if Ed owns land, or a house, or a factory, he has a strong incentive to bear costs now, if necessary, to preserve the asset's value. His wealth is tied up in its value, which reflects nothing more than the net benefits which will be available to the owner in the future. So Ed's wealth depends on his good stewardship.

4. *With private property rights, a negligent owner can be held accountable for damage to others through misuse of property.* Ed, the car owner, has a right to drive his car, but he has no right to drive in a drunken or reckless way that injures Alice. A chemical company has control over its products, but exactly for that reason, it is legally liable for damages if it mishandles the chemicals. Courts of law recognize and enforce the authority granted by ownership, but they also enforce the responsibility that goes with that authority. Once again, property rights hold accountable the person (owner) with authority over property.

These characteristics of property rights are very useful. When private property rights are not present or are not enforced, other methods must be found to provide

"Their house looks so nice. They must be getting ready to sell it."

Pepper . . . and Salt © The Wall Street Journal

the incentives for good stewardship of property, and for proper concern for others by the users of property. For example, when the owner of an automobile or a factory pollutes the air, and is not made to pay for damage done to the property of others, property rights are not being enforced. Without effective property rights, other measures may be necessary to control polluting behavior. We will return to this problem in Chapter 4.

Production Possibilities Curve: A curve that outlines all possible combinations of total output that could be produced, assuming (a) the utilization of a fixed amount of productive resources, (b) full and efficient use of those resources, and (c) a specific state of technical knowledge. The slope of the curve indicates the rate at which one product can be traded off to produce more of the other.

THE PRODUCTION POSSIBILITIES CURVE: SEPARATING THE POSSIBLE FROM THE IMPOSSIBLE

The resources of every individual are limited. Purposeful decision-making and economizing behavior imply that individuals seek to get the most from their limited resources. They do not deliberately waste resources.

The nature of the economizing problem can be made more clear by the use of a conceptual tool, the production possibilities diagram. A **production possibilities curve** reveals the maximum amount of any two products that can be produced from a fixed set of resources, and the possible tradeoffs in production between them.

Exhibit 1 illustrates the production possibilities curve for Susan, an intelligent economics major. This curve indicates the combinations of grades possible for two alternative amounts of study time—six hours and eight hours. If Susan uses her six hours of study time efficiently, she can choose any grade combination along the six-hour production possibilities curve. When her study time is limited to six hours per week, though, Susan is able to raise her grade in one of the subjects only by accepting a lower grade in the other. If she wants to improve her overall performance (raise at least one grade without lowering the other), she will have to spend more time on academic endeavors. For example, she might increase her weekly study time from six to eight hours. Of course, this would require her to give up something else—leisure.

EXHIBIT 1

The Production Possibilities Curve for Grades in English and Economics

The production possibilities for Susan, in terms of grades, are illustrated for two alternative quantities of total study time. If Susan studied six hours per week, she could attain (a) an F in English and an A in economics, (b) a D in English and a B in economics, (c) a C in both, (d) a B in English and a D in economics, or (e) an F in economics and an A in English.

Could she make higher grades in both? Yes, if she were willing to apply more resources, thereby giving up some leisure. The colored line indicates her production possibilities curve if she studied eight hours per week.

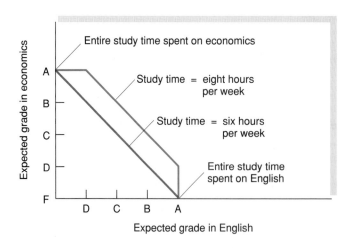

Can the production possibilities concept be applied to the entire economy? The answer is yes. Having more guns means having less butter, as the old saying goes. Beefing up the military requires the use of resources that otherwise could be used to produce nonmilitary goods. If scarce resources are being used efficiently, more of one thing means the sacrifice of others.

Exhibit 2 shows a production possibilities curve for an economy producing only two goods: food and clothing. The curve is concave or bowed out from the origin. Why? Resources are not equally well suited to produce food and clothing. Consider an economy that was using all of its resources to produce clothing. At that point (*S*), food production can be expanded by transferring those resources which are best suited for production of food (and least suitable for clothing production) from clothing to food production. Since the resources transferred are highly productive in food and not very productive in clothing, *in this range* the opportunity cost (clothing forgone) of additional food is low. However, as successively larger amounts of food are produced (moves from *S* to *A* to *B* and so on), the opportunity cost of food will rise. This results because as more and more food is produced, additional food output can be achieved only by using resources that are less and less suitable for the production of food. Thus, as food output is expanded, successively larger amounts of clothing must be forgone per unit of additional food.

What restricts the ability of an economy, once resources are fully utilized, from producing more of everything? The same thing that kept Susan from making a higher grade in both English and economics—lack of resources. There will be various maximum combinations of goods that an economy will be able to produce when:

1. it uses some fixed quantity of resources;
2. the resources are not unemployed or used inefficiently; and
3. the level of technology is constant.

When these three conditions are met, the economy will be at the perimeter of its production possibilities frontier (points such as *A*, *B*, and *C*, Exhibit 2). Pro-

EXHIBIT 2

The Concept of the Production Possibilities Curve for an Economy

When an economy is using its limited resources efficiently, production of more clothing requires the economy to give up some other goods—food in this simple example. *With time,* a technological discovery or expansion of the economy's resource base could make it possible to produce more of both, shifting the production possibilities curve outward. Or, the citizens of the economy might decide to give up some leisure for more of both goods. These factors aside, limited resources will constrain the production possibilities of an economy.

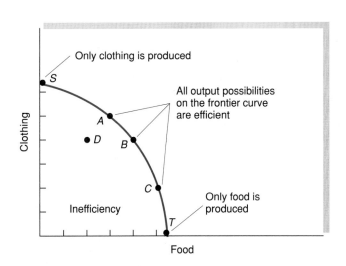

ducing more of one good, such as clothing, will necessitate less production of other goods (for example, food).

When the resources of an economy are unemployed or used inefficiently, the economy is operating at a point inside the production possibilities curve—point *D,* for example. Why might this happen? It happens because the economy is not properly solving the economizing problem. A major function of economics is to help us get the most out of available resources, to move us out to the production possibilities frontier. We will return to this problem again and again.

SHIFTING THE PRODUCTION POSSIBILITIES CURVE OUTWARD

Could an economy ever have more of all goods? Could the production possibilities curve be shifted outward? The answer is yes, under certain circumstances. There are three major methods.

1. An Increase in the Economy's Resource Base Would Expand Our Ability to Produce Goods and Services. If we had more and better resources, we could produce a greater amount of all goods. Many resources are human-made. If we were willing to give up some current consumption, we could invest more of today's resources into the production of long-lasting physical structures, machines, education, and the development of human skills. This **capital formation** would provide us with better tools and skills in the future and thereby increase our ability to produce goods and services. Exhibit 3 illustrates the link between capital formation and the future production possibilities of an economy. The two economies illustrated start with the same production possibilities curve (*RS*). However, since Economy A (Exhibit 3a) allocates more of its resources to investment than does Economy B, A's production possibilities curve shifts outward with the passage of time by a greater amount. The growth rate of A—the expansion rate of the economy's ability to produce goods—is enhanced because the economy allocates a larger share of its output to investment. Of course, more investment in machines and human skills will necessitate less current consumption.

Capital Formation: The production of buildings, machinery, tools, and other equipment that will enhance the ability to future economic participants to produce. The term can also be applied to efforts to upgrade the knowledge and skill of workers and thereby increase their ability to produce in the future.

EXHIBIT 3

Investment and Production Possibilities in the Future

Here we illustrate two economies that initially confront identical production possibilities curves (*RS*). The economy illustrated on the left allocates a larger share of its output to investment (I_a, compared to I_b for the economy on the right). As a result, the production possibilities of the high-investment economy will shift outward by a larger amount than will be true for the low-investment economy.

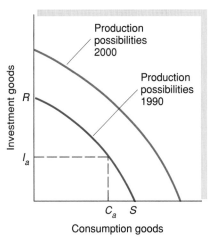

(a) Economy A, high investment

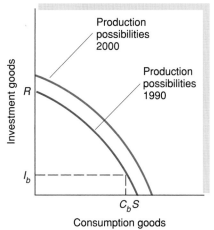

(b) Economy B, low investment

Technology: The body of skills and technological knowledge available at any given time. The level of technology establishes the relationship between inputs and the maximum output they can generate.

Invention: The discovery of a new product or process, often facilitated by the knowledge of engineering and scientific relationships.

Innovation: The successful introduction and adoption of a new product or process; the economic application of inventions.

Entrepreneur: A profit-seeking decision-maker who decides which projects to undertake and how they should be undertaken. A successful entrepreneur's actions will increase the value of resources.

2. Advancements in Technology Can Expand the Economy's Production Possibilities. **Technology** determines the maximum physical output obtainable from any particular set of resource inputs. New technology can make it possible to get more from our given base of resources.[5] An important form of technological change is **invention,** the use of science and engineering to discover new products or processes. Sending information instantly and cheaply by satellite, getting more oil from a well, and growing more corn from newly developed hybrid seed are all examples of technological advances resulting from inventions. Each one has pushed our production possibilities curve outward.

An economy can also benefit from technological change through **innovation,** the practical and effective adoption of new techniques. Such innovation is commonly carried out by an **entrepreneur**—one who seeks profit by introducing new or improved products at a low cost.[6] To prosper, an entrepreneur must convert and rearrange resources in a manner that will increase their value, thus expanding our production possibilities. Some examples will help us explain.

One entrepreneur, Henry Ford, changed car-making technology by pioneering the assembly line for making cars. With the same amount of labor and materials, Ford made more cars, more cheaply. Another entrepreneur, the late Ray Kroc, founded the McDonald's hamburger chain. In addition to a popular restaurant menu, he provided information to potential customers. By carefully designing a limited menu that could be prepared according to strict formulas, setting up a training school (Hamburger University, outside of Chicago) for managers, and providing for a regular inspection program, he could guarantee uniformity (known products and quality level) to each customer. Once the McDonald's reputation spread, hungry people knew what to expect at the "golden arches" without even having to enter the restaurant. Trying McDonald's in one location provides information on thousands of others. Nationwide franchises and quality control make it easy for McDonald's fans to find these quick, cheap meals. The same information makes it easy for those who dislike the formula to avoid it. In both cases, we benefit from Mr. Kroc's entrepreneurship—an innovative way to guarantee quality and to transmit instant information cheaply.

Another type of entrepreneur takes inventions produced by others and applies them more effectively. Steven Jobs, co-founder of the Apple Computer Corporation, is an example. He and his firm used the new computer technology to create personal- and small-business computers, and arranged for the "user friendly" software needed by most of us to use such machines. Selling the combination helped make computers useful to millions of people, both at home and on the job,

---

[5]Without modern technical knowledge, it would be impossible to produce the vast array of goods and services responsible for our standard of living. Thomas Sowell makes this point clear when he notes:

> *The cavemen had the same natural resources at their disposal as we have today, and the difference between their standard of living and ours is a difference between the knowledge they could bring to bear on those resources and the knowledge used today.*

See Thomas Sowell, *Knowledge and Decisions* (New York: Basic Books, 1980), p. 47.

[6]This French-origin word literally means "one who undertakes." The entrepreneur is the person who is ultimately responsible. Of course, this responsibility may be shared with others (partners or stockholders, for example) or it may be partially delegated to technical experts. Nevertheless, the success or failure of the entrepreneur is dependent on the outcome of the choices he or she makes.

and brought the new technology within their financial reach. Once again, entrepreneurship has expanded our production possibilities.

3. By Working Harder and Giving Up Current Leisure, We Could Increase Our Production of Goods and Services. Strictly speaking, this is not an expansion in the production frontier because leisure is also a good. We are giving up some of that good to have more of other things.

The work effort of individuals depends not only on their personal preferences but also on public policy. For example, high tax rates may induce individuals to reduce their work time. The basic economic postulate implies that as high tax rates reduce the personal payoff from working (and earning taxable income), individuals will shift more of their time to other, untaxed activities, including the consumption of leisure, moving the production possibilities curve for market goods inward. Any reduction in market work time not only reduces output directly, but it is likely also to reduce the gains from the division of labor. We turn now to look at why this is important.

DIVISION OF LABOR AND PRODUCTION POSSIBILITIES

Division of Labor: A method that breaks down the production of a commodity into a series of specific tasks, each performed by a different worker.

In a modern economy, individuals do not produce most of the items we consume. Instead, we sell our labor services (usually agreeing to do specified productive work) and use the income we get in exchange to buy what we want. We do this because the **division of labor**, together with exchange, allow us to produce far more goods and services through cooperative effort than we could if each household produced its own food, clothing, shelter, transportation, and other desired goods.

Observing the operation of a pin manufacturer more than 200 years ago, Adam Smith noted that specialization and division of labor permitted far more output. When each worker specialized in a productive function, ten workers were able to produce 48,000 pins per day, or 4,800 pins per worker. Without specialization and division of labor, Smith doubted an individual worker would have been able to produce as many as 20 pins per day.[7]

The division of labor separates production tasks into a series of related operations. Each worker performs a single task, only one of perhaps hundreds of tasks necessary to produce a commodity. There are several reasons why the division of labor often leads to enormous gains in output per worker. First, specialization permits individuals to take advantage of their existing abilities and skills. (Put another way, specialization permits an economy to take advantage of the fact that individuals have different skills.) Productive assignments can be undertaken by those individuals who are able to accomplish them most efficiently. Second, a worker who specializes in just one task (or one narrow area) becomes more experienced and more skilled in that task with the passage of time. Most importantly, the division of labor lets us adopt complex, large-scale production techniques unthinkable for an individual household. As our knowledge of technology and the potential of machinery expand, capital-intensive production procedures and the division of labor permit us to attain living standards undreamed of just a few decades ago.

---

[7]See Adam Smith, *An Inquiry into the Nature and Causes of the Wealth of Nations* (1776; Cannan's ed., Chicago: University of Chicago Press, 1976), pp. 7–16, for additional detail on the importance of the division of labor.

TRADE, COMPARATIVE ADVANTAGE, AND REALIZING OUR PRODUCTION POSSIBILITIES

Economizing means getting the most out of our available resources. How can this be accomplished? How can we reach our production possibilities frontier and get more value from our productive activities? To answer these questions, we must understand several important principles.

First, let us consider the economizing problem of Woodward and Mason, individuals in the construction business. Exhibit 4 presents certain facts about the abilities of Woodward and Mason. Woodward is highly skilled, fast, and reliable. During one month, Woodward can build either four frame houses or two brick houses. Mason is less skilled, and is slower than Woodward at building both kinds of houses. It takes Mason an entire month to build either a frame or a brick house.

Last year, Woodward spent 8 months producing 16 brick houses and the other 4 months producing 16 frame houses. Mason was able to produce only 6 frame and 6 brick houses during the year. Their joint output was 22 frame and 22 brick houses.

EXHIBIT 4 ■ Comparative Advantage and Increasing Output

The monthly production possibilities of Woodward and Mason are:

Frame Houses per Month		Brick houses per Month	
Woodward	Mason	Woodward	Mason
4	1	2	1

Initially each produced an equal quantity of both frame and brick houses. Annually, Woodward could produce 16 of each, and Mason only 6 of each. Thus, their total output could reach 22 frame and 22 brick units.

After each specialized in his area of greatest comparative advantage, Mason produced only brick houses, building 12 of them (one each month). Woodward spent 6 months building frame houses, and 6 months building brick houses, producing 24 frame (4 per month) and 12 brick units (2 per month). As the chart shows, after specialization, their total output of both frame houses and brick houses increased from 22 to 24.

If Mason trades 5 brick houses to Woodward for 7 frame houses, Woodward would end up with 17 brick and 17 frame houses, one more of each than he could achieve without specialization and trade. Similarly, Mason would be left with 7 brick and 7 frame (received in the trade with Woodward) houses. Specialization and exchange permit both parties to gain.

	Annual Output Before Specialization		Annual Output After Specialization	
	Frame Houses	Brick Houses	Frame Houses	Brick Houses
Woodward	16	16	24	12
Mason	6	6	0	12
Total	22	22	24	24

Since Woodward has an absolute advantage (Woodward can build both frame and brick houses more rapidly than Mason) in the production of houses, few observers would believe that Woodward and Mason could gain from specialization and trade of products. Potential gain, though, is clearly present. Suppose Mason specialized in the production of brick houses, while Woodward spent 6 months producing both types of house. Woodward could produce 24 frame houses (4 per month) in those 6 months, and 12 brick houses (2 per month) in another 6 months. After they became more specialized, Mason and Woodward could produce 24 frame houses (all by Woodward) and 24 brick houses (12 each) in the same 12-month period. Together, the builders would be better off. If 5 of Mason's 12 brick houses were traded to Woodward for 7 frame houses, then Mason would have 7 frame and 7 brick houses to show for his efforts, compared to last year's individual output rate of 6 frame and 6 brick. Similarly, upon receipt of the 5 brick houses from Mason in exchange for 7 frame ones, Woodward would also be left with 17 frame and 17 brick houses, definitely an improvement over last year's output of 16 frame and 16 brick. Thus, specialization and exchange could allow both Woodward and Mason to surpass last year's production rate.

Despite the fact that Woodward was better than Mason at producing both frame and brick houses, the two were able to gain from trade and specialization.[8] Was it magic? What is happening here? Our old friend, opportunity cost, will help us unravel this seemingly paradoxical result. In what sense is Woodward better at producing brick houses than Mason? True, in one month, Woodward can produce twice as many brick houses as Mason, but what is Woodward's opportunity cost of producing a brick house? Two frame ones, right? In the same time required to produce a single brick house, Woodward can produce two frame houses.

Consider Mason's opportunity cost of producing a brick house. It is only one frame house. So, who is the cheaper producer of brick houses? Mason is, because Mason's opportunity cost of producing a brick house is one frame house, compared to Woodward's opportunity cost of two frame houses.

The reason that Woodward and Mason could both gain is that their exchange allowed each of them to specialize in the production of the product that, comparatively speaking, they could produce most cheaply. Mason was the cheaper producer of brick houses. Woodward was the cheaper producer of the frame ones. They were able to economize—get more out of their resources—by trading and specializing in the thing that each did better, comparatively speaking.

This simple example demonstrates a basic truth known as the law of comparative advantage, which lies at the heart of economizing behavior for any economy. Initially developed in the early 1800s by the great English economist David Ricardo, the **law of comparative advantage** states that the total output of a group of individuals, an entire economy, or a group of nations will be greatest when the output of each good is produced by the person (or firm) with the lowest opportunity cost.

If a product, any product made, could be produced by someone else with a lower opportunity cost, the economy is giving up more than necessary. It is not

Law of Comparative Advantage: A principle that states that individuals, firms, regions, or nations can gain by specializing in the production of goods that they produce cheaply (that is, at a low opportunity cost) and exchanging those goods for other desired goods for which they are high opportunity cost producers.

[8]Throughout this section we will assume that individuals are equally content to produce either product. Dropping this assumption would add to the complexity of the analysis, but it would not change the basic principle.

economizing. Economizing, or economic efficiency, requires that output always be generated by the producer who has the lowest opportunity cost.

Perhaps one additional example will help to drive home the implications of the law of comparative advantage. Consider the situation of an attorney who can type 120 words per minute. The attorney is trying to decide whether or not to hire a secretary, who types only 60 words per minute, to complete some legal documents. If the lawyer does the typing job, it will take four hours; if a secretary is hired, the typing job will take eight hours. Thus, the lawyer has an absolute advantage in typing compared to the prospective employee. The attorney's time, though, is worth $50 per hour when working as a lawyer, whereas the typist's time is worth $5 per hour as a typist. Although a fast typist, the attorney is also a high opportunity cost producer of typing service. If the lawyer types the documents, the job will cost $200, which is the opportunity cost of four hours of lost time as a lawyer. Alternatively, if the typist is hired, the cost of having the documents typed is only $40 (eight hours of typing service at $5 per hour). The lawyer's comparative advantage thus lies in practicing law. The attorney will gain by hiring the typist and spending the additional time specializing in the practice of law.

DIVISION OF LABOR, SPECIALIZATION, AND EXCHANGE IN ACCORDANCE WITH THE LAW OF COMPARATIVE ADVANTAGE

It is difficult to exaggerate the gains derived from specialization, division of labor, and exchange in accordance with the law of comparative advantage. These factors are the primary source of our modern standard of living. Can you imagine the difficulty involved in producing one's own housing, clothing, and food, to say nothing of radios, television sets, dishwashers, automobiles, and telephone services? Yet, most families in North America, Western Europe, Japan, and Australia enjoy these conveniences. They are able to do so largely because their economies are organized in such a way that individuals can cooperate, specialize, and trade, thereby reaping the benefits of the enormous increases in output—both in quantity and diversity—thus produced. An economy not realizing the gains from specialization and division of labor is ignoring the law of comparative advantage. It is operating inside of its production possibilities curve, at a point such as *D* of Exhibit 2. This is the case for most of the less-developed economies. For various reasons, production in these economies is centered primarily in the individual household. Therefore, the output level per worker of these economies falls well below the attainable level.

When one stops to think about it, the law of comparative advantage is almost common sense. Stated in layman's terms, it simply means that if we want to accomplish a task with the least effort, each of us should specialize in that component of the task that we do best, comparatively speaking.

The principle of comparative advantage is universal. It is just as valid in socialist countries as it is in capitalist countries. Socialist planners, to get the most out of available resources, must also apply the principle of comparative advantage.

DEPENDENCE, SPECIALIZATION, AND EXCHANGE

Specialization and mutual dependence are directly related. If the United States specializes in the production of agricultural products and Middle East countries specialize in the production of oil, the two countries become interdependent. Similarly, if Texas specializes in the production of cotton and Kansas specializes in the production of wheat, interdependence results. In some cases, this dependence can have serious consequences for one or both of the parties. The potential costs of mutual dependence (for example, vulnerability to economic pressure applied by a trading partner who supplies an important economic good) and its potential benefits (for example, economic interaction that may well increase international understanding and reduce the likelihood of war) should be weighed along with the mutual consumption gains when one is evaluating the merits of specialization.

SPECIALIZATION AND WORKER ALIENATION

Specialization clearly makes it possible to produce more goods, but it may also result in many workers performing simple, boring, and monotonous functions. Our friend Woodward may get tired of building frame houses, and Mason's life may lose a certain zest because he produces only brick ones. On a more practical level, specialization often results in assembly-line production techniques. Workers

MYTHS OF ECONOMICS

"In exchange, when someone gains, someone else must lose."

People tend to think of making, building, and creating things as productive activities. Agriculture and manufacturing are like this. They create something genuinely new, something that was not there before. Trade, however, is only the exchange of one thing for another. Nothing is created. Therefore, it must be a zero-sum game in which one person's gain is necessarily a loss to another. So goes a popular myth.

A closer look at the motivation for trade helps one see through this myth. Mutual gain is the foundation for voluntary exchange. If the parties to the exchange do not anticipate that the trade will improve their well-being, they will not agree to it. Trade is productive because it increases the well-being of each trading partner.

There are three major reasons why trade is productive—why it is a positive-sum activity. First, it chan-

nels goods and services to those who value them most. People have fallen into the habit of thinking of material things as wealth, but material things are not wealth until they are in the hands of someone who values them. A highly technical mathematics book is not wealth to a longshoreman with a sixth-grade education. It becomes wealth only after it is in the hands of a mathematician. A master painting may be wealth to the collector of art, but it is of little value to the average cowboy. Wealth is created by the act of channeling goods to persons who value them highly.

Second, exchange can be advantageous to trading partners because it permits each to specialize in areas in which they have a comparative advantage. For example, exchange permits a skilled carpenter to concentrate on building house frames, while contracting for electrical and plumbing services from others who have comparative advantages in those areas.

Similarly, trade permits a country such as Canada to specialize in the production of wheat, while Brazil specializes in coffee. Such specialization enlarges joint output and permits both countries to gain from the exchange of Canadian wheat for Brazilian coffee.

Third, voluntary exchange makes it possible for individuals to produce more goods through cooperative effort. In the absence of exchange, productive activity would be limited to the individual household. Self-provision and small-scale production would be the rule. Voluntary exchange permits us to realize gains derived from the division of labor and the adoption of large-scale production methods. Production can be broken down into a series of specific operations. This procedure often leads to a more efficient application of both labor and machinery. Without voluntary exchanges, these gains would be lost.

may become quite skilled because they perform identical tasks over and over again, but they may also become bored if the work is personally unrewarding. Thus, strictly speaking, some of the gains associated with the expansion of physical output may result in worker dissatisfaction.

You may be thinking that economists consider only material goods and ignore the importance of human beings. It may seem that they do not care if a worker hates a job because it is repetitive, unchallenging, and boring. Our initial approach to the topic of specialization is vulnerable to this charge. We stressed only physical production because it makes the principle simpler to communicate. However, specialization could be considered strictly from the viewpoint of utility, in which both output and job satisfaction are economic goods.

An individual's opportunity cost of producing a good (or performing a service) includes the sacrifice of both physical production of other goods and any change in the desirability of working conditions. This approach considers both material goods for one's satisfaction and any difference in job satisfaction. It does not alter the basic principle. Individuals could still gain by producing and selling those things for which they have a comparatively low opportunity cost, including the job satisfaction component, while buying other things for which their opportunity cost is high. They would tend to specialize in the provision of those things they both do well and enjoy most. People with a strong aversion to monotonous work would be less likely to choose such work even though they might be skilled at it. Those with a smaller comparative advantage, measured strictly in terms of physical goods, might have a lower opportunity cost because they find the work more rewarding.

The consideration of working conditions and job preferences does not invalidate the basic concept. It is still true that maximum economic efficiency, in the utility sense, requires that each productive activity be performed by those persons with the lowest opportunity cost, including satisfaction given up by turning down other jobs.

PERSONAL MOTIVATION AND THE GAINS FROM SPECIALIZATION AND EXCHANGE

What motivates people to act? How does the purposeful decision-maker choose? Economic thinking implies that people will choose an option only if they expect the benefits (utility) of the choice to exceed its opportunity cost. Purposeful decision-makers will be motivated by the pursuit of personal gain. They will never knowingly choose an alternative when they expect the opportunity cost to exceed the benefits. To do so would be to make a choice with the full awareness that it meant the sacrifice of another, preferred course of action. That simply would not make sense. To say that people are motivated by personal gain does not, of course, mean that they are inconsiderate of others. Other people's feelings will often affect the personal benefit received by a decision-maker.

When an individual's interest, aptitudes, abilities, and skills make it possible to gain by exchanging low opportunity cost goods for those things that he or she could only produce at a high opportunity cost, pursuit of the potential gain will motivate the individual to trade precisely in this manner. If free exchange is allowed, it will not be necessary for people to be assigned the "right" job or to be told that, comparatively speaking, they should trade A for B because they are good at producing A but not so good at producing B. In a market setting, individuals will voluntarily specialize because they will gain by doing so. People following their own interests will produce and sell items for which they have a comparative advantage—items they can produce cheaply—and will buy those things that others can produce more cheaply.

THREE ECONOMIZING DECISIONS FACING ALL NATIONS: WHAT, HOW, AND FOR WHOM?

We have outlined several basic concepts that are important if one is to understand the economizing problem. In this section, we outline three general economizing questions that every economy, regardless of its institutions, must answer.

1. What Will Be Produced? We cannot produce as many goods as we desire. What goods should we produce and in what quantities? Should we produce more food and less clothing, more consumer durables and less clean air, more national defense and less leisure? Or, should we use up some of our productive resources, producing more consumer goods today even though it will mean fewer goods in the future? If our economy is operating efficiently (that is, on its production possibilities curve), the choice to produce more of one commodity will reduce our ability to produce others. Sometimes the impact may be more indirect. Production of some goods will not only require productive resources but may, as a by-product, reduce the actual availability of other goods. For example, production of warmer houses and more automobile travel may, as a by-product, increase air pollution, and thus reduce the availability of clean air (another desired good). Use of natural resources (water, minerals, trees, and so on) to produce some goods may simultaneously reduce the quality of our environment. Every economy must answer these and similar questions concerning what should be produced.

2. How Will Goods Be Produced? Usually, different combinations of productive resources can be used to produce a good. Education could be produced with less labor by the use of more television lectures, recording devices, and books. Wheat could be raised with less land and more fertilizer. Chairs could be constructed with more labor and fewer machines. What combinations of the alternative productive resources will be used to produce the goods of an economy?

The decision to produce does not accomplish the task. Resources must be organized and people must be motivated. How can the resources of an economy be transformed into the final output of goods and services? Economies may differ as to the combination of economic incentives, threats of force, and types of competitive behavior that are permissible, but all still face the problem of how their limited resources can be used to produce goods.

3. For Whom Will Goods Be Produced? Who will actually consume the available products? This economic question is often referred to as the distribution problem. Property rights for resources, including labor skills, might be established and resource owners might be permitted to sell their services to the highest bidder. Income from the sale of resource services would be used to bid for goods. Prices and resource ownership would be the determining factors of distribution. Alternatively, goods might be split on a strict per capita basis, with each person getting an equal share of the pie. Or, they might be divided according to the relative political influence of citizens, with larger shares going to those who are more persuasive and skillful than others at organizing and obtaining political power. They could be distributed according to need, with a dictator or an all-powerful, democratically elected legislature deciding the various "needs" of the citizens.

THE THREE DECISIONS ARE INTERRELATED

One thing is clear—these three questions are highly interrelated. How goods are distributed will exert considerable influence on the "voluntary" availability of productive resources, including human resources. The choice of what to produce will influence how resources are used. In reality, these three basic economic questions must be resolved simultaneously and all economies, whatever their other differences, must somehow answer them. There are many ways to set up the institutions—the "rules of the game"—by which an economy makes these decisions. Each will result in a different set of answers to the universal questions.

TWO METHODS OF MAKING DECISIONS—THE MARKET AND GOVERNMENT PLANNING

Market Mechanism: A method of organization that allows unregulated prices and the decentralized decisions of private property owners to resolve the basic economic problems of consumption, production, and distribution.

Collective Decision-making: The method of organization that relies on public-sector decision-making (voting, political bargaining, lobbying, and so on). It can be used to resolve the basic economic problems of an economy.

Capitalism: An economic system based on private ownership of productive resources and allocation of goods according to the signals provided by free markets.

Socialism: A system of economic organization in which (a) the ownership and control of the basic means of production rest with the state and (b) resource allocation is determined by centralized planning rather than by market forces.

Two prominent ways to organize economic activity are through the **market mechanism** and **collective decision-making.** Let us briefly consider each of these methods.

Private ownership, voluntary contracts (often these contracts are verbal), and reliance upon market prices are the distinguishing characteristics of markets, or capitalist economies as they are often called. Under market **capitalism,** people have private ownership rights to consumption goods, their labor, and productive assets.[9] Private parties are permitted to buy and sell ownership rights at mutually agreeable prices in unregulated markets. The role of government is limited to that of a referee—a neutral party enforcing the rules of the game. The government defines and protects private ownership rights, enforces contracts, and protects people from fraud. But the government is not an active player; the political process will not be used to modify market outcomes or favor some at the expense of others. The government will not prevent a seller from using price reductions and quality improvements to compete with other sellers. Nor will the government prevent a buyer from using a higher price to bid a product or productive resource away from another potential buyer. Legal restraints (for example, government licensing) will not be used to limit potential buyers or sellers from producing, selling, or buying in the marketplace. Under market organization, planning by a central authority is absent. The three basic economic questions are answered through the market coordination of the decentralized choices of buyers and sellers.

The major alternative to market organization is the *collective decision-making process,* the use of political organization and government planning to allocate resources. In some cases, the government may own the income-producing assets (machines, buildings, and land) and directly determine what goods they will be used to produce. This form of economic organization is referred to as **socialism.** Alternatively, the government may maintain private ownership in name, but use taxes, subsidies, and regulations to answer the basic economic questions. In both

---

[9]Capitalism is a term coined by Karl Marx.

instances, political powers rather than market forces are used to direct the economy. In both cases, the decision to expand or contract the output of education, medical services, automobiles, electricity, steel, consumer durables, and thousands of other commodities is made by government officials and planning boards. This is not to say that the preferences of individuals are of no importance. If the government officials and central planners are influenced by the democratic process, they have to consider how their actions will influence their election prospects. If they do not, like the firm that produces a product consumers do not want, their tenure of service is likely to be a short one.

In most economies, including that of the United States, a large number of decisions are made both through the decentralized pricing system and through public-sector decision-making. Both exert considerable influence on how we solve fundamental economic problems. Although the two arrangements are different, in each case the choices of individuals acting as decision-makers are important. Economics is about how people make decisions; the tools of economics can be applied to both market- and public-sector action. Constraints on the individual and incentives to pursue various types of activities will differ according to whether decisions are made in the public sector or in the marketplace. Still, people are people; changes in personal costs and benefits will influence their choices. In turn, the acts of political participants—voters, lobbyists, and politicians—will influence public policy and its economic consequences.

LOOKING AHEAD

The next chapter presents an overview of the market sector. Chapter 4 focuses on how the public sector, the democratic collective decision-making process, functions. It is not enough merely to study how the pricing system works. To understand the forces influencing the allocation of economic resources in a country such as the United States, we must apply the tools of economics to both market- and public-sector choices.

We think this approach is important, fruitful, and exciting. How does the market sector really work? What does economics say about which activities should be handled by government? What types of economic policies are politically attractive to democratically elected officials? Is sound economic policy sometimes in conflict with good politics? We will tackle all these questions.

CHAPTER SUMMARY

1. Because of scarcity, when an individual chooses to do, to make, or to buy something, that individual must simultaneously give up something else that might otherwise have been chosen. The highest valued activity sacrificed is the opportunity cost of the choice.

2. Trade is productive. Voluntary exchange creates value by channeling goods into the hands of people who value them most. Recognition of this fact exposes the physical fallacy, which incorrectly assumes that a good or a service has a given value, regardless of who uses it and how it is used. Trade is a positive-sum game that improves the economic well-being of each voluntary participant.

3. The production possibilities curve reveals the maximum combination of any two products that can be produced with a fixed quantity of resources, assuming that the level of technology is constant. When an individual or an economy is operating at maximum efficiency, the combination of output chosen will be on the production possibilities curve. In such cases, greater production of one good will necessitate a reduction in the output of other goods.

4. The production possibilities curve of an economy can be shifted outward by (a) current investment that expands the future resource base of the economy, (b) technological advancement, and (c) the forgoing of leisure and an increase in work effort. The last factor indicates that the production possibilities constraint is not strictly fixed, even during the current time period. It is partly a matter of preference.

5. Production can often be expanded through division of labor and cooperative effort among individuals. With division of labor, production of a commodity can be broken down into a series of specific tasks. Specialization and division of labor often lead to an expansion in output per worker because they (a) permit productive tasks to be undertaken by the individuals who can accomplish those tasks most efficiently, (b) lead to improvement in worker efficiency as specific tasks are performed numerous times, and (c) facilitate the efficient applications of machinery and advanced technology to the production process.

6. Joint output of individuals, regions, or nations will be maximized when goods are exchanged between parties in accordance with the law of comparative advantage. This law states that total output is maximized when parties specialize in the production of goods for which they are low opportunity cost producers and exchange these for goods for which they are high opportunity cost producers. Pursuit of personal gain will motivate people to specialize in those things they do best (that is, for which they are low opportunity cost producers) and sell their products or services for goods for which they are high opportunity cost producers.

7. Every economy must answer three basic questions: (a) What will be produced? (b) How will goods be produced? (c) How will the goods be distributed? These three questions are highly interrelated.

8. There are two basic methods of making economic decisions: The market mechanism and public-sector decision-making. The decisions of individuals will influence the result in both cases. The tools of economics are general. They are applicable to choices that influence both market- and public-sector decisions.

CRITICAL ANALYSIS QUESTIONS

1. If Jones trades $2,000 to Smith for a used car, the items exchanged must be of equal value. (True, false, or uncertain.)

*2. Economists often argue that wage rates reflect productivity. Yet, the wages of housepainters have increased nearly as rapidly as the national average, even though these workers use approximately the same methods that were applied 50 years ago. Can you explain why the wages of painters have risen substantially even though their productivity has changed so little?

3. It takes one hour to travel from New York City to Washington, D.C., by air, but it takes five hours by bus. If the air fare is $55 and the bus fare $35, which would be cheaper for someone whose opportunity cost of travel time is $3 per hour? for someone whose opportunity cost is $5 per hour? $7 per hour?

4. Explain why the percentage of college-educated women employed outside the home exceeds the percentage of women with eight years of schooling who are engaged in outside employment.

5. Explain why parking lots in downtown areas of large cities often have several decks, whereas many of equal size in suburban areas cover only the ground level.

*6. "People in business get ahead by exploiting the needs of their consumers. The gains of business are at the expense of suffering imposed on their customers." (Statement from the producer of a prime-time television program.) Evaluate this statement.

*Asterisk denotes questions for which answers are given in Appendix C, Selected Answers.

7. (a) Do you think that your work effort is influenced by whether or not there is a close link between personal output and personal compensation (reward)? Explain.

   (b) Suppose the grades in your class were going to be determined by a random draw at the end of the course. How would this influence your study habits?

   (c) How would your study habits be influenced if everyone in the class were going to be given an A grade? if grades were based entirely on examinations composed of the multiple-choice questions in the *Coursebook* for this textbook?

   (d) Do you think the total output of goods in the United States is affected by the close link between productive contribution and individual reward? Why or why not?

8. In many states, the resale of tickets to sporting events at prices above the original purchase price ("ticket scalping") is prohibited. Who is helped and who is hurt by such prohibitions? Can you think of ways ticket owners who want to sell might get around the prohibition? Do you think it would be a good idea to extend the resale prohibition to other things—automobiles, books, works of art, or stock shares, for example? Why or why not?

*9. Does a 60-year-old tree farmer have an incentive to plant and care for Douglas fir trees which will not reach optimal cutting size for another 50 years?

*10. What forms of competition does a private property, market-directed economy authorize? What forms does it prohibit?

11. With regard to the use of resources, what is the objective of the entrepreneur? What is the major function of the middleman? Is the middleman an entrepreneur?

*12. Do private property rights permit owners to use their property selfishly to the detriment of others? Do private property rights protect owners against the selfishness of others? Explain.

13. "The rancher, who owns his grazing land, may over-graze it (let the cattle eat so much of the grass that erosion ruins the land) if he is desperate to make money now. Private ownership of land is dangerous." Evaluate.

*14. "Really good agricultural land should not be developed for housing. Food is far more important." Evaluate.

3

SUPPLY, DEMAND, AND THE MARKET PROCESS

I am convinced that if it [the market system] were the result of deliberate human design, and if the people guided by the price changes understood that their decisions have significance far beyond their immediate aim, this mechanism would have been acclaimed as one of the greatest triumphs of the human mind.[1]

Nobel Laureate
Friedrich Hayek

CHAPTER FOCUS

- What do economists mean when they talk about the laws of supply and demand?

- How do market prices respond to changes in supply and demand?

- As buyers and sellers respond to changes in supply and demand, what role does time play in the adjustment process?

- Why are waiting lines, "sold out" signs, and huge inventories seldom observed in market economies? What is the invisible hand?

- What happens when prices are fixed above or below the market level?

Consider the awesome task of coordinating the economic activity of the United States, a nation with 246,000,000 people and more than 64,000,000 families. The labor force is composed of approximately 120,000,000 workers, each possessing various skills and job preferences. There are about 18,000,000 business firms, which currently produce a vast array of products ranging from hairpins to jumbo jets.

How can the actions of these economic participants be coordinated in a sensible manner? How do producers know how much of each good to produce? What keeps them from producing too many ballpoint pens and too few bicycles with reflector lights? Who directs each labor force participant to the job that best fits his or her skills and preferences? How can we be sure that business firms will choose the correct production methods? In this chapter, we analyze how a market-directed pricing system answers these questions.

In the ideal market economy, no individual or planning board tells the participants what to do. Markets are free, some would say competitive, in the sense that there are no legal restrictions limiting the entry of either buyers or sellers. The economic role of government is limited to defining property rights, enforcing contracts, protecting people from fraud, and similar activities that establish the rules of the game. Although centralized planning is absent, the participants are not without direction. As we shall see, the decentralized decision-making of market participants provides direction and leads to economic order.

In the real world, even economies that are strongly market-oriented, such as the United States economy, use a combination of market- and public-sector answers to the basic economic questions. In all economies, the institutions provide a mixture of market-sector and government allocation. Nevertheless, it is still quite useful to understand how a free-market pricing system functions, how it motivates people, and how it allocates goods and resources.

SCARCITY NECESSITATES RATIONING

Rationing: An allocation of a limited supply of a good or resource to users who would like to have more of it. Various criteria, including charging a price, can be utilized to allocate the limited supply. When price performs the rationing function, the good or resource is allocated to those willing to give up the most "other things" in order to obtain ownership rights.

When a good (or resource) is scarce, some criterion must be set up for deciding who will receive the good (or resource) and who will do without it. Scarcity makes **rationing** a necessity.

There are several possible criteria that could be used in rationing a limited amount of a good among citizens who would like to have more of it. If the criterion were first-come, first-served, goods would be allocated to those who were fastest at getting in line or to those who were most willing to wait in line. If beauty were used, goods would be allocated to those who were thought to be most beautiful. The political process might be used, and goods would be allocated on the basis of political status and ability to manipulate the political process to personal advantage. One thing is certain: Scarcity means that methods must be established to decide who gets the limited amount of available goods and resources.

[1]Friedrich Hayek, "The Use of Knowledge in Society," *American Economic Review* 35, (September, 1945), pp. 519–530.

COMPETITION IS THE RESULT OF SCARCITY

Competition is not unique to a market system. Rather, it is a natural outgrowth of scarcity and the desire of human beings to improve their conditions. Competition exists both in capitalist and in socialist societies. It exists both when goods are allocated by price and when they are allocated by other means—collective decision-making, for example.

Certainly the rationing criterion will influence which competitive techniques will be used. When the rationing criterion is price, individuals will engage in income-generating activities that enhance their ability to pay the price. The market system encourages individuals to provide services to others in exchange for income. In turn, the income will permit them to procure more of the scarce goods.

A different rationing criterion will encourage other types of behavior. When the appearance of sincerity, broad knowledge, fairness, good judgment, and a positive TV image are important, as they are in the rationing of elected political positions, people will use resources to project these qualities. They will hire makeup artists, public relations experts, and advertising agencies to help them compete. We can change the form of competition, but no society has been able to eliminate it, because no society has been able to eliminate scarcity and the resulting necessity of rationing. When people who want more scarce goods seek to meet the criteria established to ration those goods, competition occurs.

The market is one method of producing and rationing scarce goods and resources. Let us investigate how it works.

CONSUMER CHOICE AND THE LAW OF DEMAND

Since our desire for goods is generally far greater than the purchasing power of our income, we have to make choices. How do consumers decide which things to buy and which things to forgo? Economizing behavior suggests that to get the most satisfaction from spending their money, rational consumers will buy the things from which they expect the most satisfaction per dollar spent. Given personal tastes, they will choose the best alternatives that their limited incomes will permit. Prices influence consumer decisions. An increase in the price of a good will increase a consumer's opportunity cost of consuming it. More of other things must be given up if the consumer chooses the higher-priced commodity.

According to a basic postulate of economics, an increase in the cost of an alternative will reduce the likelihood that it will be chosen. This basic postulate implies that higher prices will discourage consumption. Lower prices will reduce the cost of choosing a good, stimulating consumption of it. This inverse relationship between the price of a good and the amount of it that consumers choose to buy is called the **law of demand.**

Law of Demand: A principle that states that there is an inverse relationship between the price of a good and the amount of it buyers are willing to purchase.

The availability of substitutes—goods that perform similar functions—helps to explain the logic of the law of demand. No single good is absolutely essential. Margarine can be substituted for butter. Wood, aluminum, bricks, and glass can take the place of steel. Car pools, slower driving, bicycling, and smaller cars are substitutes for gasoline, allowing households to reduce their gas consumption. When the price (and therefore the consumer's opportunity cost) of a good in-

The Law of Demand

As the price of VCRs fell during 1979–1986, consumers purchased more of them. The consumption level of VCRs (and other products) is inversely related to their price.

Source: *Statistical Abstract of the United States, 1988* (p. 730) and *1985* (p. 777).

creases, people have a greater incentive to turn to substitute products and economize on their use of the more expensive good. Prices really do matter.

Exhibit 1 is a graphic presentation of the law of demand. Looking at what happened, we will assume that the price changes that occurred resulted from decreasing costs facing suppliers, and that consumers did not change their desire for video cassette recorders (VCRs) during this period. This allows us to estimate the influence of price on quantity demanded by constructing a demand curve. To do so, economists measure price on the vertical or *y*-axis, and the amount demanded on the horizontal or *x*-axis. The demand curve will slope downward to the right, indicating in this case that the number of VCRs demanded will increase as price declines. During 1979–1986, the price of VCRs fell sharply. Consumers happily responded by purchasing more of them. In 1979, when the average price of a VCR was $1,362 (in 1986 dollars), manufacturers sold less than half a million (478,000) of them. But costs dropped, and the price fell steadily. By 1983 the average VCR sold for only $630. In fact this reduction in average price understates the price drop, since quality and features also were improving at the same time. Sales climbed and by 1983 reached 4,020,000 units. The downward fall of price continued, and at the 1986 price of just under $400, people were watching a lot of movies at home! VCR sales in 1986 were 12,685,000. People are willing to use far more VCRs when the cost of doing so declines.

Some commodities are much more responsive to change in price than others. Consider a good for which there are several viable substitutes—a Florida vacation. If the price of a Florida vacation increases, perhaps because of higher air fares, consumers will substitute more movies, local camping trips, baseball games, TV programs, and other recreational activities for the Florida vacation. Exhibit 2 il-

EXHIBIT 2

Responsiveness of Demand to a Price Change

A 15 percent increase in the price of Florida vacations (D_1) caused the quantity demanded to decline from Q_0 to Q_1, a 50 percent reduction. In contrast, a 15 percent increase in the price of physician services (D_2) resulted in only a 5 percent reduction in quantity demanded (from Q_0 to O_2).

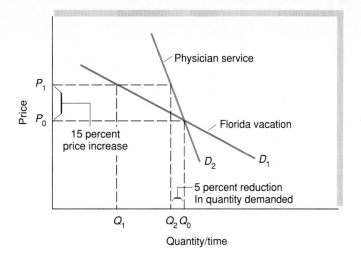

lustrates that, since good substitutes are available, an increase in the price of Florida vacations will cause a sharp reduction in quantity demanded. The quantity of Florida vacations demanded is quite responsive to a change in price.[2]

Other goods may be much less responsive to a change in price. Suppose the price of physician services were to rise 15 percent, as indicated by Exhibit 2. What impact would this price increase have on the quantity demanded? The higher prices would cause some people to prescribe their own medications for colds, flu, and minor illnesses. Others might turn to painkillers, magic potions, and faith healers for even major medical problems. Most consumers, though, would consider these to be poor substitutes for the services of a physician. Thus, higher medical prices would cause a relatively small reduction in the quantity demanded. The amount of physician services demanded is relatively unresponsive to a change in price.

However, despite differences in the degree of responsiveness, the fundamental law of demand holds for all goods. A price increase will induce consumers to turn to substitutes, leading to a reduction in the amount purchased. In contrast, a price reduction will make a commodity relatively cheaper, inducing consumers to purchase more of it as they substitute it for other goods.

The demand schedule is not something that can be observed directly by decision-makers of a business firm or planning agency. Nevertheless, when prices are used to ration goods, consumer reactions to each price communicate information about the preferences of consumers—how they value alternative commodities. The height of the unseen demand curve indicates the maximum price that consumers are willing to pay for *an additional unit* of the product. If consumers value *additional units* of a product highly, they will be willing to pay a large amount (a high price) for it. On the other hand, if their valuation of *additional units* of the good is low, they will be willing to pay only a small amount for it.

---

[2]The technical term for price responsiveness is elasticity. For those in a microeconomics course, this concept will be explored in the chapter on demand and consumer choice.

NEEDS AND WANTS VERSUS DEMAND

When discussing purchasing decisions, noneconomists often speak of what they "need" or "want." For example, people say: "I need a new pair of shoes" or "I want to see the movie." Two points should be recognized with regard to the relationship between (a) needs and wants and (b) demand. First, there are no critical needs, minimum requirements, or absolute necessities in the sense that one must have some fixed amount of a good or service, regardless of its price. We live in a world of substitutes. There are alternative ways of satisfying needs. Therefore, the amount needed, or more precisely, the amount demanded, is very much dependent upon price. The vertical demand curve (indicating that a fixed amount will be purchased regardless of price) is a myth. Second, just because one needs or wants a good, it does not follow that he or she should purchase (demand) it. Needs and wants are unlimited. There are literally millions of goods or services that each of us would like to have more of. The authors want ("need") backyard tennis courts, vacations in the Far East, and summer homes in the mountains, but we have not purchased any of them. Why? Because, given the restrictions imposed by our finite incomes and limited time, our desire for other goods is even greater.

We live in a world of scarcity that restricts our consumption possibilities. Therefore, we must choose to forgo many needs and wants so that we will have the resources to satisfy other needs that are even more urgent. Demand is important precisely because it provides information about the preferences of people—how much they value alternative scarce goods. After all, the choice of a consumer to purchase a good reveals that he or she values (needs or wants) that good more than other needs and wants which must now remain unfulfilled as the result of the purchase.

PRODUCER CHOICE AND THE LAW OF SUPPLY

How does the market process determine the amount of each good that will be produced? We cannot answer this question unless we understand the factors that influence the choices of those who supply goods. Producers of goods and services, often using the business firm:

1. organize productive inputs, such as labor, land, natural resources, and intermediate goods;
2. transform and combine these factors of production into goods desired by households; and
3. sell the final products to consumers for a price.

Profit: An excess of sales revenue relative to the cost of production. The cost component includes the opportunity cost of all resources, including those owned by the firm. Therefore, profit accrues only when the value of the good produced is greater than the sum of the values of the individual resources utilized.

Production involves the conversion of resources into commodities and services. Producers have to pay the owners of scarce resources a price that is at least equal to what the resources could earn elsewhere. Stated another way, each resource employed has to be bid away from all other uses; its owner will have to be paid its opportunity cost. The sum of the amounts paid by the producer for each productive resource, including the cost of production coordination and management, will equal the product's opportunity cost. That cost represents the value of those things given up by society to produce the product.

All economic participants have a strong incentive to undertake activities that generate profit. **Profit** is a residual "income reward" earned by decision-makers who produce a good or service that is valued more highly than the resources that were required for its production. It is what is left over after all costs have been paid. If an activity is to be profitable, the revenue derived from the sale of the product must exceed the cost of employing the resources that have been diverted from other uses to make the product. Sometimes decision-makers use resources unwisely. They divert resources to production of an output that consumers value less than the opportunity cost of the resources used. Losses result, since the sales revenue derived from the project is insufficient to pay the opportunity cost of the resources.

Loss: Deficit of sales revenue relative to the cost of production, once all the resources used have received their opportunity cost. Losses are a penalty imposed on those who use resources in lower, rather than higher, valued uses as judged by buyers in the market.

Losses discipline even the largest of firms. For example, in January of 1984, IBM introduced a small personal computer, the PC Jr. The company expected it to be profitable, but 15 months later, it announced that it would quit making the machines. Of IBM's $46 billion in 1984 revenue, only $150 million was accounted for by the PC Jr. Even a $40 million Christmas advertising campaign did not help. IBM could not sell enough units at a price high enough to cover its opportunity costs. So, "Big Blue," as the firm is called, threw in the towel, announcing in March of 1985 that the line had been discontinued.

Also in 1985, the Coca-Cola Company announced its carefully planned multimillion-dollar strategy to replace its main product, Coca-Cola, with "New Coke," which had a slightly different taste. There was a lukewarm reception to the new product and an insistent demand by fans of the "old Coke" to reverse the action. Within the year, the company had reversed itself and reintroduced the older product, calling it "Coke Classic" to be sold alongside New Coke. The market had once again disciplined a giant company, despite its huge advertising campaign to sell what it had thought would be a more popular product. The company had made a mistake, but was smart enough to correct it quickly in the face of strong consumer demand.

As we learned in the last chapter, entrepreneurs undertake production organization, deciding what to produce and how to produce it. The business of the entrepreneur is to figure out which projects will, in fact, be profitable. Since the profitability of a project will be affected by the price consumers are willing to pay for a product, the price of resources required to produce it, and the cost of alternative production processes, successful entrepreneurs must either be knowledgeable in each of these areas or obtain the advice of others who have such knowledge.

To prosper, entrepreneurs must convert and rearrange resources in a manner that will increase their value. An individual who purchases 100 acres of raw land, puts in a street and a sewage disposal system, divides the plot into one-acre lots, and sells them for 50 percent more than the opportunity cost of all resources used is clearly an entrepreneur. This entrepreneur "profits" because the value of the resources has been increased. Sometimes entrepreneurial activity is less complex. For example, a 15-year-old who purchases a power mower and sells lawn service to the neighbors is also an entrepreneur seeking to profit by increasing the value of resources. In a market economy, profit is the reward to the entrepreneur who discovers and acts upon an opportunity to produce a good or service that is valued more highly than the resources required for its production. It also provides an incentive for rival entrepreneurs to enter the market.

How will producer-entrepreneurs respond to a change in product price? Other things constant, a higher price will increase the producer's incentive to supply the good. New entrepreneurs, seeking personal gain, will enter the market and begin supplying the product. Established producers will expand the scale of their operations, leading to an additional expansion in output. Higher prices will induce producers to supply a greater amount. The direct relationship between the price of a product and the amount of it that will be supplied is termed the **law of supply.**

Law of Supply: A principle that states that there will be a direct relationship between the price of a good and the amount of it offered for sale.

Exhibit 3 presents a graphic picture of this law. The supply curve summarizes information about production conditions. Unless the profit-seeking producer receives a price that is at least equal to the opportunity cost of the resources employed, the producer will not continue to supply the good. The height of the supply curve indicates both (a) the minimum price necessary to induce producers to supply a specific quantity and (b) the valuation of the resources used in the production of the marginal unit of the good. This minimum supply price will be high (low) if the opportunity cost of supplying the marginal unit is high (low).

MARKETS COORDINATE SUPPLY AND DEMAND ACTIVITIES

Market: An abstract concept that encompasses the trading arrangements of buyers and sellers that underlie the forces of supply and demand.

Consumer-buyers and producer-sellers make decisions independent of each other, but markets coordinate their choices and influence their actions. To the economist, a market is not a physical location. A **market** is an abstract concept that encompasses the forces generated by the buying and selling decisions of economic participants. A market may be quite narrow (for example, the market for razor blades). Alternatively, it is sometimes useful to aggregate diverse goods into a single market, such as the market for ''consumer goods.'' There is also a broad range of sophistication among markets. The New York Stock Exchange is a highly computerized market in which buyers and sellers who never formally meet exchange each weekday shares of corporate ownership worth billions of dollars. In contrast, the neighborhood market for lawn-mowing services may be highly informal, since it brings together buyers and sellers primarily by word of mouth.

Equilibrium: A state of balance between conflicting forces, such as supply and demand.

Equilibrium is a state in which conflicting forces are in perfect balance. When there is a balance—an equilibrium—the tendency for change is absent.

EXHIBIT 3
The Supply Curve

As the price of a product increases, *other things constant,* producers will increase the amount of the product supplied.

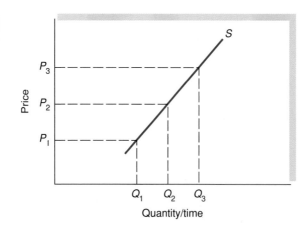

Before a market equilibrium can be attained, the decisions of consumers and producers must be coordinated. Their buying and selling activities must be brought into harmony with one another.

SHORT-RUN MARKET EQUILIBRIUM

Short-Run: A time period of insufficient length to permit decision-makers to adjust fully to a change in market conditions. For example, in the short-run, producers will have time to increase output by using more labor and raw materials, but they will not have time to expand the size of their plants or to install additional heavy equipment.

The great English economist Alfred Marshall pioneered the development of supply and demand analysis. From the beginning, Marshall recognized that time plays a role in the market process. Marshall introduced the concept of the **short run**, a time period of such short duration that decision-makers do not have time to adjust fully to a change in market conditions. During the short run, producers are able to alter the amount of a good supplied only by using more (or less) labor and raw materials with their existing plant and heavy equipment. In the short run, there is insufficient time to build a new plant or to obtain new "made-to-order" heavy equipment for the producer's current facility.

As Exhibit 1 illustrates, the amount of a good demanded by consumers will be inversely related to its price. On the other hand, a higher price will induce producers to use their existing facilities more intensively in the short run. As Exhibit 3 depicts, the amount of a good supplied will be directly related to its market price.

The market price of a commodity will tend to change in a direction that will bring the rate at which consumers want to buy into balance with the rate at which producers want to sell. This means that unless the quantity supplied by producers is already precisely equal to the quantity demanded by consumers, there will be a tendency for the market price to rise or fall until a balance is reached.

Exhibit 4 illustrates both supply and demand curves in the short run for a hypothetical commodity—smoos. At a high price, $12 for example, smoo producers will plan to supply 600 units per month, whereas consumers will choose to purchase only 450. An excess supply of 150 units will result. Production exceeds sales, so inventories of smoo producers will rise. To reduce undesired inventories, some smoo producers will increase their sales by cutting their price. Other firms will have to lower their price also, or sell even fewer smoos. The lower price will make smoo production less attractive to producers. Some of the marginal producers will go out of business, and others will reduce their current output. How low will the smoo price go? When the price has declined to $10, the quantity supplied by producers and the quantity demanded by consumers will be in balance at 550 units per month. At this price ($10), coordination of buyer and seller desires is achieved. The production plans of producers are in harmony with the purchasing plans of consumers.

What will happen if the price of smoos is low—$8, for example? The amount demanded by consumers (650 units) will exceed the amount supplied by producers (500 units). An excess demand of 150 units will be present. Some consumers who are unable to purchase smoos at $8 per unit because of the inadequate supply would be willing to pay a higher price. Recognizing this fact, producers will raise their price. As the price increases to $10, producers will expand their output and consumers will cut down on their consumption. At the $10 price, short-run equilibrium will be restored.

LOCAL, NATIONAL, AND WORLD MARKETS

Consider a typical breakfast of an American consumer. It is likely to include coffee from Brazil, bananas from Honduras, jelly from Switzerland, and strawberries, apples, and milk produced by farmers hundreds, if not thousands, of miles

EXHIBIT 4

Supply and Demand

The table below indicates the supply and demand conditions for smoos. These conditions are also illustrated by the graph on the right. When the price exceeds $10, an excess supply is present, which places downward pressure on price. In contrast, when the price is less than $10, an excess demand results, which causes the price to rise. Thus, the market price will tend toward $10, at which point supply and demand will be in balance.

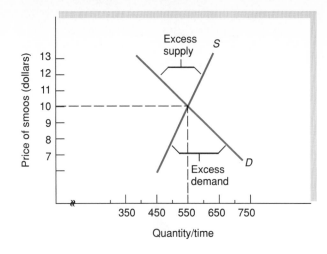

Price of Smoos (dollars)	Quantity Supplied (per month)	Quantity Demanded (per month)	Condition in the Market	Direction of Pressure on Price
13	625	400	Excess supply	Downward
12	600	450	Excess supply	Downward
11	575	500	Excess supply	Downward
10	550	550	Balance	Equilibrium
9	525	600	Excess demand	Upward
8	500	650	Excess demand	Upward
7	475	700	Excess demand	Upward

away. This remarkable diversity is a reflection of low transportation costs, which expand the opportunity for gains for specialization and exchange. During the last 200 years, dramatic reductions in the cost of transporting goods have changed our lives and linked markets around the world.

When there are no trade barriers (legal restrictions limiting exchange), transportable goods will tend to trade for the same price in all markets, except for price differences caused by transportation costs and taxes. This **price equalization principle** reflects the fact that any inequality in the price of a good, for reasons other than taxes and transport costs, creates a profit opportunity for entrepreneurs. One could profit by buying the good in the market where its price is low and selling it in the high-price market. But the additional buying will push the good's price upward in the low-price market and the additional supply will drive its price down in the high-price market. Therefore, as entrepreneurs act on the opportunity for profit, they tend to equalize the price of each good across all markets, except for price differences reflecting transport costs and taxation among markets.

The price equalization principle explains why if it costs 5 cents to transport oranges from Florida to Wisconsin, oranges will not sell for 25 cents in Florida and 50 cents in Wisconsin. If those prices were present, entrepreneurs would buy the oranges at the cheap Florida price and ship them to Wisconsin until the price differential between the two locations was reduced to only the cost of transportation (assuming similar tax treatment between the two states).

Price Equalization Principle: The tendency for markets, when trade restrictions are absent, to establish a uniform price for each good throughout the world (except for price differences due to transport costs and differential tax treatment of the good).

The principle is just as applicable to international markets, as to a regional or national market. It explains why the price of a good, transportable at a relatively low cost, will not be cheap in one market and expensive in another if free trade is present. In fact, when the costs of transportation are low, the presence of substantial price differences between two markets is evidence that there are either substantial trade barriers or differences in the taxation of the good in the markets.

LONG-RUN MARKET EQUILIBRIUM

Long-Run: A time period of sufficient length to enable decision-makers to adjust fully to a market change. For example, in the long-run, producers will have time to alter their utilization of all productive factors, including the heavy equipment and physical structure of their plants.

Rate-of-Return Equalization Principle: The tendency for capital investment in each market to move toward a uniform or normal rate of return. An abnormally high return in a market will attract additional investment which will drive returns down. Conversely, an abnormally low return will result in investment flight from the market which will eventually lead to the restoration of normal returns.

In the **long run,** decision-makers will have time to adjust fully to a change in market conditions. With the passage of time, producers will be able to alter their output; not only will they use their current plant more intensively, but given sufficient time, they will be able to change the size of their production facility. The long run is a time period long enough to permit producers to expand the size of their capital stock (the physical structure and heavy equipment of their plant).

A balance between amount supplied and amount demanded will bring about market equilibrium in the short run. However, if the current market price is going to persist in the future, an additional condition must be present: The opportunity cost of producing the product must also be equal to the market price.

If the market price of a good is greater than the opportunity cost of producing it, suppliers will gain from an expansion in production. Profit-seeking entrepreneurs will be attracted to the industry. Investment capital will flow into the industry and output (supply) will expand until the additional supply lowers the market price sufficiently to eliminate the profits.[3] In contrast, if the market price is less than the good's opportunity cost of production, suppliers will lose money if they continue to produce the good. The losses will drive producers from the market and capital will flow away from the industry. Eventually the decline in supply and shrinkage in the capital base (durable productive assets) of the industry will push prices upward and eliminate the losses.

In a market economy, characterized by freedom of entry and exit, there will be a tendency for the *after-tax* rate of return on investment to move toward a uniform rate, the competitive or normal-profit return. Neither abnormally high nor abnormally low after-tax returns will persist for long periods of time. This tendency for returns on investment capital to move toward a uniform, normal rate is sometimes referred to as the **rate-of-return equalization principle.**

It is easy to see why there is a tendency for abnormal investment returns—that is, both profits and losses—to be eliminated with the passage of time in a competitive environment. Suppose the after-tax investment return on capital was abnormally high in the retail clothing industry and abnormally low in the publishing industry. The high return in retail clothing would attract additional investors (rival suppliers). Supply in the clothing industry would expand, causing both prices and returns on investment to decline. Eventually, normal returns would be restored in the clothing industry. Conversely, the abnormally low return in the

[3]Bear in mind that economists use the opportunity cost concept for *all* factors of production, including those owned by the producers. Therefore, the owners are receiving a return equal to the opportunity cost of their investment capital even when profits are zero. Zero profits therefore mean that the capital owners are being paid precisely their opportunity cost, precisely what they could earn if their resources were employed in the highest valued alternative that must be forgone as the result of current use. Far from indicating that a firm is about to go out of business, zero economic profits imply that each factor of production, including the capital owned by the firm and the managerial skills of the owner-entrepreneur, is earning the market rate of return.

publishing industry would cause investment flight and a reduction in supply. This shrinkage of the capital base and decline in supply in the publishing industry would lead to higher prices until eventually the remaining firms in the industry could once again earn normal returns.

The rate-of-return equalization principle enhances our understanding of supply changes and capital movements when the market price of a good differs from its opportunity cost of production. However, the principle also explains why it will be very difficult for public policy to alter the market returns to any activity over the long term. Suppose the government tries to enhance the returns of farmers (or small business operators, or any other group). For example, it might provide low-cost loans, tax breaks, and subsidies in other forms. Such a policy might initially increase the returns in farming, but it will fail to do so in the long run. If the subsidies increase the returns in farming, capital would flow into the industry, driving commodity prices down (or production costs up) until normal returns are restored. In the long run, the subsidies do not enhance the profitability of investment in farming.

Conversely, consider what would happen if the government imposes higher taxes or discriminatory regulations on an industry. Returns in the industry may temporarily fall below normal. But if they do, capital flight and reductions in supply will push prices upward and eventually restore normal returns.

SHIFTS IN DEMAND AND CHANGES IN QUANTITY DEMANDED

A demand curve isolates the impact that price has on the amount of a product purchased. Of course, factors other than price—for example, consumer income, tastes, prices of related goods, and expectations as to the future price of a product—also influence the decisions of consumers. Until now, we have assumed that these factors stay the same. If one of them changes, though, the entire demand curve will shift. Economists refer to such shifts in the demand curve as a change in *demand*.

Let us take a closer look at some of the factors that would cause the demand for a product to change. Expansion in income makes it possible for consumers to purchase more goods at current prices. They usually respond by increasing their spending on a wide cross-section of products. Changes in prices of closely related products also influence the choices of consumers. If the price of butter were to fall, many consumers would substitute it for margarine. The demand for margarine would decline (shift to the left) as a result. If coffee and cream are frequently used together, a rise in the price of coffee may decrease the demand for cream, since less coffee will be consumed at the higher price.

Our expectations about the future price of a product also influence our current decisions. For example, if you think that the price of automobiles is going to rise by 20 percent next month, this will increase your incentive to buy now, before the price rises. In contrast, if you think that the price of a product is going to decline, you will demand less now, as you attempt to extend your purchasing decision into the future, when prices are expected to be lower.

Failure to distinguish between a change in *demand* and a change in *quantity demanded* is one of the most common mistakes made by introductory economics

OUTSTANDING ECONOMIST

**Alfred Marshall
(1842–1924)**

Early economists such as Adam Smith and David Ricardo thought that the price of a good was determined by its cost of production. Later, other economists, known as the "marginalists," emphasized the importance of demand and consumer preferences. Alfred Marshall put these two ideas together in 1890 when he introduced the concept of supply and demand.

Marshall noted that "the greater the amount to be sold, the smaller must be the price at which it is offered in order that it may find purchasers." Similarly, he argued that the supply of a commodity reflects the cost of the resources required to produce the good. In turn, the price of the commodity is determined by the balancing of these two forces—supply and demand.

In a famous analogy, Marshall likened the importance of supply and demand to the blades of a pair of scissors. When discussing which was more important, he wrote:

> We might reasonably dispute whether it is the upper or the under blade of a pair of scissors that cuts a piece of paper, as whether value is governed by utility [consumer demand] or cost of production [supply].[5]

Although it is true that the blades of supply and demand operate jointly to determine price, Marshall recognized that the passage of time affects the relative importance of the supply and demand sides of the market in its response to change. In the short run, both supply and demand are highly significant, interacting to determine price. In contrast, in the long run, the supply side of a market is more important. As Marshall pointed out nearly a century ago, "the longer the time period, the more important will be the influence of cost of production" on price.

Alfred Marshall's father wanted him to enter the ministry, but young Marshall turned down a theological scholarship at Oxford in order to study mathematics at Cambridge. Marshall's serious study of economics began in 1867. In 1885, he was appointed to the Chair of Political Economy at Cambridge, a position he occupied for almost a quarter of a century.

In his *Principles of Economics* (1890), Marshall introduced many of the concepts and tools that form the core of modern microeconomics. Elasticity, the short run, the long run, equilibrium—all of these concepts were initially developed by Marshall. More than any other English economist, Marshall turned economics into a science. His influence was so great during the first 25 years of the twentieth century that this period is sometimes referred to as the "Age of Marshall." Clearly, his legacy is still accepted and honored today.

[5]Alfred Marshall, *Principles of Economics,* 8th ed. (London: Macmillan, 1920), p. 348.

students.[4] A change in demand is a shift in the entire demand curve. A change in quantity demanded is a movement along the same demand curve.

Exhibit 5 clearly demonstrates the difference between the two. The demand curve D_1 indicates the initial demand (the entire curve) for doorknobs. At a price of \$3, consumers would purchase Q_1. If the price declined to \$1, there would be an increase in quantity demanded from Q_1 to Q_3. Arrow *A* indicates the change in

---

[4]Questions designed to test the ability of students to make this distinction are favorites of many economics instructors. A word to the wise should be sufficient.

EXHIBIT 5

The Difference Between a Change in Demand and a Change in Quantity Demanded

Arrow *A* indicates a change in *quantity demanded*, a movement along the demand curve D_1, in response to a change in the price of doorknobs. The *B* arrows illustrate a change in *demand*, a shift of the entire curve.

Quantity of doorknobs per unit time

quantity demanded—a movement along demand curve D_1. Now, suppose that there were a 20 percent increase in income that caused a housing boom. The demand for doorknobs would increase from D_1 to D_2. As indicated by the *B* arrows, the entire demand curve would shift. At the higher income level, consumers would be willing to purchase more doorknobs at $3, at $2, at $1, and at every other price than was previously true. The increase in income leads to an increase in demand—a shift in the entire curve.

How does the market react to a change in demand? What happens to price and the amount supplied of a good if demand increases? Exhibit 6 will help to answer these questions while yielding insight into real-world events. From 1970 to 1981, there was a sharp rise in the price of gasoline. Many car owners attempted to economize on their use of the more expensive fuel by substituting smaller cars for their heavier, gas-guzzling models. There was an increase in demand for compact cars. The demand curve for such cars shifted to the right (from D_1 to D_2). At the original equilibrium price ($6,000, in our example), there was

EXHIBIT 6

A Shift in Demand

As conditions change over time, the entire demand curve for a product may shift. Facing higher gasoline prices after the large increases of 1979 and 1980, many consumers decided to purchase compact cars. The *demand* for compact cars increased, causing both an increase in price and greater sales.

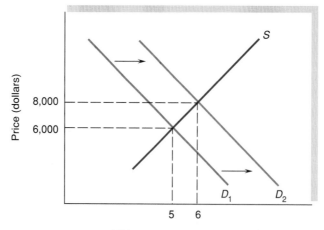

Millions of compact cars per year

an excess demand for compact cars—a shortage. This caused the price of compact cars to rise. Market forces eventually brought about a new balance between supply and demand, establishing a new equilibrium price, $8,000, at a higher sales level. The pricing system responded to the increase in demand by granting (a) producers a stronger incentive to supply more compact cars and (b) consumers an incentive to search for additional, cheaper ways to conserve gasoline other than buying compact cars.

SHIFTS IN SUPPLY

The decisions of producers lie behind the supply curve. Other things constant, the supply curve summarizes the willingness of producers to offer a product at alternative prices. As with demand it is important to note the difference between (a) a change in quantity supplied and (b) a change in supply. A change in quantity supplied is a movement along the same curve in response to a change in price. A change in supply indicates a shift in the entire supply curve.

What factors would cause a shift in the entire supply curve? How does the market for consumer goods adjust to a shift in supply? We now turn to an analysis of these two questions.

We previously indicated that a profit-seeking entrepreneur will produce a good only if the sales price of the good exceeds its opportunity cost. Factors that increase the opportunity cost of producers will discourage production and thereby decrease supply (shift the entire curve to the left). Conversely, changes that decrease the opportunity cost of producers will increase supply (shift the entire curve to the right).

Let us consider a number of important factors that will shift the supply curve.

Changes in Resource Prices. Resource and product markets are closely linked. Firms demand labor, machines, and other resources because they contribute to the production of goods and services. In turn, individuals supply resources in order to earn income.

As in product markets, the demand curve is typically downward-sloping and the supply curve upward-sloping in resource markets. An inverse relationship will exist between the amount of a resource demanded and its price because businesses will substitute away from a resource as its price rises. Less of the resource will be used at higher prices. In contrast, there will be a direct relationship between the amount of a specific resource supplied and its price. An increase in the price of a resource, for example the labor services of an automotive mechanic, will make it more attractive to supply the resource. Some people, who would choose to do other things when the wage (price) of automotive mechanics is low, will be willing to supply the resource (or more of the resource) when the payoff from doing so improves.

Just as in markets for consumer goods, prices will coordinate the choices of business firms and households in resource markets. There will be a tendency for the price of each resource to move toward an equilibrium, where the amount of the resource supplied by households is in balance with the amount demanded by businesses.

How will an increase in the price of a resource affect product markets? Higher resource prices will increase the opportunity cost of producing consumer goods that use the resource. The higher costs will reduce supply and increase price in the product market. Exhibit 7 illustrates this point. Many economists are forecasting that the wages of low-skill workers will increase substantially in the next few years, primarily because there will be fewer youthful workers (teenagers and persons in their early twenties). As Exhibit 7a illustrates, a reduction in the supply of low-skill workers will push their wage rates upward (from $4.35 to $5.25). The higher price of this resource will increase the opportunity cost of hamburgers at fast-food restaurants such as McDonald's and Wendy's. In turn, the higher opportunity cost will reduce supply (from S_1 to S_2) and increase hamburger prices at fast-food establishments (Exhibit 7b).

Of course, lower resource prices would exert the opposite effect in the product market. A reduction in resource prices will reduce costs and expand the supply (a shift to the right) of consumer goods using the lower priced resources. The increase in supply will lead to a lower price in the product market.

Changes in Technology. Technological improvements—the discovery of new, lower cost production techniques—will reduce the opportunity cost of production and increase supply (shift the supply curve to the right) in the product market. Previously, we indicated that consumers increased their purchases of VCRs as prices for those items declined between 1979 and 1986 (see Exhibit 1). Exhibit 8 illustrates why VCR prices fell. Technological improvements substantially reduced the opportunity cost of producing VCRs between 1979 and 1986. The reduction in cost made it more attractive for entrepreneurs to produce VCRs. Established firms expanded output. New firms began production, further contributing to the expansion of supply. The supply curve shifted to the right (from S_{79} to S_{86}). At the old $1,362 price (an average for VCRs sold in 1979, adjusted to 1986 dollars), consumers would not buy the larger supply of VCRs. A reduction in price was necessary to bring the desires of producers to expand production into line with consumers' willingness to purchase the output. By 1986, the average VCR was not only a much better machine, but its price had fallen to about $400. At that price, coordination of buyer and seller decisions was achieved.

EXHIBIT 7

Resource Prices and the Opportunity Cost of Consumer Goods

Suppose a reduction in the supply of low-skill labor pushes the wage rates of workers hired by fast-food restaurants upward. In the product market, the higher wage rates will increase the restaurant's opportunity cost, causing a reduction in supply (frame b, shift from S_1 to S_2), leading to higher hamburger prices.

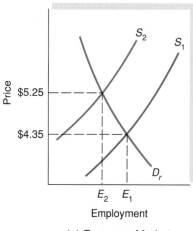

(a) Resource Market
(low skilled labor)

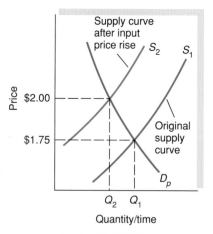

(b) Product Market
(fast food hamburgers)

EXHIBIT 8

Improved Technology and a Shift in the Supply Curve

In 1979, VCRs were selling for $1,362 (in 1986 dollars). Improved technology and manufacturing substantially reduced their production cost, shifting the supply curve to the right (from S_{79} to S_{86}). Prices declined, inducing consumers to purchase a larger quantity.

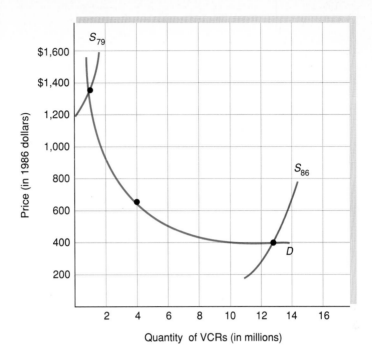

Natural Disasters and Political Disruptions. Natural disasters and changing political conditions may also alter supply, sometimes dramatically. For example, in 1986 a drought hit Brazil, destroying a substantial portion of that year's coffee crop. War and political unrest in Iran exerted a major impact on the supply of oil in the late 1970s.

In the early 1980s, there was substantial overfishing in the Atlantic haddock fishery of Georges Bank, off the coasts of New England and Canada. No one owned the fishery; no one controlled access. As a result, too many fishing boats took too many fish. The breeding stock fell, and by 1986 the catch was much smaller than it had been. At the 1981 price, there would have been an excess

THUMBNAIL SKETCH

These factors increase (decrease) the demand for a good:

1. A rise (fall) in consumer income
2. A rise (fall) in the price of a good used as a substitute
3. A fall (rise) in the price of a complementary good often used with the original good
4. A rise (fall) in the expected future price of the good

These factors increase (decrease) the supply of a good:

1. A fall (rise) in the price of a resource used in producing the good
2. A technological change allowing cheaper production of the good
3. Favorable weather (bad weather or a disruption in supply due to political factors, or war)

A Decrease in Supply

Overfishing of the Atlantic haddock fishery off Georges Bank in the early 1980s caused the number of haddock to decline dramatically. Supply was reduced—the supply curve shifted upwards, so that 1986 prices were more than double those of 1981. The smaller supply was rationed to buyers willing to pay the higher prices.

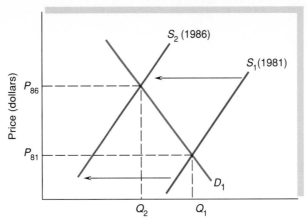

demand for haddock. In response to the reduction in supply (shift from S_1 to S_2), price rose sharply (Exhibit 9). Consumers cut back on their consumption of the more expensive good. Some switched to substitutes—in this case probably other fish. By 1986, the price of haddock had risen to more than twice its 1981 level, rationing the smaller supply of haddock to those most willing to pay the higher price. Balance was maintained in the market, despite the sharp drop in the supply of haddock. The accompanying Thumbnail Sketch summarizes the major factors causing shifts in demand and supply.

TIME AND THE ADJUSTMENT PROCESS

The signals that the pricing system sends to consumers and producers will change with market conditions. The market adjustment process will not be completed instantaneously, though. Sometimes various signals are sent out and understood only gradually, with the passage of time.

The response of consumers to a change in market conditions will generally be more pronounced as time passes. Consider the response of consumers when gasoline prices nearly doubled from 1978 to 1980 (corrected for inflation, gasoline prices rose more than 50 percent during the two-year period). Initially consumers responded by cutting out some unnecessary trips and leisure driving. Some drove more slowly in order to get better gasoline mileage. As Exhibit 10 illustrates, these adjustments led to some reduction in gasoline consumption. However, while the rise in gasoline prices persisted, new car purchases began to shift toward smaller cars that used less gas. Since people usually waited for their current gas-guzzler to wear out before they bought a new, smaller car, the adjustment was still taking place years later, when gasoline prices began to drop in 1982. But, while the shift to higher-mileage automobiles was taking place, gasoline consumption declined more and more. The adjustment process for gasoline is a typical one. The demand response to a price change will usually be less in the short run than over a longer period of time.

Similarly, the adjustments of producers to changing market conditions take time. Suppose there is an increase in demand for radios. How will this change be

EXHIBIT 10

Time and the Buyer's Response to a Price Increase

Usually, the shorter the time period, the less responsive is consumption to a change in price. The gasoline price increases of 1979–1980 illustrate the point. Gasoline consumption declined from 7.4 million barrels per day to 7.0 million during the first year as the price of gasoline rose. The second year, consumption dropped to 6.6 million barrels. If the price had remained at the 1980 level for another four years, we would have expected a further decline, perhaps to Q_3, as consumers adjusted more fully. (The price fell after 1980.)

reflected in the market? Initially, retailers will note a decline in their inventories as radios move off their shelves more rapidly. They will increase their wholesale orders, causing producer inventories to decline. At first, producers may be unsure whether the increase in demand is a random, temporary phenomenon or a lasting change. In either case, some will use a price increase to ration their limited supplies among the increased number of buyers.

A few alert entrepreneurs may have anticipated the expansion in demand and developed plans early to increase their production. With the passage of time, other producers, initially oblivious to the increase in demand, will take note of the strong demand for radios. To bring more resources into radio production, some resource prices will have to be bid higher, raising costs. For this reason also, manufacturers will raise their prices. Retailers will soon pass the higher wholesale prices on to consumers.

Once the increase in demand is widely perceived by suppliers, the price of radios will rise sharply. Profits will exist in the industry. Astute entrepreneurs who anticipated the increase in demand will have expanded their production capacity. They will be rewarded with substantial profits. Other radio suppliers will hastily attempt to expand their production in order to increase their profits. A rapid increase in production, however, will be costly for producers who failed to anticipate (and plan for) the higher level of demand. Such firms will have to resort to overtime payments, air shipments of raw materials, and/or the employment of inexperienced workers to increase their output rapidly. Producers whose apt foresight gives them more time to expand their output in an orderly fashion can do so at a lower cost.

Although producers will expand their output at different rates, the profitable opportunities will induce additional supply, which will eventually moderate the price rise. All of these responses will take time, however, even though economists sometimes talk as if the process were instantaneous.

REPEALING THE LAWS OF SUPPLY AND DEMAND

Buyers often believe that prices are too high, and sellers generally perceive prices as too low. Unhappy with prices established by market forces, individuals may seek to have prices set by legislative action. Fixing prices seems like a simple, straightforward solution. Simple, straightforward solutions, though, often have unanticipated repercussions. Do not forget the secondary effects.

Price Ceiling: A legally established maximum price that sellers may charge.

Price ceilings are often popular during a period of inflation, a situation in which prices of most products are continually rising. Many people mistakenly believe that the rising prices are the cause of the inflation rather than just one of its effects. Exhibit 11a illustrates the impact of fixing a price of a product below its equilibrium level. Of course, the price ceiling does result in a lower price than market forces would produce, at least in the short-run. However, that is not the end of the story. At the below-equilibrium price, producers will be unwilling to supply as much as consumers would like to purchase. A shortage ($Q_D - Q_S$, Exhibit 11a) of the goods will result. A shortage is a situation in which the quantity demanded by consumers exceeds the quantity supplied by producers *at the existing price*. Normally, competing buyers would bid up the price. Fixing the price will prevent that, but will not eliminate the rationing problem. Nonprice factors will now become more important in the rationing process. Producers must discriminate on some basis other than willingness to pay as they ration their sales to eager buyers. Sellers will be partial to friends, to buyers who do them favors, and even to buyers who are willing to make illegal black-market payments.

Shortage: A condition in which the amount of a good offered by sellers is less than the amount demanded by buyers at the existing price. An increase in price would eliminate the shortage.

In addition, the below-equilibrium price reduces the incentive of sellers to expand the future supply of the good. Fewer resources will flow into the production of this good. Higher profits will be available elsewhere. With the passage of time, the shortage conditions will worsen as suppliers direct resources away from production of this commodity and into other areas.

EXHIBIT 11

The Impact of Price Ceilings and Price Floors

Frame a illustrates the impact of a price ceiling. When price is fixed below the equilibrium level, shortages will develop. Frame b illustrates the effects of a price floor. If price is fixed above its equilibrium level, then a surplus will result. When ceilings and floors prevent prices from bringing about a market equilibrium, nonprice factors will play a more important role in the rationing process.

(a) Price ceiling

(b) Price floor

What other secondary effects can we expect? In the real world, there are two ways that sellers can raise prices. First, they can raise their money price, holding quality constant. Or, second, they can hold the money price constant while reducing the quality of the good. Confronting a price ceiling, sellers will rely on the latter method of raising prices. Rather than do without the good, some buyers will accept the lower-quality product. It is not easy to repeal the laws of supply and demand. (See Myths of Economics box.)

It is important to note that a shortage is not the same as scarcity. *Scarcity is inescapable.* Scarcity exists whenever people want more of a good than Nature has provided. This means, of course, that almost everything of value is scarce. *Shortages, on the other hand, are avoidable if prices are permitted to rise.* A higher, unfixed price (P_0 rather than P_1 in Exhibit 11a) would (a) stimulate additional production, (b) discourage consumption, and (c) ration the available supply to those willing to give up the most in exchange; that is, to pay the highest prices. These forces, an expansion in output and a reduction in consumption, would eliminate the shortage.

Exhibit 11b illustrates the case of a **price floor,** which fixes the price of a good or resource above its equilibrium level. At the higher price, sellers will want to bring a larger amount to the market, while buyers will choose to buy less of the good. A **surplus** ($Q_S - Q_D$) will result. Agricultural price supports and minimum wage legislation are examples of price floors. Predictably, nonprice factors will again play a larger role in the rationing process than would be true without a price floor. Buyers can now be more selective, since sellers want to sell more than buyers, in aggregate, desire to purchase. Buyers can be expected to seek out sellers willing to offer them favors (discounts on other products, easier credit, or better service, for example). Some sellers may be unable to market their product or service.[6] Unsold merchandise and underutilized resources will result.

Note that a surplus does not mean the good is no longer scarce. People still want more of the good than is freely available from Nature, even though they desire less, *at the current price,* than sellers desire to bring to the market. A decline in price would eliminate the surplus but not the scarcity of the item.

Price Floor: A legally established minimum price that buyers must pay for a good or resource.

Surplus: A condition in which the amount of a good that sellers are willing to offer is greater than the amount that buyers will purchase at the existing price. A decline in price would eliminate the surplus.

HOW THE MARKET ANSWERS THE THREE BASIC ECONOMIC QUESTIONS

How does the market's pricing mechanism resolve the three basic economic questions—what goods will be produced, how will they be produced, and for whom will they be produced?

In a market economy, what will be produced is determined by the consumer's evaluation of a good (demand) relative to its opportunity cost (supply). If consumers value a good (in terms of money) more than its opportunity cost, they will choose to purchase it. Simultaneously, profit-seeking producers will supply a good as long as consumers are willing to pay a price that is sufficient to cover the

---

[6]Our theory indicates that minimum wage legislation (a price floor for unskilled labor) will generate an excess supply of inexperienced, low-skilled workers. The extremely high unemployment rate of teenagers—a group with little work experience—supports this view.

opportunity cost of producing it. The result: There is an incentive to produce those goods, and only those goods, to which consumers attach a value at least as high as the production costs of the goods.

How goods will be produced is determined by the economizing behavior of suppliers. Suppliers have a strong incentive to use production methods that minimize costs, because lower costs will mean larger profits. Thus, producers can be expected to organize production efficiently—to use a division of labor, to discover and adapt new technologies, and to choose labor-capital combinations that will result in lower production costs.

What assurances are there that producers will not waste resources or exploit consumers by charging high prices? Competition provides the answer. Inefficient

MYTHS OF ECONOMICS

"Rent controls are an effective method of ensuring adequate housing at a price the poor can afford."

When rents (a price for a good) are set below the equilibrium level, the amount of rental housing demanded by consumers will exceed the amount landlords will make available. Initially, if the mandated price is not set too much below equilibrium, the impact of rent controls may be barely noticeable. With the passage of time, however, their effects will grow. Inevitably, controls will lead to the following results.

1. *The Future Supply of Rental Houses Will Decline.* The below-equilibrium price will discourage entrepreneurs from constructing new rental housing units. Private investment will flow elsewhere, since the controls have depressed the rate of return in the rental housing market. The current owners of such housing may be forced to accept the lower price. However, potential future suppliers of rental housing have other alternatives. Many of them will opt to use their knowledge and resources in other areas.

2. *Shortages and Black Markets Will Develop.* Since the quantity of housing supplies will fail to keep pace with the quantity demanded, some persons who value rental housing highly will be unable to find it. Frustrated by the shortage, they will seek methods by which they may induce landlords to rent to them. Some will agree to prepay their rent, including a substantial damage deposit. Others will resort to tie-in agreements (for example, they might also agree to rent or buy the landlords' furniture at an exorbitant price) in their efforts to evade the controls. Still others will make under-the-table payments to secure the cheap housing.

3. *The Quality of Rental Housing Will Deteriorate.* Economic thinking suggests that there are two ways to raise prices. The nominal price can be increased, quality being held constant. Alternatively, quality can be reduced, while the same nominal price is maintained. When landlords are prohibited from adopting the former, they will use the latter. They will paint rental units less often. Normal maintenance and repair service will deteriorate. Tenant parking lots will be eliminated (or rented). Cleaning and maintenance of the general surroundings will be neglected. Eventually, the quality of the rental

housing will reflect the controlled price. Cheap housing will be of cheap quality.

4. *Nonprice Methods of Rationing Will Increase in Importance.* Since price no longer plays its normal role, other forms of competition will develop. Prohibited from price rationing, landlords will rely more heavily on nonmonetary discriminating devices. They will favor friends, persons of influence, and those with life-styles similar to their own. In contrast, applicants with many children, unconventional life-styles, or perhaps dark skin will find fewer landlords who cater to their personal requirements. Since the cost to landlords of discriminating against those with characteristics they do not like has been reduced, such discrimination will become more prevalent in the rationing process.

5. *Inefficient Use of Housing Space Will Result.* The tenant in a rent-controlled apartment will think twice before moving. Why? Even though the tenant might want a larger or smaller space, or even though the tenant might want to move closer to work, he or she will be less likely to move because it is much more difficult to find a vacancy if rent control

producers will have higher costs. They will find it difficult to meet the price competition of sellers who use resources wisely. Similarly, in a market with many sellers, competition among firms will, on the whole, keep prices from straying much above production costs. When prices are above the opportunity costs of a good, profits for the producers will result. As we have discussed, the profits will attract additional suppliers into the market, driving the price downward.

To whom will the goods be distributed? Goods will be allocated to consumers willing and able to pay the market price. Of course, some consumers will be better able to pay the market price—they have larger incomes (more "dollar votes") than others. The unequal distribution of income among consumers is directly related to what is produced and how. The income of individuals will reflect the

ordinances are in effect. As a result, turnover will drop somewhat, and people will end up living in apartments not quite suited to their needs.

6. *Long-term Renters Will Benefit at the Expense of Newcomers.* People who stay for lengthy time periods in the same apartment often pay rents substantially below market value (because the controls restrict rent increases), while newcomers are forced to pay exorbitant prices for the limited supply of newly constructed (and therefore temporarily unrestricted) apartments. This results in distortions and inequities. Journalist William Tucker, in a study of New York rent-controlled apartments, found that actress Mia Farrow's 10-room apartment, for which others would be willing to pay $12,000 to $15,000 per month (the market rent), cost her only $1,870.[7] State Senate Minority Leader Manfred Ohrenstein, a strong supporter of rent control, pays less than $1,800 monthly for ten rooms overlooking Central Park. New York City Mayor Koch also has a great deal, paying only $351.60 for a large Greenwich Village one-bedroom unit that could easily rent for $1,500. Many others who have resided in the same location for many years have

similar bargains. Meanwhile, others search for the restricted supply of housing in a market with one of the lowest vacancy rates in the United States.

During the inflation-plagued 1970s, the popularity of rent controls increased. Washington, D.C., San Francisco, Los Angeles, and several other cities experimented with various types of control schemes.[8] Studies indicated that a three-pronged pattern emerged after the imposition of rent controls. First, investment in new construction came to a standstill after the controls were imposed. Even in cases where newly constructed buildings were exempt from the controls, construction was adversely affected; landlords feared the imposition of the controls once a new apartment dwelling was in place. Second, the rent controls induced many landlords to convert their apartment buildings to condominium complexes. In New York, for example, it was estimated that in 1984, 25,000 apartments were held off the market, or "warehoused," simply to make them more easily available for developers of condominiums and cooperative apartments. Far more than that, of course, had already been con-

verted. Finally, vacancy rates declined as the rent-control communities began to feel the developing housing shortage.

Although rent controls may appear to be a simple solution, the truth of the matter is that a decline in the supply of rental housing, poor maintenance, and shortages are the inevitable results. Controls may initially lead to lower housing prices for some, but in the long-run the potential for the deterioration of urban life is almost unlimited. In the words of Swedish economist Assar Lindbeck: "In many cases rent control appears to be the most efficient technique presently known to destroy a city—except for bombing."[9] Though this may overstate the case somewhat, economic analysis suggests that the point is well-taken.

---

[7]This paragraph uses information from Paul La Rosa, "High Life at a Low Rent" *New York Daily News,* May 25, 1986.

[8]The information in the following section is from Peter Navarro, "Rent Control in Cambridge, Mass.," *The Public Interest,* No. 78, Winter 1985, pp. 83–100.

[9]Assar Lindbeck, *The Political Economy of the New Left, 1970* (New York: Harper and Row, 1972), p. 39.

extent of their provision of resources to others. Those who supply large amounts of highly valued resources—resources for which market participants are willing to pay a high price—will have high incomes. In contrast, those who supply few resources or resources that are not valued highly by others will have low incomes.

As long as the preferences and productive abilities of individuals differ, a market solution will lead to unequal incomes. Many people are critical of the pricing system because of the income inequality that results. But, unequal incomes are not unique to a market economy. In virtually all systems, unequal income shares exist and provide at least some of the incentive for individuals to undertake productive activities. Since efforts to alter the allocation of income will also affect supply conditions, this issue is highly complex. As we proceed, we will investigate it in more detail.

THE INVISIBLE HAND PRINCIPLE

The market system is a mechanism for social cooperation. As Adam Smith (see the Outstanding Economist box in chapter one) noted more than 200 years ago, the remarkable thing about a market economy—an economy based on private property and freedom of contract—is that market prices will bring the actions of self-interested individuals into harmony with the general welfare. Emphasizing his point, Smith stated:

> Every individual is continually exerting himself to find out the most advantageous employment for whatever capital he can command. It is his own advantage, indeed, and not that of the society which he has in view. But the study of his own advantage naturally, or rather necessarily, leads him to prefer that employment which is most advantageous to society. . . . He intends only his own gain, and he is in this, as in many other cases, led by an invisible hand to promote an end which was not part of his intention. By pursuing his own interest he frequently promotes that of the society more effectually than when he really intends to promote it.[10]

Invisible Hand Principle:
The tendency of market prices to direct individuals pursuing their own interests into productive activities that also promote the economic well-being of the society.

Economists refer to the tendency of market prices to *communicate* information, *coordinate* the actions of self-interested individuals, and *motivate* them into engaging in activities that promote the general welfare as the **invisible hand principle.** An efficiently operating economy must communicate, coordinate, and motivate the actions of decision-makers. Let us take a closer look at how the invisible hand of market prices performs these functions.

COMMUNICATING INFORMATION TO DECISION-MAKERS

Communication of information is one of the most important functions of a market price. We cannot *directly* observe the preferences of consumers. How highly do consumers value tricycles relative to attic fans, television sets relative to trampolines, or automobiles relative to swimming pools? Product prices and quantities sold communicate up-to-date information about consumers' valuation of additional units of these and numerous other commodities. Similarly, we cannot turn to an engineering equation in order to calculate the opportunity cost of alternative com-

---

[10]Adam Smith, *An Inquiry into the Nature and Causes of the Wealth of Nations* (New York: Modern Library, 1937), p. 423.

modities. But, resource prices tell the business decision-maker the relative importance others place on production factors (skill categories of labor, natural resources, and machinery, for example). With this information, in addition to knowledge of the relationship between potential input combinations and the output of a product, producers can make reliable estimates of their opportunity costs.

Without the information provided by market prices, it would be impossible for decision-makers to determine how intensively a good was desired relative to its opportunity costs—that is, relative to other things that might be produced with the resources required to produce the good. Markets collect and register bits and pieces of information reflecting the choices of consumers, producers, and resource suppliers. This vast body of information, which is almost always well beyond the comprehension of any single individual, is tabulated into a summary statistic—*the market price*. This summary statistic provides market participants with information on the relative scarcity of products.

When weather conditions, consumer preferences, technology, political revolution, or natural disasters alter the relative scarcity of a product or resource, market prices communicate this information to decision-makers. Direct knowledge of why conditions were altered is not necessary for making the appropriate adjustments. A change in the market price provides sufficient information to determine whether an item has become more or less scarce.

COORDINATING THE ACTIONS OF MARKET PARTICIPANTS

Market prices coordinate the choices of buyers and sellers, bringing their decisions into line with each other. If producers are currently supplying a larger amount than consumers are willing to purchase at the current price, then the excess supply will lead to falling prices, which discourage production and encourage consumption and thereby eliminate the excess supply. Alternatively, if consumers want to buy more than producers are willing to supply at the current price, then the excess demand will lead to price increases. The price rise will encourage consumers to economize on their uses of the good and encourage suppliers to produce more of it. Eventually, these forces will eliminate the excess demand and bring the choices of market participants into harmony.

Prices also direct entrepreneurs to undertake the production projects that are demanded most intensely (relative to their cost) by consumers. Entrepreneurial activity is guided by the signal lights of profits and losses. If consumers really want more of a good—for example, luxury apartments—the intensity of their demand will lead to a market price that exceeds the opportunity cost of constructing the apartments. A profitable opportunity will be created. Entrepreneurs will soon discover this opportunity for gain, undertake construction, and thereby expand the availability of the apartments. In contrast, if consumers want less of a good—very large cars, for example—the opportunity cost of supplying such cars will exceed the sales revenue from their production. Entrepreneurs who undertake such unprofitable production will be penalized by losses.

An understanding of the importance of the entrepreneur also sheds light on the market adjustment process. Since entrepreneurs, like the rest of us, have imperfect knowledge, they will not be able to instantaneously identify profitable opportunities and the disequilibrium conditions that accompany them. With the passage of time, however, information about a profitable opportunity will become more widely disseminated. More and more producers will move to supply a good that is intensely desired by consumers relative to its cost. Of course, as entrepreneurs expand supply, they will eventually eliminate the profit.

The move toward equilibrium will typically be a groping process. With time, successful entrepreneurial activity will be more clearly identified. Successful methods will be copied by other producers. Learning-by-doing and trial-and-error will help producers sort out attractive projects from "losers." The process, though, will never quite be complete. By the time entrepreneurs discover one intensely desired product (or a new, more efficient production technique), change will have occurred elsewhere, creating other unrealized profitable opportunities. The wheels of dynamic change never stop.

MOTIVATING THE ECONOMIC PLAYERS

As many leaders of centrally planned economies have discovered, people must be motivated to act before production plans can be realized. One of the major advantages of the pricing system is its ability to motivate people. Market prices establish a reward–penalty (profit–loss) structure that induces the participants to work, cooperate with others, use efficient production methods, supply goods that are intensely desired by others, and invest for the future.

No government agency needs to tell business decision-makers to use resources wisely and thereby minimize the cost of producing their product. The pursuit of profit will encourage them to economize, and if they do not they will be unable to compete successfully with more cost effective rivals. No control authority has to force the farmer to raise wheat, the construction firm to build houses, or the furniture manufacturer to produce chairs. When the market prices of these and literally millions of other products indicate that consumers value them as much or more than their production costs, producers seeking personal gain will supply them.

Similarly, no one has to tell resource suppliers to invest and develop productive resources. Why are many young people willing to undertake the necessary work, stress, late hours of study, and financial cost to acquire a medical or law degree, a doctoral degree in economics or physics, or a master's degree in business administration? Why do others seek to master a skill requiring an apprentice program? Why do individuals save to buy businesses, machines, and other capital assets? Although many factors undoubtedly influence one's decision to acquire skills and capital assets, the expectation of financial reward is an important stimulus. Without this stimulus, the motivation to work, create, develop skills, and supply capital assets to those productive activities most desired by others would be weakened.

PRICES AND MARKET ORDER

How is it that grocery stores in thousands of different locations have approximately the right amount of milk, bread, vegetables, and other goods—an amount sufficiently large that the goods are nearly always available but not so large that spoilage and waste are a problem? How is it that refrigerators, automobiles, and VCRs, produced at diverse places around the world, are supplied in the U.S. market in approximately the same amount that they are demanded by consumers? Why are long waiting lines and "sold out until next week" signs that are commonplace in centrally planned economies almost completely absent in market economies? In each case, the answer is that the invisible hand of market prices directs self-interested individuals into cooperative action and brings their choices into harmony.

The market process works so automatically that most people fail to grasp the concept—they fail to understand the source of the social coordination. Perhaps an illustration will help the reader grasp the concept. Visualize a busy limited-access highway with four lanes of traffic moving in each direction. There is not a central planning agency that assigns lanes and directs traffic. No one tells drivers when to shift to the right, middle, or left lane. Drivers are left to choose for themselves. Nonetheless, they do not all try to drive in the same lane. Drivers are alert for adjustment opportunities that offer personal gain. When traffic in a lane slows due to congestion, some drivers will shift to other lanes and thereby smooth out the flow of traffic among the lanes. Even though central planning is absent, this process of mutual adjustments by the individual drivers results in order and social cooperation. In fact, the degree of social cooperation is generally well beyond what could be achieved if central coordination was attempted; if for example, each vehicle were assigned a lane.

Market participation is a lot like driving on the freeway. It is often necessary to alter one's actions in light of the choices made by others. Success is dependent upon one's ability to act upon opportunities. Like the degree of traffic in a lane, profits and losses provide market participants with information concerning the advantages and disadvantages of alternative economic activities. Losses indicate that an economic activity is congested, and as a result, producers are unable to cover their costs. Successful market participants will shift away from such activities. Conversely, profits are indicative of an open lane, the opportunity to experience gain if one shifts into an activity where price is currently high relative to costs. As producers and resource suppliers shift away from activities characterized by congestion and into those characterized by the opportunity for gain (profit), they smooth out economic activity and enhance its flow. Order is the result, even though central authority is absent. This order in the absence of central planning is precisely what Adam Smith was referring to more than 200 years ago when he spoke of the "invisible hand" of market coordination.

QUALIFICATIONS

In this chapter, we have focused on the operation of a market economy. The efficiency of market organization is dependent on (a) competitive markets and (b) well-defined private property rights. Competition, the great regulator, can protect both buyer and seller. The presence (or possible entry) of independent alternative suppliers protects the consumer against a seller who seeks to charge prices substantially above the cost of production. The existence of alternative resource suppliers protects the producer against a supplier who might otherwise be tempted to withhold a vital resource unless granted exorbitant compensation. The existence of alternative employment opportunities protects the employee from the power of any single employer. Competition can equalize the bargaining power between buyers and sellers.

Understanding the information, coordination, and motivation results of the market mechanism helps us see all the more clearly the importance of property rights, the things actually traded in markets. Although property rights are often associated with selfishness, they are more properly viewed as an arrangement to (a) force resource users to bear fully the cost of their actions and (b) prohibit persons from engaging in destructive forms of competition. When property rights are well-defined, secure, and tradeable, suppliers of goods and services will be required to pay resource owners the opportunity cost of each resource employed.

They will not be permitted to seize and use scarce resources without compensating the owner; that is, without bidding the resources away from alternative users.

Similarly, secure property rights eliminate the use of violence as a competitive weapon. A producer you do not buy from (or work for) will not be permitted to burn down your house. Nor will a competitive resource supplier whose prices you undercut be permitted to slash your automobile tires or threaten you with bodily injury.

Lack of competition and poorly defined property rights will alter the operation of a market economy. As we proceed, we will investigate each of these problems in detail.

CHAPTER SUMMARY

1. Because people want more of scarce goods than Nature has made freely available, a rationing mechanism is necessary. Competition is the natural outgrowth of the necessity for rationing scarce goods. A change in the rationing mechanism used will alter the form of competition, but it will not eliminate competitive tactics.

2. The law of demand holds that there is an inverse relationship between price and the amount of a good purchased. A rise in price will cause consumers to purchase less because they now have a greater incentive to use substitutes. On the other hand, a reduction in price will induce consumers to buy more, since they will substitute the cheaper good for other commodities.

3. The law of supply states that there is a direct relationship between the price of a product and the amount supplied. Other things constant, an increase in the price of a product will induce established firms to expand their output and new firms to enter the market. The quantity supplied will expand.

4. Market prices will bring the conflicting forces of supply and demand into balance. If the quantity supplied to the market by producers exceeds the quantity demanded by consumers, price will decline until the excess supply is eliminated. On the other hand, if the quantity demanded by consumers exceeds the quantity supplied by producers, price will rise until the excess demand is eliminated.

5. If there are no restrictions on the movement of a good, the good will tend to sell for the same price in all markets, except for price differences resulting from differences in transport costs and taxes among markets. This price equalization principle applies to regional, national, and global markets.

6. When a market is in long-run equilibrium, supply and demand will be in balance and the producer's opportunity cost will equal the market price. If the opportunity cost of supplying the good is less than the market price, profits will accrue. However, competition will tend to erode profit (abnormally high returns). The profits will attract additional suppliers, cause lower prices, and push the market toward an equilibrium. On the other hand, if the opportunity cost of producing a good exceeds the market price, suppliers will experience losses. The losses will induce producers to leave the market, causing price to rise until equilibrium is restored.

7. Changes in consumer income, prices of closely related goods, preferences, and expectations as to future prices will cause the entire demand curve to shift. An increase (decrease) in demand will cause prices to rise (fall) and quantity supplied to increase (decline).

8. Changes in input prices, technology, and other factors that influence the producer's cost of production will cause the entire supply curve to shift. An increase (decrease) in supply will cause prices to fall (rise) and quantity demanded to expand (decline).

9. The constraint of time temporarily limits the ability of consumers to adjust to changes in prices. With the passage of time, a price increase will usually elicit a larger reduction in quantity demanded. Similarly, the market supply curve shows more responsiveness to a change in price in the long-run than during the short term time period.

10. When a price is fixed below the market equilibrium, buyers will want to purchase more than sellers are willing to supply. A shortage will result. Nonprice factors such as waiting lines, quality deterioration, and illegal transactions will play a more important role in the rationing process. When a price is fixed above the market equilibrium level, sellers will want to supply a larger amount than buyers are willing to purchase at the current price. A surplus will result.

11. The pricing system answers the three basic allocation questions in the following manner.
    (a) What goods will be produced? Additional units of goods will be produced only if consumers value them more highly than the opportunity cost of the resources necessary to produce them.
    (b) How will goods be produced? The methods that result in the lowest opportunity cost will be chosen. Since lower costs mean larger profits, markets reward producers who discover and utilize efficient (low-cost) production methods.
    (c) To whom will the goods be distributed? Goods will be distributed to individuals according to the quantity and price of the productive resources they supplied in the marketplace. A large quantity of goods will be allocated to persons who are able to sell a large quantity of highly valued productive resources; few goods will be allocated to persons who supply only a small quantity of low-valued resources.

12. Market prices communicate information, coordinate the actions of buyers and sellers, and provide the incentive structure that motivates decision-makers to act. The information provided by prices instructs entrepreneurs as to (a) how to use scarce resources and (b) which products are intensely desired (relative to their opportunity cost) by consumers. Market prices establish a reward–penalty system, which induces individuals to cooperate with each other and motivates them to work efficiently, invest for the future, supply intensely desired goods, economize on the use of scarce resources, and use efficient production methods. Even though decentralized individual planning is a characteristic of the market system, there is a harmony between personal self-interest and the general welfare, as Adam Smith noted long ago. The efficiency of the system is dependent on (a) competitive market conditions and (b) securely defined private-property rights.

CRITICAL ANALYSIS QUESTIONS

*1. Which of the following do you think would lead to an increase in the current demand for beef: (a) higher pork prices, (b) higher incomes, (c) higher feed grain prices, (d) a banner-year corn crop, (e) an increase in the price of beef?

2. How many of the following ''goods'' do you think conform to the general law of supply: (a) gasoline, (b) cheating on exams, (c) political favors from legislators, (d) the services of heart specialists, (e) children, (f) legal divorces, (g) the services of a minister? Explain your answer in each case.

3. **What's Wrong with this Way of Thinking?**
   ''Economists argue that lower prices will necessarily result in less supply. However, there are exceptions to this rule. For example, in 1970, 10-digit electronic calculators sold for $100. By 1985, the price of the same type of calculator had declined to less than $15. Yet business firms produced and sold five times as many calculators in 1985 as in 1970. Lower prices did *not* result in less production and a decline in the number of calculators supplied.''

*4. A drought during the summer of 1988 sharply reduced the 1988 output of wheat, corn, soybeans, and hay. Indicate the expected impact of the drought on the following:
   (a) prices of feed grains and hay during the summer of 1988

---

*Asterisk denotes questions for which answers are given in Appendix C, Selected Answers.

(b) price of cattle during the summer and fall of 1988

(c) price of cattle during the summer and fall of 1989

5. The County Commission recently voted $15 million for the construction of a new civic center. The chairperson of the Commission stated, "We are undertaking this project because the community needs a civic center and the 500 new jobs the project will create." (News item)

    (a) Does a "need" for a project mean it should be undertaken?

    (b) What is the opportunity cost of the project?

    (c) Will the project expand employment by 500 workers?

*6. If a price ceiling is "meaningful," the ceiling must be below the market price. Conversely, a meaningful price floor must be above the market price. What impact will a meaningful price ceiling have on the quantity exchanged? What impact will a meaningful price floor have on the quantity exchanged? Explain.

7. Which of the following statements are true? Explain your answer.

    (a) The high excise tax on cigarettes reduces the profitability of cigarette manufacturers.

    (b) Government-subsidized, low-interest loans to farmers increase the profitability of farming.

    (c) A tariff (tax) that restricts the supply of textile products to the domestic market pushes up domestic prices and increases the profitability of domestic textile manufacturers.

*8. "The future of our industrial strength cannot be left to chance. Somebody has to develop notions about which industries are winners and which are losers." (Newspaper columnist) Is this statement true? Who is the "somebody"?

9. What is the "invisible hand principle"? Does the invisible hand principle indicate that "good intentions" are necessary if one's actions are going to be beneficial to others?

*10. "Production should be for people and not for profit."

    (a) If production is profitable, are people helped or hurt? Explain.

    (b) Are people helped more if production results in a loss than if it leads to profit?

    (c) Is there a conflict between production for people and production for profit?

11. Suppose a disease destroys half of the cattle herds in Kansas and Missouri. Should we expect shortages and sky-high beef prices in these states as the result of the disease?

*12. Suppose a drought destroyed half of the wheat crop in France. What is the expected impact on the market price of wheat in France?

13. If there is a surplus of a good, does this mean that the good is not scarce? Indicate what the supply and demand curves would look like for a good that was not scarce.

*14. When the price of a commodity (for example, rental housing or campus parking) is below equilibrium, then waiting in line rather than monetary payments will play a greater role in the allocation of the good. What is a major disadvantage of rationing by waiting in line rather than price. (Hint: How do the alternative methods affect future supply?)

15. "Economists claim that when the price of something goes up, producers bring more of it to the market. But the last year in which the price was really high for oranges, there were not nearly as many oranges as usual. The economists are wrong!" How would an economist respond?

4 SUPPLY AND DEMAND FOR THE PUBLIC SECTOR

Democracy is the worst form of government, except for all the rest.

Winston Churchill

CHAPTER FOCUS

■ What does the economic way of thinking have to say about economic efficiency?

■ When do markets fall short of the ideal of economic efficiency?

■ What role does the government play in guiding economic activity?

■ Why does government activity sometimes fail to meet ideal efficiency standards?

■ What can economics tell us about how individuals act in the public sector?

The economic role of government is pivotal. The government sets the rules of the game. It establishes and defines property rights, which are necessary for the smooth operation of markets. As we shall soon see, public policy is also an important determinant of economic stability. The government sometimes uses subsidies to encourage the production of some goods while it applies special taxes to reduce the availability of others. In a few cases—education, the mail service, and local electric power, for example—the government becomes directly involved in the production process.

Because of government's broad economic role, it is vital that we understand how it works and the circumstances under which it contributes to the efficient allocation of resources. Recent work in economics, particularly in the area of public choice, is relevant if we are seeking intelligent answers to the questions posed in the Chapter Focus.

In this chapter, we examine the shortcomings of the market and the potential of government policy as an alternate means for resolving economic problems. Issues involving market- and public-sector organization will be discussed repeatedly throughout this book. Political economy—how the public sector works, and how its workings compare with those of the market—is an integral and exciting aspect of economic analysis.

IDEAL ECONOMIC EFFICIENCY

Economic Efficiency: Economizing behavior. When applied to a community, it implies that (a) an activity should be undertaken if the sum of the benefits to the individuals exceeds the sum of their costs and (b) no activity should be undertaken if the costs borne by the individuals exceed the benefits.

We need a criterion by which to judge alternative institutional arrangements—market- and public-sector policies. Economists use the standard of economic efficiency. The central idea is straightforward. It simply means that for any given level of effort (cost), we want to obtain the largest possible benefit. A corollary to this is that we want to obtain any specific level of benefits with the least possible effort. Economic efficiency simply means getting the most out of the available resources—making the largest pie from the available set of ingredients, so to speak.

Why efficiency? Economists acknowledge that each individual does not have the efficiency of the economy as a primary goal. Instead, each person wants the largest possible "piece of the pie." All might agree that a bigger pie is preferred, however, particularly if they and those they care most about will get a larger slice as a result. Not only will most people agree that efficiency is good in the abstract, but an alternative that is more efficient can potentially make more people better off than an inefficient alternative.

What does efficiency mean when applied to the entire economy? Individuals are the final decision-makers of an economy. Individuals will bear the costs and reap the benefits of economic activity. When applied to the entire economy, two conditions are necessary for ideal economic efficiency to exist:

Rule 1. *Undertaking an economic action will be efficient if it produces more benefits than costs for the individuals of the economy.* Such actions result in gain—improvement in the well-being of at least some individuals without creating reductions in the welfare of others. Failure to undertake such activities means that potential gain has been forgone.

Rule 2. *Undertaking an economic action will be inefficient if it produces more costs than benefits to the individuals.* When an action results in greater total costs than benefits, somebody must be harmed. The benefits that accrue to those who gain are insufficient to compensate for the losses imposed on others. Therefore, when all persons are considered, the net impact of such an action is counterproductive.

When either rule 1 or rule 2 is violated, economic inefficiency results. The concept of economic efficiency applies to each and every possible income distribution, although a change in income distribution may alter the precise combination of goods and services that is most efficient. Positive economics does not tell us how income should be distributed. Of course, we all have ideas on the subject. Most of us would like to see more income distributed our way. For each kind of income distribution, though, there will be an ideal resource allocation that will be most efficient.

A closer look at supply and demand when competitive pressures are present will help you to understand the concept of efficiency. The supply curve reflects the producer's opportunity costs. Each point along the supply curve indicates the minimum price for which the units of a good could be produced without a loss to the seller. Each point along the demand curve indicates the consumer's valuation of an extra unit of the good—the maximum amount the consumer of each unit is willing to pay for the unit. Any time the consumer's valuation exceeds the producer's opportunity cost—the producer's minimum supply price—producing and selling more of the good can generate mutual gain.

When only the buyer and seller are affected by production and exchange, competitive markets directed by the forces of supply and demand are efficient. Exhibit 1 illustrates why this is true. Suppliers of a good, bicycles in this example, will produce additional units as long as the market price exceeds the production cost. Similarly, consumers will gain from the purchase of additional units as long as their benefits, revealed by the height of the demand curve, exceed the market price. Market forces will result in an equilibrium output level of Q: All units for which the benefits to consumers exceed the costs to suppliers will be produced. Rule 1 is met; all potential gains from exchange (the shaded area) between consumers and producers are fully realized. Production beyond Q, however, will

EXHIBIT 1

What Is Good About Idealized Market Exchange?

When competitive forces are present, price will tend toward the supply-demand intersection P. At that price, the seller's opportunity cost of producing the last unit will just equal the buyer's evaluation of that unit. All potential mutual gains from production and exchange are realized.

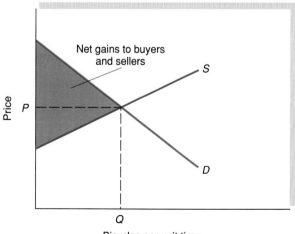

prove inefficient. If more than Q bicycles are produced, rule 2 is violated; consumers value the additional units less than their cost. With competitive markets, suppliers will find it unprofitable to produce units beyond Q because the cost of the additional units will exceed revenues.

Consumers and producers alike will thus be guided by the pricing system to output level Q, just the right amount. The market works beautifully. Individuals, pursuing their own interests, are guided as if by an invisible hand to promote the general welfare. This was the message of Adam Smith, more than 200 years ago.

WHY MIGHT THE INVISIBLE HAND FAIL?

Is the invisible hand still working today? Why might it fail? There are four important factors that can limit the ability of the invisible hand to perform its magic.

LACK OF COMPETITION

Competition is vital to the proper operation of the pricing mechanism. It is competition that drives the prices for consumer goods down to the level of their cost. Similarly, competition in markets for productive resources prevents (a) sellers from charging exorbitant prices to producers and (b) buyers from taking advantage of the owners of productive resources. The existence of competitors reduces the power of buyers and sellers alike to rig the market in their own favor.

Modern mass production techniques, marketing, and distributing networks often make it possible for a large-scale producer to gain a cost advantage over smaller competitors. In several industries—automobiles, aircraft, and aluminum, for example—a few large firms produce the entire output. Because an enormous amount of capital investment is required to enter these industries, existing large-scale producers may be partially insulated from the competitive pressure of new rivals.

Since competition is the enemy of high prices, sellers have a strong incentive to escape from its pressures by colluding rather than competing. Competition is something that is good when the other guy faces it. Individually, each of us would prefer to be loosened from its grip. Students do not like stiff competitors at exam time, when seeking entry to graduate school, or in their social or romantic lives. Similarly, sellers prefer few real competitors.

Exhibit 2 illustrates how sellers can gain from collusive action. If a group of sellers could eliminate the competition from new entrants to the market, they would be able to raise their prices. The total revenue of sellers is simply the market price multiplied by the quantity sold. The sellers' revenues may well be greater, and their total costs would surely be lower, if the smaller, restricted output Q_2 were sold rather than the competitive output Q_1. The artificially high price P_2 is in excess of the competitive opportunity cost of supplying the good. The price of the good does not reflect its actual level of scarcity.

It is in the interest of consumers and the community that output be expanded to Q_1, the output consistent with economic efficiency. It is in the interest of sellers, though, to make the good artificially scarce and raise its price. If sellers can use collusion, government action, or other means of restricting supply, they can gain. However, the restricted output level would violate rule 2. Inefficiency would result. There is a conflict between the interests of sellers and what is best for the entire community.

EXHIBIT 2
Rigging the Market

If a group of sellers can restrict the entry of competitors and connive to reduce their own output, they can sometimes obtain more total revenue by selling fewer units. Note that the total sales revenue $P_2 Q_2$ for the restricted supply exceeds the sales revenue $P_1 Q_1$ for the competitive supply, in this case.

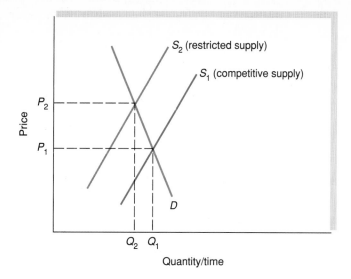

When there are only a few firms in the industry and competition from new entrants can be restrained, sellers may be able to rig the market in their favor. Through collusion, either tacit or overt, suppliers may be able to escape competitive pressures. What can the government do to preserve competition? Congress has enacted a series of antitrust laws, most notably the Sherman Antitrust Act and the Clayton Act, making it illegal for firms to collude or attempt to monopolize a product market. Congress also established the Federal Trade Commission, which prohibits "unfair methods of competition in commerce," such as false advertising, improper grading of materials, and deceptive business practices.

For the most part, economists favor the principle of government action to ensure and promote competitive markets, but there is considerable debate about the effectiveness of past public policy in this area. Few economists are satisfied with the government's role as a promoter of competition.

Two general criticisms are voiced. Many economists suggest government should pursue a more vigorous antitrust policy. They believe antitrust action should be taken to expand the number of rivals in several industries—automobiles and steel, for example—that are currently dominated by a few firms. On the other hand, other critics argue that antitrust policy and business regulation, both past and present, have often, paradoxically, restricted competition. These critics argue that government regulatory policy has been part of the problem rather than part of the solution.

Externalities: The side effects of an action that influence the well-being of nonconsenting parties. The nonconsenting parties may be either helped (by external benefits) or harmed (by external costs).

EXTERNALITIES—WHAT HAVE YOU BEEN DOING TO YOUR NEIGHBOR?

Production and consumption of some goods will result in spillover effects that the market will fail to register. These spillover effects, called **externalities,** are present when the actions of one individual or group affect the welfare of others without their consent.

Examples of externalities abound. If you live in an apartment house and the noisy stereo of your next-door neighbors keeps you from studying economics, your neighbors are creating an externality. Their actions are imposing an unwanted cost on you. Driving your car during rush hour increases the level of congestion, thereby imposing a cost on other motorists.

The existence of externality implies the lack of property rights, or of enforcement of those rights. The apartment dweller who is bothered by a neighbor's noise either does not have a right to quiet, or is unable to enforce the right. In either case, the maker of noise need not take into account the resulting discomfort of neighbors. Similarly, each motorist adding his or her car to heavy traffic will not be forced to consider the effects on others, unless there is a highway access fee reflecting the costs of congestion. When enforceable property rights are not present, externality is a normal result.

Not all externalities result in the imposition of a cost. Sometimes human actions generate benefits for nonparticipating parties. The home-owner who keeps a house in good condition and maintains a neat lawn improves the beauty of the entire community, thereby benefitting community members. A flood-control project built by upstream residents for their benefit will also generate gains for those who live downstream. Scientific theories benefit their authors, but the knowledge gained also contributes to the welfare of others. Again, a lack of enforceable property rights causes the problem. The producers of the goods or the services which provide the positively valued externalities do not have property rights in them. They cannot expect to be paid for the benefits of their services, and so those benefits may not influence their decision-making.

Why do externalities create problems for the market mechanism? Exhibit 3 can help answer this question. With competitive markets in equilibrium, the cost of a good (including the opportunity cost borne by the producer) will be paid by consumers. Unless consumer benefits exceed the opportunity cost of production, the goods will not be produced. What happens, though, when externalities are present?

Suppose that a business firm discharges smoke into the air or sewage into a river. Valuable resources, clean air and pure water, are used essentially for garbage-removal services. Neither the firm nor the consumers of its products, how-

EXHIBIT 3

Externalities and
Problems for the Market

When external costs are present (a), the output level of a product will exceed the desired amount. In contrast, market output of goods that generate external benefits (b) will be less than the ideal level.

(a) External costs

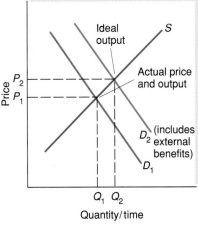

(b) External benefits

ever, will pay for these costs. As Exhibit 3a shows, the supply curve will understate the opportunity cost of production when these external costs are present. Since the producer only has to consider the cost to the firm, and can ignore the cost imposed on secondary parties, supply curve S_1 will result. If all costs were considered, supply would be S_2. The actual supply curve S_1 will not reflect the opportunity cost of producing the good. The producer will be misled into thinking that the opportunity cost is low enough to merit an increase in supply. Output will be expanded beyond Q_2 (to Q_1), even though the community's valuation of the additional units is less than their cost. The second efficiency condition, rule 2, is violated. Inefficiency in the form of excessive air and water pollution results. In the total picture, the harm caused by the added pollution outweighs the benefits to some of the people involved.

As Exhibit 3b shows, external benefits often result in opportunities forgone. When they are present, the market demand curve D_1 will not fully reflect the total benefits, which include those going to parties who receive the benefits without payment. They may be unwilling to pay, since they already receive benefits without payment. Output Q_1 will result. Could the community gain from a greater output of the product? Yes. The demand curve D_2 reflects both the direct benefits to paying consumers and the benefits bestowed on secondary, nonpaying parties. Expansion of output beyond Q_1 to Q_2 would result in net gain to the community. But, since neither producers nor paying consumers can capture the secondary benefits, consumption level Q_1 will result. The potential net gain from the greater output level Q_2 will be lost. Rule 1 of our ideal efficiency criterion is violated.

Competitive markets will fail to give consumers and producers the correct signals when externalities are present. The market will tend to underallocate resources to the production of goods with external benefits and overallocate resources to the production of goods that impose external costs on nonconsenting parties.

PUBLIC GOODS—MORE PROBLEMS FOR THE MARKET

Public Goods: Jointly consumed goods. When consumed by one person, they are also made available to others. National defense, poetry, and scientific theories are all public goods.

Some goods cannot be provided through the marketplace because there is no way to exclude nonpaying customers. Goods that must be consumed jointly by all are called **public goods.** National defense, the judicial and legal systems, and the monetary system are examples of public goods. The national defense that protects you also protects others. Unlike candy bars, national defense cannot be provided to some citizens but not to others. Similarly, the actions of a central monetary authority are a public good. The monetary system that influences the prices of things you buy and sell also influences the prices and incomes of others.

Why are public goods troublesome for the market? Typically, in the marketplace, there is a direct link between consumption and payment. If you do not pay, you do not consume. Similarly, the payments of consumers provide the incentive to supply products. Public goods, however, are consumed jointly. If a public good is made available to one person, it is simultaneously made available to others. Since people cannot be excluded, their incentive to pay or even to reveal their true valuation of the good is destroyed. Why would you voluntarily pay your "fair share" for national defense, the courts, or police protection if these goods were provided in the market? If others contribute a large amount, the public good will be provided pretty much regardless of what you do. If others do not pay, your actions will not make much difference anyway. Each person thus has an incentive to opt out, to refuse to help pay voluntarily for the public good.

When everybody opts out, what happens? Not very much of the public good is produced. This is precisely why the market cannot handle public goods very well. Resources will be underallocated to the production of public goods because many people, following their self-interest, will refuse to pay for them. Because of their very nature, public goods cause a conflict between self-interest and the public interest of economic efficiency.

ECONOMIC INSTABILITY

If markets are to function well, a stable monetary exchange system must be provided. Many market exchanges involve a time dimension. Houses, cars, consumer durables, land, buildings, equipment, and many other items are paid for over a period of months or even years. If the purchasing power of the monetary unit, the dollar in the United States, gyrated wildly, few would want to make transactions involving long-term commitments because of the uncertainty. The smooth functioning of the market would be retarded. Many economists believe that without the help of government, the economy would be less stable than it is.

The government's spending and monetary policies exert a powerful influence on economic stability. If properly conducted, these policies contribute to economic stability, full and efficient utilization of resources, and stable prices. Improper stabilization polices, though, can cause massive unemployment, rapidly rising prices, or both.

Economists are not in complete agreement on the extent to which public policy can stabilize the economy and promote full employment. They often debate the impact of various policy tools. All agree, however, that a stable economic environment is vital to a market economy. Those pursuing a course in macroeconomics will find both the potential and the limitations of government action as a stabilizing force in the economy discussed further in Part Two.

THE ECONOMICS OF COLLECTIVE ACTION

The pricing system will fail to meet our ideal efficiency standards if (a) markets are not competitive, (b) externalities are present, (c) public goods necessitate joint consumption, or (d) the aggregate economy is characterized by instability and the resultant uncertainty. If public-sector action can correct these deficiencies, net gains for the community are possible. Public policy does not have to be a zero-sum game.

Just because it is possible to visualize that public-sector action will promote economic welfare, it does not follow that real-world governments, including those organized democratically, will necessarily institute sound policies. Government is *not* a supraindividual that will always make decisions in the ''public interest,'' however that nebulous term might be defined. Neither is it a corrective device available for use when market organization fails to achieve a desired outcome. It is instead an alternative method of social organization—an institutional process through which individuals collectively make choices and carry out activities.

Public Choice Analysis: The study of decision-making as it affects the formation and operation of collective organizations, such as governments. The discipline bridges the gap between economics and political science. In general, the principles and methodology of economics are applied to political science topics.

If we are going to make meaningful comparisons between market allocation and collective action, we need to develop a sound theory that will help us understand both forms of economic organization. **Public choice analysis** has significantly advanced our understanding of the collective decision-making process in recent years. Something of a cross between economics and political science, public choice theory applies the principles and methodology of economics to collective choices.

In a democratic setting, individual preferences will influence the outcome of collective decisions, just as they influence outcomes in the market. Public choice theory postulates that individual behavior in the political arena will be motivated by considerations similar to those that influence market behavior. If self-interest is a powerful motivator in the marketplace, there is every reason to believe it will also be a motivating factor when choices are made collectively. If market choices are influenced by changes in projected personal costs relative to benefits, we can expect that such changes will also influence political choices. Public choice theory, in other words, suggests that the number of saints and sinners in the two sectors will be comparable.

In analyzing the behavior of people in the marketplace, economists develop a logically consistent theory of behavior that can be tested against reality. Through theory and empirical testing, we seek to explain various economic actions of decision-makers and, in general, how the market operates.

In the public sphere, our purpose should be the same: to explain how the collective decision-making process really operates. This means developing a log-

APPLICATIONS IN ECONOMICS

Perspectives on the Cost of Political Competition

We all have our own ideas concerning how government should be run. Since government is such an extremely important force in our economy and in our lives, individuals and groups try to influence election outcomes by voting, by contributing to political campaigns, and by ringing doorbells, among other activities. In addition, legislative and executive branch decisions can be influenced directly, by lobbying.

Competition for elective office is fierce, and campaigns are expensive. In preparation for the 1986 elections, for example, candidates for House and Senate positions spent more than $450 million. Unlike bidders in a market auction, winners and losers alike pay the full costs of the election bid. It is common for lobbying groups to donate to opposing candidates in a close race.

During and after the election, lobbying groups compete for the attention—the ear—of elected officials. In fact, the greatest portion of campaign funds raised by incumbents is not raised at election time; rather, it accrues over their entire term in office. A large campaign contribution may not be able to "buy" a vote, but it certainly enhances the lobbyist's chance to sit down with the elected official to explain the power and the beauty of a client's position. In the competitive world of politics, the politician who does not at least listen to helpful "friends of the campaign" is less likely to survive.

Campaign contributions are only the tip of the lobbying iceberg. In Washington, D.C., alone, thousands of offices and tens of thousands of individuals, many of them extremely talented, hard-working, and well-paid, are dedicated to lobbying Congress and the executive branch of the federal government. Trade associations, for example, have more than

3,000 offices and 80,000 employees in Washington.[1] Another indicator of the enormous amount of time and effort allocated to influencing government is that 65 percent of Fortune 200 Chief Executive Officers travel to Washington at least every two weeks, on average. Billions of dollars in budgets, in taxes, and in expenditures required by regulation are at stake, in addition to such emotional issues as gun control and abortion. The natural result is huge expenditures designed to influence governmental policy.

[1]More details on campaign finance can be found in Michael Barone and Grant Ujifusa, *The Almanac of American Politics: 1988* (Washington, D.C.: National Journal, 1988). See also David Boaz, "Spend Money to Make Money," *Wall Street Journal*, November 13, 1983.

ically consistent theory linking individual behavior to collective action, analyzing the implications of that theory, and testing these implications against events in the real world.

Since the theory of collective decision-making is not as well developed as our theory of market behavior, our conclusions will, of course, be less definitive. In the last 25 years, however, social scientists have made great strides in our understanding of resource allocation by the public sector.[2] Currently, this subject is often dealt with at a more advanced academic level. Even on an introductory level, though, economic tools can be used to shed light on how the public sector handles economic activities.

DIFFERENCES AND SIMILARITIES BETWEEN MARKET AND COLLECTIVE ACTION

There are some basic characteristics that influence outcomes in both the market and the public sectors.[3] As we have noted, there is reason to believe that the motivational factors present in both sectors are similar. There are, however, basic structural differences. Voluntary exchange coordinated by prices is the dominant characteristic of a market economy (although, of course, when externalities are present, involuntary exchange may also result). In a democratic setting, the dominant characteristic of collective action is majority rule, effective either directly or through legislative procedures. Let us take a look at both the differences and similarities between the two sectors.

1. Competitive Behavior Is Present in Both the Market and Public Sectors. Although the market sector is sometimes referred to as "the competitive sector," it is clear that competitive behavior is present in both sectors. Politicians compete with each other for elective office. Bureau chiefs and agency heads compete for additional taxpayer dollars. Public-sector employees, like their counterparts in the private sector, compete for promotions, higher incomes, and additional power. Lobbyists compete to secure funds, to receive favorable rulings, and to secure legislation for the interest groups they represent—including both private and governmental clients. (See Applications in Economics box on p. 89.) The nature of the competition and the criteria for success do differ between the two sectors. Nonetheless, competitive behavior is present in both sectors.

2. Public-Sector Organization Can Break the Individual Consumption-Payment Link. In the market, a consumer who wants to obtain a commodity must be willing to pay the price. For each person, there is a one-to-one correspondence between consuming the commodity and paying the purchase price. In this respect, there is a fundamental difference between market and collective action. The government usually does not establish a one-to-one relationship between the individual's payment and receipt of a good.

Your tax bill will be the same whether you like or dislike the national defense, agriculture, or antipoverty policies of the government. You will be taxed for subsidies to higher education, sugarbeet growers, airlines, cultural centers, and

[2]The contributions of Kenneth Arrow, James Buchanan, Duncan Black, Anthony Downs, Mancur Olson, Robert Tollison, and Gordon Tullock have been particularly important.
[3]The "Public Choice" section of this book analyzes the topics of alternative forms of economic organization—market versus collective action—in more detail.

Political Good: Any good (or policy) supplied by the political process.

many other **political goods**[4] regardless of whether or not you consume or use them. In some cases, you may receive very large benefits (either monetary or subjective) from a governmental action without any significant impact on your tax bill. The direct link between individual consumption of the good and individual payment for the good is not required in the public sector.

3. Scarcity Imposes the Aggregate Consumption-Payment Link in Both Sectors. Although the government can break the link between an individual's payment for a good and the right to consume the good, the reality of the *aggregate consumption-aggregate payment* link will remain. Provision of scarce goods requires sacrificing alternatives. Someone must cover the cost of providing scarce goods, regardless of the sector used to produce (or distribute) them. There are no free lunches in either the private or the public sector. Free goods provided in the public sector are ''free'' only to individuals. They are most certainly not free from the viewpoint of society.

An increase in the amount of goods provided by the public sector will mean an increase in the total costs of government. Given the fact of scarcity, the link between aggregate consumption and aggregate costs of production cannot be broken by public-sector action.

4. The Element of Compulsion Is Present in the Public Sector. As we have already discussed, voluntary exchange is the dominant characteristic of market organization. Except when externalities are present, involuntary exchange is absent. In the marketplace, a minority need not yield to the majority. For example, the views of the majority, even an overwhelming majority, do not prevent minority consumers from purchasing desired goods.

Governments possess an exclusive right to the use of coercion. Large corporations like Exxon and General Motors are economically powerful, but they cannot require you to buy their products. In contrast, if the majority (either directly or through legislative process) decides on a particular policy, the minority must accept the policy and help pay for its cost, even if that minority strongly disagrees. If representative legislative policy allocates $10 billion for the development of a superweapon system, the dissenting minority is required to pay taxes that will help finance the project. Other dissenting minorities will be compelled to pay taxes for the support of welfare programs, farm subsidies, foreign aid, or hundreds of other projects on which reasonable people will surely differ. When issues are decided in the public sector, dissidents must, at least temporarily, yield to the current dominant view.

5. When Collective Decisions Are Made Legislatively, Voters Must Choose Among Candidates Who Represent a Bundle of Positions on Issues. On election day, the voter cannot choose the views of Representative Free Lunch on poverty and business welfare and simultaneously choose the views of challenger Ms. Austerity on national defense and tariffs. Inability to separate a candidate's views on one issue

---

[4]''Political good'' is a broad term used to designate any action supplied through the public sector. Note that political goods may be either private goods or public goods.

from his or her views on another greatly reduces the voter's power to register preferences on specific issues. Since the average representative is asked to vote on roughly 2,000 different issues during a two-year term, the enormity of the problem is obvious.

To the average individual, choosing a representative is a bit like choosing an agent who will control a substantial portion of one's income and also regulate one's activities. Even if this individual voter could personally elect the agent, it would be impossible for the voter to select one agent's views on issue X and another agent's views on issue Y. Looked at another way, deciding to vote for (or against) a candidate on the basis of one issue essentially means being disenfranchised on all others. As a result of the "bundle-purchase" nature of the political process, the likelihood that a collective decision will reflect the precise views of an individual voter is low.

6. Income and Power Are Distributed Differently in the Two Sectors.   Individuals who supply more highly valued resources in the marketplace have larger incomes. The number of dollar votes available to an individual reflect her or his abilities, ambitions, skills, perceptiveness, past savings, inheritance, and good fortune, among other things. An unequal distribution of consumer power is the result.

In the public sector, ballots call the tune when decisions are made democratically. One citizen, one vote is the rule. This does not mean, however, that political goods and services—those resources that make up political power or political income—are allocated equally to all citizens by the collective decision-making process. Some individuals are much more astute than others at using the political process to obtain personal advantage. The political process rewards those who are most capable of delivering votes—not only their own individual votes but those of others as well. Persuasive skills (that is, lobbying, public speaking, public relations), organizational abilities, financial contributions, and knowledge are vital to success in politics. Persons who have more of these resources—and are willing to spend them in the political arena—can expect to benefit more handsomely, in terms of both money and power, from the political process than individuals who lack them.

THE SUPPLY OF AND DEMAND FOR PUBLIC-SECTOR ACTION

Consumers use their dollar votes to demand goods in the marketplace. Producers supply goods. The actions of both are influenced by self-interest. In a democratic political system, voters and legislators are counterparts to consumers and producers. Voters demand political goods using their political resources—votes, lobbying, contributions, and organizational abilities. Vote-conscious legislators are suppliers of political goods.

How does a voter decide which political supplier to support? Since there is no evidence that entrance into a voting booth or participation in the political process causes a personality transformation, there is sound reason to believe that the motivation of participants in the market and political processes is similar. The voter who selects among political alternatives is the same person who selects among market alternatives. If Jones is influenced by expected personal benefits and costs when he makes choices in the department store, it makes sense that he will be similarly influenced by personal benefits and costs when he makes choices in the voting booth.

Other things constant, voters will support those candidates whom they expect to provide them with the most benefits, net of cost. The greater the expected gains from a candidate's election, the more voters will do to ensure the candidate's success. A voter, like the consumer in the marketplace, will ask the supplier, "What can you do for me and how much will I pay?"

The goal of the political supplier is to put together a majority coalition—to win the election. Vote-seeking politicians, like profit-seeking business decision-makers, will have a strong incentive to cater to the views of politically active constituents. The easiest way to win votes, both politically and financially, is to give the constituents, or at least appear to give them, what they want. A politician who pays no heed to the views of his or her constituents is as rare as a business-person selling bikinis in the Arctic.

There are two major reasons that voters are likely to turn to public-sector economic organization: (a) to reduce waste and inefficiency stemming from non-competitive markets, externalities, public goods, and economic instability and (b) to redistribute income. Public-sector action that corrects, or appears to correct, the shortcomings of the market will be attractive. If properly conducted, it will generate more benefits than costs to the community. Much real-world public policy is motivated by a desire to correct the shortcomings of the market. Antitrust action is designed to promote competition. Government provision of national defense, crime prevention, a legal system, and flood-control projects is related to the public-good nature of these activities. Similarly, externalities help justify public-sector action in such areas as pollution control, education, pure research, and no-fault insurance. Clearly, the tax, spending, and monetary policies of the government are used to influence the level of economic activity in most Western nations.

Demand for public-sector action may also stem from a desire to change the income distribution. There is no reason to presume that the unhampered market will lead to the most desirable distribution of income. In fact, the ideal distribution of income is largely a matter of personal preference. There is nothing in positive economics that tells us that one distribution of income is better than another. Some people may desire to see more income allocated to low-income citizens. The most common scientific argument for redistribution to the poor is based on the "public-good" nature of adequate income for all. Alleviation of poverty may help not only the poor but also those who are well-off. Middle- and upper-income recipients, for example, may benefit if the less fortunate members of the community enjoy better food, clothing, housing, and health care. If the rich would gain, why will they not voluntarily give to the poor? For the same reason that individuals will do little to provide national defense voluntarily. The antipoverty efforts of any single individual will exert little impact on the total amount of poverty in the community. Because individual action is so insignificant, each person has an incentive to opt out. When everyone opts out, the market provides less than the desired amount of antipoverty action.

Others may desire public-sector redistribution for less altruistic reasons— they may seek to enhance their own personal incomes. This poses a problem: How can government engage in income redistribution based on the "public-good" nature of antipoverty transfers and at the same time restrain income transfers based on the political clout of various interest groups? This is an important question because there is reason to believe that economic waste is a side effect of substantial government involvement in the determination of income shares. There are three major reasons why large-scale redistribution is likely to reduce the size of the economic pie.

First, such redistribution weakens the link between productive activity and reward. When taxes take a larger share of one's income, tax revenues are spread among all beneficiaries, so the benefits derived from hard work and productive service are reduced. The basic economic postulate suggests that when benefits allocated to producers are reduced (and benefits of nonproducers are raised), less productive effort will be supplied.

Rent Seeking: Actions by individuals and interest groups designed to restructure public policy in a manner that will either directly or indirectly redistribute more income to themselves.

Second, as public policy redistributes a larger share of income, individuals will allocate more resources to **rent seeking.**[5] Rent seeking is a term used by economists to classify actions designed to change public policy—tax structure, composition of spending, or regulation—in a manner that will redistribute income to oneself. Resources used for lobbying and other means of rent seeking (perhaps "favor seeking" would be more descriptive) will not be available to increase the size of the economic pie.

Third, higher taxes to finance income redistribution and an expansion in rent-seeking activities will induce taxpayers to engage in protective action. Taxpayers will be encouraged to take steps to protect their income. More accountants, lawyers, and tax-shelter experts will be retained as people seek to limit the amount of their income that is redistributed to others. Like the resources allocated to rent seeking, resources allocated to protecting one's wealth from public policy will also be wasted. They will not be available for productive activity. Therefore, given the incentive structure generated by large-scale redistribution policies, there is good reason to expect that such policies will reduce the size of the economic pie.

CONFLICTS BETWEEN GOOD ECONOMICS AND GOOD POLITICS

What reason is there to believe that political action will result in economic inefficiency? Current economic and political research is continually yielding knowledge that will help us answer this question more definitively. We deal with it in more detail in a later chapter, but three important characteristics of the political process are introduced here.

THE RATIONALLY IGNORANT VOTER

Rational Ignorance Effect: Voter ignorance that is present because people perceive their individual votes as unlikely to be decisive. Voters rationally have little incentive to inform themselves so as to cast an informed vote.

Less than one half of the American electorate can correctly identify the names of their congressmen and women, much less state where their representatives stand on various issues. Why are so many people ignorant of the simplest facts regarding the political process? The explanation does not lie with a lack of intelligence on the part of the average American. The phenomenon is explained by the incentives confronting the voter. Most citizens recognize that their vote is unlikely to determine the outcome of an election. Since their vote is highly unlikely to resolve the issue at hand, citizens have little incentive to seek costly information that will help them cast an intelligent vote. Economists refer to this lack of incentive as the **rational ignorance effect.**

[5]See Charles K. Rowley, Robert D. Tollison, and Gordon Tullock, *The Political Economy of Rent-Seeking* (Boston: Kluewer Academic Publishers, 1988) for additional details on rent seeking.

The rationally ignorant voter is exercising good judgment as to how his or her time and effort will yield the most personal benefits. There is a parallel between the voter's failure to acquire political knowledge and the farmer's inattention to the factors that determine the weather. Weather is probably the most important factor determining the income of an individual farmer, yet it makes no sense for the farmer to invest time and resources attempting to understand atmospheric science. An improved knowledge of how weather systems work will seldom enable the farmer to avoid their adverse effects. So it is with the average voter. The voter stands to gain little from acquiring more information about a wide range of issues that are decided in the political arena. Since the resolution of these issues, like the weather, is out of the individual voter's hands, he or she has little incentive to become more informed.

Because of this fact, most voters simply rely on information that is supplied to them freely by candidates and the mass media. Conversations with friends and information acquired at work, from newspapers, from TV news, and from political advertising are especially important because the voter has so little incentive to spend personal time and effort gathering information. It is not surprising, then, that few voters are able to accurately describe the consequences of raising tariffs on automobiles or of abolishing the farm price support program. In using their time and efforts in ways other than studying these policy issues, voters are merely responding to economic incentives.

THE PROBLEM OF SPECIAL INTEREST

Special Interest Issue: An issue that generates substantial individual benefits to a small minority while imposing a small individual cost on many other voters. In total, the net cost to the majority might either exceed or fall short of the net benefits to the special interest group.

A **special interest issue** is one that generates substantial personal benefits for a small number of constituents while imposing a small individual cost on a large number of other votes. A few gain a great deal individually, whereas a large number lose a little as individuals.

Special interest issues are very attractive to vote-conscious politicians (that is, to those most eager and most likely to win elections). Voters who have a small cost imposed on them by a policy favoring a special interest will not care enough about the issue to examine it, particularly if it is complex enough that the imposition of the cost is difficult to identify. Because information is costly, most of those harmed will not even be aware of the legislator's views on such an issue. Most voters will simply ignore special interest issues. Those representing the special interest, though, will be vitally concerned. They will let the candidate (or legislator) know when an issue is important to them. They will give financial and other help to politicians receptive to their ideas, and will oppose those who are not.

What would you do if you wanted to win an election? Support the special interest groups. Milk them for financial resources. Use those resources to "educate" the uniformed majority of voters to the fact that you support policies of interest to them. You would have an incentive to follow this path even if the total community benefits from the support of the special interest were less than the cost. The policy might cause economic inefficiency, but it could still be a political winner.

Why stand up for a large majority? Even though the total cost may be very large, each person bears only a small cost. Most voters are uninformed on the issue. They do not care much about it. They would do little to help you get elected even if you supported their best interests on this issue. Astute politicians will support the special interest group if they plan to be around for very long.

The political process tends to work in favor of special interest groups, even when their programs are inefficient. This means that there is sometimes a conflict between good politics (winning elections) and ideal public policy. Throughout, as we consider public policy alternatives, we will remind you to consider how public policy is likely to operate when special interest influence is strong.

POLITICAL GAINS FROM SHORTSIGHTED POLICIES

The complexity of many issues makes it difficult for voters to identify the future benefits and costs. Will a tax cut reduce the long-run rate of unemployment? Are wage-price controls an efficient means of dealing with inflation? Can pro-union legislation raise the real wages of workers? These questions are complex. Few voters will analyze the short-run and long-run implications of policy in these areas. Instead, voters will have a tendency to rely on current conditions. To the voter, the best indicator of the success of a policy is, "How are things now?"

Politicians seeking reelection have a strong incentive to support policies that generate current benefits in exchange for future costs, particularly if the future costs will be difficult to identify on election day. Public-sector action will therefore be biased in favor of legislation that offers immediate (and easily identifiable) current benefits in exchange for future costs that are complicated and difficult to identify. Simultaneously, there is a bias against legislation that involves immediate and easily identifiable costs (for example, higher taxes) while yielding future benefits that are complex and difficult to identify. Economists refer to this bias inherent in the collective decision-making process as the **shortsightedness effect.**

Shortsightedness Effect:
Misallocation of resources that results because public-sector action is biased (a) in favor of proposals yielding clearly defined current benefits in exchange for difficult-to-identify future costs and (b) against proposals with clearly identifiable current costs yielding less concrete and less obvious future benefits.

The nature of democratic institutions restricts the planning horizon of elected officials. Positive results must be observable by the next election, or the incumbent is likely to be replaced by someone who promises more rapid results. Policies that will eventually pay off in the future (after the next election) will have little attractiveness to vote-seeking politicians if those policies do not exert a beneficial impact by election day. As we shall subsequently see, the shortsighted nature of the political process reduces the likelihood that it will be able to promote economic stability and a noninflationary environment.

What if shortsighted policies lead to serious problems after an election? This can be sticky for politicians, but is it not better to be an officeholder explaining why things are in a mess than a defeated candidate trying to convince people who will not listen why you were right all the time? The political entrepreneur has a strong incentive to win the next election and worry about the problems, as they arise, later.

IMPLICATIONS OF PUBLIC CHOICE

It is important to distinguish between ordinary politics and constitutional rules. Constitutions establish the procedures that will be utilized to make decisions. They also may limit the boundary of ordinary politics—place certain matters (for example, the taking of private property without compensation, restrictions on freedom of speech or worship, and various restrictions on voting) beyond the reach of majority rule or normal legislative procedures.

Both bad news and good news flow from public choice analysis. The bad news is that for certain classes of economic activity, unconstrained democratic government will predictably be a source of economic waste and inefficiency. Not only does the invisible hand of the market sometimes fail to meet our ideal efficiency criteria, so too, does political decision-making. But there is also some good news arising from public choice theory: properly structured constitutional rules can improve the expected result from government.

Whether political organization leads to desirable or undesirable economic outcomes is critically dependent upon the structure of the political (constitutional) rules. When the structure of the political rules brings the self-interest of individual voters, politicians, and bureaucrats into harmony with the general welfare, government will promote economic prosperity. On the other hand, if the rules fail to bring about this harmony, politically determined outcomes will often conflict with economic efficiency. The challenge before us is to develop political economy institutions that are more consistent with economic prosperity. As we proceed, we will discuss several modifications of the political rules that public choice theory indicates would improve the economic effectiveness of the political process. Needless to say, this general topic—modifications in the structure of government that will make it more consistent

OUTSTANDING ECONOMIST

James Buchanan
(1919–   )

Thirty years ago, most economists were content to concentrate on the workings of the marketplace, its shortcomings, and what government action might do to correct these deficiencies. Political scientists and economists alike envisioned the public sector as a type of supra-individual, a creature making decisions in the public interest. James Buchanan was determined to change all this. He, perhaps more than anyone else, is responsible for what some have called the "public choice revolution." For this and related contributions, he was awarded the 1986 Nobel Prize in Economics.

Buchanan refers to himself as a "constitutional political economist," which he differentiates from a "public policy economist." Buchanan argues that it is constitutional restraints and political rules, rather than the people elected to office or the experts advising them, that determine the pattern of political outcomes. Public choice theory maintains that politicians and bureaucrats are guided by essentially the same motives as consumers and business decision-makers. Therefore, unless we design rules that bring the self-interest of the political players into harmony with the wise use of resources, the process will go awry. Waste and stagnation will result.

Much of Buchanan's research has focused on how alternative political decision rules (simple majority, supra-majority, legislative procedures, and so on) work. Buchanan's most famous work on this topic is *The Calculus of Consent* (1962), coauthored with Gordon Tullock.[6] Indeed, *The Calculus* has become a modern-day classic.

Buchanan and Tullock founded the Center for Study of Public Choice in 1969. Located on the campus of George Mason University, the Center is a focal point of public choice scholarship. Currently a Distinguished Professor of Economics at George Mason and general Director of the Center, Buchanan continues his work as a prolific writer and innovative scholar.

---

[6]J. M. Buchanan and G. Tullock, *The Calculus of Consent* (Ann Arbor: University of Michigan Press, 1962).

with economic efficiency and general prosperity—is one of the most exciting and potentially fruitful areas of study in economics.

LOOKING AHEAD

In the next chapter, we will examine the government's actual spending and tax policies. In subsequent chapters, the significance of economic organization and issues of political economy will be highlighted. The tools of economics are used with a dual objective. We will point out what government ideally might do, but we will also focus on what government can be expected to do. Not surprisingly, these two are not always identical. Political economy—the use of economic tools to explain how both the market and the public sectors actually work—is a fascinating subject. It helps us to understand the "why" behind many of today's current events. Who said economics is the dismal science?

CHAPTER SUMMARY

1. Economic efficiency—creating as much value as possible from a given set of resources—is a goal by which alternative institutions and policies can be judged. Two conditions must be met to achieve economic efficiency: (a) all activities that produce more benefits than costs for the individuals within an economy must be undertaken and (b) activities that generate more costs than benefits to the individuals must not be undertaken. If only the buyer and the seller are affected, production and exchange in competitive markets are consistent with the ideal efficiency criteria.

2. Lack of competition may make it possible for a group of sellers to gain by restricting output and raising prices. There is a conflict between (a) the self-interest of sellers that leads them to collude, restrict output, and raise product prices above their production costs and (b) economic efficiency. Public-sector action—promoting competition or regulating private firms—may be able to improve economic efficiency in industries in which competitive pressures are lacking.

3. The market will tend to underallocate resources to the production of goods with external benefits and overallocate resources to those products that generate external costs.

4. Public goods are troublesome for the market to handle because nonpaying customers cannot easily be excluded. Since the amount of a public good that each individual receives is largely unaffected by whether he or she helps pay for it, many individuals will contribute little. The market will thus tend to undersupply public goods.

5. The public sector can improve the operation of markets by providing a stable economic environment.

6. The public sector is an alternative means of organizing economic activity. Public-sector decision-making will reflect the choices of individuals acting as voters, politicians, financial contributors, lobbyists, and bureaucrats. Public choice analysis applies the principles and methodology of economics to group decision-making to help us understand collective organizations.

7. Successful political candidates will seek to offer programs that voters favor. Voters, in turn, will be attracted to candidates who reflect the voters' own views and interests. In a democratic setting, there are two major reasons why voters will turn to collective organization: (a) to reduce waste and inefficiency stemming from noncompetitive markets, externalities, public goods, and economic instability and (b) to alter the income distribution.

8. Public-sector action may sometimes improve the market's efficiency and lead to an increase in the community's welfare, all individuals considered. However, the political process is likely to conflict with ideal economic efficiency criteria when (a) voters have little knowledge of an issue, (b) special interests are strong, and/or (c) political figures can gain from following shortsighted policies.

CRITICAL ANALYSIS QUESTIONS

1. Explain in your own words what is meant by external costs and external benefits. Why may market allocations be less than ideal when externalities are present?

*2. If producers are to be provided with an incentive to produce a good, why is it important for them to be able to prevent nonpaying customers from receiving the good?

3. Do you think real-world politicians adopt political positions to help their election prospects? Can you name a current political figure who consistently puts "principles above politics"? If so, check with three of your classmates and see if they agree.

4. Do you think special interest groups exert much influence on local government? Why or why not? As a test, check the composition of the local zoning board in your community. How many real-estate agents, contractors, developers, and landlords are on the board? Are there any citizens without real-estate interests on the board?

*5. "Economics is a positive science. Government by its very nature is influenced by philosophical considerations. Therefore, the tools of economics cannot tell us much about how the public sector works." Do you agree or disagree? Why?

*6. Which of the following are public goods: (a) an antimissile system surrounding Washington, D.C.; (b) a fire department; (c) tennis courts; (d) Yellowstone National Park; (e) elementary schools? Explain, using the definition of a public good.

7. "A democratic government is a corrective device which can be used to remedy problems and inefficiencies that arise if market allocation is not working well." (True or false; explain)

8. Incentives are important in both the market and political sectors. Discuss the similarities and differences in the incentives of the following pairs of people to use resources efficiently and provide value to others.

   (a) the President of General Motors and the President of a large state university.

   (b) a member of the Board of Directors of IBM and a congressional representative.

   (c) the General Manager of a Walt Disney World and the Superintendant of Yellowstone National Park.

   (d) the President of a textbook publishing company and the Superintendent of public schools in your state.

*9. How can you determine if a market action is efficient? How can you determine if a government action is efficient? If the majority of the citizens favor a project, does this indicate it is productive?

10. English philosopher John Locke argued that the protection of each individual's person and property was the primary function of government. Why is the secure protection of each individual's person and property acquired without the use of violence, theft, or fraud important to the efficient operation of an economy?

*11. Does the democratic political process incorporate the invisible hand principle? Is the presence or absence of the invisible hand principle important? Why or why not?

*12. "The average person is more likely to make an informed choice when he or she purchases a personal computer than when he or she votes for a congressional candidate." Evaluate this view.

---

*Asterisk denotes questions for which answers are given in Appendix C, Selected Answers.

5

GOVERNMENT SPENDING AND TAXATION

*Our Constitution is in actual operation; everything appears
to promise that it will last; but in this world nothing is
certain but death and taxes.*

Benjamin Franklin (1789)

CHAPTER FOCUS

■ How big is government? What goods and services do we provide through
government? How are they financed?

■ Why has the size of government grown more rapidly than our economy during
the last several decades? Does government now provide more goods and
services than it did in the past? Does it redistribute more income?

■ How did legislation passed during the 1980s modify the structure of the
income tax? How did it affect the taxes paid by the rich?

■ How do taxes influence the choices of taxpayers? If a tax rate is increased by
10 percent, will revenue from the tax increase by 10 percent?

■ How does the size of government in the United States compare with the size
of government in other countries?

Whether the setting is the halls of Congress, the classroom, or a social gathering, a discussion of the economic role of government generally means controversy. Governments levy taxes and organize the production of goods and services. The role of government in the economy, though, is not limited to its taxation and spending activities. Governments set the rules of the game. Public policy defines property rights, enforces contracts, regulates business activities, and establishes a monetary framework. These legal and regulatory activities influence how markets work and the degree of cooperation and conflict among economic participants. In fact, the role of government as the rule-maker and referee probably exerts more influence on the economic prosperity of a nation than does its function as a producer of goods and services. Nevertheless, taxation and government expenditures are the most direct means by which the government influences the economy. Analysis of the government's spending policies and methods of finance will reveal a great deal about the size and economic character of government.

THE GROWTH OF GOVERNMENT

Federal, state, and local government expenditures generally amounted to less than 10 percent of gross national product (GNP) in the United States prior to the 1930s.[1] As Exhibit 1 illustrates, since 1930, the size of government has increased substantially relative to the size of the economy. In the midst of the defense effort

EXHIBIT 1

The Growth of Governmental Expenditures, 1902–1988

Between 1902 and 1929, governmental spending rose from 7.7 percent to 10 percent of total output. Since 1930, governmental expenditures have increased substantially as a proportion of total output. In 1988 governmental spending summed to 34 percent of total output. Federal spending alone accounts for 23.0 percent of the total output in the United States.

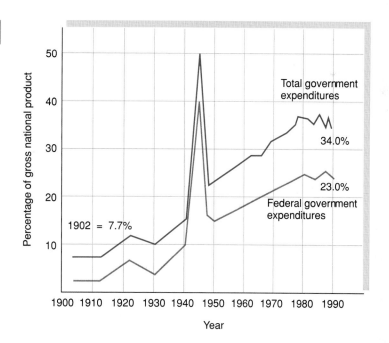

---

[1]The gross national product (GNP) is discussed in Chapter 6. For now, it can be thought of as a measure of total output produced during a period.

during World War II, government expenditures consumed approximately 50 percent of total output. At the conclusion of the war, however, they dropped back to only about 20 percent of GNP. Since the late 1940s, both the relative and absolute size of government have expanded substantially. By 1975, 34.5 percent of our total output was channelled through government, up sharply from the 21.3 percent in 1950. Since 1975, the upward trend in the size of government as a share of the economy has slowed. In fact, total government expenditures as a proportion of GNP were approximately the same in 1988 as they were in 1975.

WHAT DO FEDERAL, STATE, AND LOCAL GOVERNMENTS DO?

In recent decades, federal expenditures have accounted for a little less than two-thirds of the total spending by governments. The more than 82,000 state and local governmental units account for about one-third of the spending. The responsibilities of the three levels of government in the United States differ considerably. A breakdown of expenditures and revenue sources will highlight some of these differences.

Exhibit 2 shows the broad categories of federal expenditures for fiscal year 1988. The federal government is solely responsible for national defense. A little more than 30 percent of federal expenditures went for defense and related areas (space, veterans' benefits, and foreign affairs) in 1988. The largest item in the federal budget was cash income maintenance—social security, unemployment payments, and public assistance to the poor and the disabled. These income trans-

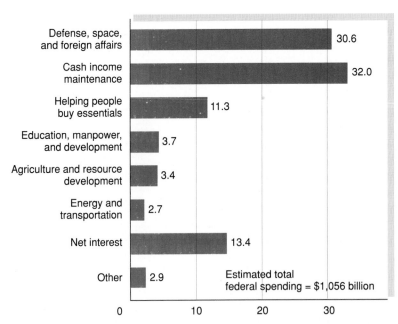

EXHIBIT 2

How the Federal Government Spends Your Tax Dollar

The breakdown of the 1988 fiscal year federal budget is presented here. Defense accounted for 30.6 percent of federal spending. Approximately 50 percent of the federal tax dollar was spent on cash income maintenance, helping people buy essentials, and manpower development.

Defense, space, and foreign affairs — 30.6
Cash income maintenance — 32.0
Helping people buy essentials — 11.3
Education, manpower, and development — 3.7
Agriculture and resource development — 3.4
Energy and transportation — 2.7
Net interest — 13.4
Other — 2.9

Estimated total federal spending = $1,056 billion

0　　10　　20　　30

Percentage of total federal expenditures, 1988

Source: *Economic Report of the President, 1988*, Table B–77.

fers accounted for 32.0 percent of the total federal budget. Programs to help people buy essentials (medical care, housing, food, and so on) made up 11.3 percent of all federal spending in 1988. This category differs from cash income maintenance in that people must purchase specific goods in order to qualify for the assistance. Expenditures on education, manpower development, agriculture, energy, and transportation also constitute major items in the federal budget from year to year. Interest payments on the national debt for 1988 constituted 13.4 percent of total federal outlays.

Exhibit 3 is a graphic presentation of state and local government expenditures. In the United States, public education has traditionally been the responsibility of state and local governments. Twenty-nine percent of state and local governmental expenditures were allocated to education during the fiscal year 1985. State governments supplement federal allocations in the areas of social welfare, public welfare, and health. These social welfare expenditures composed 18 percent of the total spending of state governments during 1985. Highways, utilities, insurance trusts, law enforcement, and fire protection are other major areas of expenditure for state and local governments.

GOVERNMENT PURCHASES AND TRANSFER PAYMENTS

Government Purchases:
Current expenditures on goods and services provided by federal, state, and local governments; They exclude transfer payments.

It is important to distinguish between (a) government purchases of goods and services and (b) transfer payments. **Government purchases** are expenditures incurred when goods and services are supplied through the public sector. Govern-

What State and Local Governments Buy

Education, public welfare, and general administrative expenditures comprise the major budget items of state and local governments.

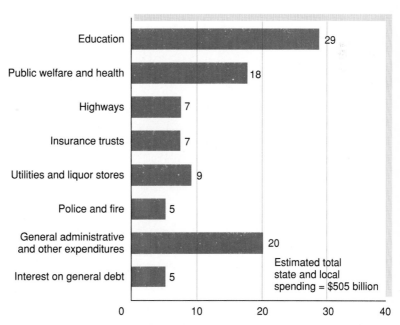

Percentage of state and local expenditures, fiscal year 1985

Source: U.S. Department of Commerce.

ment purchases include items such as jet planes, missiles, highway construction and maintenance, police and fire protection, and computer equipment. Governments also purchase the labor services of teachers, clerks, lawyers, accountants, and public relation experts to produce goods ranging from public education to administrative services. Since they consume resources with alternative uses, government purchases directly reduce the supply of resources available to produce private goods and services.

Transfer payments are transfers of income from taxpayers to recipients who do not provide current goods and services in exchange for these payments. Simply put, transfer payments take income from some to provide additional income to others. Social security benefits, pensions of retired government employees, and Aid to Families with Dependent Children (AFDC) are examples of transfer payments.

Unlike governments purchases, transfer payments do not *directly* reduce the resources available to the private sector. They do, however, alter the incentive structure of the economy and almost certainly exert an indirect impact on the size of the economic pie. The taxes necessary to finance transfer payments reduce the personal payoff from saving, investing, and working. If receipt of transfer payments is inversely related to income level, they will also reduce the recipient's incentive to earn taxable income. As we proceed, we will investigate the link between aggregate output and the incentive structure in more detail.

Transfer Payments:
Payments to individuals or institutions that are not linked to the current supply of a good or service by the recipient.

ALTERNATIVE MEASURES OF GOVERNMENT'S SIZE

Exhibit 4 presents four alternative measures of governmental size. In 1988, the purchases of federal, state, and local governments amounted to $958.5 billion, or 19.7 percent of total U.S. output. Government purchases thus consumed a little more than one-fifth of our resources. Government employment offers a second gauge by which we can measure the size of government. In 1988, approximately one out of every seven workers (14.9 percent) was employed by a governmental unit.

As we have already pointed out, government purchases fail to tell the whole story. Governments not only employ people and provide goods and services, they

EXHIBIT 4   ■   Four Measures of the Size of Government (Federal, State, and Local), 1988

1. Government purchases of goods and services	a) Billions of dollars	958.5
	b) Percentage of GNP	19.7
2. Government employment	a) Millions of employees	16.7
	b) Percentage of total employment	14.9
3. Total government expenditures including transfer payments	a) Billions of dollars	1,643.8
	b) Percentage of GNP	34.0
4. Total taxes and other revenues	a) Billions of dollars	1,571.5
	b) Percentage of GNP	32.3

Source: *Facts and Figures on Government Finance—1988–1989* and *The Economic Report of the President, 1989* (Washington, D.C.: U.S. Government Printing Office, 1989). Intergovernmental transfer payments (i.e., federal grants to state and local governments) are not counted twice.

also tax the income of some and transfer it to others. Once transfer payments are included (the third measure of size), total government expenditures in 1988 amounted to $1,643.8 billion, or 34.0 percent of the gross national product (GNP).[2] The total tax bill (the fourth measure of size) was slightly less, amounting to 32.3 percent of GNP. Therefore, during 1988, approximately one-third of the national output was channeled through the public sector.

On a per capita basis, government expenditures were equal to $6,680 in 1988. If government expenditures in 1988 had been divided equally among the 90 million households in the United States, each household would have received $18,265.

THE CHANGING COMPOSITION OF GOVERNMENT

The federal government has traditionally been responsible for national defense in the United States. Since defense is a classic example of a public good, it is not surprising that this good is supplied through the public rather than through the private sector. Police and fire protection, road maintenance, and education have traditionally been financed and distributed by state and local governments. Each of these goods either generates external "spillover effects" or exhibits public-good characteristics. The police and fire departments available to help protect my life and property are also available for your protection. At least until congestion becomes a problem, my use of the roadways does not diminish their availability to you. Education contributes to the feasibility of a modern democratic society, thereby generating a benefit to persons other than those educated.

For many years, government has been involved in the provision of national defense, police and fire protection, roads, education, and other jointly consumed goods and services. Given the characteristics of such goods, government involvement in these areas is not surprising. Interestingly, these traditional public-sector functions are not responsible for the growth of government in recent years. As Exhibit 5a illustrates, government purchases of goods and services have fluctuated within a narrow band, around 20 percent of GNP, for more than three decades. Surprising perhaps to some, *federal* purchases of goods and services consume a smaller percent of GNP today than they did in the mid-1950s. As Exhibit 5a shows, federal purchases of goods and services as a share of GNP were 8.5 percent in 1988, down from 11.1 percent in 1955.

The expansion in the relative size of the public sector during the last three decades is almost exclusively the result of increased governmental involvement in income transfer activities. The government has emerged as a major redistributor of income from one group to another—from the working population to retirees, from the employed to the unemployed, from the taxpayer to disadvantaged groups (such as low-income households with dependent children). In 1955, income transfers were 4.5 percent of the GNP. Since the mid-1970s, the government has been redistributing more than 10 percent of total output away from current producers to income-transfer recipients.

Most of the expansion in the size of the transfer sector has taken place at the federal level. As a result, there has been a major change in the composition of activities undertaken by the federal government. Exhibit 5b illustrates this point.

---

[2]The public administration costs associated with income transfer programs do involve the direct use of resources and they therefore are counted as government purchases. Only the redistribution portion is counted as a transfer payment.

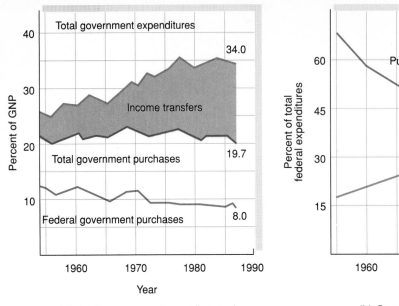

(a) Total government spending and
income transfers as a
share of GNP

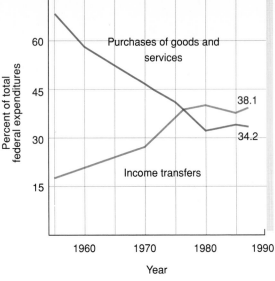

(b) Government purchases and
transfers as a share of
the federal budget

EXHIBIT 5

Government Purchases,
Transfer Payments, and
the Changing Function of
Government

State, local, and federal purchases of goods and services have accounted for approximately 20 percent of total output throughout the last three decades (frame a). The growth of transfer payments have accounted for the growth in the relative size of the public sector during this period. Frame b shows how government purchases and transfer payments have changed as a share of federal spending during the last three decades. Clearly, the federal government now plays a larger role as a redistributor of income and a smaller role as a purchaser of goods and services.

In 1988, only one-third of all federal expenditures was for the purchase of goods and services, down from two-thirds in 1955. On the other hand, income transfers consumed 38 percent of the federal budget in 1988, compared to less than 20 percent in 1955. It is clear that the federal government is now more heavily involved in income-redistribution activities than it is in the provision of public-sector goods and services.

FINANCING GOVERNMENT EXPENDITURES

If the government is going to supply goods, services, or income transfers, then these activities must be financed. Governments use three major sources of funds to pay for their expenditures: (1) taxes (2) user charges, and (3) borrowing.[3] In the United States, taxes are by far the largest source of governmental revenue. The power to tax sets governments apart from private businesses. Of course, a

---

[3]In addition to borrowing from private sources, the federal government also may borrow from its central bank. As we will see later, borrowing from a central bank is equivalent to the finance of government via the creation of money.

private business can put whatever price tag it wishes on its products; but no private business can force you to buy. With its power to tax, a government can force citizens to pay, regardless of whether or not they receive a "good" of equal or greater value in return.

Let's take a closer look at the taxes levied by governments and at the other sources of revenue available for the finance of government activities.

PERSONAL INCOME TAXES

Progressive Tax: A tax that requires those with higher taxable incomes to pay a larger percentage of their incomes to the government than those with lower taxable incomes.

Average Tax Rate: One's tax liability divided by one's taxable income.

The largest single source of revenue for governments is the personal income tax. The income tax is particularly important at the federal level, where it accounts for 41 percent of federal budget receipts (Exhibit 6). Since the Second World War, the income tax has also become an important source of revenue at the state level, where it now accounts for almost one-fifth of the tax receipts collected by the states. Only six states (Florida, Nevada, South Dakota, Texas, Washington, and Wyoming) now fail to levy a state income tax.

The structure of the federal income tax is progressive, although less so than in the past. A **progressive tax** takes a larger percentage from high-income recipients. For example, using the rate structure applicable to income in 1987, the tax liability of a single person with $10,000 of taxable income is $1,432. The **average tax rate** (ATR) can be expressed as follows:

$$ATR = \frac{\text{tax liability}}{\text{taxable income}}$$

(a) Federal government

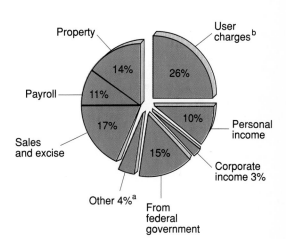

(b) State and local governments

Source: Tax Foundation, *Facts and Figures on Government Finance, 1988–89* (Baltimore: Johns Hopkins University Press, 1988), Table A11.

[a]Primarily motor vehicle and inheritance taxes.
[b]Revenues from government operated utilities and liquor stores are included in this category.

EXHIBIT 6

Sources of Government Revenue, 1985

Personal income and payroll taxes are the major sources of revenue for the federal government. User charges, sales taxes, and grants from the federal government provide the major revenue sources for state and local governments.

A married couple's average tax rate on $10,000 of income is 14.3 percent ($1,432/$10,000). Since the federal income tax structure is progressive, the average tax rate will increase with taxable income. For example, the tax liability (1987) of a single person with a taxable income of $20,000 is $3,351, resulting in an average tax rate of 16.8 percent, higher than the ATR for $10,000 of taxable income.

The economic way of thinking stresses that what happens at the margin is of crucial importance in personal decision-making. The **marginal tax rate** (MTR) can be expressed as follows:

$$MTR = \frac{\text{change in tax liability}}{\text{change in income}}$$

The marginal tax rate reveals both how much of one's additional income can be retained and how much must be turned over to the tax collector. For example, when the marginal tax rate is 25 percent, $25 of every $100 of additional earnings must be paid to the taxing authority. The individual is permitted to keep $75 of his or her additional income.

Marginal Tax Rate: Additional tax liability divided by additional income. Thus, if $100 of additional earnings increases one's tax liability by $30, the marginal tax rate would be 30 percent.

PAYROLL TAXES

Although income from all sources is covered by the income tax, only earnings derived from labor are subject to the payroll tax. Interest, dividends, rents, and other income derived from capital are not subject to payroll taxes. Payroll taxes on the earnings of employees and self-employed workers are used to finance social security (including Medicare) and unemployment compensation benefits. Payroll taxes constitute the second largest and most rapidly expanding source of tax revenue. In 1985, payroll taxes comprised 31 percent of all federal revenues, compared to only 16 percent in 1960.

Payroll taxes are often criticized because of their regressive structure. Actually, the payroll tax encompasses proportional and regressive features. A **proportional tax** is one that takes the same percentage of income from all taxpayers, regardless of income level. Until the maximum taxable income ceiling is reached, the payroll tax is proportional. For example, in 1989, each employee pays a tax rate of 7.51 percent on earnings up to $45,000. Beyond that taxable income ceiling, no additional payroll tax is levied. So, a worker earning $10,000 incurs a payroll tax of $751, whereas one earning $20,000 is taxed twice that amount, or $1,502. Until the taxable income ceiling is met, all workers pay exactly the same tax rate.

Proportional Tax: A tax for which individuals pay the same percentage of their income (or other tax base) in taxes, regardless of income level.

A **regressive tax** takes a smaller *percentage* of income from those in high-earnings brackets than it does from low-income recipients. Since the social security payroll tax does not apply beyond the maximum income ceiling, it is regressive for incomes beyond that point. For example, a person with an income twice the taxable ceiling will pay exactly the same amount of payroll taxes (and only one-half the average tax rate) as another individual whose earnings are equal to the taxable ceiling. All people with earnings above the taxable ceiling will pay a lower average tax rate than people with earnings below the ceiling. Thus, since the payroll tax does not apply to earnings above the ceiling, its basic structure can be considered regressive.

Regressive Tax: A tax that takes a smaller percentage of one's income as one's income level increases. Thus, the proportion of income allocated to the tax would be greater for the poor than for the rich.

SALES AND EXCISE TAXES

Taxes levied on the consumption expenditures for a wide range of goods and services are called sales taxes. A tax levied on specific commodities, such as gasoline, cigarettes, or alcoholic beverages, is called an excise tax. There is little difference between the two, except that one is a general tax and the other is quite specific.

Sales and excise taxes provided 17 percent of the revenue for state and local governments in 1985. They are particularly important at the state level where they account for almost a third of the revenue raised by state governments.

PROPERTY TAXES

Despite their unpopularity, property taxes still constitute the bulk of local tax revenues. In 1985, 74 percent of the tax revenue raised by local governments was generated from this source. Property taxes are often criticized because they are cumbersome. The assessor must set a value on taxable property. This generally involves a certain amount of judgment and arbitrariness. During a period of rising prices, property that has recently been exchanged is likely to command a higher valuation than similar property without an easily identifiable indicator of current value. High administration costs and problems associated with providing equal treatment for similarly situated taxpayers reduce the attractiveness of property taxes.

CORPORATE INCOME TAX

The corporate income tax is levied on the accounting profits of the business firm. Its structure is relatively simple. In 1988, the first $50,000 of corporate profit was taxed at a rate of 15 percent. Corporate earnings in the range from $50,000 to $75,000 were taxed at a rate of 25 percent. All corporate earnings above $75,000 were taxed at a flat rate of 34 percent. Corporate incomes in the United States have been taxed since 1909. The tax currently generates approximately 8 percent of all federal tax receipts and 3 percent of the revenue of state and local governments (see Exhibit 6).

Inadvertently, the corporate income tax encourages debt financing rather than equity ownership. This results because no adjustment is made for factors of production owned by the firm and the equity capital invested by the owners. A corporation that uses debt financing will incur an interest cost, which will reduce its accounting profits and tax liability. In contrast, if the same firm uses equity financing (that is, raises financial capital by issuing additional stock), the interest cost will not appear on the firm's accounting statement. Therefore, even though there is an opportunity cost of capital, regardless of whether it is raised by equity financing or by debt, only the latter will reduce the firm's tax liability.

USER CHARGES

Not all government revenue comes from taxes. For some services, governments charge consumers a price, just as private businesses do. User charges differ from taxes in that one's payment is directly linked to the consumption of a good or service. Citizens who do not consume the government-provided good or service do not have to pay for it. User charges are particularly important at the state and local level where they account for 26 percent of government revenue. Local governments often provide utility services, garbage pick-up, hospital care, and bus transportation. These government-operated businesses—many of which are in competition with private firms—are often partially or entirely financed by prices charged to the users of these services. In general, when the nature of the good permits, economists favor the use of charges rather than taxes, since the former provide better information on whether consumers value the good or service produced more than its cost of production.

Sometimes taxes can be used to approximate the effects of a user charge. For example, an excise tax on gasoline used to finance roads imposes the cost of the roads on individuals roughly in proportion to their consumption (use). Similarly, if a civic auditorium is operated by the government, a ticket tax used to finance the arena's cost approximates a user charge.

BORROWING

In addition to taxes and user charges, government has one other method of financing expenditures: borrowing. When the total spending exceeds revenue from taxes and user charges, the government will have to borrow to cover its budget deficit. Governments generally borrow by issuing interest-bearing bonds. In effect, the bonds commit the government to higher future taxes in order to meet the interest obligations on the bonds.

In recent years, the federal government has borrowed funds to cover a major proportion—approximately 20 percent during the 1980s—of its expenditures. Constitutional provisions often limit the borrowing powers of state governments. Thus, state and local governments borrow much less than the federal government. In fact, state and local governments in aggregate have run substantial budget surpluses in recent years.

THE ISSUES OF EFFICIENCY AND EQUITY

There are two major factors to consider when choosing among taxation alternatives. First, taxes should be consistent with the concept of economic efficiency. Taxes should not encourage people to use scarce resources wastefully. A tax system is inconsistent with economic efficiency if it encourages individuals (a) to buy goods costing more than their value to consumers and/or (b) to channel time into tax-avoidance activities.

Second, a tax system should be equitable; that is, it should be consistent with widely accepted principles of fairness. Economists often speak of "horizontal" and "vertical" equity. Horizontal equity means equal treatment of equals. If two parties earn equal incomes, for example, horizontal equity implies that the two should be taxed equally. The corollary concept of vertical equity requires that persons who are situated differently should be taxed differently. It encompasses what economists refer to as the **ability-to-pay principle,** the seemingly straightforward idea that taxes should be levied according to the ability of the taxpayer to pay. Deciding exactly what this means, however, is at least partially subjective. Most people find it reasonable that the rich should pay more taxes than the poor. This would be in the case under a proportional tax system since high-income taxpayers would pay the flat (constant) rate on a larger tax base. Many find it reasonable that the rich should pay a *higher proportion* of their income (or wealth or consumption) in taxes than the poor. Of course, progressive taxation incorporates this concept. But, how much higher should the rate be for those with higher incomes? At this point, the consensus breaks down. There is little agreement among either laymen or professional economists about the proper degree of tax progressivity.

A tax system must take equity into account if it is to succeed. The cost of enforcing a system widely presumed to be unreasonable or unfair is certain to be extremely high. Equity, though, must be balanced with efficiency. A tax system that ignores economic efficiency will also be extremely costly to an economy .

Ability-to-Pay Principle: The equity concept that people with larger incomes (or more consumption or more wealth) should be taxed at a higher rate because their ability to pay is presumably greater. The concept is subjective and fails to reveal how much higher the rate of taxation should be as income increases.

TAXES AND ECONOMIC EFFICIENCY

Neutral Tax: A tax that does not (a) distort consumer buying patterns or producer production methods or (b) induce individuals to engage in tax avoidance activities. There will be no excess burden if a tax is neutral.

An ideal tax system would not alter the incentive of individuals to allocate their time and income into those areas that yield them the most satisfaction. A tax of this kind is called a **neutral tax.** A neutral tax would not encourage individuals to spend more of their income on business travel, housing, medical service, or professional association publications, and less of their income on food and clothing because the former are tax-deductible and the latter are not. Similarly, a neutral tax would not encourage an individual to allocate more time and money to investments that reduce the tax burden (depreciable assets, municipal bonds, tax-free retirement plans, and so on), and less time and money to savings and work activities that generate taxable income.

Head Tax: A lump-sum tax levied on all individuals, regardless of their income, consumption, wealth, or other indicators of economic well-being.

There is a problem, though, with the concept of a neutral tax. Probably the only tax that would meet the hypothetical ideal of neutrality is a **head tax,** a tax imposing an equal lump-sum tax on all individuals. A head tax would impose the same dollar tax liability on the poor as it would on the rich (or the same liability on those who consume few goods as on those who consume many goods). Since a head tax conflicts with the concept of vertical equity—the view that persons who are situated differently should be taxed differently—it fails to pass our test of fairness.

Thus, we generally tax things such as income, consumption, and property. However, taxes on these items distort pricing signals and thereby cause individuals to forgo productive activities. Economists refer to this inefficiency and the accompanying reduction in private-sector output over and above the tax revenue collected as the **excess burden of taxation.** It is easy to think of cases that illustrate the excess burden of taxation. For example, if two individuals decide to forgo a mutually advantageous exchange because a tax makes the transaction unprofitable, they incur a burden from the taxation even though they do not pay a tax, because the transaction did not take place. Similarly, if a taxpayer decides to allocate more time to leisure or to household production and less time to market work—because the tax system limits the individual's ability to retain income generated by market work—a burden over and above tax revenues collected from the individual is imposed. Income from market work is lost to the individual, and whatever benefits for others that might have resulted from the work are sacrificed. Excess burdens reflect economic inefficiency, relative to our hypothetical ideal. They impose a **deadweight loss** on an economy, because they reflect a cost imposed on some individuals without any offsetting benefit to others.

Excess Burden of Taxation: A burden of taxation over and above the burden associated with the transfer of revenues to the government. An excess burden usually reflects losses that occur when beneficial activities are forgone because they are taxed.

Deadweight Loss: A net loss associated with the forgoing of an economic action. The loss does not lead to an offsetting gain for other participants. It thus reflects economic inefficiency.

Exhibit 7 illustrates the distinction between the tax burden associated with the transfer of purchasing power and the excess burden of taxation. Here we show the impact of a 40-cent tax imposed on each pack of cigarettes. Prior to the imposition of the tax, 35 billion packs of cigarettes were produced and sold to consumers at a market price of 80 cents per pack. The cigarette tax increases the cost of supplying and marketing cigarettes by 40 cents per pack. Thus, the supply curve of cigarettes shifts vertically by the amount of the tax. Consumers, however, would not continue to purchase as many cigarettes if the full burden of the tax were passed on to them in the form of a 40-cent increase in the per-pack price. So, when the supply curve shifts vertically, the market price of cigarettes rises by less than the amount of the tax. Since the number of cigarettes demanded is thus

EXHIBIT 7

The Impact of a Tax on Economic Activity

Here we illustrate the impact of a 40-cent tax (per pack) on cigarettes. Since the tax increases the cost of supplying cigarettes for consumption, the supply curve is shifted vertically by the amount of the tax. At the higher price, however, consumers reduce their consumption. The equilibrium price increases from 80 cents to $1 per pack. Consumers pay 20 cents more per pack and sellers receive 20 cents less as the result of the 40-cent tax. In addition, consumers and producers lose the mutual gains from exchange (triangle ABC) that would be realized if the tax did not reduce the volume of trade between cigarette producers and consumers.

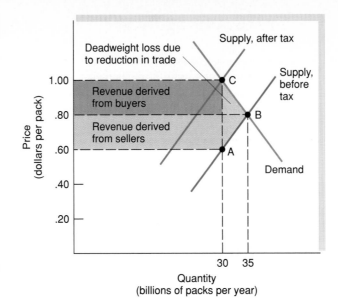

responsive to the higher price, some of the tax burden will fall on cigarette producers. In our hypothetical example, the new equilibrium price for cigarettes will become $1 per pack, with an annual output rate of 30 billion packs of cigarettes. The tax will raise $12 billion (40 cents times 30 billion packs) of revenue. Buyers will pay 20 cents more per pack for the 30 billion packs of cigarettes purchased after the tax is imposed. Simultaneously, sellers will receive 20 cents less per pack. The tax thus transfers $12 billion of revenue from cigarette buyers and sellers to the government. Note, though, that the quantity of cigarettes produced and consumed has fallen by 5 billion packs. The mutually advantageous gains that would have accrued to producers and consumers from these unrealized trades (the triangle ABC) are lost. (Remember that trade is a positive-sum game, so a reduction in the volume of trade will result in economic loss.) This loss of welfare (triangle ABC) associated with the unrealized exchanges imposes an excess burden on buyers and sellers over and above the burden accompanying the transfer of revenue to the government. Clearly, the triangle ABC is a deadweight loss, since it is not accompanied by an offsetting gain in the form of additional tax revenue for the government.

In our example, the burden of the tax was divided equally between sellers and buyers. This will not always be the case. If the demand curve were steeper (and the supply curve flatter), the price of the taxed good would rise by a larger amount, imposing more of the burden on buyers. In contrast, if the demand curve were flatter (and the supply curve steeper), the market price would rise by a smaller amount, and a larger share of the tax burden would fall on sellers.

Tax Incidence: The manner in which the burden of the tax is distributed among economic units (consumers, employees, employers, and so on). The tax burden does not always fall on those who pay the tax.

The burden of taxes is not always borne by the person who writes a check to the Internal Revenue Service. Economists use the term **tax incidence** when discussing the question of how the burden of a tax is distributed among parties. Since the distribution of the tax burden is dependent on the slope of the supply and demand curves for the activity being taxed, it is not easy to determine how it is distributed among parties.

THE TAX POLICY DEBATE OF THE 1980s

The 1980s were a period of substantial change in tax policy in the United States. In many respects, economic conditions during the 1970s provided the foundation for the modifications. The 1970s were characterized by rising prices and wages. This "inflating" of prices was rapidly pushing the money incomes of families and individuals upward, even though the purchasing power of their income was increasing much more slowly. Under a progressive tax structure, increases in money income push taxpayers into higher tax brackets, even if the higher money incomes merely reflect the general increase in prices. This is precisely what happened during the 1970s. As Exhibit 8 illustrates, the marginal tax rate of a four-person family earning the median income rose from 17 percent in 1965 to 24 percent in 1980. The growth in the marginal tax rates was even more dramatic at higher incomes: a family with twice the median income confronted a marginal tax rate of 43 percent in 1980, nearly double that of a similar family in 1965. During the 1980 presidential campaign, Ronald Reagan promised to cut tax rates and thereby provide relief from the inflation-induced, nonlegislated tax increases of the 1970s.

TAX RATES, WORK EFFORT, AND TAX AVOIDANCE

The debate concerning the wisdom of cutting tax rates, particularly the highest marginal rates, focused on the impact of these rates on the incentive to work, the incentive to engage in tax avoidance activities, economic efficiency, and aggregate output. In the past, most economists believed that tax rates on income exerted little adverse influence on the incentive of individuals to engage in productive activity. According to this traditional view, workers lack viable alternatives to the earning of taxable income. Because of this, they will be unable, or virtually unable, to shift from current work to other income-generating activities in order to partially avoid the tax burden.

During the late 1970s and early 1980s, the traditional view underwent a serious reevaluation. Challengers to the traditional view argued that high marginal tax rates induced taxpayers to reduce their work time and engage in more tax avoid-

---

EXHIBIT 8 ■ Changes in Marginal Tax Rates for Four-Person Families, 1965–1988

	Marginal Tax Rate for Four-Person Family		
Year	Family Income Equal to One-Half of Median Family Income	Family Income Equal to the Median Family Income	Family Income Is Twice the Median Family Income
1965	14	17	22
1970	15	20	26
1975	17	22	32
1980	18	24	43
1986	14	22	38
1988	15	15	28

Source: Council of Economic Advisers, *Economic Report of the President, 1987*, Table 2–1.

Underground Economy:
Unreported barter and cash transactions that take place outside recorded market channels. Some are otherwise legal activities undertaken to evade taxes. Others involve illegal activities such as trafficking in drugs, prostitution, extortion, and similar crimes.

ance, and even illegal tax evasion. The proponents of this view argued that when high marginal tax rates take a major share of the income from additional work, some individuals will respond by increasing their vacation time and absenteeism, while reducing their overtime hours. Others will allocate more time to untaxed household activities, such as fixing their cars, painting their houses, and producing additional home-prepared meals, rather than allocating more time to working, purchasing new cars, buying new houses, and eating meals at restaurants. Still others will take jobs with lower pay but higher nonmonetary benefits and allocate more time to real-estate investments with attractive tax benefits. Business ventures designed to show an accounting loss to shelter taxable income will also flourish. These alternatives are perfectly legal. However, some individuals will also use illegal means to evade the payment of taxes. Participation in the **underground economy** is one device that many believe is widely used to avoid or reduce taxes (see "The Underground Economy" box). If this view is correct—if there are fairly good, feasible alternatives to the payment of the higher tax rates—the

MEASURES OF ECONOMIC ACTIVITY

The Underground Economy

High marginal tax rates increase the incentive of individuals to participate in the underground economy to escape taxation. The underground economy encompasses unreported production and exchange, often conducted in cash to avoid possible detection.

There are two major components of the underground economy: (a) production and distribution of illegal goods and services and (b) the nonreporting of transactions involving legal goods and services. Drug trafficking, smuggling, prostitution, and other criminal activities are examples of the first component. Income from such activities is generally unreported to avoid detection by law enforcement authorities.

Of course, even when the work activity is legal, it is illegal to earn income and not report it to the taxing authorities. However, the likelihood of detection by authorities is very small for certain types of activities. Since cash transactions are difficult to trace, they provide the life-blood of

the underground economy. The participants in the legal-if-reported portion of the underground economy are diverse. Taxicab drivers and waitresses may pocket fees and tips. Small-business proprietors may fail to ring up cash sales. Craft and professional workers may fail to report cash income. All of these individuals are participating in the underground economy.

In addition, it is estimated that millions of employees, ranging from farm laborers to bartenders, are paid in cash. Company books fail to record their employment. Neither income taxes nor social security deductions are withheld. The employer evades the payroll taxes, while employees pocket "tax-free" cash wage payments without endangering their eligibility for welfare or unemployment benefits.

For obvious reasons, it is difficult to accurately measure the size of the underground economy. Based on data from its special audits, the IRS estimates that underground activities

constitute approximately 10 percent of the U.S. economy. Peter Gutmann of Baruch College believes the U.S. underground economy is even larger, closer to 15 percent.[4]

The underground economy is not a problem unique to the United States. In fact, available evidence indicates it is even more widespread in Western Europe, where tax rates are higher. The Organization for Economic Cooperation and Development estimates that between 3 and 5 percent of the total labor force in Western Europe is working "off the books" and thereby evading taxes. In Italy, Great Britain, and Sweden, the estimated size of the underground economy ranges from 10 to 30 percent of the national income. Apparently, the underground economy has become a sizable sector of Western economies.

[4]Peter M. Gutmann, "The Subterranean Economy," *Taxing and Spending*, April, 1979.

amount of labor supplied to taxable work activities will decrease significantly as marginal tax rates rise.

Exhibit 9 uses supply and demand analysis to illustrate the economics of this debate as it relates to the issue of work effort. Here we consider a labor market in which workers earn an equilibrium wage of $6 per hour in the absence of income taxation. Forty hours of work per week are supplied by each worker in this market at the $6 hourly wage. Now, consider the impact of a flat 20 percent tax rate on income (or payroll). Just as the cigarette tax made it more costly to supply that product, so, too, will the income tax make it more costly to supply labor. The supply curve of labor will then decline (shift vertically) by the amount of the tax. According to the traditional view, illustrated by Exhibit 9a, the income tax will exert relatively little impact on hours worked, since the aggregate supply curve of labor is vertical (or almost vertical). The equilibrium wage, including the tax, will only be slightly higher ($6.30 per hour), and the after-tax wage rate of workers will decline substantially (to $5.04). Since the labor supply curve is almost vertical, the burden of the income tax will fall primarily on workers. Furthermore, this will be true regardless of whether the tax is paid directly by the individuals (as in the case of the personal income tax) or whether the check to the IRS is made out by their employer (as in the case of the payroll tax).

The challengers to the traditional view argue that when marginal tax rates are extremely high, say 40 percent or more, the supply curve for labor will be flatter, as illustrated by Exhibit 9b. If this is the case, the vertical shift in the labor supply curve will cause a larger decline in the work time allocated to activities that generate taxable income. For example, hours might decline from 40 per week to 36 per week (rather than to only 39 hours per week in the traditional view). Simultaneously, the higher tax rates will lead to an increase in tax-avoidance activities. Waste and sizable deadweight losses will be incurred. The triangle ABC (Exhibit 9b), which indicates only the inefficiency stemming from lost hours of work, is

EXHIBIT 9

The Controversy Concerning the Incentive Effects of the Income Tax

Here we illustrate two alternative outcomes associated with the imposition of a 20 percent tax on income. According to the traditional view (a), when the aggregate labor supply curve is vertical, or nearly vertical, the tax will result in only a small reduction in work effort (from 40 to 39 hours per week). In contrast, according to a more recent view (b), if the labor supply curve is flatter, the tax will lead to a larger reduction (from 40 to 36 hours per week) in time spent generating taxable income.

(hours per week generating taxable income)

(a)

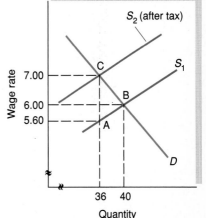

(hours per week generating taxable income)

(b)

one measure of allocative inefficiency. However, it actually understates society's excess burden since it ignores work intensity, rent seeking, and other factors related to both the cost and value of output.

TAX RATES, TAX REVENUES, AND THE LAFFER CURVE

Tax Rate: The per-unit or percentage rate at which an economic activity is taxed.

Tax Base: The level of the activity that is taxed. For example, if an excise tax is levied on each gallon of gasoline, the tax base is the number of gallons of gasoline sold. Since higher tax rates generally make the taxed activity less attractive, the size of the tax base is inversely related to the rate at which the activity is taxed.

Laffer Curve: A curve illustrating the relationship between tax rates and tax revenues. The curve reflects the fact that tax revenues are low for both very high and very low tax rates.

It is important to distinguish between a change in **tax rates** and a change in tax revenues. The quantity or level of an activity that is taxed—the **tax base**—is inversely related to the rate at which the activity is taxed. An increase in a tax rate will lead to a less-than-porportional increase in tax revenues. Higher tax rates will make it more costly to engage in the activity, thereby inducing individuals to shift to substitutes. If there are attractive substitutes, the decline in the activity due to the tax may be substantial. Perhaps a real-world example will help clarify this point. In 1981, the District of Columbia increased the tax rate on gasoline from 10 cents to 13 cents per gallon, a 30 percent increase. Tax revenues, however, did not increase by 30 percent—they expanded by only 12 percent. Why? The higher tax rate discouraged motorists from purchasing gasoline in the District of Columbia. There was a pretty good alternative to the purchase of the more highly taxed (and therefore higher-priced) gasoline—the purchase of gasoline in Virginia and Maryland, where the tax rates (and therefore prices) were slightly lower. Because of this, the quantity of gasoline sold in Washington, D.C., declined. The revenue gains associated with the higher tax rates were partially eroded by a decline in the tax base.

Economist Arthur Laffer has popularized the idea that higher tax rates can sometimes shrink the tax base so much that tax revenues will decline despite the higher tax rates. As the result of Laffer's efforts, the curve illustrating the relationship between tax rates and tax revenues is now called the **Laffer curve.** Exhibit 10 illustrates the concept of the Laffer curve for the taxation of income-generating activity. Obviously, tax revenues would be zero if the tax rate were zero. What is not so obvious is that tax revenues would also be zero (or at least very close to zero) if the tax rate were 100 percent. Confronting a 100 percent tax

EXHIBIT 10

The Laffer Curve

Since taxation affects the amount of the activity being taxed, a change in tax rates will not lead to a proportional change in tax revenues. As the Laffer curve indicates, beyond some point (B), an increase in tax rates may actually cause tax revenues to fall. Since large tax rate increases will lead to only a small expansion in tax revenue as B is approached, there is no presumption that point B is an ideal rate of taxation.

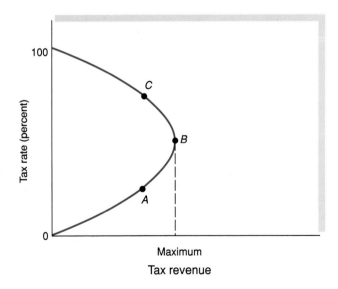

rate, most individuals would go fishing or find something else to do rather than engage in taxable productive activity, since the 100 percent tax rate would completely remove the material reward derived from earning taxable income. Production in the taxed sector would come to a halt, and without production, tax revenues would plummet to zero.

As tax rates are reduced from 100 percent, the incentive to work and earn taxable income increases, income expands, and tax revenues rise. Similarly, as tax rates increase from zero, tax revenues expand. Clearly, at some rate greater than zero but less than 100 percent, tax revenues will be maximized (point *B*, Exhibit 10). This is not to imply that the tax rate that maximizes revenue is ideal. In fact, as the maximum revenue point (*B*) is approached, relatively large tax rate increases will be necessary to expand tax revenues. In this range, the excess burden of taxation will be substantial.

Have tax rates in the United States ever been so high that *lower* rates would have led to an *increase* in tax revenue, implying that taxpayers were on the backward-bending portion *(BC)* of the Laffer curve? For the economy as a whole, tax cuts have generally led to a reduction in tax revenues (adjusted for inflation). This was true during the 1980s. There is some evidence, though, that taxpayers in the highest tax brackets may have been on the backward-bending portion of the Laffer curve prior to the rate reduction of the 1980s. For example, the tax revenue (adjusted for inflation) collected from the top 10 percent of taxpayers rose during 1981–85, even though the tax rates of these taxpayers were reduced substantially (see ''Applications in Economics'' box).

CHANGES IN TAX POLICY DURING THE 1980s

Indexing: The automatic increasing of money values as the general level of prices increases. Economic variables that are often indexed include wage rates and tax brackets.

Concern about the impact of high marginal tax rates on work effort, tax avoidance, and economic growth provided the foundation for the changes in the structure of the personal income tax during the 1980s. At the beginning of the decade, the personal income tax structure encompassed 14 different brackets, ranging from a beginning rate of 14 percent to a top rate of 70 percent. The Economic Recovery Tax Act of 1981 reduced marginal tax rates in each bracket by approximately 23 percent over a three year period. The top marginal rate was cut from 70 to 50 percent. The beginning rate was sliced from 14 percent to 11 percent.

The 1981 legislation also provided for indexing of the personal income tax structure. **Indexing** adjusts money income figures for the effects of inflation and thereby prevents rising prices from pushing people into higher tax brackets. With indexing, tax brackets are widened each year to compensate for the inflation-induced component of a rising money income (see box, ''How Does Indexing Work?''). The act also included substantial investment incentives, primarily in the form of accelerated depreciation allowances. While these incentives were later scaled back somewhat, they lowered the effective tax on income from most capital investments.

The Tax Reform Act of 1986 built on the earlier modifications. The 1986 Act (1) reduced marginal rates; (2) broadened the taxable income base; and (3) substantially increased the personal exemption. The 1986 legislation collapsed the tax structure into just two tax brackets with marginal rates of l5 and 28 percent. For single taxpayers, taxable income of up to $17,850 is taxed at the 15 percent rate, while the 28 percent rate applies to all additional income. For joint returns, the 28 percent rate takes effect at $29,750. However, the legislation also calls for a phasing out of the personal exemption and the 15 percent rate above certain in-

APPLICATIONS IN ECONOMICS

Tax Rate Changes and the Taxes Paid by the Rich and Others

A reduction in marginal tax rates decreases the incentive to engage in tax avoidance activities. However, when rates are reduced by a similar proportion, these incentive effects will generally be far more important in the highest tax brackets.

Consider the impact of a reduction in a marginal tax rate from 70 percent to 50 percent on the incentive of a high-income professional or business executive to earn *taxable* income. When confronting a 70 percent marginal tax rate, the taxpayer gets to keep only 30 cents of each additional dollar earned by cutting costs, producing more, or investing more wisely. However, after the tax cut, take-home pay from each dollar of taxable income jumps to 50 cents—a whopping 67 percent increase in the incentive to earn. Predictably, high-income taxpayers will then spend more time finding ways to cut business costs and increase sales and less time on the tennis courts and on seeking out tax avoidance. Similarly, they will spend less money on tax-deductible expenditures, such as plush offices, Hawaii business conferences, and various fringe benefits (for example, a luxury company automobile, business entertainment, and a company retirement plan).

In contrast, consider the incentive effects of an *identical* percentage rate reduction in lower tax brackets. Suppose the 14 percent marginal rate were cut to 10 percent. Take-home pay, per dollar of additional earnings, would expand from 86 cents to 90 cents, only a 5 percent increase. Compared with the incentive effects in the upper brackets, the same percentage tax cut in the lower tax brackets would lead to a much smaller increase in take-home pay and thus a much smaller increase in the incentive

to earn more taxable income.

Since the incentive effects of a proportional rate reduction (one that cuts all rates by the same percent) will be greater in the upper tax brackets, taxable income will increase most in these brackets. The growth in the taxable income base will offset, at least partially, revenue losses emanating from the lower rates. As the Laffer curve analysis indicates, if the incentive effects are strong, it is even possible for lower rates to lead to an increase in tax revenue. Clearly, this is most likely to be the case for high income taxpayers confronting high tax rates.

The Kennedy-Johnson tax cut was consistent with this view. This 1964 tax cut sliced the top marginal bracket from 91 percent to 70 percent, leading to a 233 percent increase (from 9 cents to 30 cents per additional dollar of earnings) in take-home pay from marginal income in this bracket. The bottom rate was cut

from 20 percent to 14 percent—about the same proportional tax reduction. But, after-tax income, per dollar of additional earnings, in the bottom bracket, rose from 80 cents to 86 cents, an increase of only 7.5 percent.

Just as one would expect, given the incentive effects accompanying the rate reductions, *taxable incomes* grew rapidly in the upper tax brackets after the tax cut. This growth in the tax base partially offset revenue losses due to the rate reductions, particularly in the highest tax brackets. Exhibit 11 presents data on tax revenue before and after the 1964 tax cut, according to percentile income groupings. Adjusted for inflation, the tax liability of the bottom 95 percentile of returns fell. For these taxpayers, lower tax rates meant less tax revenue. The negative impact of the rate reduction on tax revenues was dominant over the positive impact of income growth on tax revenues.

However, the picture for the top 5

EXHIBIT 11 ■ The Change in Federal Income Tax Revenue Derived from Various Income Groupings, 1963–1965

The tax revenues are ranked according to adjusted gross income prior to and subsequent to the 1964 reduction in tax rates.

Percentile of All Returns (ranked from lowest to highest income)	Tax Revenues Collected from Group (in billions of 1963 dollars)[a]		Percent Changes
	1963	1965	
Bottom 50 percent	$ 5.01	$ 4.55	−9.2
50th and 75th percentile	10.02	9.61	−4.1
75th to 95th percentile	16.00	15.41	−3.7
Top 5 percent	17.17	18.49	+7.7
Total	$48.20	$48.06	−0.3

[a]These estimates were derived by interpolation.

Source: Internal Revenue Service, *Statistics of Income: Individual Income Tax Returns* (1963 and 1965).

percent of taxpayers was quite different. Despite the roughly 20 percent lower tax rates, measured in constant dollars, the revenues collected from the top 5 percent of earners rose from $17.17 billion in 1963 to $18.49 billion in 1965, a healthy increase of 7.7 percent. Tax revenue collected from these high-income taxpayers grew because the rapid expansion in their taxable income more than offset the loss of tax revenue associated with the rate reductions.

The tax rate reductions of the 1980s provide us with another experiment that sheds light on the relationship between tax rates and tax revenue. The 1981 tax legislation reduced rates across the board by approximately 23 percent over a 3-year period. In addition, the top tax bracket was reduced from 70 percent to 50 percent, effective during the first year of the rate reduction. Exhibit 12 presents data on the personal income taxes paid according to income groupings during the 1981–1985 period. As the rates were sliced, the tax revenues in real dollars declined substantially for the bottom 90 percent of

earners. In 1985, after the 23 percent rate reductions were fully phased in, real tax revenues collected from the bottom 90 percent of earners were 9.1 percent lower than in 1981. Once again, however, the experience of high-income (and therefore high marginal tax rate) taxpayers was different. Measured in constant dollars, the tax revenue collected from the top 10 percent of earners rose from $161.1 billion in 1981 to $168.6 billion in 1985, an increase of 4.7 percent. The tax revenues paid by the top 1 percent and top 5 percent of earners grew even more rapidly.

The data of Exhibits 11 and 12 highlight the importance of distinguishing between changes in tax rates and tax revenues. Failing to consider the "incentive effect" adjustments of taxpayers, many commentators charged that the lower tax rates of the 1980s shifted the burden of the income tax from the rich to the poor. Clearly, the revenue figures paint a different picture. They indicate that the rate reductions of the 1980s increased the income tax revenue collected from the rich and reduced the

taxes paid by others.

It is interesting to view the evidence of Exhibits 11 and 12 within the framework of the Laffer curve. The evidence indicates that most taxpayers are on the upward-sloping portion (the AB range of Exhibit 10) of the Laffer curve. In this range, changes in tax rates and tax revenues are directly related. However, the data also indicate that in high tax brackets, say tax rates of 40 percent or more, the incentive effects of rate changes are very important.[5] Reduction in tax rates in this range will result in very little revenue loss, and may possibly even lead to increases in tax revenues.

As recently as 1980, the top marginal tax rate imposed at the federal level in the United States was 70 percent. In 1986, it was 50 percent. In 1988, the top effective marginal rate fell to 33 percent. This dramatic reduction in marginal tax rates reflects the view that high marginal tax rates—for example, rates of 40 percent or more—raise little revenue and that they retard economic efficiency and growth. The substantial rate reductions in the United Kingdom, New Zealand, and several other countries (see Exhibit 11) are also reflective of this view.

EXHIBIT 12 ■ The Change in Federal Income Tax Revenue Derived from Various Income Groups, 1981–1985

| Income Group | Tax Revenue Collected from Group (in billions of 1985 dollars) | | |
	1981	1985	Percent Change 1981–1985
Top 10 percent of Earners	161.1	168.6	+ 4.7
Top 1 percent	60.3	72.1	+19.6
Top 5 percent	116.6	131.4	+12.7
All Other	172.8	157.0	− 9.1
Total	333.9	325.6	− 2.5

Source: U.S. Department of Treasury, Internal Revenue Service

[5]A study for the National Bureau of Economic Research by Harvard professor Lawrence Lindsey estimates that, in the United States, marginal personal income rates above 43 reduce tax revenues. See Lawrence Lindsey, *Estimating the Revenue Maximizing Top Personal Tax Rate* (New York: National Bureau of Economic Research—Working Paper 1761, 1985). Also see James E. Long and James D. Gwartney, "Income Tax Avoidance: Evidence from Individual Tax Returns" *National Tax Journal,* December 1987, for additional evidence on this topic.

come levels—$56,000 for single taxpayers and $92,000 for joint returns. This results in an effective marginal tax rate of 33 percent for a broad range of income. As Exhibit 8 illustrates, the 1986 legislation reduces the marginal tax rate of most Americans to the approximate levels that prevailed in the mid-1960s.

In order to offset revenue losses from the lower marginal tax rates, the 1986 legislation eliminated various deductions and exclusions from the taxable income base. The deductibility of state and local sales taxes, nonmortgage consumer interest expenses, and contributions to Individual Retirement Accounts was eliminated. Long-term capital gains income on the sale of assets was fully included (previously only 40 percent of capital gains income was included) in the tax base. Limitations were imposed on net losses from passive investments and from active real-estate investments in the case of high-income taxpayers. The permissible allowances for the depreciation of assets were decelerated, reversing the effects of the 1981 Act. This combination of factors—lower marginal tax rates and the more stringent limitations on the deductibility of investment losses—substantially reduces the attractiveness of investments driven by tax considerations rather than income-generating potential.

Finally, the 1986 legislation also increased the personal exemption allowance for each taxpayer, spouse, and dependent from $1,080 to $2,000. The standard deduction (the income allowance to taxpayers who do not itemize their deductions) was increased from $2,480 to $3,670. Therefore, a family of four can now earn at least $11,670 (four personal exemptions of $2,000 plus the $3,670 standard deduction) without confronting any federal income tax liability. Increases in the personal exemption allowance and standard deduction reduce the average tax liability of low-income recipients more than those with higher income. Thus, these modifications contribute to the progressivity of the overall structure, partially offsetting the decline in progressivity implied by the sharp reduction in the highest marginal tax rates.

MEASURES OF ECONOMIC ACTIVITY

How Does Indexing Work?

Since 1985, the personal-income-tax-structure in the United States has been indexed. Indexing expands the tax brackets (and personal-exemption allowance) in proportion to the increase in prices.

An example will help clarify how indexing works. Suppose a marginal tax rate of 10 percent is applied to the initial income bracket of $0 to $5,000, and also suppose that higher marginal tax rates are applicable at higher levels of income. In the absence of indexing, taxpayers whose incomes merely keep pace with inflation are pushed into higher tax brackets. For example, if a 10 percent inflation rate expands the taxable income of a worker from $5,000 to $5,500, it pushes that taxpayer into a higher tax bracket. Both the taxpayer's average and marginal tax rates are increased, even though the expansion in income merely reflects the general rise in prices. Indexing widens the tax brackets for the effects of inflation and thereby keeps inflation from pushing taxpayers with incomes of constant purchasing power into higher tax brackets. With indexing, the $0–$5,000 income bracket would be expanded to $0–$5,500, when prices increase by 10 percent. So, when inflation increases the income of a taxpayer by 10 percent, the taxpayer's average and marginal tax rates remain constant. Indexing thus protects individuals from unlegislated tax increases that, under a progressive tax system, would otherwise be automatically imposed by inflation.

Cuts in Top Marginal Tax Rates

As the accompanying chart illustrates, several nations reduced their top marginal tax rates during the latter half of the 1980s.

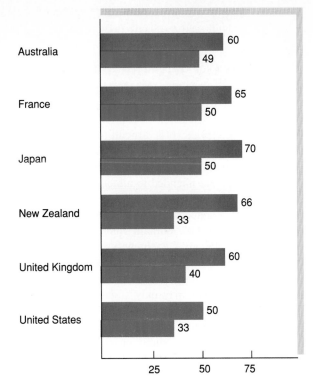

Highest marginal tax rate

The Tax Reform Act of 1986 also reduced the corporate tax rate from 46 percent to 34 percent. This rate reduction was more than offset by other modifications that broadened the tax base. The tax credit for new investment expenditures was repealed. The deductibility of expenses on business meals and entertainment, which were previously fully deductible, was cut to 80 percent. The deceleration in depreciation allowances also broadens the business tax base. Overall, a slight increase in corporate tax revenue is expected as the result of these changes.

In summary, major tax legislation during the 1980s fundamentally altered the structure of the federal income tax. Both the personal and corporate income tax bases were broadened and the tax rates were substantively reduced. During the decade, the top marginal tax rate was sliced from 70 percent to 33 percent for the personal income tax and from 46 percent to 34 percent for the corporate income tax. The logic underpinning the changes was the increasingly widespread view that high marginal tax rates, say rates in excess of 40 percent, discourage work effort and the productive use of resources.

The United States was not the only country that significantly reduced high marginal tax rates on personal income in the late 1980s. As Exhibit 13 illustrates, there were also sharp reductions in the top tax rate in Australia, France, Japan, New Zealand, and the United Kingdom.

WHO PAYS THE TAX BILL?

How is the overall burden of taxation distributed among income groupings? This is not an easy question to answer. As we have discussed, several different types of taxes are levied. It is difficult to identify who actually bears the burden of many taxes. In some cases, taxes are designed to act as a proxy for a user charge for public services. Motor fuel taxes to finance roads provide an example. Thus, taxes of this type are intended to allocate costs to users, independent of income.

The two most comprehensive studies concerning the overall incidence of taxes have been conducted by Joseph Pechman of the Brookings Institution and by Edgar Browning and William Johnson of Texas A&M and the University of Virginia, respectively.[6] Pechman's findings support the conclusion that the U.S. tax structure is within the proportional-to-mildly progressive range. Even Pechman's assumptions that yielded his most progressive estimates projected that high-income recipients pay only slightly higher average tax rates—27.3 percent compared with 20.6 percent—than households with much lower incomes.

Browning and Johnson dispute these findings. Their study implies that the U.S. tax structure is highly progressive. According to Browning and Johnson, the overall average tax rate of high-income groups is approximately three times the average rate of low-income groups. Neither of these studies reflects the drastic changes in the tax structure that took place during the 1980s.

A recent study of the federal tax structure by the Congressional Budget Office (CBO) indicates that the federal taxes are quite progressive, though somewhat less so than during the 1970s.[7] The CBO study estimated the incidence of the federal personal income, corporate income, payroll, and excise taxes. These four taxes account for 95 percent of the federal tax revenue. According to CBO projections, federal taxes will consume between 25 percent and 26.6 percent of the income of the top 20 percent of wage earners in 1988, compared with slightly less than 10 percent for the bottom decile of earners. Taxpayers in middle-income groupings are projected to pay average rates ranging from 13 percent (the third decile) to 24 percent (the ninth decile). The CBO study indicates that the progressivity of federal taxes declined during the 1980s. For example, in 1977 the CBO estimates that federal taxes took between 26.7 percent and 29.5 percent of the income of the top decile of earners, compared to approximately 8 percent for the bottom decile. Given the sharp reduction in the top rates and the accompanying reduction in incentive for tax avoidance, the estimated decline in progressivity during the 1980s is unsurprising.

[6]Joseph Pechman, *Who Paid the Taxes, 1966–85?* (Washington, D.C.: The Brookings Institution, 1985); and Edgar K. Browning and William R. Johnson, *The Distribution of the Tax Burden* (Washington, D.C.: American Enterprise Institute, 1979).
[7]Congressional Budget Office, *The Changing Distribution of Federal Taxes: 1975–1990* (Washington, D.C.: U.S. Government Printing Office), October 1987.

With regard to the burden of taxation, two additional points should be noted. First, middle- and upper-middle-income taxpayers earn the bulk of income and pay the bulk of the tax bill. In 1988, 55 percent of households in the United States had incomes between $30,000 and $75,000. These households earned approximately 70 percent of the total income and they shouldered slightly more than 70 percent of the tax burden. The findings of both Pechman and Browning-Johnson are consistent with this view.

Second, people pay all taxes. Politicians sometimes speak of imposing taxes on businesses, as if part of the tax burden could be transferred from individuals to nonpersons (business firms). The assumptions of this viewpoint are incorrect. Like all other taxes, business taxes are paid by individuals. A corporation or business firm may write the tax check to the government, but it does not pay the taxes. The business firm merely collects the money from someone else—its customers, employees, or stockholders—and transfers it to the government. It makes good political rhetoric to talk about "businesses" paying taxes, but the hard facts are that individuals provide all tax revenues.

THE COST OF GOVERNMENT

Do taxes measure the cost of government? Interestingly, the answer to this question is, "Not entirely." Our old friend—the opportunity cost concept—will help

"THIS NEW TAX PLAN SOUNDS PRETTY GOOD... WE GET A 9% CUT AND BUSINESS PICKS UP THE BURDEN...."

By John Trever, Albuquerque Journal © by and permission of News America Syndicate.

us understand why. There are three types of costs incurred when governments provide goods and services.

First, there is the opportunity cost of the resources used to produce goods supplied through the public sector. When governments purchase missiles, education, highways, health care, and other goods, resources to provide these goods must be bid away from private-sector activities. If these resources were not tied-up producing goods supplied through the public sector, they would be available to produce private-sector goods. Note that this cost is incurred regardless of whether the provision of the public-sector goods is financed by current taxes, an increase in government debt, or money creation. This cost can only be diminished by reducing the size of governmental purchases.

Second, there is the cost of resources expended in the collection of the tax. Tax laws must be enforced. Tax returns must be prepared and monitored. Resources used to prepare, monitor, and enforce tax legislation are unavailable for the production of either private- or public-sector goods. In the United States, studies indicate that these compliance costs amount to between 5 percent and 7 percent of the tax revenue raised.

EXHIBIT 14

The Size of Government—An International Comparison

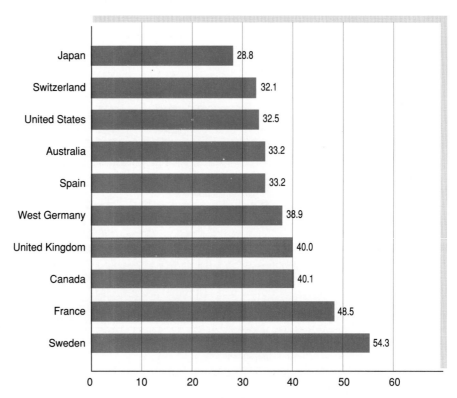

Government spending as a percentage of gross domestic product, 1985

Source: *OECD Economic Outlook* (December 1988) and Tax Foundation, *Facts and Figures on Government Finance, 1988–1989.*

Finally, there is the excess burden cost due to price distortions emanating from the levying of taxes (and the provision of transfers). Less output will result because the tax-transfer structure will cause individuals to forgo productive activities and engage in counterproductive action (for example, tax-avoidance activities).

In essence, the cost of government activities is the sum of (a) the opportunity cost of resources used to produce government supplied goods and services, (b) the cost of tax compliance, and (c) the excess burden cost of taxation. Thus, government purchases of goods and services generally cost the economy a good bit more than either the size of the tax bill or the level of budget expenditures imply.

THE SIZE OF GOVERNMENT IN OTHER COUNTRIES

How does the size of the public sector in the United States compare with the size of the public sector in other countries? Exhibit 14 helps to answer that question. In Canada, public-sector spending accounted for 40.1 percent of total output in 1985, significantly greater than the 32.5 percent for the United States. The size of the public sectors in Japan, Switzerland, Australia, and Spain are approximately the same as in the United States. On the other hand, compared to the United States, government spending accounts for a substantially larger share of total output in the United Kingdom, West Germany, France, and Sweden. The higher level of government spending in these countries primarily reflects greater public-sector involvement in the provision of housing, health care, retirement insurance, and aid to the poor and unemployed. In Sweden, 54.3 percent of national output was either produced or channeled through the public sector in 1985, the largest figure for any democratic industrial nation.

LOOKING AHEAD

Government expenditures and tax rates are important determinants of an economy's output and employment. They also influence the price and output of consumer goods and income of resource suppliers. As we proceed, we will investigate these topics in greater detail.

CHAPTER SUMMARY

1. Governmental expenditures have grown more rapidly than the U.S. economy during this century. In 1902, government spending accounted for only 7.7 percent of GNP. By 1929, the figure had risen to 10 percent. Since 1929, the relative size of government expenditures has expanded every decade. In the late 1980s, more than one-third of the total output of the United States was channeled through the public sector.

2. Government purchases of goods and services constitute approximately 20 percent of the national output. Slightly less than one out of every seven Americans works for the local, state, or federal government. Taking into account transfer payments, total government expenditures amounted to 39 percent of the gross national product in 1988.

3. During the last three decades, government spending in traditional areas such as national defense, highways, police and fire protection, and the provision of other goods and services has changed very little relative to the size of the economy. The growth of government in recent decades is almost exclusively the result of increased governmental involvement in the redistribution of income.

4. Personal income taxes, payroll taxes, and corporate income taxes are the major sources of federal tax revenues. Sales taxes provide the major tax base for state government, whereas local governments still rely primarily on property taxes for their revenue.

5. Payroll taxes constitute the most rapidly expanding source of tax revenues. In 1985, payroll taxes comprised 31 percent of the total tax revenue at the federal level. The social security payroll tax is a regressive tax because it is not levied on income beyond a designated maximum.

6. As the marginal tax rates increase, the proportion of income individuals are permitted to keep for private use declines. Since it determines the share of earnings available for private expenditures, the marginal tax rate exerts a major impact on the incentive of individuals to earn taxable income.

7. Both efficiency and equity should be considered when choosing among taxation alternatives. A tax system that induces inefficient behavior will be costly to a society. Similarly, it will be costly to induce compliance with a tax system that is perceived as unreasonable or unfair.

8. Ideally, we would all prefer a neutral tax system—one that does not distort prices or induce individuals to channel scarce resources into tax-avoidance activities. However, a tax on productive activity will always alter some prices. Our goal should be to adopt an equitable system that will minimize the inefficiency effects.

9. It is important to distinguish between a change in tax rates and a change in tax revenues. The size of the tax base will generally be inversely related to the rate of taxation. Therefore, an increase in tax rates will lead to a less-than-proportional increase in tax revenues, particularly if there are viable substitutes for those things that are taxed.

10. At very high rates of taxation, it is possible that an increase in tax rates will cause a reduction in tax revenues, because such a large number of people will shift away from the activity that is being taxed. The Laffer curve illustrates this possibility.

11. Tax legislation passed during the 1980s fundamentally altered the federal income tax structure. Both the personal and corporate income tax bases were broadened and the marginal tax rates reduced substantially. The tax policy of the 1980s was based on the belief that the lower tax rates will reduce tax avoidance and economic distortions and thereby promote economic growth. In addition to the United States, several other countries substantially reduced their top marginal tax rates during the latter half of the 1980s.

12. The cost of government activities encompasses the following components: (a) the opportunity cost of resources used to produce public-sector goods and services, (b) the compliance costs of taxation, and (c) the excess burden costs associated with price distortions and inefficiencies emanating from taxation. Generally, these costs will exceed both the size of the government budget and the dollar amount of the tax revenue collected.

13. The size of government as a share of the economy in the United States is approximately the same as for Japan, Australia, and Switzerland, but significantly smaller than for Canada and most Western European nations.

CRITICAL ANALYSIS QUESTIONS

1. Major categories of governmental spending include (a) national defense, (b) education, and (c) income transfers and antipoverty expenditures. Why do you think the public sector has become involved in these activities? Why not leave them to the market?

*2. People can avoid local taxes and, to a lesser degree, state taxes by moving. In comparison with the federal government, how does this characteristic influence people's ability to achieve value for their tax dollar at these levels of government?

*3. "User charges are simply another name for taxes. It makes no difference whether a government activity is financed by taxes or user charges." Evaluate.

4. "Transfer payments exert no influence on our economy because they merely transfer income from one group of individuals to another." Evaluate.

5. Do you think the indexing of the U.S. tax structure was a good idea? Why or why not? Will indexing make it easier or more difficult for Congress to increase tax revenues without voting for a tax increase? Explain. Do you think Congress may want to repeal indexing in the future? Why or why not?

*6. "A government project financed by taxation should be undertaken only if the expected value of the project is somewhat greater than the outlay necessary for its finance." Evaluate.

*7. How would a reduction in marginal tax rates influence the incentive of a taxpayer to incur a tax deductible expenditure?

8. Why do tourists and environmental groups generally favor taxation rather than entrance fees as a method of covering the operation and maintenance costs of national parks?

9. Do you think your college should cover the cost of providing campus parking through user charges, higher tuition for all students, or taxation? Should waiting in line (that is, time spent hunting for a parking space) play a substantial role in the allocation of parking spaces? Discuss.

*10. A popular sticker on trucks reads: "This truck pays $6,775 (or some other figure) in annual road-use taxes." Is this statement true?

11. How would each of the following affect the ability of the invisible hand to bring self-interest and helping others into harmony?

    a. A tax transfer system that equalized incomes.

    b. High tax rates and a large public sector that allocated most goods and services.

---

*Asterisk denotes questions for which answers are given in Appendix C, Selected Answers.

TWO

MICROECONOMICS

6 DEMAND AND CONSUMER CHOICE

Wisdom, whose lessons have been represented as so hard to learn by those who were never at her school, only teaches us to extend a simple maxim universally known. And this is, not to buy at too dear a price.[1]

Henry Fielding

CHAPTER FOCUS

■ How do economists analyze consumer choice? What assumptions do they make?

■ What role does time play in the consumption of goods?

■ What factors will cause a demand curve to shift?

■ What determines the demand for a specific item? Is advertising effective? Is it useful, or just misleading?

■ What is demand elasticity, and what factors determine its size? How is the elasticity concept used?

Macroeconomics focuses on aggregate markets—the big picture. Aggregate outcomes are, of course, the result of many individual decisions. We cannot understand or successfully influence the big picture without a solid knowledge of how microeconomic decisions are made. In this section, we will break down the aggregate product market into microeconomic markets for specific products.

Microeconomics focuses on how changes in *relative* prices influence consumer decisions. As we stressed in Chapter 3, the price system guides individuals in their production and consumption decisions.[2] Prices coordinate the vast array of individual economic activities by signaling relative wants and needs, and by motivating market participants to bring their own activities into harmony with those of others. Changes in one market affect conditions in others. In this chapter, we take a closer look at (a) the inter-relationships among markets and (b) the factors underlying the demand for specific products.

CHOICE AND INDIVIDUAL DEMAND

Exhibit 1 shows how consumers allocated their spending among alternative goods in 1950 and 1987. Why did consumers spend more on transportation than on medical care, or more on alcoholic beverages than on religious and welfare activities? Why have consumer expenditures on food declined (as a percentage of the total), while spending on housing has expanded? If we are to answer these questions, we will need to know something about the factors that influence the behavior of consumers.

When analyzing the choices of consumers, economists usually make the following assumptions.

1. *Limited Income Necessitates Choice.* Most of us are all too aware that our desire for goods far exceeds our limited incomes. People do not have enough resources to produce everything they would like. A limited income forces each of us to make choices. When one good or service is purchased, many others must be sacrificed. That is precisely the meaning of cost.

2. *Consumers Make Decisions Purposefully.* Consumption decisions are made with the desire to upgrade one's personal welfare in mind. A foolish purchase means giving up something more worthwhile. The purpose or goal behind a consumer decision can usually be met in many different ways, so that careful consideration of alternatives is useful. Consumers generally choose the alternative that is expected to enhance their personal welfare the most, relative to cost. They do not *intentionally* choose a lesser-valued alternative when they know that another of equal cost but greater projected benefit is available.

3. *One Good Can Be Substituted for Another.* Consumers have many goals, each with alternative means of satisfaction. No single good is so precious that some of it will not be given up in exchange for a large enough quantity of other goods. For example, consumers will give up some fried chicken to have more pizza, hamburgers, fish, ham sandwiches, or apple pie. Similarly, reading, watching movies and television, or playing cards can be substituted for playing football.

---

[1]Henry Fielding, *Tom Jones,* Book VI, Chapter III.
[2]You may want to review Chapter 3 before beginning the study of microeconomics.

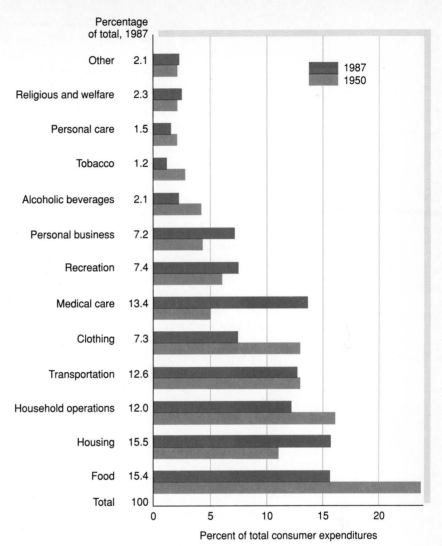

EXHIBIT 1

How Consumers Spent Their Income, 1950 and 1987

Percentage of total, 1987

Category	%
Other	2.1
Religious and welfare	2.3
Personal care	1.5
Tobacco	1.2
Alcoholic beverages	2.1
Personal business	7.2
Recreation	7.4
Medical care	13.4
Clothing	7.3
Transportation	12.6
Household operations	12.0
Housing	15.5
Food	15.4
Total	100

Percent of total consumer expenditures

U.S. Department of Commerce. *Survey of Current Business*, July 1988.

How about our "need" for basic commodities such as water or energy? The "need" of a person for an item is closely related to its cost—what must be given up to obtain the item. Southern California residents "need" water from the north, but the individual resident, when faced with a high water cost, finds that cactus gardens can be substituted for lawns, a plumber's bill for a faucet drip, and flow constrictors for full-force showers. The need for water depends on its cost. People living in Montana, where household electricity costs about twice as much as in nearby Washington, use half as much electricity per household. Montanans reduce their "need" for electricity by substituting gas, fuel oil, insulation, and wool sweaters, which cost about the same as in Washington.

4. *Consumers Must Make Decisions without Perfect Information, but Knowledge and Past Experience Will Help*. No human being has perfect foresight. Na-

poleon did not anticipate Waterloo; Julius Caesar did not anticipate the actions of Brutus. Consumers will not always correctly anticipate the consequences of their choices.

Consumer choices, however, are not made in a vacuum. You have a pretty good idea of what to expect when you buy a cup of coffee, five gallons of gasoline, or lunch at your favorite café. Why? Because you have learned from experience—your own and that of others. When you buy a product, your expectations may not be fulfilled precisely (for example, the coffee may be stronger than expected or the gasoline may make your car knock), but even these experiences will give you valuable information that can be used in making future decisions.

5. *The Law of Diminishing Marginal Utility Applies: As the Rate of Consumption Increases, the Utility Derived from Consuming Additional Units of a Good Will Decline.* Utility is a term economists use to describe the subjective personal benefits that result from an action. The **law of diminishing marginal utility** states that the **marginal** (or additional) **utility** derived from consuming successive units of a product will *eventually* decline as the rate of utilization increases. For example, the law implies that even though you might like ice cream, your marginal satisfaction from *additional* ice cream will eventually decline. Ice cream at lunchtime might be great. An additional helping for dinner might be even better. However, after you have had it for evening dessert and a midnight snack, ice cream for breakfast will begin to lose some of its attraction. The law of diminishing marginal utility will have set in, and thus the marginal utility derived from the consumption of additional units of ice cream will decline.

Law of Diminishing Marginal Utility: A basic economic principle, which states that as the consumption of a commodity increases, the marginal utility derived from consuming more of the commodity (per unit of time) will eventually decline. Marginal utility may decline even though total utility continues to increase, albeit at a reduced rate.

Marginal Utility: The additional utility received by a person from the consumption of an additional unit of a good within a given time period.

MARGINAL UTILITY AND CONSUMER CHOICE

Consumer choices, like other decisions, are influenced by changes in benefits and costs. If a consumer wants to get the most out of his or her expenditures, how much of each good should be purchased? As more of a good is consumed per unit of time, the law of diminishing marginal utility states that the consumer's marginal benefit per unit of time will decline. A consumer will gain by purchasing more of a product as long as the benefit, or marginal utility (MU), derived from the consumption of an additional unit exceeds the cost of the unit (the expected marginal utility from other consumption alternatives that must now be given up).

Given a fixed income and specified prices for the commodities to be purchased, consumers will maximize their satisfaction (or total utility) by ensuring that the last dollar spent on each commodity purchased yields an equal degree of marginal utility. If consumers are to get the most for their money, the last dollar spent on product A must yield the same utility as the last dollar spent on product B (or any other product).[3] After all, if tickets for football games, for example,

---

[3]Mathematically, this implies that the consumer's total utility is at a maximum when limited income is spent on products such that

$$\frac{MU_a}{P_a} = \frac{MU_b}{P_b} = \ldots = \frac{MU_n}{P_n}$$

where MU represents the marginal utility derived from the last unit of a product, and P represents the price of the good. The subscripts a, b, . . ., n indicate the different products available to the consumer. In the continuous case, the above expression implies that the consumer will get the most for his or her money when the consumption of each product is increased only to the point at which the marginal utility from one more unit of the good is equal to the marginal utility obtainable from the best alternative purchase that must now be forgone. For more advanced students, this proposition is developed in an alternative, more formal manner in the Addendum on indifference curves.

yielded less marginal utility *per dollar* than did opera tickets, the obvious thing for a consumer to do would be to cut back spending on football games and allocate more funds for opera tickets. If people really attempt to spend their money in a way that yields the greatest amount of satisfaction, the applicability of the consumer decision-making theory outlined above is difficult to question.

PRICE CHANGES AND CONSUMPTION DECISIONS

Demand is the schedule of the amount of a product that consumers would be willing to purchase at alternative prices during a specific time period. The first law of demand states that the amount of a product purchased is inversely related to its price. Why? First, as the price of a product declines, the lower opportunity cost will induce consumers to buy more of it. What will happen to the marginal utility derived from the product, though, as they increase their rate of consumption? It will fall. Each additional unit consumed adds less to total utility. Thus, as more of the product is consumed, a point is reached where the benefits (marginal utility) derived from the consumption of still more units will again be less than the cost. Purposeful decision-makers will not choose such units. A price reduction will thus induce consumers to purchase more of a product, but the response will be limited because of the law of diminishing marginal utility. Economists refer to this tendency to substitute a product that has become relatively cheaper for goods that are now more expensive as the **substitution effect.**

Substitution Effect: That part of an increase (decrease) in amount consumed that is the result of a good being cheaper (more expensive) in relation to other goods because of a reduction (increase) in price.

Income Effect: That part of an increase (decrease) in amount consumed that is the result of the consumer's real income (the consumption possibilities available to the consumer) being expanded by a reduction in the price of a good.

Second, since the money income of consumers is constant, a reduction in the price of a product will increase their real income—the amount of goods and services they are able to purchase. Typically, consumers will respond by purchasing more of the cheaper product (as well as other products) because they can now better afford to do so. This factor is referred to as the **income effect.** (Both the income and substitution effects are derived graphically in the addendum to this chapter, entitled "Consumer Choice and Indifference Curves.")

Of course, the substitution and income effects will generally induce consumers to purchase less of a good if its price rises. Why will consumers curtail their consumption of a product that has risen in price? The rising opportunity cost of consuming the product makes it a less attractive buy. However, as consumption is reduced, remaining units have a higher marginal utility. If the price increase is not so great as to price the consumer out of the market completely, a sufficient fall in the rate of consumption will raise the product's marginal utility enough to again equal its new, higher opportunity cost. With moderate increases in price, the consumer's reduction in consumption will be limited. We must also bear in mind that if the consumer's money income is constant, the price increase reduces the individual's real income. A reduction in real income will tend to result in a reduction in the consumption of many goods, generally including the good that has increased in price.

Exhibit 2 illustrates the adjustment of consumers to a higher price. During 1985–1986, gasoline prices fell rapidly in the United States. As demand theory would predict, consumers increased their rate of consumption. As gasoline prices fell from $1.20 to $.80, Jones's average weekly consumption rose from 16 gallons to 20 gallons. The availability of less expensive fuel resulted in his postponement of a costly tuneup on his car, which would have saved some fuel. He went to the grocery store a little more often, rather than waiting as usual to combine shopping trips with other business near the shopping center. He and his family took a vacation by car, which would have been much more expensive at the 1985 gasoline

EXHIBIT 2

Gas Prices, Consumption, and Marginal Utility

An individual, Jones in this case, will increase his rate of consumption of a product as long as MU exceeds its opportunity cost (principally the price of the good). Higher prices will induce him to consume less, but the reduction in consumption will be limited because the MU of the product will rise as consumption falls.

price level. At the higher rate of use, the marginal utility of gasoline fell, bringing it into line with the lower price.

Still lower gasoline prices would cause an even greater increase in consumption. The additional decline in price would allow consumers to enjoy still more slightly lower valued uses of gasoline. Lower prices bring on further consumption increases, but the response is limited because the marginal utility of gasoline falls as consumption rises.

TIME COST AND CONSUMER CHOICE

The monetary price of a good is not always a complete measure of its cost to the consumer. Consumption of most goods requires time as well as money. Time, like money, is scarce to the consumer. A lower time cost, like a lower money price, will make a product more attractive to consumers.[4]

Some commodities are demanded primarily because of their ability to reduce the consumer's time cost. Consumers are often willing to pay higher money prices for such goods. The popularity of automatic dishwashers, prepared foods, air travel, and taxi service is based partly on their low time cost in comparison with substitutes.

What is the cost of a college education? Tuition payments and the price of books comprise only a small component. The major cost of a college education is the time cost—approximately 4,000 hours. Even if a student's time is valued at only $3 per hour, the time cost of a college education is $12,000!

Time costs, unlike money prices, differ among individuals. They are higher for persons with greater earning power. Other things being equal, high-wage consumers choose fewer time-intensive (and more time-saving) commodities than persons with a lower time cost. High-wage consumers are overrepresented among air and taxicab passengers but underrepresented among television watchers, chess players, and long-distance automobile travelers. Can you explain why?

---

[4]For a technical treatment of the importance of time as a component of cost from the vantage point of the consumer, see Gary Becker, ''A Theory of the Allocation of Time,'' *Economic Journal* (September 1965), pp. 493–517.

You can, if you understand how both money and time cost influence the choices of consumers.

CONSUMER CHOICE AND MARKET DEMAND

The market demand schedule is the amount demanded by all the individuals in the market area at various prices. Since individual consumers purchase less at higher prices, the amount demanded in a market area is also inversely related to price.

Exhibit 3 illustrates the relationship between individual demand and market demand for a hypothetical two-person market. The individual demand curves for both Jones and Smith are shown. Jones and Smith each consume 20 gallons of gasoline weekly at 80 cents per gallon. The amount demanded in the two-person market is 40 gallons. If the price rises to $1.20 per gallon, the amount demanded in the market will fall to 28 gallons, 16 demanded by Jones and 12 by Smith. The market demand is simply the horizontal sum of the individual demand curves.

Market demand reflects individual demand. Individuals buy less as price increases. Therefore, the total amount demanded in the market declines as price increases.

CONSUMER SURPLUS

Consumer Surplus: The difference between the maximum amount a consumer would be willing to pay for a unit of a good and the payment that is actually made.

The demand curve reveals how many units consumers will purchase at various prices. In so doing, it reveals consumers' evaluation of units of a good. The height of the demand curve indicates how much consumers value an added unit. The difference between the amount that consumers would be willing to pay and the amount they actually pay for a good is called consumer surplus. As Exhibit 4 illustrates, it is measured by the area under the demand curve but above the market price.

Previously, we indicated that voluntary exchange is advantageous to buyer and seller alike. Consumer surplus is a measure of the net gain to the buyer/consumer. Consumer surplus also reflects the law of diminishing marginal utility. Consumers will continue purchasing additional units of a good, each yielding less marginal utility than the previous unit, until the marginal utility is just enough to

EXHIBIT 3
Individual and Market Demand Curves

The market demand curve is merely the horizontal sum of the individual demand curves. The market demand curve will slope downward to the right just as the individual demand curves do.

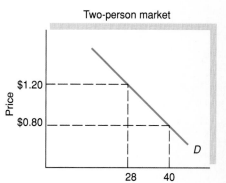

Weekly gasoline consumption (gallons)

EXHIBIT 4
Consumer Surplus

As the shaded area indicates, the difference between the largest amount consumers would be willing to pay for each unit and the price they actually pay for the unit is called consumer surplus.

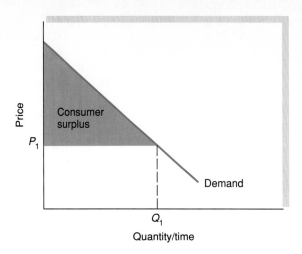

justify paying the market price. Up to that point, however, consumption of each unit generates a surplus for the consumer, since the value of the unit generally exceeds the market price. In aggregate, the total value (utility) to consumers of a good may be far greater than the total cost to them.

The size of the consumer surplus is affected by the market price. A reduction in the market price will lead to an expansion in quantity purchased and a larger consumer surplus. Conversely, a higher market price will reduce the amount purchased and shrink the surplus (net gain) of consumers.

WHAT CAUSES THE DEMAND CURVE TO SHIFT?

The demand schedule isolates the impact of price on the amount purchased, assuming other factors are held constant. What are these "other factors"? How do they influence demand?

Changes in the Income of Consumers Influence the Demand for a Product.[5] The demand for most products is positively related to income. As their income expands, individuals typically spend more on consumption. The demand for most products increases. Conversely, a reduction in consumer income usually causes the demand for a product to fall.

Changes in the Distribution of Income Influence the Demand for Specific Products. If more income were allocated to alcoholics and less to vegetarians, the demand for liquor would increase, whereas the demand for vegetables would fall. Consider another example. Suppose a law were passed that taxed all inheritances over $500,000 at a 90 percent rate. If the law effectively reduced the income of sons and daughters of the wealthy, it would also reduce their demand for yachts, around-the-world cruises, diamonds, and perhaps even Harvard educations. If the revenues from the tax were redistributed to persons with incomes below $10,000,

---

[5]Do not forget that a change in *quantity demanded* is a movement along a demand curve in response to a change in price, but a change in *demand* is a shift in the entire demand curve. Review Chapter 3 if you find this point confusing.

the demand for hamburgers, used cars, moderately priced housing, and other commodities that low-income families purchase would increase relative to yachts, cruises, and diamonds.

Substitutes: Products that are related such that an increase in the price of one will cause an increase in demand for the other (for example, butter and margarine, Chevrolets and Fords).

Complements: Products that are usually consumed jointly (for example, lamps and light bulbs). An increase in the price of one will cause the demand for the other to fall.

The Prices of Closely Related Goods Influence the Demand for a Product. Related goods may be either substitutes or complements. When two products perform similar functions or fulfill similar needs, they are **substitutes.** There is a direct relationship between the price of a product and the demand for substitutes. For example, margarine is a substitute for butter. Higher butter prices will increase the demand for margarine as consumers substitute it for more expensive butter. Similarly, higher coffee prices will increase the demand for such substitutes as cocoa and tea. On the other hand, if technology, good weather, or some other factor reduces the price of a good, then the demand for its substitutes will decline. A substitute relationship exists between beef and pork, pencils and pens, apples and oranges, and so forth.

Other closely related products are consumed jointly. Goods that "go together," so to speak, are called **complements.** With complements, there is an inverse relationship between the price of one and the demand for the other. For example, as the experiences of the 1970s illustrate quite well, higher gasoline prices cause the demand for large automobiles to decline. Gasoline and large automobiles are complementary. Similarly, lower prices in 1986 for video cassette recorders increased the demand for video cassettes. Ham and eggs are complementary items, as are tents and camping equipment.

Changes in Consumer Preferences Influence Demand. Why do preferences change? Preferences change because people change. New information, for example, might change their valuation of a good. How did consumers respond to new information linking cigarette smoking to cancer in the mid-1960s? They responded by purchasing and smoking fewer cigarettes. Annual per capita consumption, which had been increasing, fell more than 6 percent between 1965 and 1970. As more consumers learned that cigarettes were "cancer sticks," many of them changed their preferences.

Changes in Population and Its Composition Influence the Demand for Products. The demand for products in a market area is directly related to the number of consumers. Because of this, changes in the composition of the population may also have an impact on demand. If a higher percentage of the population is between 16 and 21 years of age, the demand for movies, stereo equipment and records, sports cars, and college educations will be positively affected. An increase in the number of elderly people will positively affect the demand for medical care, retirement housing, and vacation travel.

Expectations Influence Demand. When consumers expect the future price of a product to rise (fall), their current demand for it will expand (decline). "Buy now, before the price goes even higher" becomes the order of the day. When the price of coffee rose sharply in 1986, how did shoppers respond? Initially, current sales increased; consumers hoarded the product because they expected its price to continue rising. Conversely, if consumers thought the price of automobiles, for example, would be 10 percent lower next year, would their actions be influenced? Yes. Many consumers would defer their automobile purchases until next year, waiting for bargain prices.

An economist constructing a demand schedule for a product assumes that factors other than the price of the product are held constant. As Exhibit 5 shows, a change in any of these other factors that influence consumer decisions will cause the entire demand curve to shift. The accompanying Thumbnail Sketch (a) points out that *quantity demanded* (but not demand) will change in response to a change in the price of a product and (b) summarizes the major factors that cause a change in *demand* (a shift of the entire curve.)

THUMBNAIL SKETCH

Change in Quantity Demanded and Change in Demand

A change in this factor will cause the quantity demanded (but not demand) to change:

1. The current price of the product

Changes in these factors will cause the entire demand curve to shift:

1. Consumer income
2. The distribution of consumer income
3. Price of related products (substitutes and complements)
4. Consumer preferences
5. Population in the market area
6. Expectations about the future price of the product

EXHIBIT 5

Price Is Not All That Matters

Other things constant, the demand schedule will slope downward to the right. However, changes in income and its distribution, the prices of closely related products, preferences, population, and expectations about future prices will also influence consumer decisions. Changes in these factors will cause the entire demand curve to shift (for example, increase from D_1 to D_2).

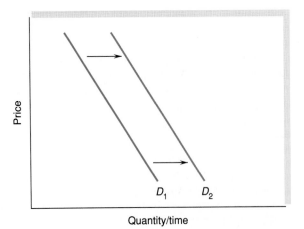

DETERMINANTS OF SPECIFIC PREFERENCES— WHY DO CONSUMERS BUY *THAT?*

Did you ever wonder why a friend spent hard-earned money on something that you would not have even if it were free? Tastes differ, and as we have already shown, they influence demand. What determines preferences? Why do people like one thing but not another? Economists have not been able to explain very much about how preferences are determined. The best strategy has generally been to take preferences as given, using price and other demand-related factors to explain and predict human behavior. Still, there are some observations about consumer preferences worth noting.

First, the preferences behind any one choice are frequently complex. The person looking for a house wants far more than just a shelter: an attractive setting, a convenient location, quality of public services, and a great many other factors will enter the housing decision. Each person may evaluate the same attribute differently. For example, living near a school may be a high priority for a family with children but a nuisance to a retired couple.

Second, the individual consumer's choice is not always independent of other consumers. Not wanting to be left out, a person might buy an item to "get on the bandwagon"—just because others are buying the same item. Or, a good may have "snob appeal," setting owners apart from the crowd or elevating them into an exclusive group. Even relatively inexpensive items, such as old army jackets or faded sweat shirts, sometimes have snob appeal.[6]

A third factor influencing consumer choice is advertising. Advertisers would not spend tens of billions of dollars each year if they did not get results. How does advertising affect consumers? Does it simply provide valuable information about product quality, price, and availability? Or, does it use repetition and misleading information to manipulate consumers? Economists are not of one opinion. Let us take a closer look at this important issue.

ADVERTISING—HOW USEFUL IS IT?

What does advertising do for Americans? What were the results of the $110 billion spent on advertising in 1987? Advertising is often used as a sponsoring medium; it reduces the purchase price of newspapers, magazines, and, most obviously, television viewing. It is the consumer of the advertised products who indirectly pays for these benefits, though. Advertising thus cannot be defended solely on the basis of its sponsorship role.

Advertising does convey information about product price, quality, and availability. New firms or those with new products, new hours, new locations, or new services use advertising to keep consumers informed. Such advertising facilitates trade and increases efficiency. But, what about those repetitious television commercials that offer little or no information? Critics charge that such advertising is wasteful, misleading, and manipulative. Let us look at each of these charges.

---

[6]See Harvey Leibenstein, "Bandwagon, Snob, and Veblen Effects in the Theory of Consumer Demand," *Quarterly Journal of Economics* (May 1950), pp. 183–207; and R. Joseph Monsen and Anthony Downs, "Public Goods and Private Status," *Public Interest* (Spring 1971), pp. 64–76, for a more complete discussion of bandwagon and snob effects.

Is Advertising Wasteful? A great deal of media advertising simply seems to say "We are better" without providing supportive evidence. An advertiser may wish to take customers from a competitor or establish a brand name for a product. A multimillion-dollar media campaign by a soap, cigarette, or automobile manufacturer may largely be offset by a similar campaign waged by a competitor. The consumers of these products end up paying the costs of these battles for their attention and their dollars. We must remember, however, that consumers are under no obligation to purchase advertised products. If advertising results in higher prices with no compensating benefits, consumers can turn to cheaper, nonadvertised products.

A brand name in which people have confidence, even if it has been established by advertising, has another function. It is an asset at risk for the seller. People value buying from sellers in whom they have confidence, and will pay a premium to do so. If something happens to damage a brand name, the willingness of consumers to pay falls, and the value of the brand name falls, too. When brand names are not allowed, as in the case of alcoholic beverages during the Prohibition era, consumers often suffer. Without brand names to protect, anonymous moonshiners sometimes were careless and allowed dangerous impurities into the moonshine. Some consumers of moonshine were blinded, and others died. Today the situation is different. Those who buy Jack Daniels or Jim Beam whiskey know that besides skill and integrity, the distillers have an enormous sum of money tied up in their brands. A brand-name distiller would spend a large amount of money to avoid even one death from an impure batch. Is a brand name, promoted by costly advertising, worthwhile to the customer? The customer must decide.

Is Advertising Misleading? Unfair and deceptive advertising—including false promises, whether spoken by a seller or packaged by an advertising agency—is illegal under the Federal Trade Commission Act. The fact that a publicly advertised false claim is easier to establish and prosecute than the same words spoken in private is an argument for freedom in advertising. But, what about general, unsupported claims that a product is superior to the alternative or that it will help one enjoy life more? Some believe that such noninformational advertising should be prohibited. They would establish a government agency to evaluate the "informativeness" of advertising. But if consumers are misled by slick advertisers to part with their money without good reason, might they not also be misled by a slick media campaign to support politicians and regulatory policies that are not in their interest? Why should we expect consumers to make poor decisions when they make market choices, but wise decisions when they act in the political (and regulatory) arena? Clearly, additional regulation is not a cure-all. Like freedom in advertising, it has some defects.

Does Advertising Manipulate the Preferences of Consumers? The demand for some products would surely be much lower without advertising. Some people's preferences may, in fact, be shaped by advertising. However, in evaluating the manipulative effect of advertising, we must keep two things in mind. First, business decision-makers are likely to choose the simplest route to economic gain. Generally, it is easier for business firms to cater to the actual desires of consumers than attempt to reshape their preferences or persuade them to purchase an undesired product. Second, even if advertising does influence preferences, does it follow that this is bad? Economic theory cannot provide an answer. Economists may have an opinion, but they have no analytical answer to that question.

THE ELASTICITY OF DEMAND

Price Elasticity of Demand:
The percent change in the quantity of a product demanded divided by the percent change in the price causing the change in quantity. Price elasticity of demand indicates the degree of consumer response to variation in price.

If the tuition charges at your school go up 50 percent next year, how many of your classmates will be back? If the price of salt doubles, how much less will you purchase? These are questions about price elasticity of demand.

Price elasticity of demand[7] is defined as:

$$\frac{\text{Percent change in quantity demanded}}{\text{Percent change in price}}$$

This ratio is called the elasticity coefficient. Elasticity of demand refers to the flexibility of consumers' desires for a product—the degree of their responsiveness to a change in a product's price. If a small rise in price causes consumers to choose a much smaller amount of a product, the demand for the product is elastic. In contrast, if a substantial increase in price results only in a small reduction in quantity demanded, the demand is inelastic. On an elastic demand curve, the quantity demanded is highly sensitive to a change in price. In contrast, an inelastic demand curve indicates inflexibility or little consumer response to variation in price.

The precise distinction between elastic and inelastic can be determined by the elasticity coefficient. When the elasticity coefficient is greater than 1 (ignoring the sign), demand is elastic. An elasticity coefficient of less than 1 means that demand is inelastic. "Unitary elasticity" is the term used to denote a price elasticity of 1. Although the sign of the coefficient of price elasticity is often ignored, it is always negative, since a change in price causes the quantity demanded to change in the opposite direction.

GRAPHIC REPRESENTATION OF DEMAND ELASTICITY

Exhibit 6 presents demand curves of varying elasticity. A demand curve that is completely vertical is termed "perfectly inelastic." The addict's demand for heroin or the diabetic's demand for insulin might *approximate* perfect inelasticity over a range of prices, although no demand curve will be perfectly inelastic at all prices (Exhibit 6a).

The more inelastic the demand, the steeper the demand curve *over any specific price range*. Inspection of the demand for cigarettes (Exhibit 6b), which is

---

[7]You might want to distinguish between (a) the elasticity at a point on the demand curve and (b) the *arc* elasticity *between* two points on the demand curve. The formula for point elasticity is:

$$\frac{\text{Change in quantity demanded}}{\text{Initial Quantity demanded}} \div \frac{\text{Change in Price}}{\text{Initial Price}}$$

The formula for arc elasticity is:

$$[(q_0 - q_1)/(q_0 + q_1)] \div [(P_0 - P_1)/(P_0 + P_1)]$$

where the subscripts 0 and 1 refer to the respective prices and amounts demanded at two alternative points on a specific demand curve. The arc elasticity is really the point elasticity at the midpoint of a line between the two points on the curve. See William Sher and Rudy Pinola, *Modern Microeconomics* (Amsterdam, North-Holland, 1986), pp. 167–169.

EXHIBIT 6
Demand Elasticity

(a) *Perfectly inelastic*—Despite an increase in price, consumers still purchase the same amount. The price elasticity of an addict's demand for heroin or a diabetic's demand for insulin might be approximated by this curve.

(b) *Relatively inelastic*—A percent increase in price results in a smaller percent reduction in sales. The demand for cigarettes has been estimated to be highly inelastic.

(c) *Unitary elasticity*—The percent change in quantity demanded is equal to the percent change in price. A *curve* of decreasing slope results. Sales revenue (price times quantity sold) is constant.

(d) *Relatively elastic*—A percent increase in price leads to a larger percent reduction in purchases. Consumers substitute other products for the more expensive good.

(e) *Perfectly elastic*—Consumers will buy all of farmer Jones's wheat at the market price, but none will be sold above the market price.

highly inelastic, and the demand for portable television sets (Exhibit 6d), which is relatively elastic, indicates that the inelastic curve tends to be steeper. When demand elasticity is unitary, as Exhibit 6c illustrates, a demand curve that is convex to the origin will result. When a demand curve is completely horizontal, an economist would say that it is perfectly elastic. Demand for the wheat of a single wheat farmer, for example, would approximate perfect elasticity (Exhibit 6e).

Since elasticity is a relative concept, the elasticity of a straight-line demand curve will differ at each point along the line. As Exhibit 7 illustrates, the elasticity of a straight-line demand curve (one with a constant slope) will range from highly elastic to highly inelastic. For Exhibit 7, when the price rises from $10 to $11, sales decline from 20 to 10. According to the arc elasticity formula, the price elasticity of demand is –7.0. Demand is very elastic in this region. In contrast, demand is quite inelastic in the $1 to $2 price range. As the price increases from $1 to $2, the amount demanded declines from 110 to 100. The arc elasticity of demand in this range is only –0.14; demand is highly inelastic.

Why do we bother with elasticity? Why not talk only about the slope of a demand curve? We use elasticities because they are independent of the units of measure. Whether we talk about dollars per gallon or cents per quart, the elasticities, given in percentages, remain the same. This is appropriate because people do not care what units of measurement are used; their response depends on the actual terms of exchange.

DETERMINANTS OF ELASTICITY OF DEMAND

Economists have estimated the price elasticity of demand for many products. Exhibit 8 presents some of these estimates, which vary a great deal. The demand for several products—salt, toothpicks, matches, light bulbs, or newspapers, for example—is highly inelastic. On the other hand, the demand for fresh tomatoes, Chevrolet automobiles, or fresh green peas is highly elastic. What factors explain this variation? Why is demand highly responsive to changes in price for some products but not for others?

The Availability of Substitutes. This factor is the most important determinant of demand elasticity. When good substitutes for a product are available, a price rise simply induces consumers to switch to other products. Demand is elastic. **For**

EXHIBIT 7

The Slope of a Demand Curve Is Not the Same as the Price Elasticity

With this straight-line (constant-slope) demand curve, demand is more elastic in the high-price range. The formula for arc elasticity (see footnote 7) shows that when price rises from $1 to $2 and quantity falls from 110 to 100, demand is inelastic. A price rise of the same magnitude (but of a smaller percentage), from $10 to $11, leads to a decline in quantity of the same size (but of a larger percentage), so that elasticity is much greater. (Price elasticities are negative, but we typically ignore the sign and look only at the absolute value.)

EXHIBIT 8   ■   The Estimated Price Elasticity of Demand for Selected Products

Inelastic	
Salt	0.1
Matches	0.1
Toothpicks	0.1
Airline travel, short-run	0.1
Gasoline, short-run	0.2
Gasoline, long-run	0.7
Residential natural gas, short-run	0.1
Residential natural gas, long-run	0.5
Coffee	0.25
Fish (cod) consumed at home	0.5
Tobacco products, short-run	0.45
Legal services, short-run	0.4
Physician services	0.6
Taxi, short-run	0.6
Automobiles, long-run	0.2
Approximate unitary elasticity	
Movies	0.9
Housing, owner occupied, long-run	1.2
Shellfish, consumed at home	0.9
Oysters, consumed at home	1.1
Private education	1.1
Tires, short-run	0.9
Tires, long-run	1.2
Radio and television receivers	1.2
Elastic	
Restaurant meals	2.3
Foreign travel, long-run	4.0
Airline travel, long-run	2.4
Fresh green peas	2.8
Automobiles, short-run	1.2–1.5
Chevrolet automobiles	4.0
Fresh tomatoes	4.6

Hendrik S. Houthakker and Lester D. Taylor, *Consumer Demand in the United States, 1929–1970* (Cambridge: Harvard University Press, 1966, 1970); Douglas R. Bohi, *Analyzing Demand Behavior* (Baltimore: Johns Hopkins University Press, 1981); and Hsaing-tai Cheng and Oral Capps, Jr. "Demand for Fish," *American Journal of Agricultural Economics,* August 1988; and U.S. Department of Agriculture.

example, if the price of fountain pens increased, many consumers would simply switch to pencils, ballpoint pens, and felt-tip pens. If the price of Chevrolets increased, consumers would substitute Fords, Volkswagens, and other cars.

When good substitutes are unavailable, the demand for a product tends to be inelastic. Medical services are an example. When we are sick, most of us find witch doctors, faith healers, palm readers, and cod-liver oil to be highly imperfect substitutes for a physician. Not surprisingly, the demand for physician services is inelastic.

The availability of substitutes increases as the product class becomes more specific, thus enhancing price elasticity. For example, as Exhibit 8 shows, the price elasticity of Chevrolets, a narrow product class, exceeds that of the broad class of automobiles in general.

The Share of Total Budget Expended on the Product. If the expenditures on a product are quite small relative to the consumer's budget, demand tends to be more inelastic. Compared to one's total budget, expenditures on some commodities are almost inconsequential. Matches, toothpicks, and salt are good examples. Most consumers spend only $1 or $2 per year on each of these items. A doubling of their price would exert little influence on the family budget. Therefore, even if the price of such a product were to rise sharply, consumers would still not find it in their interest to spend much time and effort looking for substitutes.

Time and Adjustment to a Price Change. It takes time for consumers to recognize and to respond fully to a change in the price of a product. Initially, not all consumers are aware of the price change. Many are slow to change their buying and consumption habits. But over time, people learn of the price change; they learn how to conserve more effectively on newly expensive items, and how to use cheaper items more effectively. New habits of consumption are formed, and the quantity demanded adjusts to the new price pattern.

Generally, the longer a price change persists, the greater the price elasticity of demand. The direct relationship between the elasticity coefficient of demand and the length of the time period allowed for consumer adjustment is often referred to as the second law of demand. According to this law, the elasticity of demand for a product is generally greater in the long run than in the short run.

Gasoline consumption patterns in the 1970s and 1980s provide a vivid illustration of the second law of demand. When gasoline prices rose from 35 cents to 60 cents during 1973–1975, did consumers *immediately* stop driving their 350-horsepower, gas-guzzling automobiles? No. When their full-sized cars wore out, though, many consumers did switch to compact cars giving higher gas mileage. In the short run consumers responded to higher gas prices by reducing speeds, forming car pools, and driving less often. Given more time, however, they also substituted compact cars for full-sized models, reducing gasoline consumption even more. As Exhibit 8 shows, then, the long-run demand for gasoline (0.7) proved more elastic than the short-run demand (0.2).

The same process occurred in reverse when gasoline prices fell from $1.20 to 80 cents during 1985–1986. Cheaper fuel allowed consumers to pay more attention to convenience and speed, and less attention to carpools and gas mileage. With time, people gradually replaced many small cars with larger cars that delivered more performance, comfort, and safety. As the lower fuel prices persisted into the late 1980s, even small cars were redesigned to take advantage of gasoline that was much cheaper than it had been earlier in the decade. Once again the response proved to be greater when consumers (and producers too) had more time to react to the price change.

Even though the demand for most products will be more elastic in the long run than in the short run, there can be some exceptions, primarily among durable consumer goods. Often, such purchases can initially be delayed into the future as prices rise. Repairs to existing goods can at first be a substitute for a purchase; repairing the old washing machine one more time is an example. Thus, higher prices result in a greater reduction in quantity demanded in the short run than is possible over an extended time period.

ELASTICITY AND TOTAL EXPENDITURES

Price elasticity shows us the relationship between a change in price and the resulting change in total expenditure on the product. When demand is inelastic, the percent change in unit sales is less than the percent change in price. Since quantity demanded changes by a smaller amount than price, the change in price will exert a larger impact on total expenditures than will the change in quantity demanded. Therefore, total expenditures will change in the same direction as price when demand is inelastic. For example, a higher product price will lead to an increase in expenditures on the product. Suppose that when the price of beef rises from $2 to $2.40 (a 20 percent increase), the quantity demanded by an average consumer falls from 100 pounds to 90 pounds (a 10 percent reduction) per year. Since the percent reduction in quantity demanded is less than the percent increase in price, we know that demand is inelastic.[8] At the $2 price, the average person spends $200 annually on beef. When the price rises to $2.40, the average annual expenditures rise to $216. The higher beef prices cause total expenditures to increase because demand is inelastic.

When demand is elastic, on the other hand, quantity demanded is more responsive to a change in price. The percent decline in quantity demanded will exceed the percent increase in price. The loss of sales will exert a greater influence on total expenditures than the rise in price. Therefore, a price increase will reduce total expenditures when the demand for a product is inelastic.

Exhibit 9 summarizes the relationship between changes in price and total expenditures for demand curves of varying elasticity. When demand is inelastic, a change in price will cause total expenditures to change in the same direction. If demand is elastic, price and total expenditures will change in opposite directions. For unitary elasticity, total expenditures will remain constant as price changes.

HOW DOES INCOME INFLUENCE DEMAND?

As income expands, the demand for most goods will increase. **Income elasticity** indicates the responsiveness of the demand for a product to a change in income. It is defined as:

$$\frac{\text{Percent change in quantity demanded}}{\text{Percent change in income}}$$

Income Elasticity: The percent change in the quantity of a product demanded divided by the percent change in consumer income. It measures the responsiveness of the demand for a good to a change in income.

As Exhibit 10 shows, the income elasticity coefficients for products vary; they are normally positive, however. In general, goods that people regard as "necessities" will have a low income elasticity of demand. Therefore, it is understandable that items such as fuel, electricity, bread, tobacco, economy clothing, and potatoes have a low income elasticity. A few commodities, such as navy beans, low-quality meat cuts, and bus travel have a negative income elasticity. Economists refer to goods with a negative income elasticity as **inferior goods.** As income expands, the demand for inferior goods will decline.

Inferior Goods: Goods for which the income elasticity is negative. Thus, an increase in consumer income causes the demand for such a good to decline.

Goods that consumers regard as "luxuries" generally have a high (greater than 1) income elasticity. For example, private education, new automobiles, recreational activities, expensive foods, swimming pools, and air travel are all income-elastic. As income increases, the demand for these products thus expands even more rapidly.

---

[8]Calculate the elasticity coefficient as an exercise. Is it less than 1?

EXHIBIT 9 ■ Demand Elasticity, Change in Price, and Change in Total Expenditures		
Price Elasticity of Demand	Numerical Elasticity Coefficient[a]	The Impact of a Change in Price on Total Expenditures (and Sales Revenues)
Elastic	1 to ∞	Price and total expenditures change in opposite directions
Unitary	1	Total expenditures remain constant as price changes
Inelastic	0 to 1	Price and total expenditures change in the same direction

[a]The sign of the elasticity coefficient is negative.

EXHIBIT 10 ■ The Estimated Income Elasticity of Demand for Selected Products	
Low income elasticity	
Margarine	−0.20
Fuel	0.38
Electricity	0.20
Fish (Haddock)	0.46
Food	0.51
Tobacco	0.64
Hospital care	0.69
High income elasticity	
Private education	2.46
New cars	2.45
Recreation and amusements	1.57
Alcohol	1.54

Hendrik S. Houthakker and Lester D. Taylor, *Consumer Demand in the United States, 1929–1970* (Cambridge: Harvard University Press, 1966); L. Taylor, "The Demand for Electricity: A Survey," *Bell Journal of Economics* (Spring 1975); F. W. Bell, "The Pope and the Price of Fish." *American Economic Review*, vol. 58 (December 1968).

USING THE CONCEPT OF ELASTICITY—THE BURDEN OF A TAX

When a tax is placed on the sale of a good, who pays it? How much does the price rise? How much is paid by the seller, rather than being passed on to the customer in the form of a higher price? When the price of a good rises, we have seen that the effect on revenue and on sales depends on the price elasticity of demand. In determining the relative burden of a tax, price elasticity again plays a major role.

Sellers would like to pass the entire tax on to buyers, raising price by the full amount of the tax, rather than paying any part of it themselves. However, as price rises, customers respond by purchasing less. Sales decline and sellers must then lower their price, accepting part of the tax burden themselves by receiving less revenue. In Chapter 5 we learned that when taxes increase the amount paid by consumers and reduce the *net* (after-tax) price received by sellers, both share in the tax burden. Using the concept of elasticity, we can now say more about how the burden is divided and the size of the deadweight loss associated with the tax. (Now would be a good time for the reader to review the "Taxes and Economic Efficiency" section, pages 111–113.)

Exhibit 11 illustrates the results of a new tax on gasoline. Panel (a) shows the result in the short run, when the price elasticity of demand is 0.2. Panel (b) shows the result in the long run, when demand elasticity is 0.7. In order to demonstrate what happens when demand elasticity changes but supply is the same, in panel (b) we temporarily assume the same supply curve applies in the long run as in the short.

In panel (a) the equilibrium price of gasoline before the new tax is $1 per gallon. The $.20 tax shifts the supply upward by the amount of the tax. Since they must turn over $.20 to the government for each gallon sold, sellers must receive the old price plus $.20 per gallon in order to maintain their prior incentive

EXHIBIT 11(a)

A Gasoline Tax When Demand Is Highly Inelastic

When a $.20 gasoline tax is imposed, the supply curve shifts vertically by the amount of the tax. Since consumers will buy less as the price increases, sellers will not be able to pass all of the tax along to consumers. The new short-run equilibrium will be at a price of $1.15. As the result of the tax, consumers pay $.15 more and sellers receive $.05 less.

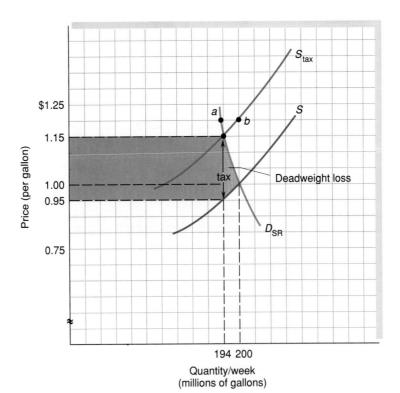

to produce. This is precisely what happens when the pre-tax supply curve is shifted vertically by the $.20 tax.

Of course, sellers would like to raise prices to $1.20 and pass the entire amount of the tax onto motorists. However, they will be unable to do so since motorists reduce their purchases in response to higher prices. If the price of gasoline rose to $1.20, then an excess supply (ab) would result. Therefore, sellers are only able to increase the price to $1.15, where they are able to sell 194 million gallons, 6 million fewer than before the tax was imposed. *Short-run equilibrium* is present at that price ($1.15) and output (194 million). In the short run, the buyers pay $.15 more and the sellers receive $.05 less per gallon.

There are relatively few ways that buyers can substitute away from the more expensive gasoline in the short run. Since their responsiveness—the price elasticity of their demand—is relatively small in the short run, consumers shoulder most of the tax burden.

In the long run, though, consumers will find more ways to economize on the more expensive gasoline (for example, they will shift to smaller cars). As consumer purchases decline by a larger amount, sellers must further decrease the price they will accept (reducing the quantity they will supply). As Exhibit 11b illustrates, in the long run the equilibrium price will decline to $1.10, and quantity exchanged will fall to 186 million gallons per week. In this case, buyers and sellers divide the burden of the $.20 tax equally. Comparing Exhibit 11a with Exhibit 11b, where supply is the same but the elasticities of demand differ, we can see that *ceteris paribus, when demand is more elastic, buyers pay a smaller share of the tax burden.* This makes good intuitive sense. When consumers find

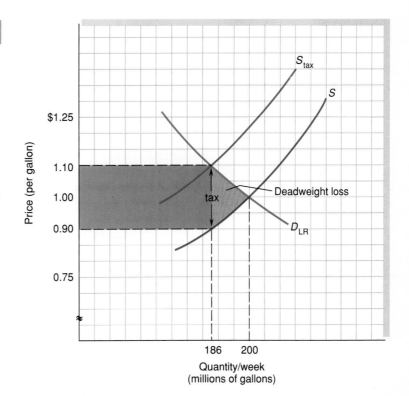

EXHIBIT 11(b)

A Gasoline Tax with More Elastic Demand

When demand is more elastic, consumers reduce their purchases by greater amounts. As a result, sellers must reduce price further [to $1.10 in this case, compared with $1.15 in panel (a)], and the tax burden falls more heavily on sellers, due to the greater demand elasticity. Here we assume that supply is unchanged.

more ways to economize when they reduce their purchases more in response to the higher price—in the long run, they put more pressure on sellers to lower the price they will accept.

Elasticity of Supply: The percentage change in quantity supplied, divided by the percentage change in the price that causes that change in quantity supplied.

Exhibit 11c introduces the other factor determining the burden of a tax: the elasticity of supply. The **elasticity of supply** is the percentage change in quantity supplied, divided by the percentage change in the price that causes the change. Since it measures the responsiveness of sellers to a change in price, it is analogous to the price elasticity of demand. In the next two chapters we will discuss the factors that determine supply elasticity. For now, it is important simply to recognize the concept of supply elasticity, and the fact that suppliers (like buyers) will be more responsive to price changes when they have more time to react to a change in price.

Earlier, in going from panel (a) to panel (b), we allowed demand to become more elastic, since panel (b) represented the long run. However, we unrealistically assumed that the elasticity of supply was the same in the long run as in the short run in order to isolate what would happen if only demand changed. Exhibit 11c shows the more realistic case in which supply, like demand, is more elastic in the long run. By comparing panels (b) and (c), we can see that when supply elasticity is greater (and demand is the same), a smaller share of the tax burden is borne by suppliers. Here, supply is drawn so the gasoline price, tax included, happens to rise to $1.15, just as it did in the short-run case. That would not necessarily be the case in the real world. In general, however, *when supply is more elastic, ceteris paribus, suppliers will bear a smaller part of the tax burden.*

EXHIBIT 11(c)

A Gasoline Tax with More Elastic Demand and Supply

When supply is more elastic, resources have other good alternative uses, so suppliers are less willing to reduce the price they receive in respone to a tax. Instead, quantity supplied is reduced by a greater amount. The price to consumers rises from $1.00 to $1.15. Compared with panel (b), where demand is the same as in (c), the greater supply elasticity in (c) causes less of the tax burden to be placed on suppliers.

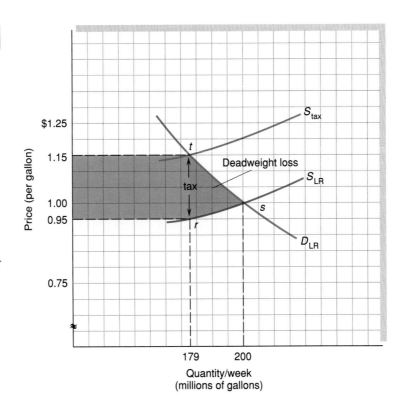

ELASTICITY AND THE DEADWEIGHT LOSS DUE TO A TAX

We have seen that elasticity of supply and demand play an important part in determining how the burden of a tax is distributed between buyer and seller. Exhibit 11 also illustrates how these elasticities influence the size of the excess burden, or deadweight loss caused by the tax. As we saw in Chapter 5 (Exhibit 7), reducing trade by taxing it not only transfers revenue (amount of the tax per unit, multiplied by the number of units sold after the tax) from buyers and sellers to the government; it reduces the gains from trade for both buyers and sellers by the transferred amount, plus somewhat more. Trades which would take place without the tax are eliminated by the presence of the tax. When either demand or supply is inelastic, so that few trades are eliminated when the tax is imposed, the excess burden is smaller. Exhibit 11a illustrates this point in the case of a highly inelastic demand. Since demand is highly inelastic, the quantity of gasoline traded declines by only 6 million gallons as the result of the $.20 tax.

In contrast, when both demand and supply are elastic as in Exhibit 11c, more trades are cut off by the tax. Given the more elastic demand and supply curves of Exhibit 11c, the quantity of gasoline produced and sold declines by 21 million gallons (from 200 million to 179 million). As the triangle *rst* illustrates, the excess burden of a tax increases as it cuts off more exchanges. Therefore, the burden of excise taxes will be less if they are levied on goods and services for which either demand or supply are highly inelastic.

LOOKING AHEAD

In this chapter, we outlined the mechanism by which consumers' wants and tastes are communicated to producers. Consumer choices underlie the market demand curve. Discovering the market demand for a product tells producers how strongly consumers desire each commodity relative to others. In the following chapter, we turn to costs of production, which arise because resources have alternative uses. In fact, the cost of producing a good tells the producer how badly the resources are desired in *other* areas. An understanding of these two topics—consumer demand and cost of production—is essential if we are to understand how markets allocate goods and resources.

CHAPTER SUMMARY

1. The demand schedule indicates the amount of a good that consumers would be willing to buy at each potential price. The first law of demand states that the quantity of a product demanded is inversely related to its price. A reduction in the price of a product reduces the opportunity cost of consuming it. At the lower price. many consumers will substitute the now cheaper good for other products. In contrast, higher prices will induce consumers to buy less as they turn to substitutes that are now *relatively* cheaper.
2. The market demand curve reflects the demand of individuals. It is simply the horizontal sum of the demand curves of individuals in the market area.
3. In addition to price, the demand for a product is influenced by the (a) level of consumer income, (b) distribution of income among consumers, (c) price of related products (substitutes and complements), (d) preferences of consumers, (e) population in the market area, and (f) consumer expectations about the future price of the product. Changes in any of these six factors will cause the *demand* for the product to change (the entire curve to shift).
4. Consumers usually gain from the purchase of a good. The difference between the amount that consumers would be willing to pay for a good and the amount they ac-

tually pay is called consumer surplus. It is measured by the area under the demand curve but above the market price.

5. Time, likely money, is scarce for consumers. Consumers consider both time and money costs when they make decisions. Other things constant, a reduction in the time cost of consuming a good will induce consumers to purchase more of the good.

6. Both functional and subjective factors influence the demand for a product. Some goods are chosen because they have "snob appeal." Goods may also have a "bandwagon effect," fulfilling a consumer's desire to be fashionable. Observation suggests that goods are demanded for a variety of reasons.

7. The precise effect of advertising on consumer decisions is difficult to evaluate. The magnitude of advertising by profit-seeking business firms is strong evidence that it influences consumer decisions. Advertising often reduces the amount of time consumers must spend looking for a product and helps them make more informed choices. However, a sizable share of all advertising expenditures is largely for noninformational messages. Although this is a controversial area, it is clearly much easier to point out the shortcomings of advertising than to devise an alternative that would not have similar imperfections.

8. Price elasticity reveals the responsiveness of the amount purchased to a change in price. When there are good substitutes available and the item forms a sizable component of the consumer's budget, its demand will tend to be more elastic. Typically, the price elasticity of a product will increase as more time is allowed for consumers to adjust to the price change. This direct relationship between the size of the elasticity coefficient and the length of the adjustment time period is often referred to as the second law of demand.

9. The concept of elasticity is useful in explaining the effects of a policy change, such as the imposition of a sales tax. When demand is more elastic, buyers bear less of the tax burden; when supply is more elastic, sellers bear less of the burden. When either is inelastic, the excess burden of the tax is smaller.

CRITICAL ANALYSIS QUESTIONS

*1. What impact did the substantially lower gasoline prices of the mid-1980s have on (a) the demand for big cars, (b) the demand for small cars, (c) the incentive to experiment and develop electric and other non-gas-powered cars, (d) the demand for gasoline (*Be careful*), and (e) the demand for vacations by automobile in Florida?

2. "As the price of beef rises, the demand of consumers will begin to decline. Economists estimate that a 5 percent rise in beef prices will cause demand to decline by 1 percent." Indicate the two errors in this statement.

*3. The following chart presents data on the price of fuel oil, the amount of it demanded, and the demand for insulation. (a) Calculate the price elasticity of demand for fuel oil as its price rises from 30 cents to 50 cents; from 50 cents to 70 cents. (b) Are fuel oil and insulation substitutes or complements? How can you tell from the figures alone?

	Fuel Oil	Insulation
Price per Gallon (cents)	Quantity Demanded (millions of gallons)	Quantity demanded (millions of tons)
30	100	30
50	90	35
70	60	40

4. "Since the same price rise causes a reduction in the demand of each consumer, and since market demand is the sum of individual demands, the demand elasticity for the

---

*Asterisk denotes questions for which answers are given in appendix C, Selected Answers.

market must be much greater than for any individual. The same percentage price change brings about a much larger quantity change in the market.'' Evaluate this statement.

5. ''As soon as they heard about the shortage of peaches in this year's crop, suppliers of canned peaches raised the price of peaches already on the shelf! This price increase serves no economic purpose, since those on the shelf now were from last year's plentiful crop.'' Explain why this statement is false.

6. ''Economists recommend that taxes be levied on goods with inelastic demand. This means that consumers have no place to go. Their demand is inelastic, so no good substitutes exist for such goods. Taxing such goods hurts market participants, rather than helps them.'' Evaluate.

7. Residential electricity in the state of Washington costs about half as much as in nearby Montana. A study showed that in Washington, the average household used about 1200 kilowatt-hours per month, whereas Montanans used about half that much per household. Do these data provide us with two points on the average household's demand curve for residential electricity in this region? Why or why not?

*8. **What's Wrong with this Way of Thinking?**
''Economics is unable to explain the value of goods in a sensible manner. A quart of water is much cheaper than a quart of oil. Yet water is essential to both animal and plant life. Without it, we could not survive. How can oil be more valuable than water? Yet economics says that it is.''

*9. The wealthy are widely believed to have more leisure time than the poor. However, even though we are a good deal wealthier today than our great-grandparents were 100 years ago, we appear to live more hectic lives and have less free time. Can you explain why?

10. Recently, two researchers used variables such as hospital beds and doctors per capita, expenditures on public education, and percent of income expended on highways to construct an index of ''livability.'' Florida ranked as one of the ''least desirable'' places to live. Yet, the migration rate to Florida is one of the highest in the nation. What conclusions would you draw from these facts?

11. Most systems of medical insurance substantially reduce the costs of physician services and hospitalization. Some reduce these costs to zero. How does this method of payment affect the consumption levels of medical services? Might this method of organization result in ''too much'' consumption of medical services? Discuss.

*12. Indicate whether the following statements are true or false. Explain.
  a. A 10 percent reduction in price that leads to a 15 percent increase in amount purchased indicates a price elasticity of more than one.
  b. A 10 percent reduction in price that leads to a 2 percent increase in total expenditures indicates a price elasticity of more than one.
  c. If the percent change in price is less than the resultant percent change in quantity demanded, demand is elastic.

*13. a. If you really like pizza, should you try to consume as much pizza as possible?
  b. If you want to succeed, should you try to make the highest possible grade in your economics class?

*14. Sue loves ice cream but cannot stand yogurt. In contrast, Carole cannot tell the difference between ice cream and yogurt. Who will have the more elastic demand for yogurt?

*15. ''If all the farmers reduced their output to one-half of the current rate, farm incomes would increase, the total utility derived from farm output would rise, and the nation would be better off.'' True or false? Evaluate.

16. Can you think of any circumstances under which an *increase* in price might temporarily lead to an *increase* in amount purchased?

17. Can you think of any reason why the prices of shares of stock of a specific company,

gold, and other commodities for which the supply is (approximately) fixed will fluctuate more than the prices of goods that are reproduceable at a constant cost?

*18. ''Market competition encourages deceitful advertising and dishonesty.'' True or false? Explain.

*19. What is the nature of the deadweight loss accompanying sales taxes? Why is it often referred to as an ''excess burden'' of the tax?

ADDENDUM

CONSUMER CHOICE AND INDIFFERENCE CURVES

In the text of this chapter, we used marginal utility analysis to develop the demand curve of an individual. In developing the theory of consumer choice, economists usually rely on a more formal technique—indifference curve analysis. Since this technique is widely used at a more advanced level, many instructors like to include it in their introductory course. In this addendum, we use indifference curve analysis to develop the theory of demand in a more formal—some would say more elegant—manner.

WHAT ARE INDIFFERENCE CURVES?

Indifference Curve: A curve, convex from below, that separates the consumption bundles that are more preferred by an individual from those that are less preferred. The points *on* the curve represent combinations of goods that are equally preferred by the individual.

There are two elements in every choice: (a) preferences (the desirability of various goods) and (b) opportunities (the attainability of various goods). The **indifference curve** concept is useful for portraying a person's preferences. An indifference curve simply separates better (more preferred) bundles of goods from inferior (less preferred) bundles. It provides a diagrammatic picture of how an individual ranks alternative consumption bundles.

In Exhibit A-1, we assume that Robinson Crusoe is initially consuming 8 fish and 8 breadfruit per week (point A). This initial bundle provides him with a certain level of satisfaction (utility). He would, however, be willing to trade this initial bundle for certain other consumption alternatives if the opportunity presented itself. Since he likes both fish and breadfruit, he would especially like to

EXHIBIT A-1

The Indifference Curve of Robinson Crusoe

The curve generated by connecting Crusoe's "I do not care" answers separates the combinations of fish and breadfruit that he prefers to the bundle A from those that he judges to be inferior to A. The I points map out an indifference curve.

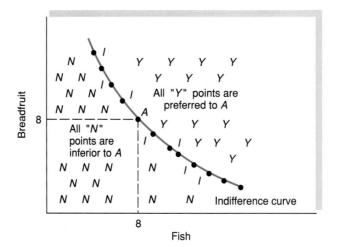

obtain bundles to the northeast of *A*, since they represent more of both goods. However, he would also be willing to give up some breadfruit if in return he received a compensatory amount of fish. Similarly, if the terms of trade were right, he would be willing to exchange fish for breadfruit. The trade-offs he is just willing to make lie *along* the indifference curve. Of course, he is quite willing to move to any bundle on a higher indifference curve.

Starting from point *A* (8 fish and 8 breadfruit), we ask Crusoe if he is willing to trade that bundle for various other bundles. He answers "Yes" (*Y*), "No" (*N*), or "I do not care" (*I*). Exhibit A-1 illustrates the pattern of his response. Crusoe's "I do not care" answers indicate that the original bundle (point *A*) and each alternative indicated by an *I* are valued equally by Crusoe. These *I* points, when connected, form the indifference curve. This line separates the preferred bundles of fish and breadfruit from the less valued combinations. Note that such a curve may be entirely different for any two people. The preferences of different individuals vary widely.

We can establish a new indifference curve by starting from any point not on the original curve and following the same procedure. If we start with a point (a consumption bundle) to the northeast of the original indifference curve, all points on the new curve will have a higher level of satisfaction for Crusoe than any on the old curve. The new curve will probably have about the same shape as the original.

CHARACTERISTICS OF INDIFFERENCE CURVES

In developing consumer theory, economists assume that the preferences of consumers exhibit certain properties. These properties enable us to make statements about the general pattern of indifference curves. What are these properties, and what do they imply about the characteristics of indifference curves?

1. More Goods Are Preferable to Fewer Goods—Thus, Bundles on Indifference Curves Lying Farthest to the Northeast Are Always Preferred. Assuming the consumption of only two commodities, since *both* commodities are desired, the individual will always prefer to have more of at least one of the goods without loss of any of the others. This means that combinations to the northeast of a point on the diagram will always be preferred to points lying to the southwest.

2. Goods Are Substitutable—Therefore, Indifference Curves Slope Downward to the Right. As we indicated in the text of this chapter, individuals are willing to substitute one good for another. Crusoe will be willing to give up some breadfruit if he is compensated with enough fish. Stated another way, there will be some amount of additional fish such that Crusoe will stay on the same difference curve, even though his consumption of breadfruit has declined. However, in order to remain on the same indifference curve, Crusoe must always acquire more of one good to compensate for the loss of the other. The indifference curve for goods thus will always slope downward to the right (run northwest to southeast).

3. The Valuation of a Good Declines As It Is Consumed More Intensively—Therefore, Indifference Curves Are Always Convex When Viewed from Below. The slope of the indifference curve represents the willingness of the individual to substitute one good for the other. Economists refer to the amount of one good that is just sufficient to compensate the consumer for the loss of a unit of the other good as the

Marginal Rate of Substitution: The change in the consumption level of one good that is just sufficient to offset a unit change in the consumption of another good without causing a shift to another indifference curve. At any point on an indifference curve, it will be equal to the slope of the curve at that point.

marginal rate of substitution. The marginal rate of substitution is equal to the slope of the indifference curve. Reflecting the principle of diminishing marginal utility, the marginal rate of substitution of a good will decline as the good is consumed more intensively relative to other goods. Suppose Crusoe remains on the same indifference curve while continuing to expand his consumption of fish relative to breadfruit. As his consumption of fish increases (and his consumption of breadfruit declines), his valuation of fish relative to breadfruit will decline. It will take more and more units of fish to compensate for the loss of still another unit of breadfruit. The indifference curve will become flatter and flatter, reflecting the decline in the marginal rate of substitution of fish for breadfruit as Crusoe consumes more fish relative to breadfruit.

Of course, just the opposite will happen if Crusoe's consumption of breadfruit increases relative to that of fish—if he moves northwest along the same indifference curve. In this case, as breadfruit is consumed more intensively, Crusoe's valuation of it will decline relative to that of fish, and the marginal rate of substitution of fish for breadfruit will rise (the indifference curve will become steeper and steeper). Therefore, since the valuation of each good declines as it is consumed more intensively, indifference curves must be convex when viewed from the origin.

4. Indifference Curves Are Everywhere Dense. We can draw an indifference curve through any point on the diagram. This simply means that any two bundles of goods can be compared by the individual.

5. Indifference Curves Cannot Cross—If They Did, Rational Ordering Would Be Violated. If indifference curves crossed, our postulate that more goods are better than

EXHIBIT A-2

Indifference Curves Cannot Cross

If the indifference curves of an individual crossed, it would lead to the inconsistency pictured here. Points X and Y must be equally valued, since they are both on the same indifference curve (i₁). Similarly, points X and Z must be equally valued, since they are both on indifference curve i₂. If this is true, Y and Z must also be equally preferred, since they are both equally preferred to X. However, point Y represents more of both goods than Z, so Y has to be preferred to Z. When indifference curves cross, this type of internal inconsistency always arises.

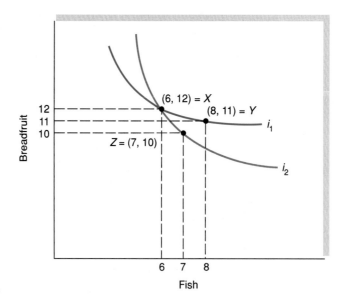

fewer goods would be violated. Exhibit A-2 illustrates this point. The crossing of the indifference curves implies that points *Y* and *Z* are equally preferred, since they both are on the same indifference curve as *X*. Consumption bundle *Y*, though, represents more of both fish and breadfruit than bundle *Z*, so *Y* must be preferred to *Z*. Whenever indifference curves cross, this type of internal inconsistency (irrational ranking) will arise. So, the indifference curves of an individual must not cross.

THE CONSUMER'S PREFERRED BUNDLE

Consumption Opportunity Constraint: The constraint that separates the consumption bundles that are attainable from those that are unattainable. In a money income economy, it is usually called a budget constraint.

Together with the opportunity constraint of the individual, indifference curves can be used to indicate the most preferred consumption alternatives available to an individual. The **consumption opportunity constraint** separates consumption bundles that are attainable from those that are unattainable.

Assuming that Crusoe could produce only for himself, his consumption opportunity constraint would look like the production possibilities curves discussed in Chapter 2. What would happen if natives from another island visited Crusoe and offered to make exchanges with him? If a barter market existed that permitted Crusoe to exchange fish for breadfruit at a specified exchange rate, his options would resemble those of the market constraint illustrated by Exhibit A-3. First, let us consider the case where Crusoe inhabits a barter economy in which the current market exchange rate is 2 fish equal 1 breadfruit. Suppose as a result of his expertise as a fisherman, Crusoe specializes in this activity and is able to bring 16 fish to the market per week. What consumption alternatives will be open to him? Since 2 fish can be bartered in the market for 1 breadfruit, Crusoe will be able to consume 16 fish, or 8 breadfruit, or any combination on the market constraint indicated by the line between these two points. For example, if he trades 2 of his 16 fish for 1 breadfruit, he will be able to consume a bundle consisting of 14 fish and 1 breadfruit. Assuming that the set of indifference curves of Exhibit

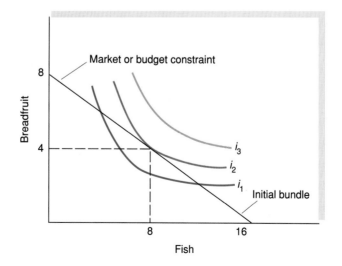

EXHIBIT A-3

Consumer Maximization—Barter Economy

Suppose that the set of indifference curves shown here outlines Crusoe's preferences. The slope of the market (or budget) constraint indicates that 2 fish trade for 1 breadfruit in this barter economy. If Crusoe produces 16 fish per week, he will trade 8 fish for 4 breadfruit in order to move to the consumption bundle (8 fish and 4 breadfruit) that maximizes his level of satisfaction.

A-3 outlines Crusoe's preferences, he will choose to consume 8 fish and 4 bread-fruit. Of course, it would be possible for Crusoe to choose many other combinations of breadfruit and fish, but none of the other attainable combinations would enable him to reach as high a level of satisfaction. Since he is able to bring only 16 fish to the market, it would be impossible for him to attain an indifference curve higher than i_2.

Crusoe's indifference curve and the market constraint curve will coincide (they will be tangent) at the point at which his attainable level of satisfaction is maximized. At that point (8 fish and 4 breadfruit), the rate at which Crusoe is *willing* to exchange fish for breadfruit (as indicated by the slope of the indifference curve) will be just equal to the rate at which the market will *permit* him to exchange the two (the slope of the market constraint).[9] If the two slopes differ at a point, Crusoe will always be able to find an attainable combination that will permit him to reach a *higher* indifference curve. He will always move down the market constraint when it is flatter than his indifference curve, and up if the market constraint is steeper.[10]

CRUSOE IN A MONEY ECONOMY

Budget Constraint: The constraint that separates the bundles of goods that the consumer can purchase from those that cannot be purchased, given a limited income and the prices of products.

As far as the condition for maximization of consumer satisfaction is concerned, moving from a barter economy to a money income economy changes little. Exhibit A-4 illustrates this point. Initially, the price of fish is $1, and the price of breadfruit $2. The market therefore permits an exchange of 2 fish for 1 breadfruit, just as was the case in Exhibit A-3. In Exhibit A-4, we assume Crusoe's money income is $16. At this level of income, he confronts the same market constraint (usually called a **budget constraint** in an economy with money) as for Exhibit A-3. Given the product prices and his income, Crusoe can choose to consume 16 fish, or 8 breadfruit, or any combination indicated by a line (the budget constraint) connecting these two points. Given his preferences, Crusoe will again choose the combination of 8 fish and 4 breadfruit if he wishes to maximize his level of satisfaction. As was true for the barter economy, when Crusoe maximizes his satisfaction (moves to the highest attainable indifference curve), the rate at which he is willing to exchange fish for breadfruit will just equal the rate at which the

---

[9]This actually is required only if the two goods are available in completely divisible amounts, not just as whole fish or whole breadfruit. For simplicity, we assume here that fractional availability is not a problem.

[10]Mathematically, the satisfaction of the consumer is maximized when the marginal rate of substitution of fish for breadfruit is equal to the price ratio. In utility terms, the marginal rate of substitution of fish for breadfruit is equal to the MU of fish divided by the MU of breadfruit. Therefore, the following expression is a condition for maximum consumer satisfaction:

$$\frac{MU_f}{MU_b} = \frac{P_f}{P_b}$$

This can be rewritten as follows:

$$\frac{MU_f}{P_f} = \frac{MU_b}{P_b}$$

Note that this is precisely the condition of consumer maximization that we indicated earlier in this chapter (see footnote 3).

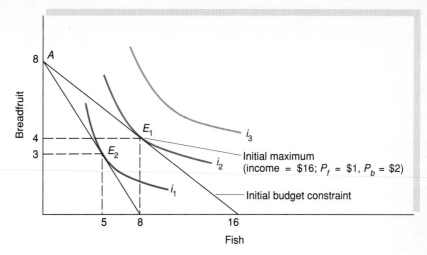

EXHIBIT A-4

Consumer
Maximization—Money
Income Economy

Suppose that Crusoe's income is $16 per day, the price of fish (P_f) is $1, and the price of breadfruit (P_b) is $2. Thus, Crusoe confronts exactly the same price ratio and budget constraint as in Exhibit A-3. Assuming that his preferences are unchanged, he will again maximize his satisfaction by choosing to consume 8 fish and 4 breadfruit. What will happen if the price of fish rises to $2? Crusoe's consumption opportunities will be reduced. His budget constraint will turn clockwise around point A, reflecting the higher price of fish. Crusoe's fish consumption will decline to 5 units. (Note: since Crusoe's real income has been reduced, his consumption of breadfruit will also decline.)

market will permit him to exchange the two goods. Stated in more technical terms, when his level of satisfaction is at a maximum, Crusoe's marginal rate of substitution of fish for breadfruit, as indicated by the slope of the indifference curve at E_1, will just equal the price ratio (P_f/P_b, which is also the slope of the budget constraint).

What will happen if the price of fish increases? Exhibit A-4 also answers this question. Since the price of breadfruit and Crusoe's money income are constant, a higher fish price will have two effects. First, it will make Crusoe poorer, even though his *money* income will be unchanged. His budget constraint will turn clockwise around point A, illustrating that his consumption options are now more limited—that is, his real income has declined. Second, the budget line will be steeper, indicating that a larger number of breadfruit must now be sacrificed to obtain an additional unit of fish. It will no longer be possible for Crusoe to attain indifference curve i_2. The best he can do is indifference curve i_1, which he can attain by choosing the bundle of 5 fish and 3 breadfruit.

Using the information supplied by Exhibit A-4, we can now locate two points on Crusoe's demand curve for fish. When the price of fish was $1, Crusoe chose 8 fish; when the price rose to $2, Crusoe reduced his consumption to 5 (see Exhibit A-5). Of course, other points on Crusoe's demand curve could also be located if we considered other prices for fish.

The demand curve of Exhibit A-5 is constructed on the assumption that the price of breadfruit remains $2 and that Crusoe's money income remains constant at $16. If either of these factors were to change, the entire demand curve for fish, illustrated by Exhibit A-5, would shift.

Crusoe's Demand for Fish

As Exhibit A-4 illustrates, when the price of fish is $1, Crusoe chooses 8 units. When the price of fish increases to $2, he reduces his consumption to 5 units. This gives us two points on Crusoe's demand curve for fish. Other points on the demand curve could be derived by confronting Crusoe with still other prices of fish. [Note: Crusoe's money income ($16) and the price of breadfruit ($2) are unchanged in this analysis.]

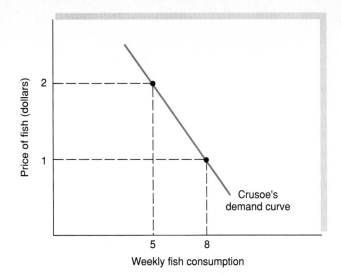

THE INCOME AND SUBSTITUTION EFFECTS

The indifference curve approach is a useful way to illustrate how a person with a fixed budget chooses between two goods. In the real world, of course, people have hundreds, or even thousands, of goods to choose from, and the doubling of only one price usually has a small impact on a person's overall consumption and satisfaction possibilities. In our simple example, the twofold increase in the price of fish makes Crusoe much worse off, since he spends a large portion of his budget on the item.

In the text, we indicated that when the price of a product rises, the amount consumed will change as a result of both an "income effect" and a "substitution effect." Indifference curve analysis can be used to separate these two effects. Exhibit A-6 is similar to Exhibit A-4. Both exhibits illustrate Crusoe's response to an increase in the price of fish from $1 to $2 when money income ($16) and the price of breadfruit ($2) are held constant. Exhibit A-6 however, breaks down his total response into the substitution effect and the income effect. The reduction in the consumption of fish solely because of the substitution (price) effect, holding Crusoe's real income (level of utility) constant, can be found by constructing a line tangent to Crusoe's original indifference curve (i_2), and having a slope indicating the higher price of fish. This line (the broken line of Exhibit A-6), which is parallel to Crusoe's actual budget constraint (the line containing point E_2), reflects the higher price of fish. It is tangent to the original indifference curve i_2, so Crusoe's real income is held constant. As this line indicates, Crusoe's consumption of fish will fall from 8 to 7, due strictly to the fact that fish are now more expensive. This move from E_1 to F is a pure substitution effect.

Real income, though, has actually been reduced. As a result, Crusoe will be unable to attain point F on indifference curve i_2. The best he can attain is point E_2, which decreases his consumption of fish by another 2 units to 5. Since the broken line containing F and the budget constraint containing E_2 are parallel, the relative prices of fish and breadfruit are held constant as Crusoe moves from F to E_2. The move from F to E_2 is thus a pure income effect. The reduction in the

EXHIBIT A-6

The Income and Substitution Effects

Here we break down Crusoe's response to the rise in the price of fish from $1 to $2 (see Exhibit A-4) into the substitution and income effects. The move from E_1 to F illustrates the substitution effect, whereas the move from F to E_2 reflects the income effect.

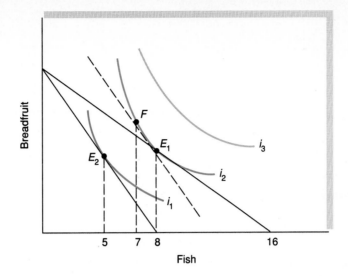

consumption of fish (and breadfruit) is due entirely to the decline in Crusoe's real income.

Indifference curve analysis highlights the assumptions and considerations that enter into consumer decisions. The logic of the proof that there is an inverse relationship between the price and the amount demanded is both elegant and reassuring. It is elegant because of the internal consistency of the logic and the precision of the analysis. It is reassuring because it conforms with our expectations, which are based on the central postulate of economics—that incentives matter in a predictable way.

7

COSTS AND THE SUPPLY OF GOODS

Opportunity cost is the value of the best alternative that must be sacrificed in order to engage in an activity. This is the only relevant cost in economic analysis because it is based on the very nature of the science—the formulation of principles for maximum satisfaction of human wants and scarce resources. The supply curve of any commodity or service consequently reflects opportunity costs which are determined indirectly by consumers clamoring for a myriad of goods.[1]

Marshall Colberg

CHAPTER FOCUS

■ Why are business firms used by societies everywhere to organize production?

■ How are firms organized in market economies? What internal incentive problems must they solve?

■ What are explicit and implicit costs, and what role do they play in guiding the behavior of the firm?

■ How does economic profit differ from accounting profit? What is the role of profit for a firm, and for an industry?

■ How do short-run costs differ from long-run costs for the firm?

■ What factors can shift the firm's cost curves?

Demand and supply interact to determine the market price of a product. In the last chapter, we illustrated that the demand for a product reflects the preferences of consumers. In this chapter, we focus on costs of production, which are the major determinants of both the nature and the position of the supply curve for a good. If the cost of producing a good exceeds its price, producers will not continue to supply it. Most persons recognize that supply and cost of production are closely linked. For example, if it costs $400 to produce a stereo set, manufacturers will not supply the sets, at least not for very long, at a price of $200. In the long run, the sets will be supplied only if they can command a price of at least $400.

In this chapter, we lay the foundation for a detailed investigation of the link between costs and market supply. The nature and function of costs are central to economic analysis. The economist's use of the term ''costs'' differs sometimes from that of business decision-makers and accountants. What do economists mean by costs? Why are costs so important? What is the function of costs in a market economy? We discuss these and related questions in this chapter.

ORGANIZATION OF THE BUSINESS FIRM

The business firm is an entity designed to organize raw materials, labor, and machines with the goal of producing goods and/or services. Firms (a) purchase productive resources from households and other firms, (b) transform them into a different commodity, and (c) sell the transformed product or service to consumers.

Economies may differ in the amount of freedom they allow business decision-makers. They may also differ in the incentive structure used to stimulate and guide business activity. Nevertheless, every society relies on business firms to organize resources and transform them into products. In Western economies, most business firms choose their own price, output level, and productive techniques. In socialist countries, government policy often establishes the selling price and constrains the actions of business firms in various other ways. In any case, the central position of the business firm as the organized productive unit is universal to capitalist and socialist economies alike.

INCENTIVES, COOPERATION, AND THE NATURE OF THE FIRM[2]

Residual Claimant: Individual in a firm who receives the excess of revenues over costs. A residual claimant gains if the firm's costs are reduced and if revenues are increased.

Most firms are privately owned in capitalist countries. The owners, who may or may not act as entrepreneurs, are the individuals who risk their wealth on the success of the business. If the firm is successful and makes profits, these financial gains go to the owners. Conversely, if things go badly and the firm suffers losses, the owners must bear the consequences. Because the owners gain (or lose) what remains after the revenue of the firm is used to pay the costs, they are called **residual claimants.** Their wealth is directly influenced by the success or failure of the firm. More than anyone else in the firm, they have an incentive to see that resources are used efficiently.

Business firms rely primarily on two organizational methods when producing

---

[1]Marshall R. Colberg, Dascomb R. Forbush, and Gilbert R. Whitaker, *Business Economics* (Homewood, Illinois: Irwin, 1980), p. 12.

[2]A classic article on this topic is Ronald Coase, ''The Nature of the Firm,'' *Economica,* (1937), pp. 386–405. See also Armen Alchian and Harold Demsetz, ''Production, Information Costs, and Economic Organization,'' *American Economic Review,* (Dec. 1972), pp. 777–795.

Shirking: Working at less than a normal rate of productivity, thus reducing output. Shirking is more likely when workers are not monitored, so that the cost of lower output falls on others.

Principal-Agent Problem: The incentive problem arising when the purchaser of services (the principal) lacks full information about the circumstances faced by the seller (the agent) and thus cannot know how well the agent performs the purchased services. The agent may to some extent work toward objectives other than those sought by the principal paying for the service.

a good or service: team production and contracting. In team production, employees work together under the supervision of the owner, or the owner's representative. The owner must direct the efforts of the employees, maintain morale and provide an incentive system, and monitor the work of each employee to prevent shirking. Team members are shirking if they are reducing output by working at less than a normal rate of productivity. Taking long work breaks, paying more attention to worker convenience than to results, and wasting time when diligence is called for are examples of shirking. A worker will shirk more when the costs of doing so are shifted to other members of the team. Hired managers, even including those at the top, must be monitored and provided with incentives.

When team production is utilized, the problem of imperfect monitoring and incentives is difficult, and it is always present. It is part of a larger class of problems called "principal-agent" problems. (See Applications in Economics box, "The Principle-Agent Problem.") The owner's gains from the firm depend directly on successful monitoring techniques and incentive management, as well as on wise choices of outputs and production techniques.

Contracting is another option, used by many firms when producing goods or services. The Boeing Company, for example, hires many employees, but when it builds a giant 747 airliner, it also contracts with hundreds of other firms to provide many of the needed parts and services. This reduces the employee monitoring problem for Boeing. The company only has to monitor the product of the contractor supplying the jet engines, rather than monitor all the engine-building workers.

APPLICATIONS IN ECONOMICS

The Principal-Agent Problem

In recent years, economists have focused a great deal of attention on a class of problems in which one individual is hired to act on behalf of another. A *principal-agent problem* arises when the purchaser of services (the principal) lacks full information about the circumstances faced by the seller (the agent), and thus cannot know how well the agent performs the purchased services. As a result, the agent may to some extent work toward objectives other than those sought by the principal, who is paying for the services. Because the agent exercises judgment in performing the work and cannot be completely monitored, he or she has opportunities to shirk, and, in general, to serve the agent's own ends rather

than those of the principal.

We all run into the principal-agent problem when we pay a dentist, a mechanic, or a lawyer to perform services for us. The agents we hire know more than we do about their work and about the circumstances of the specific job we pay them to do. We cannot be sure that they are doing the best possible job for us. The owner of a business firm faces similar incentive problems with every employee hired. A large firm has many managers who spend a good deal of time monitoring the work of employees and providing them with the incentive to work efficiently. But they cannot monitor perfectly and, in any case, who will monitor the monitors?

Even top-level executives hired to

manage a firm do not have the same objectives as owners—primarily profit maximization—unless, of course, the managers *are* the owners. So the judgments of executives, too, are influenced by what is in their personal best interests. They want perquisites, personal job security, and other benefits that may not be consistent with profit maximization for the firm. The problem is more serious as firms grow larger and acquire more managers and employees. Ultimately it is the job of the owners, as residual claimants, to develop an incentive structure that minimizes the principal-agent problem. For the owner, the saying "the buck stops here" always applies.

This adds some additional transactions costs, though, since it must search out reliable suppliers, and negotiate and enforce contracts.

How do owners share the risks and liabilities of the firm? How do they carry out or participate in the decision-making? There are three major legal structures under which business firms may be organized—proprietorships, partnerships, or corporations. The role of residual claimants (owners), and the liability faced by them, differs in each of the three structures.

PROPRIETORSHIPS

A proprietorship is a business firm that is owned by a single individual who is fully liable for the debts of the firm. In addition to assuming the responsibilities of ownership, the proprietor often works directly for the firm, providing managerial and other labor services. Many small businesses, including neighborhood grocery stores, barbershops, and farms, are business proprietorships. As Exhibit 1 shows, proprietorships comprised 70 percent of all business firms in 1985. Because most proprietorships are small, however, they generated only 7 percent of all business receipts for that year.

PARTNERSHIPS

A partnership consists of two or more persons acting as co-owners of a business firm. The partners share risks and responsibilities in some pre-arranged manner. There is no difference between a proprietorship and a partnership in terms of owner liability. In both cases, the owners are fully liable for all business debts incurred by the firm. Many law, medical, and accounting firms are organized along partnership lines. This form of business structure accounts for only 10 percent of the total number of firms and 4 percent of all business receipts.

CORPORATIONS

Measured in terms of business receipts, the corporate business structure is by far the most important. Even though corporations comprised only 20 percent of all business firms in 1985, they accounted for 89 percent of all business receipts. What are the distinctive characteristics of the corporation? What accounts for its attractiveness?

First, the stockholders of the corporation are the legal owners of the firm.

EXHIBIT 1

How Business Firms Are Organized

Nearly three out of every four firms is a proprietorship, but only 7% of all business revenue is generated by proprietorships. Corporations are only one out of every five firms, but generate 89% of all revenues.

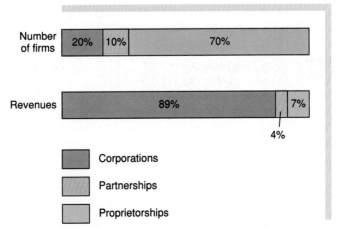

Source: *Statistical Abstract of the United States: 1989*, Table 848 (Data are for 1985).

Any profits of the firm belong to them. Their liability, however, is strictly limited. They are liable for corporate debts only to the extent of their explicit investment. If a corporation owes you money, you cannot directly sue the stockholders. You can, of course, sue the corporation. But, what if it goes bankrupt? You and others to whom the firm owes money will simply be out of luck.

Second, the limited liability makes it possible for corporations to attract investment funds from a large number of "owners" who do not participate in the day-to-day management of the firm. The stockholders of many large corporations simply hire managers to operate the firm. Corporations are thus often characterized by a separation of ownership and operational management.

Third, ownership can easily be transferred. The shares, or ownership rights, of an owner who dies can be sold by the heirs to another owner without disrupting the business firm. Because of this, the corporation is an ongoing concern. Similarly, any stockholders who become unhappy with the way a corporation is run can bail out merely be selling their stock.

The mangers of a large corporation might be thought of as trained experts hired by the stockholders to run the firm. The decisions of stockholders to buy and sell shares of stock mirror the confidence of investors in the management of the firm. If enough current and prospective stockholders alike come to believe that the managers will do a good job, the demand for the firm's stock will increase. Rising stock prices will reflect this increase in demand. Conversely, when the

Applications in Economics

Corporate Takeovers: Harmful or Productive?

Since the early 1970s, the number of corporate mergers and takeovers has increased substantially. There is an ongoing debate on whether or not this trend is good for the economy. Are these takeovers actually attempts by new owners to use resources more productively, or are they primarily a financial game, where stock prices are manipulated and purely speculative gains pursued? One careful look at this question was taken in 1987 by Lichtenberg and Siegel.[3]

Examining data on more than 20,000 manufacturing plants, owned by nearly 6,000 firms and accounting for two-thirds of total U.S. manufacturing shipments, the two economists found evidence to support the hypothesis that productivity gains were intended, and indeed were achieved.

In their view, the economic performance of many operating plants deteriorates over time as conditions change. When this happens, potential new owners may be better situated than current owners to deal with the new conditions. In such cases, a sale of the plants could be productive.

When Lichtenberg and Siegel examined the productivity of plants that changed ownership, the results were striking. They found that, controlling for other factors, these plants had previously been significantly less productive, on average, than plants that did not change ownership, Also, relative productivity in the plants destined for ownership change had been deteriorating prior to the change, but starting about a year after the change, productivity figures be-

gan to increase, rising until they nearly matched those of plants with no ownership change.

Such studies as this can never be totally conclusive, because there are always other factors which are not included, and not all cases, in all years, can be fully examined. This study was large and carefully done, however, and does provide some important evidence in support of those who say that corporate takeovers are not just financial games, but are an important way in which resources in the economy can be moved to higher-valued uses.

[3]Frank Lichtenberg and Donald Siegel, "Productivity and Changes of Ownership of Manufacturing Plants," *Brookings Papers on Economic Activity*, Vol. 3, 1987, pp. 643–673.

number of investors wanting to hold shares in the firm declines because they are dissatisfied with the current management, the stock's price will tumble. Falling stock prices will often lead to a shake-up in the management of the firm. (See Applications in Economics box, ''Cost, Sensitivity to Consumers, and the Structure of the Modern Corporation.'')

THE ROLE OF COSTS

Consumers would like to have more economic goods, but resources to produce them are scarce. We cannot produce as much of all goods as we would like. The use of resources to make one commodity takes resources from the production of other desired goods. The desire for product A must be balanced against the desire for other items which must be sacrificed to produce A. Every economic system must make these balancing judgments. When decisions are made in the political arena, the budget process performs this balancing function. Congress (or the central committee, or the king) decides which goods are most highly valued compared to others. Taxes and budgets are set accordingly.

In a market economy, consumer demand and cost of production are central to the performance of this balancing function. The desire of consumers for a specific good must be balanced against the desire for *other goods* that could be produced with the resources. Since resources have alternative uses, the use of resources to produce one good necessitates a reduction in the output of other goods. The most highly valued of these forgone opportunities when a good is produced comprise the good's costs of production. The owner of a resource employed in the production of one good must be paid at least as much as the resource would be worth in alternative uses that must be forgone. The production cost of a good reveals the value of the resources used to produce it, in terms of other opportunities forgone.

The demand for a product can be thought of as the voice of consumers instructing firms to produce a good. On the other hand, costs of production represent the voice of consumers saying that other items that could be produced with the resources are also desired. The demand for a product indicates the intensity of consumers' desires for the item. The cost of producing a product indicates the desire of consumers for other goods that must now be forgone because the necessary resources have been employed in the production of the first item.

Explicit Costs: Money paid by a firm to purchase the services of productive resources.

Implicit Costs: The opportunity costs associated with a firm's use of resources that it owns. These costs do *not* involve a direct money payment. Examples include wage income and interest forgone by the owner of a firm who also provides labor services and equity capital to the firm.

CALCULATING ECONOMIC COSTS AND PROFITS

Business firms, regardless of their size, give primary attention to profits. What is profit? Most people, including many businesspeople, think of profit as that portion of their sales revenues that remains after they have paid for raw materials, labor, machines, and similar inputs. Unfortunately, this concept of profit, which stems from accounting procedures, generally ignores some of the firm's costs.

The key to understanding the economist's concept of profit is our old friend— opportunity cost. The firm incurs a cost whenever it uses a resource, thereby requiring the resource owner to forgo the highest valued alternative. These costs may either be explicit or implicit. Explicit costs result when the firm makes a monetary payment to resource owners. Money wages, interest, and rental payments are a measure of what the firm gives up to employ the services of labor and capital resources. Firms also usually incur implicit costs—costs associated with the use of resources owned by the firm. Since implicit costs do not involve a

Total Cost: The costs, both explicit and implicit, of all the resources used by the firm. Total cost includes an imputed normal rate of return for the firm's equity capital.

direct money or contractual payment, they are sometimes excluded from accounting statements. For example, the owners of small proprietorships often supply labor services to their businesses. There is an opportunity cost associated with the use of this resource; other opportunities have to be given up because of the time spent by the owner in the operation of the business. The highest valued alternative forgone is the opportunity cost of the labor service provided by the owner. The total cost of production is the sum of the explicit and implicit costs incurred by the employment of all resources involved in the production process.

APPLICATIONS IN ECONOMICS

Costs, Sensitivity to Consumers, and the Structure of the Modern Corporation

How can we be sure that business firms will operate efficiently and respond to the interests of customers? In the case of owner-managed firms, clearly there is a strong incentive for efficient management, cost-effective production, and sensitivity to the interest of consumers. Offering consumers value at a low cost is the ticket to profitability. Since owner-managers are residual income claimants, they have a strong incentive to manage firms wisely.

However, in the case of a large corporation with millions of stockholders, the situation is more complex. While the stockholders hold the legal claim to residual income, professional managers direct the operation of the firm. There is a separation between ownership and management. The objectives of managers may conflict with those of stockholders. For example, managers may prefer high salaries, large offices, and first-class travel. They may also prefer the power and prestige of business expansion, even if it reduces profitability.

Can the stockholders control the actions of managers and direct them toward the pursuit of profitability? For large corporations, *direct* control is unlikely. Most large corporations are owned by shareholders, none of whom owns more than a tiny fraction of the firm's outstanding stock.

While they elect a Board of Directors, which in turn appoints high-level managers, individual stockholders have neither the incentive nor the information to exercise direct control. Most find it too expensive even to attend the annual shareholder's meeting. They can, of course, send a "proxy"—a designated person to vote their shares. But management generally solicits the proxies of shareholders prior to the annual meeting. If they do not throw it in the wastebasket, most stockholders turn their proxy over to the present management, and thereby provide management with the votes to reelect themselves.

Given this organizational structure, what keeps managers from using corporate resources as a personal feifdom? What prevents management from pursuing its own objectives at the expense of stockholders and consumers? There are three major factors that promote cost efficiency and retard the power of corporate managers. Let us consider each.

Competition for Investment Funds and Customers

Nobody forces stockholders to invest in corporations. Unless they are able to earn a competitive return, shareholders will invest their funds elsewhere—in bonds, real estate, or personal business activities, for

example. Similarly, no one forces consumers to buy the products of a corporation. Unless a corporate firm is able to supply products and services at a competitive price, consumers will take their business elsewhere. The corporate form of business organization must meet the competition. This limits the ability of managers to pursue objectives at the expense of either stockholders or customers.

Compensation and Management Incentives

The compensation of managers can be structured in a manner that will bring the interest of managers into harmony with shareholders. Market determination of managerial salaries will help achieve this objective. The market tends to reward managers who establish a track record of business profitability. In contrast, the demand for managers associated with losing enterprises and business failures is weak.

Internally, corporate firms can, and generally do, tie the compensation of managers to the market success of the business. Salary increases and bonuses can be directly related to the firm's profitability. Senior managers can be paid in part with shares of corporate stock that will encourage them to follow policies that maximize the wealth holdings of all shareholders. Many firms have designed stock

PROFIT AND THE OPPORTUNITY COST OF CAPITAL

Opportunity Cost of Capital: The implicit rate of return that must be paid to investors to induce them to continuously supply the funds necessary to maintain a firm's capital assets.

The most important implicit cost generally omitted from accounting statements is the cost of capital. Persons who supply equity capital to a firm expect their financial investment to yield at least a normal rate of return, which could be derived from other investment opportunities. If investors do not earn this normal rate of return on their investment, they will not continue to supply financial capital to the business.

This normal rate of return is the opportunity cost of capital. If the normal rate of return on equity capital is 10 percent, investors will not continue to supply

option-to-buy plans available to management that are extremely valuable if the market value of the firm's shares rise, but worthless if they fall. All of these factors tend to reduce the conflict between the interests of managers and shareholders.

The Threat of a Corporate Takeover

Managers who do not serve the interest of their shareholders are vulnerable to a *takeover*, a move by an outside person or group to gain the control of the firm. As we previously noted, shareholders who lose confidence in management can "fire" management by selling their shares. When a significant number of shareholders follows this course of action, the market value of the firm's stock will decline. This will increase the attractiveness of the firm to takeover specialists shopping for a poorly run business, the value of which could be substantially increased by a new management team.[4]

Consider a firm, currently earning $1.50 per share. Reflecting current earnings, the market value of the firm's stock is $15 per share (assuming a 10 percent interest rate). If the earnings of the firm are reduced because the current management team is pursuing its own objectives at the expense of profitability, then a corporate takeover could lead to sub-

stantial gain. Suppose an outside person or group believes that they could restructure the firm, improve the management, and thereby increase the firm's earnings to $3 per share. Therefore, they tender a takeover bid—an offer to buy shares of the firm's stock—for $20 per share. If the takeover team is correct, and if it is able to increase the firm's earnings to $3 per share, then the stock value of the firm will rise accordingly (to $30 per share).

Of course, the current management has an incentive to resist the takeover. After all, the current operating plans are their own, and the jobs they now hold are the best available to them. The outsiders who say that the current management is wrong and should be replaced will seldom be welcomed with open arms.

If the takeover specialists are right—if the new management is able to improve the cost efficiency and profitability of the firm—they will experience a handsome profit. Of course, they may sometimes be wrong and experience losses as a consequence. However, the important point is that the potential of a takeover acts as a check against managerial strategies that conflict with profit maximization. Managers who pursue their own interest at the expense of stockholders make themselves vulnerable to a takeover. The

mere potential of the takeover reduces the likelihood that managers will stray too far from the profit maximum strategy.

Concluding Thought

How efficient is the corporate business structure? Perhaps history provides the best answer. If the corporate structure were not an efficient form of business organization, it would not continue to survive. Rival forms of business organization, including proprietorships, partnerships, consumer cooperatives, employee ownership, and mutually owned companies can and do compete in the marketplace. In certain industries, some of the alternative forms of business organization are dominant. Nonetheless, in most industries, the corporate structure is the dominant form of business organization (see Exhibit 1). This is strong evidence that, despite its defects, it is generally a cost efficient, consumer sensitive form of organization. If it were not, it would not be so prevalent.

---

[4]For a discussion of corporate takeovers from various points of view, see John C. Coffee, Jr., Joseph A. Grundfest, Roberta Romano, and Murray Weidenbaum, "Corporate Takeovers: Who Wins; Who Loses; Who Should Regulate?" p. 23. *Regulation*, 1988, No. 1 (Journal of the American Enterprise Institute).

funds to firms unable to earn a 10 percent rate of return on capital assets. As a result, earning the normal rate of return—that is, covering the opportunity cost of capital—is vital to the survival of a business firm.

ACCOUNTING PROFIT AND ECONOMIC PROFIT

Economic Profit: The difference between the firm's total revenues and total costs.

Accounting Profits: The sales revenues minus the expenses of a firm over a designated time period, usually one year. Accounting profits typically make allowances for changes in the firm's inventories and depreciation of its assets. No allowance is made, however, for the opportunity cost of the equity capital of the firm's owners, or other implicit costs.

Since economists seek to measure the opportunities lost due to the production of a good or service, they include both explicit and implicit costs in total cost. **Economic profit** is equal to total revenues minus total costs, including both the explicit and implicit cost components. Economic profits will be present only if the earnings of a business are in excess of the opportunity cost of using the assets owned by the firm. Economic losses result when the earnings of the firm are insufficient to cover explicit and implicit costs. When the firm's revenues are just equal to its costs, both explicit and implicit, economic profits will be zero.

Remember that zero economic profits do not imply that the firm is about to go out of business. On the contrary, they indicate that the owners are receiving exactly the market rate of return on their investment (assets owned by the firms).

Since accounting procedures often omit implicit costs, such as those associated with owner-provided labor services or capital assets, the accounting costs of the firm generally understate the opportunity costs of production. This understatement of cost leads to an overstatement of profits. Therefore, the **accounting profits** of a firm are generally greater than the firm's economic profits (see Applications in Economics box, "Economic and Accounting Cost—A Hypothetical Example"). When the omission of the costs of owner-provided services is unimportant, as is the case for most large corporations, accounting profits approximate the returns to the firm's equity capital. High accounting profits (measured as a rate of return on a firm's assets), relative to the average for other firms, suggest that a firm is earning an economic profit. Correspondingly, a low rate of accounting profit implies economic losses.

SHORT RUN AND LONG RUN

Short Run (in Production): A time period so short that a firm is unable to vary some of its factors of production. The firm's plant size typically cannot be altered in the short run.

A firm cannot instantaneously adjust its output. Time plays an important role in the production process. Economists often speak of the **short run** as a time period so short that the firm is unable to alter its present plant size. In the short run, the firm is "stuck" with its existing plant and heavy equipment. They are "fixed" for a given time period. The firm can alter output, however, by applying larger or smaller amounts of variable resources, such as labor and raw materials. The firm's existing plant capacity can thus be used more or less intensively in the short run.

In sum, we can say that the short run is that period of time during which at least one factor of production, usually the size of the firm's plant, cannot be varied.

How long is the short run? The length varies from industry to industry. In some industries, substantial changes in plant size can be accomplished in a few months. In other industries, particularly those that use assembly lines and mass production techniques (for example, aircraft and automobiles), the short run might be a year or even several years.

Long Run (in Production): A time period long enough to allow the firm to vary all factors of production.

The **long run** is a time period of sufficient length to allow a firm the opportunity to alter its plant size and capacity and all other factors of production. All resources of the firm are variable in the long run. In the long run, from the viewpoint of an entire industry, new firms may be established and enter the industry; other firms may dissolve and leave the industry.

Perhaps an example will help to clarify the distinction between the short- and long-run time periods. If a battery manufacturer hired 200 additional workers and ordered more raw materials to squeeze a larger output from the existing plant, this would be a short-run adjustment. In contrast, if the manufacturer built an additional plant (or expanded the size of its current facility) and installed additional heavy equipment, this would be a long-run adjustment.

COSTS IN THE SHORT RUN

Fixed Costs: Cost that does not vary with output. However, fixed cost will be incurred as long as a firm continues in business and the assets have alternative uses.

Average Fixed Costs: Fixed cost divided by the number of units produced. It always declines as output increases.

We have emphasized that in the short run some of a firm's factors of production, such as the size of the plant, will be fixed. Other productive resources will be variable. In the short-run, then, we can break the firm's costs into these two categories—fixed and variable.

Fixed costs will remain unchanged even though output is altered. A firm's insurance premiums, its property taxes, and, most significantly, the opportunity cost of using its fixed assets will be present whether the firm produces a large or a small rate of output. Nor will costs vary with output. These costs are "fixed" as long as the firm remains in business. Fixed costs will be present at all levels of output, including zero. They can be avoided only if the firm goes out of business.

What will happen to average fixed cost (AFC) as output expands? Remember

---

APPLICATIONS IN ECONOMICS

Economic and Accounting Cost—A Hypothetical Example

The revenue-cost statement for a corner grocery store owned and operated by Terry Smith is presented below.

Terry works full-time as the manager, chief cashier, and janitor. Terry has $30,000 worth of refrigeration and other equipment invested in the store. Last year, Terry's total sales were $85,000; suppliers and employees were paid $50,000. Terry's revenues exceed explicit costs by $35,000. Did Terry make a profit last year? The accounting statement for the store will probably show a net profit of $35,000. However, if Terry did not have a $30,000 personal investment in equipment, these funds could be collecting 10 percent interest. Thus, Terry is forgoing $3,000 of interest each year. Similarly, if the

building that Terry owns was not being used as a grocery store, it could be rented to someone else for $500 per month. Rental income thus forgone is $6,000 per year. In addition, since Terry is tied up working in the grocery story, a $28,000 managerial position with the local A&P is forgone. Considering the interest, rental, and salary income that Terry had to forgo in order to operate the grocery store last year, Terry's implicit costs were $37,000. The total costs were $87,000. The total revenue of Terry's grocery store was less than the opportunity cost of the resources utilized. Terry incurred an economic loss of $2,000, despite the accounting profit of $35,000.

Total revenue		**$85,000**
Sales (groceries)		
Total (explicit costs)		
Groceries, wholesale	$38,000	
Utilities	2,000	
Taxes	3,000	
Advertising	1,000	
Labor services (employees)	6,000	
Total (explicit) costs		$50,000
Net (accounting) profit		$35,000
Additional (implicit) costs		
Interest (personal investment)		$ 3,000
Rent (Terry's building)		6,000
Salary (Terry's labor)		28,000
Total implicit costs		$37,000
Total explicit and implicit costs		**$87,000**
Economic profit (**total revenue minus explicit and implicit costs**)		-$2,000

EXHIBIT 2

General Characteristics of
the Short-run Cost Curves

(a) Average fixed cost

(b) Marginal cost

(c) Average total cost

Average fixed costs (a) will be high for small rates of output, but they will always decline as output expands. Marginal cost (b) will rise sharply as the plant's production capacity q is approached. As graph (c) illustrates, ATC will be a U-shaped curve, since AFC will be high for small rates of output and MC will be high as the plant's production capacity is approached.

that the firm's fixed cost will be the same whether output is 1, 100, or 1,000. The average fixed cost is simply fixed cost divided by output. AFC will decline as output is increased (see Exhibit 2a).

Variable costs are those costs that vary with output. For example, additional output can usually be produced by hiring more workers and expending additional funds on raw materials. Variable costs involve expenditures on these and other variable inputs. At any given level of output, the firm's **average variable cost** is the total variable cost divided by output.

We have noted that total cost includes explicit and implicit costs. The total cost of producing a good is also the sum of the fixed and variable costs at each output level. At zero output, total cost will equal fixed cost. As output expands from zero, variable cost and fixed cost must be added to obtain total cost. **Average total cost** (ATC), sometimes referred to as "unit cost," can be found by dividing total cost by the total number of units produced. Average total cost is also equal to the sum of the average fixed and average variable costs.

The economic way of thinking emphasizes the importance of what happens "at the margin." How much does it cost to produce an additional unit? **Marginal cost** is the change in total cost that results from the production of one additional unit. In the short run, as illustrated by Exhibit 2, marginal costs will generally decline if output is increased, then eventually reach a minimum, and then increase. The rising marginal costs simply reflect the fact that it becomes increasingly difficult to squeeze additional output from a plant as the facility's maximum capacity (the dotted line of Exhibit 2b) is approached. The Thumbnail Sketch summarizes the interrelationships among a firm's various costs.

As a firm alters its rate of output in the short run, how will unit cost be affected? First, let us look at this question intuitively. In the short run, the firm can vary output by using its fixed plant size more (or less) intensively. As Exhibit 2 illustrates, there are two extreme situations that will result in a high unit cost of output. First, when the output rate of a plant is small relative to its capacity, it is obviously being underutilized. Under these circumstances, average fixed cost will be high, and therefore average total cost will also be high. It will be costly and

Variable Costs: Costs that vary with the rate of output. Examples include wages paid to workers and payments for raw materials.

Average Variable Cost: The total variable cost divided by the number of units produced.

Average Total Cost: Total cost divided by the number of units produced. It is sometimes called per unit cost.

Marginal Cost: The change in total cost required to produce an additional unit of output.

THUMBNAIL SKETCH

Relationships among a Firm's Costs

1. Total cost includes both explicit and implicit costs.
2. Total cost = fixed cost + variable cost.
3. Marginal cost = change in total cost per added unit of output.
4. Average total cost = total cost ÷ output.
5. Average fixed cost = fixed cost ÷ output.
6. Average variable cost = variable cost ÷ output.
7. Average total cost = average fixed cost + average variable cost.

---

inefficient to operate a large plant substantially below its production capacity. At the other extreme, overutilization can also result in high unit cost. An overutilized plant will mean congestion, time spent by workers waiting for machines, and similar costly delays. As output approaches the maximum capacity of a plant, overutilization will lead to high marginal costs and therefore to high average total costs.

Thus, the average total cost curve will be U-shaped, as pictured in Exhibit 2c. Average total cost will be high for both an underutilized plant (because AFC is high) and an overutilized plant (because MC is high).

DIMINISHING RETURNS AND PRODUCTION IN THE SHORT RUN

Law of Diminishing Returns: The postulate that as more and more units of a variable resource are combined with a fixed amount of other resources, employment of *additional* units of the variable resource will eventually increase output only at a decreasing rate. Once diminishing returns are reached, it will take successively larger amounts of the variable factor to expand output by one unit.

Our analysis of the link between unit cost and output rate is corroborated by a long-established economic law, the law of diminishing returns. The **law of diminishing returns** states that as more and more units of a variable factor are applied to a fixed amount of other resources, output will eventually increase by smaller and smaller amounts. Therefore, in terms of their impact on output, the returns to the variable factor will diminish.

The law of diminishing returns is as famous in economics as the law of gravity is in physics. The law is based on common sense. Have you ever noticed that as you apply a single resource more intensively, the resource eventually tends to accomplish less and less? Consider a farmer who applies fertilizer more and more intensively to an acre of land (a fixed factor). At some point, the application of additional 100-pound units of fertilizer will expand the wheat yield by successively smaller amounts.

Essentially, the law of diminishing returns is a constraint imposed by Nature. If it were not valid, it would be possible to raise all the world's foodstuffs on an acre of land, or even in a flowerpot. Suppose we did *not* experience diminishing returns when we applied more labor and fertilizer to land. Would it ever make sense to cultivate any of the less fertile land? Of course not. We would be able to increase output more rapidly simply by applying another unit of labor and fertilizer to the world's most fertile flowerpot! But, of course, that would be a fairy tale; the law of diminishing returns applies in the real world.

Exhibit 3 illustrates the law of diminishing returns numerically. Column 1 indicates the quantity of the variable resource, labor in this example, that is combined with a specified amount of the fixed resource. Column 2 shows the **total**

EXHIBIT 3   ■   The Law of Diminishing Returns (hypothetical data)

(1) Units of the Variable Resource, Labor (per Day)	(2) Total Product (Output)	(3) Marginal Product	(4) Average Product
0	0		—
1	8	8	8.0
2	20	12	10.0
3	34	14	11.3
4	46	12	11.5
5	56	10	11.2
6	64	8	10.7
7	70	6	10.0
8	74	4	9.3
9	75	1	8.3
10	73	−2	7.3

Total Product: The total output of a good that is associated with alternative utilization rates of a variable input.

Marginal Product: The increase in the total product resulting from a unit increase in the employment of a variable input. Mathematically, it is the ratio of (a) change in total product to the (b) change in the quantity of the variable input.

Average Product: The total product (output) divided by the number of units of the variable input required to produce that output level.

product that will result as the utilization rate of labor increases. Column 3 provides data on the marginal product, the change in total output associated with each additional unit of labor. Without the application of labor, output would be zero. As additional units of labor are applied, total product (output) expands. As the first three units of labor are applied, total product increases by successively larger amounts (8, then 12, then 14). Beginning with the fourth unit, however, diminishing returns are confronted. When the fourth unit is added, marginal product—the change in the total product—declines to 12 (down from 14, when the third unit was applied). As additional units of labor are applied, marginal product continues to decline. It is increasingly difficult to squeeze a larger total product from the fixed resources (for example, plant size and equipment). Eventually, marginal product becomes negative (beginning with the tenth unit).

Column 4 of Exhibit 3 provides data for the average product of labor. The average product is simply the total product divided by the units of labor applied. Note the average product increases as long as the marginal product is greater than the average product. This is true through the first four units. The marginal product of the fifth unit of labor, though, is 10, less than the average product for the first four units of labor (11.5). Therefore, beginning with the fifth unit, average product declines as additional labor is applied. When marginal productivity is below the average, it brings down the average product.

Using the data from Exhibit 3, Exhibit 4 illustrates the law of diminishing returns graphically. Initially, the total product curve (Exhibit 4a) increases quite rapidly. As diminishing marginal returns are confronted (beginning with the fourth unit of labor), total product increases more slowly. Eventually, a maximum output (75) is reached with the application of the ninth unit of labor. The marginal prod-

(a) Total product curve

(b) Average and marginal product curve

EXHIBIT 4

The Law of Diminishing Returns

As units of the variable input (labor) are added to a fixed input, total product will increase, first at an increasing rate and then at a declining rate (frame a). This will cause both the marginal and average product curves (frame b) to rise at first and then decline. Note that the marginal product curve intersects the average product curve at its maximum (when 4 units of labor are used). The smooth curves indicate that labor can be increased by amounts of less than a single unit.

uct curve (Exhibit 4b) reflects the total product curve. Geometrically, marginal product is the slope—the rate of increase—of the total product curve. That slope, the marginal product, reaches its maximum with the application of three units of labor. Beyond three units, diminishing returns are present. Eventually, at ten units of labor, the marginal product become negative. When marginal product becomes negative, total product is necessarily declining. The average product curve rises as long as the marginal product curve is above it, since each added unit of labor is raising the average. The average product reaches its maximum at four units of labor. Beyond that, each additional unit of labor brings down the average product, and the curve declines.

DIMINISHING RETURNS AND COST CURVES

What impact will diminishing returns have on a firm's costs? Once a firm confronts diminishing returns, larger and larger additions of the variable factor are required to expand output by one unit. Marginal costs rise until, eventually, they exceed average total cost. When marginal costs are greater than ATC, ATC increases. It is easy to see why. What happens when an above-average student is added to a class? The class average goes up. What happens if a unit of above-average cost is added to output? Average total cost rises. The firm's marginal cost curve therefore crosses the ATC curve at the ATC's lowest point. For output rates beyond the minimum ATC, the rising marginal cost causes average total cost to increase. Again, the average total cost curve is U-shaped.

Exhibit 5 numerically illustrates the implications of the law of diminishing returns for a firm's short-run cost curve. Here, we assume that Royal Roller Skates, Inc., combines units of a variable input with a fixed factor to produce units of output (pairs of skates). Columns 2, 3, and 4 indicate how total cost schedules vary as output is expanded. Total fixed costs, representing the oppor-

EXHIBIT 5 ■ Numerical Short-Run Cost Schedules of Royal Roller Skates, Inc.

(1)	(2)	(3)	(4)	(5)	(6)	(7)	(8)
	Total Cost Data (per Day)			Average/Marginal Cost Data (per Day)			
Output per Day	Total Fixed Cost	Total Variable Cost	Total Cost, (2)+(3)	Average Fixed Cost, (2)÷(1)	Average Variable Cost, (3)÷(1)	Average Total Cost, (4)÷(1)	Marginal Cost, Δ(4)÷Δ(1)
0	$50	$ 0	$ 50	—	—	—	—
1	50	15	65	$50.00	$15.00	$65.00	$15
2	50	25	75	25.00	12.50	37.50	10
3	50	34	84	16.67	11.33	28.00	9
4	50	42	92	12.50	10.50	23.00	8
5	50	52	102	10.00	10.40	20.40	10
6	50	64	114	8.33	10.67	19.00	12
7	50	79	129	7.14	11.29	18.43	15
8	50	98	148	6.25	12.25	18.50	19
9	50	122	172	5.56	13.56	19.11	24
10	50	152	202	5.00	15.20	20.20	30
11	50	202	252	4.55	18.36	22.91	50

tunity cost of the fixed factors of production, are $50 per day. For the first four units of output, total variable costs increase at a *decreasing rate*. Why? In this range, there are increasing returns to the variable input. Beginning with the fifth unit of output, however, diminishing marginal returns are present. From this point on, total variable costs and total costs increase by successively larger amounts as output is expanded.

Columns 5 through 8 of Exhibit 5 reveal the general pattern of the average and marginal cost schedules. For small output rates, the average total cost of producing skates is high, primarily because of the high AFC. Initially, marginal costs are less than ATC. When diminishing returns set in for output rates beginning with five units, however, marginal cost rises. Beginning with the sixth unit of output, marginal cost exceeds average variable cost, causing AVC to rise. Beginning with the eighth unit of output, MC exceeds ATC, causing it also to rise. ATC thus reaches a minimum at seven units of output. Observe the data of Exhibit 5 carefully to ensure that you fully understand the relationships among the various cost curves.

Using the numeric data of Exhibit 5, Exhibit 6 graphically illustrates both the total and the average/marginal cost curves. Note that the marginal cost curve intersects both the average variable cost and average total cost curves at the minimum points (Exhibit 6b). As marginal costs continue to rise above average total cost, unit costs rise higher and higher as output increases beyond seven units.

In sum, the firm's short-run cost curves are merely a reflection of the law of diminishing marginal returns. Assuming that the price of the variable resource is constant, marginal costs decline so long as the marginal product of the variable input is rising. This results because, in this range, smaller and smaller additions of the variable input are required to produce each extra unit of output. This situation is reversed, however, when diminishing returns are confronted. Once dimin-

EXHIBIT 6

Costs in the Short run

Using data of Exhibit 5, frame a illustrates the general shape of the firm's short-run total cost curves; frame b illustrates the general shape of the firm's average and marginal cost curves. Note that when output is small (for example, 2 units), average total cost will be high because the average fixed costs are so high. Similarly, when output is large (for example, 11 units) per unit cost (ATC) will be high because it is extremely costly to produce the marginal units. Thus, the short-run ATC curve will be U-shaped.

(a) Total cost data

(b) Average/marginal cost data

ishing returns set in, more and more units of the variable factor are required to generate each additional unit of output. Marginal cost will rise, because the marginal product of the variable resources is declining. Eventually, marginal costs exceed average variable and average total costs, causing these costs also to rise. A U-shaped short-run average total cost curve results.

COSTS IN THE LONG RUN

The short-run analysis relates costs to output *for a specific size of plant*. Firms, though, are not committed forever to their existing plant. In the long run, a firm can alter its plant size and all other factors of production. All resources used by the firm are variable in the long run.

How will the firm's choice of plant size affect production costs? Exhibit 7 illustrates the short-run average total cost curves for three plant sizes, ranging from small to large. If these three plant sizes were the only possible choices,

EXHIBIT 7

The Long-run Average Cost

The short-run average cost curves are shown for three alternative plant sizes. If these three were the only possible plant sizes, the long-run average curve would be *ABCD*.

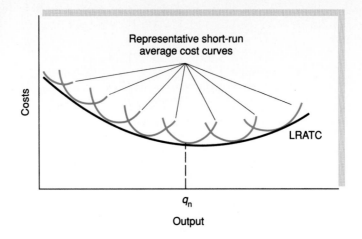

which one would be best? The answer depends on the rate of output the firm expects to produce. The smallest plant would have the lowest cost if an output rate of less than q_1 were produced. The medium-sized plant would provide the least-cost method of producing output rates between q_1 and q_2. For any output level greater than q_2, the largest plant would be the most cost-efficient.

The long-run average total cost curve shows the minimum average cost of producing each output level when the firm is free to choose among all possible plant sizes. It can best be thought of as a "planning curve," because if reflects the expected per unit cost of producing alternative rates of output while plants are still in the blueprint stage.

Exhibit 7 illustrates the long-run average total cost curve when only three plant sizes are possible. The planning curve *ABCD* is mapped out. Given sufficient time, of course, firms can usually choose among many plants of various sizes. Exhibit 8 presents the long-run planning curve under these circumstances. A smooth planning curve results. Each short-run average total cost curve will be tangent to the long-run planning curve.[5]

It is important to keep in mind that no single plant size could produce the alternative output rates at the costs indicated by the planning curve. Any of the planning curve options are available before a plant size is chosen and the plant is built, but while the firm can plan for the long run, choosing among many options, it can only *operate* in the short run. The LRATC outlines the possibilities available in the planning stage, indicating the expected average costs of production for each of a large number of plants, which differ in size.

SIZE OF FIRM AND UNIT COST IN THE LONG RUN

Do larger firms have lower minimum unit costs than smaller ones? The answer to this question depends on which industries are being considered. There is a sound basis, though, for *initially* expecting some cost reductions from large-scale production methods. Why? Large firms typically produce a large total volume of output.[6] Volume of output denotes the total number of units of a product that the firm expects to produce.[7] There are three major reasons why unit costs initially decline as firms plan a larger total volume of output (and a larger size of plant).

---

[5]The tangency, though, will occur at the least-cost output level for the short run only when the long-run curve is parallel to the *x*-axis, as in q_n, Exhibit 8.

1. Adoption of Mass Production Techniques. Large firms are often able to use mass production techniques that are economical *only* when large volumes of output are planned. Mass production usually involves large development and setup costs. Once the production methods are established, though, marginal costs are low. Because of the large setup costs, mass production techniques are uneconomical for small volumes of output. For example, the use of molds, dies, and assembly line production methods reduce the per unit cost of automobiles only when the planned volume is in the millions. Machines designed to make five times as many welds on the assembly line per day (and five times as many over their lifetime) will probably not be five times as costly. High volume methods, although cheaper to use for high rates of output and high volumes, will typically be far more costly if utilized for low volumes of production.

2. Specialization. Large-scale operation results in greater opportunity for specialized use of labor and machines. Adam Smith noted 200 years ago that the output of a pin factory is much greater when one worker draws the wire, another straightens it, a third cuts it, a fourth grinds the point, a fifth makes the head of the pin, and so on.[8] In economics, the whole can sometimes be greater than the sum of the parts. Specialization provides the opportunity for people to become exceptionally proficient at performing small but essential functions. When each of them acts as a specialist, more is produced than if each made the final product from start to finish.

Economies of Scale:
Reductions in the firm's per unit costs that are associated with the use of large plants to produce a large volume of output.

3. Learning by Doing. Workers and managers in a firm that has made more units have probably learned more from their experience. Improvements in the production process result. Baseball players improve by playing, and musicians improve by performing. Similarly, workers and management improve their skills as they ''practice'' productive techniques. This factor has been found to be tremendously important in the aircraft and automobile industries, among others.

ECONOMIES AND DISECONOMIES OF SCALE

Economic theory suggests that compared to smaller firms, larger firms have lower unit costs. When unit costs declines as output expands, economies of scale are present over the initial range of outputs. The long-run average total cost curve is falling.

---

[6]Throughout this section, we assume that firms with larger plants necessarily plan a larger volume of output than do their smaller counterparts. Reality approximates these conditions. Firms choose large plants because they are planning to produce a large volume.

[7]Note the distinction between rate and volume of output. *Rate* of output is the number of units produced during a specific period (for example, the next six months). *Volume* is the total number of units produced during all time periods. For example, Boeing might produce two 767 airplanes per month (rate of output) while planning to produce a volume of two hundred 767s during the expected life of the model. Increasing the rate (reducing the time period during which a given output is produced) tends to raise costs, whereas increasing the volume (total amount produced) tends to lower costs. For additional information on production and costs, see Armen Alchian, ''Costs,'' in *International Encyclopedia of the Social Sciences* (New York: Macmillan, 1968), pp. 404–415, and Jack Hirshleifer, ''The Firm's Cost Function: A Successful Reconstruction,'' *Journal of Business* (July 1962), pp. 235–255.

[8]Smith went on to state: ''I have seen a small manufactory of this kind where ten men only were employed, and where some of them consequently performed two or three distinct operations. Those ten persons, therefore, could make among them upwards of forty-eight thousand pins in a day. But if they had all wrought separately and independently, and without any of them having been educated to this peculiar business, they certainly could not each of them have made twenty, perhaps not one pin in a day,'' (Adam Smith, *An Inquiry into the Nature and Causes of the Wealth of Nations,* 1776 [Cannan's edition, Chicago: University of Chicago Press, 1976], pp. 8–9).

Are diseconomies of scale possible—that is, are there ever situations in which the long-run average costs are greater for larger firms than they are for smaller ones? The economic justification for diseconomies of scale is less obvious (and less tenable) than that for economies of scale. However, as a firm gets bigger and bigger, bureaucratic inefficiencies *may* result. Code-book procedures tend to replace managerial genius. Motivating the work force and carrying out managerial directives is also more complex when the firm is larger. Principal-agent problems grow as there are more employees and more levels of monitoring to be done. Coordinating more people and conveying information to them is more difficult. These factors combine to cause rising long-run average total costs in some, but certainly not all, industries.

Economies and diseconomies of scale stem from different sources than do increasing and diminishing returns. Economies and diseconomies of scale are long-run concepts. They relate to conditions of production when all factors are variable. In contrast, increasing and diminishing returns are short-run concepts. They are applicable only when the firm has a fixed factor of production.

Exhibit 9 outlines three different long-run average total cost (LRATC) curves that describe real-world conditions in differing situations. For Exhibit 9a, both economies and diseconomies of scale are present. Higher per unit costs will result if the firm chooses a plant size other than the one that minimizes the cost of producing output q, the ideal size of plant in this situation. If each firm in an industry faces the same cost conditions, we can generalize and say that any plants that are larger or smaller than this ideal size will experience higher unit costs. A very narrow range of plant sizes would be possible in industries with LRATC depicted by Exhibit 9a. Some lines of retail sales and agriculture might approximate these conditions.

Exhibit 9b demonstrates the general shape of the LRATC that economists believe is present in most industries. Initially, economies of scale exist, but once a minimum efficient scale is reached, wide variation in firm size is possible. Firms smaller than the minimum efficient size would have higher per unit costs, but firms larger than that would not gain a cost advantage. **Constant returns to scale** are present for a broad range of output rates (between q_1 and q_2). This situation is consistent with real-world conditions in many industries. For example, small firms can be as efficient as larger ones in such industries as apparel, lumber, shoes, publishing, and in many lines of retailing.

Exhibit 9c indicates that economies of scale exist for all relevant output levels. The larger the firm size, the lower the per unit cost. The LRATC in the local telephone service industry may approximate the curve of Exhibit 9c.

Constant Returns to Scale:
Unit costs are constant as the scale of the firm is altered. Neither economies nor diseconomies of scale are present.

EXHIBIT 9

Three Different Types of Long-run Average Cost Curves

Frame a indicates that for output levels less than q, economies of scale are present. Immediately beyond q, diseconomies of scale dominate. Frame b indicates that economies of scale are important until some minimum output level q_1 is attained. Once the minimum has been attained, there is a wide range of output levels (q_1 to q_2) that are consistent with the minimum ATC for the industry. Frame c indicates that economies of scale exist for all relevant output levels. As we will see later, this type of long-run ATC curve has important implications for the structure of the industry.

(a)

(b)

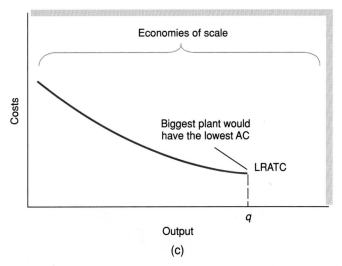

(c)

WHAT FACTORS CAUSE THE FIRM'S COST CURVES TO SHIFT?

In outlining the general shapes of a firm's cost curves in both the long run and short run, we assumed that certain other factors remained constant, not changing with the firm's output. What are those other factors, and how will they affect production costs?

1. *Prices of Resources.* If the price of resources used should rise, the firm's cost curves will shift upward, as Exhibit 10 illustrates. Higher resource prices will increase the cost of producing each alternative output level. For example, what happens to the cost of producing automobiles when the price of steel rises? The cost of producing automobiles also rises. Conversely, lower resource prices will result in cost reductions. Thus, the cost curves for any specific plant size will shift downward.

2. *Taxes.* Taxes are a component of firm's cost. Suppose that an excise tax of 20 cents were levied on each gallon of gasoline sold by a service station. What would happen to the seller's costs? They would increase, just as they did in Exhibit 10. The firm's average total and marginal cost curves would shift upward by the amount of the tax.

3. *Technology.* Technological improvements often make it possible to produce a specific output with fewer resources. For example, the printing press drastically reduced the number of labor-hours required to print newspapers and books. The spinning wheel reduced the labor-hours necessary to weave cotton into cloth. More recently, computers and robots have reduced costs in many industries. As Exhibit 11 shows, a technological improvement will shift the firm's cost curves downward, reflecting the reduction in the amount of resources used to produce alternative levels of output.

EXHIBIT 10

Higher Resource Prices and Cost

An increase in resource prices will cause the firm's cost curves to shift upward.

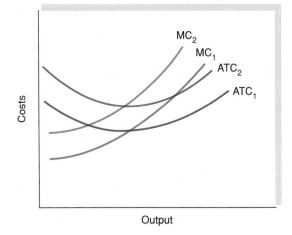

EXHIBIT 11

Egg Production, Costs, and Technological Change

Suppose that an egg producer discovers (or develops) a "super" mineral water that makes it possible to get more eggs from the same number of chickens. Because of this technological improvement, various output levels of eggs can now be produced with less feed, space, water, and labor. Costs will be reduced. The egg producer's ATC and MC curves will shift downward.

COST AND THE ECONOMIC WAY OF THINKING

When analyzing the firm's costs, economists often present a highly mechanical—some would say unrealistic—view. The role of personal choice tends to be glossed over.

It is important to keep in mind that costs are incurred when choices are made. When business decision-makers choose to purchase raw materials, hire new employees, or renew the lease on a plant, they incur costs. All these decisions, like other choices, must be made under conditions of uncertainty. Of course, past experience acts as a useful guide, yielding valuable information. Because of this, business decision-makers will have a good idea of the costs that will be associated with alternative decisions.

Opportunity costs are usually "expected costs"—they represent that which the decision-maker expects to give up as the result of a choice. Think for a moment of what the cost curves developed in this chapter really mean. The firm's short-run marginal cost curve represents the opportunity cost of expanding output, *given the firm's current plant size*. The firm's long-run average total cost curve represents the opportunity cost per unit of output associated with varying plant sizes and rates of output, *given that the alternative plants are still on the drawing boards*. Opportunity costs look forward, reflecting expectations—often based on the past record—as to what will be forgone as a result of current decisions. At decision time, neither the short-run marginal cost nor the long-run average total cost can be determined from accounting records. Accounting costs look backward. They yield valuable information about historical costs.

SUNK COSTS

Sunk Costs: Costs that have already been incurred as a result of past decisions. They are sometimes referred to as historical costs.

Historical costs associated with past decisions—economists call them sunk costs—should exert no direct influence on current choices. The outcome of past choices will provide knowledge relevant to current decisions, but the specific costs themselves are no longer relevant. Past choices cannot be reversed; money that has been spent is gone for good. Current choices should be based on the costs and benefits expected in relation to *current* market conditions.

If they are to minimize costs, business decision-makers must recognize the irrelevance of sunk costs. Let us consider a simple example that emphasizes this point. Suppose that the firm of Exhibit 5 pays $100,000 to purchase and install a skate-producing machine. The machine is expected to last ten years. The company's books record the cost of the machine as $10,000 each year under the heading of depreciation. The machine can be used only to make roller skates. Since dismantling and reinstallation costs are high, the machine cannot be leased or sold to another firm. It has no scrap value. In other words, there are no alternative uses for the machine. The machine's annual production of roller skates will generate $50,000 of revenues for the firm when it is employed with raw materials and other factors of production that cost $45,000.

Should the firm continue to use the machine? The annual depreciation cost of the machine suggests that the firm loses $5,000 annually on the output of the

MYTHS OF ECONOMICS

"A good business decision-maker will never sell a product for less than its production costs."

This statement contains a grain of truth. A profit-seeking entrepreneur would not *undertake* a project knowing that the costs could not be covered. However, this view fails to emphasize (a) the time dimension of the production process and (b) the uncertainty associated with business decisions. The production process takes time. Raw materials must be purchased, employees hired, and plants equipped. Retailers must contract with suppliers. As these decisions are made, costs result. Many of the firm's costs of production are incurred long before the product is ready for marketing.

Even a good business decision-maker is not always able to predict the future correctly. Market conditions may change in an unexpected manner. At the time the product is

ready for sale, buyers may be unwilling to pay a price that will cover the seller's past costs of production. These past costs, however, are now sunk costs and no longer relevant. Current decisions must be made on the basis of current cost and revenue considerations.

Should a grocer refuse to sell oranges that are about to spoil because their wholesale cost cannot be covered? The grocer's current opportunity cost of selling the oranges may be nearly zero. The alternative may be to throw them in the garbage next week. Almost any price, even one far below past costs, would be better than letting the oranges spoil.

Consider another example. Suppose a couple who own a house plan to relocate temporarily. Should they refuse to rent their house for

$200 (if this is the best offer available) because their monthly house payment is $240? Of course not. The house payment will go on, regardless of whether or not they rent the house. If the homeowners can cover their opportunity costs, perhaps a $60 monthly fee for a property management service, they will gain by renting rather than leaving the house vacant.

Past mistakes provide useful lessons for the future, but they cannot be reversed. Bygones are bygones, even if they resulted in business loss. Only current revenue and cost considerations are relevant to current decisions about prices and profitability. There is no need to fret over spilt milk, burnt toast, or yesterday's business losses.

machine. The depreciation cost, however, is a sunk cost. It was incurred when the machine was installed. The current opportunity cost of the machine is precisely zero. The firm is not giving up anything by continuing to operate it. Since the machine generates $5,000 of additional net revenue, the firm should continue using it. Of course, if current market conditions are expected to continue, the firm will not purchase a similar machine or replace the machine when it wears out, but this should not influence the decision of whether or not to continue operating the current one. The irrelevance of sunk costs helps explain why it often makes sense to continue operating older equipment (it has a low opportunity cost), even though it might not be wise to purchase similar equipment again.

COST AND SUPPLY

Economists are interested in cost because they seek to explain the supply decisions of firms. A strictly profit-maximizing firm will compare the expected revenues derived from a decision or a course of action with the expected costs. If the expected revenues exceed costs, the course of action will be chosen because it will expand profits (or reduce losses).

In the short run, the marginal cost of producing additional units is the relevant cost consideration. A profit-maximizing decision-maker will compare the expected marginal costs with the expected additional revenue from larger sales. If the latter exceeds the former, output (the quantity supplied) will be expanded.

Whereas marginal costs are central to the choice of short-run output, the expected average total cost is vital to a firm's long-run supply decision. *Before entry into an industry,* a profit-maximizing decision-maker will compare the expected market price with the expected long-run average total cost. Profit-seeking potential entrants will supply the product if, and only if, they expect the market price to exceed their long-run average total cost. Similarly, existing firms will continue to supply a product only if they expect that the market price will enable them at least to cover their long-run average total cost.

LOOKING AHEAD

In this chapter, we outlined several basic principles that affect costs for business firms. We will use these basic principles when we analyze the price and output decisions of firms under alternative market structures in the chapters that follow.

CHAPTER SUMMARY

1. The business firm is used to organize productive resources and transform them into goods and services. There are three major business structures—proprietorships, partnerships, and corporations. Proprietorships are the most numerous, but most of the nation's business activity is conducted through corporations. To solve the principal-agent problem, which tends to reduce worker efficiency in team production, every firm must provide work incentives and monitoring.

2. The demand for a product indicates the intensity of consumers' desires for the item. The (opportunity) cost of producing the item indicates the desire of consumers for other goods that must now be given up because the necessary resources have been used in the production of the item. In a market economy, these two forces—demand and costs of production—balance the desire of consumers for more of a good against the reality of scarce resources, which requires that other goods be forgone as more of any one specific item is supplied.

3. Economists employ the opportunity cost concept when figuring a firm's costs. Therefore, total cost includes not only explicit (money) costs but also implicit costs associated with the use of productive resources owned by the firm.

4. Since accounting procedures generally omit the opportunity cost of the firm's equity capital and sometimes (in the case of owner-operated firms) omit the cost of owner-provided services, accounting costs understate the opportunity cost of producing a good. As a result of these omissions, the accounting profits of a firm are generally larger than the firm's economic profits.

5. Economic profit (loss) results when a firm's sales revenues exceed (are less than) its total costs, both explicit and implicit. Firms that are making the market rate of return on their assets will therefore make zero economic profit. Firms that transform resources into products of greater value than the opportunity cost of the resources used will make an economic profit. On the other hand, if the opportunity cost of the resources used exceeds the value of the product, losses will result.

6. The firm's short-run average total cost curve will tend to be U-shaped. When output is small (relative to plant size), average fixed cost (and therefore ATC) will be high. As output expands, however, AFC (and ATC) will fall. As the firm attempts to produce a larger and larger rate of output using its fixed plant size, diminishing returns will eventually set in, and marginal cost will rise quite rapidly as the plant's maximum capacity is approached. Thus, the short-run ATC will also be high for large output levels because marginal costs are high.

7. The law of diminishing returns explains why a firm's short-run marginal and average costs will eventually rise as the rate of output expands. When diminishing marginal returns are present, successively larger amounts of the variable input will be required to increase output by one more unit. Thus, marginal costs will eventually rise as output expands. Eventually, marginal costs will exceed average total costs, causing the latter to rise, also.

8. The ability to plan a larger volume of output often leads to cost reductions. These cost reductions associated with the scale of one's operation result from (a) a greater opportunity to employ mass production methods, (b) specialized use of resources, and (c) learning by doing.

9. The LRATC reflects the costs of production for plants of various sizes. When economies of scale are present (that is, when larger plants have lower per unit costs of production), LRATC will decline. When constant returns to scale are experienced, LRATC will be constant. A rising LRATC is also possible. Bureaucratic decision-making and other diseconomies of scale may in some cases cause LRATC to rise.

10. In analyzing the general shapes of a firm's cost curves, we assumed that the following factors remained constant: (a) resource prices, (b) technology, and (c) taxes. Changes in any of these factors would cause the cost curves of a firm to shift.

11. In any analysis of business decision-making, it is important to keep the opportunity cost principle in mind. Economists are interested in costs primarily because costs affect the decisions of suppliers. Short-run marginal costs represent the supplier's opportunity cost of producing additional units with the existing plant facilities of the firm. The long-run average total cost represents the opportunity cost of supplying alternative rates of output, given sufficient time to vary all factors, including plant size.

12. Sunk costs are costs that have already been incurred. They should not exert a *direct* influence on current business choices. However, they may provide a source of information that will be useful in making current decisions.

CRITICAL ANALYSIS QUESTIONS

*1. What is economic profit? How might it differ from accounting profit? Explain why firms that are making zero economic profit are likely to continue in business.

*2. Which of the following do you think reflect sound economic thinking? Explain your answer.

*Asterisk denotes questions for which answers are given in Appendix C, Selected Answers.

a. "I paid $200 for this economics course. Therefore, I'm going to attend the lectures even if they are useless and boring."
b. "Since we own rather than rent, housing doesn't cost us anything."
c. "I own 100 shares of stock that I can't afford to sell until the price goes up enough for me to get back at least my original investment."
d. "It costs to produce private education, whereas public schooling is free."

3. Suppose a firm produces bicycles. Will the firm's accounting statement reflect the opportunity cost of producing bicycles? Why or why not? What costs would an accounting statement reveal? Should current decisions be based on accounting costs? Explain.

4. Suppose that Ajax, Inc., is the target of a takeover attempt by the management of Beta Corporation, which is offering to buy stock from any Ajax stockholder who wants to sell, at 20 percent above its current rate. Explain how the resistance of Ajax management to the takeover attempt might illustrate the principal-agent problem. Is it possible that the Beta Corporation management's action is itself an illustration of the principal-agent problem? Explain.

5. Explain the factors that cause a firm's short-run average total costs to decline initially, but eventually to increase, as the rate of output rises.

6. Which of the following are relevant to a firm's decision to increase output: (a) short-run average total cost; (b) short-run marginal cost; (c) long-run average total cost? Justify your answer.

7. Economics students often confuse (a) diminishing returns to the variable factor and (b) diseconomies of scale. Explain the difference between the two and give one example of each.

8. **What's Wrong with This Way of Thinking?**
"The American steel industry cannot compete with German and Japanese steel producers. After the Second World War, these countries rebuilt modern, efficient mills that made use of the latest technology. In contrast, American mills are older and less efficient. Our costs are higher because we are stuck with old facilities."

*9. Is profit maximization consistent with the self-interest of corporate owners? Is it consistent with the self-interest of corporate managers? Is there a conflict between the self-interest of owners and of managers?

*10. What is the opportunity cost of (a) borrowed funds and (b) equity capital? Under current tax law, firms can take the opportunity cost of borrowed funds, but not equity capital, as an expense. How does this tax feature affect the debt/equity ratio of business firms?

*11. "If a firm maximizes profit it must minimize the cost of producing the profit-maximum output." True or false? Explain.

12. Why do economists consider normal returns to capital as a cost? How does economic profit differ from normal returns (or "normal profit")?

*13. Draw a U-shaped short-run average total cost curve for a firm. Construct the accompanying marginal cost and average variable cost curves.

14. a. Prior to legislation passed in 1986, appreciation in the market value of a stock was taxed at a lower rate than dividends from the stocks. How would this affect the incentive of firms to use internal financing relative to debt?
b. Subsequent to the 1986 legislation, capital gains (appreciation in the stock) and dividends were taxed at identical rates. The 1986 legislation was followed by a rash of takeover moves against firms with low debt/equity ratios. Did the 1986 tax change contribute to these moves? Why or why not?

15. In 1967, Congress passed the Williams Act, which mandated that any investor acquiring 5 percent or more of a company's stock must register this fact with the Securities Exchange Commission and thereby disclose the takeover possibility. How did the Williams Act affect the ability of the takeover market to impose discipline on inefficient corporate management?

190 PART TWO ■ Microeconomics

16. What are implicit costs? Do implicit costs contribute to the opportunity cost of production? Should an implicit cost be counted as cost? Give three examples of implicit costs. Does the firm's accounting statement take implicit costs into account? Why or why not?

*17. Consider a machine purchased one year ago for $12,000. The machine is being depreciated $4,000 per year over a three-year period. Its current market value is $5,000, and the expected market value of the machine one year from now is $3,000. If the interest rate is 10 percent, what is the expected cost of holding the machine during the next year?

*18. Investors seeking to take over a firm often bid a positive price for the business even though it is currently experiencing losses. Why would anyone ever bid a positive price for a firm operating at a loss?

8

THE FIRM UNDER PURE COMPETITION

Competition is conducive to the continuous improvements of industrial efficiency. It leads some producers to eliminate wastes and cut costs so that they may undersell others. It compels others to adopt similar measures in order that they may survive. It weeds out those whose costs remain high and thus operates to concentrate production in the hands of those whose costs are low.[1]

Clair Wilcox

CHAPTER FOCUS

■ What does the term ''competition'' mean in economics?

■ What is the purely competitive model and why is it important?

■ What determines the output of a competitive firm?

■ How do competitive firms change their output when price changes, in the short run? In the long run?

■ What is the role of time in determining the elasticity of supply?

■ How is the competitive model related to economic efficiency?

In the last chapter, we outlined some basic principles that determine the general relationship between output and costs of production for any firm. Of course, a firm's output decisions will be influenced by its costs and its revenues. In this and the next two chapters, we will illustrate how the structure of an industry affects the revenues and output levels of firms. We will analyze four models of industrial structure: (a) pure competition, (b) monopoly, (c) monopolistic competition, and (d) oligopoly. These models will help us understand the role of competitive forces under various market conditions. This chapter focuses on pure competition.

THE PROCESS OF COMPETITION

Competition as a Dynamic Process: A term that denotes rivalry or competitiveness between or among parties (for example, producers or input suppliers), each of which seeks to deliver a better deal to buyers when quality, price, and product information are all considered. Competing implies a lack of collusion among sellers.

Before we introduce the model of pure competition, a few comments about the use of the term ''competition'' are in order. It is important not to lose sight of the function of competition as a dynamic process to explain the mechanics of alternative forms of industrial structure. The competitive process emphasizes the rivalry among firms—the effort on the part of a seller to outperform the alternative suppliers. Competing firms may use a variety of methods—quality of product, style, convenience of location, advertising, and price—to attract consumers. Independent action and rivalry are the essential ingredients of the competitive process.

Markets serve consumers well when they are open to rival sellers, so that each is under intense competition to cater to consumer preferences. Open markets have both rewards and risks for producers. Profits are possible for entrepreneurs who are alert in finding ways to satisfy consumer wants better or more cheaply, and who successfully implement them. But producers who offer only low quality at a high price find that their customers turn to rival sellers.

As the introductory quotation from Professor Wilcox indicates, competition also places pressure on producers to operate efficiently and to avoid waste. Competition weeds out the inefficient—those who are incapable of providing consumers with quality goods at low prices. Competition also keeps producers on their toes in other areas. The production techniques and product offerings that lead to success today will not necessarily pass the competitive market test tomorrow. Producers who survive in a competitive environment cannot be complacent. They must be forward-looking and innovative. They must be willing to experiment and quick to adopt improved methods.

Each competitor is, of course, in business to make a profit. Rival firms struggle for the dollar votes of consumers. Competition, though, is the taskmaster that forces producers to serve the interests of consumers and to do so at the lowest possible level of profit. As Adam Smith noted more than 200 years ago, competition harnesses the profit motive and puts it to work, elevating our standard of living and directing our resources toward the production of those goods that we desire most intensely relative to their cost. Smith pointed out that aggregate output would be vastly expanded if individuals specialized in those things they did best and cooperated with others desirous of their services. He believed that self-interest

[1]Clair Wilcox, *Competition and Monopoly in American Industry,* Monograph no. 21, Temporary National Economic Committee, Investigation of Concentration of Economic Power, 76th Congress, 3rd session (Washington, D.C.: U.S. Government Printing Office, 1940).

directed by competitive markets would generate precisely these two ingredients—specialization and cooperation. Smith emphasized this theme in Book 1 of *The Wealth of Nations:*

> It is not from the benevolence of the butcher, the brewer, or the baker, that we expect our dinner, but from their regard to their own self-interest. We address ourselves, not to their humanity but to their self-love, and never talk to them of our own necessities, but of their advantages.[2]

In Smith's time, as today, many thinkers erred because they did not understand that productive action and voluntary exchange offer the potential for mutual gain. Both parties to an economic exchange generally gain (see Myths of Economics box, p. 00). Bridled by competition, self-interest leads to economic cooperation and provides a powerful fuel for the benefit of humankind. Paradoxical as it seems, even though benevolence may be the more admirable attitude, it cannot generate the cooperative effort that is a natural outgrowth of self-interest directed by competition. Unilateral giving does not generate the information and feedback to buyers and sellers inherent in the competitive market process. Thus, the competitive process occupies center stage in economic analysis, as one of the forces directing the economic behavior of human beings.

Before we move on to more technical material, two additional points should be addressed. First, a dual usage of the term "competition" has evolved through the years. The term is used to describe a rivalry or competitiveness among sellers, as we have already noted. In addition, the term "competition," or more precisely, "pure competition," is used to describe a hypothetical model of industrial structure characterized by independent firms and a large number of sellers. This dual usage can sometimes be confusing. It is important to recognize that firms can be competitive in the sense of rivalry even through they may not be competitive in the industrial structure sense. To avoid confusion, we will use the complete expression "pure competition" when we discuss the competitive model of industrial structure.

Second, we have emphasized the role of competition as the taskmaster forcing sellers to obey the desires of consumers. Nobody likes a taskmaster, and sellers often try to escape the discipline imposed by competitive forces. The models of industrial structure that we examine are useful because they provide a framework for analyzing both the likelihood of a business firm escaping the directives of competition and the economic implications of its doing so.

Pure Competition: A model of industrial structure characterized by a large number of small firms producing a homogeneous product in an industry (market area) that permits complete freedom of entry and exit.

Homogeneous Product: A product of one firm that is identical to the product of every other firm in the industry. Consumers see no difference in units of the product offered by alternative sellers.

THE PURELY COMPETITIVE MODEL

Pure competition presupposes that the following conditions exist in a market.

1. *All Firms in the Market Are Producing a Homogeneous Product.* The product of firm A is identical to the product offered by firm B and all other firms. This presupposition rules out advertising, location preferences, quality difference, and other forms of nonprice competition.

2. *A Large Number of Independent Firms Produce the Product.* The indepen-

---

[2]Adam Smith, *An Inquiry into the Nature and Causes of the Wealth of Nations* (1776; Cannan's ed., Chicago: University of Chicago Press, 1976), p. 18.

dence of the firms rules out joint actions designed to restrict output and raise prices.

3. *Each Buyer and Seller Is Small Relative to the Total Market.* Therefore, no single buyer or seller is able to exert any noticeable influence on the market supply and demand conditions. For example, a wheat farmer selling 5,000 bushels annually would not have a noticeable impact on the U.S. wheat market, in which 2,500,000,000 bushels are traded annually.

4. *There Are No Artificial Barriers to Entry into or Exit from the Market.* Under pure competition, any entrepreneur is free either to produce or fail to produce in the industry. New entrants need not obtain permission from the government or the existing firms before they are free to compete. Nor does control of an essential resource limit market entry.

Barriers to Entry: Obstacles that limit the freedom of potential rivals to enter an industry.

The purely competitive model, like other theories, is abstract. Keep in mind that the test of a theory is not the realism of its assumptions but its ability to make *predictions* that are consistent with the real world (see Chapter 1). Assumptions are made and ideas are simplified so that we can better organize our thoughts. Models, based on simplifications and assumptions, can often help us develop the economic way of thinking.

WHY IS PURE COMPETITION IMPORTANT?

Previously, we discussed how supply and demand jointly determine market price. The model of pure competition is another way of looking at the operation of market forces. This model will help us understand the relationship between the decision-making of individual firms and market supply. If we familiarize ourselves with the way in which economic incentives influence the supply decisions of firms within the competitive model, we will be better able to understand the behavior of firms in markets that are less than purely competitive.

There are other reasons for the model's importance. Its conditions are approximated in a few important industries, most notably in many parts of agriculture. The model will help us understand these industries. In addition, as we will show later, the equilibrium conditions in the competitive model yield results that are identical with the conditions necessary for ideal static efficiency. Many economists thus use the competitive model as a standard by which to judge other industrial structures.

THE WORKINGS OF THE COMPETITIVE MODEL

Since a competitive firm by itself produces an output that is small relative to the total market, it cannot influence the market price. A purely competitive firm must accept the market price if it is to sell any of its product. Competitive firms are sometimes called price takers, because they must take the market price in order to sell.

Price Takers: Sellers who must take the market price in order to sell their product. Because each price taker's output is small relative to the total market, price takers can sell all of their output at the market price, but are unable to sell any of their output at a price higher than the market price. Thus, they face a horizontal demand curve.

Exhibit 1 illustrates the relationship between market forces (frame b) and the demand curve facing the purely competitive firm (frame a). If a pure competitor sets a price above the market level, consumers will simply buy from other sellers. Why pay the higher price when the identical good is available elsewhere at a lower price? For example, if the price of wheat were $4 per bushel, a farmer would be unable to find buyers for wheat at $4.50 per bushel. A firm could lower its price, but since it is small relative to the total market, it can already sell as

EXHIBIT 1

The Firm's Demand Curve
Under Pure Competition

The market forces of supply and
demand determine price (b).
Under pure competition,
individual firms have no control
over price. Thus, the demand for
the product of the firm is
perfectly elastic (a).

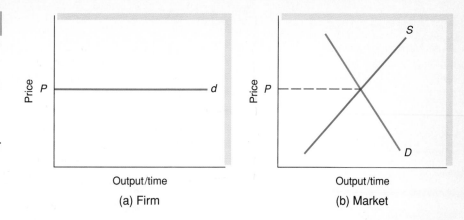

(a) Firm   (b) Market

much as it wants at the market price. A price reduction would merely reduce
revenues. A purely competitive *firm* thus confronts a perfectly elastic demand for
its product.

DECIDING HOW MUCH TO PRODUCE—THE SHORT RUN

The firm's output decision is based on comparison of benefits with costs. If a firm
produces at all, it will continue expanding output as long as the benefits (additional revenues) from the production of the additional units exceed their marginal
costs.

How will changes in output influence the firm's costs? In the last chapter, we
discovered that the firm's short-run marginal costs will *eventually* increase as the
firm expands its output by working its fixed plant facilities more intensively. The
law of diminishing marginal returns assures us that this will be the case. *Eventually,* both the firm's short-run marginal and average total cost curves will turn
upward.

What about the benefits or additional revenues from output expansion? **Mar-
ginal revenue** (MR) is the change in the firm's total revenue per unit of output.
It is the additional revenue derived from the sale of an additional unit of output.
Mathematically,

$$MR = \frac{\text{Change in total revenue}}{\text{Change in output}}$$

Since the purely competitive firm sells all units at the same price, its marginal
revenue will be equal to the market price.

In the short run, the purely competitive firm will expand output until marginal
revenue (its price) is just equal to marginal cost. This decision-making rule will
maximize the firm's profits (or minimize its losses).

Exhibit 2 helps explain why. Since the firm can sell as many units as it would
like at the market price, the sale of one additional unit will increase revenue by
the price of the product. As long as price exceeds marginal cost, revenue will
increase more than cost as output is expanded. Since profit is merely the difference between total revenue and total cost, profit will increase as output is expanded as long as each extra unit adds more to revenue than it does to cost. This
happy state of affairs comes to an end when MC has risen enough to make MC
= MR = *P*. For the pure competitor then, profit will be at a maximum when *P*
= MR = MC. In Exhibit 2, this occurs at output level *q*.

Marginal Revenue: The
incremental change in total
revenue derived from the sale
of one additional unit of a
product.

EXHIBIT 2

Profit Maximization and the Purely Competitive Firm

The purely competitive firm would maximize profits by producing the output level q, where P = MC.

Why would the firm not expand output beyond q? The cost of producing such units is given by the height of the MC curve. The sale of these units would increase revenues only by P, the price of the product. Production of units beyond q would add more to cost than to revenue. Therefore, production beyond q, the P = MC output level, would reduce the firm's profits.

A profit-maximizing firm with the cost curves indicated by Exhibit 2 would produce exactly q. The total revenue of the firm would be the sales price P multiplied by output sold q. Geometrically, the firm's total revenues would be $POqB$. The firm's total cost would be found by multiplying the average total cost by the output level. Geometrically, total costs are represented by $COqA$. The firm's total revenues exceed total costs, and the firm is making short-run economic profit (the shaded area).

In the real world, of course, decisions are not made by entrepreneurs who sit around drawing curves labeled MC and P. Many have not even heard of these concepts. Our model also ignores the problem of uncertainty. Very often, businesspeople must make decisions without complete knowledge of what costs or product price will be. In addition, there may be problems of "lumpiness." The manager may prefer to use 1.7 machines and 2.5 people to carry out a production process. Managers, however, know that machines and people alike come in discrete "lumps," or whole units. They may not be able to approximate what they want even by renting, or changing the machine size they use, or hiring part-time employees.

Despite the inconvenient and uncertain facts of real life, our simple model does make fairly accurate predictions. A business decision-maker who has never heard of the P = MC rule for profit maximization probably has another rule that yields approximately the same outcome. For example, the rule might be: Produce those units, and only those units, that add more to revenue than to cost. This ensures maximum profit (or minimum loss). It also takes the firm to the point at which P = MC. Why? To stop short of that point would mean not producing some profitable units—units that would add more to revenue than to cost. Similarly, failing to produce units whose cost is greater than the revenue they would add, ensures that production will not exceed the P = MC output level. This common sense rule thus leads to the same outcome as the competitive model, even when the decision-maker knows none of the technical jargon of economics. No wonder economics is sometimes thought of as "organized common sense."

Just how accurate is the purely competitive model in predicting behavior in real markets? Do other models, which assume that sellers collude to eliminate competition, make better predictions? Direct scientific evidence bearing on such questions is highly desirable. As the Applications in Economics box, "Experimental Economics—Testing the Purely Competitive Model," indicates, such evidence has been produced repeatedly in recent decades by the relatively new subdiscipline of experimental economics. The evidence supports the purely competitive model surprisingly well under a variety of circumstances.

PROFIT MAXIMIZING—A NUMERIC EXAMPLE

Exhibit 3 uses numeric data to illustrate profit-maximizing decision-making for a competitive firm. The firm's short-run total and marginal cost schedules have the general characteristics we discussed in the previous chapter. Since the firm confronts a market price of $5 per unit, its marginal revenue is $5. Total revenue thus *increases* by $5 per additional unit of output. The firm maximizes its profit when it supplies an output of 15 units.

There are two ways of viewing this profit-maximizing output rate. First, we could examine the difference between total revenue and total cost, identifying the output rate at which this difference is greatest. Column 6, the profit data, provides this information. For small output rates (less than 11), the firm would actually experience losses. But, at 15 units of output, an $11 profit is earned ($75 total revenue minus $64 total cost). Inspection of the profit column indicates that it is impossible to earn a profit larger than $11 at any other rate of output.

EXHIBIT 3 ■ Profit Maximization of a Competitive Firm—A Numeric Illustration

(1) Output (per Day)	(2) Total Revenue	(3) Total Cost	(4) Marginal Revenue	(5) Marginal Cost	(6) Profit (TR − TC)
0	$ 0.00	$ 25.00	$0.00	$ 0.00	− 20.00
1	5.00	29.80	5.00	4.80	− 24.80
2	10.00	33.75	5.00	3.95	− 23.75
3	15.00	37.25	5.00	3.50	− 22.25
4	20.00	40.25	5.00	3.00	− 20.25
5	25.00	42.75	5.00	2.50	− 17.75
6	30.00	44.75	5.00	2.00	− 14.75
7	35.00	46.50	5.00	1.75	− 11.50
8	40.00	48.00	5.00	1.50	− 8.00
9	45.00	49.25	5.00	1.25	− 4.25
10	50.00	50.25	5.00	1.00	− 0.25
11	55.00	51.50	5.00	1.25	3.50
12	60.00	53.25	5.00	1.75	6.75
13	65.00	55.75	5.00	2.50	9.25
14	70.00	59.25	5.00	3.50	10.75
15	75.00	64.00	5.00	4.75	11.00
16	80.00	70.00	5.00	6.00	10.00
17	85.00	77.25	5.00	7.25	7.75
18	90.00	85.50	5.00	8.25	4.50
19	95.00	95.00	5.00	9.50	0.00
20	100.00	108.00	5.00	13.00	− 8.00
21	105.00	125.00	5.00	17.00	− 20.00

APPLICATIONS IN ECONOMICS

Experimental Economics—Testing the Purely Competitive Model

Do individual decision-makers, without any economics training, behave as if they understand marginal cost? Do they act according to the competitive model, even though not all of the assumptions of that model are satisfied? Or when there are only a few sellers, do they collude successfully so as to raise price above marginal cost?

Answering such questions is important, but verifying economic principles and comparing alternative economic models by scientific testing is not an easy task. Simply observing people's economic behavior to see whether they behave as economic principles suggest is not completely satisfying. Since a normal economic event that we can observe is the result of more than one cause, the economist trying to isolate the impact of one causal factor must try to be sure that other factors influencing the outcome do not vary, or else try to take them into account in the analysis. To isolate the impact of a change in the price of a product on consumer behavior for example, the economist must somehow account for the impact of all other price changes, income changes, and so on, that may have occurred. In other disciplines, scientists use experiments in the laboratory, with all factors controlled, to tackle this problem. They test the principles on which their science is built, using carefully detailed methods, so that other scientists can replicate the experiment.

Beginning about the middle of the twentieth century, economists began to conduct laboratory experiments, too. A good many experiments have been conducted to investigate the predictive power of the purely competitive model. In one of the earliest, conducted in 1956 by Vernon Smith of the University of Arizona, individual subjects were brought into a laboratory setting and arbitrarily assigned roles as buyers and sellers, in a game-like setting.

Each buyer was given a different "limit price" (that is, a maximum price he or she was allowed to pay) for a paper asset. If the buyer could purchase the paper commodity for less than the limit price, he or she received a cash payment equal to the difference between the limit price and the amount actually paid. So, as in other markets, each buyer gained financially by purchasing at lower prices. The sellers were treated in a parallel fashion. Each had a "limit price" (a minimum selling price) and received in cash any extra revenue above that price.

Buyers and sellers were free to make oral offers to buy or sell. How did markets develop in this "double oral auction?" Did the outcomes resemble a competitive market, or did sellers collude, controlling the market price for their own benefit, so that a monopoly model would better describe the outcome?

The competitive model predicts that trades among buyers and sellers will occur at a market price, which will allow every efficient trade to take place. The market price equates the quantity demanded with the quantity willingly supplied.

Prior to the work in experimental economies, many economists thought the competitive model was relevant only under highly restrictive conditions. The experimental work indicates that this is not the case. The wide applicability of the purely competitive model surprised many observers. As Vernon Smith a leading experimental economist points out, "Since 1956, several hundred experiments using different supply and demand conditions, experienced as well as inexperienced subjects, buyers and sellers with multiple unit trading capacity, a great variation in the numbers of buyers and sellers, and different trading institutions have established the replicability and robustness of these results [competitive outcomes]."[3]

The experimental approach allows researchers to test theories under a wide range of conditions. By changing the number of sellers, the type of trading rules, and so on, researchers can find out whether predicted outcomes hold only in special cases or under a wide variety of circumstances. Without the control that is possible in the laboratory, questions about the relevance of a theory might lead only to heated debate, with little light shed on the topic.

Experimental economics, like laboratory work in other sciences, cannot answer all questions about what might happen in nonlaboratory settings. But it has already provided a great deal of precision and certainty to a world of economics needing just those things. And its contributions undoubtedly will continue.

[3]See Vernon L. Smith, "Experimental Methods in Economics," in *The New Palgrave: A Dictionary of Economics*, ed. by John Eatwell, et al., (London: Macmillan Press Ltd., 1987), pp. 241–249 for a good overview of experimental economics.

Exhibit 4a presents the total revenue and total cost approach in graph form. (However, the curves are drawn smoothly, as though output could be increased in any amounts including tiny amounts, not just in whole unit increments as shown in Exhibit 3.) Profits will be maximized when the total revenue line exceeds the total cost curve by the largest vertical amount. That takes place, of course, at 15 units of output.

The marginal approach also can be used to determine the profit-maximizing rate of output for the competitive firm. Remember, as long as price (marginal revenue) exceeds marginal cost, production and sale of additional units will add to the firm's profit (or reduce its losses). Inspection of columns 4 and 5 of Exhibit 3 indicates that MR is greater than MC for the first 15 units of output. Production of these units will expand the firm's profit. In contrast, the production of each unit beyond 15 adds more to cost than to revenue. Profit will therefore decline if output is expanded beyond 15 units. Given the firm's cost and revenue schedule, the profit-maximizing manager will choose to produce 15, and only 15, units per day.

EXHIBIT 4

Profit Maximization—The Total and Marginal Approaches

Utilizing the data of Exhibit 3, here we provide two alternative ways of viewing profit maximization. As frame (a) illustrates, the profits of the competitive firm are maximized at the output level at which total revenue exceeds total cost by the maximum amount. Frame (b) demonstrates that the maximum-profit output can also be identified by comparing marginal revenue and marginal cost.

(a) Total revenue/total cost approach

(b) Marginal revenue/marginal cost approach

EXHIBIT 5

Operating with Short-run Losses

A firm making losses will operate in the short run if it (a) can cover its variable costs now and (b) expects price to be high enough in the future to cover all its costs.

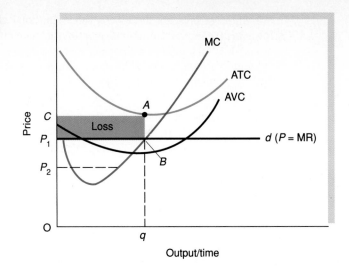

Exhibit 4b graphically illustrates the marginal approach. Note here that the output rate (15 units) at which the marginal cost and marginal revenue curves intersect coincides with the output rate in Exhibit 4a at which the total revenue curve exceeds the total cost curve by the largest amount.

LOSSES AND GOING OUT OF BUSINESS

Suppose changes take place in the market that depress the price below a firm's average total cost. How will a profit-maximizing (or loss-minimizing) firm respond to this situation? The answer to this question depends on both the firm's current sales revenues relative to its *variable cost* and its expectations about the future. The firm has three options—it can (a) continue to operate in the short run, (b) shut down temporarily, or (c) go out of business.

If the firm anticipates that the lower market price is temporary, it may want to continue operating in the short run as long as it is able to cover its variable cost.[4] Exhibit 5 illustrates why. The firm shown in this exhibit would minimize its loss at output level q, where $P = $ MC. At q, total revenues ($OqBP_1$) are, however, less than total costs ($OqAC$). The firm confronts short-run economic losses. Even if it shuts down completely, it will still incur fixed costs, *unless it goes out of business.* If the firm anticipates that the market price will increase enough that it will be able to cover its average total costs in the future, it may not

---

[4]In thinking about this issue, we must keep in mind the opportunity cost concept. The firm's fixed costs are *opportunity costs* that do not vary with the level of output. They can be avoided if, and only if, the firm goes out of business. Following this course releases the fixed-cost resources to their best alternative use, and thus eliminates the fixed costs. Fixed costs are *not* (as some economics texts have stated) the depreciated value of the firm's fixed assets. Such accounting measures may have little to do with the firm's opportunity cost of those fixed assets. To specify fixed costs, we need to know (a) how much the firm's fixed assets would bring if they were sold or rented to others and (b) any other costs, such as operating license fees and debts, which could be avoided if the firm declared bankruptcy and/or went out of business. Although these costs can be avoided if the firm goes out of business, the firm could not operate even in the short run if it cannot cover its fixed costs (unless it expects conditions to improve; then it would have to pay extra costs to get back into business at that future time.) See Marshall Colberg and James King, "Theory of Production Abandonment," *Revista Internazionale di Scienze Economiche e Commerciali* 20 (1973), pp. 961–1072.

Shutdown: A temporary halt in the operation of a business. The firm does *not* sell its assets. Its variable cost will be eliminated, but the firm's fixed costs will continue. The shut-down firm anticipates a return to operation in the future.

Going Out of Business: The sale of a firm's assets, and its permanent exit from the market. By going out of business, a firm is able to avoid fixed cost, which would continue during a shutdown.

want to sell out. It may choose to produce q units in the short run, even though losses are incurred. At price P_1, production of output q is clearly more advantageous than shutting down, because the firm is able to cover its variable costs and pay some of its fixed costs. If it were to shut down, *but not sell out,* the firm would lose the entire amount of its fixed cost.

What if the market price declines below the firm's average variable cost (for example, P_2)? Under these circumstances, a temporary shutdown is preferable to short-run operation. If the firm continues to operate in the short run, operating losses merely supplement losses resulting from the firm's fixed costs. Therefore, even if the firm expects the market price to increase, enabling it to survive and prosper in the future, it will shut down in the short run when the market price falls below its average variable cost.

The firm's third option is going out of business immediately. After all, even the losses resulting from the firm's fixed costs (remember that if they are costs of doing business, they must be avoidable by not doing business) can be avoided if the firm sells out. If it does not expect market conditions to change for the better, this is the preferred option.

THE COMPETITIVE FIRM'S SHORT-RUN SUPPLY CURVE

The competitive firm that intends to stay in business will maximize profits (or minimize losses) when it produces the output level at which $P = MC$ and variable costs are covered. Therefore, the portion of the firm's short-run marginal cost curve that lies above its average variable cost is the short-run supply curve of the firm.

Exhibit 6 illustrates that as the market price increases, the competitive firm will expand output along its MC curve. If the market price were less than P_1, the firm would shut down immediately because it would be unable to cover even its variable costs. If the market price is P_1, however, a price equal to the firm's average variable cost, the firm may supply output q_1 *in the short run.* Economic losses will result, but the firm would incur similar losses if it shut down completely. As the market price increases to P_2, the firm will happily expand output along its MC curve to q_2. At P_2, price is also equal to average total costs. The firm is making a "normal rate of return," or zero economic profits. Higher prices

The Supply Curve for the Firm and the Market

When resource prices are constant, the short-run market supply is merely the sum of the supply produced by all the firms in the market area (b).

(a) Representative firm

(b) Market

will result in a still larger short-run output. The firm will supply q_3 units at market price P_3. At this price, economic profits will result. At still higher prices, output will be expanded even more. As long as price exceeds average variable cost, the firm will expand supply along its MC curve, which therefore becomes the firm's short-run supply curve.

THE SHORT-RUN MARKET SUPPLY CURVE

The short-run market supply curve corresponds to the total amount supplied by all of the firms in the industry. For a purely competitive industry, the short-run market supply curve is the horizontal summation of the marginal cost curves (above the level of average variable cost) for all firms in the industry. Since individual firms will supply a larger amount at a higher price, the short-run market supply curve will slope upward to the right.

Exhibit 6 illustrates this relationship. As the price of the product rises from P_1 to P_2 to P_3, the individual firms expand their output along their marginal cost curves. Since the individual competitive firms supply a larger output as the market price increases, the total amount supplied to the market also expands.

Our construction of the short-run market supply curve assumes that the prices of the resources used by the industry are constant. When the entire industry (rather than just a single firm) expands output, resource prices may rise. If this does happen, the short-run market supply curve (reflecting the higher prices of purchased inputs) will be slightly more inelastic (steeper) than the sum of the supply curves of the individual firms.

The short-run market supply curve, together with the demand curve for the industry's product, will determine the market price. At the short-run equilibrium market price, each of the firms will have expanded output until marginal costs have risen to the market price. They will have no desire to change output, *given their current size of plant.*

OUTPUT ADJUSTMENTS IN THE LONG RUN

In the long run, firms have the opportunity to alter their plant size and enter or exit from an industry. As long-run adjustments are made, output in the whole industry may either expand or contract.

LONG-RUN EQUILIBRIUM

In addition to the balance between quantity supplied and quantity demanded necessary for short-run equilibrium, the firms in a competitive industry must earn the normal rate of return, and only the normal rate, before long-run equilibrium can be attained. If economic profit is present, new firms will enter the industry, and the current producers will have an incentive to expand the scale of their operations. This will lead to an increase in supply, placing downward pressure on prices. In contrast, if firms in the industry are suffering economic losses, they will leave the market. Supply will decline, placing upward pressure on prices.

Therefore, as Exhibit 7 illustrates, when a competitive industry is in long-run equilibrium, (a) the quantity supplied and the quantity demanded will be equal at the market price, and (b) the firms in the industry will be earning normal (zero) economic profit (that is, their minimum ATC will just equal the market price).

EXHIBIT 7

Long-run Equilibrium in a Competitive Market

The two conditions necessary for equilibrium in a competitive market are depicted here. First, quantity supplied and quantity demanded must be equal in the market (b). Second, the firm must earn zero economic profit, that is, the "normal rate of return," at the established market price (a).

(a) Firm

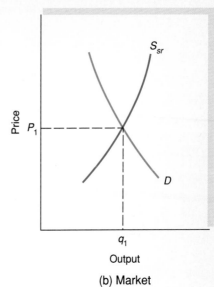

(b) Market

ADJUSTING TO AN EXPANSION IN DEMAND

Suppose a purely competitive market is in equilibrium. What will happen if there is an increase in demand? Exhibit 8 presents an example. An entrepreneur introduces a fantastic new candy product. Consumers go wild over it. However, since it sticks to one's teeth, the market demand for toothpicks increases from D_1 to D_2. The price of toothpicks rises from P_1 to P_2. What impact will the higher market price have on the output level of toothpick-producing firms? It will increase (from q_1 to q_2, Exhibit 8a) as the firms expand output along their marginal cost curves. In the short run, the toothpick producers will make economic profits. The profits will attract new toothpick producers to the industry and cause the existing firms to expand the scale of their plants.[5] Hence, the market supply will increase (shift from S_1 to S_2) and eventually eliminate the short-run profits. If cost conditions are unchanged in the industry, the market price for toothpicks will return to its initial level, even though output has expanded to Q_3.

ADJUSTING TO A DECLINE IN DEMAND

Economic profits attract new firms to an industry; economic losses (those expected to continue) encourage capital and entrepreneurship to move out of the industry and into other areas where the profitability potential is more favorable. Economic losses mean that the owners of capital in the industry are earning less than the market rate of return. The opportunity cost of continuing in the industry exceeds the gain.

Exhibit 9 illustrates how market forces react to economic losses. Initially, an equilibrium price exists in the industry. The firms are able to cover their average

[5]If the *long-run* average total cost curve results in only one possible minimum-cost output level (see Exhibit 9a of the previous chapter), the expansion in the long-run supply will be generated entirely by the entry of new firms. However, when the long-run average total cost is such that a wide range of minimum-cost output levels is possible (see Exhibit 9b of the previous chapter), both the entry of new firms and expansion by the established firms will contribute to the increase in supply.

(a) Firm   (b) Market

EXHIBIT 8

How the Market Responds
to an Increase in Demand

The introduction of a new candy product that sticks to one's teeth causes the demand for toothpicks to increase to D_2 (frame b). Toothpick prices rise to P_2, inducing firms to expand output. Toothpick firms make short-run profits (frame a), which draw new competitors into the industry. Thus, the toothpick supply expands (shifts from S_1 to S_2). If cost conditions are unchanged, the expansion in supply will continue until the market price of toothpicks has declined to its initial level P_1.

EXHIBIT 9

Impact of a Decline in
Demand

A reduction in market demand will cause price to fall and short-run losses to occur. The losses will cause some firms to go out of business and others to reduce their scale. Thus, the market supply will fall, causing the market price to rise. The supply will continue to decline and price will continue to rise until the short-run losses have been eliminated (S_2).

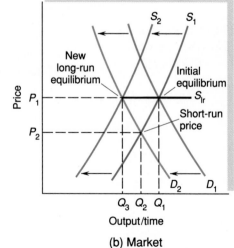

(a) Firm   (b) Market

costs of production. Now, suppose there is a reduction in consumer income, causing the market demand for the product to decrease and the market price to decline. At the new, lower price, firms in the industry will not be able to cover their costs of production. In the short run, they will reduce output along their MC curve. This reduction in output by the individual firms results in a reduction in the quantity supplied in the market.

In the face of short-run losses, there will be a reduction even in replacement capital into this industry. Some firms will leave the industry as their fixed costs become variable when they are no longer able to cover their variable cost at the prevailing price. Others will reduce the scale of their operations. These factors will cause the industry supply to decline, to shift from S_1 to S_2. What impact will this have on price? It will rise. In the long run, the market supply will decline until the price rises sufficiently to permit "normal profits" in the industry.

THE LONG-RUN SUPPLY CURVE

The long-run market supply curve indicates the minimum price at which firms will supply various market output levels, given sufficient time both to adjust plant size (or other fixed factors) and to enter or exit from the industry. The shape of the long-run market supply curve is dependent on what happens to the cost of production as the output of an industry is altered. Three possibilities emerge, although one is far more likely than the other two.

If factor prices remain unchanged, the long-run market supply curve will be perfectly elastic. In terms of economics, this describes a **constant cost industry.** Exhibits 8 and 9 both picture constant cost industries. As Exhibit 8 illustrates, an expansion in demand causes prices to increase *temporarily*. The high prices and profits stimulate additional production. The short-run market supply continues to expand (the entire schedule shifts to the right) until the market price returns to its initial level and profits return to their normal level. In the long run, the larger supply will not require a permanent price increase. The *long-run* supply curve (S_{lr}) is thus perfectly elastic. Exhibit 9 illustrates the impact of a decline in demand in a constant cost industry. Again, the long-run supply curve is perfectly elastic, reflecting the basically unchanged cost at the lower rate of industry output.

A constant cost industry is most likely to arise when the industry's demand for resource inputs is quite small relative to the total demand for these resources. For example, since demand of the matches industry for wood, chemicals, and labor is so small relative to the total demand for these resources, doubling the output of matches would exert only a negligible impact on the price of the resources used by the industry. Matches therefore approximate a constant cost industry.

For most industries, called increasing cost industries by economists, an expansion in total output causes a firm's production cost to rise. As the output of an industry increases, demand for resources used by the industry expands. This usually results in higher resource prices, which cause the firm's cost curves to shift upward. For example, an increase in demand for housing place upward pressure on the prices of lumber, roofing, window frames, and construction labor, causing the cost of housing to rise. Similarly, an increase in demand (and market output)

Constant Cost Industry: An industry for which factor prices and costs of production remain constant as market output is expanded. Thus, the long-run market supply curve is horizontal.

Increasing Cost Industries: Industries for which costs of production rise as the industry output is expanded. Thus, the long-run quantity supplied to the market is directly related to price.

INCREASING COST INDUSTRIES

for beef may cause the prices of feed grains, hay, and grazing land to rise. Thus, the production costs of beef rise as more of it is produced.

In some industries, additional demand may lead to industrial congestion, which will reduce the efficiency of the industry and cause costs to rise, even though resource prices are constant. For example, as the demand for lobster increases, additional fishermen are attracted to the industry. However, the increase in the number of fishermen combing lobster beds typically leads to congestion, which reduces the catch per hour of individual fishermen. The production cost in the lobster industry therefore rises as output per labor-hour declines.

For an increasing cost industry, an expansion in market demand will bid up resource prices and/or lead to industrial congestion, causing the per unit cost of

APPLICATIONS IN ECONOMICS

A Shift in Demand—The Impact of Papal Decree on the Price of Fish[6]

Sometimes changes in institutions, legal restrictions, or regulatory policies influence the demand for a product. The 1966 papal decree lifting the Catholic Church's ban on the eating of meat on Fridays provides an interesting illustration of this point. Prior to the lifting of the ban, most of the nearly 600 million Roman Catholics consumed fish on Fridays. After the decree, many shifted to substitute goods such as beef, pork, and chicken. The demand for fish therefore declined. As our analysis indicates, a decline in demand will lead to a lower market price in the short-run.

Economist Frederick Bell of Florida State University estimated the impact of the reduction in demand on the market price of fish in the Northeast United States, an area where Catholics comprise a large proportion of the total population. As we discussed earlier, changes in personal income and the price of related commodities (beef, pork, and poultry in this case) will influence the demand for a good. Bell utilized statistical techniques to adjust for these factors. This permitted him to isolate the independent effect of the papal decree on the price of fish.

Bell estimated the impact of the decree on the price of seven different species of fish during the period following the decree. As Exhibit 10 shows, his analysis indicates that the price of each variety of fish fell. In the case of large haddock, the price was 21 percent lower after the papal decree than for the 10 years prior to the lifting of the ban. In other instances, the decline in price was smaller. On average, Bell estimates,

the price of fish in the Northeastern United States fell by 12.5 percent as the result of the papal decree. Just as economic theory indicates, a reduction in demand for a product leads to a lower price in the short run (see Exhibit 9).

[6]Frederick W. Bell, "The Pope and The Price of Fish," *American Economic Review, 58* (December 1968), pp. 1346–1350.

EXHIBIT 10   ■   The Papal Decree and the Price of Fish

The papal decree lifting the ban against the eating of meat on Fridays reduced the demand for fish and resulted in lower prices for fish.

Species	Percent Change in the Price of Fish After Papal Decree
Sea scallops	−17
Yellowtail flounder	−14
Large haddock	−21
Small haddock (scrod)	−2
Cod	−16
Ocean perch	−10
Whiting	−20
All species (average)	−12.5

Source: F. W. Bell, "The Pope and The Price of Fish," *American Economic Review* (December 1968).

the firms to rise. As a result, a larger market output will be forthcoming only at a higher price. The long-run market supply curve for the product will therefore slope upward.

Exhibit 11 depicts an increasing cost industry. An expansion in demand causes higher prices and a larger market output. The presence of short-run profit attracts new competitors to the industry, expanding the market output even more. *As the industry expands,* factor prices rise and congestion costs increase. What happens to the firm's cost curves? Both the average and marginal cost curves rise (shift to ATC_2 and MC_2). This increase in production cost necessitates a higher long-run price (P_2). Hence, the long-run supply curve slopes upward to the right.

DECREASING COST INDUSTRIES

Decreasing Cost Industries: Industries for which costs of production decline as the industry expands. The market supply is therefore inversely related to price. Such industries are atypical.

Conceivably, factor prices could decline if the market output of a product were expanded. Since a reduction in factor prices would lead to a lower long-run competitive market price for the product, economists refer to such industries as **decreasing cost industries.** The long-run (but not the short-run) market supply curve for a decreasing cost industry would slope downward to the right. For example, as the electronics industry expands, suppliers of components may be able to adopt large-scale techniques that will lead to lower component prices. If this occurs, the cost curves of the electronics firms may drift downward, causing the industry supply curve for electronics products to slope downward to the right (at least temporarily). However, since expansion of an industry is far more likely to cause rising rather than falling input prices, decreasing cost industries are atypical.

EXHIBIT 11

Increasing Costs and the Long-run Supply

Most often, higher factor prices and industrial congestion will cause costs to rise as the *market* output increases. For such increasing cost industries, the long-run supply curve (S_{lr}, frame b) will slope upward to the right.

(a) Firm

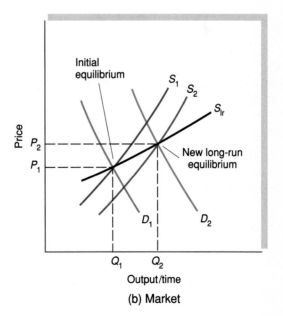

(b) Market

SUPPLY ELASTICITY AND THE ROLE OF TIME

The market supply curve is more elastic in the long run than in the short run because the firm's short-run response is limited by the "fixed" nature of some of its factors. The short- and long-run distinction offers a convenient two-stage analysis, but in the real world there are many intermediate production "runs." Some factors that could not be easily varied in a one-week time period can be varied over a two-week period. Expansion of other factors might require a month, and still others, six months. To be more precise, the cost penalty for quicker availability is greater for some production factors than for others. In any case, a faster expansion usually means that greater cost penalties are necessary to provide for an earlier availability of productive factors.

When a firm has a longer time period to plan output and adjust all of its productive inputs to the desired utilization levels, it will be able to produce any specific rate of output at a lower cost. Because it is less costly to expand output slowly in response to a demand increase, the expansion of output by firms will increase with time, as long as price exceeds cost. Therefore, the elasticity of the market supply curve will be greater when more time is allowed for firms to adjust output.

Exhibit 12 illustrates the important effect of time on the supply response of producers. When the price of a product increases from P_1 to P_2, the *immediate* supply response of the firms is small because it is costly to expand output hastily. After one week, firms are willing to expand output only from Q_1 to Q_2. After one month, due to cost reductions possible because of the longer production planning period, firms are willing to offer Q_3 units at the price P_2. After three months, the rate of output expands to Q_4. In the long run, when it is possible to adjust all inputs to the desired utilization levels (within a six-month time period, for example), firms are willing to supply Q_5 units of output at the market price of P_2. The supply curve for products is typically more elastic over a longer time period than for a shorter period. The length of time necessary to bring about large changes in quantity supplied can vary dramatically across industries. The Applications in Economics box on the dairy industry shows that the adjustment process there takes many years.

EXHIBIT 12

Time and the Elasticity of the Supply

The elasticity of the market supply curve usually increases as more time is allowed for adjustment to a change in price.

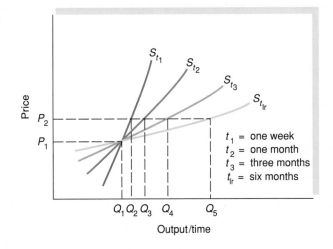

t_1 = one week
t_2 = one month
t_3 = three months
t_{lr} = six months

THE ROLE OF PROFITS IN THE COMPETITIVE MODEL

In the competitive model, profits and losses are signals sent to producers by consumers. Economic profits will be largest in those areas in which consumer wants at the margin are greatest *relative to costs of production*. Profit-seeking entrepreneurs will guide additional resources into these areas. Supply will increase, driving prices down and eliminating the profits. Free entry and the competitive process will protect the consumer from arbitrarily high prices. In the long run, competitive prices will reflect costs of production.

Economic profits result because a firm or entrepreneur increases the value of resources. The successful firm puts resources into a product valued more highly, as measured by buyers' willingness to pay, than the resources would be valued in other uses, as measured by the cost of bidding the resources away from all other users. Losses discipline the firm that produces a product that consumers value less than the resources required for its production. Losses and bankruptcies are the market mechanism's way of bringing wasteful activities to a halt.

Producers, like other decision-makers, of course, confront uncertainty and dynamic change. Entrepreneurs, at the time they must make investment decisions,

APPLICATIONS IN ECONOMICS

Increasing Milk Supplies—Slowly

When milk prices rise and are expected to remain higher, other things equal, dairies will expand their output of milk. They will retain more older cows past their prime—cows that would have been sent to slaughter. New dairy cows will be added to the herd, and more expensive feed rations may be used to boost milk output from each cow in the herd. Genetically advanced cows, capable of producing more milk, will be sought. New firms will enter the dairy business.

Some of these changes will begin immediately. Others, though, especially those that change the size and composition of dairy herds, will take years to complete. Similarly, a decrease in milk production will take many years, if milk price falls.

Just how slow is the response in the dairy industry? The supply elasticity numbers that follow, from a study published in 1985 at the University of Wisconsin, indicate that even after 25 years, some of the

long-run effects of a milk price increase are felt. A 10 percent increase in the price of milk will, after one year, lead to only a 1.2 percent increase in the quantity of milk supplied. But, after six years, the same price increase would lead to a 12 percent quantity increase, and after 10 years, the response would be 25 per-

cent. Given 20 years to react, dairies would provide a 50 percent increase in the quantity of milk supplied, in response to the same 10 percent price increase. After 30 years, the response would be greater still. On the dairy farm, at least, changes can take a great deal of time.

Supply Elasticities for Milk	
Length of Run (Years)	Percent Change in the Quantity of Milk Supplied Due to a 10% Rise in the Price of Milk
1	1.2
3	2.3
6	11.7
10	24.6
15	39.0
20	50.3
25	59.5
30	67.0

Source: Richard Klemme and Jean-Paul Chavas, "The Effects of Changing Milk Price on Milk Supply and National Dairy Herd Size," *Economic Issues,* University of Wisconsin, June 1985.

cannot be sure of either future market prices or costs of production. They must base their decisions on expectations. Within the framework of the competitive model, however, the reward-penalty system is clear. Firms that efficiently produce and correctly anticipate the products and services for which future demand will be most urgent (relative to production cost) will make economic profits. Those that are inefficient and incorrectly allocate resources into areas of weak future demand will be penalized with losses.

EFFICIENCY AND THE COMPETITIVE MODEL

Economists often seem to be enchanted by the purely competitive model. They sometimes use it as the standard by which to judge other models. What accounts for the special significance of pure competition? Most economists agree that under rather restrictive assumptions resource allocation within the purely competitive model is ideal from society's viewpoint. In what sense can we say that it is "ideal"?

PRODUCTION EFFICIENCY (P = ATC)

In the long run, competition forces firms to minimize their average total cost of production and to charge a price just sufficient to cover production costs. Competitive firms must use production methods that minimize costs if they are going to survive. In addition, they must choose a scale of operation that minimizes their long-run average total cost of production. Consumers of competitively produced goods will benefit, since they will receive the largest quantity at the lowest possible price, given the prevailing cost conditions. Competitive markets will eliminate waste and production inefficiency. Inefficient, high-cost producers will confront economic losses and be driven from a competitive industry.

ALLOCATIVE EFFICIENCY (P = MC)

Allocative Efficiency: The allocation of resources to the production of goods and services most desired by consumers. The allocation is "balanced" in such a way that reallocation of resources could not benefit anyone without hurting someone else.

Allocative efficiency refers to the balance achieved by the allocation of available resources to the production of goods and services most desired by consumers, given their incomes. Allocative efficiency is present when all markets are in long-run competitive equilibrium. Each good is produced as long as consumers value it more than the alternative goods that might be produced with the same resources. Conversely, no unit of the good is produced if a more valuable alternative must be forgone. Therefore, no reallocation of resources toward production of different goods—or different combinations of goods—could benefit any one person without simultaneously hurting someone else.

The profit-maximization rule (P = MC) assures allocative efficiency within the competitive model. The market demand (price) reflects consumers' valuation of an additional unit of a good. The seller's marginal cost indicates the value of the resources (in their alternative uses) necessary to produce an additional unit of the good. When the production of each good is expanded so long as price exceeds marginal cost, each good will be produced if, and only if, consumers value it more than the alternatives that might have been produced. In purely competitive markets, therefore, profit-maximizing producers will be led to produce the combination of goods most desired by consumers.

PURE COMPETITION AND THE REAL WORLD

In the purely competitive model, the "invisible hand" that Adam Smith spoke of does its job very well indeed. Producers who are motivated purely by the desire to make a profit act no differently than they would if they cared only about the efficient satisfaction of consumers' desires. Because of the resulting price structure, even the desire of a very selfish consumer for a consumption item is balanced against the value of the good (and the resources embodied within it) to other people. In other words, prevailing prices provide each person with the information and incentive to heed the wishes of others. An incredibly complex array of consumer desires, production possibilities, and resource availabilities can be optimally coordinated in the model. No central person or group need know or understand all the aspects of the model. A few market prices condense the needed information and convey it to each decision-maker.

However, remember that pure competition is a hypothetical model. Even though it predicts fairly well in many circumstances, it ignores some important features of real markets. First, in many industries, the production costs of large firms are less than those of small firms, due to economies of scale. Under these circumstances, it may not be economical to have the industry's output divided among a large number of small producers.

Second, the preferences of consumers differ widely with regard to product design, quality, and location of purchase. Sometimes consumers want variety rather than the homogeneous products implied by the purely competitive model.

Third, we live in a dynamic world. Frequent changes in knowledge and technology bring about a continual parade of new products that are better, or cheaper,

OUTSTANDING ECONOMIST

Friedrich A. von Hayek
(1899–   )

For six decades, Professor Hayek has been a consistent eloquent defender of classical liberalism, even when most of the world was moving toward central planning and big government. Born in Vienna, Hayek was a lecturer in Austria during the 1920s. In 1931, he accepted a professorship of economics at the London School of Economics. After the Second World War, he joined the faculty of the University of Chicago, where he taught for many years.

Hayek has made important contributions in areas as diverse as monetary theory, markets and knowledge, capital theory, and the theory of business cycles. In 1979, he was the joint recipient (along with Gunnar Myrdal) of the Nobel Prize in economics.

Hayek believes that the competitive process is far more important than the perfect competition which so often preoccupies economists. He argues that markets will be competitive when the government does not create artificial obstacles restricting the entry of firms. According to Hayek, competition is a process that "creates the views people have about what is best and cheapest." In the absence of entry barriers created by government, the competitive process will drive prices down to the level of production costs. "The practical lesson of all this," Hayek states, "is that we should worry much less about whether competition in a given case is perfect and worry much more whether there is competition at all."[7]

Hayek is much more than an economist—he is a social critic, philosopher, political theorist, and scholar. His recent publications include a three-volume work entitled *Law, Legislation, and Liberty,* in which he articulates his views on the importance of rules over discretionary authority, the interrelationship of economic and political freedom, and the illusory concept of social justice.

[7]Friedrich A. Hayek, *Individualism and Economic Order* (Chicago: University of Chicago Press, 1948), pp. 105–106.

or both. Adjustments take time, and disequilibrium, rather than the stable equilibrium of a purely competitive model, is normally present.

Fourth, competition in the sense of rivalry is multidimensional. Pure competition features only one dimension—price. But product quality, producer reliability, convenience, location of service, and other competitive factors are important in the real world.

LOOKING AHEAD

Pure competition is important because it can help us understand real-world markets characterized by low barriers to entry and a substantial number of independent sellers. At the opposite end of the spectrum lie markets characterized by high barriers to entry and a single seller. The following chapter focuses on the hypothetical model developed by economists to analyze markets of this type—pure monopoly.

CHAPTER SUMMARY

1. Competition as a process should not be confused with pure competition, a model of industrial structure. Competition as a process implies rivalry and entrepreneurial behavior. Rival firms use quality, style, location, advertising, and price to attract consumers. Pure competition, on the other hand, is a model of industrial structure that assumes the presence of a large number of small (relative to the total market) firms, each producing a homogeneous product in a market for which there is complete freedom of entry and exit.

2. The competitive process places producers under strong pressure to operate efficiently and heed the views of consumers. Those who do not offer quality goods at economical prices lose customers to rivals. As Adam Smith recognized long ago, self-interest is a powerful motivator of human beings. If it is bridled by competition, self-interest leads to economic cooperation and productive effort.

3. Under pure competition, firms are price takers—they face a perfectly elastic demand curve. Profit-maximizing (or loss-minimizing) firms will expand output as long as the additional output adds more to revenues than to costs. Therefore, the competitive firm will produce the output level at which marginal revenue (and price) equals marginal cost.

4. The firm's short-run marginal cost curve (above its average variable cost) is its supply curve. Under pure competition, the short-run *market* supply curve is the horizontal sum of the marginal cost curves (when MC is above AVC) for all firms in the industry.

5. If a firm (a) is covering its average variable cost and (b) anticipates that the price is only temporarily below average total cost, it may operate in the short run even though it is experiencing a loss. However, even if it anticipates more favorable market conditions in the future, loss minimization will require the firm to shut down if it is unable to cover its average variable cost. If the firm does not anticipate that it will be able to cover its average total cost even in the long run, loss minimization requires that it immediately go out of business (even if it is covering its average *variable* cost) so that it can at least avoid its fixed cost.

6. When price exceeds average total cost, a firm will make economic profits. Under pure competition, profits will attract new firms into the industry and stimulate the existing firms to expand. The market supply will increase, pushing price down to the level of average total cost. Competitive firms will be unable to make long-run economic profits.

7. Losses exist when the market price is less than the firm's average total cost. Losses will cause firms to leave the industry or reduce the scale of their operations. Market

supply will decline until price rises sufficiently for firms to earn normal (that is, zero economic) profits.

8. As the output of an industry expands, marginal costs will increase in the short run, causing the short-run market supply curve to slope upward to the right. If the price of resources purchased by the industry remain unchanged, as the market output is expanded, the long-run supply curve will be perfectly elastic. However, as the output of an industry expands, rising factor prices and industrial congestion will normally cause the firm's cost curve to shift upward. The long-run market supply curve for such an increasing cost industry will slope upward to the right.

9. Within the framework of the purely competitive model, firms that efficiently produce and correctly anticipate those goods for which future demand will be most urgent (relative to costs of production) will make profits. Firms that inefficiently produce and incorrectly allocate resources to the production of goods for which future demand turns out to be weak (relative to costs of production) will be penalized with losses. In the short run, firms might make either profits or losses, but in the long run, competitive pressures will eliminate economic profits (and losses).

10. Economists often argue that pure competition leads to ideal economic efficiency because (a) average costs of production are minimized and (b) output is expanded to the level at which the consumer's evaluation of an additional unit of a good is just equal to its marginal cost.

CRITICAL ANALYSIS QUESTIONS

*1. Farmers are often heard to complain about the high cost of machinery, labor, and fertilizer, suggesting that these costs drive down their profit rate. Does it follow that if, for example, the price of fertilizer fell by 10 percent, farming (a highly competitive industry with low barriers to entry) would be more profitable? Explain.

*2. If the firms in a competitive industry are making short-run profits, what will happen to the market price in the long run? Explain.

3. What factors will cause the supply curve for a product to slope upward in the long run? Be specific.

4. A sales tax collected from the seller, will shift the firm's cost curves upward. Outline the impact of a sales tax within the framework of the competitive model. Use diagrams to indicate both the short-run and long-run impact of the tax. Who will bear the burden of the sales tax?

5. "In the model of perfect competition, there is no room for the entrepreneuer." How would you defend this position? Is it always true? Is it true in equilibrium?

*6. "In long-run equilibrium for a competitive industry, the firms in the industry are just able to cover their cost of production. Economic profit is zero. Therefore, if there were a reduction in demand causing prices to go down even a little bit, all of the firms in the industry would be driven out of business." Evaluate.

7. "Under pure competition, the average total cost of production determines the price of each good." True or false?

*8. Within the framework of the pure competition model, how will an unanticipated increase in demand for a product affect each of the following in a market that was initially in long-run equilibrium?
   a. the short-run market price of the product.
   b. industry output in the short run.
   c. profitability in the short run.
   d. the long-run market price in the industry.

*Asterisk denotes questions for which answers are given in Appendix C, Selected Answers.

e. industry output in the long run.

f. profitability in the long run.

*9. Suppose that the development of a new drought-resistant hybrid seed corn leads to a 50 percent increase in the average yield per acre without increasing the cost to the farmers who use the new technology. If the conditions in the corn production industry are approximated by the pure competition model, what will happen to the following:

a. the price of corn.

b. the profitability of corn farmers who quickly adopt the new technology.

c. the profitability of corn farmers who are slow to adopt the new technology.

d. the price of soybeans, a substitute product for corn.

10. Indicate whether the following statements are true or false:

a. "If the demand for a product is inelastic, a technological change that reduces the production cost of the good will lead to a reduction in the expenditures on the good."

b. "If the demand for a product is inelastic, a reduction in the good's cost of production will reduce the total utility derived from the good."

*11. Explain why the firms in a highly competitive industry are unable to earn long term economic profit. Since long-run economic profit in a competitive industry is absent, does it follow that profits and losses are unimportant in industries that are competitive? Why or why not?

12. "In a competitive market, if a business operator produces efficiently—that is, if the cost of producing the good is minimized—the operator will be able to make at least a normal profit." True or false?

13. During the summer of 1988, drought conditions throughout much of the United States substantially reduced the size of the corn, wheat, and soybean crops, three commodities for which demand is inelastic. Use the competitive model to determine how the drought affected (a) grain prices, (b) revenue from the three crops, and (c) the profitability of farming.

*14. Suppose that the government of a large city levies a 5 percent sales tax on hotel rooms. How will the tax affect (a) prices of hotel rooms, (b) the profits of hotel owners, and (c) gross (including the tax) expenditures on hotel rooms.

15. Explain why the market supply curve is slightly less elastic than the summation of the marginal cost curves for the firms in a competitive industry.

*16. "Competition is never between the buyer and the seller. It is always between a seller and other sellers (both actual and potential) and a buyer and other buyers (both actual and potential)." True or false?

*17. The following table presents the expected cost and revenue data for the Tucker Tomato Farm. The Tuckers produce tomatoes in a greenhouse and sell them wholesale in a purely competitive market. (a) Fill in the firm's marginal cost, average variable cost, average total cost, and profit schedules. (b) If the Tuckers are profit maximizers, how many tomatoes should they produce when the market price is $500 per ton? Indicate their profits. (c) Indicate the firm's output level and maximum profit if the market price of tomatoes increases to $550 per ton. (d) How many units would the Tucker Tomato Farm produce if the price of tomatoes declined to $450? Indicate the firm's profits. Should the firm continue in business? Explain.

Cost and Revenue Schedules—Tucker Tomato Farm, Inc.

Output (Tons per Month)	Total Cost	Price per Ton	Marginal Cost	Average Variable Cost	Average Total Cost	Profits (Monthly)
0	$1000	$500	—	—	—	—
1	1200	500	————	————	————	————
2	1350	500	————	————	————	————
3	1550	500	————	————	————	————
4	1900	500	————	————	————	————
5	2300	500	————	————	————	————
6	2750	500	————	————	————	————
7	3250	500	————	————	————	————
8	3800	500	————	————	————	————
9	4400	500	————	————	————	————
10	5150	500	————	————	————	————

9

MONOPOLY AND HIGH BARRIERS TO ENTRY

Competitive industries have their monopolistic aspects; monopolized industries have their competitive aspects. The most that can be said today is that competition is far too common to justify the thesis that the competitive system is approaching extinction, and that monopoly is far too common to justify its treatment as an occasional exception to the general rule.[1]

Clair Wilcox

CHAPTER FOCUS

■ What, exactly, is a monopoly? What are the barriers that allow monopoly to exist?

■ What price will a monopolist set?

■ Why is monopoly a problem?

■ What are the reasons for trying to regulate monopolies? What problems occur when we do regulate monopolies?

■ In dealing with monopoly, what are the policy alternatives, and what can we expect from each one?

■ What impact does dynamic change have on a monopoly situation?

In the last chapter, we analyzed pure competition, a hypothetical market structure characterized by numerous sellers. We now turn to the other extreme of market structure—pure monopoly. The word "monopoly," derived from two Greek words, means "single seller." When only a single seller for a product exists, the firm will exert more control over price and output. This does not mean that the monopolist is completely free from competitive pressures. As Professor Wilcox implies, varying degrees of competition are present even under conditions of monopoly.

The absence of numerous rivals and the existence of substantial barriers restricting the entry of rivals will influence the nature of a market. The profit-maximizing price for a monopolist, the impact of monopoly on the efficiency of a market, and the potential gains from policies designed to improve the outcome of a market influenced by monopoly, will be discussed in this chapter.

DEFINING MONOPOLY

Monopoly: A market structure characterized by a single seller of a well-defined product for which there are no good substitutes and by high barriers to the entry of any other firms into the market for that product.

We will define **monopoly** as a market structure characterized by (a) high barriers to entry and (b) a single seller of a well-defined product for which there are no good substitutes. Even this definition is ambiguous because "high barriers" and "good substitutes" are both relative terms. Are the barriers to entry into the automobile or steel industries high? Many observers would argue that they are. After all, it would take a great deal of financial capital to compete successfully in these industries. However, there are no *legal* restraints that prevent an entrepreneur from producing automobiles or steel. If price is well above cost, so that substantial profits are being made, it should not be difficult to find the necessary investment capital. After all, even a tiny portion of the investors who make up the capital market would be enough to finance a full-scale steel plant, for example. And profit, it seems, draws investment capital the way honey draws bears. Then again, would the new factory, perhaps one making cars, require a new and extensive marketing network? Or could other sales outlets be enticed into carrying the new competitor? Barriers to entry are like expected profits: in both cases, assessing their size requires subjective judgments.

"Good substitutes" is also a subjective term. There is always some substitutability among products, even those produced by a monopolist. Is a letter a good substitute for telephone communication? For some purposes, legal correspondence for example, a letter is a very good substitute. In other cases, when the speed of communication and immediacy of response are important, telephone communication has a tremendous advantage over letter writing. Are there any good substitutes for electricity? Most of the known substitutes for electric lighting (candles, oil lamps, and battery lights, for example) are inferior to electric lights. Natural gas, fuel oil, and wood, though, are often excellent substitutes for electric heating.

Monopoly, then, is always a matter of degree. Pure monopoly, like pure competition, is a rare phenomenon. Nevertheless, there are two reasons why it is important to understand how markets work under pure monopoly. First, the mo-

[1]Clair Wilcox, *Competition and Monopoly in American Industry,* Monograph no. 21, Temporary National Economic Committee, Investigation of Concentration of Economic Power, 76th Congress, 3rd session (Washington, D.C.: U.S. Government Printing Office, 1940), p. 8.

nopoly model will help us understand markets dominated by only a few sellers. A dominant firm in an industry often has a tendency to behave like a monopolist. When there are only two or three producers in a market, rather than competing with each other they may seek to collude and thus together behave like a monopoly. Second, there usually is only a single producer in a few important industries. Local telephone and electricity services provide examples. The monopoly model will illuminate the operation of such markets.

BARRIERS TO ENTRY

What makes it difficult for potential competitors to enter a market? Three factors are of particular importance.

1. Legal Barriers. Legal barriers are the oldest and most effective method of protecting a business firm from potential competitors. Kings once granted exclusive business rights to favored citizens or groups. Today, governments continue to establish barriers, restricting the right to buy and sell goods. To compete in the communications industry in the United States (for example, in order to operate a radio or television station), one must obtain a government franchise. The Post Office, a government corporation, is granted the exclusive right to deliver first-class mail, although this is sometimes challenged. Potential private competitors are eliminated by law. Shops at airports frequently have exclusive franchises, as do local public utilities in most areas of the United States.

Licensing, a process by which one obtains permission from the government to enter a specific occupation or business, often limits entry. In many states, a person must obtain a license before operating a liquor store, barbershop, taxicab, funeral home, or drugstore. Sometimes, these licenses cost little and are designed to ensure certain minimum standards. In other cases, they are expensive and designed primarily to limit competition.

Patent: The grant of an exclusive right to use a specific process or produce a specific product for a period of time (17 years in the United States).

Another legal barrier to entry is a **patent,** which grants the owner a legal monopoly on the commercial use of a newly invented product or process for a limited period of time; 17 years in the United States. Once a patent has been granted, other persons are prevented from using the procedures or producing the product unless they obtain permission from the patent holder. Essentially, the patent system is designed to permit inventors to reap the benefits of their inventions. Nevertheless, patents are often used to restrict the entry of rivals into a broad market area. For example, Polaroid's control over patent rights enabled it to exclude all rivals from the instant-picture market for years, until Eastman Kodak developed a new process. Polaroid went to court, however, and forced Eastman Kodak to withdraw from that market. The new process was judged to be an infringement on Polaroid's patent.

2. Economies of Scale. In some industries, a firm is unable to produce at a low cost unless it is quite large, both in absolute terms and relative to the market. Under these circumstances, economies of scale prevent small firms from entering the market, building a reputation, and competing effectively with large firms. The existing firms are thus protected from potential competitors.

3. Control over an Essential Resource. If a single firm has sole control over a resource essential for entry into an industry, it can eliminate potential competitors. An example often cited is the Aluminum Company of America, which before the

Second World War controlled the world's known bauxite supply. Without this critical raw material, potential competitors could not produce aluminum. However, such situations are rare and seldom last long if they are profitable.

New technology, mineral exploration, and other ways to exploit profitable situations are always sought. Over time, they are usually found. Nevertheless, let us move on to see what happens when at least a temporary monopoly is gained.

THE HYPOTHETICAL MODEL OF MONOPOLY

Suppose you invent, patent, and produce a microwave device that locks the hammer of any firearm in the immediate area. This fabulous invention can be used to immobilize potential robbers or hijackers. Since you own the exclusive patent right to the device, you are not concerned about a competitive supplier in the foreseeable future. Although other products are competitive with your invention, they are poor substitutes. In short, you are a monopolist.

What price should you charge for your product? Like the purely competitive firm, you will want to expand output as long as marginal revenue exceeds marginal cost. Unlike the purely competitive firm, however, you will face a downward-sloping demand curve. Since you are the only firm in the industry, the industry demand curve will coincide with your demand curve. Consumers will buy less of your product at a higher price. At high prices, even a monopolist will have few customers.

TOTAL REVENUE, MARGINAL REVENUE, AND ELASTICITY OF DEMAND

Since the demand curve of a monopolist slopes downward, there are two conflicting influences on total revenue when the seller reduces price in order to expand output and sales. As Exhibit 1 illustrates, the resultant increase in sales (from q_1 to q_2) will, by itself, add to the revenue of the monopolist. But since the price reduction also applies to units that *would have been* sold at a higher price (P_1, rather than the lower price P_2) this factor by itself would cause a *reduction* in total revenue for the monopolist. Together, the higher quantity and the lower price produce a change in total revenue (the marginal revenue associated with the added sales) that is smaller than the price at which the added units are sold.

The marginal revenue derived from additional sales by a monopolist will be less than the sales price. Thus, as shown in Exhibit 1, the marginal revenue curve of the monopolist will lie inside (below) the demand curve of the firm.[2]

While the demand curve shows the number of units that can be sold at different prices, it also reveals how revenues vary as price and output are altered. Using a straight-line demand curve, Exhibit 2 illustrates how total and marginal revenue are related to elasticity of demand. At very high prices, the sales of the monopolist will be small and demand will tend to be elastic. As price is reduced and output is expanded on the elastic portion of the monopolist's demand curve, total revenue will rise. Marginal revenue will be positive. Suppose the monopolist charged $15 for a product and sold 25 units, yielding a total revenue of $375. If the monopolist cut the price to $10, sales would expand to 50 units. Total revenue would rise to

---

[2] For a straight-line demand curve, the marginal revenue curve will bisect any line parallel to the *x*-axis. For example, the MR curve will divide the line P_2F into two equal parts, P_2E and EF.

EXHIBIT 1

The Effect of Increases in
Sales on Revenue

When a firm faces a downward-sloping demand curve, a price reduction that increases sales
will exert two conflicting influences on total revenue. First, total revenue will rise because of an
increase in the number of units sold (from q_1 to q_2). However, revenue losses from the lower
price (P_2) on units that could have been sold at a higher price (P_1) will at least partially offset
the additional revenues due to increased sales. Therefore, the marginal revenue curve will lie
inside the firm's demand curve.

$500. A price reduction from $15 to $10 would thus increase the total revenue of
the monopolist.

Consider the output rate at which elasticity of demand is equal to unity. At
that point, total revenue reaches its maximum. Marginal revenue is equal to zero.
As price falls below $10 into the inelastic portion of the monopolist's demand
curve, total revenue declines as output is expanded. For this range of price and
output, marginal revenue will be negative. Thus, marginal revenue goes from
positive to negative as the elasticity of demand changes from elastic to inelastic
(at output 50 of Exhibit 2).

This analysis has clear implications. For a monopolist operating on the inelastic portion of its demand curve, a price increase would lead to more total
revenue *and* less total cost (since fewer units would be produced and sold). Because of this, we would never expect a profit-maximizing monopolist to push the
sales of a product into the range in which the product's demand curve becomes
inelastic.

THE PROFIT-MAXIMIZING OUTPUT

Both costs and revenues must be considered when we analyze the profit-maximizing decision rule for the monopolist. The profit-maximizing monopolist will continue expanding output until marginal revenue equals marginal cost. The price at
which that output level can be sold is given by the demand curve of the monopolist.

Exhibit 3 provides a graphic illustration of profit maximization. The monop-

EXHIBIT 2

Price, Total Revenue, and Marginal Revenue of a Monopolist

In the elastic portion of the monopolist's demand curve (prices greater than $10), a price reduction will be associated with rising total revenue (frame b) and positive marginal revenue. At unitary elasticity (output of 50 units), total revenue will reach a maximum. When the monopolist's demand curve is inelastic (output beyond 50 units), lower prices will lead to declining total revenue and negative marginal revenue.

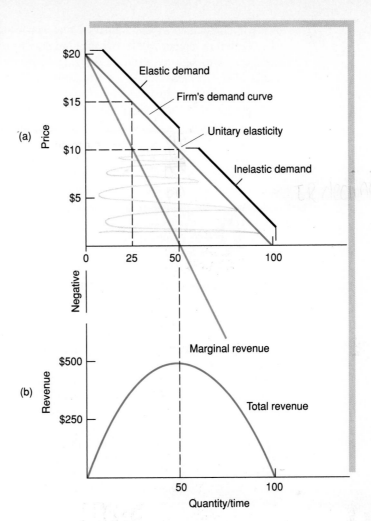

EXHIBIT 3

The Short-Run Price and Output of a Monopolist

The monopolist will reduce price and expand output as long as MR exceeds MC. Output Q will result. When price exceeds average cost at any output level, profit will accrue at that output level.

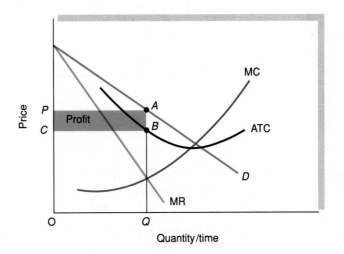

olist will continue to expand output as long as marginal revenue exceeds marginal cost. Therefore, output will be expanded to Q, where MR = MC. The monopolist will be able to sell the profit-maximizing output Q for a price indicated by the height of the demand curve. At any output less than Q, the benefits (marginal revenue) of producing the *additional* units will exceed their costs. The monopolist will gain by expanding output. For any output greater than Q, the monopolist's costs of producing *additional* units will be greater than the benefits (marginal revenue). Production of such units will reduce profits.

Exhibit 3 also depicts the profits of a monopolist. At output Q, the monopolist would charge price P. Price times the number of units sold yields the firm's total revenue ($PAQO$). The firm's total cost would be $CBQO$, the average per unit cost multiplied by the number of units sold. The firm's profits are merely total revenue less total cost, the shaded area of Exhibit 3.

Even though competitive and monopolistic firms alike expand output until MR = MC, there is one important difference. For the competitive firm, price is always equal to marginal revenue, so that price will also equal marginal cost when profit is maximized. For the monopolist, however, price is always greater than marginal revenue, so that when profit is maximized and MR = MC, price will exceed marginal cost. This difference has implications for efficiency in the market, which we will discuss later in this chapter.

Exhibit 4 provides a numeric illustration of profit-maximizing decision-making. At low output rates, marginal revenue exceeds marginal cost. The monopolist will continue expanding output as long as MR is greater than MC. Thus, an output rate of eight units per day will be chosen. Given the demand for the product, the monopolist can sell eight units at a price of $17.25 each. Total revenue will be $138, compared to a total cost of $108.50. The monopolist will make a profit of $29.50. The profit rate will be smaller at all other output rates. For

EXHIBIT 4 ■ Profit Maximization for a Monopolist						
Rate of Output (per Day) (1)	Price (per Unit) (2)	Total Revenue (1) × (2) (3)	Total Cost (per Day) (4)	Profit (3) − (4) (5)	Marginal Cost (6)	Marginal Revenue (7)
0	—	—	$ 50.00	$ − 50.00	—	—
1	$25.00	$ 25.00	60.00	− 35.00	$10.00	$ 25.00
2	24.00	48.00	69.00	− 21.00	9.00	23.00
3	23.00	69.00	77.00	− 8.00	8.00	21.00
4	22.00	88.00	84.00	4.00	7.00	19.00
5	21.00	105.00	90.50	14.50	6.50	17.00
6	19.75	118.50	96.75	21.75	6.25	13.50
7	18.50	129.50	102.75	26.75	6.00	11.00
8	17.25	138.00	108.50	29.50	5.75	8.50
9	16.00	144.00	114.75	29.25	6.25	6.00
10	14.75	147.50	121.25	26.25	6.50	3.50
11	13.50	148.50	128.00	20.50	6.75	1.00
12	12.25	147.00	135.00	12.00	7.00	− 1.50
13	11.00	143.00	142.25	.75	7.25	− 4.00

example, if the monopolist reduces the price to $16 in order to sell nine units per day, revenue will increase by $6. However, the marginal cost of producing the ninth unit is $6.25. Since the cost of producing the ninth unit is greater than the revenue it brings in, profits will decline.

Can the monopolist gain by *raising* the price, to $18.50 for example? It may surprise some that the answer is no. If price is increased to $18.50, only seven units will be sold, for a total revenue of $129.50. The cost of producing seven unit will be $102.75. The output of seven units will generate a profit of $26.75, less than could be attained at the lower price ($17.25) and larger output (eight). The highest price is not always the best price for the monopolist. Sometimes a price reduction will increase the firm's total revenue more than its total cost.

MARKET FORCES AND THE MONOPOLIST

Can market forces eliminate the profits of a monopolist? It is possible—technological change, for example, may provide low-cost substitutes for consumers. High barriers to market entry, though, insulate a monopolist from direct competitive pressures, which would otherwise lead to expanded output and reduced prices.

Does this mean that a monopolist can be assured of economic profit? Not necessarily. A monopolist's ability to make profits is limited by the demand for whatever product is produced. In some cases, even a monopolist may be unable to sell for a profit. For example, there are thousands of clever, patented items that are never produced because demand–cost conditions are not favorable. Exhibit 5 illustrates this possibility. When the average cost curve of a monopolist is always above its demand curve, economic losses will result. Even a monopolist will not want to operate under these conditions. If market conditions are expected to improve, the monopolist will produce output Q (at which MR = MC) and charge price P, *operating in the short run* as long as variable cost can be covered. If the loss-producing conditions persist, however, the monopolist will discontinue production.

EXHIBIT 5

When a Monopolist Incurs Losses

Even a monopolist will incur short-run losses if the average cost curve lies above the demand curve.

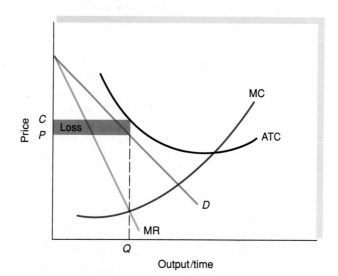

REALITY AND THE MONOPOLY MODEL

Price Searcher: A seller with imperfect information, facing a downward sloping demand curve, who tries to find the price that maximizes profit.

Thus far, we have proceeded as if monopolists always knew exactly what their revenue and cost curves looked like. Of course, this not true in the real world. A monopolist cannot be sure of the demand conditions for a product. Demand curves frequently shift, and choices must be made without the benefit of perfect knowledge.

The monopolist is, in fact, a **price searcher**; a seller trying to find the price at which profit will be maximized. How many sales will be lost if the price is raised? How many sales will be added if the price is lowered? Trial and error are often necessary to learn the answers. A firm that is a price searcher will price its produce on the basis of what it *expects* to happen if the price is changed.

The revenue and cost data illustrated in Exhibits 3, 4, and 5 might be thought of as representing *expected* revenues and costs associated with various output levels. A monopolist, of course, seldom calculates what we have called demand, marginal revenue, and cost curves. Even so, the same questions are asked: Would a lower price add more to revenue than to cost? Would a higher price decrease revenue more than cost? The profit-maximizing price is usually just approximated. However, the monopolist who *is* maximizing profits acts *as if* MR and MC had been calculated, so our model of monopoly shows what a profit-maximizing monopolist is trying to do.

PRICE DISCRIMINATION

3 conditions to Price Dis.
① downsloping Dem. Cur
② two identable groups
③ Reselling Prevented

Price Discrimination: A practice whereby a seller charges different consumers different prices for the same product or service.

... that all sellers of a product will charge each customer ... es, though, sellers can increase their revenues (and prof- ... t prices to different groups of consumers. This practice is called **price discrimination**.

If price discrimination is going to be beneficial to a seller, three conditions must be met. First, the firm must confront a downward-sloping demand curve for its product. A monopolist will meet this criterion; a pure competitor will not. Second, there must be at least two identifiable groups of consumers whose price elasticities of demand for the firm's product differ. The seller must be able to identify and separate these consumers at a low cost. Third, the sellers must be able to prevent the customers who are charged a low price from reselling the product to customers who are charged higher prices.

Exhibit 6 illustrates why sellers can sometimes gain from price discrimination. Here, there are two groups of customers for the firm's product. The demand of the first group, frame a, is less elastic than the demand of the second group, frame b. In each market, the seller will maximize profit by equating marginal cost and marginal revenue. The best price for the group with the less elastic demand is P_a, associated with the output rate at which $MR_a = MC$. Since the amount purchased by this group is relatively less sensitive to an increase in price, the higher price (P_a) will generate more revenues (and profit) from this group. In contrast, the demand of the second group, frame b, is more sensitive to price. When the price charged the second group decreases, the group purchases substantially more units. The lower price P_b thus maximizes the profit from this group.

What easily identifiable characteristics might be linked to the customer's elasticity of demand? Factors such as age, income, and sex will sometimes influence elasticity of demand. For example, the demand of children for movies, airline

Price Discrimination

Sometimes the demand of some consumers is less elastic than that of other conusmers. When this is true, a firm may be able to gain by segmenting its market and charging a higher price to the consumers with a less-elastic demand (a) and a lower price to consumers whose demand is more elastic (b).

(a) Consumers with less elastic demand

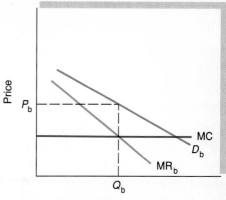

(b) Consumers with more elastic demand

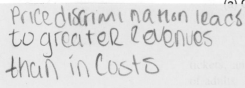

Price discrimination leads to greater revenues than in costs

...ball games is often believed to be more elastic than the demand of adults.

Can you think of any example of price discrimination? Airlines often offer discount fares to individuals willing to travel during off-peak hours, make reservations well in advance, or travel with another person paying a full fare. The demand of these consumers is thought to be more elastic than that of other customers, such as business travelers. Because of this, the group with the more elastic demand is given the discount, while other customers are required to pay the full fare. Why do the producers of professional journals usually charge individual subscribers lower rates than libraries? They generate more revenue by charging higher prices to subscribers with an inelastic demand (libraries). Why are senior citizens often charged lower prices for attending movies and baseball games? Again, price discrimination apparently leads to greater increases in revenues than in costs.

A seller need not be a pure monopolist to gain from price discrimination. Any firm that faces a downward-sloping demand curve for its product may employ the technique. In fact, differential prices accompanying discounts and economy fares are often indicative of intense rivalry among firms. We introduce the concept while discussing monopoly merely to illustrate the general point.

DEFECTS AND PROBLEMS OF MONOPOLY

> Monopolists, by keeping the market constantly understocked, by never fully supplying the effectual demand, sell their commodities much above the natural price, and raise their emoluments, whether they consist of wages or profit, greatly above their natural rate.[3]

What types of problems arise under monopoly? Can public policy improve resource allocation in markets characterized by monopoly?

---

[3]Adam Smith, *An Inquiry into the Nature and Causes of the Wealth of Nations* (1776; Cannan's ed., Chicago: University of Chicago Press, 1976), p. 69.

"And though in 1969, as in previous years, your company had to contend with spiralling labor costs, exorbitant interest rates, and unconscionable government interference, management was able once more, through a combination of deceptive marketing practices, false advertising, and price fixing, to show a profit which, in all modesty, can only be called excessive."

Drawing by Lorenz © 1970 The New Yorker Magazine, Inc.

FOUR DEFECTS OF MONOPOLY

From Adam Smith's time to the present, economists have generally considered monopoly a necessary evil at best. There are four major reasons for this view.

1. *Monopoly Severely Limits the Options Available to Consumers*. If you do not like the food at a local restaurant, you can go to another restaurant. If you do not like the wares of a local department store, you can buy good substitutes somewhere else. The competition of rivals protects the consumer from the arbitrary behavior of a single seller. What, though, are your alternatives if you do not like the *local* telephone service? You can send a letter or deliver your message in person, or you can write to your legislative representative and complain. These are not very satisfactory alternatives to the service of the monopolist, however. If the monopolist "pushes you around," you often have no feasible alternative but to accept poor service, rude treatment, or high prices.

In the absence of monopoly, the consumer can buy a product either from firm A or from a competitor. In the presence of monopoly, the option is to buy from the monopolist or do without. This reduction in the options available to the consumer greatly reduces the consumer's ability to discipline monopolists.

2. *Monopoly Results in Allocative Inefficiency*. Allocative efficiency requires that an activity be undertaken when it generates additional benefits that exceed its added costs. This requires that a firm expand output as long as price exceeds marginal cost. A profit-maximizing monopolist, however, would restrict output below this level. The monopolist will expand output only to the point where marginal revenue is equal to marginal cost, an output rate less than that at which price is equal to marginal cost.

The logic of this criticism is pictured in Exhibit 7. Demand is a measure of

EXHIBIT 7

Under-stocking in the Market

A monopolist will produce only output Q_m, even though Q_i is best for the entire community. If output were expanded from Q_m to Q_i, the benefits *to the community* would exceed the costs by *ABC*. However, since the profit of the monopolist is a maximum at Q_m, units beyond Q_m will not be produced. What is best for the monopolist (output Q_m) conflicts with what is best for the community (output Q_i).

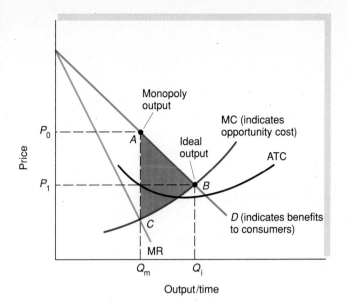

the degree to which consumers value additional units of a product. The marginal cost curve represents the opportunity cost of the resources used to produce the additional units. Ideally, economic efficiency would require output to be expanded as long as the height of the demand curve exceeded that of the marginal cost curve. From the viewpoint of the entire community, output level Q_i would be best.

The monopolist, however, would produce only Q_m units, the profit-maximizing output rate. If output were expanded beyond Q_m to Q_i, how much would consumers gain? The area under the demand curve, ABQ_iQ_m, reveals the answer. How much would it cost the monopolist to produce these units? CBQ_iQ_m reflects the monopolist's costs. The benefits of expanding output from Q_m to Q_i exceed the costs by *ABC*. The monopolist, though, would not produce these additional units because they would add less to the monopoly's revenues (assuming that all consumers are charged the same price) than to its costs. Potential gains represented by *ABC* are lost under monopoly. As Adam Smith observed 200 years ago, the monopolist understocks the market and charges prices that are too high.

3. *Under Monopoly, Profits and Losses Do Not Properly Induce Firms to Enter and to Exit from Industries.* When barriers to entry are low, profits induce firms to produce goods for which consumers are willing (because of the expected benefits) to pay prices sufficient to cover costs of production. Inefficient firms face competition and are unable to cover their costs. They are forced to either improve efficiency or leave the market. Losses also constrain firms from producing goods for which consumers are not willing to cover costs of production. Profits and losses direct resources into those activities for which consumer valuation is highest.

For the monopolist, profits play a smaller role because entry barriers are high. The discipline of close competition is missing. Even though losses will induce exit from the market, when costs are high relative to demand, the ability of profits and losses to discipline firms under monopoly is weakened. Firms that are earning profits, or that are inefficient, may nonetheless be protected from potential new competitors by barriers to entry. Their benefits are enjoyed at the consumer's expense.

4. *Legal Protection for Monopolies Encourages Rent-Seeking Activities.* We pointed out in Chapter 4 that governmental policies can be used to transfer income to organized groups and individuals. If a legally protected monopoly can raise the rate of profit above normal, we should expect potential monopolists to seek to establish such monopolies, and to be willing to compete, if necessary, to obtain the monopoly rights.

Gordon Tullouck, in a classic 1967 article,[4] pointed out that when the government restricts entry into a market, potential monopolists will compete for exclusive franchises or for other such awards of monopoly power. For example, suppose the government issues a license providing a seller with the exclusive right to sell liquor in a specific market. If this grant of monopoly power permits the licensee to earn monopoly profit, potential suppliers will expend resources trying to convince government officials that they should be granted the license. The potential monopolists will lobby government officials, make political contributions, hire representatives to do consulting studies, and undertake other action designed to convince politicians and their appointees that they can best "serve the public interest" as a monopoly supplier. Any firm that expects its rent-seeking activities to be successful will be willing to spend up to the present value of the future expected monopoly profits, if necessary, to obtain the monopoly protection. Other suppliers, of course, may also be willing to invest in rent-seeking activities. When several suppliers believe they can win, the total expenditures of all firms on rent-seeking activities may actually consume resources worth more than the economic profit expected from the monopoly enterprise.

From an efficiency standpoint, rent-seeking activities waste resources. Thus, the major social cost of legal monopolies may well be the rent-seeking activities they encourage.

WHEN CAN A MONOPOLIZED INDUSTRY BE COMPETITIVE?

The most serious problems raised by a monopoly would be avoided if the monopolist faced the threat of rivals producing the same product or even close substitutes. The presence of competitors would prevent independent firms from restricting output and raising prices.

Why not break up the monopoly into several rival units, substituting competition for monopoly? If it were not for economies of scale, this would be a very good strategy.

Exhibit 8 compares competition and monopoly, assuming that economies of scale are unimportant in the industry. The minimum-cost output conditions for purely competitive firms thus would not differ from those of monopolists. If the industry were purely competitive, price would be determined by supply and demand. As Exhibit 8a illustrates, under these conditions, competition would drive price down to P_c in the long run. An industry output of Q_c would result. The market price would just equal the *marginal* opportunity costs of production.

In contrast, if the industry were monopolized, the profit-maximizing monopolist would equate marginal revenue with marginal cost (Exhibit 8b). This would

---

[4]See Gordon Tullock, "The Welfare Costs of Tariffs, Monopolies, and Theft," *Western Economic Journal* 5 (June 1967), pp. 224–232.

EXHIBIT 8

Pure Competition and
Pure Monopoly in the
Absence of Economies of
Scale

(a) Pure competition   **(b) Pure monopoly**

Here we assume that a product can be produced by either numerous small firms or a monopolist at the same average total and marginal costs. When there are no cost disadvantages for small-scale production, competition serves to reduce price. For a purely competitive industry (a), supply and demand would dictate price P_c. The firms would just be able to cover their cost. If all the firms merged into a monopoly and *cost conditions remained the same*, the monopolist would restrict output to Q_m (where MC would equal MR). Price would rise to P_m.

lead to an output level of Q_m. The monopolist would charge P_m, a price higher than would exist in a competitive industry. When economies of scale are unimportant, imposition of competitive conditions on a monopolized industry would result in lower prices, a larger output, and improved economic efficiency.

ECONOMIES OF SCALE AND NATURAL MONOPOLY

Unfortunately, it is often unrealistic to expect similar cost conditions for pure competition and monopoly. Economies of scale may be the reason that certain industries tend to be monopolized. If economies of scale are important, larger firms will have lower per unit cost than smaller rivals. Sometimes economies of scale may be so important that per unit cost of production will be lowest when the entire output of the industry is produced by a single firm. In the absence of government intervention, the "natural" tendency will then be toward monopoly, because increases in firm size through merger, or "survival of the fittest," will lead to lower per unit cost.

Natural Monopoly: A market situation in which the average costs of production continually decline with increased output. Therefore, average costs of production will be lowest when a single large firm produces the entire output demanded.

Exhibit 9 depicts the **natural monopoly** case. The long-run average cost in the industry declines and eventually crosses the demand curve. To take full advantage of the economies of scale, given the demand for the product, the total output of the industry would have to be produced by a single firm. If the firm were an unregulated monopolist, it would produce output Q_m and charge price P_m. The firm would realize economic profits, because average cost would be less than price at the profit-maximizing output level. It would be very difficult for any firm to begin to compete with the natural monopolist; initially, while the new competitor was still small, it would have very high costs of production and would be unable to make profits at price P_m. The "natural" monopoly conditions of the industry would act as an entry barrier to potential competitors.

Therefore, when "natural" monopoly exists, a "competitive" market struc-

Monopoly and
Competition with
Economies of Scale

When economies of scale are
important, efforts to impose a
competitive market structure are
self-defeating. For an industry
with cost (and demand) curves
like those indicated here, prices
(and costs) would be lower
under monopoly than if there
were ten competitors of size Q_c.

ture will be both costly and difficult to maintain. Suppose the output of an industry
were divided among ten firms of size Q_c (see Exhibit 9). These small firms would
have per unit average costs of P_c. Even if they charged a price equal to their
average cost, the price would be higher than the monopolistic price P_m. In addition, since firms larger than Q_c would always have lower per unit costs, there
would be a strong tendency for firms to merge and become larger. Imposition of
a competitive structure would be self-defeating in cases in which monopoly "naturally" exists because of the economies of scale.

In what situations are substantial economies of scale present? It is difficult for
an observer to know, especially when technology is constantly changing. Existing
and potential suppliers sometimes have different opinions as to the importance of
scale economies, at a given time and place. However, it is commonly assumed
that delivery of local telephone service, water, and electricity exhibit natural monopoly conditions. If there were several telephone companies operating in the
same area, each with its own lines and transmission equipment, the resulting duplication would be costly. In such industries, a large number of firms might not
be feasible.

POLICY ALTERNATIVES TO NATURAL MONOPOLY

When monopoly or near monopoly results from economies of scale, there are
three policy alternatives. First, monopolists could be permitted to operate freely.
We have already pointed out that this option limits consumer choice and results
in a higher product price (and smaller output) than is consistent with ideal economic efficiency. Second, government regulation could be imposed on the monopolists. Third, the government could completely take over production in the
industry. Government operation is an alternative to private monopoly. Let us take
a closer look at the last two alternatives, and compare them with private monopoly.

**REGULATING THE
MONOPOLIST**

Can government regulation improve the allocative efficiency of unregulated monopoly? In theory, the answer to this question is clearly yes. Government regulation *can* force the monopoly to reduce its price; at the lower government-imposed
price ceiling, the monopolist will voluntarily produce a larger output.

EXHIBIT 10

Regulation of a Monopolist

If unregulated, a profit-maximizing monopolist with the costs indicated here would produce Q_0 units and charge P_0. If a regulatory agency forced the monopolist to reduce price to P_1, the monopolist would expand output to Q_1. Ideally, we would like output to be expanded to Q_2, where $P =$ MC, but regulatory agencies usually do not attempt to keep prices as low as P_2. Can you explain why?

Exhibit 10 illustrates why ideal government price regulation would improve resource allocation. The profit-maximizing monopolist sets price at P_0 and produces output Q_0, where MR = MC. Consumers, however, would value *additional* units more than the opportunity cost. How can the regulatory agency improve on the situation that would result from unregulated monopoly?

1. Average Cost Pricing. If a regulatory agency forces the monopolist to reduce price to P_1, at which the firm's ATC curve intersects with the market (and firm) demand curve, the monopolist will expand output to Q_1. Since the firm cannot charge a price above P_1, it cannot increase revenues by selling a smaller output at a higher price. Once the price ceiling is instituted, the firm can increase revenues by P_1, and by only P_1, for each unit it sells. The regulated firm's MR is constant at P_1 for all units sold until output is increased to Q_1. Since the firm's MC is less than P_1 (and therefore less than MR), the profit-maximizing, regulated monopolist will expand output from Q_0 to Q_1. The benefits from the consumption of these units (ABQ_1Q_0) clearly exceed their costs (CEQ_1Q_0). Social welfare has improved as a result of the regulative action (we will ignore the impact on the distribution of income). At that output level, revenues are sufficient to cover costs. The firm is making zero economic profit (or "normal" accounting profit).

2. Marginal Cost Pricing. Ideally, since even at the Q_1 output level marginal cost is still less than price, additional welfare gains are possible if output is increased to Q_2. However, if a regulatory agency forced the monopolist to reduce price to P_2 (so that price would equal marginal cost at the output level Q_2), economic losses would result. Even a monopolist, unless subsidized, would not undertake production if the regulatory agency set the price at P_2 or any price below P_1. Usually, problems associated with determining and allocating the necessary subsidy would make this option infeasible.

WHY REGULATION MAY GO ASTRAY

It is not easy to regulate an industry well. The cost-plus orientation toward which pricing methods gravitate weakens incentives for efficiency.[5]

Even though government regulation of monopoly seems capable of improving market results, as in the average cost pricing example above, economic analysis suggests that regulating monopolies will usually not be an ideal solution. Why? As Professor Scherer indicates in the quote above, the lack of incentive to produce at a low cost is important. Information is another factor. Together, the lack of incentives and information form a serious principal-agent problem for regulators who would act on behalf of citizens to control monopoly. Let us look at the various factors that make this such a difficult task.

Lack of Information. In discussing ideal regulation, we assumed that we knew what the firm's ATC, MC, and demand curves looked like. In reality, of course, this would not be the case. The firms themselves have difficulty knowing their costs, and especially their demand curves, with any precision.

Because estimates of demand and marginal costs are difficult to obtain, regulatory agencies usually use profits (or rate of return) as a gauge to determine whether the regulated price is too high or too low. The regulatory agency, guarding the public interest, seeks to impose a "fair" or "normal" rate of return on the firm. If the firm is making profits (that is, an abnormally high rate of return), the price must be higher than P_1 and should be lowered. If the firm is incurring losses (less than the fair or normal rate or return), the regulated price must be less than P_1, and the firm should be allowed to increase price.

The actual existence of profits, though, is not easily identified. Accounting profit, even allowing for a normal rate of profit, is not the same as economic profit. In addition, regulated firms have a definite incentive to adopt reporting techniques and accounting methods that conceal profits. This will make it difficult for a regulatory agency to identify and impose the price consistent with allocative efficiency.

Cost Shifting. When demand is sufficient, the owners of the regulated firm can expect the long-run rate of profit to be essentially fixed regardless of whether efficient management reduces costs or inefficient management allows costs to increase. If costs decrease, the "fair return" rule imposed by the regulatory agency will force a price reduction; if costs increase, the "fair return" rule will allow a price increase. Thus, the *owners* of the regulated firm have less incentive to be concerned about costs than the owners of unregulated firms. Managers will have a freer hand to pursue personal objectives. They will be more likely to fly first-class, entertain lavishly on an expense account, give their relatives and friends good jobs, grant unwarranted wage increases, and in general make decisions that increase costs, but yield personal benefits to the managers. Since monopoly means that buyers do not have a close substitute to turn to, consumers will bear the burden of managerial inefficiency. Normally, wasteful activities would be policed by the owners, but since the firm's rate of return is set by the regulatory agency, the owners have little incentive to be concerned.

---

[5]F. M. Scherer, *Industrial Market Structure and Economic Performance,* 2nd ed. (Boston: Houghton Mifflin, 1980), p. 485.

Exhibit 11 demonstrates the impact of inefficient management. If the firm's costs were effectively policed, average total cost curve ATC_1 would result. Because of production inefficiency, however, the firm's average total cost curve shifts to ATC_2. A regulatory agency, granting the firm a fair return, would then allow a price increase to P_2. Even though P_2 might be less than the unregulated profit-maximizing monopolist would charge, some of the gains of the regulatory policy would be lost to inefficiency.

Alternatively, Exhibit 11 could represent a very different situation. Suppose that the firm's costs previously were ATC_2, but now ATC_1 has been attained due to the firm's innovative and efficient operation. In this case, ironically, if the rate adjustments by the regulatory agency come only after a delay, permitting the firm temporarily to continue charging P_2 despite the lower costs, then there is a beneficial incentive effect. The temporary ability to profit from increased efficiency is a spur to generating more efficiency. In the short run, consumers may have failed to gain immediately from the lower costs, but when innovation and increased efficiency are rewarded, even temporarily, cost-reducing innovation is encouraged.

The Impact of Inflation. Regulatory lag is not always beneficial. Regulation based on normal rate of return will encounter serious difficulties during inflationary times. If the costs of labor, energy resources, and other factors of production rise along with other prices, the cost of producing the product or service of the regulated firm will increase during the period of inflation. A rate structure based on *last year's cost figures* will not permit the firm to earn a normal rate of return. Of course, as its rate of return drops below normal, the firm's case for a rate increase *next* year will be strengthened. If the inflation continues, however, the regulated firm's rate of return will continue to be below normal. The firm will be unable to earn the normal rate of return during inflationary times as long as its rate structure is based on historical costs. As a result of low earnings, the regulated firm will have difficulty raising funds in the capital market. If the normal rate of return on

EXHIBIT 11

Cost Shifting and Monopoly Regulation

Managers of a regulated firm have a greater incentive to follow policies that yield personal gain at the expense of higher cost. With time, this may cause the cost curves of the regulated monopolistic firm to rise, resulting in higher prices even though the monetary profits are still normal.

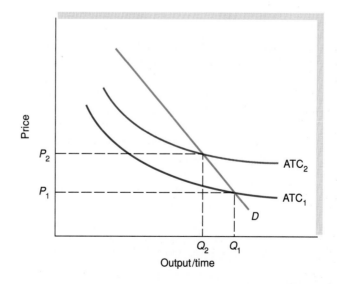

capital is 12 percent, who will want to invest with a firm that is able to earn only 9 percent? Many regulated utilities were caught in precisely this cost-regulated price squeeze as the price of energy and other resources soared during the inflation of the 1970s.

Quality Regulation. It is much easier to regulate product price than to regulate quality. Regulated firms desiring to raise the price of their product can often do so by taking cost-reducing steps that result in quality deterioration. Consider the quality dimension of a seemingly uniform good such as telephone service. The speed at which your call goes through, the likelihood that you will have to redial the desired number, how often your phone is out of order, and how quickly you can get it repaired are included in the quality of telephone service. Since these factors are hard to control, it is extremely difficult for a regulatory agency to impose a price *per constant quality unit*. During inflationary times, regulated firms caught in a cost-regulated price squeeze may be particularly tempted to lower the quality of their product.

Special Interest Effect. The difficulties of government regulation discussed thus far are practical limitations that a regulatory agency, seeking to perform its duties efficiently, would confront. But, the special interest effect suggests that regulatory authorities cannot necessarily be expected to pursue only efficiency. Regulated firms have a strong incentive to see that "friendly," "reasonable" people serve as regulators, and they will invest political and economic resources to this end. Just as rent-seeking activities designed to gain monopoly privileges can be expected, so can activities to influence regulatory decisions.

What about consumer interests? Do you know who serves on the Interstate Commerce Commission or the public utility regulatory boards? Do you know any consumer who voted against a politician because of his or her appointments to a regulatory commission? Chances are that you do not. Consumer interests are widely dispersed and disorganized. Ordinarily, consumers cannot be expected to invest time, resources, votes, and political contributions to ensure that a particular regulatory commission represents their views. The firms that are regulated can, however, be expected to make such investments.[6] Even though the initial stimulus for a regulating agency might come from consumer interests, economic theory suggests that such agencies will eventually reflect the views of the business and labor interests they are supposed to regulate.

THE GOVERNMENT-OPERATED FIRM

Government-operated firms—socialized firms such as the Post Office, the Tennessee Valley Authority, and many local public utilities—present an alternative to both private monopoly and regulation. How do socialized firms operate in the real world? The decision-makers of firms owned by the government are influenced by political and economic factors alike. With the rise of public-sector action, economists have recently expressed renewed interest in the socialized firm.

The ideal theoretical solution is straightforward. The socialized firm should

---

[6]The special interest effect will be weaker when regulatory commissions are elected rather than appointed, allowing the voter to separate this issue from other issues of greater importance.

(a) operate efficiently and (b) set price equal to marginal cost. When cost conditions are like those illustrated by Exhibit 7, the government-operated monopoly firm will ideally expand output to Q_i (where P = MC) and charge price P_1. The firm will make profits that can be channeled into the public treasury. On the other hand, marginal cost pricing may sometimes result in economic losses, requiring a subsidy for the government-operated firm. Exhibit 10 illustrates this possibility. Output should be expanded to Q_2 if the potential marginal welfare gains are to be fully realized. Price P_2 will be charged. The consumer's valuation of the marginal unit (P_2) will equal its marginal cost. Since losses result at this price and output, it will be necessary to subsidize the public enterprise.

This analysis assumes that the socialized firm will both operate efficiently and set the proper price. How realistic are these assumptions? The same "perverse" managerial incentives—incentives to ignore efficiency and pursue personal or professional objectives at the firm's expense—that regulated firms confront also tend to plague the government-operated firm. Professor John Kenneth Galbraith and others have pointed out that there is a principal-agent problem in private corporations. Poorly informed stockholders may be unable to police management inefficiency. Managers may pursue their own objectives at the expense of "owners."

The socialized firm, however, is the extreme case of a principal-agent problem. Unorganized and typically uninformed "owners" (voters) are not in a strong position to assert their ownership rights. No small group of owners can increase its wealth by causing the public enterprise to operate more efficiently. The disorganized owners (voters and taxpayers) will have neither the incentive nor the information to police the managerial decision-making of public enterprises effectively—to reward efficiency and penalize inefficiency. Higher costs result.

In much the same way, special interests also affect incentives—usually in terms of political or group gain—and result in inefficiency. The managers, employees, and specialized users of public enterprises often comprise special interest groups, particularly if the employees are well organized (for example, unionized) for political action. Should the wages of public-sector employees be raised and their working conditions improved? Should comfortable offices, lengthy coffee breaks, and lucrative fringe benefits be provided to employees? Should attractive positions in the public enterprise be provided to the politically faithful? Should management resist pressure to lay off unneeded workers (particularly at election time), abandon unprofitable service areas, and charge users low prices (that is, less than the marginal cost) when the opportunity cost of providing the service is high? On all these issues, the interests of special interest groups involved with public-sector production and its consumption will be in conflict with the interests of the disorganized, uninformed taxpayers. Under these circumstances, economic theory suggests that the views of the special interest groups will usually dominate, even when inefficiency and higher costs result.

Public enterprises can thus be expected to use at least some of their monopoly power, not to benefit the wide cross-section of disorganized taxpayers and consumers, but as a cloak for inefficient operation and actions that advance the personal and political objectives of those who exercise control over the firm. Government ownership, like unregulated monopoly and government regulation, is a less than ideal solution. It is not especially surprising that those who denounce monop-

APPLICATIONS IN ECONOMICS

Product Obsolescence, Monopoly Power, and the Dynamics of Product Development

Many Americans believe that business firms can gain by producing shoddy merchandise that wears out quickly. It is often charged that business firms, over the objections of consumers, produce goods with a short life expectancy so they can sell replacements. Economists have sometimes been at the forefront of those deploring such planned obsolescence.

Yet, a solid majority of economists believe that price indexes overstate the measured rate of inflation because they fail to make an adequate allowance for actual observed improvements in product quality. Why has the quality of products, on the average, risen, if firms have an incentive to produce shoddy, nondurable goods?

Should a Car Last a Lifetime?

There are three important points to keep in mind. First, the production of longer-lasting, higher-quality goods will increase costs. There are no free lunches. A car that lasts 15 years will be more expensive than one with a shorter life expectancy. We should expect consumers to trade off lower prices for more durability. At some point, the greater durability will not be worth the price.

Second, "newness," product variability, and style changes are often valued by consumers. For example, operational reliability aside, many consumers would prefer three differently styled, new-model cars lasting 5 years each to a single car of equal cost that lasts 15 years. *Under these conditions*, the production of

goods with less than maximum life expectancy is perfectly consistent with consumer tastes.[7]

Third, goods engineered to last a relatively short time put their owners a more adaptable position. For example, buyers of new American cars in 1971–1972 preferred large cars. At the time, this made good sense because gasoline prices were low and had been falling in real terms for many years. The value of large, gas-guzzling cars dropped sharply in 1974, though, as gasoline prices soared and spot shortages developed. Years later, in the mid-1980s, the reverse happened: gasoline prices fell sharply, and buyers found it economical to buy cars with more size, comfort, and safety. If those who bought large cars in 1971–1972 and small cars in the early 1980s had paid for years of extra durability, their losses (and the nation's) would have been greater. In a dynamic world, one decision every ten years is less flexible (and, if wrong, more costly to correct) than a decision every five years.

Durability of Products and Producer Choices

In a competitive environment, producers have a strong incentive to cater to the preferences of consumers. Product quality, including durability, is a competitive weapon. If customers really want longer-lasting products, competitive firms have a strong incentive to introduce them. If consumers are willing to pay the price for greater durability, firms that cater to their views can gain. Durability, however, is only one facet of a prod-

uct that is attractive to consumers. Low prices, newness, and product variation are also preferred by many people. Much of our planned obsolescence undoubtedly stems from the choice of consumers to give up some of the former (durability) to have more of the latter.

The Monopolist and the Durability of Products

Will a monopolist ever introduce a new, improved, longer-lasting product, even if the new product is expected to drive the existing profitable product off the market? Strange as it may seem, a monopolist will introduce the new product if two conditions are met.

1. The product must be a genuine improvement—it must give the consumer more service per dollar of opportunity cost (to the monopolist) than the monopolist's current product.

2. The monopolist must be able to enforce property rights over gains from the new product. A patent preventing others from copying the innovative idea serves this purpose.

If these two conditions are met, the monopolist will be able to price the new product such that it will be profitable to introduce, even though it may eventually replace the monopolist's current product line. Two examples will help to clarify this point.

Super Sharp: The Better Blade

Suppose Super Sharp Razor, Inc., has a monopoly on razor blades, which sell for 5 cents and give one week of comfortable shaves. Currently, Super Sharp makes a 3-cent profit (return above opportunity cost) on each blade. Assume the firm discovers (and quickly patents) a blade made with the same machines at the same cost but with a slightly different metal alloy.[8] It gives two weeks of comfortable shaves instead of one. Will the firm market the new blade, even though it will lose one half of its weekly sales of blades? Yes! Customers will gladly pay up to 10 cents per blade for the new blades, which last twice as long. Instead of making 3 cents net profit per customer per week, the firm now will make up to 8 cents per customer every two weeks. Profits will rise. In fact, a price of 9 cents per blade will benefit the buyer *and* Super Sharp alike.

Would Monopoly Oil Sell the Miracle Carburetor?

For years, it has been rumored that a much more efficient "miracle carburetor" for automobiles has been discovered, but that the big oil companies have plotted to keep it off the market because it would reduce their profits from the sale of gasoline.

Suppose an oil cartel, Monopoly Oil, sells all the oil and gasoline in the world. This hypothetical organization has also obtained the patent on a miracle carburetor. The real improvement is simply a little plastic gizmo that can be inserted into ordinary carburetors. The gizmo can be made in quantity for 1 cent each, and each gizmo lasts just long enough (one year, on average) to save its buyer 1,000 gallons of gas. If Monopoly Oil makes 5 cents per gallon

economic profit on each gallon of gasoline, the sale lost *per gizmo* will cost the firm $50 per year. Will Monopoly Oil sell the gizmo? Of course! If gas sells for 95 cents per gallon (but the opportunity cost of crude oil, refining, and so on is only 90 cents), the cartel will *increase* its profit by selling the gizmo (cost 1 cent), which replaces 1,000 gallons of gasoline, as long as the price of the gizmo exceeds $50.01. The consumer would certainly pay far more than $50.01 to save 1,000 gallons of gas. Indeed, any price below $950 per gizmo would help the motorist.[9]

Do Patents Help or Hurt the Consumer?

A patent right is crucial, of course, to both of the above examples. If firms could not at least partially capture the gains to be made from introducing a new product, they might prefer to keep it off the market and thereby prevent other firms from cutting into their profits by copying the new idea.

The patent system has a dual impact on the allocation of resources. First, the patent monopoly grants, as any monopoly does, the patent owner the ability (for a limited time) to keep the price of the patented item higher than costs of production warrant. Thus, *for patented inventions that have already been introduced,* consumers would be better off if competition replaced patent monopolies.

There is, however, a second effect. The fact that one can patent a new product or production process encourages the development of im-

proved, lower-cost goods. Public policy in the United States allows temporary patent monopolies, which are costly to consumers in the short-run, in order to provide firms (and individuals) with a strong incentive to undertake the risk and effort involved in the development of technological improvements, which may lead to lower costs and greater efficiency in the long-run.

---

[7]Both the authors and reader may disagree with such "vulgar taste." We should be aware, however, that such disagreement stems from our views about how consumers should behave and does not necessarily mean that the system that caters to that taste is defective.

[8]If the blade requires new and different machines that render the firm's current machines obsolete, the firm will still introduce the product. It will do so, however, at a slower pace, because the cost associated with new machines is higher than the zero *opportunity cost* (assuming the old machines have no alternative use) of using existing machines. Phasing in the new product so that the existing machines may be more fully used could be a cheaper alternative for Super Sharp. If so, it will also be cheaper for society.

[9]If the gizmo were invented by someone other than Monopoly Oil, the inventor would have an even stronger incentive to introduce the product. However, the introduction of the product *by someone else* would detract from the net profit of Monopoly Oil. The latter would have an incentive to suppress the product, if possible. The cartel might attempt to use political power or extra legal methods to keep the product off the market. Of course, such actions would conflict with the efficient use of resources.

oly in, for instance, the telephone industry seldom point to a government-operated monopoly—such as the Post Office—as an example of how an industry should be run.[10]

SUMMARY

The policy implications that can legitimately be drawn from an analysis of monopoly are more limited than might initially appear. We may not like monopolistic power or its effects, but the alternatives are not terribly attractive. Monopoly power based on economies of scale poses a particularly troublesome problem. When average total costs decline with the size of firm, per unit costs will be minimized if a single firm produces the entire market output. However, if a monopolist is permitted to dominate the market, inefficiency will arise because a monopolist will restrict output and charge a price in excess of marginal cost. Since smaller firms have higher per unit costs, restructuring the industry to increase the number of firms is unattractive. Neither is regulation an ideal solution. Since regulators do not possess the information necessary to impose an efficient outcome and since the special interest effect indicates that regulators are susceptible to manipulation by the industrial interests, regulation is unlikely to achieve our hypothetical ideal efficiency conditions. Finally, since public-sector managers are likely to pursue political objectives at the expense of economic efficiency, public ownership is also a less than ideal solution. Thus, economic theory indicates that there are no ideal solutions when natural monopoly is present. Choices must be made among alternatives, all of which are imperfect.

DYNAMIC CHANGE, MONOPOLY POWER, AND RESOURCE ALLOCATION

We have analyzed monopoly within a static framework and emphasized the lack of competition (sellers of alternative products) *within the industry*. No firm, though, is an island unto itself. Each firm competes with every other firm for the dollar votes of consumers. Dynamic change is present in the real world and the expectation of monopoly profit may influence its speed. Competitors will seek to develop and market substitutes for products offered by profitable firms. If a monopoly is profitable, it will attract rivals that produce substitute products. Actual and potential substitutes exist for almost every product. With the passage of time, the development of substitutes is a threat to the market power of even an entrenched monopoly.

High monopoly prices will encourage development of substitutes. For example, the high price of natural rubber spurred the development of synthetic rubber. High rail-shipping rates accelerated the development of long-distance trucking. The strong exercise of monopoly power by the Organization of Petroleum Exporting Countries (OPEC) subjected oil to vastly intensified competition from coal, solar energy, and other nonpetroleum energy sources, as well as from greatly expanded exploration efforts. The result was a long tumble in the price OPEC

---

[10]For an analysis of potential cost savings in the case of the U.S. Postal Service, see *Privatization: Toward More Effective Government*, Report of the President's Commission on Privatization, (March 1988), Chapter 7, pp. 101–128.

could charge for its oil. What seemed to be a secure monopoly position for OPEC turned out to be something very different.

This dynamic competition from substitute products and suppliers, both actual and potential, is important for two reasons. First, a monopolist will sometimes choose to produce a larger output and charge a lower price—lower than the short-run profit-maximizing price—to discourage potential rivals from developing substitutes. When this happens, the allocative inefficiency associated with monopoly will be less than our static model implies. Second, the expectation of monopoly profits may spur product development. In fact, the patent system is based on this premise. When a new product or production method is patented, monopoly power is granted to the patent owner for a period of 17 years. Others are prohibited from copying the product or technique. If this "reward" of temporary monopoly power and profit did not exist, businesses would be less inclined to undertake research designed to reduce costs and improve product quality (see Applications in Economics on product obsolescence). Thus, even though these dynamic competitive forces will operate more slowly than when barriers to entry into an industry are low, the development of substitutes will nonetheless tend with the passage of time to erode the market power of a monopolist.

LOOKING AHEAD

Most markets do not fit neatly into either the pure competition or pure monopoly models. Many markets are characterized by low barriers to entry and competition on the basis of product quality, design, convenience of location, and producer reliability. Other markets involve a small number of rival firms, operating under widely varying entry conditions. In the next chapter, we will investigate market structures that lie between pure competition and monopoly.

CHAPTER SUMMARY

1. Pure monopoly is a market structure characterized by (a) high barriers to entry and (b) a single seller of a well-defined product for which there are no good substitutes. Pure monopoly is at the opposite end of the market-structure spectrum from pure competition.

2. Analysis of pure monopoly is important for two reasons. First, the monopoly model will help us understand the operation of markets dominated by a few firms. Second, in a few important industries, such as local telephone services and utilities, there is often only a single producer in a market area. The monopoly model will help us understand these markets.

3. The three major barriers to entry into a market are legal restrictions, economies of scale, and control of an essential resource.

4. The monopolist's demand curve is the market demand curve. It slopes downward to the right. The marginal revenue curve for a monopolist will lie inside the demand curve because of revenue losses from the lower price for units that could have been sold at a higher price.

5. For the elastic portion of a monopolist's demand curve, a lower price will increase total revenue. For the inelastic portion of the monopolist's demand curve, a price reduction will cause total revenue to decline. A profit-maximizing monopolist will not operate on the inelastic portion of the demand curve because in that range it is always possible to increase total revenue by raising the price and producing fewer units.

6. A profit-maximizing monopolist will lower price and expand output as long as marginal revenue exceeds marginal cost. At the maximum-profit output, MR will equal

MC. The monopolist will charge the price on its demand curve corresponding to that rate of sales.

7. If losses occur in the long run, a monopolist will go out of business. If profit results, high barriers to entry will shield a monopolist from competitive pressures. Therefore, *long run* economic profits for a monopoly are sometimes possible.

8. Economists are critical of a monopoly because (a) it severely limits the role of demand in the market for a good and thus consumers' "control" over the producer; (b) the unregulated monopolist produces too little output and charges a price in excess of the marginal cost; (c) profits are less able to stimulate new entry, which would expand the supply of the product until price declined to the level of average production costs; and (d) legal monopoly encourages rent-seeking activity.

9. Natural monopoly exists when long-run average total costs continue to decline as firm size increases (economies of scale). Thus, a larger firm always has lower costs. Cost of production will be lowest when a single firm generates the entire output of an industry.

10. In the presence of natural monopoly, there are three policy alternatives: (a) private, unregulated monopoly; (b) private, regulated monopoly; and (c) government ownership. Economic theory suggests that each of the three will fail to meet our criteria for ideal efficiency. Private monopoly will result in higher prices and less output than would be ideal. Regulation will often fail to meet our ideal efficiency criteria because (a) the regulators will not have knowledge of the firm's cost curves and market demand conditions; (b) firms have an incentive to conceal their actual cost conditions and take profits in disguised forms; and (c) the regulators often end up being influenced by the firms they are supposed to regulate. Under public ownership, managers often derive personal gain from policies that conflict with cost control and cater to the views of special interest groups (for example, well-organized employees and specialized customers) who will be able to help them further their political objectives.

11. Even a monopolist is not completely free from competitive pressures. All products have some type of substitute. Monopolists who raise the price of their products provide encouragement for other firms to develop substitutes, which may eventually erode the market power of the monopolist. Some monopolists may charge less than the short-run, profit-maximizing price to discourage *potential* competitors from developing substitute products.

12. Monopoly profits derived from patents have two conflicting effects on resource allocation. *Once a product or process has been discovered,* the monopoly rights permit the firm to restrict output and raise price above the current marginal (and average) cost of production. However, the possibility of future monopoly rights granted by a patent encourage entrepreneurs to improve products and develop lower-cost methods of production.

CRITICAL ANALYSIS QUESTIONS

*1. "Barriers to entry are crucial to the existence of long-run profits, but they cannot guarantee the existence of profits." Evaluate.

2. "Monopoly is good for producers but bad for consumers. The gains of the former offset the losses of the latter. On balance, there is no reason to think that monopoly is bad for the economy." Evaluate.

*3. Do monopolists charge the highest prices for which they can sell their products? Do they maximize their average profit per sale? Are monopolistic firms always profitable? Why or why not?

4. The retail liquor industry is potentially a competitive industry. However, the liquor retailers of a southern state organized a trade association that sets prices for all firms.

---

*Asterisk denotes questions for which answers are given in Appendix C, Selected Answers.

For all practical purposes, the trade association transformed a competitive industry into a monopoly. Compare the price and output policy for a purely competitive industry with the policy that would be established by a profit-maximizing monopolist or trade association. Who benefits and who is hurt by the formation of the monopoly?

5. Does economic theory indicate that a monopoly forced by an ideal regulatory agency to set prices according to either marginal or average cost would be more efficient than an unregulated monopoly? Explain. Does economic theory suggest that a regulatory agency *will* follow a proper regulation policy? What are some of the factors that complicate the regulatory function?

6. Is a monopolist subject to any competitive pressures? Explain. Would an unregulated monopolist have an incentive to operate and produce efficiently? If so, why?

*7. If a university has some monopoly power, explain why it would allocate more of its financial aid to students from low-income families than those from richer families if it seeks to maximize revenue.

8. Explain why it is impossible to draw a supply curve for a monopolist.

*9. "The patent system provides a monopoly to the producer and raises consumer prices. It is inefficient." Evaluate, giving economic arguments for and against this point of view.

10. Which of the following are monopolists: (a) your local newspaper, (b) Boston Celtics, (c) General Motors, (d) U.S. Postal Service, (e) Johnny Carson, (f) American Medical Association? Is the definition of an industry or market area important in the determination of a seller's monopoly position? Explain.

11. How can a firm, through rent-seeking activities, hope to "buy" monopoly profits? Is there competition for monopoly-seller positions? How does competition among rent seekers for monopoly profit influence the efficiency of resource allocation?

*12. Suppose that there is an increase in demand for a product such that a monopolist confronting a straight line demand curve is able to sell a 10-percent-larger quantity at each price. If the product is produced at a constant marginal cost, will the increase in demand cause the monopolist to raise its price? Explain.

*13. In the midst of the sharply higher oil prices of the 1970s, it was often charged that (a) the big oil companies colluded and set prices as if they were a monopolist and (b) the higher prices of petroleum products failed to reduce consumption. Is there a conflict between these two propositions?

14. Once a manuscript is supplied to the publisher, the personal services of the author are a sunk cost. Generally, authors bear none of the production cost and are paid a percentage of total revenue. Given this arrangement, would authors generally prefer a lower sales price for the book than would their publishers? Explain.

*15. Historically, the real cost of transporting both goods and people has declined substantially. What impact does a reduction in transportation cost have on the monopoly power of producers? Do you think the U.S. economy is more or less competitive today than it was 100 years ago? Explain.

16. Is price discrimination harmful to the U.S. economy? How does price discrimination affect the gains from exchange? Why do firms often charge students, the elderly, or people with coupons different prices than others? Explain.

10

THE INTERMEDIATE CASES: MONOPOLISTIC COMPETITION AND OLIGOPOLY

Difference in tastes, desires, incomes and locations of buyers, and differences in the uses which they wish to make of commodities all indicate the need for variety and the necessity of substituting for the concept of a "competitive ideal" an ideal involving both monopoly and competition.[1]

Edward H. Chamberlin

CHAPTER FOCUS

■ What are the characteristics of monopolistic competition?

■ How do consumers fare, under monopolistic competition? How large should we expect producer profits to be?

■ How is oligopoly different from monopolistic competition?

■ Why have economists been unable to construct a general theory of oligopoly?

■ What is the theory of contestable markets? What can we say about the outcomes in such markets?

■ What do we know about competitiveness within the U.S. economy, and how it has changed over the last several decades?

■ How large are accounting profits, and what changes have occurred in profit levels over the years? What would happen if accounting profits were eliminated.

Most real-world firms operate in markets that fall between the extremes of pure competition and pure monopoly. These firms do not confront numerous competitors all producing a homogenous product sold at a single price; neither do most firms produce a good or service that is unavailable from other sellers. Instead, most firms face varying degrees of competition. In some cases, there are competitors offering roughly the same product; in other instances, the competitor's product is merely an attractive substitute. There may be numerous competitors, or there may be only a few other sellers in a given market. The models of monopolistic competition and oligopoly have been developed by economists to describe markets that are neither purely competitive nor purely monopolistic.

Monopolistically competitive and oligopolistic firms have different degrees of freedom in setting prices, altering quality, and choosing a marketing strategy than do firms in purely competitive or purely monopolistic markets. Most firms, unlike those under purely competitive conditions, will lose some *but not all* of their customers when they increase the price of their product. These firms face a downward-sloping demand curve. Like monopolists, they are price searchers: they must search for the price most consistent with their overall goal—maximum profit, for example. As we have indicated, though, just as they are not pure competitors, most price searchers are not monopolists, either. Thus, their freedom to raise prices is limited by the existence of actual and potential competitors offering similar products. The difference between monopolistic competition and oligopoly is in one sense a difference in the degree to which a price searcher is limited by competition.

CHARACTERISTICS OF MONOPOLISTIC COMPETITION

During the 1920s, many economists believed that neither pure competition nor pure monopoly was descriptive of markets such as retail sales, construction, service businesses, and small manufacturing, which were generally characterized by numerous firms offering different but closely related products or services. The need for a more accurate model for markets of this type led to the theory of **monopolistic competition.** The theory was developed independently by Joan Robinson, a British economist, and Edward Chamberlin, an American economist. The major works of Robinson and Chamberlin were both published in 1933.[2] These economists outlined three distinguishing characteristics of monopolistic competition.

Monopolistic competitors offer **differentiated products** to consumers. Goods and services of one seller are differentiated from those of another by convenience of location, product quality, reputation of the seller, advertising, and various other product characteristics.

Monopolistic Competition: A situation in which there are a large number of independent sellers, each producing a differentiated product in a market with low barriers to entry. Construction, retail sales, and service stations are good examples of monopolistically competitive industries.

Differentiated Products: Products distinguished from similar products by such characteristics as quality, design, location, and method of promotion.

PRODUCT DIFFERENTIATION

---

[1]Edward H. Chamberlin, *The Theory of Monopolistic Competition* (Cambridge: Harvard University Press, 1948), p. 214.
[2]See Joan Robinson, *The Economics of Imperfect Competition* (1933, reprint ed., New York: St. Martin's, 1969), and Edward H. Chamberlin, *The Theory of Monopolistic Competition* (Cambridge: Harvard University Press, 1933).

Since the product of each monopolistic competitor is slightly different from that of its rivals, the individual firm faces a downward-sloping demand curve. A price reduction will enable the firm to attract new customers. Alternatively, the firm will be able to increase its price by a small amount and still retain many of its customers, who prefer the location, style, dependability, or other product characteristics offered by the firm. The demand curve confronted by the monopolistic competitor is highly elastic, however. Even though each firm has some control over price, that control is extremely limited, since the firm faces competition from rivals offering very similar products. The availability of close substitutes and the ease with which consumers can turn to rival firms (including new firms that are free to enter the market) force a monopolistically competitive firm to think twice before raising its price.

LOW BARRIERS TO ENTRY

Under monopolistic competition, firms are free to enter into or exit from the market. There are neither legal barriers nor market obstacles hindering the movement of competitors into and out of a monopolistically competitive market. Monopolistic competition resembles pure competition in this respect; firms in both these types of markets confront the constant threat of competition from new, innovative rivals.

MANY INDEPENDENT FIRMS

A monopolistic competitor faces not only the potential threat posed by new rivals but competition from many current sellers as well. Each firm is small relative to the total market. No single firm or small group of firms is able to dominate the market.

Retailing is perhaps the sector of our economy that best typifies monopolistic competition. In most market areas, there are a large number of retail stores offering similar products and services. Rivalry is intense, and stores are constantly trying new combinations of price and quality of service (or merchandise) to win customers. The *free entry* that typifies most retailing makes for rapid change. Yesterday's novelty can quickly become obsolete as new rivals develop still better (or more attractive) products and marketing methods.

PRICE AND OUTPUT UNDER MONOPOLISTIC COMPETITION

How does a monopolistic competitor decide what price to charge and what level of output to produce? Like a pure monopolist, a monopolistic competitor will face a downward-sloping demand curve for its product. Additional units can be sold only at a lower price. Therefore, the marginal revenue curve of the monopolistic competitor will always lie below the firm's demand curve.

Any firm can increase profits by expanding output as long as marginal revenue exceeds marginal cost. Therefore, a monopolistic competitor will lower its prices and expand its output until marginal revenue is equal to marginal cost.

Exhibit 1 illustrates the profit-maximizing price and output under monopolistic competition. A profit-maximizing monopolistic competitor will expand output to q, where marginal revenue is equal to marginal cost and price P can be charged. Beyond q, to sell more output would require a reduction in price so large that profit would be reduced. For any output level less than q (for example, R), a price reduction and sales expansion will add more to total revenues than to total costs. At output R, marginal revenues exceed marginal costs. Thus, profits will

EXHIBIT 1

The Monopolistic Competitor's Price and Output

A monopolistic competitor maximizes profits by producing output *q*, for which MR = MC, and charging price *P*. The firm is making economic profits. What impact will they have?

be greater if price is reduced so output can be expanded. On the other hand, if output exceeds *q* (for example, *S*), sale of additional units beyond *q* will *add* more to costs (MC) than the revenues (MR). The firm will therefore gain by raising the price to *P*, even though the price rise will result in the loss of customers. Profits will be maximized by charging price *P* and producing the output level *q*, where MC = MR.

The firm pictured by Exhibit 1 is making economic profit. Total revenues *PAqO* exceeds the firm's total costs *CBqO* at the profit-maximizing output level. Since barriers to entry in monopolistically competitive markets are low, profits will attract rival competitors. Other firms will attempt to duplicate the product (or service) offered by the profit-making firms.

What impact will the entry of new rivals have on the demand for the products of profit-making firms already in the market? These new rivals will draw customers away from existing firms. As long as monopolistically competitive firms can make economic profits, new competitors will be attracted to the market. This pressure will continue until the competition among rivals has shifted the demand curve for monopolistic competitors inward far enough to eliminate economic profits. In the long run, as illustrated by Exhibit 2, a monopolistically competitive firm will just be able to cover its production costs. It will produce to the MR = MC output level, but the entry of new competition will force the price down to the average per unit cost.

If losses exist in a monopolistically competitive industry, some of the existing firms in the industry will go out of business over a period of time. As firms leave the industry, some of their previous customers will buy from other firms. The demand curve facing the remaining firms in the industry will shift out until the economic losses are eliminated and the long-run, zero-profit equilibrium illustrated by Exhibit 2 is again restored.

Under monopolistic competition, profits and losses play precisely the same role as they do under pure competition. Economic profits will attract new competitors to the market. The increased availability of the product (and similar products) will drive the price down until the profits are eliminated. Conversely, economic losses will induce competitors to exit from the market. The decline in the availability of the product (supply) will allow the price to rise until firms are once again able to cover their average cost.

Monopolistic Competition and Long-Run Normal Profit

Since entry and exit are free, competition will eventually drive prices down to the level of average total cost.

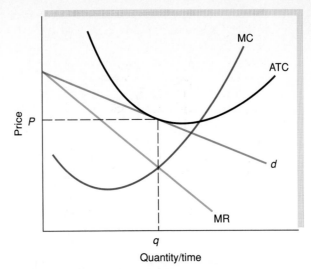

In the short run, a monopolistic competitor may make either economic profits or losses, depending on market conditions. In the long run, however, only a normal profit rate (that is, zero economic profits) will be possible because of competitive conditions and freedom of entry.

COMPARING PURE AND MONOPOLISTIC COMPETITION

As you can see, determination of price and output under monopolistic competition is in some ways very similar to that under pure competition. Also, since the long-run equilibrium conditions under pure competition are consistent with ideal economic efficiency, it is useful to compare and contrast other market structures with pure competition. There are both similarities and differences between pure and monopolistic competition.

SIMILARITIES BETWEEN PURE AND MONOPOLISTIC COMPETITION

Since barriers to entry are low, neither pure nor monopolistic competitors will be able to earn long-run economic profit. In the long run, competition will drive the price of pure and monopolistic competitors down to the level of average total cost.

In each case, entrepreneurs have a strong incentive to manage and operate their businesses efficiently. Inefficient operation will lead to losses and forced exit from the market. Pure and monopolistic competitors alike will be motivated to develop and adopt new cost-reducing procedures and techniques because lower costs will mean higher profits (or at least smaller losses).

The response of pure and monopolistic competitors to changing demand conditions is very similar. In both cases, an increase in market demand leads to higher prices, short-run profits, and the entry of additional firms. With the entry of new producers, and the concurrent expansion of existing firms, the market supply will increase. The process will continue until the market price falls to the level of average total cost, squeezing out all economic profit. Similarly, a reduction in demand will lead to lower prices and short-run losses, causing output to fall and some firms to exit. The remaining firms can raise prices until short-run losses are eliminated. Profits and losses will direct the activities of firms under both pure and monopolistic competition.

DIFFERENCES BETWEEN PURE AND MONOPOLISTIC COMPETITION

As Exhibit 3 illustrates, the pure competitor confronts a horizontal demand curve; the demand curve faced by a monopolistic competitor is downward-sloping. This is important because it means that the marginal revenue of the monopolistic competitor will be less than, rather than equal to, price. So, when the profit-maximizing monopolistic competitor expands output until MR = MC, price will still exceed marginal cost (Exhibit 3b). In contrast, in long-run equilibrium, the price charged by the pure competitor will *equal* marginal cost (Exhibit 3a). Also, for a firm in monopolistic competition, unlike one in pure competition, the equilibrium (zero economic profit) output rate fails to minimize the firm's long-run average total cost, as Exhibit 3 illustrates. The monopolistic competitor would have a lower per unit cost (97 cents rather than $1.00) if a larger output were produced.

ALLOCATIVE EFFICIENCY UNDER MONOPOLISTIC COMPETITION

The efficiency of monopolistic competition has been the subject of debate among economists for years. At one time, the dominant view seemed to be that allocative inefficiency results because monopolistic competitors fail to operate at an output level that minimizes their long-run average total cost. Due to the proliferation in the number of monopolistic competitors, the sales of each competitor fall short of their least-cost capacity level. The potential social gain associated with the expansion of production to the $P = MC$ output rate is lost. The advocates of this view point out that if there were fewer producers, they would each be able to operate

---

Comparing Pure and Monopolistic Competition

The long-run equilibrium conditions of firms under pure and monopolistic competition are illustrated here. In both cases, price is equal to average total cost, and economic profit is absent. However, since the monopolistically competitive firm confronts a downward-sloping demand curve for its product, its equilibrium price exceeds marginal cost, and equilibrium output is not large enough to minimize average total cost. *For identical cost conditions,* the price of the monopolistic competitor will be slightly higher than that of the pure competitor. Chamberlin referred to this slightly higher price as the premium a society pays for variety and convenience (product differentiation).

(a) Pure competition

(b) Monopolistic competition

at a minimum-cost output rate. Instead, there is costly duplication—too many producers each operating below their minimum-cost output capacity. According to this traditional view, the location of two or more filling stations, restaurants, grocery stores, or similar establishments side by side is indicative of the economic waste generated by monopolistic competition.

In addition, the critics of monopolistic competition argue that it often leads to self-defeating, wasteful advertising. Firms have an incentive to use advertising to promote artificial distinctions between similar products. Each firm bombards consumers with advertisements proclaiming (or implying) that its own product is fancier, has greater sex appeal, and/or brings quicker relief than any product of rival firms. Firms that do not engage in such advertising can expect their sales to decline. Advertising, though, results in higher prices for consumers and thus is costly from society's point of view.

In recent years, this traditional view has been seriously challenged. Many economists now believe that such a view is mechanistic and fails to take into account the significance of dynamic competition. Most important, the traditional view assumes that consumers place no value on the wider variety of qualities and styles that results from monopolistic competition. Prices might very well be slightly lower if there were fewer gasoline stations, located farther apart, and offering a more limited variety of service and credit plan options. Similarly, the prices of groceries might very well be slightly lower if there were fewer supermarkets, each a bit more congested and located less conveniently for some customers. However, since customers value product diversity as well as lower prices, they might be better off under the conditions created by monopolistic competition. Edward Chamberlin, one of the developers of the theory, argues that higher prices (and costs) are simply the premium consumers pay for variety and convenience. When consumers receive utility from product diversity, one cannot conclude that pure competition with a lower price, but less variety from which to select, would be preferable to monopolistic competition.

The defenders of monopolistic competition also deny that this leads to excessive, wasteful advertising. They point out that advertising often reduces the consumer's search time and provides valuable information on prices. If advertising really raises prices, it must provide the consumer with something valuable. Otherwise, the consumer will purchase lower-priced, nonadvertised goods. When consumers really prefer lower prices and less advertising, firms offering that combination do quite well. In fact, proponents argue that monopolistic competitors actually do often use higher quality service and lower prices to compete with rivals who advertise heavily.

The debate among economists has helped clarify this topic's issues. Nevertheless, the efficiency of monopolistic competition continues to be one of the unresolved issues of economics.

REAL-WORLD MONOPOLISTIC COMPETITORS

In our model, we assume that firms have perfect knowledge of their costs and demand conditions. Real-world firms do not have such information. They must rely on past experience, market surveys, experimentation, and other business skills when they make price, output, and production decisions. (See the Applications in Economics box, ''The Left-Out Variable: Entrepreneurship.'')

Despite their high hopes, many firms go out of business every year. In recent years, among corporate establishments alone, the number of firms going out of business has generally exceeded 250,000 annually. A great many of these unsuccessful businesses are small, monopolistically competitive firms that are forced out of business by losses stemming from market competition.

Why do losses occur in the real world? Since business decisions must be made with imperfect information, mistakes sometimes result. A firm may mistakenly produce a good for which consumers are unwilling to pay a price that will enable the producer to cover the costs of production. Losses are the market's method of bringing such activities to a halt. Economic losses signal that the resources would be valued more highly if they were put to other uses. That is, the opportunity cost of production exceeds the value of the output. Losses also provide the incentive to correct this allocative inefficiency.

CHARACTERISTICS OF OLIGOPOLY

Oligopoly: A market situation in which a small number of sellers comprise the entire industry. It is competition among the few.

"Oligopoly" means "few sellers." When there are only a few firms in an industry, the industrial structure is called an **oligopoly.** In the United States, the great majority of output in such industries as automobiles, steel, cigarettes, and aircraft is produced by five or fewer dominant firms. In addition to a small number of producers, there are several other characteristics that oligopolistic industries have in common.

OUTSTANDING ECONOMIST

Joan Robinson
(1903–1983)

Along with Edward Chamberlin, Joan Robinson is given credit for developing the theory of monopolistic competition. In her book *The Economics of Imperfect Competition* (1933), she redefined the market demand curve to account for interdependence among firms. Following Alfred Marshall, she used differences among products to define an industry. Essentially, she viewed each firm as a monopolist facing a downward-sloping demand curve that is affected by the behavior of other "monopolists" in the industry. Unlike Chamberlin, she did not introduce product differentiation and quality competition *within an industry* into her analysis.

Professor Robinson's contribution to economics goes far beyond her role in developing the theory of monopolistic competition. A long-time professor emerita of economics at Cambridge University, she was one of a select group of economists who worked with Keynes during the developmental stage of his *General Theory.* Her work in economics ran the gamut. Capital theory, international trade, Marxian economics, growth theory, and comparative systems are among the many areas that felt the touch of her pen.

During the latter years of her life, Professor Robinson was a vocal critic of the capitalist system. Nevertheless, her scholarly work was highly acclaimed by economists of all persuasions. The *Collected Economic Papers* of Professor Robinson fill four volumes.[3]

---

[3]Joan Robinson, *Collected Papers,* 4 vols. (New York: Humanities Press, 1960–1972).

INTERDEPENDENCE AMONG FIRMS

Since the number of sellers in an oligopolistic industry is small, each firm must take the potential reactions of rivals into account when it makes business decisions. The decisions of one seller often influence the price of products and the profits of rival firms. In an oligopoly, the welfare of each seller is dependent on the policies followed by its major rivals.

APPLICATIONS IN ECONOMICS

The Left-Out Variable: Entrepreneurship[4]

To help us understand facts and make predictions, a scientific model must simplify what it describes, and draw attention to the most important relationships. Economic models are no exception. Our model of decision-making in business firms is designed to highlight for us the decision-making elements common to all firms, and it performs this job quite well. But it leaves out some important steps in the decision-making process of real-world firms. Typically, a great many judgments are needed before the process we describe can even begin.

Would profits increase if prices were raised, or would lower prices lead to larger profits? Real-world decision-makers cannot go into the back room and look at their demand-cost diagram to answer these questions. They must search for clues, experiment with actual price changes, and interpret what they see, often using a great deal of "seat-of-the-pants" judgment. The successful entrepreneur will search and find (or at least approximate) the profit-maximizing price—the MR = MC price and output combination that our model shows so simply.

For real-world entrepreneurs, the problem of uncertainty goes well beyond setting the profit-maximizing price and output. How can an entrepreneur decide whether demand and cost conditions will make entry into a monopolistically competitive field profitable? How large should the plant be? How should production be organized? How much variety, and what combination of qualities should be built into the firm's product or service? What location will be best? What forms of advertising will be most effective? These questions and many more require entrepreneurial judgment. The essence of entrepreneurial judgment is that there is no decision rule that can be applied and which uses only information that is freely available. For this reason, the entrepreneurial function has not been put into economic models. There simply is no way to model such judgmental decisions. All we can do is note their importance and recognize that our models are limited by the fact that they are missing this critical element of successful business decision-making.

The Entrepreneur: A Job Description

If we cannot put entrepreneurship into our models, what can we say about its function? One way to answer this question is to consider a generalized job description for an entrepreneurial position. An investor who lacks the desire, or perhaps the skill, to be an entrepreneur, but nonetheless wants to be in business, may well seek someone to act as the business entrepreneur, while the investor provides some of the capital. A newspaper ad to find such a person (while perhaps not the usual way for the investor to search) might read as follows:

> **Wanted: Entrepreneur.** Must have many qualities: 1) Alert to new business opportunities and to new problems before they become obvious. 2) Willing to back judgments with investments of hard work and creative effort before others recognize correctness of judgments. 3) Able to make correct decisions and to convince others of their correctness, so as to attract additional financial backing. 4) Able to recognize own inevitable mistakes and to back away from incorrect decisions without wasting additional resources. Exciting, exhausting, high risk position. Pay will be very good for success, and very poor for failure.

Entrepreneurship is not for the faint-hearted or the lazy. Entrepreneurs are at the center of the action in the real world, even if they do not have a place in most economic models.

---

[4]For a more complete overview of entrepreneurship, and references on the topic, see Mark Crosson, "Entrepreneurship," in *The New Palgrave: a Dictionary of Economics* edited by John Eatwell, et. al., (New York: Stockton Press, 1987) pp. 151–53.

SUBSTANTIAL ECONOMIES OF SCALE

In an oligopolistic industry, large-scale production (relative to the total market) is necessary to attain a low per unit cost. Economies of scale are significant. A small number of the large-scale, cost-efficient firms will meet the demand for the industry's product.

Using the automobile industry as an example, Exhibit 4 illustrates the importance of economies of scale as a source of oligopoly. It has been estimated that each firm must produce approximately one million automobiles annually before its per unit cost of production is minimized. However, when the selling price of automobiles is barely sufficient for firms to cover their costs, the total quantity demanded from these producers is only six million. To minimize costs, then, each firm must produce at least one sixth (one million of the six million) of the output demanded. In other words, the industry can support no more than five or six domestic firms of cost-efficient size.

SIGNIFICANT BARRIERS TO ENTRY

As with monopoly, barriers to entry limit the ability of new firms to compete effectively in oligopolistic industries. Economies of scale are probably the most significant entry barrier. A potential competitor will be unable to start out small and gradually grow to the optimal size, since a firm in an oligopolistic industry must gain a large share of the market before it can minimize per unit cost. The manufacture of refrigerators, diesel engines, as well as automobile production, seems to fall into this category.

Other factors, including patent rights, control over an essential resource, and government-imposed monopoly may also prevent new competitors from entering profitable oligopolistic industries. Without substantial barriers to entry, oligopolistic competition would be similar to monopolistic competition.

PRODUCTS MAY BE EITHER HOMOGENEOUS OR DIFFERENTIATED

The products of sellers in an oligopolistic industry may be either homogeneous or differentiated. When firms produce identical products, there is less opportunity for nonprice competition. On the other hand, rival firms producing differentiated products are more likely to use style, quality, and advertising as competitive weapons.

EXHIBIT 4

Economies of Scale and Oligopoly

Oligopoly exists in the automobile industry because firms do not fully realize the cost reductions from large-scale output until they produce approximately one-sixth of the total market.

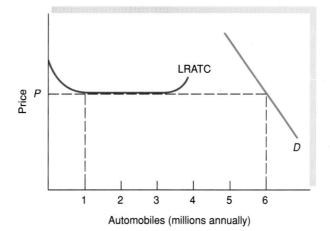

PRICE AND OUTPUT UNDER OLIGOPOLY

Unlike a monopolist or a pure competitor, an oligopolist cannot determine the product price that will deliver maximum profit simply by estimating market demand and cost conditions. An oligopolist must also predict how rival firms (that is, the rest of the industry) will react to price (and quality) adjustments. Since each oligopolist confronts such a complex problem, it is impossible to determine the precise price and output policy that will emerge in oligopolistic industries. Economics does, however, indicate a potential range of prices, and the factors that will determine whether prices in the industry will be high or low relative to costs of production.

Consider an oligopolistic industry in which seven or eight rival firms produce the entire market output. Substantial economies of scale are present. The firms produce identical products and have similar costs of production. Exhibit 5 depicts the market demand conditions and long-run costs of production of the individual firms for such an industry.

What price will prevail? We can answer this question for two extreme cases. First, suppose that each firm sets its price independently of the other firms. There is no collusion, and each competitive firm acts independently, seeking to maximize profits by offering consumers a better deal than its rivals. Under these conditions, the market price would be driven down to P_c. Firms would be just able to cover their per unit costs of production. What would happen if a *single firm* raised its price? Its customers would switch to rival firms, which would now expand to accommodate the new customers. The firm that raised its price would lose out. It would be self-defeating for any one firm to raise its price if the other firms did not raise theirs.

What would happen if supply conditions were such that the market price was above P_c? Since the demand curve faced by each *individual firm* is highly elastic, rival sellers would have a strong incentive to reduce their price. Any firm that

EXHIBIT 5

The Range of Price and Output under Oligopoly

If oligopolists competed with one another, price-cutting would drive price down to P_c. In contrast, perfect cooperation among firms would lead to a higher price P_m and a smaller output (Q_m rather than Q_c). The shaded area shows profit if firms collude.

reduced its price slightly, by 1 percent, for example, would gain numerous customers. The price-cutting firm would attract some new buyers to the market, but more importantly, that firm would also lure many buyers away from rival firms charging higher prices. Total profit would expand as the price-cutter gained a larger share of the total market. But, what would happen if all firms attempted to undercut their rivals? Price would be driven down to P_c, and the economic profit of the firms would be eliminated.

When rival oligopolists compete (pricewise) with one another, they drive the market price down to the level of costs of production. This is not always the case, however. There is a strong incentive for oligopolists to collude, raise price, and restrict output.

Suppose the oligopolists, recognizing their interdependence, acted cooperatively to maximize their joint profit. They might form a **cartel,** such as OPEC, to accomplish this objective. Alternatively, they might collude without the aid of a formal organization. Under federal antitrust laws, collusive action to raise price and raise the joint profit of the firms would, of course, be illegal. Nevertheless, let us see what would happen if oligopolists followed this course. Exhibit 5 shows the marginal revenue curve that would accompany the market demand D for the product. Under perfect cooperation, the oligopolists would refuse to produce units for which marginal revenue was less than marginal cost. Thus, they would restrict joint output to Q_m, where MR = MC. Market price would rise to P_m. With collusion, substantial joint profits (the shaded area of Exhibit 5) could thus be attained. The case of perfect cooperation would be identical with the outcome under monopoly.

In the real world, however, the outcome is likely to fall between the extremes of price competition and perfect cooperation. Oligopolists generally recognize their interdependence and try to avoid vigorous price competition, which would drive price down to the level of per unit costs. But, there are also obstacles to collusion. Thus, prices in oligopolistic industries do not rise to the monopolistic level. Oligopolistic prices are typically above the purely competitive level but below that for pure monopoly.

Cartel: An organization of sellers designed to coordinate supply decisions so that the joint profits of the members will be maximized. A cartel will seek to create a monopoly in the market.

OBSTACLES TO COLLUSION

Collusion: Agreement among firms to avoid various competitive practices, particularly price reductions. It may involve either formal agreements or merely tacit recognition that competitive practices will be self-defeating in the long run. Tacit collusion is difficult to detect. The Sherman Act prohibits collusion and conspiracies to restrain interstate trade.

Collusion is the opposite of competition. It involves cooperative actions by sellers to turn the terms of trade in favor of the group, and against buyers. Since oligopolists can profit by colluding to restrict output and raise price, economic theory suggests that they will have a strong incentive to do so.

Each *individual* oligopolist, though, also has an incentive to cheat on collusive agreements. Exhibit 6 will help us understand why. An undetected price cut will enable a firm to attract (a) customers who would not buy from any firm at the higher price *and* (b) those who would normally buy from other firms. The demand facing the oligopolistic *firm* will thus be considerably more elastic than the industry demand curve. As Exhibit 6 shows, the price P_i that maximizes the industry's profits will be higher than the price P_f that is best for each individual oligopolist. If a firm can find a way to undercut the price set by the collusive agreement, while other sellers maintain the higher price, expanded sales will more than make up for the reduction in per unit profit margin.

In oligopolistic industries, there are two conflicting tendencies. An oligopolistic firm has a strong incentive to cooperate with its rivals so that joint profit can be maximized. However, it also has a strong incentive to cheat secretly on any

EXHIBIT 6
Gaining from Cheating

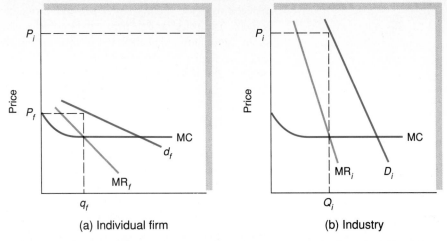

(a) Individual firm   (b) Industry

The industry demand (D_i) and marginal revenue curves are shown in frame b. The joint profits of oligopolists would be maximized at Q_i, where $MR_i = MC$. Price P_i would be best for the industry as a whole. However, the demand curve (d_f) facing each firm (frame a) would be much more elastic than D_i. Given the greater elasticity of its demand curve, an individual firm would maximize its profit by cutting its price to P_f and expanding output to q_f, where $MR_f = MC$. Thus, individual oligopolists could gain by secretly shaving price and cheating on the collusive agreement.

collusive agreement in order to increase its share of the joint profit. Oligopolistic agreements therefore tend to be unstable. This instability exists whether the co-operative behavior is formal, as in the case of a cartel, or informal.

There are certain situations in which it is difficult for oligopolists to collude. Five major obstacles can limit collusive behavior.

When the Number of Oligopolists Is Larger, Effective Collusion Is Less Likely. Other things constant, as the number of major firms in an industry increases, it becomes more costly for the oligopolists to communicate, negotiate, and enforce agreements among themselves. Developing and maintaining collusive agreements become more difficult. In addition, the greater the number of firms, the more likely it is that the objectives of individual firms will conflict with those of the industry. Each firm will want a bigger slice of the pie. Opinions about the best collusive price arrangement will differ because marginal costs, unused plant capacity, and estimates of market demand elasticity are likely to differ among firms. Aggressive, less mature firms may want to expand their share of total output. These conflicting interests contribute to the breakdown of collusive agreements.

When It Is Difficult to Detect and Eliminate Price Cuts, Collusion Is Less Attractive. Unless a firm has a way of policing the pricing activities of its rivals, it may be the "sucker" in a collusive agreement. Firms that secretly cut prices may gain a larger share of the market, while others maintain their higher prices and lose customers and profits. Price-cutting can sometimes be accomplished in ways that are difficult for the other firms to identify. For example, a firm might provide better credit terms, faster delivery, and other related services "free" to improve slightly the package offered to the consumer.[5]

When firms sell a differentiated product, improvements in quality and style can be used as competitive weapons. "Price cuts" of this variety are particularly attractive to an oligopolist because they cannot be easily and quickly duplicated by rivals. Competitors can quickly match a reduction in money price, but it will take time for them to match an improvement in quality. When firms can freely use improvements in quality to gain a larger share of the market, collusive agreements on price are of limited value. When cheating (price-cutting) is profitable and difficult for rivals to police, it is a good bet that oligopolistic rivals will be induced to cheat.

Low Entry Barriers Are an Obstacle to Collusion. Unless potential rivals can be excluded, oligopolists will be unable to make unusually large profits. Successful collusion will merely attract competitors into the industry, which will eliminate the profits. Even with collusion, long-run profits will not be possible unless entry into the industry can be blocked.

Local markets are sometimes dominated by a few firms. For example, many communities have only a small number of ready-mix concrete producers, bowling alleys, accounting firms, and furniture stores. In the absence of government restrictions, however, entry barriers into these markets are often low (see Applications in Economics box on Contestable Markets). The threat of potential rivals reduces the gains from collusive behavior under these conditions.

Unstable Demand Conditions Are an Obstacle to Collusion. Demand instability tends to increase the honest differences of opinion among oligopolists about what is best for the industry. One firm may want to expand because it anticipates a sharp increase in future demand, while a more pessimistic rival may want to hold the line on existing industrial capacity. Greater differences in expectations about future demand create greater conflict among oligopolistic firms. Successful collusion is more likely when demand is relatively stable.

Vigorous Antitrust Action Increases the Cost of Collusion. Under existing antitrust laws, collusive behavior is prohibited. Secret agreements are, of course, possible. Simple informal cooperation might be conducted without discussions or collusive agreements. However, like other illegal behavior, all such agreements are not legally enforceable by any firm. Vigorous antitrust action can discourage firms from making such illegal agreements. As the threat of getting caught increases, participants will be less likely to attempt collusive behavior.

THE KINKED DEMAND CURVE

As we noted earlier, the demand for an oligopolistic firm's product depends not only on market conditions but also on the reaction of rival firms, so the oligopolist must predict the reactions of rivals. How will rivals react to a price change? When

---

[5]See Marshall R. Colberg, Dascomb Forbush, and Gilbert R. Whitaker, *Business Economics,* 5th ed. (Homewood: Irwin, 1975), for an extensive discussion of the alternative methods by which business firms are able to alter price.

there is a dominant firm in an industry, rivals may be willing to follow the leadership of the larger firm. For example, if General Motors raises its prices by 5 percent, the other major automobile manufacturers might cooperate by raising their prices by a similar amount. Oligopolists, though, can never be sure what rivals will do. Sometimes prospective price increases are announced simply to observe the reactions of competitors.

The response of rivals is more difficult to predict when there is no single

APPLICATIONS IN ECONOMICS

Contestable Markets: Low Entry Barriers May Yield Competitive Results

Markets with few sellers are sometimes more competitive than they seem. Consider the case of the airline route between Salt Lake City, Utah, and Albuquerque, New Mexico. Only two airlines serve this route directly, since it has so little traffic. Further, there would seem to be high barriers to entry, since it takes multimillion dollar airplanes to compete, as well as facilities for reservations, ticketing, baggage handling and so on. The two airlines are well aware of the rivalry (with or without competition) between them, and they both charge the same price. One might expect that price to be high, perhaps close to the monopoly level. But, there is reason to believe that the two airlines, much as they would like to collude and drive up the price, will not be able to do so, as long as other airlines are free to enter this market.

Contestable Market: A market in which the costs of entry and exit are low, so that a firm risks little by entering. Efficient production and zero economic profits should prevail in a contestable market. A market can be contestable even if capital requirements are high.

To compete on an airline route may require millions of dollars in equipment, but the barriers to entry are much lower than that fact suggests. The Salt Lake City–Albuquerque market, for example, can be entered simply by shifting aircraft, personnel, and equipment from other locations. The aircraft can even be rented or leased. By the same token, if a new entrant (or an established firm) wants to leave that market, nearly all the invested capital values can be recovered, through shifting the aircraft and other capital equipment to other routes, or leasing them to other firms. An airline route then, in the absence of legal barriers, is a classic case of a **contestable market:** the costs of entry and exit are low, so that a firm risks little by entering.[6] If entry is later judged to be a mistake, exit is relatively easy because fixed costs are not sunk costs, but are instead recoverable. Entry into a contestable market may require the use of large amounts of capital, but so long as the capital is recoverable, and not a sunk cost, the large capital requirement is not a high barrier to entry.

In a contestable market, potential competition, as well as actual entry, can discipline firms selling in the market. When entry and exit are not expensive, even a single seller in a market faces the serious prospect of

competition. Contestable markets yield two important results: (a) prices will not for long be higher than the level necessary to achieve zero economic profits, and (b) least-cost production will occur. The reason is that both inefficiency and prices above costs present a profitable opportunity to new entrants. Potential competitors who see an opportunity for economic profit can be expected to enter and move the market toward the perfectly competitive result.

These results do have a policy implication: if policy-makers want to correct an oligopoly (or monopoly) situation, they should consider what might be done to make the market in question contestable. Much of the enthusiasm of economists for deregulation can be traced to the fact that regulation often is the primary restraint to entry. Many economists believe that deregulation permitting new entry can make many markets contestable, achieving lower prices and more efficiency than can direct regulation of producers. We will have more to say about this in the next chapter.

───────────────

[6]The classic article on this topic is William J. Baumol's "Contestable Markets: An Uprising in the Theory of Industry Structure," *American Economic Review* 72 (March 1982), pp. 1–15.

dominant firm in an industry. However, it may be that rivals are more likely to match a price reduction than a price increase. If a nondominant firm increases its price, other firms could expand their market shares by maintaining their current prices. The sales of the firm that increases its price may fall substantially. On the other hand, when a single oligopolist lowers its price, it seems likely that rivals will respond. If they do not, their sales may fall sharply. If the price reduction is matched by the other firms of the industry, however, it is not likely to increase sales substantially for any single firm.

Kinked Demand Curve: A demand curve that is highly elastic for a price *increase* but inelastic for a price *reduction*. These differing elasticities are based on the assumption that rival firms will match a price reduction but not a price increase.

The hypothesis of the **kinked demand curve** is based on these assumptions about the reactions of rival firms. The essential idea of the kinked demand curve is that the oligopolist's demand curve will be (a) very *elastic* for a price increase, because customers would be lost to other firms, who will maintain their price, but (b) very inelastic for a price reduction because the other firms, seeking to maintain their market share, will respond by lowering their price.

Exhibit 7 illustrates the kinked demand curve. Since the demand curve is kinked at output Q, the marginal revenue curve will be discontinuous. This means that marginal costs could vary substantially at output Q while continuing to equal marginal revenue. For example, both MC_1 and MC_2 intersect the MR curve at output Q. Therefore, despite these changes in cost, the profit-maximizing price of the oligopolist will remain at P. When the demand curve of a firm is kinked, the firm's profit-maximizing price may remain unchanged despite substantial changes in cost conditions. Thus, the theory implies that prices in oligopolistic markets are likely to be quite stable.

Economists continue to debate the importance of the kinked demand curve hypothesis. Initially, the widespread use of price lists and categories that estab-

EXHIBIT 7

The Kinked Demand Curve

Here we illustrate the demand curve of an oligopolist when rivals match a price reduction but fail to respond to a price increase. Under these assumptions, if an oligopolistic firm increases its price, it will lose many customers to rival firms. In contrast, a price reduction, since it will be matched by competitors, will lead to few additional customers. Thus, the oligopolist's demand curve is kinked, and the corresponding MR curve is discontinuous, as shown. The oligopolist will not change price even if MC fluctuates between E and F.

lished prices in oligopolistic industries for a significant time period was thought to be consistent with the concept of a kinked demand and stable prices. Recent studies suggest, however, the price stability in oligopolistic industries may be more apparent than real. These studies have found that even when the *list* price of a product is stable, firms use such factors as discounts, credit terms, and delivery conditions to alter ''price'' in response to changing market conditions. In any event, it is clear that the kinked demand theory does not offer a complete explanation of price determination. Even though the theory predicts tendencies *once a price is established,* it does not explain how the initial price is set.

LIMITS OF THE OLIGOPOLY MODEL

Market Power: The ability of a firm that is not a pure monopolist to earn unusually large profits, indicating that it has some monopoly power. Because the firm has few (or weak) competitors, it has a degree of freedom from the discipline of vigorous competition.

Uncertainty and imprecision characterize the theory of oligopoly. We know that firms will gain if they can successfully agree to restrict output and raise price. However, collusion also has its costs. We have outlined some of the conflicts and difficulties (costs) associated with the establishment of perfect cooperation among oligopolistic firms. In some industries, these difficulties are considerable, and the **market power** of the oligopolists is therefore relatively small. In other industries, oligopolistic cooperation, although not perfect, may raise prices significantly. Economists would say that such firms have market power, indicating that even though these firms are not pure monopolists, they do have some monopoly power. Analysis of the costs and benefits of collusive behavior, while it does not yield precise predictions on oligopoly pricing, at least allows us to determine when discipline by competitive pressures is more likely for an oligopolist.

CONCENTRATION AND REAL-WORLD OLIGOPOLISTIC POWER

Concentration Ratio: The total sales of the four (or sometimes eight) largest firms in an industry as a percentage of the total sales of the industry. The higher the ratio, the greater is the market dominance of a small number of firms. The ratio can be seen as a measure of oligopolistic power.

Which industries are dominated by a small number of firms? How important is oligopoly? Economists have traditionally used a tool, the concentration ratio, to help answer these questions.

The **concentration ratio** is the percentage of total industry sales made by the four (or sometimes eight) largest firms of an industry. This ratio can vary from nearly zero to 100, with 100 indicating that the sales of the four largest firms comprise those of the entire industry.

The concentration ratio can be thought of as a broad indicator of competitiveness. In general, the higher (lower) the concentration ratio, the more (less) likely that the firms of the industry will be able to successfully collude against the interests of consumers. This ratio, though, is by no means a perfect measure of competitiveness. Since the sales of foreign producers are excluded, it overstates the degree of concentration in industries in which foreign firms compete. Neither does the concentration ratio reveal the elasticity of demand for products, even though concentration is not as great a problem if good substitutes for a product are available. For example, the market power of aluminum producers is partially limited by competition from steel, plastics, copper, and similar products. Similarly, the monopoly power of commercial airlines is substantially reduced by the availability of automobiles, buses, chartered private flights, and even conference telephone calls. Concentration ratios tend to conceal such competitiveness among products.

The concentration ratio can also overstate the competitiveness in instances in which the relevant market area is a city or region. For example, consider the case of newspaper publishing companies. In 1982, there were more than 7500 such companies in the United States. Sales of the four largest companies amounted to only 22 percent of the national market. Most cities, however, were served by only one or two newspapers. In most market areas, newspaper publishing is a highly concentrated industry, even though this is not true nationally. In this instance, the low concentration ratio for the nation in the newspaper publishing industry probably understates the market power of most newspapers in their local markets.

What do concentration ratios reveal about the U.S. economy? Exhibit 8 presents concentration data for several manufacturing industries in 1947 and in 1982, the most recent year for which the Census Bureau concentration ratios for industries economy-wide are available. Several industries, including the automobile, steel, aircraft, telephone and telegraph, computer equipment, and soap industries, are dominated by a few firms. They are oligopolistic. At the other end of the spectrum, the "big four" accounted for less than 20 percent of the sales of sporting goods, saw mill products, bottled and canned soft drinks, and commercial printing.

Most research suggests that there has been, if anything, an increase in business competitiveness over the last several decades. *Within specific industries,*

EXHIBIT 8 ■ Concentration Ratios for Selected Manufacturing Industries in 1947 and 1982

Industry	1947	1982	Change
High concentration (40 or more)			
Motor vehicles and car bodies	71	92	+21
Blast furnaces and steel mills	50	42	− 8
Tires and inner tubes	70[a]	66	− 4
Aircraft and parts	72	64	− 8
Telephone and telegraph	92	76	−16
Farm machinery	36	53	+17
Soap and other detergents	72[a]	60	−12
Photographic equipment and supplies	61	74	+13
Electronic computing equipment	66[a]	43	−23
Medium concentration (20–39)			
Petroleum	37	28	− 9
Bread, cake, and related products	16	34	+18
Periodicals	34	20	−14
Gray iron foundries	16	29	+13
Toilet preparations	24	34	+10
Pharmaceuticals	28	26	− 2
Newspapers	21	22	+ 1
Meat packing	41	29	−12
Low concentration (less than 20)			
Bottled and canned soft drinks	12[a]	14	+ 2
Commercial printing	13[a]	7	− 6
Sporting and athletic goods	24	17	− 7
Sawmills	11[a]	17	+ 6

[a]Data are for 1963.

Source: U.S. Bureau of the Census, *Census of Manufacturing, 1947* and *1982*.

there are cases of both increases and decreases in the degree of concentration. For example, concentration increased in the motor vehicle, farm machinery, and photographic equipment industries between 1947 and 1982. On the other hand, the degree of concentration in aircraft, computer equipment, steel, telephone and telegraph equipment, and meat packing has declined significantly in recent years.

CONCENTRATION AND MERGERS

Horizontal Merger: The combining of the assets of two or more firms engaged in the production of *similar products* into a single firm.

At some points in American history, especially during the early developmental stages of American manufacturing, mergers had an important influence on the structure of our economy. The desire of oligopolistic firms to merge is not surprising. A **horizontal merger,** the combining of two or more firms' assets under the same ownership, provides the firms with an alternative to both the rigors of competition and the insecurity of collusion.

There have been two great waves of horizontal mergers. The first occurred between 1887 and 1904; the second between 1916 and 1929. Many corporations whose names are now household words—U.S. Steel, General Electric, Standard Oil, General Foods, General Mills, and American Can, for example—are products of mergers formed during these periods. Mergers led to a dominant firm in manufacturing industries such as steel, sugar refining, agricultural implements, leather, rubber, distilleries, and tin cans.

Analysis of these horizontal mergers leads to two interesting observations. First, horizontal mergers can create a highly profitable dominant firm, even if there is freedom of entry into an industry. The entry of new competitors takes time. A firm formed by merger that controls a substantial share of the market for a product can often realize oligopolistic profits for a period of time before the entry of new firms drives prices back down to the level of average cost. Of course, if entry barriers can be established to limit or retard the entry of new rivals, the incentive to merge is further strengthened.[7] Second, with the passage of time, competitive forces have generally eroded the position of the dominant firms created by horizontal mergers. Almost without exception, the market share of the dominant firms created by horizontal mergers began to decline soon after the mergers were consummated. Smaller firms gained ground relative to the dominant firm. This suggests that temporary profits stemming from market power, rather than economies of scale, were the primary motivation for the horizontal mergers. In 1950, the Celler-Kefauver Act made it substantially more difficult to use horizontal mergers as a means of developing oligopolistic power. Today, mergers involving large firms seldom involve former competitors.

Vertical Merger: The creation of a single firm from two firms, one of which was a supplier or customer of the other—for example, a merger of a lumber company with a furniture manufacturer.

Another type of merger, the **vertical merger,** joins a supplier and a buyer— for example, an automobile maker and a steel producer. A vertical merger might simplify the long-range planning process for both firms and reduce the need for costly legal contracting between the two. Even though vertical mergers generally do not increase concentration within industries, some economists are concerned that such mergers may reduce competition if either the buyer or the supplier grants a market advantage to the other.

Conglomerate Merger: The combining under one ownership of two or more firms that produce *unrelated products*.

A **conglomerate merger** combines two firms in unrelated industries. The stated intent is usually to introduce new and superior management into the firm

---

[7]See George Stigler, ''Monopoly and Oligopoly by Merger,'' *American Economic Review* (May 1950), pp. 23–34, for a detailed analysis of this issue.

being absorbed. This type of merger results in increased size but not necessarily in reduced competition. Since the 1960s, when some very large corporations were formed by conglomerate merger, some observers have expressed concern that the concentration of political power created by such mergers and the enormous financial assets available to the operating units may be potentially dangerous. Others have argued that conglomerate mergers often lead to more efficient management and increased competitiveness within specific industries.

CONCENTRATION AND PROFITS

The model of oligopoly implies that if the firms in concentrated industries cooperate with one another, they can *jointly* exercise monopoly power. Is there a relationship between industrial concentration and profitability in the real world? Researchers in this area have not been able to arrive at a definite conclusion. An early study by Joe Bain showed a distinctly positive relationship between concentration and profitability. George Stigler, in a detailed study of manufacturing industries, found that from 1947 to 1954 "the average [profit] rate in the concentrated industries was 8.00 percent, while that in the unconcentrated industries was 7.16 percent." Later, both a study by William Shepherd covering the period from 1960 to 1969 and the White House Task Force on Antitrust Policy presented evidence that the rate of profitability is higher in concentrated industries.

More recent research results indicate that greater profits for larger firms are likely to come from greater efficiency, so that prices are lower. As Sam Peltzman concluded in his 1977 study, "Briefly, more concentration raises profitability not because prices rise, but because they fall less than costs."[8] Other researchers are not fully convinced. In any case, the weight of the evidence is that the profit rate of firms in concentrated industries is only slightly higher than the profit rate of other firms. Demand conditions, efficient management and superior entrepreneurship are the main determinants of profitability. Thus, the odds are only a little better than 50–50 that a more concentrated industry will be more profitable than a less concentrated one.

MARKET POWER AND PROFIT—THE EARLY BIRD CATCHES THE WORM

In the last chapter, we saw that under certain conditions an unregulated monopolist can earn economic profit, even in the long run. Similarly, our analysis of oligopoly suggests that if barriers to entry are high, firms might be consistently able to earn above-average profits, even in the long run. Suppose a well-established firm, such as Exxon or General Motors, is able to use its market power to earn consistent economic profits. Do its current stockholders gain because of its monopoly power? Surprisingly, the answer is no. The ownership value of a share of corporate stock for such a corporation long ago began to reflect its market power and profitability. Many of the *present* stockholders paid high prices for their stock because they expected the firm to be highly profitable. In other words, they paid for any above-normal economic profits that the firm was expected to earn because of its monopoly power.

Do not expect to get rich buying the stock of monopolistic or oligopolistic

---

[8]Sam Peltzman, "The Gains and Losses from Industrial Concentration," *Journal of Law and Economics* 20 (Oct. 1977): 257. For a detailed analysis of this issue, see Leonard W. Weiss, "The Concentration—Profits Relationship and Antitrust," in H. J. Goldschmid et al., eds. *Industrial Concentration: the New Learning*. Boston: Little, Brown, 1974. 184–232; and John S. McGee, *Industrial Organization*. Englewood Cliffs: Prentice Hall, 1988, 332–37.

MYTHS OF ECONOMICS

"The prices of most goods are unnecessarily inflated by at least 25 percent as a result of the high rate of profit of producers."

Profits are about as popular with consumers as failing grades are with stu-

dents at the end of a term. When food prices rise, the profits of farmers, meat processors, and food store chains are heavily publicized by the news media. If gasoline prices jump, many people believe that they are being pushed up by greedy profiteer-

ing on the part of the major oil companies. The casual observer might easily be left with the impression that large profits are the major source of the high cost of living.

This issue is clouded by the fact that both the size of profits and their

EXHIBIT 9
How Great Are Profits?

After-tax corporate profits average about 12 percent of stockholder equity and 5 percent of sales in the United States.

(a) Corporate after-tax profits as a percentage of stockholder equity

(b) Corporate after-tax profits as a percentage of corporate sales

Source: *Economic Report of the President, 1988.* As the result of changes in definitions and accounting procedures, the data for one period may not be perfectly comparable to the figures for other periods.

firms known to be highly profitable. You are already too late. The early bird catches the worm. Those who owned the stock when these firms initially developed their market position have already captured the gain. The value of their stock increased at that time. After a firm's future prospects are widely recognized, subsequent stockholders fail to gain a higher-than-normal rate of return on their financial investment.

LOOKING AHEAD

The competitiveness of a market economy is influenced not only by the various market structures operating within it but also by public policy. Business activity is often directly regulated by the government. In the next chapter, we will invesfunction are largely misunderstood by most people. Surveys show that young people believe the after-tax profits of corporations comprise between 25 and 30 percent of sales. A national sample poll of adults conducted by Opinion Research of Princeton found that the average person thought profits comprised 29 cents of every dollar of sales in manufacturing. In reality, as Exhibit 9b shows, the after-tax accounting profits of manufacturing corporations are about 4 to 5 percent of sales. Thus, the public believes that the rate of profit as a percentage of sales is nearly six times as great as the actual figure!

Why are people so misinformed on this issue? The popular media are one source of confusion. They nearly always report the accounting profits of firms in dollar terms, instead of comparing them to sales, stockholder equity, or the value of the firms' assets. A favorite device is to report that profits, either annually or quarterly, were up by some astonishing percentage.[9] Unless we know whether profits were high, normal, or low during the previous period, this type of statement tells little or nothing about the firm's earnings rate on its capital assets. For example, suppose a corporation with $100 million of assets earned a profit of $2 million last year, a 2 percent rate of return on its capital assets. Now, suppose the firm's earnings this year are $4 million, generating only a 4 percent rate of return. It would not be unusual for the popular media to report, "The profits of corporation X soared to $4 million, a 100 percent increase over last year." What this statement conceals is that the profits of the firm as a percentage of its capital assets were less than one could earn on a savings account.

Not only is the average person misinformed about the size of profits, but most people do not understand their function. Many believe that if profits were eliminated, our economy would continue to operate as if nothing had happened. This erroneous view indicates a misunderstanding of what accounting profits are. Accounting profits are primarily a monetary return to those who have invested in machines, buildings, and nonhuman productive resources. Investment in physical capital involves both risk and the forgoing of current consumption. If profits were eliminated, the incentive of persons to invest and provide the tools that make the American worker the most productive in the world would be destroyed. Who would invest in either physical or human capital (for example, education) if such investments did not lead to an increase in future income—that is, if investment did not lead to accounting profit?

Profits play an important role in our economy. People who increase the value of resources—who produce something that is worth more than the resources that went into it—are rewarded with economic profit (and generally an above-average accounting profit). Those who allocate resources to a venture producing outputs that consumers value less than the venture's opportunity cost will experience economic losses (below-average accounting profits). Without this reward-penalty system, individuals (and firms) would have neither the information nor the incentives to use resources wisely and produce the goods that consumers desire most, relative to the goods' opportunity costs.

---

[9]This is equally true for large wage increases. Apparently, the extreme example rather than the norm helps to sell newspapers. We should note that such reports do not imply an antibusiness bias. The *Wall Street Journal*, not noted for such bias, regularly headlines it stories in the same manner.

tigate the business structure of the U.S. economy and consider the impact of regulatory activities.

CHAPTER SUMMARY

1. The distinguishing characteristics of monopolistic competition are (a) firms that produce differentiated products, (b) low barriers to entry into and exit from the market, and (c) a substantial number of independent, rival firms.

2. Monopolistically competitive firms face a gently downward-sloping demand curve. They often use product quality, style, convenience of location, advertising, and price as competitive weapons. Since all rivals within a monopolistically competitive industry are free to duplicate another's products (or services), the demand for the product of any one firm is highly elastic.

3. A profit-maximizing firm will expand output as long as marginal revenue exceeds marginal cost. Thus, a firm under monopolistic competition will lower its price so that output can be expanded until MR = MC. The price charged by the profit-maximizing monopolistic competitor will be greater than its marginal cost.

4. If monopolistic competitors are making economic profits, rival firms will be induced to enter the market. They will expand the supply of the product (and similar products), enticing some customers away from established firms. The demand curve faced by an individual firm will fall (shift inward) until the profits have been eliminated.

5. Economic losses will cause monopolistic competitors to exit from the market. The demand for the products of each remaining firm will rise (shift outward) until the losses have been eliminated.

6. Since barriers to entry are low, firms in a monopolistically competitive industry will make only normal profits in the long run. In the short run, they may make either economic profits or losses, depending on market conditions.

7. Traditional economic theory has emphasized that monopolistic competition is inefficient because (a) price exceeds marginal cost at the long-run equilibrium output level; (b) long-run average cost is not minimized; and (c) excessive advertising is sometimes encouraged. However, other economists have argued more recently that this criticism is misdirected. According to the newer view, firms under monopolistic competition have an incentive to (a) produce efficiently; (b) undertake production if and only if their actions will increase the value of resources used; and (c) offer a variety of products.

8. Although standard economic models do not include the judgments made under uncertainty by entrepreneurs, economists generally recognize that the world is not so simple as our models indicate, and that entrepreneurial judgments are, in fact, important.

9. Oligopolistic market structure is characterized by (a) an interdependence among firms, (b) substantial economies of scale that result in only a small number of firms in the industry, and (c) significant barriers to entry. Oligopolists may produce either homogeneous or differentiated products.

10. There is no general theory of price, output, and equilibrium for oligopolistic markets. If rival oligopolists acted totally independently of their competitors, they would drive price down to the level of cost of production. Alternatively, if they used collusion to obtain perfect cooperation, price would rise to the level that a monopolist would charge. The actual outcome lies between these two extremes.

11. Collusion is the opposite of competition. Oligopolists have a strong incentive to collude and raise their prices. However, the interests of individual firms will conflict with those of the industry as a whole. Since the demand curve faced by individual firms is far more elastic than the industry demand curve, each firm could gain by cutting its price (or raising product quality) by a small amount so that it could attract customers from rivals. If several firms tried to do this, however, the collusive agreement would break down.

12. Oligopolistic firms are less likely to collude successfully against the interests of consumers if (a) the number of rival firms is large; (b) it is costly to prohibit competitors from offering secret price cuts (or quality improvements) to customers; (c) entry barriers are low; (d) market demand conditions tend to be unstable; and/or (e) the threat of antitrust action is present.

13. Competition can come from potential, as well as actual rivals. If entry and exit are not expensive, and if there are no legal barriers to entry, the theory of contestable markets indicates that competitive results may occur even if only one or a few firms are actually in the market.

14. The kinked demand curve helps explain why oligopolistic prices may tend to be inflexible. Under the basic assumption of the kinked demand curve—rivals will match

price reductions but not increases—a firm's price rise leads to a sharp reduction in its sales, but a price reduction attracts a few new customers. Thus, once a price is established, it remains inflexible for extended periods of time.

15. Analysis of concentration ratios suggest that, on balance, there has been an increase in the competitiveness of the U.S. economy in recent decades.

16. Accounting profits as a share of stockholder equity are probably slightly greater in highly concentrated industries than in those that are less concentrated. The relationship between profits and concentration, however, is not a close one. This suggests that several other factors, such as changing market conditions, quality competition, risk, and ability to exclude rivals, are the major determinants of profitability.

17. The after-tax accounting profits of business firms average about 5 cents of each dollar of sales, substantially less than most Americans believe to be the case. Accounting profits average approximately 12 percent of stockholder equity. This rate of return (accounting profit) provides investors with the incentive to sacrifice current consumption, assume the risk of undertaking a business venture, and supply the funds to purchase buildings, machines, and other assets.

CRITICAL ANALYSIS QUESTIONS

1. Street-corner vendors using pushcarts have sometimes engaged in price wars at popular locations within Washington, D.C. Each vendor would like to drive out the other sellers and have the prime location to himself. Explain why a strategy of cutting price below cost in order to drive out other vendors would not make sense, if there are no legal barriers to entry.

*2. Suppose that a group of investors wants to start a business operated out of a popular Utah ski area, and the group is considering either building a new resort or starting a new local airline serving that market. Each new business would require about the same amount of capital and personnel hiring. The group believes each to have the same profit potential. Which is the safer (less likely to result in a substantial capital loss) investment? Why? Is there an offsetting advantage to the other investment?

3. "Monopolistic competition is inefficient. Not only are prices higher than marginal cost, and average cost above the minimum in long-run equilibrium, the firms do not make long-run profits! Consumers lose, and even the firms don't gain." Evaluate.

4. "The important functions of entrepreneurs cannot be put into an economic model. The models therefore are useless." Evaluate.

*5. "My uncle just bought stock in Mammoth Insurance, Incorporated. It has long been one of the most profitable firms in the business. I have a smart uncle!" Evaluate.

*6. Why is oligopolistic collusion more difficult when there is product variation than when the products of all firms are identical?

7. "Market conditions in the world oil market are constantly changing. This makes it difficult for the Organization of Petroleum Exporting Countries (OPEC) to collude successfully and hold price far above the marginal cost of oil." Evaluate.

8. "World markets are impossible to control, because you cannot keep out new competitors. Brazil, once a major oil importer, illustrated the problem when it reached a production level of 600,000 barrels a day. OPEC, the oil cartel, will never again be able to raise prices as they did for a time at the beginning, and again at the end, of the 1970s." Evaluate.

*9. "A high concentration ratio virtually guarantees monopoly pricing and excess profits." Evaluate.

10. We have a theory to explain the equilibrium price and output for monopoly, but not for oligopoly. Why?

---

*Asterisk denote questions for which answers are given in Appendix C, Selected Answers.

11. "Successful collusion by a group of oligopolists contains the seeds of its own destruction, generating incentives that will destroy cooperation." Evaluate.

*12. What determines the *variety* of styles, designs, and sizes of different products? Why do you think there are only a few different varieties of toothpicks, but lots of different types of napkins on the market?

*13. How would the imposition of a fixed, per unit tax of $2,000 on new automobiles affect the average *quality* of automobiles, if the proceeds of the tax were used to subsidize a government operated lottery?

14. What is the primary function of the entrepreneur? Some economists have charged that the major market-structure models of economic theory assume away the function of the entrepreneur. In what sense is this true? Is the function of the entrepreneur important? Discuss.

15. Is quality and style competition as important as price competition? Would you like to live in a country where government regulation restricted the use of quality and style competition? Why or why not? Do you think you would get more or less for your consumer dollar if quality and style competition were restricted? Discuss.

16. Suppose that a monopolistic competitor is currently charging a price that maximizes the firm's total revenue. Will this price also maximize the firm's profit? Why or why not? Explain.

Business Structure, Regulation, and Deregulation

If we can avoid the creation of undue market power, by and large we expect to achieve better market performance— better in terms of lower prices, higher quality products and innovations both in product and technology.[1]

Donald F. Turner, Former Chief of the Antitrust Division,
U.S. Department of Justice

CHAPTER FOCUS

■ How is the U.S. economy structured? In particular, what role does big business play? How important is competition?

■ What forms of antitrust legislation are important? What are its policy objectives? How effective has it been?

■ What new directions have appeared for antitrust policy in recent years?

■ What theories do economists put forth to explain and predict government regulation of business?

■ What has been the history of traditional economic regulation? What changes have been occurring?

■ What is "the new social regulation," and how does it differ from traditional economic regulation? What can we say about its costs and benefits?

Most contemporary economists believe, just as Adam Smith did, that competition and rivalry among business firms provide benefits to consumers and workers alike. Competition forces producers to operate efficiently and to supply consumers with the goods they most intensely desire (relative to costs). Similarly, competition for resources forces each producer to treat workers and other resource suppliers fairly, offering them pay rates and work environments that are attractive relative to those available elsewhere.

But, despite widespread agreement on the desirability of competition, there are two major aspects of competition about which there is a great deal of disagreement: the strength and extent of real-world competitive pressures and the actual effectiveness of governmental regulatory policy. As we have discussed, both the nature of competition and its intensity vary according to the structure of the industry under consideration. For example, as we have seen, competitive elements will eventually be introduced into even highly concentrated oligopolistic industries; at the same time, tendencies toward collusion must also be considered. Economists often disagree on the ability of unregulated markets to provide for a strong competitive environment.

As for the argument concerning the effects of regulation on competition, some economists point out that regulatory policy, by limiting various types of noncompetitive behavior, effectively increases the discipline of the market. Others charge that past regulatory policies have often reduced market competitiveness, contributed to economic inefficiency, and in general, ignored major concerns of consumers and workers. In this chapter, we will analyze the structure of the U.S. economy and consider the effects of regulatory policy on economic behavior in the light of these controversies.

THE STRUCTURE OF THE U.S. ECONOMY

The structure of the U.S. economy is extremely diverse. There are approximately 18 million business firms in the United States. Of these, most are small. In 1985, about 9 million nonfarm, sole proprietorships made money, averaging perhaps $65,000 in receipts. On the other hand, about 10,000 corporations each employed thousands of individuals, and each corporation had business receipts of more than $50 million.

The structure of our economy has changed significantly over the years. In 1870, 50 percent of all workers were employed in agriculture, 24 percent were in service industries, and 18 percent worked in manufacturing. By 1987, agricultural employment had declined to only 3 percent, services had risen gradually to 67 percent, and manufacturing, which had risen to a peak of 35 percent in 1948, totaled 19 percent. These changes have been pronounced since 1950, and the decline in manufacturing employment has prompted concern that the United States may be dying as an industrial power, becoming, instead, a nation of hamburger cooks and laundry workers. (See Applications in Economics box, ''Is U.S. Manufacturing on Its Death Bed?'')

[1]Donald F. Turner, ''The Antitrust Chief Dissents,'' *Fortune* (April 1966), p. 113.

Output in these sectors has not changed in the same way as employment. Labor productivity grew so much in manufacturing that its share of output has stayed nearly constant, about 19 to 24 percent, for the past 70 years—despite its rising, then falling share of employment. The services sector, which includes transportation, communications, wholesale and retail trade, finance, and other industries, has had little productivity increase; so despite its steadily increasing share of the labor force, its share of output has risen only from about 56 percent in 1870 to 67 percent in the late 1980s.

HOW MUCH OF OUR ECONOMY IS COMPETITIVE?

The question, "how much of our economy is competitive," is a difficult one to answer. In a very real sense, every firm competes with every other one for the consumer's additional dollar of spending. Competition is everywhere; the seller of compact discs, for example, competes with the book store and the local restaurant for our entertainment budgets.

As we have discussed, competition, even within an industry, is multidimensional. Dynamic innovation, entrepreneurship, and product-quality competition may be important even in highly concentrated industries. The concentration ratio of an industry, as we found in the previous chapter, provides an indication of competitiveness, but it is an imperfect measure. Available substitutes reduce the monopoly power of firms in some concentrated industries. Other firms are restrained by the threat of entry from potential rivals. Still others face stiff competition from foreign producers.

Product-quality competition may also account for strong rivalry even among a limited number of competitors. Moreover, in a firm as big as General Motors, even the rivalry among divisions (Buick versus Oldsmobile, for example) may be intense. Direct price competition within the firm is presumably controlled, but competition involving quality remains. Leaders in each division compete for recognition and advancement, and each is judged by monthly sales and profit figures. Thus, competitive forces are not entirely absent even in a concentrated industry.

The relative importance of competitive and noncompetitive sectors within the economy changes with time. Moreover—and perhaps most important—it is not clear where the line should be drawn between competitive and noncompetitive industries. Most economists would probably classify unregulated industries in which the four largest firms produce less than 20 or 25 percent of the market as competitive. On the other hand, industries in which the largest firms produce more than half of the output would generally be classified as oligopolistic, suggesting the presence of noncompetitive elements. These categories, however, are arbitrary.

Economist William G. Shepherd has examined the structure of the U.S. economy in depth, and uses four categories to classify the structure of various industries. He has also looked at how much of the U.S. national income is produced by firms in each category, and how those percentages have changed over time. As Exhibit 3 shows, he finds that firms in competitive industries have produced a rising share of national income, while monopolies have produced a falling share. The intermediate categories have also declined in importance. Shepherd attributes the sharp increase in competition from 1958 to 1980 to antitrust policy, increased import competition, and deregulation. Other economists also point to reductions in transportation costs as a contributing factor to the increase in competition.

APPLICATIONS IN ECONOMICS

Is U.S. Manufacturing on Its Deathbed?

Many observers of the United States economy, noting the decline in manufacturing employment over the past four decades, have expressed concern that the United States is becoming a service nation—its workers reduced to hamburger cooks and people who do each other's laundry. Is U.S. manufacturing dying? Clearly, there has been a decline in manufacturing employment (see Exhibit 1). But a careful look at the evidence indicates that this is only part of the story.[2]

Exhibit 1, which graphs the falling proportion of the U.S. workforce in manufacturing since 1960, also indicates that the value of manufacturing output has remained roughly constant throughout the period. The growth in labor productivity has been greater in manufacturing than in other sectors. The fact that the same output share can be maintained with a falling manufacturing workforce means that additional growth can occur in other sectors. From 1960 to 1986, the period covered by Exhibit 1, workers benefitted as real hourly earnings rose by 17 percent.

Another way to look at the changes in the labor force is to look not at which *industries* (service, manufacturing, or agriculture, for example) people work in, but rather at workers' *occupations*. Federal Reserve Bank economist Mack Ott researched changes in the labor force over more than 100 years. (Some of his findings are shown in Exhibit 2.) Dividing workers' occupations into three categories, Ott found a very long and steady trend in the United States away from direct, physical production work—including such occupations as farmers and farm work-

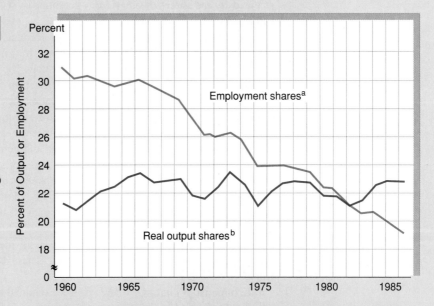

EXHIBIT 1

Real Output and Employment Shares in Manufacturing

While manufacturing took a smaller share of the workforce over the period 1960 to 1986, its share of real output stayed roughly constant. Labor productivity rose substantially, so that fewer workers were required to produce the same output. This made possible additional output (and higher real wages) in the economy as a whole.

[a] Manufacturing as a percent of nonfarm payroll employment.
[b] Manufacturing as a percent of real gross domestic product less agriculture, forestry, and fisheries.

Source: *Economic Report of the President, 1988*. p. 65.

ers, craftspeople, factory supervisors, machine operators, and nonfarm laborers—which we usually think of as "blue collar" work.

Blue collar workers declined from 73 percent of the workforce in 1900 to only 34 percent in 1980. Rather than a large movement toward food service employment or laundry work—classified here as "noninformation" service workers, along with police, firefighters, and building maintenance personnel—the shift was primarily toward "information provision/decision-making" occupations, or "white collar" jobs. This category includes professional and technical workers, managers, clerks,

and sales workers. White collar workers rose from an 18 percent share of the workforce in 1900 to a 53 percent share in 1980. As these large, but gradual changes took place, annual earnings per worker rose more than 500 percent! Meanwhile the noninformational service workforce rose much less, from 9 percent to 13 percent during the same period.

In summary, the shift from manufacturing to service jobs has been occurring for a very long period of time. It represents a shift from blue collar to white collar occupations, and it does not imply a loss of our manufacturing base. Most impor-

tantly perhaps, it has been accompanied by sustained growth in the annual real incomes of U.S. workers and consumers.

[2]The evidence cited in this box is largely from Mack Ott, "The Growing Share of Services in the U.S. Economy—Degeneration or Evolution?" *Review,* Federal Reserve Bank of St. Louis, Vol. 69. No. 6, June/July 1987; *The Statistical History of the United States, from Colonial Times to the Present,* Basic Books, 1976, pp. 164, 165; *Economic Report of the President, 1988,* pp. 60-75; and Dave M. O'Neil, "We're Not Losing Our Industrial Base," *Challenge,* May-June 1986, pp. 19–25.

EXHIBIT 2

More White Collars, Fewer Blue Collars, in America's Work Force

A dramatic shift has steadily occurred over the past century and more, from direct production, or blue collar jobs, to white collar occupations that provide information or decision-making services. At the same time, annual earnings per worker rose more than 500 percent.

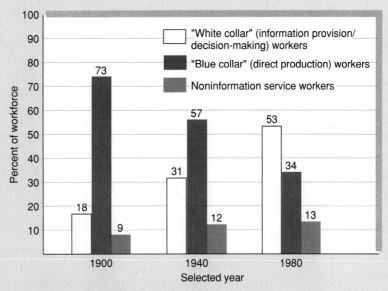

Source: Mack Ott, "The Growing Share of Services in the U.S. Economy—Degeneration or Evolution?" *Review,* Federal Reserve Bank of St. Louis, vol. 69, No. 6, June/July 1987. (Derived from Table 5.)

EXHIBIT 3 ■ The Increasing Competitiveness of the U.S. Economy, 1939–1980

This chart presents the findings of a study by William Shepherd, an industrial economist from the University of Michigan. Shepherd found that the share of national income produced by the competitive sectors of the U.S. economy has been rising for several decades, while the share produced in less competitive markets has been falling. The "single dominant firm" here is one with more than a 50 percent market share, high barriers to entry, and the ability of the dominant firm to control pricing and to influence innovation. A "tight oligopoly" means a 4-firm concentration ratio above 60 percent and stable market shares, or government-regulated firms with the ability to strongly influence the regulated prices.

Market Structure Category	Percentage Shares of National Income Produced in Each Category		
	1939	1958	1980
1. Pure Monopoly	6.2	3.1	2.5
2. Single Dominant Firm	5.0	5.0	2.8
3. Tight Oligopoly	36.4	35.6	18.0
4. Effectively Competitive	52.4	56.3	76.7
Total	100.0	100.0	100.0

Source: William G. Shepherd, "Causes of Increased Competiton in the U.S. Economy, 1939–1980," *Review of Economics and Statistics,* November 1982, p. 618.

PUBLIC POLICY AND BIG BUSINESS IN THE U.S. ECONOMY

The stated objective of public policy has been to restrain various aspects of big business activity, especially when competition seems threatened. Many believe that antitrust action can help promote efficiency and keep political power and income more equally distributed. To what extent does the economic and political power of large corporations threaten competitiveness? To what extent does this power need to be restrained? Some observers argue that large firms threaten our decentralized economic institutions and our democratic political structure. Certainly, public choice theory indicates that concentrated business interests, like other special interest organizations, often exert a disproportional influence on the political process. This notwithstanding, we should keep three points in mind as we evaluate this issue and the effectiveness of the government's antitrust policies.

First, bigness and absence of competition are not necessarily the same thing. A firm can be big and yet function in a highly competitive industry. For example, Sears and Montgomery Ward are both large, but they are also part of a highly competitive industry—retail sales.

Second, large size does not ensure greater profitability. The real-world data indicate that profits as a percentage of stockholder equity are unrelated to corporate size.[3] Many of the companies formed by conglomerate mergers discovered this when their earnings took a nose dive during the 1970s.

Third, the firms that comprise the largest 100 or 200 corporations are heterogeneous and constantly changing. As successful management and the vagaries of

---

[3]See William G. Shepherd, *The Economics of Industrial Organization* (Englewood Cliffs: Prentice-Hall), pp. 270–272, for evidence on this issue. Shepherd found that large corporate size had a mild *negative* impact on the rate of profit of firms during the period from 1960 to 1969.

business fortune exert their influences, some firms are pushed out of the top group and others enter. Following the fate of various firms over time is not easy, since mergers occur and names change, but historical research indicates that of the largest 100 manufacturing corporations in 1909, only 36 remained on the list in 1948. Of the 50 largest in 1947, only 25 remained on the list in 1972, and 5 failed to make even the top 200. Of the top 50 firms in 1954 *Fortune* 500, fifteen did not appear in the 1988 top 50. With time even giants tumble and fall, as technology and preferences change.

ANTITRUST LEGISLATION—THE POLICY OBJECTIVES

Antitrust legislation seeks to (a) ensure that the economy is structured such that competition exists among firms in the same industry (or market area) and to (b) prohibit business practices that tend to stifle competition. Once these objectives are accomplished, it is assumed that market forces can be relied on to allocate goods and services.

There are numerous tactics business entrepreneurs might use to avoid the rigors of competition. We have already stressed that collusion and price agreements are potential weapons with which to turn trade in favor of the seller. Potential competitors might also decide to divide a market geographically, agreeing not to compete in certain market areas. Large, diversified firms might use **predatory pricing,** a practice by which a firm *temporarily* reduces its price below cost in certain market areas in order to damage or eliminate weaker rivals. Once the rivals have been eliminated, the firm uses its monopoly power to raise prices above costs. A competitor might also use exclusive contracts and reciprocal agreements to maintain an advantage over rivals. An **exclusive contract** (or dealership) is an arrangement whereby the manufacturer of a line of products prohibits retailers from selling any of the products of rival producers. An established firm offering many product lines might use this tactic to limit the entry by rivals into retail markets offering only narrow product lines. A **reciprocal agreement** is a situation in which the buyer of a product requires the seller to purchase another product as a condition of sale. For example, General Motors was charged in 1963 with telling railroads that if they did not buy GM locomotives, GM would not ship its automobiles by rail. These business practices involve the use of market power rather than superior performance to gain at the expense of rivals. In one form or another, they are all illegal under current antitrust legislation.

A society that organizes economic activity on the basis of competitive markets rather than on detailed regulation or socialized planning may need to pursue an antitrust policy. The United States, to a greater extent than most Western countries, has adopted antitrust legislation designed to promote competitive markets. Three major legislative acts—the Sherman Act, the Clayton Act, and the Federal Trade Commission Act—form the foundation of antitrust policy in the United States.

The Sherman Act. The Sherman Act was passed in 1890, largely in response to a great wave of mergers. The infamous tobacco, sugar, and Standard Oil trusts

---

Predatory Pricing: The practice by which a dominant firm in an industry temporarily reduces price to damage or eliminate weaker rivals, so that prices can be raised above the level of costs at a later time.

Exclusive Contract: An agreement between manufacturer and retailer that prohibits the retailer from carrying the product lines of firms that are rivals of the manufacturer. Such contracts are illegal under the Clayton Act when they ''lessen competition.''

Reciprocal Agreement: An agreement between firms whereby the buyer of a product requires the seller to purchase another product as a condition of sale. The practice is illegal under the Clayton Act when it substantially reduces competition.

MAJOR ANTITRUST LEGISLATION

enraged Congress and the American people. Action against business concentration was necessary. The most important provisions of the act are the following:

> Section 1: Every contract, combination in the form of trust or otherwise, or conspiracy, in restraint of trade or commerce among the several states or with foreign nations, is hereby declared illegal.
>
> Section 2: Every person who shall monopolize, or conspire with any other person or persons to monopolize any part of the trade or commerce among the several states, or with foreign nations, shall be guilty of a misdemeanor.

The language of the Sherman Act is vague and subject to interpretation. What does it mean to attempt to "monopolize" or combine or "conspire" with another person? Initially, the courts were hesitant to apply the act to manufacturing corporations. In 1911, however, the Supreme Court ruled that Standard Oil and American Tobacco had used "unreasonable" tactics to restrain trade. At the time, the Standard Oil trust controlled 90 percent of the country's refinery capacity. American Tobacco controlled three-fourths of the tobacco manufacturing market. Both firms were broken up into several smaller rival firms.

The Supreme Court, however, did not prohibit monopoly *per se*. It was the tactics used by Standard Oil and American Tobacco that caused the Court to rule against them. In later cases, the Supreme Court refused to break up other trusts (U.S. Steel and American Can, for example) because it could not be proved that they had followed "unfair or unethical" business practices. The Sherman Act, though, does not clearly define unfair or unethical business practices, and the courts were reluctant to enforce it. The act was ineffective, and two other antitrust laws were passed in 1914.

The Clayton Act.   The Clayton Act was passed in an effort to spell out and prohibit specific business practices. The following are prohibited by the Clayton Act when they "substantially lessen competition or tend to create a monopoly": (a) *price discrimination*—charging purchasers in different markets different prices that are unrelated to transportation or other costs; (b) *tying contracts*—a practice whereby the seller requires the buyer to purchase another item; (c) *exclusive dealings*—agreements whereby the seller of a good is forbidden to sell to a competitor of the purchaser; (d) *interlocking stockholding*—one firm purchasing the stock of a competing firm; (e) *interlocking directorates*—the same individual(s) serving on the boards of directors of competing firms.

Although somewhat more specific than the Sherman Act, the Clayton Act is still vague. At what point do the prohibited actions actually become illegal? Under what circumstances do these actions "substantially lessen competition"? The task of interpreting this ambiguous phrase still remains with the courts.

The Federal Trade Commission Act.   The Federal Trade Commission Act declared unlawful all "unfair methods of competition in commerce." The Federal Trade Commission (FTC), composed of five members appointed by the president to seven-year terms, was established to determine the exact meaning of "unfair methods." However, a 1919 Supreme Court decision held that the courts, not the FTC, had the ultimate responsibility for interpreting the law. Today, the FTC is concerned primarily with (a) enforcing consumer protection legislation, (b) prohibiting deceptive advertising, a power it acquired in 1938, and (c) preventing overt collusion.

When a complaint is filed with the FTC, usually by a third party, the commission investigates. If there is a violation, the FTC initially attempts to settle the dispute by negotiation between the parties. If the attempts to negotiate a settlement fail, a hearing is conducted before one of the commission's examiners. The decision of the hearing examiner may be appealed to the U.S. Court of Appeals. The great majority of cases brought before the FTC are now settled by mutual consent of the parties involved.

MORE RECENT ANTITRUST LEGISLATION

Additional antitrust legislation was passed in the 1930s. The Robinson-Patman Act of 1936 prohibits selling "at unreasonably low prices" when such practices reduce competition. The section of the Clayton Act dealing with price discrimination was aimed at eliminating predatory pricing. The Robinson-Patman Act went beyond this. It was intended to protect competitors not just from stronger rivals who might temporarily sell below cost but also from more efficient rivals who were actually producing at a lower cost. Chain stores and mass distributors were the initial targets of the legislation. Economists have often been critical of the Robinson-Patman Act, since it has tended to eliminate price competition and protect inefficient producers.

In 1938, Congress passed the Wheeler-Lea Act, which was designed to strengthen sectors of the Federal Trade Commission Act that had been weakened by restrictive court decisions. Before the passage of the act, the courts were reluctant to prohibit unfair business practices, such as false and deceptive advertising, unless there was proof of damages to either consumers or rival firms. The Wheeler-Lea Act removed this limitation and gave the FTC extended powers to prosecute and ban false or deceptive advertising.

In 1950, Congress passed the Celler-Kefauver Act (sometimes referred to as the antimerger act), which prohibits a firm from acquiring the assets of a competitor if the transaction substantially lessens competition. The Clayton Act, though it prohibits mergers through stock acquisition, proved unable to prevent business combinations from being formed by sale of assets. The Celler-Kefauver Act closed this loophole, further limiting the ability of firms to combine to escape competitive pressures.

Since the intent of the Celler-Kefauver Act is to maintain industrial competition, its applicability to mergers between large firms in the same industry is obvious. The act also prohibits vertical mergers between large firms if competition is reduced by such mergers. For example, the merger of a publishing company with a paper producer is now illegal if the courts find that it lessens competition. However, the applicability of the Celler-Kefauver Act to conglomerate mergers remains ambiguous, primarily because there has not been a clear-cut court decision in this area.

CURRENT ANTITRUST POLICY

Under the Reagan administration, both the Justice Department and the Federal Trade Commission moved toward an emphasis on consumer protection in the enforcement of antitrust laws. There is now less emphasis on the idea that concentration and bigness are bad in themselves. More attention is paid to arguments that emphasize efficiency in production and the possibility of lower consumer prices. The new policy emphasis was signaled by the announcement of the Justice Department's 1982 Merger Guidelines, which recognize the potential value of mergers for efficiency purposes, and call for a challenge to a proposed merger only if it is likely to result in harm to consumers.

THUMBNAIL SKETCH

Antitrust Legislation

Antitrust laws prohibit the following:

1. Collusion—contracts and conspiracies to restrain trade (Sherman Act, Sec. 1)
2. Monopoly and attempts to monopolize any part of trade or commerce among the several states (Sherman Act, Sec. 2)
3. Persons serving on the board of directors of competing firms with more than $1 million of assets (Clayton Act, Sec. 8)
4. Unfair and deceptive advertising (Federal Trade Commission Act as amended by Wheeler-Lea Act)
5. Price discrimination if the intent is to injure a competitor (Robinson-Patman Act)

The following practices are also illegal when they substantially lessen competition or tend to create a monopoly:

1. Tying contracts (Clayton Act, Sec. 3)
2. Exclusive dealings (Clayton Act, Sec. 3)
3. Interlocking stockholdings and horizontal mergers (Clayton Act, Sec. 7, as amended by Celler-Kefauver Act)
4. Interlocking directorates (Clayton Act, Sec. 8)

Herfindahl Index: A measure of industry concentration, calculated by squaring the percentage share of each firm in the industry, then summing the squares. The index can range from zero to 10,000. It is a more sophisticated measure of concentration than the traditional concentration ratio, and is used by the Justice Department in antitrust policy.

The new merger policy uses a relatively new tool, the Herfindahl index, to measure market concentration. The new index measures market power in a way that strongly emphasizes any existing large market share, and gives relatively little weight to any firms holding small market shares, compared with the traditional concentration ratio. (See the Measures of Economic Activity box.) For example, the older measure of concentration does not distinguish between a market in which four firms divide the market equally, and one in which one firm has a large market share, and there are three other much smaller firms. The Herfindahl index gives the latter market a much larger index number, indicating a larger possibility of the presence of significant market power.

The 1982 Merger Guidelines, as clarified and extended in 1984 by the Justice Department—and agreed upon in effect by the Federal Trade Commission—indicate that if a merger results in a Herfindahl index of less than 1,000, then the resulting market is unconcentrated, and the merger generally will not be challenged. If the index would be above 1,000 after the merger, and the merger would add at least 100 points to the index, then a challenge is likely.

Other factors also are considered under the guidelines, especially in borderline cases. A merger is less likely to be challenged if, for the industry:

1. foreign firms are an important source of competition;
2. one of the firms might otherwise go out of business;
3. products are not homogeneous (so quality competition is likely); and
4. a higher price is likely to bring forth new competitors.

In general, the purpose of the new guidelines is to bring a challenge against only those mergers likely to harm consumers by significantly increasing the market power of affected firms. The guidelines have proved to be quite lenient. During the 1979–1980 period, federal agencies tried to block 2.5 percent of proposed mergers. In the years 1982–1986, only 0.7 percent were challenged.

MEASURES OF ECONOMIC ACTIVITY

The Herfindahl Index

The Herfindahl index measures market concentration in a way that gives a great deal of weight to the share of the largest one or two firms in the market. It does so by squaring the percentage each firm has in the market, and summing the squares. If there are n firms in the market, then

H, the Herfindahl index, is:

$$H = S_1^2 + S_2^2 + S_3^2 + \cdots + S_n^2$$

where S_1 in the formula is the percentage share of the largest firm in the market, S_2 is the percentage share of the second largest firm, and so on. Each S can vary from 100 (a pure monopoly, with only one firm in the market) down to almost zero. For a pure monopoly,

$$H = (100)^2 = 10,000$$

This is the largest possible value for the Herfindahl index. By contrast, if there are 100 firms in a market, each with an equal 1 percent share, then

$$H = (1)^2 + (1)^2 + (1)^2 + \cdots + (1)_2 = 100$$

The Herfindahl index is a more sophisticated tool for measuring market power than is the traditional concentration ratio, which treats a market with four firms of equal size the same as a market with four firms, one of which has 70 percent of the market and three that have 10 percent each. The Herfindahl index assigns the equal-shares market an index of 2,500 (4×25^2) and the unequal-shares market an index of 5,200 ($70^2 + 10^2 + 10^2 + 10^2$), indicating the larger potential for market power when one firm has a 70 percent share of the market. Only the shares of the larger firms are needed to approximate the index, since firms with small shares add little to the Herfindahl index.

NEW DIRECTIONS IN ANTITRUST POLICY— THE AT&T AND IBM CASES

Since the days of the Standard Oil trust nearly a century ago, antitrust policy has been strongly influenced by the notion that ideal competitive conditions are characterized by a large number of small firms. This emphasis on the number and size of rival firms has sometimes been pursued with little regard as to how well the interests of consumers are served by a given industry or firm. In the early 1980s the focus of antitrust policy shifted away from the "bigness is bad" syndrome and toward consumer protection. Even before the 1982 Merger Guidelines were announced, this shift became obvious with the settlements in the IBM and AT&T cases on the same day: January 8, 1982. In both cases, the government had previously sought to break the firms into a large number of small firms. Both cases had dragged on for years. The filing of the case against IBM in 1969 was one of the last significant acts of the Johnson administration. The AT&T case was filed in 1975 by the Ford administration. The estimated combined costs of these suits to the government and the companies ran in excess of $500 million.

As part of its settlement, AT&T agreed to divest itself of its 22 local telephone companies with assets of $80 billion. These companies continued to operate as regulated public utilities. In return, AT&T was permitted to enter the fastgrowing electronic data and computer fields, from which it had been barred since 1956.

In the early 1980s, new competitors were severely testing the dominance of AT&T in the telecommunications industry. Even though AT&T had maintained substantial market power in the telephone communications industry, technological developments were eroding its position in the broader electronic communications area. Thus, under the terms of the settlement, the research and development arm of AT&T began to operate within the forces of market pressure, while the telephone communication arm separated and continued to operate in the regulated sector. (See the Applications in Economics box, "AT&T and Cross-subsidies.")

While AT&T operated as a regulated utility, IBM did not. By the late 1960s,

IBM was far and away the dominant firm in the computer-manufacturing industry. Like AT&T, IBM had established an image as an aggressive, innovative company. According to the government's position, IBM was hindering competition by charging prices that were too low for the corporation's smaller rivals to meet. The government, though, failed to adequately prove that consumers had been harmed by IBM's dominant share of the market.

The passage of time and the competitive process played important roles in the resolution of both of these cases. In the late 1960s, it was quite possible that the competitiveness of the computer-manufacturing industry was being endangered by the near-monopoly position of IBM; by the latter half of the 1970s, this was no longer true. Technological innovations, foreign competition, and the presence of strong rivals (Wang and Control Data, for example) were eroding IBM's market position. It was not even clear that any American firm would be the leader in the future computer-manufacturing market. It was against this background that the Reagan administration laid the IBM case to rest.

THE EFFECTIVENESS OF ANTITRUST POLICY— THE DOMINANT VIEW

Few economists are completely satisfied with all aspects of antitrust policy, but most observers believe it has exerted a positive, though probably not dramatic, influence on competitive markets. The Sherman and Clayton Acts prohibit the most efficient methods of collusion (for example, mergers, interlocking boards of directors, and interlocking stockholdings) and thereby raise the costs of colluding. Also, since current collusive agreements must thus be tacit and unenforceable, rivals are more likely to cheat. The expected benefits of collusion have been effectively reduced, and economic theory suggests that the magnitude of anticompetitive collusive business practices should therefore be reduced. In addition, counterproductive (from the viewpoint of society) competitive tactics—exclusive contracts, price discrimination, and tying contracts, for example—have been made more costly. Prohibiting such practices has probably served to reduce entry barriers into markets. Since the passage of the Celler-Kefauver Act, most observers believe that antitrust legislation has effectively limited the power of firms to reduce competition *within an industry* through merger. Today, in contrast with earlier periods in American history, the probability of mergers contributing to industrial concentration—and hindering the competition that tends to erode it—is substantially lower.

ANTITRUST POLICY— THE DISSENTING VIEW

Antitrust, like most other areas of policy, has its critics. Some of the dissenting views are only partially critical. Many economists, though in agreement with overall objectives, disagree with specific aspects of antitrust policy. Many people in business argue that current legislation is vague and that it is therefore difficult to determine whether or not a firm is in compliance.

There are three major dissenting schools of thought on antitrust policy, which include (a) those individuals who would like deconcentration policies to be pursued more vigorously, (b) those who believe that the strength of competitiveness renders antitrust policy unnecessary, and (c) those who believe that antitrust policy is simply incapable of attacking industrial concentration. We will look briefly at each of these views.

Antitrust Policies Should Be More Vigorously Enforced. The proponents of this position argue that greater effort is required to ensure the existence of competitive markets. They often point out that antitrust policy has functioned primarily as a holding action. That is, it prevents large firms from *increasing* their market share, but it is ineffective as a means for *reducing* industrial concentration. Policy can end up working against its own objectives. For example, an established firm controlling 50 or 60 percent of a market is generally left untouched, whereas two smaller firms with a combined market share of as little as 10 percent may be prohibited from merging. Current policy, therefore, often protects strong, established firms while weakening their smaller rivals. Those who view current policy as self-defeating typically favor an antitrust policy that would more thoroughly restructure concentrated industries, dividing large firms into smaller, independent units.

The advocates of this position argue that antitrust legislation places too much emphasis on the number of competitors without recognizing the positive role of dynamic competition. They believe an antitrust policy that limits business concentration will often promote inefficient business organization and will therefore encourage higher prices. They reject the notion that pure competition is a proper standard of economic efficiency.[4] As Joseph Schumpeter, an early proponent of this view of competition and regulation, emphasized two decades ago:

> It . . . is a mistake to base the theory of government regulation of industry on the principle that big business should be made to work as the respective industry would work in perfect competition.[5]

Like Schumpeter, current advocates of this position believe innovative activity is at the heart of competition. An ingenious innovator may forge ahead of competitors, but competition from other innovators will always be present. Competition is a perpetual game of leapfrog, not a process that is dependent on the number of firms in an industry. Bigness is a natural outgrowth of efficiency and successful innovation. One of the leading proponents of this position, John McGee, of the University of Washington, argues that concentration is neither inefficient nor indicative of a lack of competition:

> Take an industry of many independent producers, each of which is efficiently using small scale and simple methods to make the same product. . . .Suppose that a revolution in technology or management techniques now occurs, so that there is room in the market for only one firm using the new and most efficient methods. Whether it occurs quickly through merger or gradually through bankruptcy, an atomistic industry is transformed into a "monopoly," albeit one selling the same product at a lower price than before. If expected long-run price should rise, resort can still be had to the old and less efficient ways, which were compatible with . . . small firms. It would be incomplete and misleading to describe that process as a "decline of competition."[6]

The third group of critics argues that antitrust policy is simply incapable of dealing with a modern economy already dominated by a few hundred industrial giants. The leading proponent of

[4]See Dominick T. Armentano, *Antitrust and Monopoly: Anatomy of a Policy Failure* (New York: John Wiley, 1982), for an excellent presentation of this viewpoint.
[5]Joseph Schumpeter, *Capitalism, Socialism and Democracy* (New York: Harper Torchbooks, 1950), p. 106.
[6]John S. McGee, *In Defense of Industrial Concentration* (New York: Praeger, 1971), pp. 21–22.

this position, John Kenneth Galbraith, charges that monopoly power is far too prevalent for one to expect that market forces could be imposed on large corporations. Galbraith argues that even if this were possible, competition would hinder, not help, economic development. Galbraith states his case against antitrust and competition as follows:

> But it will also be evident that the antitrust laws, if they worked as their proponents hoped, would only make problems worse. Their purpose is to stimulate competition, lower prices, otherwise unshackle resource use and promote a more vigorous expansion of the particular industry. But the problem of the modern economy is not inferior performance of the planning system—of the monopolistic or oligopolistic sector, to revive the traditional terminology. The problem is the greater development here as compared with the market system. And the greater the power, the greater the development. Where the power is least—where economic organization conforms most closely to the goals envisaged by the antitrust laws—the development is least. If they fulfilled the hopes of their supporters and those they support, the antitrust laws would make development more unequal by stimulating development further in precisely those parts of the economy where it is now greatest.[7]

THEORIES OF REGULATION AND REGULATORY POLICY

Antitrust policy seeks to assure that the structure of an industry is competitive. Regulatory policies tend to be somewhat more direct and specific, often dictating pricing or operational policies for business firms. What does economics tell us about how regulation can be expected to work? To date, economists have been unable to develop a complete theory of regulation. Given the complex array of political and economic factors involved, this should not be surprising. In regulated markets, predicting what sellers will offer and how much consumers will be willing to buy at various prices is not enough. The regulatory process also must take account of (a) buyers who are unwilling to pay the full cost; (b) sellers who are inefficient producers; (c) politicians who are simultaneously considering thousands of pieces of legislation; and (d) voters, many of whom are "rationally uninformed" on regulatory issues. It is not easy to predict how such a complex system will deal with economic problems.

We can, however, facilitate our discussion of regulation by breaking it down into two major types: traditional economic regulation and the newer social regulation. We can also draw some conclusions about the decision-making of economic and political participants in the regulatory process. Economic analysis indicates that decision-makers in the regulatory process, like those in other areas, respond to incentives. There are three incentive-related characteristics of the regulatory process that should be kept in mind.

1. *The Demand for Regulation Often Stems from the Special Interest Effect and Redistribution Considerations Rather Than from the Pursuit of Economic Efficiency.* The wealth of an individual (or business firm) can be increased by an

[7]John Kenneth Galbraith, *Economics and the Public Purpose* (Boston: Houghton Mifflin, 1973), pp. 216–217.

APPLICATIONS IN ECONOMICS

AT&T and Cross-subsidies

Cross-subsidies are a perennial issue in regulation. When a regulated firm serves more than one market, regulators must allocate fixed costs to each market if they are to set prices according to the average (or total) costs of production. In economics, there is no logical way to allocate such joint costs between the two markets. An unregulated firm has no need to do so. Based on marginal costs and marginal revenues, the firm charges a price to maximize profit (or minimize loss) in each market. Any economic profit leads to more entry, until the price is driven down to average cost. When price (and entry) are regulated, however, the arbitrary division of joint costs is necessary, and consumers in one market may be required to subsidize those in the other market. So it was in the case of telephones.

Local telephone lines are a fixed cost of providing both local and long-distance services. Until the AT&T divestiture settlement in 1982, state and federal regulators had agreed to load much of the fixed cost of the local lines onto the long-distance bills, which were charged according to minutes of use by customers. Rather than recognize the fixed nature of these costs (the same wires had to be in place and maintained regardless of how many minutes they were used, and whether or not any long-distance calls were made) and charge each customer the true (fixed) cost, fixed charges were kept low. Long-distance rates were set high enough to make up the difference.

The result of this system was to provide large subsidies to local service at the expense of long-distance telephone customers. Those who used more than 50 minutes per month[8] of long-distance service paid more than their share of the combined system's costs, while those using less than 50 minutes (a large majority) paid less than the costs they generated. In general, businesses and a few other users paid far more than their share.

The system was politically very popular at the state and local level, because as telephone customers paid their bills each month, they had detailed information before them. Seldom was there a situation in which consumers knew just who to blame in case of a rate increase. In large numbers, they complained to their state regulatory commissions whenever commissioners allowed those bills to rise. The large users were unable to counter the popular pressure on politically selected commissioners. The majority was understandably less upset when others paid the higher bills. This system was very inefficient, however. Long-distance calls costing only 7 to 9 cents a minute at the margin were charged at 30 to 40 cents, so everyone used far less than the optimal amount of long-distance service. The net result was an estimated loss to the economy of $10 to $14 billion. AT&T did not mind the cross-subsidy of local service by long distance, since it provided both, and was assured a fixed rate of return by the regulators.

When technological advances made it possible for new suppliers to enter the industry and serve large customers at a lower rate, the system began to come apart. If the new suppliers could offer a better deal to the biggest customers, the source of the cross-subsidies would disappear. Regulators could keep newcomers out, but now the really huge size of the penalties paid by large users was becoming obvious, and the politics of continuing the system of cross-subsidies became less attractive.

Following the divestiture agreement, AT&T continued to provide long-distance service at rates regulated by the Federal Communications Commission, but MCI, GTE Sprint, and other competitors were also allowed into the market. State regulators still would like to keep local rates low and load costs onto long-distance users, but now AT&T and the other long-distance suppliers, not owning the local firms, are hurt by such an arrangement and will fight it. Lower long-distance rates and a higher fixed cost for local service are observable effects of the competitive forces now in place.

---

[8]This estimate, and the others in this feature, were reported by Professor John T. Wenders in ". . . And Now Learn to Love the Chaos," *Wall Street Journal*, Nov. 29, 1985.

improvement in efficiency and an expansion in production. Regulation introduces another possibility. Sellers can gain if competition in their market is restricted. Buyers can gain, at least in the short-run, if a legal requirement forcing producers to supply goods below cost is passed. Regulation opens up an additional avenue whereby those most capable of bending the political process to their advantage can increase their wealth.

Our earlier analysis suggested that special interest groups, such as well-organized, concentrated groups of buyers or sellers, exert a disproportionate influence on the political process. In addition, the regulators themselves often comprise a politically powerful interest group. Bureaucratic entrepreneurs are key figures in the regulatory process. Their cooperation is important to those who are regulated. In exchange for cooperation, politicians and bureaucrats are offered all manner of political support.

These factors suggest that there will be demand for economic regulation even if it contributes to economic inefficiency. The wealth of specific groups of buyers, sellers, and political participants may be enhanced, even though the total size of the economic pie is reduced. This is particularly true if the burden of economic inefficiency is widely dispersed among rationally uninformed taxpayers and groups of consumers.

2. *Regulation Is Inflexible—It Often Fails to Adjust to Changing Market Conditions.* Dynamic change often makes regulatory procedures obsolete. The introduction of the truck vastly changed the competitiveness of the ground transportation industry (previously dominated by railroad interests). Nevertheless, the regulation of price, entry, and routes continued for years, even though competitive forces had long since eliminated the monopoly power of firms in this industry. Similarly, city building codes that may have been appropriate when adopted have become obsolete and now retard the introduction of new, more efficient materials and procedures. In many cities, for example, regulatory procedures have prevented builders from introducing such cost-saving materials as plastic pipes, pre-constructed septic tanks, and prefabricated housing units. Why does the process work this way? In contrast with the market process, regulatory procedures generally grant a controlling voice to established producers. The introduction of new, more efficient products would reduce the wealth of the existing producers of protected products. The political (regulatory) process is often responsive to these producers' charges that substitute materials (or new producers) would create unfair competition, violate safety codes, or generally be unreliable. Hearings are held. Lawsuits are often filed. Regulatory commissions meet and investigate—again and again. These procedures result in costs, delay, and inflexibility.

3. *With the Passage of Time, Regulatory Agencies Often Adopt the Views of the Business Interests They Are Supposed to Regulate.* Although the initial demand for regulatory action sometimes originates with disorganized groups seeking protection from practices they consider unfair or indicative of monopolistic power, forces are present that will generally dilute or negate the impact of such groups in the long-run. Individual consumers (and taxpayers) have little incentive to be greatly concerned with regulatory actions. Often, they are lulled into thinking that since there is a regulatory agency, the "public interest" is served. In contrast, firms (and employees) in regulated industries are vitally interested in the structure and composition of regulatory commissions. Favorable actions by the commission could lead to larger profits, higher-paying jobs, and insulation from the uncertain-

ties of competition. Thus, firms and employee groups, recognizing their potential gain, invest both economic and political resources to influence the actions of regulatory agencies.

How do vote-maximizing political entrepreneurs behave under these conditions? The payoffs from supporting the views of an apathetic public are small. Clearly, the special interest effect is present. When setting policy and making appointments to regulatory agencies, political entrepreneurs have a strong incentive to support the position of well-organized business and labor interests—often the very groups the regulatory practices were originally designed to police.

Regulatory activity in the United States has expanded substantially since the mid-1960s. As Exhibit 4 shows, federal expenditures for regulatory activities increased rapidly in the 1970s, dropped in the early 1980s, then resumed their expansion in the late 1980s. Total regulatory costs, including both enforcement expenditures and compliance costs, are estimated to be about $100 billion annually.[9]

TRADITIONAL ECONOMIC REGULATION

Economic Regulation:
Regulation of product price or industrial structure, usually imposed on a specific industry. By and large, the production processes used by the regulated firms are unaffected by this type of regulation.

Regulation of business activity is not a new development. In 1887, Congress established the Interstate Commerce Commission (ICC), providing it with the authority to regulate the railroad industry and, later, the trucking industry. Commissions were established to regulate the commercial airline and broadcasting industries (the Civil Aeronautics Board and the Federal Communications Commission, respectively). State commissions have regulated the generation of electrical power for many years. These activities focus on what has been called **economic regulation.**

There are several important elements of traditional economic regulation. First, it is generally industry-specific. For whatever reason, it has been deemed that unregulated market forces create various problems in an industry. Sometimes the problem is monopoly. In other cases, excess supply stemming from "cutthroat" competition is alleged to be a problem. In general, it is believed that regulation of the industry is necessary to protect the interests of the public and to provide for orderly competition. Second, traditional regulation often involves *both* the fixing of price (rates) and the protection of existing firms from potential rivals. Third, as the regulation evolves, it often takes on a cartel-like structure. This is not surprising. As we have discussed, two factors limit the effectiveness of collusive agreements among cartel members. Means must be found to (a) block the entry of potential new competitors and (b) prevent cartel members from cheating on agreements to fix prices. Regulatory agencies are sometimes used to help business firms in a specific industry accomplish both of these objectives.

During the 1970s, widespread dissatisfaction with the traditional regulatory approach developed in several industries. Major steps toward deregulation were taken in the ground and air transportation industries.

Deregulation in the Trucking Industry. The ICC was initially established to regulate rates in the railroad industry. Actually, much of the railroad industry supported the ICC's establishment. For many years, the commission regulated rates and

---

[9]See "Rethinking Regulation," in the *Economic Report of the President, 1989,* for a summary analysis of the economics of regulation. See also the various articles in *Regulation,* No. 3, 1988, for series of updates on various types of federal regulation in the U.S. economy.

EXHIBIT 4

Federal Outlays for Regulatory Activities (in constant 1982 dollars)

One index of federal regulatory activity is the expenditures by the government on those activities. This measure of regulation rose rapidly in the 1970s, reached a peak in 1980, declined, then rose again in the late 1980s.

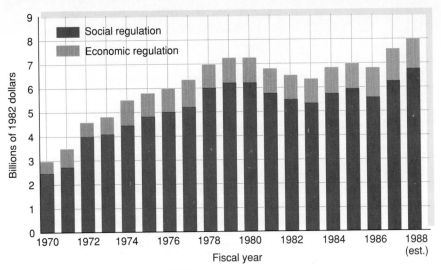

Source: *Economic Report of the President, 1989.*

allocated hauls to various rail shippers. Beginning in the 1930s, however, the railroads began to confront stiff competition from the developing trucking industry. Since the trucking industry could be entered with relative ease, competitive forces were pushing rates downward. In response to the demands of railroad and large trucking interests, in 1935, the regulatory control of the ICC was extended to include the trucking industry.

The ICC influenced the structure of the ground transportation industry in several ways. First, it limited the number of shippers in interstate commerce. Rail and truck shippers were required to obtain licenses from the ICC before they were permitted to compete in the interstate transportation industry. The ICC issued such licenses only when the proposed new service was deemed "necessary for the public convenience." Established shippers were granted the opportunity to present the ICC with counter-evidence attesting that the entry of a new shipper was unnecessary or even harmful. The ICC's policies severely limited entry into the trucking industry.

Second, the ICC regulated shipping rates and permitted the rail and truck industries to establish price-fixing rate bureaus. Competitors who wanted to *reduce* their prices below the schedule established by the rate bureau had to ask the ICC to hear the cases. Typically, it would take six to eight months to obtain a ruling from the ICC. These arrangements strongly discouraged price competition in interstate shipping.

Third, the ICC limited the products that carriers could haul, the routes they could travel, and the number of cities along the route they could serve. Carriers were prohibited from using price reductions as a means to arrange a "return haul." A carrier that was granted a license to haul from St. Louis to Denver might simultaneously have been prohibited from hauling a return shipment along the way, from Kansas City. A carrier's assigned route from New Orleans to Chicago might have required an intermediate stop in Atlanta. The result: miles of wasteful travel and trucks that were empty nearly 40 percent of the time.

"OF COURSE YOU MAY REGISTER A COMPLAINT ABOUT ALL THE GOVERNMENT PAPERWORK, SIR... BUT IT HAS TO BE IN WRITING."

Dunagin's People by Ralph Dunagin © Field Enterprises, Inc. 1977. Permission of News America Syndicate.

The ICC's strict regulation of the trucking industry has been relaxed considerably in recent years. The Motor Carrier Act of 1980 allows freer entry. The number of ICC-authorized carriers rose from about 18,000 in 1980 to 33,548 in 1984. Generally, the act permits competitors to reduce rates as much as 10 percent without obtaining the ICC's approval. The ICC was instructed to eliminate its prohibition on carriers from serving intermediate points along a route and its restrictions that limited the ability of carriers to arrange return-trip haulage. The antitrust immunity of the rate-setting bureaus was removed.

A study by the Federal Trade Commission indicates that the relaxation of entry barriers and rate-fixing policies has exerted a significant impact on the trucking industry.[10] During the first year after passage of the trucking deregulation legislation, the ICC granted 27,960 additional routes to new and existing carriers, compared to only 2,710 during fiscal year 1976. Some 2,452 new firms entered the trucking industry. Discount rates were widespread, and in general, freight rates fell between 5 and 20 percent during 1980–1981. By 1986, revenue per ton for a truckload had fallen by 22 percent. Non-price competition also occurred, as schedule reliability increased, and truckers made more specialized equipment available. There was an influx of small, primarily nonunion carriers into the industry. Price competition led to the acceptance of a temporary wage freeze by the Teamsters union. The influx of competition led to a shakeout in the trucking industry. As the profitability rates of trucking firms fell sharply, failure rates in-

---

[10]A summary of deregulation results, including trucking deregulation, is provided in the *Economic Report of the President—1986*, Ch. 5. See also Thomas Gale Moore, "Transportation Policy," *Regulation*, No. 3, 1988.

creased. According to the American Trucking Associations, 1,400 trucking companies failed in 1984, more than four times the annual rate that occurred in the 1970s.[11]

Deregulation in the Airline Industry. The history of the airline industry has followed a similar pattern. For decades, the airline business was operated under the close supervision of the Civil Aeronautics Board (CAB).[12] In effect, the regulatory powers of the CAB imposed a monopolistic structure on the industry. The CAB blocked competitive entry and outlawed competitive pricing. Any carrier that wanted to compete in an interstate route had to convince the CAB that its services were needed. To say that the CAB limited entry on major routes would be an understatement. Despite more than 150 requests, the CAB did not grant a single trunk (long-distance) route to a new carrier between 1938 and 1978. CAB policy also stifled price competition. Carriers that wanted to lower prices were required to present an application to the CAB. A hearing would be held, at which time the firm's competitors would have ample opportunity to indicate why the impending rate reduction was unfair or potentially harmful to their operations.

At least partially in response to evidence that regulatory policies were leading to excessive fares, half-empty planes, and a uniform product offering, airline regulatory policies in the United States were substantially relaxed in the late 1970s. Under the direction of economist Alfred Kahn, the CAB moved toward deregulation. Carriers were permitted to raise prices by as much as 10 percent and lower them by as much as 70 percent merely by giving the CAB notice 45 days in advance. In 1978, Congress passed the Airline Deregulation Act, which reduced the restrictions on price competition and entry into the industry.

What has been the result of the move toward deregulation? A 1986 Brookings Institution study by Clifford Winston and Stephen Morrison concluded that airline passengers gained about $11.5 billion annually, in 1988 dollars, from deregulation. The airline industry has expanded, with employment growing about one-third from 1977 to 1986.[13] During the same period, flights increased 28 percent and miles flown by paying passengers rose 61 percent. Despite the large increase in the number of flights, safety has improved. Free entry into the airline industry has also meant an expansion of air service to small communities.

Deregulation substantially increased airline efficiency. With higher, regulated fares, airlines competed partly by increased frequency of flights on lucrative routes. This meant that planes flew nearly half empty on those flights. After deregulation, however, lower fares and new entrants were allowed, and efficiency became critical to each firm's survival. The average passenger load factor (percent of seats filled) increased from about 54 to about 60 percent. The loads hauled per employee rose nearly 20 percent on the major airlines.

[11]See Daniel Machalaba, "More Companies Push Freight Haulers to Get Better Rate, Service" *Wall Street Journal*, December 18, 1985.
[12]Many people incorrectly associate the CAB with regulation of air safety, a function that it did perform in the past. However, since 1958, the Federal Aviation Agency has been responsible for air safety rules.
[13]See Thomas Gale Moore, "Transportation Policy," *Regulation*, No. 3, 1988, p. 59, and the *Economic Report of the President, 1988*, pp. 199–229 for more details.

THE NEW SOCIAL REGULATION

Social Regulation:
Legislation designed to improve the health, safety, and environmental conditions available to workers and/or consumers. The legislation usually mandates production procedures, minimum standards, and/or product characteristics to be met by producers and employers.

Along with movement toward deregulation of industrial structure and prices, there has been a sharp increase in what economists call social regulation. In the late 1960s and early 1970s, people had great faith in the ability of government to improve the quality of life. The economy was prospering, and people turned their attention more toward reducing health hazards, preserving the environment, and reducing the negative impacts of new technologies and the booming economy. The new social regulation was one result. It consists of a body of laws in the areas of health, safety, and the environment. Agencies such as the Occupational Safety and Health Administration (OSHA), Consumer Product Safety Commission (CPSC), Food and Drug Administration (FDA), and Environmental Protection Agency (EPA) grew rapidly. These new agencies as a group are now larger, in terms of number of employees and size of budgets, than the older regulatory agencies.

There are several significant differences between the two types of regulation. The older economic regulation focuses on a specific industry, whereas the new social regulation applies to the entire economy. Also, though more broadly based, social regulation is much more involved than economic regulation in the actual details of an individual firm's production. Economic regulation confines its attention to price and product quality—the final outcomes of production. The social regulatory agencies, on the other hand, frequently specify in detail the engineering processes to be followed by regulated firms and industries.

The major cost of social regulation is generally felt in the form of higher production costs and higher prices. Social regulation requires producers to alter production techniques and facilities in accordance with dictated standards—to install more restrooms, to emit less pollution, or to reduce noise levels, for example—and most of the mandated changes increase costs. Of course, there are costs associated with the process of regulation itself; employment and operating costs of regulatory agencies must be met, which means higher taxes. The higher cost stemming from mandated regulations can also be seen as a tax. As Exhibit 5

EXHIBIT 5

The Regulation "Tax"

Regulation that requires businesses to adopt more costly production techniques is similar to a tax. If the regulation increases per unit costs by t, the supply curve shifts upward by that amount. Higher prices and a smaller output result.

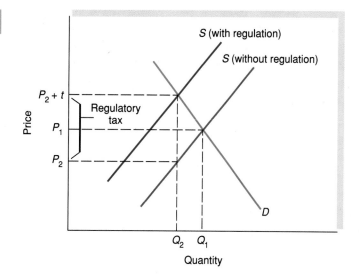

illustrates, the higher cost shifts the supply curve for a good affected by the regulation to the left. Higher prices and a decline in the output of the good result.

Who pays the cost? As with any tax, the burden is shared by buyers and sellers according to the elasticity of supply and demand. When consumers have more options to the taxed good, so that their demand is more elastic, they will pay a smaller portion of the tax. In Exhibit 5, the new price $(P_2 + t)$ will be closer to P_1 when demand is more elastic. Sellers will pay a smaller portion when the supply curve is more elastic, meaning that they have other options. In the short run, suppliers of goods may have few options for the use of capital already committed to the production process. Therefore, the short-run supply is likely to be inelastic. In the long-run, of course, capital is quite mobile among uses, and the supply should be more elastic.

Sometimes the opportunity cost of social regulation is nearly impossible to calculate. For example, the FDA often bans the sale of a new drug until years of tests costing millions of dollars are completed, demonstrating that the drug is safe. Two important costs of this regulation, if the drug finally proves (or would have

APPLICATIONS IN ECONOMICS

Buying Fuel Conservation—Expensively

In 1975, Congress, which had imposed price controls on gasoline to keep costs down for consumers, established CAFE (Corporate Average Fuel Economy) standards to force auto companies to make their cars more fuel-efficient. Automakers were told that by model year 1978 their fleet of cars would have to meet an average fuel economy standard of 18 miles per gallon, and by model year 1985 would have to average 27.5 miles per gallon.

Forcing auto companies to provide more fuel-efficient cars may at first sound reasonable, and, indeed, the CAFE standards were initially quite popular among policy-makers. But the regulatory approach poses problems.

For example, by mandating fuel-efficient cars while temporarily keeping controls on gasoline prices, Congress limited people's options for conserving fuel. Higher gasoline prices encourage people to adjust their habits in ways that suit them

best individually and are least costly to them. Some consumers will simply drive less; others will buy more tune-ups, or smaller cars. Some people who must drive long distances to work may save on gasoline by buying larger cars and car-pooling. Others may move so they can walk to work. But the CAFE standards used the requirement for fuel-efficient new cars as a substitute for allowing a higher gasoline price to spur conservation.

Furthermore, using fuel-efficient cars can itself be costly in many ways. To meet the standards, automakers have reduced the weight of domestically made cars. Robert W. Crandall of the Brookings Institution and John Graham of the Harvard School of Public Health have estimated that model year 1989 cars are, on average, 500 pounds lighter than they would have been without the CAFE standards. These lighter cars are less safe than larger cars. Crandall and Graham estimate that 2,200 to 3,900 lives will be lost over a ten-

year period as a result of the application of CAFE standards to 1989 cars.[14]

To sell enough small cars to raise the fuel economy average, the auto makers reduced small car prices and raised prices for large cars. Buying decisions were distorted, and consumers paid more on balance for their cars. Andrew Kleit of the Federal Trade Commission estimated that if a proposed 1.5 mile-per-gallon increase in fuel efficiency had been adopted, consumers would have paid $3.4 billion more in one year because of the higher prices for large cars. That represents a cost of $4.87 for each gallon of gasoline saved.

The CAFE standards also distorted automakers' decisions. Congress required the car companies to calculate average fuel economy separately for their domestic-manufactured cars and their imports so that they cannot use their smaller, more fuel-efficient imports to bring down the domestic fleet's average. This enproven) to be safe, are: (a) some drugs are never developed because of the expensive tests and delays, and (b) people who could have been helped by the drug have to forgo it for several years. These opportunity costs may be very large, but they do not show up as expenditures.

Even when the costs of a regulation are measurable largely in cash, it is frequently difficult to assess the costs per unit of results. For example, proponents of mandatory airbags to reduce passenger injuries in auto crashes estimate that the bags can be produced for $200 to $300 per car, while automakers say the cost would be $700 to $800. Perhaps more important (since lives, not airbags are fundamentally at stake) is the cost per life saved. Those estimates range from $0.5 million to $5 million per life.[15] Who is right? And, is the cost worthwhile? One important question becomes: are there cheaper ways to save lives on the highway?

[15]These estimates are reported in John D. Graham, "Secretary Dole and the Future of Automobile Airbags," *The Brookings Review*, Vol. 15, No. 4 (Summer, 1985), pp. 10–15.

courages small-car production in the United States even though production might be cheaper overseas, and it has led Ford Motor Co. to threaten to move some of its large-car production out of the country.

Were the CAFE standards effective? The price of gasoline, when it was allowed to rise, has probably had more impact on the sales of fuel-efficient cars than the CAFE standards did. Sales of small cars closely track real gasoline prices. Since there is a lag of at least four years between the design and introduction of new models, an increase in fuel efficiency before 1979 cannot be attributed to CAFE. Yet, according to the *1986 Economic Report of the President*, average fuel economy in the United States increased by 43 percent between 1973 and 1979, as consumers bought more fuel-efficient cars in response to higher fuel prices. Indeed, Crandall and Graham believe that the CAFE standards had no impact on the design of cars until model year

1986. Then, the standards did have an effect—but at a time when the declining cost of gasoline meant that bigger cars made sense for many consumers.

Several factors reduce the effect of the CAFE standards. With large cars more expensive as a result of the standards, some people are likely to keep their old cars running longer, increasing gas consumption (and pollution). The lower prices of small cars may increase the total number of cars, and more cars on the road means greater fuel consumption—because the marginal cost of driving in a small car is lower than in a large car, and smaller car sizes lead people to share fewer rides. A tax on gasoline would not have had this particular distortion.

Another outcome of the CAFE regulations was to set in motion a big lobbying effect in Washington, D.C.—taking creative skills and energy away from productive activity. General Motors and Ford have lob-

bied hard to keep the government from making the standards so tight that they will have to either severely distort their product prices and offerings or pay the heavy penalties prescribed by law. In contrast, Chrysler Corporation, which specializes in small cars, has a vested interest in keeping the standards, to make competitors' cars more expensive. The lobbying will undoubtedly continue. Once individuals and companies adjust to regulations, the rules can be changed only with great economic pain and political acrimony. This is the case even though evidence shows that they do not accomplish what is intended and place costly burdens on society.

—Jane S. Shaw, Senior Associate, Political Economy Research Center, Bozeman, Montana.

[14]Robert W. Crandall and John D. Graham, "The Effect of Fuel Economy Standards on Automobile Safety," *Journal of Law and Economics*, Vol. 32, No. 1 (April 1989) pp. 97–118.

While there is strong disagreement about the costs and benefits of proposed new regulations for automobile safety, a study by the Brookings Institution[16] indicates that the auto safety regulations prevailing in the early 1980s probably provided enough benefits to at least offset their costs. The same study, however, concluded that regulations requiring emission controls to reduce air pollution, and requiring increases in fuel efficiency for automobiles have been very costly, while yielding few, if any benefits. An unintended result of the increased regulatory costs of buying and operating new automobiles has been to reduce their sales, keeping older cars on the road longer. The earlier design of these older cars, and the wear they have experienced, increase the pollution they emit while decreasing the safety and fuel efficiency they provide. The study criticizes the lack of coordination among the many regulations on automobiles. Rules requiring greater fuel economy, for example, make cars smaller, lighter, and less safe. Emission controls often reduce fuel economy, while safety requirements increase weight and decrease performance and fuel economy. Yet, each regulation is established with little regard to these conflicting impacts on the desirability of autos.

The new social regulation is costly, but it can have important benefits. The primary goal of social regulation is the attainment of a cleaner, safer, healthier environment. Nearly everyone agrees that this is a worthy objective. There is, however, considerable disagreement about the procedures that are most likely to accomplish this objective and the price that should be paid to make improvements. Resources are scarce. More social regulation will mean less of other things.

It should not be any more surprising that people differ with regard to the proper consumption level of environmental amenities than it is that they differ with regard to the proper consumption level of ice cream, for example. If 100 people were asked the best rate of consumption for strawberry ice cream, there would be a wide variety of answers. Similarly, the extent to which we should bear costs to make our air and water cleaner, and drugs safer, for example, is a question that each person may answer quite differently. One's preferred consumption rate for these benefits, like the preferred rate for strawberry ice cream, will depend in part on the expected cost and who pays that cost. Those who expect others to foot the bill will naturally prefer more of any valued good, whether it is ice cream or safety.

Differing preferences as to how many other goals should be given up to attain a safer, cleaner, healthier environment comprise only part of the problem faced by regulators. An important characteristic of most socially regulated activities is a lack of information about their effects. This is not a coincidence. In most cases, the lack of information contributes directly to the demand for the regulation. For example, if consumers knew exactly what the effect of a particular drug would be, there would be little need for the FDA to regulate its availability. Many people, though, are unaware of the precise effects of drugs, air pollution, or workplace hazards, even when the information is available to experts. It is costly to communicate information, particularly highly technical information. A case can be made, therefore, that we should let the experts decide which drugs, how much air pollution, and what forms of work-place safety should be sought. A lack of solid information generates much of the demand for social regulation. Of course,

---

[16]See Robert W. Crandall, Howard K. Gruenspecht, Theodore E. Keeler, and Lester B. Lave, *Regulating the Automobile* (Washington, D.C.: The Brookings Institution, 1986).

the lack of information also makes it difficult to evaluate the effectiveness of the regulatory activity.

Future Directions. Most people concede that regulation, both economic and social, is an imperfect solution. It is quite difficult, however, to separate beneficial regulations from those that are counterproductive. Even though there is strong support for the continuation and expansion of social regulatory activities, recent experience indicates that forces favoring deregulation are also present. Improved empirical evidence on the effectiveness of specific social regulation programs may very well emerge during the next decade.

CHAPTER SUMMARY

1. For more than a century, the relative size of the agricultural sector has declined, while the service sector has expanded. Manufacturing rose in importance, employing an increasing fraction of the labor force until 1948, but a declining fraction since then.
2. Even though manufacturing employment has declined, manufacturing output as a share of the total has been approximately constant during the last several decades. This pattern reflects the rising productivity in the manufacturing sector.
3. An increasing portion of the U.S. economy has become competitive over the past several decades, probably due to antitrust policy, rising import competition, and deregulation.
4. Antitrust legislation seeks to (a) maintain a competitive structure in the unregulated private sector and (b) prohibit business practices that are thought to stifle competition.
5. The Sherman, Clayton, and Federal Trade Commission Acts form the foundation of antitrust policy in the United States. The Sherman Act prohibits conspiracies to restrain trade and/or monopolize an industry. The Clayton Act prohibits specific business practices, such as price discrimination, tying contracts, exclusive dealings, and mergers and acquisitions (as amended), when they ''substantially lessen competition or tend to create a monopoly.'' As it has evolved through the years, the Federal Trade Commission is concerned primarily with enforcing consumer protection legislation, prohibiting deceptive advertising, and investigating industrial structure.
6. Most economists believe that antitrust policy in the United States has promoted competition and reduced industrial concentration, but not to any dramatic extent.
7. The breakup of AT&T reduced the cross-subsidy of local telephone service by long-distance ratepayers, although the dispute about how much fixed cost should be paid by long-distance users remains unsettled.
8. To date, economists have been unable to develop a complete theory of regulation. However economic analysis does suggest that: (a) the demand for regulation often stems from special interest and redistribution considerations rather than from the pursuit of economic efficiency; (b) regulation often fails to adjust to changing market conditions; and (c) with the passage of time, regulatory agencies are likely to adopt the views of the interest groups they are supposed to regulate.
9. Traditional economic regulation has generally sought to fix prices and/or influence industrial structure. During the 1970s, changing market conditions and empirical studies generated widespread dissatisfaction with economic regulation. Significant moves toward deregulation were made in the late 1970s, particularly in the trucking and airline industries. New entrants, intense competition, and discount prices have accompanied the deregulation of these industries.
10. In recent years, economic regulation has been relaxed, and social regulatory activities have expanded rapidly. Social regulation seeks to provide a cleaner, safer, healthier environment for workers and consumers. Pursuit of this objective is costly—higher product prices and higher taxes accompany such regulation. Since the costs and particularly the benefits are often difficult to measure and evaluate, the efficiency of social regulatory programs is a controversial topic, and the subject of much current research.

CRITICAL ANALYSIS QUESTIONS

*1. ''Manufacturing is dying in the U.S. economy. We are becoming a nation of service workers—hamburger flippers and people who take in each others' laundry—and inevitably a second-rate economy.'' Evaluate.

2. ''Big business is taking over the U.S. economy. Giant firms decide what we can buy, and even what government does.'' Evaluate.

3. Does the fact that a firm is large indicate that it does not face important competition? Are large firms always unusually profitable?

*4. ''Any merger that reduces competition hurts consumers and clearly should be stopped.'' Evaluate.

5. ''Efficiency requires large-scale production. Yet big businesses mean monopoly power, high prices, and market inefficiency. We must choose between production efficiency and monopoly.'' Evaluate.

*6. Legislation mandating stronger automobile bumpers has presumably made cars both safer and more expensive, as would proposed legislation requiring air bags for front-seat drivers and passengers. Should these laws be imposed? Why or why not?

7. ''Without legal safety requirements, products such as lawn mowers would always be produced cheaply, but be unsafe.'' Evaluate.

*8. Will social legislation mandating work-place and product safety reduce the profitability of the regulated firms? Who bears the cost, and who gains the benefits of such legislation?

*9. If tariff and quota barriers for foreign imports are lifted, making imports easier to obtain, does this strengthen or weaken the case for strict antitrust legislation and enforcement?

10. AT&T, which sells long-distance service but no longer is in the local phone service business, now opposes the higher long-distance rates it previously supported. Why?

11. ''Voters in our state should insist on state utility regulators who are tough on business. Consumers will benefit if prices are kept from rising above the per unit cost of production.'' Evaluate.

*12. With rate regulation and control of routes, as the Civil Aeronautics Board imposed on interstate airlines before deregulation, new entry was permitted only when it was shown to be ''necessary.'' What definitions of ''necessary'' would you expect to hear from (a) existing airlines and (b) customers? Which one would you expect to prevail, and why?

13. In 1975, AT&T had a regulated monopoly on telephone service between Los Angeles and New York. Several airlines at that time shared a regulated cartel serving those two cities. In both cases, price was well above marginal cost of serving customers between the two cities. Relative to a no-regulation situation, what pressure would you expect on quality of service in each of the regulated industries in 1975? Why would the pressure be different in the two cases?

14. ''We owe it to our coal miners to see that mines become much safer. Regulations can accomplish this and the mine owners will pay. Since users of coal have many sources of supply, they will not pay for these regulations. Workers will clearly be better off.'' Explain the logic here, and show what additional assumptions must be made about mine owners, and about workers, before the statement can be true.

*15. ''If we force increased safety measures in the workplace by regulation, business may bear the cost in the short run, but capital will receive that market rate of return in the long run.'' Evaluate and explain.

16. ''Regulations on the introduction of new drugs should be strengthened. Fewer people would die if more research were required prior to the introduction of new drugs. Only

---

*Asterisk denotes questions for which answers are given in Appendix C, Selected Answers.

an economist could possibly disagree. Sure, it would cost more, but saving even one life would surely be worth more than whatever it costs.'' Evaluate.

*17. ''People cannot be expected to make good decisions on their own regarding auto safety. Only experts know enough to make such decisions.'' Evaluate.

18. ''Safety regulation is not an economic question. Where lives and health are at stake, economics has no place.'' Evaluate.

THREE

FACTOR
MARKETS AND
INCOME
DISTRIBUTION

12

THE SUPPLY OF AND DEMAND FOR PRODUCTIVE RESOURCES

It is . . . necessary to attach price tags to the various factors of production . . . in order to guide those who have the day-to-day decisions to make as to what is plentiful and what is scarce.[1]

Professor James Meade

CHAPTER FOCUS

■ Why do business firms demand labor, machines, and other resources?

■ Why is the demand for a productive resource inversely related to its price?

■ How do business firms decide how many skilled laborers, unskilled laborers, machines, and other factors of production to employ?

■ How is the quantity supplied of a resource related to its price in the short run? . . . in the long run?

■ What determines the market price in resource markets?

Resource Markets: Markets in which business firms demand factors of production (for example, labor, capital, and natural resources) from household suppliers. The resources are then used to produce goods and services. These markets are sometimes called factor markets.

Thus far we have focused on markets for consumer goods and services. These markets (a) allocate goods and services among competing consumers and (b) determine which consumer goods will be produced. We now turn to an analysis of **resource markets,** or, as they are sometimes called, factor markets. Resource markets coordinate the choices of business employers and resource suppliers. Prices in resource markets provide individuals with an incentive to engage in productive activity and allocate productive resources among competing employers.

As in consumer-good markets, the interplay of supply and demand determines prices in resource markets. Resources are demanded because they contribute to the production of goods and services. Since resources must be bid away from competitive firms seeking to put them to alternative uses, costs are incurred whenever resources are employed. Profit-seeking firms will find it advantageous to hire a resource if it adds more to the firm's revenue than it does to costs. Conversely, income payments motivate individuals to supply resources. When choosing among alternative employment opportunities, utility-maximizing resource suppliers will seek out those options they believe to be most advantageous.

HUMAN AND NONHUMAN RESOURCES

Nonhuman Resources: The durable, nonhuman inputs that can be used to produce both current and future output. Machines, buildings, land, and raw materials are examples. Investment can increase the supply of nonhuman resources. Economists often use the term "physical capital" when referring to nonhuman resources.

Broadly speaking, there are two different types of productive inputs—nonhuman and human resources. **Nonhuman resources** are further broken down into the categories of physical capital, land, and natural resources. Capital consists of man-made goods used to produce other goods. Tools, machines, and buildings are part of the capital stock.

Net investment can increase the supply of nonhuman resources. Increasing the available stock of nonhuman resources, though, involves the sacrifice of current consumption goods. Resources that are used to produce machines, upgrade the quality of land, or discover natural resources could be used to produce current goods and services directly. Why take the round-about path? The answer is that sometimes indirect methods of producing goods are less costly in the long run. Robinson Crusoe found he could catch more fish by taking some time off from hand-fishing to build a net. Even though his intial investment in the net reduced his current catch, once the net was completed he was able to more than make up for his earlier loss of output.

Additions to capital stock, whether they are fishing nets or complex machines, involve current sacrifices. Capital-intensive methods of production are adopted only when decision-makers expect the benefits of a larger future output to more than offset the current reduction in the production of consumption goods.

Just as the supply of machines can be increased, so too can wise land-clearing and soil conservation practices be used to upgrade both the quantity and quality of land. Similarly, the supply of natural resources can be increased (within limits) by the application of more resources to discovery and development.

Human Resources: The abilities, skills, and health of human beings that can contribute to the production of both current and future output. Investment in training and education can increase the supply of human resources.

The future productivity of **human resources** can also be increased. Investment in such things as education, training, health, skill-building experience, and

---

[1]James E. Meade, "Economic Efficiency and Distributional Justice," in *Contemporary Issues in Economics,* ed. Robert W. Crandall and Richard S. Eckaus (Boston: Little, Brown, 1972), p. 319.

Investment in Human Capital: Expenditures on training, education, and skill development designed to increase the productivity of an individual.

migration to areas where jobs are more readily available involves current sacrifices to increase future productivity (and income). Economists refer to such activities as **investment in human capital.**[2]

Decisions to invest in human capital involve all the basic ingredients of other investment decisions. Consider the decision of whether or not to go to college. For most people, it is partly an investment decision. As many of you will testify, an investment in a college education requires the sacrifice of current earnings as well as payment for direct expenses such as tuition and books. The investment is expected to lead to a better job, considering both monetary and nonmonetary factors, and other benefits associated with a college education. The rational investor will weigh the current costs against the expected future benefits. College will be chosen only if the latter are greater than the former.

Some may find it offensive to refer to human beings as though they were machines. No ethical connotations are implied by the term "human capital." Men and women are, of course, not factors of production. They are human beings.

---

[2]The contributions of T. W. Schultz and Gary Becker to the literature on human capital have been particularly significant. See Daniel S. Hamermesh and Albert Rees, *The Economics of Work and Pay* (New York: Harper & Row, 1988), Chapter 3, for additional detail on human capital theory.

OUTSTANDING ECONOMIST

Gary Becker
(1930—   )

This innovative economist is perhaps best known for his ingenious application of economics to several areas that many had previously considered noneconomic by nature. Before his pioneering book, *The Economics of Discrimination*,[3] research by economists in this area was scanty. Apparently, many felt that something as irrational as prejudice was beyond the realm of a rational science like economics. Becker's book proved otherwise. In it, he developed a general theory that could be used to analyze (and measure) the impact of discrimination in several areas on the status of minorities and women. His work laid the foundation for the burgeoning of research interest in the economics of discrimination that took place during the 1960s and 1970s.

Later, Becker applied economic analysis to such seemingly noneconomic subjects as crime prevention, family development, an individual's allocation of time, and even the selection of a marriage partner.[4] The human capital approach underlies much of Becker's research. His widely acclaimed book, *Human Capital*,[5] is already a classic. The work developed a theoretical foundation for human investment decisions in education, on-the-job training, migration, and health.

Becker is a past president of the American Economic Association and a recipient of the organization's prestigious John Bates Clark Award.

---

[3]Gary Becker, *The Economics of Discrimination* (Chicago: University of Chicago Press, 1957).
[4]Gary Becker, *The Economic Approach to Human Behavior* (Chicago: University of Chicago Press, 1976), and Gary Becker and W. M. Landes, *Essays in the Economics of Crime and Punishment* (New York: Columbia University Press, 1974).
[5]Gary Becker, *Human Capital* (New York: Columbia University Press, 1964).

However, the effort, skill, ability, and ingenuity of individuals can be applied productively. They can be used to improve human welfare. It is these productive resources that we refer to as human resources, or human capital.

Human resources differ from nonhuman resources in two important respects. First, human capital is embodied in the individual. Choices concerning the use of human resources are vitally affected by working conditions, location, job prestige, and similar nonpecuniary factors. Although monetary factors influence human capital decisions, individuals have some leeway in trading off money income for better working conditions. Second, human resources cannot be bought and sold in nonslave societies. However, the *services* of human resources are bought and sold daily. Individuals have the right to quit, to sell their labor services to another employer, or to use them in an alternative manner in a nonslave society.

In competitive markets, the price of resources, like the price of products, is determined by supply and demand. To develop the theory of price for resource markets, we must first develop a theory for each of these determining factors. Let us begin by focusing on the demand for resources, both human and nonhuman.

THE DEMAND FOR RESOURCES

Derived Demand: Demand for an item based on the demand for products the item helps to produce. The demand for resources is a derived demand.

Producers employ laborers, machines, raw materials, and the other resources required to produce goods and services they hope to sell for a profit. The demand for a resource exists because there is a demand for goods that the resource helps to produce. The demand for each resource is thus a **derived demand**; it is derived from consumers' demands for products.

For example, a service station hires mechanics because customers demand repair service, not because the service station owner receives benefits simply from having mechanics around. If customers did not demand repair service, mechanics would not be employed for long. Similarly, the demand for such inputs as carpenters, plumbers, lumber, and glass windows is derived from the demand of consumers for houses and other consumer products these resources help to make.

Most resources contribute to the production of numerous goods. For example, glass is used to produce windows, ornaments, dishes, light bulbs, and mirrors, among other things. The total demand for a resource is the sum of the derived demand for it in each of its uses. Consequently, when economists study the demand for factors of production, they must trace changes in resource prices to their impact in the product market.

How will firms respond to an increase in the price of a resource? In the long run, the higher price of a resource will lead to two distinct adjustments, which will ensure an inverse relationship between price and the amount of the resource demanded. First, firms will seek to reduce their use of the now more expensive input by substituting other resources for it. Second, the increase in the price of the resource will lead to both higher costs and higher product prices. Consumers will buy less of the higher-priced product and substitute other goods for it, leading to a decline in the demand for resources used to make it. Therefore, the amount demanded of a factor of production will decline as its price increases. The demand curve for a resource will slope downward.

Let us look a little more closely at both of these adjustments.

Substitution in Production. Firms will use the input combination that minimizes their costs. When the price of a resource goes up, cost-conscious firms will use lower-cost substitutes. The degree to which such substitution can take place will vary. Resources that are good substitutes may exist even though they are not currently being used. Sometimes the style and dimensions of a product can be altered in a manner that will conserve on the use of a more expensive input. The presence of good substitutes in production ensures not only that quantity demanded will be inversely related to price but also that the demand for the resource will be highly elastic.

Substitution in Consumption. An increase in the price of a resource will lead to higher prices for products that the input helps to produce. The higher product prices will encourage consumers to purchase substitute goods, reducing the consumption of the more expensive product. When less of that product is produced, however, producer demand for resources (including the one that has risen in price) will decline. The experience of the American automobile industry in the early 1980s illustrates the point. Throughout much of the 1970s, wages in the U.S. automobile industry increased quite rapidly. The higher wages placed upward pressure on the prices of American-made automobiles. However, as auto prices rose, many consumers switched to substitute products. American auto sales declined, causing a reduction in quantity of labor demanded in the automobile industry and therefore widespread layoffs.

Other things constant, the more elastic the demand for the product, the more elastic the demand for the resource. This relationship stems from the derived nature of resource demand. An increase in the price of a product for which the demand is highly elastic will cause a sharp reduction in the sales of the good. There will thus also be a relatively sharp decline in the demand for the resources used to produce the good.

TIME AND THE DEMAND FOR RESOURCES

It will take time for producers to adjust fully to a change in the price of a resource. Typically, a producer will be unable to alter a production process or the design of a product immediately to conserve on the use of a more expensive input or to use more efficiently an input whose price has declined. Similarly, consumers may be unable to alter their consumption patterns immediately in response to price changes. Thus, the short-run demand for resources is typically less elastic than the demand in the long run.

Using steel as an example, Exhibit 1 illustrates the relationship between time and the demand for resources. Initially, higher steel prices may lead to only a small reduction in usage. If the high price of steel persists, however, automobile manufacturers will alter their designs, moving toward lighter-weight cars that require less steel. Architectural firms will design buildings that permit more substitution of plastics, wood, aluminum, glass, and other resources for steel. Products made with steel will increase in price, which will encourage consumers to find more and more ways to cut back on their use. However, these adjustments will not take place instantaneously. Therefore, the demand (D_{sr}) for steel, like that for most other products, will be more inelastic in the short run than in the long run.

EXHIBIT 1

Time and the Demand Elasticity of Resources

An increase in the price of steel will lead to a much larger reduction in consumption in the long run than in the short run. Typically, the demand for resources will be more inelastic in the short run.

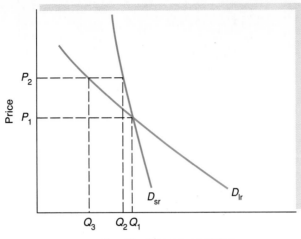

Quantity of steel per unit time

SHIFTS IN THE DEMAND FOR RESOURCES

Marginal Product: The change in total output that results from the employment of one additional unit of a factor of production—one workday of skilled labor, for example.

The entire demand curve for a resource, like that for a product, may shift, for one of three reasons.

1. *A Change in the Demand for a Product Will Cause a Similar Change in the Demand for the Resources Used to Make the Product.* Anything that increases the demand for a consumer good simultaneously increases the demand for resources required to make it; a decline in product demand and price will reduce the demand for resources embodied in the product. During the 1970s, the demand for small automobiles increased sharply, primarily because of higher gasoline prices. The increase in demand for small cars led to an increase in demand for workers to produce them. Employment at plants producing small cars expanded during the 1970s, even while auto workers were being laid off at plants producing large cars. Falling gasoline prices in the mid-1980s reversed this situation. Propelled by lower gasoline prices, the demand for larger automobiles increased, while the demand for small cars declined. Reflecting the demand in product markets, employment at automobile plants making full-size cars expanded, while employment at plants producing small cars fell.

2. *Changes in the Productivity of a Resource Will Alter the Demand for the Resource.* The higher the productivity of a resource, the greater the demand for it. Several factors combine to determine the productivity of a resource. First, the **marginal product** of any resource will depend on the amount of other resources with which it is working. In general, additional capital will tend to increase the productivity of labor. For example, someone with a lawn mower can mow more grass than the same person with a pair of shears. A student working with a textbook, class notes, and tutor can learn more economics than the same student without these tools. The quantity and quality of the tools with which we work significantly affects our productivity.

Second, technological advances can improve the productivity of resources, including labor. Advances in the computer industry illustrate this point. Working with computer technology, an accountant and a data-entry person can maintain business records and create bookkeeping reports that previously would have required 10 to 15 workers. Similarly, computers have vastly increased the productivity of typesetters, telephone operators, quality-control technicians, and workers in many other occupations.

Third, improvements in the quality (skill level) of a resource will increase productivity and therefore the demand for the resource. As workers obtain valuable new knowledge and/or upgrade their skills, they enhance their productivity. In essence, such workers move into a different skill category, where demand is greater.

All these factors help explain why wage rates in the Untied States, Canada, Western Europe, and Japan are higher than in most other areas of the world. Given the skill level of workers, the technology, and the capital equipment with which they work, individuals in these countries produce more goods and services per hour of labor. The demand for labor (relative to supply) is greater because of labor's increased productivity. Essentially, the workers' greater productivity leads to higher wage rates.

3. *A Change in the Price of a Related Resource Will Affect the Demand for the Original Resource*. An increase in the price of a substitute resource will lead to an increase in demand for the given resource. For example, when the wage rates of unionized workers in a given field or industry increase, demand for non-union workers will expand. Conversely, an increase in the price of a resource that is a complement to a given resource will decrease the demand for the given resource. For example, higher prices for computers would most likely cause the demand for computer programmers to fall.

MARGINAL PRODUCTIVITY AND THE FIRM'S HIRING DECISION

How does a producer decide whether or not to employ additional units of a resource? We noted previously that the marginal product of a resource is the increase in output that results when the employment of a resource is expanded by one unit. The resource's marginal product multiplied by the marginal revenue of the product being produced yields what is known as the **marginal revenue product**, or MRP. The MRP is simply the change in the firm's total revenue brought about by the employment of one extra unit of a resource. It reveals how much the employment of the resource adds to revenues.

A profit-maximizing firm will, of course, continue to expand output as long as marginal cost is less than marginal revenue. This rule can be generalized to include the firm's employment of resources. Since firms are usually price takers when they buy resources, the price of a resource is its marginal cost. When a firm has a fixed factor of production—its plant size, for example—the marginal product of a resource will decline as its employment increases, according to the law of diminishing returns. To maximize profit, employment of a resource should be expanded as long as MRP exceeds the price of the resource.

Thus, a profit-maximizing firm will hire units of a variable resource up to the employment level at which the price of the resource (its marginal cost) is just equal to the marginal revenue product of the resource. This decision rule applies to all firms, pure competitors and price searchers alike.

The marginal product of a resource multiplied by the selling price of the product yields the resource's **value marginal product** (VMP). When a firm sells

Marginal Revenue Product: The change in the total revenue of a firm that results from the employment of one additional unit of a factor of production. The marginal revenue product of an input is equal to its marginal product multiplied by the marginal revenue (price) of the good or service produced.

Value Marginal Product: The marginal product of a resource multiplied by the selling price of the product it helps to produce. Under perfect competition, a firm's marginal revenue product will be equal to the value marginal product.

its product in a competitive market, the selling price and the marginal revenue of the product are equal. Under pure competition, therefore, the marginal revenue product of a resource is equal to its value marginal product.

Exhibit 2 illustrates how a firm decides how much of a resource to employ. Compute-Accounting, Inc., uses computer equipment and data-entry operators to supply clients with monthly accounting statements. The firm sells its service in a competitive market for $200 per statement. Given the fixed quantity of computer equipment owned by Compute-Accounting, column 2 relates the employment of data-entry operators to the expected total output (quantity of accounting statements). One data-entry operator can process five statements per week. When two operators are employed, nine statements can be completed. Column 2 indicates how total output is expected to change as additional data-entry operators are employed. Column 3 presents the marginal product schedule for data-entry operators. Column 6, the marginal revenue product schedule, shows how the employment of each additional operator affects total revenues.

Since Compute-Accounting sells its service competitively, both the marginal revenue product and the value marginal product of labor equal MP (column 3) times the sales price per accounting statement (column 4). What if the firm is not a perfect competitor? The marginal revenue product must always equal MR multiplied by MP. When the firm confronts a downward-sloping demand curve for its product, the marginal revenue of the product will be less than its price. When this is the case, the marginal revenue product of a resource will be less than its value marginal product.

How does Compute-Accounting decide how many operators to employ? Additional operators will increase output, which will expand total revenue (column

EXHIBIT 2 ■ The Short-run Demand Schedule of a Firm

Compute-Accounting, Inc., uses computer technology and data-entry operators to provide accounting services in a competitive market. For each accounting statement processed, the firm receives a $200 fee (column 4). Given the firm's current fixed capital, column 2 shows how total output changes as additional data-entry operators are hired. The marginal revenue product schedule (column 6) indicates how hiring an additional operator affects the total revenue of the firm. Since a profit-maximizing firm will hire an additional employee if, and only if, the employee adds more to revenues than to costs, the marginal revenue product curve is the firm's short-run demand curve for the resource (see Exhibit 3).

Units of the Variable Factor (data-entry operators) (1)	Total Output (Accounting Statements Processed per week) (2)	Marginal Product [Change in (2) divided by Change in (1)] (3)	Sales Price per Statement (4)	Total Revenue (2)×(4) (5)	Marginal Revenue Product (3)×(4) (6)
0	0.0	—	$200	$ 0	—
1	5.0	5.0	200	1,000	$1,000
2	9.0	4.0	200	1,800	800
3	12.0	3.0	200	2,400	600
4	14.0	2.0	200	2,800	400
5	15.5	1.5	200	3,100	300
6	16.5	1.0	200	3,300	200
7	17.0	0.5	200	3,400	100

EXHIBIT 3

The Firm's Demand Curve for a Resource

The firm's demand curve for a resource will reflect the marginal revenue product of the resource. In the short run, it will slope downward because the marginal product of the resource will fall as more of it is used with a fixed amount of other resources. The location of the MRP curve will depend on (a) the price of the product, (b) the productivity of the resource, and (c) the quantity of other factors working with the resource.

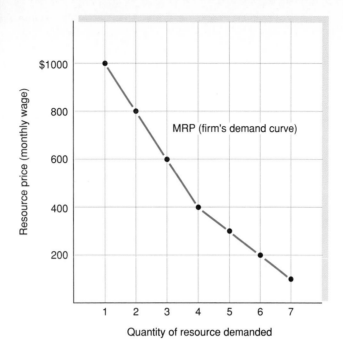

5). Employment of additional operators, though, will also add to production costs since the operators must be paid. If Compute-Accounting is going to maximize profit, it will hire additional operators as long as their employment adds more to revenues than to costs. Thus, as Exhibit 3 illustrates, the marginal revenue product curve of operators (Exhibit 2, column 6) is also the firm's short-run demand curve for the resource.[6] At a weekly wage of $1,000, Compute-Accounting would hire only one operator. If the weekly wage dropped to $800, two operators would be hired. At still lower wage rates, additional operators would be hired.

The location of the firm's MRP curve depends on (a) the price of the product, (b) the productivity of the resource, and (c) the amount of other resources with which the resource is working. Changes in any one of these three factors will cause the MRP curve to shift. For example, if Compute-Accounting obtained additional computer equipment that made it possible for the operators to complete more statements each week, the MRP curve for labor would increase. This increase in the quantity of the other resources working with labor would increase labor's productivity.

ADDING OTHER FACTORS OF PRODUCTION

Thus far, we have analyzed the firm's hiring decision, assuming that it employed one variable resource (labor) and one fixed resource. Production, though, usually involves the use of many resources. When a firm employs multiple resources, how should the resources be combined to produce the product? We can answer this question by considering either the conditions for profit maximization or the conditions for cost minimization.

---

[6]Strictly speaking, this is true only for a variable resource that is employed with a fixed amount of another factor.

Profit Maximization When Multiple Resources Are Employed. The same decision-making considerations apply when the firm employs several factors of production. The profit-maximizing firm will expand its employment of a resource as long as the marginal revenue product of the resource exceeds its employment cost. If we assume that resources are perfectly divisible, the profit-maximizing decision rule implies that, in equilibrium, the marginal revenue product of each resource will be equal to the price of the resource. Therefore, the following conditions will exist for the profit-maximizing firm:

MRP of skilled labor $= P_{SL}$ (wage rate of skilled labor)

MRP of unskilled labor $= P_{UL}$ (wage rate of unskilled labor)

MRP of machine $= P_M$ (explicit or implicit rental price of machine A)

and so on, for all other factors.

Cost Minimization When Multiple Resources Are Employed. If the firm is maximizing profits, clearly it must produce the profit-maximizing output at the least possible cost. If the firm is minimizing costs, the marginal dollar expenditure for each resource will have the same impact on output as every other marginal resource expenditure. Factors of production will be employed such that the marginal product per last dollar spent on each factor is the same for all factors.

Suppose that a dollar expenditure on labor caused output to rise by ten units, whereas an additional dollar expenditure on machines generated only a five-unit expansion in output. Under these circumstances, five more units of output (at no added cost) would result if the firm spent $1 less on machines and $1 more on labor. The firm's per unit cost would be reduced if it substituted labor for machines.

If the marginal dollar spent on one resource increases output by a larger amount than a dollar expenditure on other resources, costs can always be reduced by substituting resources with a high marginal product per dollar for those with a low marginal product per dollar expenditure. This substitution continues to add profit until the marginal product per dollar expenditure is equalized—that is, until the resource combination that minimizes cost is attained. When this is true, the proportional relationship between the price of each resource and its marginal product will be equal for all resources.

Therefore, the following condition exists when per unit costs are minimized:

$$\frac{\text{MP of skilled labor}}{\text{price of skilled labor}} = \frac{\text{MP of unskilled labor}}{\text{price of unskilled labor}}$$
$$= \frac{\text{MP of machine A}}{\text{price (rental value) of machine A}}$$

and so on, for the other factors.

In the real world, it is sometimes difficult to measure the marginal product of a factor. Businesspeople may not necessarily think in terms of equating the marginal product/price ratio for each factor of production. Nevertheless, if they are minimizing cost, this condition will be present. Real-world decision-makers may use experience, trial and error, and intuitive rules but the question always is: "Can we reduce costs by using more of one resource and less of another?" However, when profits are maximized and the cost-minimization method of production is attained, regardless of the procedures used, the outcome will be as if the employer had followed the profit-maximization and cost-minimization decision-making rules just discussed.

MARGINAL PRODUCTIVITY, DEMAND, AND ECONOMIC JUSTICE

According to the law of diminishing marginal returns, as the employment level of a resource increases, other things constant, the marginal product (and marginal revenue product) of the resource will decline. As we have just seen, a profit-maximizing employer will expand the use of a resource until its marginal revenue product is equal to the price of the resource. If the price of the resource declines, employers will increase their utilization level of that resource. Therefore, as Exhibit 4 shows, the marginal productivity approach can be used to illustrate the inverse relationship between quantity demanded and resource price.

Some observers, noting that under pure competition the price of each resource is equal to the value of what it produces (that is, input price equals the marginal product of the input multiplied by the price of the product), have argued that competitive markets are "just" or "equitable" because each resource gets paid exactly what it is worth. There is a major defect in this line of reasoning, however. The "marginal productivity" of labor (or any other factor) cannot be determined independently of the contribution of other factors. When a product is produced by a combination of factors, as is almost invariably the case, it is impossible to assign a specific proportion of the total output to each resource. For example, if one uses a tractor, an acre of land, and seed to produce wheat, one cannot accurately state that labor (or the seed or the land) produced one half or any other proportion of the output. Hence, those who argue that the factor payments generated by competitive markets are just, because each resource gets paid according to its productive contribution, assume that one can assign a specific

EXHIBIT 4

Marginal Productivity and Demand

Other things constant, an increase in the employment level will cause the MRP of a resource to decline. The larger quantity of the resource can be employed only at a lower price.

proportion of the total output to each resource. This is impossible when output is produced by a combination of factors. The marginal product can be used as a measure of the change in total output associated with the use of an additional unit of a resource, but this measurement does not directly link one resource with one segment of output.

The marginal productivity theory is really a theory about the demand for resources. The central proposition of the theory is that profit-maximizing employers will never pay more for a unit of input, whether it is skilled labor, a machine, or an acre of land, than the input is worth to them. The worth of a unit of input to the firm is determined by how much additional revenue (marginal revenue product) is generated (or seems to be generated) when the unit is used. That is, pursuit of profit will induce employers to hire additional units of each resource as long as the units' marginal productivity generates revenues in excess of costs. Resource prices will tend to reflect—though somewhat roughly in the real world—the marginal productivity of the resource.

However, the price of each resource is determined by conditions of supply as well as conditions of demand. Even though marginal productivity theory helps us understand the demand side of the market, it reveals nothing about the share of the total product produced by a resource or the justice of a resource price. We must analyze the supply of resources in order to complete the picture.

THE SUPPLY OF RESOURCES

As in the case of demand, the supply response in resource markets may vary between the short run and long run. The short run is a period so brief that there is insufficient time to alter the availability of a resource through investment in human and physical capital. In contrast, in the long run, resource suppliers have time to fully adjust their investment choices to a change in resource prices. Let us begin by focusing on supply in the short run.

SHORT-RUN SUPPLY

Resource Mobility: A term that refers to the ease with which factors of production are able to move among alternative uses. Resources that can easily be transferred to a different use or location are said to be highly mobile. In contrast, when a resource has few alternative uses, it is immobile. For example, the skills of a trained rodeo rider would be highly immobile, since they cannot be easily transferred to other lines of work.

Most resources have alternative uses; they can be used to perform a variety of functions. The principle of utility maximization implies that resource owners will use their factors of production in a manner that leads to their greatest net advantage. As a result, prices will influence the quantity of a resource applied to a specific use.

An increase in the price of a resource will attract potential resource suppliers into the market. In contrast, resource suppliers will shift into other activities when the price of a resource falls. Thus, the supply curve for a specific resource (for example, engineering services, craft labor, or wheat farm land) will slope upward to the right in the short run.

The elasticity of supply to a particular use will be dependent on **resource mobility**. Resources that can be easily transferred from one use to another in response to changing price incentives (in other words, those resources with a great many alternative uses or locations) are said to be highly mobile. The supply of such factors to any specific use will be elastic. Factors that have few alternative uses are said to be immobile and will have an inelastic short-run supply.

What can we say about resource mobility in the real world? First, let us consider the mobility of labor. When labor skills can be transferred easily and quickly, human capital is highly mobile. Within skill categories (for example, plumber, store manager, accountant, and secretary), labor will be highly mobile within the same geographical area. Movements between geographical areas and from one skill category to another are more costly to accomplish. Labor will thus be less mobile for movements of this variety.

What about the mobility of land? Land is highly mobile among uses when location does not matter. For example, the same land can often be used to raise either corn, wheat, soybeans, or oats. Thus, the supply of land allocated to production of each of these commodities will be highly responsive to changes in their relative prices. Undeveloped land on the outskirts of cities is particularly mobile among uses. In addition to its value in agriculture, such land might be quickly subdivided and used for a housing development or a shopping center. However, since land is totally immobile physically, supply is unresponsive to changes in price that reflect the desirability of a location.

Machines are typically not very mobile among uses. A machine developed to produce airplane wings is seldom of much use in the production of automobiles, appliances, or other products. Steel mills cannot easily be converted to produce aluminum. There are, of course, some exceptions. Trucks can typically be used to haul a variety of products. Building space can often be converted from one use to another. In the short run, however, immobility and inelasticity of supply are characteristic of much of our physical capital.

LONG-RUN SUPPLY

In the long run, the supply of resources can change substantially. Machines wear out, human skills depreciate, and even the fertility of land declines with use and erosion. These factors reduce the supply of resources. Through investment, though, the supply of productive resources can be expanded. Current resources can be invested to expand the stock of machines, buildings, and durable assets. Alternatively, current resources can be used to train, educate, and develop the skills of future labor force participants. The supply of both physical and human resources in the long run is determined primarily by investment and depreciation.

Price incentives will, of course, influence the investment decisions of firms and individuals. Considering both monetary and nonmonetary factors, investors will choose those alternatives they believe to be most advantageous. Higher resource prices will induce utility-maximizing individuals to undertake investments that will permit them to supply more of the higher priced resource. In contrast, other things constant, lower resource prices will reduce the incentive of individuals to invest and expand the future supply of a resource. Thus, resource prices will influence the incentive to invest and acquire resources and thereby lead to a direct relationship between the price of a resource and quantity supplied in the long run.

The theory of long-run resource supply is general. The expected payoff from an investment alternative will influence the decisions of investors in human, as well as physical, capital. For example, the higher salaries of physical and space scientists employed in the expanding space program during the early 1960s induced an expanding number of college students to enter these fields. Similarly, attractive earning opportunities in accounting and law led to an increase in investment and quantity supplied in these areas during the period from 1965 to 1975. During the last decade, job opportunities for computer programmers, systems analysts, and computer technicians have been highly attractive as the computer revolution spread throughout our economy. As salaries in these areas rose, the number of students in computer science and technology courses expanded substantially. As in other markets, suppliers respond to changing incentives in resource markets.

Considering both monetary and nonmonetary factors, investors will not knowingly invest in areas of low return when higher returns are available elsewhere. Of course, since human capital is embodied in the individual, nonpecuniary considerations will typically be more important for human than for physical capital. Nevertheless, expected monetary payoffs will influence investment decisions in both areas.

The long run, of course, is not a specified length of time. Investment can increase the availability of some resources fairly quickly. For example, it does not take very long to train additional bus drivers. Thus, in the absence of barriers to entry, the quantity of bus drivers supplied will expand rapidly in response to higher wages. However, the gestation period between expansion in investment and an increase in quantity supplied is substantially longer for some resources. It takes a long time to train physicians, dentists, lawyers, and pharmacists. Higher earnings in these occupations may have only a small impact on their current availability. Additional investment will go into these areas, but it will typically be several years before there is any substantial increase in the quantity supplied in response to higher earnings for these resources.

Because supply can be substantially expanded over time by investment, the supply of a resource will be much more elastic in the long run than in the short run. This is particularly true when there is a lengthy gestation period between an increase in investment and an actual increase in the availability of a resource.

Using engineering services as an example, Exhibit 5 illustrates the relationship between the short- and long-run supply of resources. An increase in the price

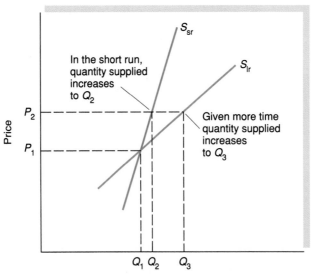

EXHIBIT 5

Time and the Elasticity of Supply for Resources

The supply of engineering services (and other resources that require a substantial period of time between current investment and expansion in the future quantity supplied) will be far more inelastic in the short run than in the long run.

of engineering services (the wage rate of engineers) will result in some immediate increase in quantity supplied. Persons currently employed as engineers may choose to work more hours. In addition, the higher wage may induce workers with engineering skills currently employed in mathematics, physics, or similar fields to switch to engineering. While these adjustments are important, they may fail to substantially increase the quantity supplied in the short run. With time, however, the more attractive earning opportunities in engineering will raise the level of investment in human capital in this area. More students will enter engineering programs. It takes time, though, to acquire an engineering degree. Several years may pass before the additional newly acquired engineering degrees exert a major impact on supply. Nevertheless, the expanded human capital investments will eventually exert important effects. Thus, in the long run, the quantity of engineering services may be quite elastic, even though supply is highly inelastic in the short run.

SUPPLY, DEMAND, AND RESOURCE PRICES

The theories of supply and demand for resources have been analyzed. This is all we need to develop the theory of resource pricing in competitive markets. When factor prices are free to vary, resource prices will bring the choices of buyers and sellers into line with each other. Continuing with our example of engineers, Exhibit 6 illustrates how the forces of supply and demand push the market price toward equilibrium, where quantity demanded and quantity supplied are equal. Equilibrium is achieved when the price (wage) of engineering services is P_1. Given the market conditions illustrated by Exhibit 6, excess supply is present if

Equilibrium in a Resource Market

The market demand for a resource such as engineering services is a downward sloping curve reflecting the declining marginal revenue product of the resource. The market supply slopes upward since higher resource prices (wage rates) will induce individuals to supply more of the resource. Resource price P_1 brings the choices of buyers and sellers into harmony. At the equilibrium price (P_1), the quantity demanded will just equal the quantity supplied.

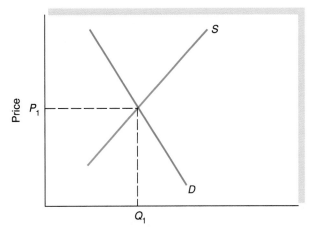

Quantity of engineering services—hours

the price of engineering services exceeds P_1. Some resource owners are unable to sell their services at the above-equilibrium price. Responding to this situation, they will cut their price (wage) and thereby push the market toward equilibrium. In contrast, if the resource price is less than P_1, excess demand is present. Employers are unable to obtain the desired amount of engineering services at a below-equilibrium resource price. Rather than doing without the resource, employers will bid the price up to P_1 and thereby eliminate the excess demand.

How will a resource market adjust to an unexpected change in market conditions? As is true for product markets, adjustment to changes do not take place instantaneously in resource markets. Our analysis of short-run and long-run responses makes the nature of the adjustment process clear. Suppose there is an unanticipated increase in demand for a resource. As Exhibit 7 illustrates, an increase in market demand (from D_1 to D_2) initially leads to a sharp rise in the price of the resource (from P_1 to P_2), particularly if the short-run supply is quite inelastic. However, at the higher price, the quantity of the resource supplied will expand with time. If it is a natural resource, individuals and firms will put forth a greater effort to discover and develop the now more valuable productive factor. If it is physical capital (for example a building or machine), current suppliers will have greater incentive to work intensively to expand production. New suppliers will be drawn into the market. Higher prices for human capital resources will also lead to an expansion in the quantity supplied. With time, more people will acquire the training, education, and experience necessary to supply the service that now commands a higher price. The expansion of the supply will eventually moderate the price rise. Because of these forces, as Exhibit 7 illustrates, the long-run price increase will be less than the short-run increase.

The market adjustment to an unexpected reduction in demand for a resource is symmetrical. A reduction in demand will cause the price of the resource to fall further in the short run than over a longer period of time. At the lower price, some resource suppliers will use their talents in other areas. The incentive for

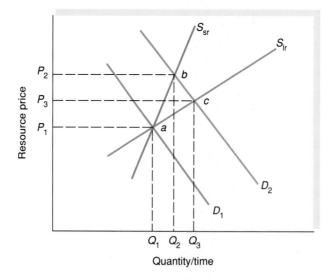

EXHIBIT 7

Adjusting to Dynamic Change

An increase in demand for a resource will typically cause price to rise more in the short run than in the long run. Can you explain why?

potential new suppliers to offer the resource will be reduced by the fall in price. With time, the quantity of the resource supplied will decline, making the long-run decline in price more moderate. Those with the poorest alternatives (that is, lowest opportunity cost) will continue to provide the resource at the lower prices. Those with better alternatives will move to other areas.

LOOKING AHEAD

Now that we have outlined the theoretical underpinnings of factor markets, we can apply the analysis to a broad range of economic issues. The next chapter will focus on the labor market and the determination of wage rates. Later, we will focus on the capital market and the allocation of resources over time. The operation of these two markets plays an important role in determining the distribution of income, a topic that will also be analyzed in detail in a subsequent chapter.

CHAPTER SUMMARY

1. Factor markets, where productive resources and services are bought and sold, help to determine what is produced, how it is produced, and how the distribution of income (output) is accomplished. There are two broad classes of productive resources—nonhuman capital and human capital. Both are durable in the sense that they will last into the future, thereby enhancing future productive capabilities. Both yield income to their owners. Investment can expand the future supply of both.

2. The demand for resources is derived from demand for products that the resources help to produce. The quantity of a resource demanded is inversely related to its price. There are two reasons why if the price of a resource increases, less of it will be used. First, producers will substitute other resources for the now more expensive input (substitution in production). Second, the higher resource price will lead to higher prices for products that the resource helps to make, inducing consumers to reduce their purchases of those goods (substitution in consumption).

3. The short-run market demand curve will be more inelastic than the long-run curve. It will take time for producers to adjust their production process to use more of the less expensive resources and less of the more expensive resources.

4. The demand curve for a resource, like the demand for a product, may shift. The major factors that can increase the demand for a resource are (a) an increase in demand for products that use the resource, (b) an increase in the productivity of the resource, and (c) an increase in the price of substitute resources.

5. Profit-maximizing firms will hire additional units of a resource as long as the marginal revenue product of the resource exceeds its hiring cost, usually the price of the resource. If resources are perfectly divisible, firms will expand their usage of each resource until the marginal revenue product of each resource is just equal to its price.

6. When a firm is minimizing its costs, it will employ each factor of production up to the point at which the marginal product per last dollar spent on the factor is equal for all factors. This condition implies that the marginal product of labor divided by the price of labor must equal the marginal product of capital (machines) divided by the price of capital, and that this ratio (MP_i/P_i) must be the same for all other inputs used by the firm. When real-world decision-makers minimize per unit costs, the outcome will be as if they had followed these mathematical procedures, even though they may not consciously do so.

7. Resource owners will use their factors of production in the manner that they consider most personally advantageous. Many resources will be relatively immobile in the short run. The less mobile a resource, the more inelastic its short-run supply. There will be a positive relationship between amount supplied and resource price even in the short run.

8. In the long run, investment and depreciation will alter resource supply. Resource owners will shift factors of production toward areas in which resource prices have risen

and away from areas in which resource prices have fallen. Thus, the long-run supply will be more elastic than the short-run supply.

9. The prices of resources will be determined by both supply and demand. The demand for a resource will reflect the demand for products that it helps make. The supply of resources will reflect the human and physical capital investment decisions of individuals and firms.

10. Changing resource prices will influence the decisions of users and suppliers alike. Higher resource prices give users a greater incentive to turn to substitutes and stimulate suppliers to provide more of the resource. Since these adjustments take time, when the demand for a resource expands, the price will usually rise more in the short run than in the long run. Similarly, when there is a fall in resource demand, price will decline more in the short run than in the long run.

CRITICAL ANALYSIS QUESTIONS

1. What is the meaning of the expression "invest in human capital"? In what sense is the decision to invest in human capital like the decision to invest in physical capital? Is human capital investment risky? Explain.

2. a. "Firms will hire a resource only if they can make money by doing so."
   b. "In a market economy, each resource will tend to be paid according to its marginal product. Highly productive resources will command high prices, whereas less productive resources will command lower prices."
   Are (a) and (b) both correct? Are they inconsistent with each other? Explain.

*3. Use the information of Exhibit 2 to answer the following:
   a. How many employees (operators) would Compute-Accounting hire at a weekly wage of $250 if it were attempting to maximize profits?
   b. What would the firm's maximum profit be if its fixed costs were $1,500 per week?
   c. Suppose there was a decline in demand for accounting services, reducing the market price per monthly statement to $150. At this demand level, how many employees would Compute-Accounting hire at $250 per week in the short run? Would Compute-Accounting stay in business at the lower market price? Explain.

*4. Are productivity gains the major source of higher wages? If so, how does one account for the rising real wages of barbers, who by and large have used the same technique for half a century? (Hint: Do not forget opportunity cost and supply.)

5. "However desirable they might be from an equity viewpoint, programs designed to reduce wage differentials will necessarily reduce the incentive of people to act efficiently and use their productive abilities in those areas where demand is greatest relative to supply." Do you agree or disagree? Why?

6. **What's Wrong with This Way of Thinking?**
   "The downward-sloping marginal revenue product curve of labor shows that better workers are hired first. The workers hired later are less productive."

7. "The demand for resources is a derived demand." What is meant by that statement? Why is the employment of a resource inversely related to its price?

*8. A dressmaker uses labor and capital (sewing machines) to produce dresses in a competitive market. The last unit of labor hired cost $1,000 per month and increased output by 100 dresses. The last unit of capital hired (rented) cost $500 per month and increased output by 80 dresses. Is the dressmaker minimizing cost? If not, what changes need to made?

9. Suppose that lawn service operators always use one worker with one mower to produce output. The resources are always used in the same proportion; there is no substi-

---

*Asterisk denotes questions for which answers are given in Appendix C, Selected Answers.

tutability between labor and capital. Under these circumstances, would a change in wages influence employment? Explain.

*10. ''The earnings of engineers, doctors, and lawyers are high because lots of education is necessary to practice in these fields.'' Evaluate this statement.

11. Other things constant, what impact will a highly elastic demand for a product have on the elasticity of demand for the resources used to produce the product? Explain.

*12. The following chart provides information on a firm that hires labor competitively and sells its product in a competitive market:

Units of Labor	Total Output	Marginal Physical Product	Product Price	Total Revenue	Marginal Revenue Product
1	14	———	$5	———	———
2	26	———	$5	———	———
3	37	———	$5	———	———
4	46	———	$5	———	———
5	53	———	$5	———	———
6	58	———	$5	———	———
7	62	———	$5	———	———

a. Fill in the missing columns.
b. How many units of labor would be employed if the market wage rate was $40? Why?
c. What would happen to employment if the wage rate rose to $50? Explain.

13 EARNINGS, PRODUCTIVITY, AND THE JOB MARKET

A fair day's-wages for a fair day's-work; it is as just a demand as governed men ever made of governing. It is the everlasting right of man.

Thomas Carlyle

CHAPTER FOCUS

■ Why do some people earn more than others?

■ Who pays for fringe benefits? Do government-mandated fringe benefits increase employee compensation?

■ Why are wages higher in the United States than they are in India or China? Why are the wages of Americans higher today than they were 50 years ago?

■ Does automation destroy jobs? Does it harm workers?

■ Can we legislate higher wages?

■ Why are the earnings of whites greater than the earnings of minorities? Why are the earnings of men greater than the earnings of women?

The major source of income for most people is labor earnings, income derived from current work. The earnings of U.S. workers are among the highest in the world and they have been increasing. The earnings of individuals, however, vary widely. An unskilled laborer may earn $5 per hour, or even less. Lawyers and physicians often earn $75 per hour. Dentists and even economists might receive $50 per hour. This chapter focuses on earnings—the source of high earnings, the explanation of why earnings vary, and the reasons why some groups earn more than others.

WHY DO EARNINGS DIFFER?

The earnings of paired individuals in the same occupation or with the same amount of education very often differ substantially. The earnings of persons with the same family background also vary widely. For example, one researcher found that the average earnings differential between brothers was $5,600, compared with $6,200 for men paired randomly.[1] In addition, the earnings of persons with the same IQ, level of training, or amount of experience typically differ. How do economists explain these variations? Several factors combine to determine the earning power of an individual. Some seem to be the result of good or bad fortune. Others are clearly the result of conscious decisions made by individuals. In the previous chapter, we analyzed how the market forces of supply and demand operate to determine resource prices. The subject of earnings differentials can be usefully approached within the framework of this model.

If (a) all individuals were homogeneous, (b) all jobs were equally attractive, and (c) workers were perfectly mobile among jobs, the earnings of all employees in a competitive economy would be equal. If, given these conditions, higher wages existed in any area of the economy, the supply of workers to that area would expand until the wage differential was eliminated. Similarly, low wages in any area would cause workers to exit until wages in that area returned to parity. However, the conditions necessary for earnings equality do not exist in the real world. Thus, earnings differentials are present.

EARNINGS DIFFERENTIALS DUE TO NONHOMOGENEOUS LABOR

All workers are clearly not the same. They differ in several important respects, which influence both the supply of and demand for their services.

Worker Productivity and Specialized Skills. The demand for employees who are highly productive—those with a higher marginal revenue product—will be greater than the demand for those who are less productive. Persons who can operate a machine more skillfully, hit a baseball more consistently, or sell life insurance policies with greater regularity will have a higher marginal revenue product than their less skillful counterparts. Because they are more productive, their services will command a higher wage from employers.

Workers can increase their productivity by investing in human capital. When education, vocational training, and other investments in human capital increase productivity, they will lead to higher earnings. In fact, the higher earnings provide

---

[1]Christopher Jencks, *Inequality* (New York: Basic Books, 1972), p. 220.

individuals with the incentive to invest in themselves and thereby upgrade their knowledge and skills. If additional worker productivity did not lead to higher earnings, individuals would have little incentive to incur the direct and indirect cost of productivity-enhancing educational and training programs.

Of course, native ability and motivation will influence the rate at which an individual can transform educational and training experience into greater productivity. Individuals differ in the amount of valuable skills they develop from a year of education, vocational school, or on-the-job training. We should not expect, therefore, a rigid relationship to exist between years of training (or education) and skill level.

Nevertheless, detailed empirical studies indicate that investment in human capital leads to higher earnings *once the person enters the labor force full-time*. For example, in 1987, the median income of college graduates age 25 and over was $34,215, compared to $20,314 for high school graduates. Some of the additional earnings of college graduates may reflect native ability, intelligence, and motivation. Research, however, indicates that a large proportion of the additional earnings also reflects knowledge and skills acquired as the result of investment in additional education. Similarly, economic research has shown that training enhances the earnings of workers.

Investment in human capital and development of specialized skills can protect high-wage workers from the competition of others willing to offer their services at a lower price. Few persons could develop the specialized skills of a Barbara Mandrell or a Bill Cosby. Similarly, skill (and human capital) factors also limit the supply of heart surgeons, trial lawyers, engineers, and business entrepreneurs. As Exhibit 1 illustrates, when the demand for a specialized resource is great relative to its supply, the resource will be able to command a high wage. In 1986 the average earnings level of engineers was $39,425, more than three times the figure for laborers. Since engineers possess specialized skills developed by both

EXHIBIT 1

Supply, Demand, and Wage Differentials

The mean number of years of education for engineers is 17.0 compared to 12.0 for laborers. Because of their specialized skills, high-wage engineers are protected from direct competition with laborers and other persons who do not possess such skills.

(a) Engineers

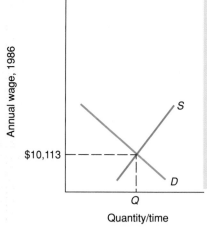

(b) Laborers (except farm)

Source: Earnings data are from the U.S. Department of Commerce.

formal education (usually between 16 and 18 years) and experience, laborers are unable to compete directly in the engineering market. In contrast, the training and skill requirements for laborers are possessed by many. Since the supply of laborers is large relative to the demand, their earnings are substantially less.

It is important to keep in mind that wages are determined by demand relative to supply. Other things constant, a skilled specialist will command a higher wage than one with less skill, but high skill will not guarantee high wages in the absence of demand. For example, expert harness makers and blacksmiths typically command low wages today, even though the supply of these workers is small—because demand even for the services of experts in these areas is low.

Worker Preferences. This very important source of earnings differentials is sometimes overlooked. People have different objectives in life. Some want to make a great deal of money. Many are willing to work long hours, undergo agonizing training and many years of education, and sacrifice social and family life to make money. Others may be "workaholics" because they enjoy their jobs. Still others may be satisfied with enough money to get by on, preferring to spend more time with their family, the Boy Scouts, the television, or the local tavern keeper.

Economics does not indicate that one set of worker preferences is more desirable than another, any more than it suggests that people should eat more spinach and less pastrami. Economics does indicate, however, that these factors contribute to differences in wages and earnings. Other things constant, persons who are more highly motivated by monetary objectives will be more likely to do the things necessary to command higher wage rates.

Race and Sex. Discrimination on the basis of race or sex contributes to earnings differences among individuals. Employment discrimination may directly limit the earnings opportunities of minorities and women. **Employment discrimination** exists when minorities or women employees are treated in a manner different from similarly productive whites or men. Of course, the earnings of minority employees, for example, may differ from whites for reasons other than employment discrimination. Nonemployment discrimination may limit the opportunity of minority groups and women to acquire human capital (for example, quality education or specialized training) that would enhance both their productivity and earnings. To isolate the impact of current employment discrimination, we must (a) adjust for the impact of education, experience, and skill factors and (b) then make comparisons *between similarly qualified groups* of employees who differ with regard to race (or sex) only. (See the Measures of Economic Activity box for additional detail on this topic.)

There are two major forms of employment discrimination—wage rates and employment restrictions. Exhibit 2 illustrates the impact of wage discrimination. When majority employees are preferred to minority and female workers, the demand for the latter two groups is reduced. The wages of blacks and women decline relative to those of white men.

Essentially, there is a dual labor market—one market for the favored group and another for the group toward whom discrimination is directed. The favored group, such as whites, is preferred, but the less expensive labor of minority workers is a substitute productive resource. Both white and minority employees are employed, but the whites are paid a higher wage rate.

Employment Discrimination: Unequal treatment of persons on the basis of their race, sex, or religion, which restricts their employment and earnings opportunities compared to others of similar productivity. Employment discrimination may stem from the prejudices of employers, consumers and/or fellow employees.

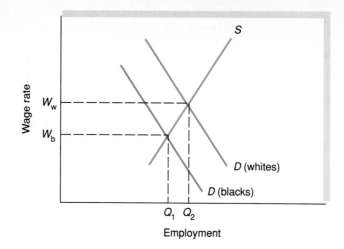

EXHIBIT 2

The Impact of Direct Wage Discrimination

If there is employment discrimination against blacks or women, the demand for their services will decline, and their wage rate will fall from W_w to W_b.

Exclusionary practices may also be an outlet for employment discrimination. Either in response to outside pressure or because of their own views, employers may primarily hire whites and males for certain types of jobs. When minority and female workers are excluded from a large number of occupations, they are crowded into a smaller number of remaining jobs and occupations. If entry restraints prevent people from becoming supervisors, bank officers, plumbers, electricians, and truck drivers, they will be forced to accept alternatives. The supply of labor in the unrestricted occupations will increase, causing wage rates to fall. The exclusionary practices will result in higher wages for white males holding jobs from which blacks and females are excluded. The outcome will be an over-representation of white males in the higher paying occupations, while a disproportionate number of blacks and women will occupy the lower-paying, nonrestricted positions. The impact will be a reduction in the earnings of minorities and women relative to white males.

While employment discrimination undoubtedly influences earning opportunities available to minorities and women, economic theory implies that discrimination is costly to employers when they are merely reflecting their own prejudices. If employers can hire *equally productive* minority employees (or women) at a lower wage than whites (or men), the profit motive gives them a strong incentive to do so. An employer who continues to hire high-wage whites, when similar minority employees are available at a lower wage, will have higher costs and lower profits than nondiscriminative employers. Since competition forces an employer to pay for prejudice with lower profits, it tends to moderate discriminatory actions.[2] Regardless of whether employers are motivated by goodwill or pursuit of profit, when a substantial proportion (it need not be all) of employers follow a nondiscriminatory policy, the wages of equally productive minority (women) and white (men) employees will approach parity.

---

[2]For empirical evidence that competition reduces the effects of employer discrimination, see James Gwartney and Charles Haworth, ''Employer Cost and Discrimination: The Case of Baseball,'' *Journal of Political Economy* (June 1974).

MEASURES OF ECONOMIC ACTIVITY

Earnings Differentials According to Race Corrected for Differences in Productivity-Related Factors

Earnings may differ among groups for reasons other than employment discrimination. If we want to isolate the impact of employment discrimination, earnings comparisons must be made between similarly productive groups. A recent study by Leonard Carlson and Caroline Swartz of Emory University uses statistical techniques to "correct" the earnings of minorities for productive characteristics that obviously affect earnings, independent of employment discrimination.[3] In essence, Carlson and Swartz calculated what the earnings of white men would be if they had the same average education, age, language (English), marital status,

native birth, annual hours worked, and regional location as minority men. The actual earnings of minority men were then compared to the "corrected" (productivity adjusted) earnings of white men.

Exhibit 3 summarizes the findings of Carlson and Swartz. The actual earnings of black men were only 67 percent the earnings of white men in 1979. However, when the work force characteristics (education, age, language, marital status, and so on) of black men were taken into account, the corrected earnings of black men rose to 83 percent of the white male earnings. Thus, productivity-related factors accounted for almost half of

the earnings differential between white and black men. Mexican-Americans constitute the second largest minority group in the United States. Even though the actual earnings of Mexican-American men were only 66 percent of the earnings of white men, their "corrected" earnings were almost equal (98 percent) to the white earnings.

This implies that if Mexican-American men possessed the same worker characteristics as white men, their earnings would be very close to parity with their white counterparts. The actual and corrected earnings for other minority groups are also presented in Exhibit 3. Interestingly, both the actual and corrected earnings of Japanese-American men were slightly greater than for their white counterparts. The two most recent arrivals among the minority groups—Cubans and Vietnamese—appear to be doing quite well, given their worker characteristics. The *corrected* relative wage of both groups was only a little less than the white wage in 1979. Clearly, differences in worker characteristics as well as employment discrimination contribute to earnings differences between white and minority men.

EXHIBIT 3 ■ The Actual and Productivity Corrected Wages of Minority Males Compared with White Males, 1979

	The Wage of Minority Men Relative to White Men, 1979	
	Actual	Corrected
White	100	100
Black	67	83
Mexican American	66	98
Japanese American	105	101
Chinese American	89	88
Puerto Rican American	63	95
American Indian	74	90
Cuban American	79	96
Vietnamese American	64	98

Source: Leonard A. Carlson and Caroline Swartz, "The Earnings of Women and Ethnic Minorities, 1959–1979," *Industrial and Labor Relations Review*, vol. 41 (July 1988). The estimates are based on 1980 census data.

[3]Leonard A. Carlson and Caroline Swartz, "The Earnings of Women and Ethnic Minorities, 1959–1979," *Industrial and Labor Relations Review*, Vol. 41 (July 1988).

EARNINGS DIFFERENTIALS DUE TO NONHOMOGENEOUS JOBS

Nonpecuniary Job Characteristics: Working conditions, prestige, variety, location, employee freedom and responsibilities, and other nonwage characteristics of a job that influence how employees evaluate the job.

When individuals evaluate employment alternatives, they consider working conditions as well as wage rates. Is a job dangerous? Does it offer the opportunity to acquire the experience and training that will enhance future earnings? Is the work strenuous and nerve-racking? Are the working hours, job location, and means of transportation convenient? These factors are what economists call nonpecuniary job characteristics. Workers are willing to trade off higher wage rates for more favorable nonpecuniary job characteristics. There are numerous examples of this. Because of the dangers involved, aerial window washers (those who hang from windows 20 stories up) earn higher wages than other window washers. Sales jobs involving a great deal of out-of-town travel typically pay more than similar jobs without such inconvenience. Electricians in contract construction are paid more than equally skilled electricians with jobs in which the work and pay are more steady. Because the majority of economists prefer the more independent work environment and intellectual stimulation offered by colleges and universities, the earnings of economists in academia are typically lower than those of economists in business.

Substantial wage differentials exist between similar jobs in (a) large and small firms and (b) urban and rural areas. Nonpecuniary factors, such as transportation costs and locational preferences, help explain these differentials. Large firms must typically draw their labor force from a wider geographical area, resulting in large average travel time to and from work. Congestion problems are more severe. These factors make employment with large firms less desirable. Because of this, they must pay higher wage rates to attract the desired size of labor force. Similarly, the lower wages in rural areas probably reflect, at least partially, employees' willingness to trade off higher wages for jobs in preferred living areas. These differences in the nonpecuniary characteristics of jobs contribute to earnings differences among individuals.

EARNINGS DIFFERENTIALS DUE TO IMMOBILITY OF LABOR

It is costly to move to a new location or train for a new occupation in order to obtain a job. Such movements do not take place instantaneously. In the real world, labor, like other resources, does not possess perfect mobility. Some wage differentials thus result from an incomplete adjustment to change.

Since the demand for labor resources is a derived demand, it is affected by changes in product markets. An expansion in the demand for a product causes a rise in the demand for specialized labor to produce the product. Since resources are often highly immobile (that is, the supply is inelastic) in the short run, the expansion in demand may cause the wages of the specialized laborers to rise sharply. This is what happened in the oil-drilling industry in the late 1970s. An expansion in demand triggered a rapid increase in the earnings of petroleum engineers, oil rig operators, and other specialized personnel. Falling oil prices triggered the opposite effect in the mid-1980s. The demand and employment opportunities of specialized resources declined substantially as output in the oil industry fell during 1985–1986. Demand shifts in the product market favor those in expanding industries but work against those in contracting industries.

Institutional barriers may also limit the mobility of labor. Licensing requirements limit the mobility of labor into many occupations—medicine, taxicab driving, architecture, and mortuary science among them. Unions may also follow policies that limit labor mobility and alter the free-market forces of supply and demand. Minimum wage rates may retard the ability of low-skill workers to obtain employment in certain sectors of the economy. These restrictions on labor mobility will influence the size of wage differentials among workers.

SUMMARY OF WAGE DIFFERENTIALS

As the Thumbnail Sketch shows, wage differentials stem from many sources. Many of them play an important allocative role, compensating people for (a) human capital investments that increase their productivity or (b) unfavorable working conditions. Other wage differentials reflect, at least partially, locational preferences or the desires of individuals for higher money income rather than nonmonetary benefits. Still other differentials, such as those related to discrimination and occupational restrictions, are unrelated to worker preferences and are not required to promote efficient production.

THUMBNAIL SKETCH

Sources of Earnings Differentials

Differences in workers:

1. Productivity and specialized skills (for example, human capital, native ability, motivation)
2. Worker preferences (trade-off between money earnings and other things)
3. Race and sex discrimination

Differences in jobs:

1. Location of jobs

2. Nonpecuniary job characteristics (for example, convenience of working hours, job safety, likelihood of temporary layoffs, and working conditions)

Immobility of resources:

1. Temporary disequilibrium resulting from dynamic change
2. Institutional restrictions (for example, occupational licensing and union-imposed restraints)

THE ECONOMICS OF FRINGE AND MANDATED BENEFITS

Fringe Benefits: Benefits other than normal money wages that are supplied to employees in exchange for their labor services.

When referring to wages or compensation, we have proceeded as if employees were compensated only with money payments. Of course, this is a simplification. There are generally two components of employee compensation: (a) money wages and (b) **fringe benefits.** Fringe benefits include items such as health care insurance, layoff benefits, on-the-premises child care services, severance benefits, use of an automobile, discounts on life and auto insurance, parental leave benefits, and paid time-off for sickness, personal business, vacation, jury duty, and holidays.

Like money wages, provision of fringe benefits will be costly to employers. When deciding whether to employ a worker, an employer will consider the *total cost* of the compensation package. Employment will be expanded as long as the employee's marginal revenue product exceeds the cost of the employee's total compensation package, including the cost of the fringe benefits. Conversely, workers will not be hired if their employment adds more to cost than to revenue.

In any specific skill category, the compensation package of employees will reflect market conditions. Employers will have to pay a compensation package equal to the market wage, or they will lose employees to rival firms. On the other hand, employees who demand a compensation package in excess of the market wage will be unable to find employment. Fringe benefits are nothing more than a component of the market-determined compensation package. Employers who offer more attractive fringe benefits will be able to attract workers with a lower money wage. Conversely, employers who offer little in the way of fringe benefits will have to pay higher money wages in order to attract workers. In essence, employees pay for fringe benefits in the form of lower money wages. Contrary to the view of some, fringe benefits are not a "gift" from the employer. Rather, they are earned by the employees as a component of their total compensation package.

Why might employers and employees find a compensation package that included fringe benefits mutually advantageous? There are two major reasons. First, it may be cheaper for the employees of a firm to purchase certain benefits as a group rather than separately as individuals. When this is the case, employees may prefer the group-purchased benefit rather than additional money wages of equal cost. Health care insurance premiums provide an example. It will often be cheaper for an insurance company to provide a single policy covering 100 employees (and their families) than it would be for workers themselves to buy 100 separate policies. Therefore, group-purchase provides the employees of a firm with a more economical insurance coverage than they could achieve if they were paid a higher wage (equal to the cost of the insurance) and bought the insurance separately. Second, compensation in the form of fringe benefits may lead to a tax savings. For example, employer-provided child care services or use of company purchased football tickets generate "income" to the employee, but such in-kind benefits are usually not taxable. Therefore, compensation in this form may increase the employee's *after-tax* compensation more than an equivalent amount of money earnings.

The cost of providing fringe benefits will vary among employers. For example, large firms may be able to provide some fringe benefits—health care insurance and child care services, for example—much more cheaply than small firms. Simultaneously, employees will vary in their personal valuation of various fringe benefits. For example, employer-provided parental leave benefits or child care services may be a highly valued benefit to one employee, while yielding little or no utility to another.

In the absence of legislation, agreement between employers and employees (and their representatives) determines the proportion of money wages and fringe benefits in the total compensation package. Employers and employees have an incentive to structure the compensation package so that it will transfer the maximum amount of value to employees for any given cost to the employer. Compensation packages of this type will attract employees, and thereby minimize the employer's labor costs.

The extent to which any given fringe benefit will be included in a compensation package will be dependent upon both the cost of the employer's provision and the employee's personal valuation of the benefit. An employer will be indifferent between paying an employee (a) $1,000 per month or (b) $800 per month plus a fringe benefit package that costs $200 per month. In both cases, the employer's monthly cost is $1,000. When the employer's cost of providing a fringe benefit is low (relative to its cost if purchased directly by the employee) and the employee's valuation of the benefit is high, employers and employees will find it mutually advantageous to substitute the fringe benefits for higher money wages. Conversely, when there is little or no advantage derived from employer-coordinated group provision, or when employees value a fringe benefit less than its cost, employees will prefer higher money wages rather than the fringe benefit. In fact, failure to include a fringe benefit in a wage package is strong evidence that it costs more than the value it provides to employees.

THE IMPACT OF MANDATED BENEFITS

Mandated Benefits:
Government mandated fringe benefits that must be included in the total compensation package of employees.

In recent years, several congressional bills have been introduced mandating that employers supply their employees with various fringe benefits, including health care insurance, parental leave, and child care services. The proponents of **mandated benefits** argue that the legislation will increase the compensation of employees, particularly those working for employers who do not provide their employees with important fringe benefits. In response, the critics often charge that mandated benefits will push up labor costs and thereby reduce employment.

In analyzing the impact of legislation mandating benefits, there are three key points to keep in mind. First, a mandated benefit is only one component of the total compensation package. Increasing a single component of the package will not necessarily increase the size of the overall package. The parties will adjust. As they adjust, money wages and other fringe benefits will be reduced *below what they would have been in the absence of the mandated benefits*. Legislation mandating benefits reduces flexibility. It forces employers and employees to include a specific item in the total compensation package even when the parties would have preferred to structure the compensation package differently. In many cases, employer-provision of a benefit—particularly provision by small firms—will cost more than the benefit is valued by employees. When this is the case, mandated benefits will increase labor costs without providing a proportional increase in value to employees.

Second, employees earn and ultimately pay for all components of their compensation package—including any benefits mandated by government. Workers will not be hired if their employment adds more to costs than to revenues. The view that fringe benefits are a gift from the employer, and that the size of the benefits package can be increased by requiring employers to include various government-mandated benefits, is purely and simply wrong.

Third, fringe benefits are often an inefficient form of compensating employees. When there are neither savings from group purchase nor tax advantages, employees will prefer money wages to in-kind benefits. When in-kind compensation is efficient—when employees value a fringe benefit more than the additional money that it costs—an employer has a strong incentive to adopt (and employees have a strong incentive to bargain for) this form of compensation. When efficient, a fringe benefit will increase the total employee compensation without increasing the employer's cost. However, failure of a fringe benefit to emerge in a given employment setting is strong evidence that it is inefficient—that employees would prefer additional money wages to the fringe benefit.

How are mandated benefits likely to affect the welfare of workers? Our analysis indicates that adjustments in other dimensions of employment contracts will erode much of their impact. Even when they alter the structure of compensation, it is unlikely that mandated benefits will significantly increase the overall level of employee compensation. (Under some circumstances, they will even reduce employee compensation by forcing inefficient forms of compensation onto employers and employees.) However, the adjustments will also minimize the adverse employment effects of mandated benefits. Thus, mandated benefits will neither exert the positive impact on employee compensation implied by their proponents, nor exert the negative impact on labor cost and employment as charged by the critics.

PRODUCTIVITY AND WAGES

Productivity and real wages are closely linked. Real earnings are vastly greater in the United States than they are in India or China, because the output per hour of U.S. workers is much greater than the output of their counterparts in India and China. The U.S. workers earn more because they produce more. Similarly, average real earnings per hour in the United States in 1987 were approximately double the earnings of U.S. workers 35 years earlier. Again, productivity explains the difference in earnings. The output of goods and services per hour of U.S. workers in 1987 was twice the level of the early 1950s.

MYTHS OF ECONOMICS

"Automation is the major cause of unemployment. If we keep allowing machines to replace people, we are going to run out of jobs."

Machines are substituted for people if, and only if, the machines reduce costs of production. Why has the automatic elevator replaced the operator, the tractor replaced the horse, and the power shovel replaced the ditch digger? Because each is a cheaper method of accomplishing a task.

The fallacy that automation

Automation: A production technique that reduces the amount of labor required to produce a good or service. It is beneficial to adopt the new labor-saving technology only if it reduces the cost of production.

causes unemployment stems from a failure to recognize the secondary effects. Employment may decline in a specific industry as the result of automation. However, lower per unit costs in that industry will lead to either (a) additional spending and jobs in other industries or (b) additional output and employment in the specific industry as consumers buy more of the now cheaper good.

Perhaps an example will help illustrate the secondary effects of automation. Suppose someone develops a new toothpaste that actually prevents cavities and sells it for half the current price of Colgate. At last, we have a toothpaste that really works. Think of the impact the invention will have on dentists, producers of the old toothpaste and their employees, and even the advertising agencies that give us those marvelous

toothpaste commercials. What are these people to do? Haven't their jobs been destroyed?

These are the obvious effects; they are seen to be the direct result of the toothpaste invention. What most people do not see are the additional jobs that will indirectly be created by the invention; assuming an inelastic demand, consumers will now spend less on toothpaste, dental bills, and pain relievers. Their real income will be higher. They will now be able to spend more on other products they would have forgone had it not been for the new invention. Their spending on clothes, recreation, vacations, swimming pools, education, and many other items will increase. This additional spending, which would not have taken place if dental costs had not been reduced by the technological advancement, will generate addi-

Differences in labor productivity—output produced per worker-hour—are the major source of variation in real wages between nations and between time periods. When the amount produced per worker-hour is high, real wages will be high.

In the last chapter, we showed that the productivity of a resource, including labor, is dependent on the amount of other resources with which it works. Contrary to what many believe, physical capital (for example, modern labor-saving machines) is not the enemy of high real wages (see the Myths of Economics box). In fact, just the opposite is true.

Machines make is possible for labor to produce more per worker-hour. Are jobs destroyed in the process? Specific jobs are sometimes eliminated, but this merely releases human resources so that they can be used to expand output in other areas. Output and productivity, not jobs, are the source of high real wages.

Not surprisingly, the *growth* of productivity and real earnings is also closely linked. The growth of real earnings is dependent upon the growth of real output. Without an expansion of output, we will be unable to increase our real earnings and improve our living standard.

Increasing productivity is brought about by a cooperative process. Investment, both in human and nonhuman capital, is vital to the growth of productivity. For several decades, the educational level of members of the work force in the United States has steadily increased. The median number of years of schooling of persons

tional demand and employment in other sectors.

When the demand for a product is elastic, a cost-saving invention can even generate an increase in employment *in the industry affected by the invention*. This was essentially what happened in the automobile industry when Henry Ford's mass production techniques reduced the cost (and price) of cars. When the price of automobiles fell 50 percent, consumers bought three times as many cars. Even though the worker-hours per car decreased by 25 percent between 1920 and 1930, employment in the industry increased from 250,000 to 380,000 during the period, an increase of approximately 50 percent.

Of course, technological advances that release labor resources may well harm specific individuals or groups. Automatic elevators reduced the job opportunities of elevator operators. Computer technology has reduced the demand for telephone operators. In the future, videotaped lectures may even reduce the job opportunities available to college professors. Thus, the earnings opportunities of specific persons may, at least temporarily, be adversely affected by cost-reducing automated methods. It is understandable why groups directly affected fear and oppose automation.

Focusing on jobs alone, though, can lead to a fundamental misunderstanding about the importance of machines, automation, and technological improvements. Automation neither creates nor destroys jobs. The real impact of cost-reducing machines and technological improvements is an increase in production. Technological advances make it possible for us to produce as much with

fewer resources, thereby releasing valuable resources so that production (and consumption) can be expanded in other areas. Other tasks can be accomplished with the newly available resources.

Since there is a direct link between improved technology and rising output, automation exerts a positive influence on economic welfare from the viewpoint of society as a whole. In aggregate, running out of jobs is not a problem. Jobs represent obstacles, tasks that must be accomplished if we desire to loosen the bonds of scarcity. As long as our ability to produce goods and services falls short of our consumption desires, there will be jobs. A society running out of jobs would be in an enviable position: It would be nearing the impossible goal—victory over scarcity.

in the labor force in 1987 was 13, compared with 10.6 years in 1949. Simultaneously, the nonhuman capital per worker has expanded (although the growth rate of capital investment per worker has slowed considerably in recent years). Both the development and innovative application of improved technological methods are also important determinants of the growth in productivity. Technological improvements make it possible to obtain a larger output from the same resource base. Of course, modern technological advancements are often linked to investments in both physical and human capital.

THE GREAT PRODUCTIVITY SLOWDOWN

What has happened to productivity in recent decades? Exhibit 4 sheds light on this question. For two decades following the Second World War, the output per worker in the United States increased at an annual rate of 3 percent or more. As would be expected, the real compensation per hour grew at a similar rate. However, since 1968 productivity has sagged badly. During the 1974–1982 period, the annual growth rate of output per hour of U.S. workers fell to less than one percent. Real compensation per hour barely grew at all during that period. Since 1982, there has been some rebound, but productivity growth still remains well below the levels achieved following the Second World War.

Productivity growth has lagged in other countries as well. Exhibit 5 presents data on the growth of per capita GNP during 1955–1973 and 1973–1987 for seven major industrial economies. In every case, the growth of GNP per capita declined substantially subsequent to 1973. For the seven countries in aggregate, per capita real GNP declined from *more than 4 percent* during the 1955–1973 period to *less than 2 percent* subsequent to 1973.

What factors explain this more than 50 percent decline in productivity and growth of real earnings? Researchers in this area believe that most, though probably not all, of the slowdown emanates from three factors. First, and probably most important, the sharply higher oil prices of the 1973–1981 period substantially reduced the efficiency of vast amounts of capital. Machines and structures designed for cost effectiveness at pre-1973 energy prices were suddenly rendered obsolete. They were too costly to operate at the higher level of energy prices. This reduction in efficiency reduced both productivity and the growth of income.

Second, increased regulation and higher tax rates during the 1970s contributed to the slowdown in productivity. As Robert Solow, the 1987 recipient of the Nobel Prize in Economics, notes:

> Since the 1970s a substantial fraction of all investment has gone into pollution control and environmental improvement. That may be very valuable, but it doesn't contribute to the output we measure for the economy.[4]

The 1970s were also a period of expanding job safety regulations and higher tax rates, regulatory factors that also adversely affect output, as it is generally measured.[5]

---

[4]Quotation is from Timothy Tregarthen, "Explaining the Great Slowdown," *The Margin* (November/December 1988).

[5]See Edward F. Denison, *Trends in American Economic Growth, 1929–1982* (Washington, D.C.: Brookings Institution, 1985) and the articles in *The Journal of Economic Perspectives* (Fall 1988) for additional details on this topic.

EXHIBIT 4
Productivity and
Employee Compensation
in the United States,
1948–1987

As illustrated in the graph,
worker productivity and
employee compensation per
hour are closely linked. During
the last two decades, The
growth rate of worker
productivity in the United States
has been sagging.

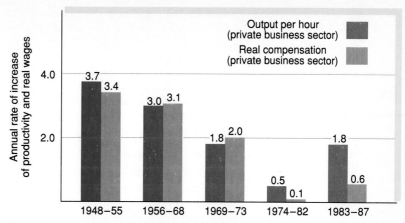

Source: *The Economic Report of the President, 1988.*

Finally, changing demographic factors in the United States also adversely affected productivity. Beginning in the latter half of the 1960s, there was a sharp influx of less experienced workers into the work force as the labor force participation of women increased and the children of the post-Second World War "baby boom" came of working age. Economics indicates that a rapid growth of the labor force—particularly the growth of inexperienced and less skilled workers—will reduce productivity.

Clearly, the lagging growth rate of productivity is a serious matter. Unless it is reversed, the future growth of income will be quite slow compared with previous historical rates. For example, a 3 percent annual growth rate means that annual earnings expand by 35 percent during a decade, while a one percent growth rate only increases earnings by a little more than 10 percent during the same period. Some of the unfavorable trends—for example, the oil price increases and the rapid growth of inexperienced workers—have reversed. Perhaps these rever-

EXHIBIT 5 ■ The Post-1973 Decline in the Growth Rates of Major Industrial Economies

	Annual Growth Rate of Per Capita GNP	
	1955–1973	1973–1987
United States	2.0	1.3
Japan	8.8	3.2
Germany	4.2	2.0
United Kingdom	2.5	1.1
Italy	4.9	2.0
France	4.6	1.9
Canada	3.0	2.0

Source: Stanley Fischer, "Symposium on the Slowdown in Productivity Growth," *Journal of Economic Perspectives*, vol. 2 (Fall 1988), Table 1. Data from the *Economic Report of the President, 1988* were used to update the figures.

sals account for the slight rise in productivity since 1982 (see Exhibit 4). However, most researchers in this area are pessimistic. Few are predicting a return to the 3 percent growth rate of productivity experienced for two decades subsequent to the Second World War.

HOW IS THE ECONOMIC PIE DIVIDED?

We have emphasized that wage rates generally reflect the availability of tools (physical capital) and the skills and abilities of individual workers (human capital). Wages tend to be high when physical capital is plentiful, technology is advanced, and the work force is highly skilled. When the equipment available to the typical worker is primitive and most workers lack education and skills, wages are low. Human capital and physical capital alike contribute to the productive process.

How is the pie divided between these two broad factors of production in the United States? Exhibit 6 provides an answer. In 1950, 81 percent of the national income was earned by employees and self-employed proprietors, the major categories reflecting the earnings of human capital. In 1988, the share of national income allocated to human capital was 81.5 percent. Income earned by nonhuman capital—rents, interests, and corporate profits—accounted for between 18 and 19 percent of the national income during both years. These earnings shares of labor and capital have been relatively constant for several decades.

CAN HIGHER WAGES BE LEGISLATED?

Minimum Wage Legislation: Legislation requiring that all workers in specified industries be paid at least the stated minimum hourly rate of pay.

In 1938, Congress passed the Fair Labor Standards Act, which provided for a national **minimum wage** of 25 cents per hour. Approximately 43 percent of the private, nonagricultural work force was covered by this legislation. During the last 40 years, the minimum wage has been increased several times, and coverage

EXHIBIT 6

The Shares of Income Going to Physical and Human Capital

Including self-employment income, approximately four-fifths of the national income is earned by owners of human capital.

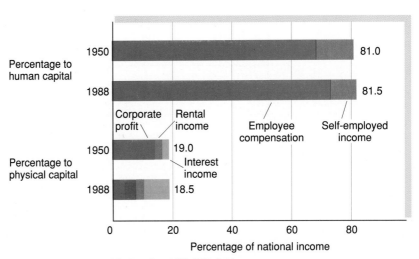

Source: *Economic Report of the President, 1988*, Table B-24.

now extends to 84 percent of the nonagricultural labor force. Currently, federal legislation requires most employers to pay wage rates of at least $3.35 per hour.

Minimum wage legislation is intended to help the working poor. There is good reason to believe, however, that such legislation has the opposite effect. Economic theory indicates that the quantity demanded of labor, particularly a specific skill category of labor, will be inversely related to its wage rate.

If a higher minimum wage increases the wage rates of unskilled workers above the level that would be established by market forces, the quantity of unskilled workers employed will fall. The minimum wage will price the services of the least productive (and therefore lowest-wage) workers out of the market.

Exhibit 7 provides a graphic illustration of the direct effect of a $3.35 minimum wage on the employment opportunities of a group of low-skill workers. Without a minimum wage, the supply of and demand for these low-skill workers would be in balance at a wage rate of $2.50. The $3.35 minimum wage makes the low-skill labor service more expensive. Employers will substitute machines and highly skilled workers (whose wages have not been raised by the minimum) for the now more expensive low-productivity employees. Jobs in which low-skill employees are unable to produce a marginal revenue product equal to or greater than the minimum will be eliminated. As the cost (and price) of goods and services produced by low-skill employees rises, consumers will rely more heavily on substitute goods produced by highly skilled labor or in foreign markets. The net effect of this substitution process will be a reduction in the quantity demanded of low-skill labor.

Of course, some low-skill workers will be able to maintain their jobs, but others will be driven into sectors not covered by the legislation or onto the unemployment and welfare rolls. Workers who retain their jobs will gain. The most adverse effects will fall on those workers who are already most disadvantaged—

EXHIBIT 7

Employment and the Minimum Wage

If the market wage of a group of employees were $2.50 per hour, a $3.35-per-hour minimum wage would (a) increase the earnings of persons who were able to maintain employment and (b) reduce the employment of others (E_0 to E_1), pushing them onto the unemployment rolls or into less-preferred jobs.

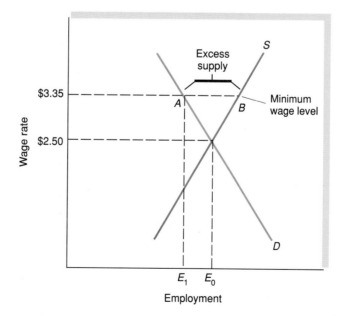

those whose market earnings are lowest relative to the minimum wage—because it will be so costly to bring their wages up to the minimum.

The direct results of minimum wage legislation are clearly mixed. Some workers, most likely the better qualified among those whose previous wages were near the minimum, will enjoy higher wages. Others, particularly those with the lowest prelegislation wage rates and skill levels, will be unable to find work.[6] They will be pushed into the ranks of the unemployed or out of the labor force.

INDIRECT EFFECTS OF THE MINIMUM WAGE

When analyzing the effects of the minimum wage, we must not forget that money wages are only one dimension of the exchange. Other aspects of the labor-service exchange will be affected by the imposition of the minimum wage. When a minimum rate pushes wages of low-skill workers above the market level, employers will have no trouble hiring workers. Therefore, they have little incentive to offer workers training, convenient working hours, continuous employment, fringe benefits, and other nonwage components of the total compensation package. Predictably, a higher minimum wage will lead to an erosion in the quality of the nonwage components of minimum wage jobs.[7] As we discussed previously, higher mandated benefits do not necessarily increase total compensation. Correspondingly, neither does a higher mandated money wage necessarily increase total compensation—at least not by the increase in the money wage.

Of the nonwage elements adversely affected by minimum wage legislation, the decline in training opportunities is particularly important. Many inexperienced workers face a dilemma: they cannot find a job without experience (or skills), but they cannot obtain experience without a job. This is particularly true for younger workers. Employment experience obtained at an early age, even on seemingly menial tasks, can help one acquire work habits (for example, promptness and self-confidence), skills, and attitudes that will enhance one's value to employers in the future. Since minimum wage legislation prohibits the payment of even a temporarily low wage, it substantially limits the employer's ability to offer employment to inexperienced workers.

In effect, the minimum wage acts as an institutional barrier limiting the on-the-job training opportunities available to low-skill workers. Therefore, most positions available to inexperienced workers are dead-end jobs. Many leading economists, including Harvard's Martin Feldstein, believe that minimum wage legislation is the major reason for the almost complete lack of skill-building jobs at the lower end of the wage spectrum.[8]

Dead-End Jobs: Jobs that offer the employee little opportunity for advancement or on-the-job training.

---

[6]The impact of minimum wage legislation could differ from the theoretical results we have outlined if labor markets were dominated by a single buyer. Economists refer to this situation as "monopsony." We choose not to present the monopsony model here because (a) in a modern society, where labor is highly mobile, the major assumptions of the model are seldom met; and (b) the bulk of the empirical evidence in this area is consistent with the competitive model.

[7]Our treatment here is parallel to that for rent controls in Chapter 3. There we noted that in response to a *below*-market price and accompanying excess demand, the quality of rental housing deteriorates because sellers (landlords) have little incentive to maintain quality in order to attract buyers (renters). Correspondingly, in response to an *above*-equilibrium price and accompanying excess supply, the nonwage characteristics of jobs deteriorate because buyers (employers) have little incentive to maintain the quality of working conditions and fringe benefits necessary to attract sellers (workers). It is hard to repeal the laws of supply and demand.

[8]It is ironic that although we subsidize formal education, we establish barriers that restrict a worker's ability to acquire training. See Martin Feldstein, "The Economics of the New Unemployment," *Public Interest* (Fall 1973), pp. 3–42.

EXHIBIT 8 ■ Changes in the Minimum Wage and the Unemployment of Black Teenagers

12 Months Prior to and Subsequent to Change in Minimum Wage	Minimum Wage	Percent of Workers Covered	Unemployment Rate	
			All Workers	Black Teenagers
March 1955–Feb. 1956	$0.75	—	4.2	15.8
March 1956–Feb. 1957	1.00	53	4.1	18.1
Sept. 1960–Aug. 1961	1.00	—	6.6	27.4
Sept. 1963–Aug. 1964[a]	1.25	62	5.4	28.4
Feb. 1966–Jan. 1967	1.25	—	3.8	25.1
Feb. 1968–Jan. 1969[a]	1.60	73	3.6	25.4
May 1973–Apr. 1974	1.60	—	4.9	30.3
Jan. 1981–Dec. 1981[a]	3.35	84	7.9	37.8

[a]The minimum wage was increased in stages. The time period is the 12 months following the final increase in the minimum wage called for by the legislation.

Source: U.S. Department of Labor, *Monthly Labor Review* (various issues).

MINIMUM WAGE AND TEENAGE UNEMPLOYMENT

Most empirical studies of the minimum wage in the United States have focused on teenagers, since there is a higher proportion of low-wage workers (reflecting their lack of skill-building experience) in this age group. There have been several studies of the impact of the minimum wage on the employment opportunities of youth. Most of these studies indicate that a 10 percent increase in the minimum wage reduces teenage employment by 1 to 3 percent.[9] Given the expected adverse impact of the minimum wage on other forms of compensation, this relatively small decline in employment is not surprising.

The minimum wage exerts its greatest impact on the employment opportunities of younger workers (ages 16–24), particularly blacks. When a minimum wage pushes earnings in a skill category above the market level, an excess supply of labor will result. Employers will be in a position to choose among a surplus of applicants for each position. They will generally choose those workers, within the low-productivity group, who have the most skill, experience, and education. These are generally not younger blacks. In addition, since all workers must be paid the minimum, the employer's incentive to hire less skilled and less favored groups is destroyed.

Exhibit 8 shows how the unemployment rate of black teenagers has changed following increases in the minimum wage during the last three decades. In March 1956, the minimum wage was increased from 75 cents to $1. During the 12 months following this increase in the minimum wage, the overall unemployment

---

[9]See Jacob Mincer, "Unemployment Effects of Minimum Wages," *Journal of Political Economy,* vol. 84 (August 1976); James Ragan, "Minimum Wages and the Youth Labor Market," *Review of Economics and Statistics,* vol. 59 (May 1977); Finis Welch, *Minimum Wages: Issues and Evidence* (Washington, D.C.: American Enterprise Institute, 1978); Charles L. Betsey and Bruce H. Dunson, "Federal Minimum Wage Laws and the Employment of Minority Youth," *American Economic Review,* vol. 71 (May 1981); and Charles Brown, Curtis Gilroy, and Andrew Kohen, "The Effect of the Minimum Wage on Employment and Unemployment," *Journal of Economic Literature,* vol. 20 (June 1982).

APPLICATIONS IN ECONOMICS

Employment Discrimination and the Earnings of Women

Since the Second World War, there has been a dramatic shift in the household/work force role of women, particularly married women. In 1986, more than half of the *married* women were in the labor force, up from less than one-fourth in 1949. As Exhibit 9 shows, the aggregate labor force participation rate of women has risen from 37.6 percent in 1960 to 55.9 percent in 1987.

While more women were working, prior to 1980 their earnings changed little relative to men. In fact, the female/male earnings ratio for *full-time workers* was approximately 60 percent throughout the 1950–1980 period. As Exhibit 9 shows, the earnings of women have improved relative to men in the 1980s. Nevertheless, women working full-time earned only 65 percent as much as their male counterparts in 1986.

Employment Discrimination and Family Specialization

Why are the earnings of women so low compared to men? Most people blame employment discrimination. A

Presidential Task Force in the 1970s concluded that widespread and pervasive discrimination accounted for the lower earnings of women relative to men. There is substantial evidence supportive of this view. In contrast with minorities relative to whites, the age, education, marital status, language, and regional locational characteristics of men and women are similar. Even after correcting for these factors, the earnings of women are only about two-thirds as great as those of men. Occupational data are consistent with the view that women are crowded into a few low-paying jobs. Until recently, more than half of all women were employed in just four occupations—clerical workers, teachers, nurses, and food service workers. High-paying professional, managerial, and craft occupations, particularly occupations where on-the-job experience leads to upward mobility, appear to be reserved primarily for men.

Despite this evidence, the case that employment discrimination is the sole or even the major source of the

earnings differential between men and women is less than airtight. First, the size of even the adjusted differential should cause one to pause. If an employer could really hire women who are *willing and able to do the same work as men* for 35 percent less, the profit motive would provide the employer with a strong incentive to do so. Remember, the average business earns a profit of about 5 percent on total sales (or total cost). If an employer could really cut labor cost 35 percent merely by hiring women (primarily) rather than men, surely many less "sexist" employers, perhaps even women employers, would jump at the chance. Of course, as more and more employers substituted women for men workers, the earnings ratio of women to men would move toward parity. This is not what is observed in the real world. There is little evidence that the 35 percent earnings differential is attracting many profit-seeking employers to substitute women for men in their work force.[10]

Second, it is important to recog-

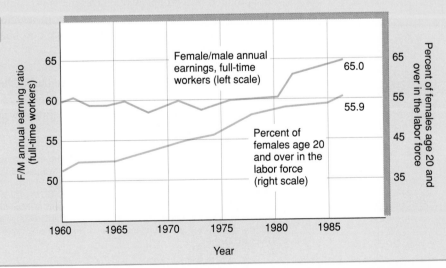

EXHIBIT 9

The Labor Force Experience of Females, 1960–1987

Between 1960 and 1987, the labor force participation of females rose from 35 to 55.9 percent. However, the F/M earning ratio fluctuated around 60 percent during the 1960–1980 period, before climbing to 65.0 percent in 1986.

F/M annual earning ratio (full-time workers)

65 — Female/male annual earnings, full-time workers (left scale) — 65.0

Percent of females age 20 and over in the labor force (right scale)

55.9

1960   1965   1970   1975   1980   1985

Year

Percent of females age 20 and over in the labor force

nize that *married* men and women have different areas of traditional specialization within the family. Married men typically pursue paid employment aggressively because they are expected to be the family's primary breadwinner. Since men envision continuous labor force participation, they are more likely to make a geographic move to improve their earnings and choose jobs for which employment experience leads to higher earnings. Given their traditional responsibility for monetary earnings, men are also more likely to accept jobs with long hours, uncertain schedules, and out-of-town travel.

In contrast, married women have generally had the primary responsibility for operating the household and caring for children. Given these areas of specialization, many women antic-ipate intermittent labor force participation. Thus, women seek different sorts of jobs than men. They seek jobs with less travel time, flexible hours, and other characteristics that are complementary with household responsibilities. Similarly, women seek jobs that will (a) be available wherever the primary earner (the husband) might locate, and (b) allow them to reenter the labor force with only a small reduction in earning power.[13] Viewed in this light, it is not particularly surprising that women find nursing, teaching, secretarial, and other jobs with easily transportable skills and credentials highly attractive.

Is there evidence in support of the view that differing areas of specialization within the family are an important source of earnings differences according to sex? Since preferences cannot be directly observed, the family specialization theory is difficult to test. However, Exhibit 10 sheds some light on its importance. Here we illustrate the median annual earnings of women relative to men, *according to marital status*. Clearly, married women earn substantially less than married men. Even when working full-time, year-round, married women earn only 59 percent as much as men. However, the earnings gap between men and women is substantially less for singles, the group least influenced by actual and potential differences in specialization within the traditional family. In 1986, the female/male annual earning ratio for full-time, full-year workers was 93 percent for singles.

Even this 7 percent disparity may not be entirely attributable to employment discrimination. Among

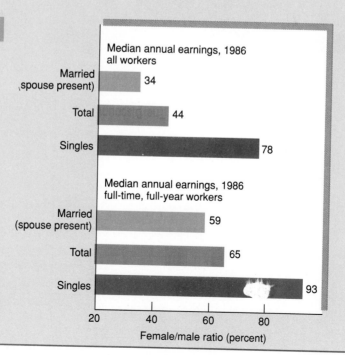

EXHIBIT 10

Female/Male Earnings According to Marital Status—1986

Although the female/male earnings ratio varies considerably according to marital status and time worked, the earnings of single women relative to the earnings of single men are much higher than the earnings of women in other marital status groupings. Source: U.S. Department of Commerce, *Current Population Reports,* Series P-60, no. 159 (Table 33).

Median annual earnings, 1986 all workers

Married (spouse present) 34
Total 44
Singles 78

Median annual earnings, 1986 full-time, full-year workers

Married (spouse present) 59
Total 65
Singles 93

Female/male ratio (percent)

current labor force participants, women are less likely than men to have studied mathematics, engineering, medicine, law, and similar fields leading to high-paying professional jobs (see Exhibit 11). Similarly, they are probably less likely than men to find construction work, coal mining, and other physically demanding jobs very attractive. Moreover, recent increases in the number of unwed mothers imply that the earnings of a significant number of never-married women are also constrained by family responsibilities.

Therefore, while a huge earnings disparity is present between married men and married women, the differential is quite small for singles. This pattern of earnings differences according to marital status implies that, although employment discrimination may well be a contributing factor, family specialization is also an important determinant of the overall earnings differential between men and women.

The Future

What can we say about the future direction of earnings according to sex? There is evidence that the career plans of young women have changed dramatically in recent years. In 1968, a national sample of women 14 to 24 years of age found that only 27 percent expected to be working at age 35. In contrast, a similar sample of young women in 1979 found that 72 percent expected to be working at age 35. Today, more than ever before, young women are preparing for a career in the labor market.[12]

Since the future labor force plans of women and men are now more similar, so, too, are their educational choices. (Exhibit 11 illustrates this point.) More and more, women are preparing for the professions, rather than for the office. For example,

women earned 49 percent of the accounting degrees in 1984–1985, up from only 10.1 percent during 1970–1971. Similar advances were made in medicine, veterinary medicine, law, architecture, pharmacy, and economics.

With the passage of time, this increased concentration on continuous labor force participation and professional skills will push the female/male earnings ratio upward.[13] In all likelihood, the growth of the female/male ratio in the early 1980s (see Exhibit 9) is the beginning of a trend that will continue in the years ahead.

---

[10]The employment and earnings data of self-employed workers are also inconsistent with the employment discrimination hypothesis. If employment discrimination is the primary cause of the low earnings of women relative to men, one would expect that many women would shift to self-employment in order to escape the effects of discrimination. As the result of employment discrimination, one would expect an over-representation of women and a higher women/men earnings ratio in self-employment occupations. In fact, the opposite results occur. See Robert L. Moore, "Employer Discrimination: Evidence from Self-Employed Workers," *Review of Economics and Statistics*, vol. LXV (August 1983).

[11]For an analysis of how family specialization influences the employment and earnings of women, see Solomon Polachek, "Discontinuous Labor Force Participation and its Effect on Women's Market Earnings," in Cynthia B. Lloyd (ed.), *Sex Discrimination and the Division of Labor* (New York: Columbia University Press, 1975), and James Gwartney and Richard Stroup, "Measurement of Employment Discrimination According to Sex," *Southern Economic Journal* (April 1973).

[12]See Chapter 7 of the *Economic Report of the President: 1987*. The numbers presented here are from Table 7–3 of the *Report*.

[13]James P. Smith and Michael P. Ward, *Women's Wages and Work in the Twentieth Century* (Los Angeles: Rand Foundation, 1984).

EXHIBIT 11 ■ Women as a Proportion of Persons Earning Selected Professional Degrees, 1970–1971 and 1984–1985

	Women as a Percentage of Persons Earning First Professional Degree in the Field	
Field of Study	1970–1971	1984–1985
Engineering	0.8	14.8
Dentistry	1.2	19.9
Optometry	2.4	27.4
Law	7.3	38.5
Veterinary Medicine	7.8	47.9
Medicine	9.2	30.1
Accounting	10.1	49.0
Economics	11.2	34.5
Architecture	12.0	35.5
Pharmacy	25.2	53.2

Source: Commission on Professionals in Science and Technology, *Professional Women and Minority* (Washington, D.C.: CPST, 1987).

rate averaged 4.1 percent, compared to 4.2 percent for the 12 months prior to the jump in the minimum wage. In contrast, the unemployment rate of black teenagers rose from 15.8 percent to 18.1 percent during the 12 months following the increase. A similar pattern was present for increases in the minimum wage during 1961–1963 and 1967–1968. In both of these cases, the unemployment rate of black teenagers rose during the period after the increase in the minimum wage even though the unemployment rate for all workers fell. During the 1974–1981 period, the minimum wage was increased seven different times, almost every year. In addition, the number of workers covered was expanded. During the 1974–1981 period, the unemployment rate of both the general labor force and black teenagers rose substantially. Nevertheless, the differential between the two continued to widen.

Much of the research documenting the adverse impact of the minimum wage on the employment opportunities of blacks has been done by black economists. Andrew Brimmer, a former member of the Federal Reserve Board, has been among the leading critics of the minimum wage. Brimmer argues:

> A growing body of statistical and other evidence accumulated by economists shows that increases in the statutory minimum wage dampen the expansion of employment and lengthen the lineup of those seeking jobs. Advances in the minimum wage have a noticeably adverse impact on young people—with the effects on black teenagers being considerably more severe.[14]

WOULD A HIGHER MINIMUM WAGE HELP THE POOR?

The composition of workers earning the minimum wage illustrates why an increase in this wage will do little to help the poor. In 1987, slightly more than 55 percent of the persons working at the minimum wage were under age 25. More than a third of the minimum wage workers were teenagers. Perhaps surprisingly to some, more than half of all of the minimum wage workers come from households with incomes above the median. Less than 7 percent of the workers earning the minimum wage were heads of families with incomes below the poverty level.

The typical minimum wage worker is a spouse or a teenage member of a household with an income well above the poverty level. Therefore, even if the adverse impact of a higher minimum wage on both employment and nonwage forms of compensation is ignored, a higher minimum wage would exert little impact on the income of the poor. This is precisely the conclusion reached in a recent study by William R. Johnson and Edgar K. Browning. Johnson and Browning estimated that a 22 percent increase in the minimum wage would add less than one-half of one percent to the income of households in the bottom 30 percent of the income distribution *even if there were no reductions in employment*.[15] The view that a higher minimum wage is an effective device with which to assist the poor is, purely and simply, incorrect.

LOOKING AHEAD

Payments to resources are of vital importance because individual incomes are determined by (a) resource prices and (b) the amount of resources that one owns. However, the purchasing power of the income received by resource owners is

---

[14] Andrew Brimmer, quoted in Louis Rukeyser, ''Jobs Are Eliminated,'' Naught News Service (August 1978).

[15] William R. Johnson and Edgar K. Browning, ''The Distributional and Efficiency Effects of Increasing the Minimum Wage: A Simulation,'' *American Economic Review* 73 (March 1983), 204–211.

dependent on productivity. There is nothing magical about the growth of real income; it is dependent on the growth of real output. The real output of a nation is strongly influenced by the capital equipment with which people work. The next chapter analyzes the factors that underlie the availability of capital and the investment choices of decision-makers.

CHAPTER SUMMARY

1. There are three major sources of wage differentials among individuals: differences in workers, differences in jobs, and degree of labor mobility. Individual workers differ with respect to productivity (skills, human capital, motivation, native ability, and so on), specialized skills, employment preferences, race, and sex. These factors influence either the demand for or the supply of labor. In addition, differences in nonpecuniary job characteristics, changes in product markets, and institutional restrictions that limit labor mobility contribute to variations in wages among workers.

2. Fringe benefits are a component of employee compensation. When the employer's cost of providing a fringe benefit is low, and the employee's personal valuation of the benefit is high, employers and employees will find it mutually advantageous to substitute fringe benefits for money wages in the total compensation package. Conversely, when these conditions are absent, money wages are the more efficient form of compensation.

3. Other forms of compensation will be scaled back as markets adjust to legislation mandating various fringe benefits. These adjustments will largely erode both the positive effects of the mandated benefits on employee compensation and the adverse effects of the benefits on labor costs and employment.

4. Productivity is the ultimate source of high wages. Workers in the United States, Canada, Japan, and other industrial countries earn high wages because their output per hour is high as the result of (a) worker knowledge and skills (human capital) and (b) the use of modern machinery (physical capital).

5. During the last 15 years, the growth of productivity in the United States and other major industrial nations has lagged well below the growth rate achieved during the two decades following the Second World War. A sharply higher world price of oil, increased regulation and high taxes, and an influx of inexperienced younger workers were important factors contributing to the slowdown in productivity in the United States. If the slowdown in productivity continues, future improvements in our standard of living will come about more slowly.

6. Approximately 80 percent of national income in the United States is allocated to human capital (labor); 20 percent is allocated to owners of physical (nonhuman) capital.

7. Automated methods of production will be adopted only if they reduce costs. Although automation might reduce revenues and employment in a specific industry, the lower cost of production will increase real income, causing demand in other industries to expand. These secondary effects will cause employment to rise in other industries. Improved technology expands our ability to produce. It is expanded production, not the number of jobs, that contributes to our economic well-being.

8. Both employment discrimination and differences in employability characteristics (the quality and quantity of schooling, skill level, prior job experience, and other human capital factors) contribute to earning differentials among groups. Economic research indicates that more than half of the earnings disparity between whites and blacks is due to differences in employability (productivity) characteristics rather than employment discrimination.

9. In the mid-1980s, women working full-time, year-round, earned only about 65 percent as much as men. Some of this differential may emanate from discrimination in the labor market. However, differences between men and women in other areas that influence earnings—particularly differences in the degree of their attachment to the labor

force and historical roles of specialization within the family—also have been important sources of earnings differences between men and women. There is evidence that the differences between men and women in these areas are eroding.

10. Minimum wage legislation increases the earnings of some low-skill workers, but others are forced to accept inferior employment opportunities, join the ranks of the unemployed, or drop out of the labor force. The direct effects, however, will be moderated by an erosion in the quality of the nonwage components of compensation in response to the minimum rate. These adjustments will moderate both (a) the increase in total compensation and (b) the adverse employment effects emanating from the minimum wage. The minimum wage exerts its most adverse affects on the employment and training opportunities of teenagers, particularly minority teenagers.

CRITICAL ANALYSIS QUESTIONS

1. What are the major reasons for the differences in earnings among individuals? Why are wages in some occupations higher than in others? How do wage differentials influence the allocation of resources? How important is this function? Explain.

*2. Why are real wages in the United States higher than in other countries? Is the labor force itself responsible for the higher wages of American workers? Explain.

3. What are the major factors that would normally explain earnings differences between (a) a lawyer and a minister, (b) an accountant and an elementary school teacher, (c) a business executive and a social worker, (d) a country lawyer and a Wall Street lawyer, (e) an experienced, skilled craftsperson and a 20-year-old high school dropout, (f) a fire fighter and a night security guard, and (g) an upper-story and a ground-floor window washer?

4. Is employment discrimination the major cause of earnings differences between whites and blacks? Is it the cause of earnings differences between males and females? Carefully justify your answer.

5. **What's Wrong with This Way of Thinking?**
"Higher wages help everybody. Workers are helped because they can now purchase more of the things they need. Business is helped because the increase in the worker's purchasing power will increase the demand for products. Taxpayers are helped because workers will now pay more taxes. Union activities and legislation mandating higher wages for workers will promote economic progress."

*6. "Jobs are the key to economic progress. Unless we create more jobs, our standard of living will fall." (True or false? Explain.)

7. If Jones has a skill that is highly valued, she will be able to achieve high market earnings. In contrast, Smith may work just as hard or even harder, and still earn only a low income.
   a. Does hard work necessarily lead to a high income?
   b. Why are the incomes of some workers high and others low?
   c. Do you think the market system of wage determination is fair? Why or why not?
   d. Can you think of a more equitable system? If so, explain why it is more equitable.

*8. People who have invested heavily in human capital (for example, lawyers, doctors, and even college professors) generally have higher wages, but they also generally work more hours than other workers. Can you explain why?

*9. Analyze the impact of an increase in the minimum wage from the current level to $6.00 per hour. How would the following be affected:
   a. employment in skill categories previously earning less than $6 per hour?
   b. the unemployment rate of teenagers?
   c. the availability of on-the-job training for low-skill workers?

*Asterisk denotes questions for which answers are given in Appendix C, Selected Answers.

d.   the demand for high-skill workers who provide good substitutes for the labor services offered by low-skill workers experiencing higher wage rates due to the increase in the minimum wage?

*10. "If individuals had identical abilities and opportunities, earnings would be equal." True or false?

11. "If it were not for employment discrimination against women, the average earnings of men and women would be equal." True or false?

*12. Other things being constant, how will the following factors influence hourly earnings?
   a.   The employee must work the midnight to 8:00 A.M. shift.
   b.   The job involves broken intervals (work 3 hours, off 2 hours, work 3 additional hours, and so on) of employment during the day.
   c.   The employer provides low-cost child care services on the premises.
   d.   The job is widely viewed as prestigious.
   e.   The job requires employees to move often from city to city.
   f.   The job requires substantial amounts of out-of-town travel.

*13. In addition to money wage compensation, some employers provide employees with health care benefits, paid time-off for sickness, vacation, and jury duty, on-the-prem-ises child care services, and severance benefits in case of termination.
   a.   How do these benefits affect the employer's cost of employment? Do you think employers offering the benefits would be willing to pay higher wages if the ben-efits were not offered?
   b.   Would you be willing to work for an employer who did not offer any of these benefits if the money wage payments were high enough?
   c.   Are these benefits "gifts" from employers offering them? Who really pays for the benefits?

14. Does it sometimes make sense for employers to pay workers with in-kind benefits (health care insurance, child care services, termination payments, and the like) rather than higher money wages? Why? Discuss.

*15. Congress is currently considering legislation that would require businesses to provide a minimum level of health insurance to all employees working more than 17.5 hours per week.
   a.   If the current money wages of part-time workers employed more than 17.5 hours per week are unchanged compared to full-time workers, how would the legisla-tion affect the cost of employing the part-time workers? How would it affect the availability of part-time (but more than 17.5 hours per week) employment?
   b.   If passed, what impact would the legislation have on the *money* wages of part-time workers employed more than 17.5 hours per week, but less than full-time?

16. "The average wage rate of women is only 59 percent of that of men. This shows that women are paid just 59 percent as much as men for doing the same work." Evaluate this statement.

*17. Consider two occupations (A and B) that employ persons with the same skill and ability. When employed, workers in the two occupations work the same number of hours *per day*. In occupation A, employment is stable throughout the year, while employment in B is characterized by seasonal layoffs. In which occupation will the *hourly* wage rate be highest? Why? In which occupation will the *annual* wage rate be highest? Why?

*18. Recognizing that one cannot support a large family at the current minimum wage, Congress passes legislation requiring that businesses employing workers with 3 or more children pay these employees at least $6 per hour. How would this legislation affect the employment level of low-skill workers with 3 or more children? Do you think some workers with large families might attempt to conceal the fact? Why?

19. Top officials of large firms already offering health care insurance, parental leaves, and

child care benefits are often at the forefront of those favoring legislation mandating that *all* firms provide these benefits. They usually argue that "good corporate citizens" should provide the benefits to their employees. Can you think of a less altruistic reason why the officials may favor the mandated benefits?

*20. In 1986, the median earnings of single men working full-time, year-round were only 61 percent those of their married counterparts. Does this indicate that there was employment discrimination against single men and in favor of married men?

14

CAPITAL, INTEREST, AND PROFIT

A greater result is obtained by producing goods in round-about ways than by producing them directly. . . .That round-about methods lead to greater results than direct methods is one of the most important and fundamental propositions in the whole theory of production.[1]

Eugen von Bohm-Bawerk

CHAPTER FOCUS

■ Why are people willing to pay interest to obtain loanable funds? How does the interest rate bring the choices of borrowers and lenders into harmony?

■ How does inflation influence the interest rate? What are the three components of the money interest rate?

■ How does an investor decide if an investment project is profitable?

■ What are the sources of economic profit? How does expected profitability influence investment decisions?

■ What role do interest and profit play in the allocation of resources?

Consumption is the objective of all production. We undertake the production of goods because we wish either to consume the good directly or use the service the good provides. All goods and services are produced by changing the form, condition, or location of raw materials through the application of human energy (human capital) and tools (physical capital).

As the Austrian economist Eugen von Bohm-Bawerk pointed out in 1884, physical capital can magnify the productivity of human beings. We can often produce a larger amount of a product with the same quantity of labor (or the same amount of a product with a lesser quantity of labor) if we first apply human energy and ingenuity to the construction of tools, machines, and even factories, and later use these constructed capital resources to produce the desired product. Economists refer to this procedure as a **roundabout method of production.**

Roundabout Method of Production: The use of productive effort to make tools and other capital assets, which are then used to produce the desired consumer good.

Through the ages, human beings have expanded both their use of tools (physical capital) and their use of knowledge about how tools can be developed and applied. This combination—more (and better) tools and the development of superior methods of production—has made it possible for us to achieve the standard of living we enjoy today.

In order to use tools and innovative methods of production to expand total production in the future, we are required to make current sacrifices. Generally speaking, we must divert resources from the production of current consumption goods in order to expand the availability of capital goods and knowledge in the future. Roundabout production methods thus require the sacrifice of current consumption. Economic efficiency requires that these costs be balanced against the future expected benefits. This chapter focuses on how a market economy directs the physical and human capital investment decisions of individuals.

THE INTEREST RATE

Interest is the additional amount a person is willing to pay to obtain a good or resource now rather than later. People generally acquire goods earlier by borrowing from a third party and making an immediate payment, rather than by simply paying the seller a larger amount at a designated date in the future. Because of this, the interest rate is often defined as the price of loanable funds. This definition is entirely proper. We should keep in mind, however, that it is the earlier availability of goods and services that can be purchased with money, not the money itself, that is desired. Willingness to pay an interest premium for loanable funds is evidence of one's desire (preference) for earlier availability.

Interest would exist even in a nonmonetary economy. Consider the economic life of a primitive economy. Suppose Robinson Crusoe wanted to obtain additional breadfruit now. If the price of breadfruit were 2 fish, Crusoe could obtain 5 breadfruit now in exchange for 10 fish. Alternatively, suppose some natives from another island would be willing to supply Crusoe the 5 breadfruit now in exchange for some amount of fish (let's say 11 fish) to be supplied one year from now. In effect, Crusoe would be paying 11 fish one year from now, rather than 10 fish

---

[1]Eugen von Bohm-Bawerk, ''Capitalist Production,'' in *The Capitalist Reader,* ed. Lawrence S. Stepelevich (New Rochelle: Arlington House, 1977), pp. 26–27.

now, to obtain the 5 breadfruit. Implicitly, he would be paying interest at a rate of 10 percent, since the breadfruit seller would not require him to pay the price (10 fish) now if he were willing to pay the price plus a 10 percent premium one year from now.

LOANABLE FUNDS: DEMAND AND SUPPLY

Positive Rate of Time Preference: The desire of consumers for goods now rather than in the future.

The demand of consumers and investors alike forms the basis of the market demand for loanable funds. Consumers demand loanable funds because they prefer earlier availability of goods. On average, individuals possess a **positive rate of time preference.** By this we mean that people subjectively value goods obtained in the immediate or near future (including the present) more highly than goods obtained in the distant future. Most people would rather have a new automobile now rather than the same automobile ten years from now.

There may be some exceptions. For example, a person with a large quantity of a perishable good, bananas, for example, might be willing to exchange 100 bananas now for fewer bananas in the future. In a modern economy, though, perishable goods can be exchanged for money, a nonperishable commodity.[2]

There is nothing irrational or even shortsighted about a positive rate of time preference. Given the uncertainties of the world in which we live, it is perfectly reasonable to prefer the reality of current consumption to the uncertainty of some larger amount (in physical or monetary terms) of future consumption. As the saying goes, "A bird in the hand is worth two in the bush." Of course, the premium that one must pay for earlier availability—the interest rate—will influence the relative amounts of current and future consumption.

Investors demand loanable funds so that they can invest in capital goods and finance roundabout methods of production that are potentially productive. Since roundabout methods of production often make it possible to produce a larger output at a lower cost, decision-makers can gain even if they have to pay an interest premium to purchase the machines, buildings, and other resources required by the production process.

Perhaps a simple example will clarify the link between the demand for loanable funds and the productivity of capital. Robinson Crusoe could pursue his fishing occupation by either (a) combining his labor with natural resources (direct production) or (b) constructing a net and eventually combining his labor with this tool (a roundabout method of production). Let us assume that Crusoe could catch 2 fish per day by hand fishing, but could catch 3 fish per day if he constructed and used a net that would last for 360 days. Suppose it would take Crusoe 5 days to build the net. The opportunity cost of constructing the net would be 10 fish (2 per day for each of the 5 days Crusoe spent building the net). If Crusoe used the roundabout method of production, his output during the next year (including the 5 days required to build the net) would be 1,080 fish (3 per day for 360 days). Alternatively, hand fishing during the year would lead to an output of only 730 (2 fish per day for 365 days). The capital-intensive, indirect method of production

---

[2]Of course, inflation may cause the purchasing power of money to diminish. The impact of inflation on the interest rate is discussed later in this chapter.

would be highly productive. Total output during the year would be expanded by 350 fish if the roundabout method of production were used.

Crusoe's fish production, though, would decline during the time he was constructing the net. Crusoe might be on the verge of starvation. Suppose a fishing crew from a neighboring island visited Crusoe and offered to lend him 10 fish so that he could undertake the capital investment project (building the net). Crusoe could gain. If Crusoe could borrow the 10 fish (the principal) in exchange for, say, 20 fish (a 100 percent interest rate) a year later, the investment project would be highly profitable.

Crusoe's—or the investor's—demand for loanable fish (or funds) stems from the productivity of the capital investment. Since construction of the net enables Crusoe to expand his total output during the year, he is willing to pay an interest premium for current availability. Crusoe's willingness to pay an interest premium for earlier availability stems directly from the productivity of capital.

An increase in the interest rate is, in essence, an increase in the cost of earlier availability. As Exhibit 1 illustrates, consumers and investors alike will curtail their borrowing in response to this increase in costs (higher interest rates). Some consumers will reduce their current consumption rather than pay the higher premium for earlier availability of consumer goods. In addition, some investment projects that would lead to gain at a lower interest rate will not be profitable at higher rates. Therefore, the amount of funds demanded is inversely related to the interest rate.

Even though higher interest rates cause the amount of borrowing to decline, they encourage lenders to provide a larger supply of funds to the market. Even individuals with a positive rate of time preference will give up current consumption to supply funds to the loanable funds market if the price is right—that is, if the interest rate is attractive. While people generally prefer earlier consumption, they also prefer more goods to fewer goods.

A rise in the interest rate increases the quantity of future goods available to persons willing to sacrifice current consumption. This increase in the quantity of future goods that can be obtained for each dollar supplied to the loanable funds market will result in a supply curve that slopes upward to the right.

EXHIBIT 1

The Determination of the Interest Rate

The demand for loanable funds stems from the consumer's desire for earlier availability and the productivity of capital. As the interest rate rises, current goods become more expensive in comparison with future goods. Therefore, borrowers will reduce the amount of loanable funds demanded. On the other hand, higher interest rates will stimulate lenders to supply additional funds to the market.

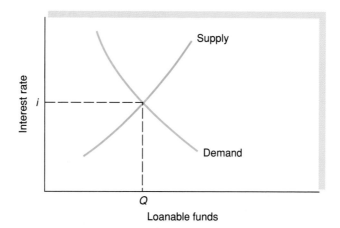

The interest rate brings the plans of borrowers into harmony with the plans of lenders. In equilibrium, the quantity of funds demanded by borrowers is equal to the amount supplied by lenders, as Exhibit 1 shows.

MONEY RATE OF INTEREST AND REAL RATE OF INTEREST

Money Rate of Interest: The rate of interest in monetary terms that borrowers pay for borrowed funds. During periods when borrowers and lenders expect inflation, the money rate of interest exceeds the real rate of interest.

Real Rate of Interest: The money rate of interest minus the expected rate of inflation. The real rate of interest indicates the interest premium, in terms of real goods and services, that one must pay for earlier availability.

We have emphasized that the interest rate is a premium borrowers are willing to pay for earlier availability. During periods of inflation, the money rate of interest, determined by the forces of supply and demand in the loanable funds market, may be a misleading indicator of how much borrowers give up to obtain earlier availability. Suppose the money rate of interest is 10 percent at a time when prices are rising at an annual rate of 5 percent. A person borrowing $100 will have to pay back $110 one year later. During that year, however, the level of prices will have increased by 5 percent. The $110 paid to the lender one year later will not buy 10 percent more goods. Instead, it will buy only 5 percent more goods than the $100 provided to the borrower one year earlier. Therefore, when the rate of inflation is taken into account, the real rate of interest is only 5 percent.

Once decision-makers anticipate rising prices, the money rate of interest will include an inflationary premium compensating lenders for the expected decline in the purchasing power of their principal and interest over the duration of the loan. The real rate of interest is equal to the money rate of interest minus the premium for the expected rate of inflation.

Recognizing the decline in the purchasing power of the dollars with which they will be repaid, lenders will reduce the amount of money supplied to the loanable funds market unless they are compensated for the anticipated rate of inflation. Simultaneously, once borrowers become fully aware that they will be paying back their loans with dollars of less purchasing power, they will be willing to pay the inflationary premium as well as the real rate of interest. If borrowers and lenders fully anticipate a 5 percent rate of inflation, for example, they will be just as willing to agree on a 10 percent interest rate as they were to agree on a 5 percent interest rate when both anticipated stable prices. Under inflationary conditions, the money rate of interest will therefore incorporate an inflationary premium reflecting the expected future increase in prices. An increase in the expected rate of inflation in the future will cause money interest rates to rise. It should not be surprising, then, that higher money interest rates are often associated with high rates of inflation. The U.S. experience during the 1970s illustrates the point. Money interest rates soared to historical highs as double-digit inflation rates were observed during the period.

THE MULTIPLICITY OF INTEREST RATES

So far, we have proceeded as though there is a single interest rate. In the real world, of course, there are many interest rates. There is a mortgage rate, a prime interest rate (the rate charged to business firms with strong credit ratings), a consumer loan rate, and a credit card rate, to name only a few. These interest rates generally differ.

The interest rate on a given loan is influenced by (a) the cost of processing, (b) the risk associated with the borrower, and (c) the duration of the loan. The accounting costs associated with a loan of several hundred thousand dollars may actually be smaller than those for a consumer loan of a few hundred dollars, if, for example, the large loan is repaid in a lump sum at a designated time in the future and the small loan is repaid monthly. Since the bookkeeping costs per

Three Components of the Money Interest

The money interest rate reflects the following three components: (a) pure interest, (b) inflationary premium, and (c) risk premium. When decision-makers expect a high rate of inflation during the period the loan is outstanding, the inflationary premium will be substantial. Similarly, the risk premium will be large when probability of default by the borrower is substantial.

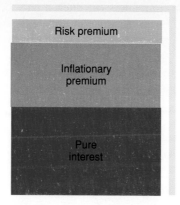

dollar loaned are generally higher for small loans, interest rates will be higher for such loans.

The interest rate on a loan is also influenced by the credit standing of the borrower and the risk associated with lending to that borrower. Banks are likely to charge an unemployed worker a higher interest rate than they charge General Motors. Since the probability of default is considerably greater for the unemployed worker than for General Motors, the former will have to pay a risk premium, which will be incorporated into the interest rate of the loan. Similarly, the interest rate on a ''secured loan,'' such as a mortgage on a house, will be less than that on a unsecured loan, such as a credit card purchase.

The degree of risk involved in a loan also varies with the loan's duration. Lenders usually require higher interest rates for longer-term loans since they involve greater risk. The longer the time period, the more likely that the financial standing of the borrower will deteriorate substantially or that market conditions will change dramatically. Also, unless rates are believed to be unusually high, borrowers are willing to pay a premium to keep the funds for a longer period of time. Thus, long-term loans usually carry a premium that compensates for the additional uncertainties and additional benefits of the longer time period.

THE COMPONENTS OF AN INTEREST RATE—A SHORT SUMMARY

As Exhibit 2 illustrates, the money rate of interest on a loan has three components. The pure interest component is the market price one must pay for earlier availability. The inflationary premium component reflects the expectation that the loan will be repaid with dollars of less purchasing power as the result of inflation. The third component—the risk premium—reflects the risk imposed on the lender by the possibility the borrower may be unable to repay the loan. The risk premium, therefore, is directly related to the probability of default by the borrower.

THE VALUE OF FUTURE INCOME

Suppose one year from now, you will have $100 in receipts. How much would that $100 be worth today? Clearly, it would be worth less than $100. If you deposited $100 today in a savings account earning 6 percent interest, you would have $106 one year from now. The interest rate connects the value of dollars (and capital assets) today with the value of dollars (and expected stream of receipts) in the future. The interest rate is used to discount the value of a dollar in the future so that its present worth can be determined today.

Net Present Value: The current worth of future income after it is discounted to reflect the fact that revenues in the future are valued less highly than revenues now.

The **net present value** (NPV) of a payment received one year from now can be expressed as follows:

$$\text{NPV} = \frac{\text{receipts one year from now}}{1 + \text{interest rate}}$$

If the interest rate is 6 percent, the current value of the $100 to be received one year from now is:

$$\text{NPV} = \frac{\$100}{1.06} = \$94.34$$

If one invested $94.34 in a savings account yielding 6 percent interest, the account would be valued at $100 one year from now.

Discounting: The procedure used to calculate the present value of future income. The present value of future income is inversely related to both the interest rate and the amount of time that passes before the funds are received.

Economists use the term **discounting** to describe this procedure of reducing the value of a dollar to be received in the future to its present worth. Clearly, the value of a dollar in the future is inversely related to the interest rate. For example, if the interest rate were 10 percent, the net present value of $100 received one year from now would be only $90.91 (100 divided by 1.10).

The net present value of $100 received two years from now is:

$$\text{NPV} = \frac{\$100}{(1 + \text{interest rate})^2}$$

If the interest rate were 6 percent, $100 received two years from now would be equal to $89 today ($100 divided by 1.06^2). In other words, $89 invested today would yield $100 two years from now.

The net present value procedure can be used to determine the current value of any future income stream. If R represents receipts received at the end of the year and i represents the interest rate, the net present value of the future income stream[3] is:

$$\text{NPV} = \frac{R_1}{(1 + i)} + \frac{R_2}{(1 + i)^2} + \cdots + \frac{R_n}{(1 + i)^n}$$

Exhibit 3 shows the net present value of $100 received at various times in the future at several different discount rates. The chart clearly illustrates two points. First, the present value of income received at a date in the future declines with the interest rate. The present value of the $100 received one year from now, when discounted at a 4 percent interest rate, is $96.15, compared to $98.04 when a 2 percent discount rate is applied. Second, the present value of the $100 also declines as the date of its receipt is set farther into the future. If the applicable discount rate is 6 percent, the present value of $100 received one year from now is $94.34, compared to $89 if the $100 is received two years from now. If the

[3]For a specific annual income stream in perpetuity, the net present value is equal simply to R/i, where R is the annual revenue stream and i the interest rate. For example, if the interest rate is 10 percent, the NPV of a $100 annual income stream in perpetuity is equal to $100/.10, or $1,000.

EXHIBIT 3 ■ The Net Present Value of $100 to be Received in the Future

The columns indicate the net present value of $100 to be received a designated number of years in the future for alternative interest rates. For example, at a discount rate of 2 percent, the net present value of $100 to be received five years from now is $90.57. Note that the net present value of the $100 declines as either the interest rate or the number of years in the future increases.

Years in the Future	Net Present Value of $100 to Be Received a Designated Number of Years in the Future for Alternative Interest Rates					
	2 Percent	4 Percent	6 Percent	8 Percent	12 Percent	20 Percent
1	98.04	96.15	94.34	92.59	89.29	83.33
2	96.12	92.46	89.00	85.73	79.72	69.44
3	94.23	88.90	83.96	79.38	71.18	57.87
4	92.39	85.48	79.21	73.50	63.55	48.23
5	90.57	82.19	74.73	68.06	56.74	40.19
6	88.80	79.03	70.50	63.02	50.66	33.49
7	87.06	75.99	66.51	58.35	45.23	27.08
8	85.35	73.07	62.74	54.03	40.39	23.26
9	83.68	70.26	59.19	50.02	36.06	19.38
10	82.03	67.56	55.84	46.32	32.20	16.15
15	74.30	55.53	41.73	31.52	18.27	6.49
20	67.30	45.64	31.18	21.45	10.37	2.61
30	55.21	30.83	17.41	9.94	3.34	0.42
50	37.15	14.07	5.43	2.13	0.35	0.01

$100 is received five years from now, its current worth is only $74.43. So, the present value of a future dollar payment is inversely related to both the interest rate and how far in the future the payment will be received.

MAKING INVESTMENT DECISIONS

Since investment projects (roundabout methods of production) involve a current sacrifice to generate a flow of output (and revenue) in the future, the discounting procedure is particularly important for investors. The value of net receipts derived from an investment project over the years can be estimated and receipts discounted to determine their current worth. This determination of the net present value of the project provides the decision-maker with an estimate of how much the project is worth now.

A worthwhile investment project must be expected to yield a rate of return equal to or greater than the opportunity cost of loanable funds. The investment discount rate, the rate at which the firm can borrow and lend funds, represents the opportunity cost of funds to the firm. If the current estimated worth (present value) of the project exceeds its cost, it would make sense to undertake the project. On the other hand, if the cost of the project exceeds the discounted value of the future net receipts, a profit-seeking firm should reject the prospective project.

Let us consider an example. Suppose a truck rental firm is contemplating the purchase of a new $40,000 truck. Past experience indicates that after the operational and maintenance expenses have been covered, the firm can rent the truck

EXHIBIT 4 ■	The Discounted Present Value of $12,000 of Truck Rental for Four Years (Interest Rate = 8 percent)		
Year (1)	Expected Future Income (Received at Year-End) (2)	Discounted Value (8 Percent Rate) (3)	Present Value of Income (4)
1	$12,000	0.926	$11,112
2	12,000	0.857	10,284
3	12,000	0.794	9,528
4	12,000	0.735	8,820
			$39,744

for $12,000 per year (received at the end of each year) for the next four years, the expected life of the vehicle.[4] Since the firm can borrow and lend funds at an interest rate of 8 percent, we will discount the future expected income at an 8 percent rate. Exhibit 4 illustrates the calculation. Column 4 shows how much $12,000 available at year-end for each of the next four years is worth today. In total, the net present value of the expected rental receipts is $39,744—less than the purchase price of the truck. The project should therefore not be undertaken.

The decision to accept or reject a prospective project is highly sensitive to the discount rate. If the discount rate in our example had been 6 percent, reflecting lower interest rates, the net present value of the future rental income would have been $41,580.[5] Since it pays to purchase a capital good whenever the net present value of the income generated exceeds the purchase price of the capital good, the project would have been profitable at the lower interest rate.

After allowance is made for risk factors, the competitive process tends to equalize the net present value of a machine (or some other capital investment project) and the purchase price of the machine (or the cost of the investment project). If the net present value of an investment project exceeds its current cost, the investor will make a profit. As more and more business decision-makers learn about the attractive opportunities for profit, they will enter the market as competitors. The entry of new competitors generally results in an increase in the price of the investment project and/or a reduction in the price of the service it provides.

---

[4]For the sake of simplicity, we assume that the truck has no scrap value at the end of four years.
[5]The derivation of this figure is shown in the following tabulation:

Year	Expected Future Income (dollars)	Discounted Value per Dollar (6% rate)	Present Value of Income (dollars)
1	12,000	0.943	11,316
2	12,000	0.890	10,680
3	12,000	0.840	10,080
4	12,000	0.792	9,504
			41,580

As we discussed previously, this process tends to erode the economic profit and equalize the net present value of the expected future revenues and the current price (or cost) of the investment.

INVESTING IN HUMAN CAPITAL

In earlier chapters, we discussed the concept of human capital. A decision to invest in human capital—to continue in school, for example—involves all the ingredients of other investment decisions. Since the returns and some of the costs normally accrue in the future, the discounting procedure helps one to assess the present value of expected costs and revenues associated with a human capital investment.

Exhibit 5 illustrates the potential human capital decision confronting Susan, an 18-year-old high school graduate contemplating the pursuit of a bachelor's degree in business administration. Just as an investment in a truck would involve a cost in order to generate a future income, so too, does a degree in business administration. If Susan does not go to college, she will be able to begin work immediately at annual earnings of E_1. Alternatively, if she goes to college, she will incur direct costs (C_d) in the form of tuition, books, transportation, and related expenses. She will also bear the opportunity cost (C_o) of lower earnings while in college. However, the study of business will expand Susan's knowledge and skills, and thereby enable her to earn a higher future income (E_2 rather than E_1). Will the higher future income be worth the cost? To answer this question,

EXHIBIT 5

Investing in Human Capital

Here we illustrate the human capital investment decision confronting Susan, an 18-year-old who just finished high school. If Susan goes to college in business administration, she will incur the direct cost (C_d) of the college education (tuition, books, transportation, and so on) plus the opportunity cost (C_o) of earnings forgone while in college. However, with a business degree, she can expect higher future earnings (B) during her career. If the discounted present value of the additional future earnings exceeds the discounted *value* of the direct and indirect cost of a college education, the business degree will be a profitable investment for Susan.

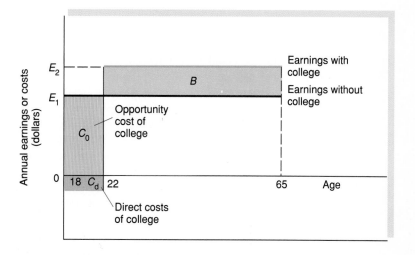

Susan must discount each year's additional income stemming from completion of the business degree and compare that with the discounted value of the cost, including the opportunity cost of earnings lost during the period of study. If the discounted value of the additional future income exceeds the discounted value of the cost, acquiring the degree is a worthwhile human capital investment.

Of course, nonmonetary considerations may also be important, particularly for human capital investment decisions, since human capital is embodied in the individual. For example, Susan's preferences might be such that she would really prefer working as a college graduate in the business world (rather than in the jobs available to high school graduates) even if she did not make more money. Thus, the nonpecuniary attractiveness of business may induce her to pursue the business degree even if the monetary rate of return is low (or even negative).

Even though human capital investments can be analyzed in the same terms as any other investment, the analysis is likely to be less precise, since it is difficult to isolate the nonmonetary aspects of these decisions. However, the same methods—the discounting procedures and the comparison of the present value of future revenues (or benefits) with costs—can apply to both human and physical capital investment decisions.

ECONOMIC PROFIT AND INVESTMENT

Why do individuals purchase long-lasting capital assets? Why do they invest in education, training, and other forms of human capital? They do so because they expect to profit—to do better than if they simply invested the funds at the market rate of interest.

Economic Profit: A return to investors that exceeds the opportunity cost of financial capital.

Economic profit is a return to investment in excess of the opportunity cost of loanable funds. There are three basic sources of economic profit: (a) uncertainty, (b) entrepreneurial alertness, and (c) monopoly.

PROFIT AND UNCERTAINTY

In a world of perfect knowledge and communication and no uncertainty, profits (and losses) would be completely absent. The real world, though, is one of change, disequilibrium markets, uncertainty, and imperfect knowledge. No one can predict the future with certainty. Unanticipated shifts in market prices or costs can cause the rate of return derived by investors to rise or fall. Investments (ownership of physical and human capital) expose one to additional uncertainty. In a sense, investing resembles a game of chance. Unanticipated changes, changes that no one could have foreseen, create winners and losers. If people did not care whether their income experienced substantial variability or not, the uncertainty accompanying investment projects would not affect the average rate of return. Most people, though, dislike uncertainty. They prefer the certain receipt of $1,000 to a 50-50 chance of receiving either nothing or $2,000. Therefore, people must be paid a premium if they are going to willingly accept the uncertainty that necessarily accompanies investments. This premium is a source of economic profit.

PROFIT AND ENTREPRENEURSHIP

While the world is characterized by uncertainty, some individuals are better than others at identifying potentially profitable opportunities. At any given time, there is virtually an infinite number of potential investment projects. Some will increase the value of resources and therefore lead to a handsome rate of return on capital. Others will reduce the value of resources, generating economic losses.

Alertness to potential opportunities to combine resources in a manner that increases their value is a source of economic profit. Economists refer to this source of profit as a return to entrepreneurship.

This component of profit reflects the ability of astute entrepreneurs to recognize and undertake economically beneficial projects that have gone unnoticed by others. Discovery of a lower-cost method of production, introduction of a new product highly valued relative to cost, development of an improved marketing technique, and the correct anticipation of a future market change provide examples of entrepreneurial behavior that markets reward with economic profit. Originality, quickness to act, and imagination are important aspects of entrepreneurship. Successful entrepreneurship involves leadership; most profits will be gone by the time the imitators arrive on the scene.

The great Harvard economist Joseph Schumpeter believed that entrepreneurship and innovative behavior were the moving forces behind capitalism. According to Schumpeter, this entrepreneurial discovery of new, improved ways of doing things led to a nation's continual improvement in its standard of living:

> The fundamental impulse that sets the capitalist engine in motion comes from the new consumer's goods, the new methods of production or transportation, and new markets, and the new forms of industrial organization that capitalist enterprise creates.[6]

Of course, entrepreneurial decision-making is always conducted in an atmosphere of uncertainty. It is important to be first and to be innovative, but it is also important to be correct. Frequently, the entrepreneur's vision turns out to have been a mirage. What appeared to be a profitable opportunity often turns out to have been an expensive illusion.

Entrepreneurship, like other resources, is scarce. Just as people differ with regard to other skills, so, too, do they possess differing amounts of entrepreneurial ability. Potential entrepreneurs are confined to using their own wealth and that of co-venturers, in addition to whatever can be borrowed. Entrepreneurs with a past record of success will be able to attract funds more readily for investment projects. Therefore, in a market economy, previously successful entrepreneurs will exert a disproportionate influence over decisions as to which projects will be undertaken and which will not.

MONOPOLY PROFIT

As we discussed in previous chapters, profits may also originate from sole ownership of a key resource (as in the diamond industry), government regulation (as in the taxicab market of many cities), or a legally granted property right to a technical innovation (as for patented products). In such cases, the monopoly rights to the key resource, privileged license, or patent are worth the present value of the future return that is in excess of what could be earned in competitive markets. In contrast with the transitory profits earned in markets with low entry restraints, monopoly profit may persist over a lengthy time period. What does economics say about monopoly profit? Two factors must be considered. First, as we pointed out previously, monopolists can gain from a "contrived" scarcity. They may choose to supply less of a product so that the price can be raised and profits

---

[6]Joseph A. Schumpeter, *Capitalism, Socialism, and Democracy* (New York: Harper Torchbooks, 1950), p. 83.

OUTSTANDING ECONOMIST

**Joseph Schumpeter
(1883–1950)**

Born in Austria, Schumpeter began his career practicing law, but soon turned to teaching of economics. In 1932, he emigrated to the United States, accepting a professorship at Harvard.

A former president of the American Economic Association (1949), Schumpeter is perhaps best known for his views on entrepreneurship and the future of capitalism. He believed that the progressive improvement in the economic well-being of the masses was the result of the creative and innovative behavior of business entrepreneurs. Entrepreneurs willing to risk their livelihood to pursue an innovative idea could be counted on to provide a steady stream of improved products at a reduced cost. These forces would generate widespread prosperity. As Schumpeter put it:

Queen Elizabeth owned silk stockings. The capitalist achievement does not typically consist in providing more silk stockings for queens but in bringing them within the reach of factory girls in return for steadily decreasing amounts of effort.[7]

Despite his admiration for a dynamic capitalist system, Schumpeter thought that the system would generate the seeds of its own destruction. Unlike Marx, who argued that capitalism would break down under the weight of its own failures, Schumpeter thought that the success of capitalism would eventually "undermine the social institutions which protect it."[8] He believed that the growth of large, technologically efficient organizations would dampen innovative zeal. The daring entrepreneur would be replaced by the organization person, the committee, and the board of directors.

In addition, Schumpeter thought that the affluence produced by a capitalist system would breed a generation of flabby business leaders incapable of defending the system against its intellectual critics, who would turn the masses toward socialism. Is Schumpeter's indictment of capitalism correct? Only the future will tell.

[7]Schumpeter, *Capitalism, Socialism, and Democracy*, p. 67.
[8]Ibid., p. 61.

increased. They may well forgo the production of units even though their marginal cost is less than the product price. If one considers only the static economic effects, allocative inefficiency will result.

Second, monopoly profit does not exist in a vacuum. In a dynamic economy, potential monopoly profit will induce competitors to follow pathways that lead to monopoly profit. If dynamic efficiency indicates that the investment resulting in monopoly profit is actually beneficial, this advantage must be weighed against the static allocative inefficiency. The protection of property rights to inventions, new products, and innovative production techniques falls in this category—economic activities of this variety, though they result in monopoly profits, can clearly lead to improvements in economic welfare. To encourage innovative activities, most countries have established a patent system, even though a temporary grant of monopoly power results.

Regardless of their source, the present value of future monopoly profits is incorporated into the value of the assets that provide the "monopoly rights." Licenses that protect their owners from competitors command high prices if they guarantee an above-market rate of return. Similarly, the market value of patent rights and specialized resources incorporates the present value of any future mo-

"My ambition is to get so good at growing things, that the government will pay me not to."

Grin and Bear It by Fred Wagner © by and Permission of News America Syndicate.

nopoly profits these assets might bestow on their owners. Once the monopoly profits are recognized by others, the market value of the monopoly-granting asset will rise until the monopoly profits have been eliminated.

INTEREST, PROFIT, AND RESOURCE ALLOCATION

Both interest and profit perform important allocation functions.[9] Interest induces people to forgo current consumption, a sacrifice that is a necessary ingredient for capital formation. Economic profit provides both human and physical capital decision-makers with the incentive to (a) undertake investments yielding an uncer-

[9]In addition to wages, interest, and profits, economists often discuss "rent" as a return to a factor of production. Economists define rent as a return to a factor the supply of which is perfectly inelastic. We have not included this discussion for two reasons. First, one can legitimately argue that the supply of all factors of production has some elasticity. After all, even the supply of usable land can be expanded through drainage, clearing, and conservation. Therefore, rent is always a matter of degree. Second, the term "rent" is used in a variety of ways, even by economists. The macroeconomic usage differs substantially from the usage in microeconomics. The term is sometimes used to define the returns to a specialized resource, such as an actor's talent, even though training plays an integral part in the supply of the resource. Rent is also sometimes applied to a factor the supply of which is temporarily fixed, even though it can clearly be expanded in the future. Since the returns to capital can be adequately discussed without introducing rent, we concluded that the cost of the ambiguity of the term exceeded the benefits of an extended discussion.

APPLICATIONS IN ECONOMICS

Can Agricultural Price Supports Make Farming More Profitable?

Since the 1930s, the government has instituted various types of **price support programs** for agricultural products. Price supports are designed to increase the prices of crops such as wheat, cotton, tobacco, peanuts, rice, and feed grains and thereby increase

Price Support Programs: Legislative action establishing a minimum price for an agricultural product. The government pledges to purchase any surplus of the product that cannot be sold to consumers at the support price.

Acreage Restriction Program: A program designed to raise the price of an agricultural product by limiting the acreage planted with the product.

farmers' incomes. However, there is good reason to question the programs' effectiveness.

Using wheat as an example, Exhibit 6 illustrates the nature of the early price support programs. These programs established a price floor (support) for wheat above the market equilibrium level and pledged that any wheat that could not be sold at the support price would be purchased by the government. Of course, the above-équilibrium price led to an excess supply of wheat. As Exhibit 6a illustrates, the excess supply was initially relatively small (A_1B_1), since both the demand for and the supply of wheat were highly inelastic in the short run. With the passage of time, however, both the demand and supply curves became more elastic. Given sufficient time to adjust, farmers both cultivated wheat land more intensively and increased the amount of land allotted to wheat. Therefore,

the excess supply the government had pledged to purchase continued to increase. (Compare the size of the excess supply of Exhibit 6b and 6a.)

The costs of storing the excess supply expanded rapidly. In fact, during the 1950s, these storage costs became a national scandal. The public outcry over the huge costs, economic waste, spoilage, and fraud eventually led to an alteration of the program.

In an effort to maintain a policy of support for farmers without creating surplus crops and the attendant problems, Congress adopted an **acreage restriction program** designed to reduce the output of agricultural products. Under this plan, price is still fixed above the market equilibrium, but the number of acres that farmers can plant is reduced to decrease supply and bring it into balance with demand at the above-equilibrium support price. Each farm is

---

EXHIBIT 6

Impact of Agricultural Price Supports

When a price support program pushes the price of an agricultural product, such as wheat, above the market equilibrium, an excess supply of the product results. Initially, the excess supply may be small (A_1B_1 of frame a). However, as farmers adjust their planting and cultivation, the long-run supply of wheat becomes increasingly elastic, causing the excess supply to expand to (A_2B_2, frame b).

Bushels of wheat per year

(a)

Bushels of wheat per year

(b)

granted an acreage allotment of wheat (and other supported products), based on the acres planted during a base year. The allotments are attached to the farm. Owners of farms are prohibited from planting more than the specified number of acres for each product.

Exhibit 7 illustrates the economics of the acreage restriction program. By restricting the number of acres planted, the supply of the product is reduced until the price of the product rises to the support level. If the government has to purchase the product at the support price, it can reduce the acreage allotments of farmers during the next period. In contrast, if the market price rises above the support level, the government can relax the allotment a little during the next period. In this manner, the government is able to bring the amount demanded and amount supplied into balance at the supported price level (for exam-

ple, as Exhibit 7 illustrates, at the $4 price floor for wheat).

The acreage restrictions make it more costly to grow any given amount of a product. Normally, farmers would minimize their cost of growing more wheat (or any other product) by using a little more of each of the factors of production (land, labor, fertilizer, machinery, and so on). The acreage restriction program prohibits them from using more land. The support price provides farmers with an incentive to produce more wheat, for example, but they must do so by using factors of production other than land more intensively. Higher costs result, shifting the supply curve of Exhibit 7 to the left (to S_2). Supply curve S_1 is unattainable once the acreage restrictions are imposed, since it would require a larger amount of land than is permissible under the allotment program.

Is farming more profitable in the long run after the imposition of the acreage restrictions and price support programs? Surprisingly, the answer is no. To the extent that price supports make farming more profitable in the short run, the demand for land with acreage allotments increases (see Exhibit 8). Competition bids up the price of land with acreage allotments until the investors receive only the normal rate of return. Just as one cannot earn an abnormally high rate of return by purchasing stock ownership rights of a firm already earning monopoly profit, neither can a farmer earn an abnormally high rate of return by purchasing the ownership rights of farms with acreage allotments.

Suppose the price support program permitted wheat growers to earn an additional $100 each year from an acre of land planted in wheat. If that were true, the net pres-

EXHIBIT 7

Acreage Restrictions and Limiting Output

Rather than permit farmers to raise an amount of wheat that would generate an excess supply at the support price, under the acreage restriction program the government restricts the number of acres allocated to the growing of wheat, causing the supply of wheat to decline to S_2. With the acreage restrictions, the excess supply is eliminated, and the $4 support price is maintained.

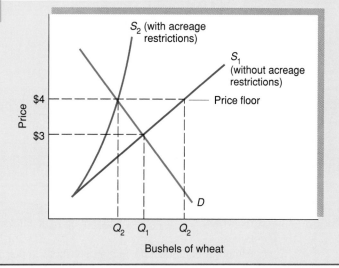

ent value (NPV) of the land with a wheat allotment would rise by $100 divided by the interest rate. At a 10 percent rate of interest, the value of the additional $100 per year would equal $1,000 (NPV = R/i = $100/.10 = $1,000). The value of an acre of land with a wheat allotment would rise by $1,000. Essentially, the value of the monopoly-profit income stream derived from the price support program would be capitalized into the

value of land with a wheat allotment.

The major beneficiaries of the price support/acreage restriction program have been the owners of land with an allotment at the time of the program's establishment. Competition for land with acreage allotments has driven the price of such land up until the rate of return on agricultural land with allotments is equal to the market rate of return. Thus, the profit rate of the current owners of the land

is no higher than it would have been had Congress never adopted any kind of price support system in the first place.[10]

_____

[10]For additional details on specific agricultural price support programs, see E. C. Pasour Jr., *Agriculture and the State: Bureaucracy and the Market Process* (San Francisco: The Independent Institute, 1989).

EXHIBIT 8
Rising Land Values and Capitalizing Profit

Since land with an acreage allotment permits one to plant wheat and sell it at the above-market-equilibrium price, the price support program makes such land more valuable. Competition drives the price of land *with an allotment* upward until the higher land values fully capture the larger profits resulting from the program. But once land values have risen, the farmer's rate of return on investment is no higher with the program than it was prior to the program's establishment. The major beneficiaries of price support programs have been those who owned land with acreage allotments *at the time the programs were established.*

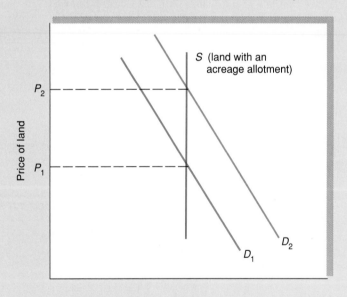

tain return and (b) discover and develop beneficial and productive investment opportunities.

Although nonmonetary factors are more important in human capital decision-making, opportunity cost and the pursuit of profit guide human capital investors just as they guide physical capital investors. As with choosing to purchase a new machine, choosing a human capital investment project (obtaining a law degree, for example) involves cost, the possibility of profit, and uncertainty. In both instances, the expected return will influence the investor. Giving due consideration to nonmonetary factors, physical and human capital investors alike seek to undertake only those projects they anticipate will yield benefits in excess of costs. To the extent they are correct, their actions will increase the value of resources—that is, they will create wealth.

LOOKING AHEAD

The agricultural price support program illustrates the importance of many of the concepts incorporated into this chapter. The competitive process and the normal rate of return, the relationship between the expected future income and the present value of an asset, and capitalization of the future value of monopoly profit—these concepts will help us understand the impact of agricultural price supports. For an analysis of this issue, see the Applications in Economics box on pages 630–32.

CHAPTER SUMMARY

1. The extensive use of tools, machinery, and other forms of physical capital sets human beings apart from other animals. An increase in the quantity (and quality) of tools and the adoption of innovative, roundabout methods of production have made our current standard of living possible.

2. Roundabout methods of production require the sacrifice of current production because resources that might otherwise be used to produce consumption goods directly are employed in the construction of tools, machines, and other constructed capital assets designed to increase future productive capability.

3. Interest is the price people are willing to pay to obtain goods and services now rather than in the future. Since earlier availability is usually attained through borrowing in the loanable funds market, the interest rate is often defined as the price of loanable funds.

4. Consumers and investors alike demand loanable funds and are willing to pay the price—the interest rate. This is so because consumers have a positive rate of time preference, and investors are willing to pay a premium for the loanable funds required to undertake potentially productive capital investment projects. If consumers did not prefer earlier availability and if capital investments were not productive, there would be no reason to expect a positive interest rate.

5. During inflationary times, the money rate of interest incorporates an inflationary premium reflecting the expected future increase in the price level. Under these circumstances, the money rate of interest exceeds the real rate of interest.

6. The money rate of interest on a specific loan reflects three basic factors—the pure interest rate, an inflationary premium, and a risk premium that is directly related to the probability of default by the borrower.

7. Since a dollar in the future is valued less than a dollar today, the value of future receipts must be discounted to calculate their current worth. The discounting procedure can be used to calculate the net present value of an expected income stream from a potential investment project. A project should be undertaken only if the net present value of the expected income from the project exceeds its current cost (purchase price).

8. The expectation of economic profit influences investment decisions in both human and physical capital. Other things constant, the higher the expected profit, the more attractive the project to an investor.

9. There are three basic sources of economic profit: (a) uncertainty, (b) entrepreneurial alertness, and (c) monopoly.
10. Since the future is uncertain, investors must expose themselves to uncertainty arising from unanticipated shifts in market demand and costs. Since most people dislike uncertainty, investors must be paid a premium (a return in excess of the interest rate) to induce them to accept the uncertainty that necessarily accompanies investment. This uncertainty premium is a source of economic profit.
11. Astute entrepreneurs are able to recognize and undertake economically beneficial investment opportunities that have gone unnoticed by others. Entrepreneurial alertness to potential opportunities to combine resources in a manner that increases their value is a source of economic profit.
12. Profits may also emanate from monopoly power—entry barriers that shield suppliers from competitive pressure. Sole ownership of a vital resource, legal restraint of entry, and patents can bestow monopoly rights on owners of assets. Monopoly profits encourage entrepreneurs to invest resources to acquire a monopoly privilege.

CRITICAL ANALYSIS QUESTIONS

1. Suppose U.S. investors are considering the construction of bicycle factories in two different countries, one in Europe and the other in Africa. Projected costs and revenues are at first identical, but the chance of guerilla warfare (and possible destruction of the factory) is suddenly perceived in the African nation. In which country will the price of bicycles (and the current rate of return to bicycle factories) probably rise? Will the investors be better off in the country with the higher rate of return? Why or why not?
*2. How would the following changes influence the rate of interest in the United States?
   a. An increase in the positive time preference of lenders.
   b. An increase in the positive time preference of borrowers.
   c. An increase in domestic inflation.
   d. Increased uncertainty about a nuclear war.
   e. Improved investment opportunities in Europe.
3. Can you discover ways to make pure economic profits from an investment by reading about currently profitable investments in the *Wall Street Journal?* Why or why not?
4. "Any return to capital above the pure interest yield is unnecessary. The pure interest yield is sufficient to provide capitalists with the earnings necessary to replace their assets and to compensate for their sacrifice of current consumption. Any return above that is pure gravy; it is excess profit." Do you agree with this view? Why or why not?
5. How are human and physical capital investment decisions similar? How do they differ? What determines the profitability of a physical capital investment? Do human capital investors make profits? If so, what is the source of profit? Explain.
*6. Suppose you are contemplating the purchase of a minicomputer at a cost of $1,000. The expected lifetime of the asset is three years. You expect to lease the asset to a business for $400 annually (payable at the end of each year) for three years. If you can borrow (and lend) money at an interest rate of 8 percent, will the investment be a profitable undertaking? Is the project profitable at an interest rate of 12 percent? Provide calculations in support of your answer.
7. How do the accounting profits of corporations differ from economic profits? Do corporate profits incorporate an interest return? A risk return? A pure profit return? A monopoly profit return? As a percentage of corporate assets, how large do think each of these returns is in most manufacturing industries? Explain.

Asterisk denotes questions for which answers are given in Appendix C, Selected Answers.

*8. According to a news item, the owner of a lottery ticket paying $3 million over 20 years is offering to sell the ticket for $1.2 million cash *now*. "Who knows?" the ticket owner explained. "We might not even be here in 20 years, and I do not want to leave it to the dinosaurs."

   a. Assuming that the ticket pays $150,000 per year at the end of each year for the next 20 years, what is the present value of the ticket if the appropriate rate for discounting the future income is thought to be 10 percent?

   b. Assuming the discount rate is in the 10 percent range, is the offer price of $1.2 million reasonable?

   c. Can you think of any disadvantages of buying the lottery earnings rather than a bond?

*9. A lender made the following statement to a borrower, "You are borrowing $1,000, which is to be repaid in 12 monthly installments of $100 each. Your total interest charge is $200, which means your interest rate is 20 percent." Is the effective interest rate on the loan really 20 percent? Explain.

10. Which of the following options would you prefer: (a) your income during the next 12 months or (b) a 50-50 chance of either zero or twice your income during the next 12 months? Would you accept (b), if someone paid you a premium? If the premium were paid, would it be improper to call it "profit"?

11. Assuming that you can borrow and lend at a 12 percent rate of interest, which would you rather have: (a) $4 million paid in $200,000 end-of-the-year installments for each of the next 20 years, or (b) $1.5 million now? (You may ignore differences in tax treatment between the two alternatives.)

*12. "Janet Jones is $20 million richer today. She just won the Florida lottery, which will pay her $1 million per year for each of the next 20 years." Evaluate. Is she really $20 million richer?

*13. A U.S. senator from a major agricultural state recently argued: "Subsidies are necessary to keep farmers in business. If all the farmers go out of business, we will starve to death."

   a. If all farm subsidies were abolished, would we have to worry about all (or even most) farmers going out of business? Why or why not?

   b. Should we subsidize automobile or shoe manufacturers for fear that, without the subsidies, all producers in these industries will go out of business and leave us with neither automobiles nor shoes?

14. Suppose the current price support/acreage allotment program for wheat were abolished. What would be the impact on (a) the value of land with a wheat allotment, (b) the cost of producing wheat, (c) the amount of wheat exported, (d) the world price of wheat, and (e) the profitability of wheat farming?

*15. Farmers are often heard to complain that they are not helped by the price support/acreage allotment program, and yet they oppose its repeal. Explain why these seemingly contradictory views are not surprising.

15 LABOR UNIONS AND COLLECTIVE BARGAINING

Analysts who have attributed national economic problems ranging from unemployment to wage inflation to low productivity to unions will have to find a new culprit to blame: unless there is a remarkable renaissance in unionism, critics won't have unions to kick around any more.[1]

Richard B. Freeman

CHAPTER FOCUS

■ How much of the U.S. work force is unionized?

■ How does the collective bargaining process work? How important is the "strike" in the bargaining process?

■ Can unions increase the wages of their members? What makes a union strong? What factors limit the power of a union?

■ Can unions increase the share of income going to labor?

■ Do unions cause inflation?

■ What impact have unions had on the legal structure of worker-management relations?

Labor Union: A collective organization of employees who bargain as a unit with employers.

In an earlier chapter, we mentioned that labor unions may be able to establish institutional arrangements that will affect supply and demand, and therefore alter wage rates. We are now prepared to examine the labor market effects of unions. A **labor union** is an organization of employees, usually working either in the same occupation or industry, who have consented to joint bargaining with employers concerning wages, working conditions, grievance procedures, and other elements of employment. The primary objective of a labor union is to improve the welfare of its members.

Unions have historically been controversial. Some believe that labor unions are a necessary shield protecting workers from the beast of employer greed. Others charge that unions are monopolies seeking to provide their members with benefits at the expense of economic efficiency, consumers, and other workers. Still others argue that the economic influence of unions—both for good and for bad—is vastly overrated. This chapter will enhance our understanding of labor unions and the economic factors that influence their ability to achieve desired objectives.

UNION MEMBERSHIP AS A SHARE OF THE WORK FORCE

Historically, the proportion of the U.S. labor force belonging to a labor union has fluctuated substantially. In 1900, less than 3 percent of the U.S. work force belonged to a labor union. From this low level, union membership expanded during the 1900–1920 period. By 1920, 12 percent of the work force was unionized. In the aftermath of the first World War, union membership declined, falling to less than 7 percent of the work force in 1935. Favorable legislation adopted during the Depression of the 1930s encouraged unions. Union membership as a share of the labor force grew rapidly during 1935–1955, reaching a peak in the mid-1950s.

During the last three decades, union membership has waned. As Exhibit 1 shows, union workers in 1986 accounted for only 17 percent of the nonfarm labor force, down from 33.2 percent in 1955.

In recent years, union workers have declined as a share of the work force in almost every industry and occupational category. There has been one significant exception: government employers. In the mid-1980s, approximately one-third of the employees in the public sector were unionized, up from 11 percent in 1960.

Why have union members declined as a share of the U.S. work force in recent decades? Several factors have contributed to the decline. First, most of the recent growth in employment has been with relatively small firms (less than 100 employees) in service and high-tech industries. Small firms are costly to organize and unions have traditionally been weak in service and high-tech industries. Second, competition has eroded union strength in several important industries. Foreign producers have increased their market share in steel, mining, automobiles, and other heavy manufacturing industries. Employment has thus been shrinking in these areas of traditional union strength. Deregulation in transportation and com-

---

[1] Richard B. Freeman, "Contraction and Expansion: The Divergence of Private Sector and Public Sector Unionism in the United States," *Journal of Economic Perspectives,* Vol. 2 (Spring, 1988), p. 86.

EXHIBIT 1

The Slide in Union
Membership as a Share
of Nonagricultural
Employment

As a proportion of nonfarm
employment, union membership
has declined from 33.2 percent
in 1955 to 17.0 percent in 1986.

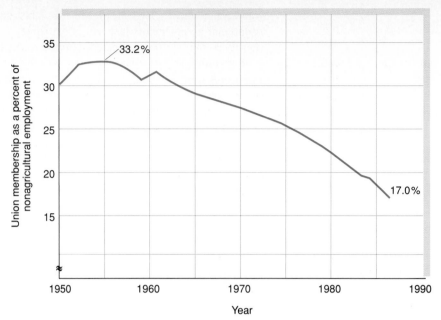

Source: *Statistical Abstract of the United States: 1981* (p. 412), and *1988* (p. 402) and *The Monthly Labor Review* (February 1985), pp. 26 and 68.

munication industries has also reduced the effectiveness of unions. As these industries have become more competitive, unionized firms have faced increased competition from nonunion producers. Finally, even regional growth patterns have adversely affected union strength. During the 1960s and 1970s, population and employment grew rapidly in the sunbelt, while stagnating in the northeast and upper middle west. Since the former is an area of union weakness and the latter an area of strength, this pattern also retarded the growth of union membership.

All of these factors, of course, have to some extent been caused by union success in raising union wages. Wages that increase more than productivity would retard the growth of employment in the geographic areas, the industries, and the classes of firms employing the high wage workers. In contrast, where wages are low relative to productivity, business investment and the growth of employment are encouraged.

THE COLLECTIVE BARGAINING PROCESS

**Collective Bargaining
Contract:** A detailed contract
between (a) a group of
employees (a labor union) and
(b) an employer. It covers
wage rates and conditions of
employment.

Each year, **collective bargaining contracts** covering wages and working conditions for six to nine million workers are negotiated. A collective bargaining contract is a union-management agreement prescribing the conditions of employment. Union negotiators, acting as agents for a group of employees, bargain with management about the provisions of a labor contract. If the union representatives are able to obtain a contract they consider acceptable, they will typically submit it to a vote of the union members. If approved by the members, the contract establishes in detail wage rates, fringe benefits, and working conditions for a future time interval, usually the next two or three years. During that time interval, union and

Union Shop: The requirement that all employees join the recognized union and pay dues to it within a specified length of time (usually 30 days) after their employment with the firm begins.

management alike must abide by the conditions of the contract. While the labor contract is between management and union, it also applies to the nonunion bargaining unit members who are employed by the firm or industry.

Some labor-management contracts contain a **union shop** provision. A union shop contract requires all workers to join the union after a specified length of employment, usually 30 days. Union proponents argue that since all workers in the bargaining unit enjoy the benefits of collective bargaining, all should be required to join and pay dues. In the absence of a union shop, individual workers might reap gains brought about by the union without incurring the costs.

Right-to-Work Laws: Laws that prohibit the union shop—the requirement that employees must join a union (after 30 days) as a condition of employment. Each state has the option to adopt (or reject) right-to-work legislation.

Opponents of the union shop argue that all employees are not helped by a union. Some unions lack the necessary power to obtain wage increases. Some employees may feel that they would be better off if they could bargain for themselves. In addition, unions often engage in political activities, either directly or indirectly. These activities may run counter to the views of individual employees. Why should an employee be forced, as a condition of employment, to support activities he or she does not approve? In 1947, Congress passed the Taft-Hartley Act; Section 14-B allows states to enact **right-to-work laws** prohibiting union shop contracts. Thus, when a state has a right-to-work statute, a union-management contract cannot require a worker to join a union as a condition of employment. Currently, 21 states, most of them in the sunbelt, have adopted right-to-work legislation.

THE STRIKE AND COLLECTIVE BARGAINING

Typically, management and labor negotiators begin the bargaining process for a new labor contract several months, or even a year, before the termination of the current agreement. The new contract is usually approved before the old contract has terminated. However, at the termination of the old labor-management agreement, if the bargaining process has broken down and there is no agreement on a new contract, either side may use its economic power to try to bring the other to terms.

Employers can withhold employment from workers at the expiration of the old contract. However, since employers can unilaterally announce their terms for continued employment, they seldom discontinue operations.

Strike: An action of unionized employees in which they (a) discontinue working for the employer and (b) take steps to prevent other potential workers from offering their services to the employer.

The major source of work stoppage is the strike. A **strike** consists of two major actions by a union: (a) employees, particularly union employees, refuse to work, and (b) steps are taken to prevent other employees from working for the employer. Both conditions are essential to a strike. Without efforts to prevent other employees, often referred to as "scabs" or "strike-breakers," from accepting jobs with the employer, a strike would merely be a mass resignation. A strike also involves picketing to restrict and discourage the hiring of other workers, actions to prevent free entry and exit from a plant, and perhaps even violence or the threat of violence against workers willing to cross the picket lines.

The purpose of a strike is to impose economic costs on an employer so that the terms proposed by the union will be accepted. When the strike can be used to disrupt the production process and interfere with the employer's ability to sell goods and services to customers, it is a very powerful weapon. Under such conditions, the employer may submit to the wage demands of the union, as a means of avoiding the costs of the strike.

Given the nature of the strike, it is not surprising that the "right to strike" has had an uneven history. At times, striking was prohibited because it was thought to interfere with the rights of nonunion workers. Before the passage of legislation in the early 1900s clearly establishing the right to strike, courts were sometimes willing to intervene and limit certain types of strikes. The role of law enforcement in strikes also has had a mixed history. In some areas, the police have given nonstrikers, who desire to continue working, protection to and from their jobs. In other cases, they have permitted pickets to block entry and have turned their backs on violence between strikers and nonstrikers. Even today, the protection a nonstriker can expect from the police varies from location to location.

The United States has established some limitations on the right to strike. The use of the strike by government employees—the single area of union growth—is substantially restricted. Most states limit the right of public employees to strike. Prohibitions against strikes by police and fire protection workers are particularly commonplace. Strikes by federal employees are also prohibited by law. When the air-traffic controllers' union called a strike during the summer of 1981, striking workers who refused to return to work were fired and eventually replaced. The Taft-Hartley Act allows the president to seek a court injunction prohibiting a private sector strike for 80 days when it is believed that the strike would create a "national emergency." During the 80-day period, work continues under the conditions of the old contract. If a settlement has not been reached during this "cooling-off" period, however, employees again have the option of using the strike weapon.

THE COST OF A STRIKE

A strike can be costly to both union and management. From the firm's viewpoint, a work stoppage may mean that it will be unable to meet the current demand for its product. It may lose customers, and they may be difficult to win back once they have turned to competitors during the strike. A strike will be more costly to the firm when (a) demand for its product is strong, (b) it is unable to stockpile its product, and (c) its fixed costs are high even during the strike. If the firm can stockpile its product in anticipation of a strike, a work stoppage may not have much impact on current sales. For example, automobile producers, particularly during slack times, often have an inventory of new cars that allows them to meet current demand during a 60- or even 90-day strike. In contrast, the shipping revenues of a trucking firm may be completely eliminated by a truckers' strike. The firm would be unable to deliver its service because of the strike, and potential customers would therefore turn to rail, air, postal, and other forms of shipping. The firm could suffer a permanent loss of sales.

Careful timing can also magnify the cost of a strike. Agricultural unions can threaten farmers with the loss of an entire year's income by striking at harvest time. Similarly, major league umpires can strengthen their position by striking at World Series time.

The nature of the product, the level of current demand, and the ability of the firm to continue to meet the requests of its customers during a strike all influence the effectiveness of the strike as a weapon. The more costly a work stoppage would be to a firm, the greater the pressure on it to yield to the demands of the union.

Strikes, particularly if they are long, are also quite costly to employees. Although a carnival attitude often prevails during the early days of a strike, a few weeks without paychecks impose an extreme hardship on most families. Strike funds are usually inadequate to deal with a prolonged strike. In recent years,

The Percentage of Work
Time Lost Due to Strikes

Since 1965, only one-tenth of 1
percent of nonfarm working
time has been lost due to labor
disputes, and the figure has
been declining.

Source: *Statistical Abstract of the United States* (annual) and *Monthly Labor Review* (various issues).

welfare benefits have been used to reduce the cost imposed on workers by the
strike.[2] Temporary employment in other areas can sometimes be arranged, but as
a strike continues, pressures build on the union to arrive at a settlement.

Strikes sometimes exert a substantial impact on secondary parties who are
unable to influence union-management relations. For example, a prolonged strike
in the steel industry might cause a loss of work time in automobile, construction,
and other industries. A teachers' strike might force a working parent to quit his
or her job to care for the children. A public transit strike in New York can para-
lyze Fun City. A coal miners' strike can leave Londoners without heat. Should
third parties be protected when strikes involve the public interest? Many would
answer this question in the affirmative. But, how can the public be protected
without interfering with the bargaining process? These questions have not yet been
fully answered.

**KEEPING WORK
STOPPAGES IN
PERSPECTIVE**

Since a strike is news, work stoppages receive considerable media exposure. Nevertheless, work stoppages due to strikes must be placed in proper perspective. The
strike, or the threat of it, forces both management and labor to bargain seriously.
Both have a strong incentive to settle without a work stoppage. This is usually
what happens. Each year an estimated 120,000 labor contracts are terminated.
Thus, during the course of a year, 120,000 labor and management bargaining
teams sit across the bargaining table from each other. They deal with the important issues of wages, fringe benefits, grievance procedures, and conditions of employment. More than 99 percent of the time, labor-management contracts are
agreed to without the use of strikes. One seldom hears about these contracts because peaceful settlements are back-page news, at best. It is the strikes that rate
the headlines.

As Exhibit 2 illustrates, very little potential work time is lost as the result of
strikes. During the last 25 years, the number of worker-hours lost because of

---

[2]The availability of welfare benefits to strikers varies among areas.

strikes was approximately one-tenth of 1 percent of the total working time—and the proportion has been falling. The amount of work time lost due to strikes is substantially less than the work time lost because of absenteeism.

HOW CAN UNIONS INFLUENCE WAGES?

The collective-bargaining process often gives one the impression that wages are established primarily by the talents of the union-management representatives who sit at the bargaining table. It might appear that market forces play a relatively minor role. However, as both union and management are well aware, market forces provide the setting in which the bargaining process is conducted. They often tip the balance of power one way or the other.

High wages increase the firm's costs. When union employers face stiff competition from nonunion producers or foreign competitors, they will be less able to pass along higher wage costs to their customers. Competition in the product market thus limits the bargaining power of a union. Changing market conditions also influence the balance of power between union and management. When the demand for a product is strong, the demand for labor will be high, and the firm will be much more willing to consent to a significant wage increase. When demand is weak, however, the product inventory level of the firm (or industry) is more likely to be high. The firm's current demand for labor will be weakened. It will be much less vulnerable to a union work stoppage. Under such conditions, wage increases will be much more difficult to obtain. (Note: When we speak of wage rates, we are referring to the total compensation package, including both fringe benefits and money wages.)

A union can use three basic strategies to increase the wages of its members: supply restrictions, bargaining power, and increase in demand. We will examine each of these in turn.

SUPPLY RESTRICTIONS

If a union can successfully reduce the supply of competitive labor, higher wage rates will automatically result. Licensing requirements, long apprenticeship programs, immigration barriers, high initiation fees, refusal to admit new members to the union, and prohibition of nonunion workers from holding jobs are all practices that unions have used to limit the supply of labor to various occupations and jobs. Craft unions, in particular, have often been able to obtain higher wages because of their successful effort to limit the entry of competitive labor. In the 1920s, unions successfully lobbied for legislation that reduced the torrent of worker-immigrants from abroad to a mere trickle. The tighter immigration laws considerably reduced the influx of new workers, reducing the growth of supply in U.S. labor markets and thus causing higher wages to prevail.

Exhibit 3a illustrates the impact of supply restrictions on wage rates. Successful exclusionary tactics will reduce supply, shifting the supply curve from S_0 to S_1. Facing the supply curve S_1, employers will consent to the wage rate W_1. Compared with a free-entry market equilibrium, the wage rate has increased from W_0 to W_1, but employment has declined from E_0 to E_1. At the higher wage rate, W_1, an excess supply of labor, AB, will result. The restrictive practices will prevent this excess supply from undercutting the above-equilibrium wage rate. Because of the exclusionary practices, the union will be able to obtain higher wages

EXHIBIT 3

Supply Restrictions, Bargaining Power, and Wage Rates

The impact of higher wages obtained by restricting supply is very similar to that obtained through bargaining power. As illustrated by frame a, when union policies reduce the supply of one type of labor, higher wages result. Similarly, when bargaining power is used in order to obtain higher wages (frame b), employment declines and an excess supply of labor results.

(a) Supply restriction

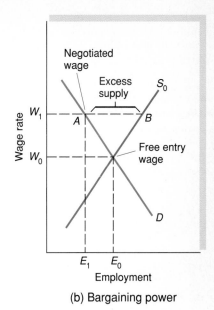

(b) Bargaining power

for E_1 employees. Other employees who would be willing to accept work even at wage rate W_0 will now be forced into other areas of employment.

BARGAINING POWER

Must unions restrict entry? Why can they not simply use their bargaining power, the strike threat, as a vehicle for raising wages? If they have enough economic power, this will be possible. A strike by even a small percentage of vital employees can sometimes halt the flow of production. For example, a work stoppage by airline mechanics can force major airlines to cancel their flights. Because the mechanics perform an essential function, an airline cannot operate without their services, even though they constitute only 10 percent of all airline employees.

If the union is able to obtain an above-free-entry wage rate, the impact on employment will be similar to a reduction in supply. As Exhibit 3b illustrates, employers will hire fewer workers at the higher wage rate obtained through bargaining power. Employment will decline below the free-entry level (from E_0 to E_1) as a result of the rise in wages. An excess supply of labor, AB, will exist, at least temporarily. More employees will seek the high-wage union jobs than employers will choose to hire. Nonwage methods of rationing jobs will become more important.

INCREASE IN DEMAND

The demand for union labor is usually determined by factors outside the union's direct control, such as the availability of substitute inputs and the demand for the product. Unions, though, can sometimes use their political power to increase the demand for their services. They may be able to induce legislators to pass laws requiring the employment of certain types or amounts of labor for a task (for example, unneeded firemen on trains, allegedly for safety reasons, or a certain number of stage engineers). Unions often seek import restrictions as a means of increasing the demand for domestic labor. For example, automobile workers generally support high tariffs and import quotas for foreign-made automobiles. Garment workers have used their political muscle to raise tariffs and reduce import

Rising Demand and Wage Increases

If a union can follow policies that will lead to an increase in the demand for its services, wages will rise automatically.

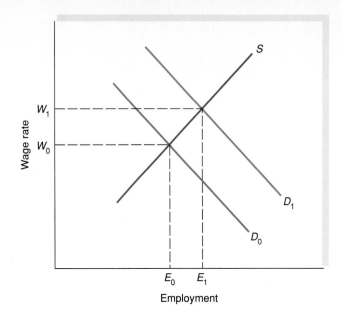

quotas for clothing goods produced abroad. Such practices increase the demand for domestic automobiles and clothing, thereby increasing the demand for domestic auto and garment workers. It is not surprising that the management and union representatives of a specific industry often join hands in demanding government tariff protection from foreign competition. As Exhibit 4 illustrates, successful union actions to increase demand for the services of union members result in both higher wages and an expansion in employment, usually at the expense of consumers.

A union in a strong bargaining position may shift the firm off its demand curve. This can happen if the union offers an ''all-or-none'' settlement in which the union specifies both wage and the quantity of labor (or restrictive work rules). To get any labor at all in this case, the firm must hire more labor at the union wage than it wants. For example, the International Typographical Union has sometimes stipulated that advertisements printed from molded mats supplied by advertisers must be set, proofread, and corrected in the newspaper's composing room. This ''bogus type'' was discarded. If the newspaper wanted any work—and no picket lines—from typesetters, it had to either pay them to do ''bogus'' work or make other bargaining concessions to induce the union to withdraw the rule. This type of ''make-work rule'' is another way in which a union may be able to loosen the connection between higher wages and lower levels of employment.

UNION POWER, EMPLOYMENT, AND MONOPSONY

Is unionization necessary to protect employees from the power of employers? When there are a large number of employers in a market area, the interest of employees will be protected by competition among employers. Under these circumstances, each employer must pay the market wage to employees to keep them from shifting to higher-paying alternative employers. In a modern society, labor is highly mobile. Most employees work in a labor market in which there are many employers. However, a few workers may confront a situation in which there is only a single employer of labor, at least for the specific skill category of labor supplied by the workers. For example, if a single large employer—perhaps a textile manufacturer or lumber mill—dominates the labor market of a small town, local workers may have few alternative employment opportunities.

Monopsony: A market in which there is only one buyer. The monopsonist confronts the market supply curve for the resource (or product) bought.

Analysis of resource markets under conditions of **monopsony** will help us understand situations in which the market is dominated by a single employer or a small number of employers. Monopsony refers to a market situation in which there is a single buyer for a specific resource; for example, a specific skill category of labor. As we previously discussed, when the seller has a monopoly, the seller can profit by restricting output and charging a price above the marginal cost of production. Under monopsony, the buyer has a monopoly. Since the alternatives available to sellers are limited, the monopsonist-buyer will be able to profit by restricting the purchase of the resource and paying a price (wage rate) that is less than the marginal revenue generated by the resource.

Marginal Factor Cost: The cost of employing an additional unit of a resource. When the employer is small relative to the total market, the marginal factor cost is simply the price of the resource. In contrast, under monopsony, marginal factor cost will exceed the price of the resource, since the monopsonist faces an upward-sloping supply curve for the resource.

Exhibit 5 illustrates the impact of monopsony in the labor market. Since the monopsonist is the only employer (purchaser of labor), its supply curve for the resource in question will coincide with the market supply curve for that resource. The supply curve for the resource will slope upward to the right because higher wages are necessary to attract the additional workers desired. For now, we will assume that both the old and new employees will be paid the higher wage rates if employment is expanded. The **marginal factor cost** (MFC) curve indicates the marginal cost of labor to the monopsonist. The marginal factor cost of labor will exceed the wage rate because the higher wages necessary to attract each additional worker must be paid to all employees. As illustrated by Exhibit 5, this means that the monopsonist's marginal factor cost curve will be steeper than the labor supply curve.

EXHIBIT 5

Labor Market Monopsony and Unionization

As frame a illustrates, the monopsonist's supply curve for labor will slope upward to the right. The marginal factor cost curve for labor will be steeper than the labor supply curve. The monopsonist will hire E_1 units of labor and pay a wage rate, W_1, along its labor supply curve. If a union establishes a wage floor, W_2 of frame b, for example, the monopsonist may hire additional workers (E_2 rather than E_1) at the higher wage rate.

(a) Monopsony (without unionization)

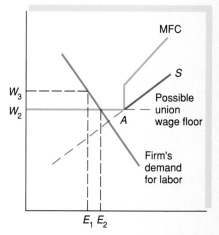

(b) Monopsony (with unionization)

How many workers should a profit-maximizing monopsony employ? The monopsonist's demand curve for labor indicates how much each additional worker adds to the firm's total revenue. The monopsonist will continue to expand employment as long as hiring additional workers adds more to total revenues than to total costs. This means that the monopsonist will choose employment level E_1, where the firm's demand curve, reflecting the marginal revenue product of labor, is just equal to the marginal factor cost of labor. A wage rate of W_1 will be sufficient to attract E_1 employees. For employment levels beyond E_1, it would cost (MFC) the monopsonist more to hire an additional worker than that worker would add to total revenue. As the result of this cost, the monopsonist firm will hire fewer employees than it would if it were not the only buyer in the labor market.

Exhibit 5b illustrates what would happen if a union established a wage floor—W_2, for example—for a monopsonist. The wage floor would prohibit the monopsonist from paying low wages even if employment dropped. The union would confront the employer with the supply curve W_2AS. In essence, the wage floor would become the firm's marginal factor cost curve until the wage floor intersected the labor supply curve at A. As long as the marginal factor cost of additional units of labor was less than the firm's demand curve, additional workers would continue to be employed. Thus, if a union imposed wage rate W_2, the monopsonist would expand employment to E_2. In this case unionization would result in both higher wages and an expansion in employment. If the union expanded the wage rate above W_3, employment would fall below E_1, the level employed by a nonunion monopsonist. But, for any wage floor less than W_3, the monopsonist would expand employment beyond E_1.

While this analysis is sound as far as it goes, there are three additional factors that should be considered.[3] First, a higher wage rate will obviously increase the firm's total costs of production. In the long run, when the firm sells its product in a competitive market, higher per unit costs will almost certainly force the firm to raise its price. A decline in the firm's market share and output is a likely result. As the firm's market share declines, employment of all factors of production, including labor, will fall.

Second, a monopsonist will often be able to confine the higher wage rates to new employees only. When this is the case, the marginal factor cost curve of the monopsonist will not differ from its labor supply curve. Rather than restricting employment to keep wages low, the firm may simply offer new employees (but not old ones) higher job classifications and more attractive employment conditions to obtain their services.

Third, given the speed of transportation, employers often draw workers from 30 to 50 miles away. In addition, many employees (particularly skilled workers, professionals, and managers) compete in a much broader labor market, a national labor market in some cases. Over a period of time, such workers will flow into and away from local labor markets. Given the mobility of labor, then, most employers will be small relative to their labor market, and their decisions to expand

---

[3]See Armen Alchian and William Allen, *Exchange and Production: Competition, Coordination, and Control* (Belmont: Wadsworth, 1983), pp. 334–339, for additional theoretical analysis of monopsony.

or contract their work force will not exert much impact on the market wage rate. Under these circumstances, marginal factor cost is nearly the same as the wage rate in the competitive market model. A rise in the wage rate will therefore almost certainly reduce employment.

The strength of these factors is enough to substantially reduce monopsony power. When economic researchers have compared the predictive power of the monopsony model with the competitive model, the latter has generally been shown to perform better. Empirical evidence thus indicates that unions normally operate in labor markets characterized by competition rather than monopsony.

WHAT GIVES A UNION STRENGTH?

Not all unions are able to raise the wages of their workers. What are the factors that make a union strong? Why are some unions able to maintain employee wages above free-entry level, while others have a negligible impact on wage rates?

Simply stated, if a union is to be strong, the demand for its labor must be inelastic. This will enable the union to obtain large wage increases while suffering only modest reductions in employment. In contrast, when the demand for union labor is quite elastic, a substantial rise in wages will mean few, if any, jobs.

There are four major determinants of the demand elasticity for a factor of production: (a) the availability of substitutes, (b) the elasticity of product demand, (c) the share of the input as a proportion of total cost, and (d) the supply elasticity of substitute inputs.[4] We now turn to the importance of each of these conditions as a determinant of union strength.

THE AVAILABILITY OF GOOD SUBSTITUTE INPUTS

When it is difficult to substitute other inputs for unionized labor when producing a good, the union is strengthened. Since nonunion labor is a good substitute for union labor, the power of unions to exclude nonunion labor is an important determinant of union strength. Unless a union can prevent nonunion employees from entering an occupation and cutting wages below the union level, it will be unable to raise wages significantly above the free-entry level.

Even if a union can successfully restrict competition from nonunion employees, the availability of machines that are good substitutes for labor will greatly reduce the power of the union. Wage increases will induce employers to mechanize. A substantial wage increase can thus mean a sharp reduction in employment. Many workers may be laid off.

A comparison of the experiences of elevator operators and airline pilots highlights the importance of substitute inputs. When the elevator operators of many large cities unionized and negotiated substantial wage increases, their gains were short-lived. Employers quickly turned to automated elevators and the employment of elevator operators fell drastically. Airline pilots, however, are able to maintain above-free-entry wage rates without much substitution in production. People do not object to riding an automated elevator, but they are not likely (at least not in the foreseeable future) to tolerate an automated airplane. Because a low-cost sub-

[4]Alfred Marshall, *Principles of Economics,* 8th ed. (New York: Macmillan, 1920).

stitute was available for elevator operators, their union was weakened. In contrast, there have historically been few substitutes for unionized airline pilots. Until the recent growth of nonunion airlines, the pilots' union was one of the strongest unions in the United States.

ELASTICITY OF DEMAND FOR THE PRODUCTS OF UNIONIZED FIRMS

Wages are a component of costs. An increase in the wages of union members will almost surely lead to higher prices for goods produced with union labor. Unless the demand for the good produced by union labor is inelastic, the output produced by unionized firms will decline if the union pushes up wages (and costs). If a union is going to have a significant impact on wages, its workers must produce a good for which the demand is inelastic.

Our analysis implies that a union will be unable to significantly increase wages above the free market rate when producing a good that competes with similar (or identical) goods produced by nonunion labor or foreign producers. The demand for the good produced by union labor will almost surely be highly elastic when the same product is available from nonunion and foreign producers. Thus, if the union pushes up wages and costs, the market share of unionized firms will shrink and the employment of union labor will fall substantially.

Both past history and recent events are consistent with this view. In the 1920s, the United Mine Workers obtained big wage gains in unionized coal fields. The union was unable to halt the growth of nonunion mining, though, particularly in the strip mines of the West. The unionized mines soon lost the major share of their market to nonunionized fields, leading to a sharp reduction in the employment of union members.

More recently, the strength of the Teamster's union was substantially eroded when deregulation subjected the unionized segment of the trucking industry to much more intense competition from nonunion firms in the early 1980s. With deregulation, nonunion firms with lower labor costs entered the industry. Given their labor-cost advantage, many of the new entrants cut prices to gain a larger share of the market. The market share of the unionized firms declined. More than 100,000 Teamsters lost their jobs. Given the sharp reduction in the employment of their members, the Teamsters eventually agreed to wage concessions and a reduction in their fringe-benefit package.[5]

Unions sometimes negotiate substantial wage increases, even though they may eventually result in significant reductions in employment. This appears to be the case in both the steel and automobile industries. As Exhibit 6 shows, the hourly earnings of production workers in these two industries rose sharply compared with other workers in the private sector during the 1970s. By 1982, the average hourly earnings of steel workers were 74 percent greater than for all private-sector workers, up from a 19 percent premium in 1969. The parallel wage premium in the automobile industry was 51 percent in 1982, up from 21 percent in 1969.

---

[5]A recent study found that after the deregulation of the trucking industry, the wage premium of unionized truckers fell from 48 percent to 30 percent in the *regulated* sector of the industry. See Barry Hirsch, "Trucking Regulation, Unionization, and Labor Earnings," *The Journal of Human Resources,* Vol. 23 (Summer 1988), pp. 296–319.

EXHIBIT 6 ■ Average Hourly Earnings of Nonsupervisory Production Workers in the Steel and Automobile Industries Compared to Other Private-Sector Workers

Year	Average Hourly Earnings (nonsupervisory production workers)				
	Private Sector	Steel Industry	Automobile Industry	Percent Premium in Steel Industry	Percent Premium in Automobile Industry
1969	$3.38	$ 4.02	$ 4.10	+19	+21
1975	5.15	6.94	6.44	+34	+25
1982	7.68	13.35	11.62	+74	+51
1987	8.98	13.78	13.55	+53	+51

Source: U.S. Department of Labor, *Monthly Labor Review*.

No doubt partially as the result of the wage and cost increases during the 1970s, foreign producers were able to expand their share of both the steel and automobile manufacturing markets in the United States. The employment of unionized labor in both industries declined. Between 1978 and 1982, membership in the United Steel Workers Union fell by 45 percent. Between 1978 and 1980, the United Automobile Workers (UAW) lost 142,000 members, nearly a 16 percent decline. Eventually, major unions representing steel and automobile workers agreed to several concessions, including the loss of various paid vacation days and scheduled cost-of-living wage increases. In addition, the UAW applied pressure that led to a reduction in Japanese imports. This combination of factors arrested, at least temporarily, the employment decline in the U.S. automobile industry. Nevertheless, the experience of steel and automobile workers during the last decade once again reveals that product market competition significantly reduces the bargaining power of even the strongest unions.

UNION LABOR AS A SHARE OF COST OF PRODUCTION

If the unionized labor input comprises only a small share of total production cost, demand for that labor will tend to be relatively inelastic. For example, since the wages of plumbers and pilots comprise only a small share of the total cost of production in the housing and air travel industries, respectively, a doubling or even tripling of the wages of plumbers or airline pilots would result in only a 1 or 2 percent increase in the cost of housing or air travel. A large increase in the price of such inputs would have little impact on product price, output, and employment. This factor has sometimes been called "the importance of being unimportant," because it is important to the strength of the union.

THE SUPPLY ELASTICITY OF SUBSTITUTE INPUTS

We have just explained that if wage rates in the unionized sector are pushed upward, firms will look for substitute inputs, and the demand for these substitutes will increase. If the supply of these substitutes (such as nonunion labor) is inelastic, however, their price will rise sharply in response to an increase in demand. The higher price will reduce the attractiveness of the substitutes. An inelastic supply of substitutes will thus strengthen the union by making the demand for union labor more inelastic.

WAGES OF UNION AND NONUNION EMPLOYEES

The precise impact of unions on the wages of their members is not easy to determine. In order to isolate the union effect, differences in other factors must be eliminated. Comparisons must be made between union and nonunion workers who have similar productivity (skills) and who are working on similar jobs.

Numerous studies have examined the effect of unions on wages. The pioneering work in this area was a 1963 study by H. Gregg Lewis of the University of Chicago.[6] Lewis estimated that, on average, union workers during the 1950s received wages between 10 and 15 percent higher than those of nonunion workers with similar productivity characteristics. The findings of other researchers using data from the 1950s and 1960s are generally consistent with the early work of Lewis.[7]

In a 1986 work, Lewis reviewed the evidence from nearly 200 studies on this topic and used more recent data to develop estimates of the union wage premium for the 1960s and 1970s.[8] Exhibit 7 summarizes the findings of Lewis's work and projects his estimates into the 1980s. Research focusing on the 1970s and early 1980s generally indicates a widening of the union-nonunion differential during that period.[9] Lewis estimates that union workers received an 18 percent premium compared to similar nonunion workers during the 1976–1979 period. During the early 1980s, the wages of union workers continued to grow more rapidly than their nonunion counterparts, leading to an estimated 20 percent differential for 1980–1982. More recently, the trend of the 1970–1982 period has reversed, resulting in a slight decline in the union premium (to an estimated 18 percent for 1986–1987).[10]

Just as our theory predicts, the empirical evidence indicates that some unions have a much greater impact on wages than others. Lewis estimated that strong unions, such as those of the electricians, plumbers, tool and die makers, metal craft workers, truckers (this was prior to the moves toward deregulation), and

[6]H. Gregg Lewis, *Unionism and Relative Wages in the United States* (Chicago: University of Chicago Press, 1963).

[7]See Albert Rees, *The Economics of Trade Unions* (Chicago: University of Chicago Press, 1967) and Michael J. Boskin, "Unions and Relative Wages," *American Economic Review,* Vol. LXII (June, 1972), pp. 466–472.

[8]H. Gregg Lewis, *Union Relative Wage Effects: A Survey* (Chicago: University of Chicago Press, 1986).

[9]See William J. Moore and John Raision, "The Level and Growth of Union/Nonunion Relative Wage Effects, 1967–1977," *Journal of Labor Research,* Vol. 4 (Winter, 1983), pp. 65–79, and Richard B. Freeman and James L. Medoff, *What Do Unions Do?* (New York: Basic Books, 1984) for evidence on this point.

[10]The studies referred to in the text compared the wages of similarly productive union and nonunion workers at a point in time. Another approach would be to compare the *change* in the wages of the same worker in cases where the worker moves from a union to a nonunion job and vice versa. Research using this approach has generally placed the union wage premium in the 10 percent range, somewhat smaller than the estimates derived from the cross-section studies. For evidence provided by studies using this methodology, see Wesley Mellow, "Unionism and Wages: A Longitudinal Analysis," *Review of Economics and Statistics,* Vol. 63 (February, 1981), pp. 43–52, and Richard B. Freeman, "Longitudinal Analysis and Trade Union Effects" *Journal of Labor Economics,* Vol. 2 (January, 1984), pp. 1–26.

EXHIBIT 7

The Wage Premium of Union Workers, 1950–1979

Most studies indicate that the wages of union workers are between 10 and 20 percent higher than similar nonunion workers. The union-nonunion differential widened during the 1970s and early 1980s, before receding in the mid-1980s.

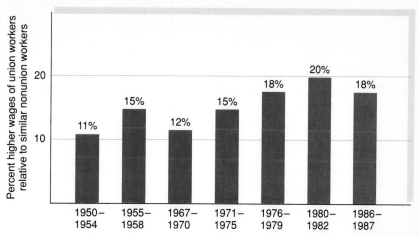

Source: H. Gregg Lewis, *Unionism and Relative Wages in the United States: An Empirical Inquiry* (Chicago: University of Chicago Press, 1963), p. 222; and H. Gregg Lewis, *Union Relative Wage Effects: A Survey* (Chicago: University of Chicago Press, 1986), p. 9. The 1980–1982 and 1986–1987 data are estimates by the authors based on the annual change in the Employment Cost Index of union and nonunion labor since 1979, as reported by the U.S. Department of Labor.

commercial airline pilots, were able to raise the wages of their members substantially more than the average for all unions. Other economists have also found substantial variation in the impact of unions on wages. In a study using 1973 data, Paul Ryscavage placed the union-nonunion wage differential at 29 percent for craft workers, 23 percent for operatives (machine operators), 44 percent for truck drivers (prior to deregulation) and 36 percent for laborers.[11]

Unionization appears to have had the least impact on the earnings of cotton textile, footwear, furniture, hosiery, clothing, and retail sales workers. In these areas, the power of the union has been substantially limited by the existence of readily available nonunion workers. Even when a union shop exists, the demands of the union are moderated by the fear of placing the unionized employer at a competitive disadvantage in relation to the nonunion employers of the industry.[12]

Above and beyond wage differences for union and nonunion workers, it is important to note that higher wages for union members do not necessarily mean an increase in the share of income going to labor in general—in other words, higher union wages do not necessarily benefit all workers. (The Myths of Economics box addresses this issue.)

In the final analysis, a general increase in the level of wages is dependent on an increase in productivity per hour. Of course, improvements in (a) technology, (b) the machines and tools available to workers (physical capital), (c) worker skills (human capital), and (d) the efficiency of economic organization provide the essential ingredients for higher levels of productivity. Higher real wages can be

---

[11]Paul M. Ryscavage, "Measuring Union-Nonunion Earnings Differences," *Monthly Labor Review,* Vol. 97 (December, 1974), pp. 3–9.
[12]For a review of the research findings on the union-nonunion wage differential, see, C. J. Parsley, "Labor Union Effects on Wage Gains: A Survey of Recent Literature," *Journal of Economic Literature,* Vol. 18 (March, 1980), pp. 1–31, and Morgan O. Reynolds, *Making America Poorer: The Cost of Labor Law* (Washington, D.C.: The Cato Institute, 1987), Chapter V.

obtained only if the production of goods and services is expanded. Although unions can increase the wages of union workers, they cannot increase the wages of all workers unless their activities increase the total productivity of labor.

DO UNIONS CAUSE INFLATION?

Labor unions are often accused of pushing up wages and thereby triggering price increases that cause inflation. Inspection of this view, however, indicates that it suffers from a major defect; it fails to incorporate the secondary effects of higher union wages. Let us consider this issue in more detail.

Suppose an economy were initially experiencing stable prices and the normal (natural) rate of unemployment. What would happen if a major union, that of the

MYTHS OF ECONOMICS

"Unions have increased the wages of workers and thereby expanded the share of income going to labor."

It is one thing for unions to increase the wages of *union members*. It is quite another for them to increase the wages of *all workers*, both nonunion and union. Neither economic theory nor empirical evidence indicates unions are able to increase the general level of wages. If unions were the primary source of high wages, the real wages of workers would be higher in highly unionized countries such as Australia, the United Kingdom, and most European counties than they are in the United States. But, this is not what we observe. For example, real wages are at least 40 percent lower in the United Kingdom

EXHIBIT 9

Labor's Share of National Income, 1930–1987

As a share of the nonfarm work force, union membership increased from less than 10 percent in the 1930s to nearly 35 percent in the mid-1950s. Since 1960, union membership declined substantially as a proportion of the U.S. labor force (see Exhibit 1). Despite these fluctuations, the share of national income allocated to labor (employee compensation and self-employment income) has been virtually constant throughout the 1930–1987 period.

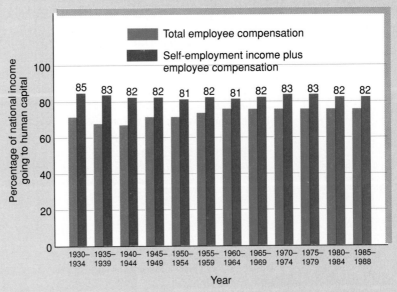

Source: Derived from the national estimates of the U.S. Department of Commerce published in *Survey of Current Business*.

automobile workers, for example, used its economic power and the threat of a strike to obtain a very substantial increase in wages? The higher wages would trigger both direct and secondary effects. The increased labor costs would push up the prices of automobiles, trucks, and buses, particularly if imports could also be restrained. The direct effect of the higher automobile prices would be an increase in the consumer price index.

However, there would also be important secondary effects that are often overlooked. Confronting the higher automobile prices, consumers must either (a) purchase significantly fewer automobiles (quality-constant units) or (b) increase their expenditures on automobiles. To the extent that consumers purchased fewer (or less expensive) automobiles, the amount of labor services required by the automobile industry would decline. Automotive employment would fall (or at least expand by an abnormally small amount). Some workers who would have been

than they are in the United States, even though half of the work force is unionized in the United Kingdom compared to less than 20 percent in the United States (see Exhibit 8).

The real source of high wages is high productivity, not labor unions. In turn, high productivity depends on abundant physical capital, the knowledge and skill of the work force, and institutional arrangements that encourage the creation of wealth.

To the extent unions increase the wages of union members, there is good reason to believe they do so primarily at the expense of nonunion workers. Higher union wages (and costs) will lead to a reduction in the output of products that intensively use union labor. This factor, along with the substitution of physical capital for labor at the higher wage rate, will cause employment in the unionized sectors to fall. What will happen to employees who are unable to find jobs in the unionized sector? They will compete for nonunion jobs, increasing supply and depressing nonunion wages. Labor economist Gregg

Lewis has estimated that the real wages of nonunion workers, four-fifths of the labor force, are 3 to 4 percent lower than they would be in the absence of unionism.[13]

If labor unions increased the wages of all workers and therefore the share of income going to labor, we would expect labor's share of income to be directly related to union membership. Again, the evidence is inconsistent with this view. Exhibit 9 presents data on labor's share of income since 1930. Total employee compensation (including the social security contribution of the employer) has increased slightly since the Second World War. However, this is primarily a reflection of the decline in the number of self-employed persons in agriculture and the corresponding increase in the proportion of employed workers. Since the earnings of self-employed proprietors such as farmers, sales personnel, accountants, and small business operators emanates primarily from their labor services, a clearer picture of the labor-property owner components of

income emerges when self-employment income is added to employee compensation. As Exhibit 9 shows, this measure of labor's share has been amazingly constant. Between 81 and 83 percent of national income in the United States has gone to labor during each five-year period since 1935. The share of national income going to labor did not rise as union membership grew as a proportion of the labor force during the 1935–1955 period. Neither has it fallen as union membership has declined since 1955.

In conclusion, while there is evidence that unions often increase the wages of their members, there is no evidence that they are able to increase the general level of real wages or the share of income earned by labor relative to physical capital.

[13]H. Gregg Lewis, *Unionism and Relative Wages in the United States* (Chicago: University of Chicago Press, 1963).

able to find jobs in the automobile industry will now be forced into other lines of employment. The labor supply in these alternative employment areas would increase, placing *downward* pressure on wages and costs in these sectors.

On the other hand, if consumers increased their expenditures on automobiles, they would have less income to spend on other things. Consumers would be forced to cut back their spending in other areas. The demand for products, the consumption of which must now be forgone as a result of the increase in expenditures on automobiles, would decline. Market adjustments would place downward pressure on prices on these areas.

Clearly, neither of these secondary effects would trigger an inflationary spiral. In fact, quite the opposite is true. Both (a) and (b) would place downward pressure on costs and prices outside of the automobile industry, which would, at least partially, offset the impact of higher automobile prices on the general price level. Of course, relative prices would change. The prices of goods requiring the services of automobile workers would rise, but the prices (and costs) of other goods would decline (or rise less rapidly). Once we consider the secondary effects, there is no reason to expect that an increase in the wages of automobile or other unionized workers would trigger a sustained increase in the general price level.[14]

UNIONISM IN OTHER COUNTIES

Exhibit 8 presents data on the level of unionism for several Western industrial economies. The data illustrates that union workers comprise a larger share of the labor force in other major industrial countries than they do in the United States. In 1984 and 1985, more than 50 percent of the nonagricultural workers in both Australia and the United Kingdom were union members. The comparable figures in both Italy and West Germany exceeded 40 percent. Correspondingly, unionization as a percent of the labor force in Canada, Japan, and France was substantially greater than in the United States.

Not only is the rate of unionization higher in other countries than for the United States, but the gap has been widening. Except for Japan (and the United States), union workers were an even larger proportion of the labor force in the mid-1980s than in 1970 for each of the countries included in Exhibit 8.

We must be cautious in our interpretation of the international data on unionism. The role of unions varies substantially among countries. In Europe, unions are often more closely tied to a political party and are more heavily involved in political activities than unions in the United States. In contrast, unions are less political and more directly involved with the firm's personnel policies in Japan. Approximately 90 percent of the union members in Japan belong to an enterprise or "company union," a type of organization that has been illegal in the United States since the passage of the Wagner Act in 1935. These variations in the role of unions contribute to the substantial differences in union membership among countries.

[14]For an in-depth analysis of the impact of unions on inflation, see Daniel J. Mitchell, *Unions, Wages, and Inflation* (Washington, D.C.: Brookings Institution, 1980).

EXHIBIT 8 ■ Union Membership: An International Comparison

	Union Membership as a Percent of Nonagricultural Employment	
Country	1970	1984–1985
Australia	52	57
United Kingdom	51	52
Italy	39	45
West Germany	37	42
Canada	32	37
Japan	35	29
France	22	28
United States	31	18

Source: Richard B. Freeman, "Contraction and Expansion: The Divergence of Private Sector and Public Sector Unionism in the United States," *Journal of Economic Perspectives* Vol. 2 (Spring, 1988).

THE CONTRIBUTION AND SIGNIFICANCE OF UNIONS

If one talks to any worker long enough, and candidly enough, one discovers that his loyalty to the union is not simply economic. One may even be able to show him that, on a strictly cost-benefit analysis, measuring income lost from strikes and jobs lost as a result of contract terms, the cumulative economic benefits are delusions. It won't matter. In the end, he will tell you, the union is the only institution that ensures and protects his "dignity" as a worker.[15]

Irving Kristol

Economists generally focus on wages and employment when discussing the impact of unions. The data suggest that many unions are able to raise the wages of their members, but, as we have seen, there is little evidence that unions have been able to significantly influence labor's share of total income. It is also clear that rising production, not union power, is the primary source of the increasing real wages of modern industrial society.

The great contribution of unions in the United States has been their role in defending employees against a sense of powerlessness, unimportance, alienation, and insecurity. The union movement has established a system of on-the-job civil rights and what Summer Slichter has called "industrial jurisprudence" to protect workers' rights.

A union provides the worker with a strong defense against the whim, arbitrary actions, and excesses of a foreman or management representative. Because of the power of the union, even in cases where only a portion of the workers are unionized, management has a greater incentive to treat workers with dignity and to grant them a sense of individual importance. These worker benefits are, for the

---

[15]Irving Kristol, "Understanding Trade Unionism," *Wall Street Journal* (October 23, 1978). Reprinted with permission of the *Wall Street Journal*.

most part, nonpecuniary and difficult to measure, but they are nevertheless extremely important.

In an industrial society, it is easy to see how individual employees could acquire a sense of helplessness. After all, what does one employee mean to General Motors, General Electric, or Boeing? If workers were unorganized, foremen, supervisors, and personnel managers would possess a great deal of power. In such a case, it would not be difficult to believe stories about employees being fired because they refused to contribute to the foreman's personal Christmas fund or because they won half of their supervisor's paycheck on a lunch-hour craps game. Analysis of economic incentives suggests that when the foreman is king and the worker is a replaceable cog in the wheel, management arbitrariness, worker insecurity, and alienation will result.

The union movement set out nearly a century ago to relieve the helplessness of the individual worker. Today, labor contracts define a worker's civil rights and provide the worker with a series of industrial appeal courts. Specifically, a worker cannot be fired without good cause, which must be proved to the satisfaction of his or her union representative. Actions the worker considers arbitrary or unfair can be taken to a shop steward, appealed through labor-management channels, and eventually brought to an objective outside arbitrator. When a union brings a grievance to the attention of management, management listens. Production at multimillion-dollar plants has been brought to a halt because a single worker's civil rights, as specified by the labor contract, were violated. Collective bargaining gives management a greater incentive to see that supervisors use discretion in dealing with each worker.[16]

This is not to say that the worker is always right in disputes involving labor and management. But, it is important for the self-esteem, morale, and human dignity of workers that they are able to have their say, that they are not powerless, and that they can take their grievances to a neutral third party. Unions have played a vital role in establishing these worker rights and in promoting a sense of community among workers.

LOOKING AHEAD

The previous four chapters have analyzed markets for human and physical resources. Wages, prices, and employment levels in these markets determine our personal incomes. The next chapter will focus on the distribution of income among individuals.

CHAPTER SUMMARY

1. Union membership grew rapidly during the 1935–55 period. In 1955, approximately one out of three nonfarm workers in the United States belonged to a union. Since the mid-1950s, union membership has waned. In 1986, only one in six nonfarm workers were union members.

---

[16]Of course, when a union is large enough to deal effectively with management and the government, individual workers may not exert much control within the union. There are occasional problems with corrupt and arbitrary actions by union officials, at both the local and the national levels. Opposition to union leadership from within the union is sometimes risky. On the whole, however, unions have worked effectively to give their members a greater voice in determining how their place of work is managed. For a discussion of these problems and how they are handled, see Lloyd G. Reynolds, Stanley H. Masters and Colletta H. Moser, *Economics of Labor* (Englewood Cliffs: Prentice-Hall, 1987), Chapter 14.

2. The strike is a major source of union power. A strike can cause the employer to lose sales while incurring continuing fixed cost. The threat of a strike, particularly when inventories are low, is an inducement for the employer to consent to the union's terms.

3. A strike is also costly to employees. Strike funds are usually inadequate to deal with a prolonged strike. The loss of just a few paychecks can impose extreme hardship on most families. The potential cost of a strike to both union and management provides each with an incentive to bargain seriously to avoid a work stoppage.

4. Agreement on most collective bargaining contracts is reached without a work stoppage. Since the Second World War, the number of work hours lost due to strikes is approximately one-tenth of one percent of the total work time—and the proportion of work time lost due to strikes has been declining.

5. There are three basic methods a union can use to increase the wages of its members: (a) restrict the supply of competitive inputs, including nonunion workers; (b) apply bargaining power enforced by a strike or threat of one; and (c) increase the demand for the labor service of union members.

6. When a large number of employers compete in the market for labor services, each employer will have to pay the market wage rate to keep employees from shifting to higher-wage alternatives. However, when monopsony is present, the single purchaser of labor may be able to profit by restricting employment and paying a wage rate that is less than the marginal revenue generated by the labor. Under these circumstances, a wage floor established by a union can result in both higher wages and increased employment.

7. If a union is going to increase the wages of its members without experiencing a significant reduction in employment, the demand for union labor must be inelastic. The strength of a union is enhanced if (a) there is an absence of good substitutes for this service, (b) the demand for the good it produces is highly inelastic, (c) the union labor input is a small share of the total cost of production, and/or (d) the supply of any available substitute is highly inelastic. An absence of these conditions weakens the power of the union.

8. Studies suggest that the earnings of union members exceed those of similar nonunion members by between 10 and 20 percent. Research using data from the 1970s and 1980s tends to place the differential closer to the higher figure. The most powerful unions have been able to obtain even larger wage gains for their members. Some weaker unions, unable to restrict the supply of nonunion workers (or products made by them), have had little impact on wages. Most of real wage increases of union workers have probably been obtained at the expense of nonunion workers and consumers.

9. Union workers are a substantially larger proportion of the work force in other industrial counties than they are in the United States. Since the role of unions varies among countries, this factor may contribute to the variation in the level of unionism among countries.

10. There is no indication that unions have significantly increased the share of national income going to labor in general. The real wages of workers are a reflection of their productivity rather than the result of union action or power. There is little reason to believe that unions enhance worker productivity—they may even retard it.

11. An increase in the wages of union members will either reduce expenditures on goods produced by nonunion labor or increase the supply of nonunion labor. In either case, the secondary effects of higher union wages will tend to reduce prices in the nonunion sector. Thus, there is no reason to believe that unions cause sustained increases in the general price level (inflation).

12. Unions in the United States have helped defend employees against a sense of powerlessness, unimportance, alienation, and insecurity, and against arbitrary behavior by management. The union movement is primarily responsible for our system of "indus-

trial jurisprudence.'' Many think these nonpecuniary factors are far more important than the impact of unions on wages.

CRITICAL ANALYSIS QUESTIONS

1. Assume that the primary objective of a union is to raise wages.
   a. Discuss the conditions that will help the union achieve this objective.
   b. Why might a union be unable to meet its goal?

*2. Suppose that Florida migrant farm workers are effectively unionized. What will be the impact of the unionization on (a) the price of Florida oranges, (b) the profits of Florida fruit growers in the short run and in the long run, (c) the mechanization of the fruit-picking industry, and (d) the employment of fruit pickers?

*3. Unions in the North have been vigorously involved in efforts to organize lower-wage workers in the South. Union leaders often express their compassion for the low-money-wage southern workers. Can you think of a reason, other than compassion, for northern union leaders' (and workers') interest in having the higher union scale extended to the South? Explain.

4. ''Unions have brought a decent living to working men and women. Without unions, employers would still be paying workers a starvation wage.'' Analyze.

5. a. ''An increase in the price of steel will be passed along to consumers in the form of higher prices of automobiles, homes, appliances, and other products made with steel.'' Do you agree or disagree?
   b. ''An increase in the price of craft-union labor will be passed along to consumers in the form of higher prices of homes, repair and installation services, appliances, and other products that require craft-union labor.'' Do you agree or disagree?
   c. Are the interests of labor unions in conflict primarily with the interests of union employers? Explain.

6. ''The purpose of unions is to push the wage rate above the competitive level. By their very nature, they are monopolists. Therefore, they will necessarily cause resources to be misallocated.'' Do you agree or disagree? Explain.

*7. ''If a union is unable to organize all the major firms in an industry, it is unlikely to exert a major impact on the wages of union members.'' Indicate why you either agree or disagree.

8. The Retail Clerks Union has organized approximately one-third of the department stores in a large metropolitan area. Do you think the union will be able to significantly increase the wages of its members? Explain.

*9. ''When an industry is highly unionized, higher labor costs will reduce industry profitability. Unions benefit workers at the expense of capitalists.'' True or false?

*10. ''In the absence of unions, employers would be able to pay workers whatever they wanted.'' True or false?

11. Suppose that the United Automobile Workers (UAW) is able to substantially increase wages in the auto industry. What impact will the higher wages in the auto industry have on:
    a. the wages of nonunion workers outside of the automobile industry?
    b. the price of automobiles made by the UAW?
    c. the demand for foreign produced automobiles?
    d. the profitability of U.S. automobile manufacturers?

*12. Even though the wage scale of union members is substantially greater than the minimum wage, unions have generally been at the forefront of those lobbying for higher minimum rates. Why do you think unions fight so hard for a higher minimum wage?

*13. Suppose that Congress were considering the following revenue measures: (a) a 10 cent per gallon increase in the gasoline tax or (b) an increase in the tariff (tax) on imported

---

*Asterisk denotes questions for which answers are given in Appendix C, Selected Answers.

automobiles that would raise an equivalent amount of revenue. Which of the two options would the United Auto Workers be most likely to favor? Which would American automobile manufacturers be most likely to favor? Explain.

14. a. With whom do union workers compete?
    b. When union workers restrict entry into a market, who are they trying to keep out?
    c. How did the deregulation of the trucking and airline industries affect the wage premium of union workers in these industries?

*15. A survey of firms in your local labor market reveals that the average hourly wage rate of unionized production workers is $1.50 higher than the average wage rate of non-union production workers. Does this indicate that unionization increases the wage rates of workers in your area by $1.50? Why or why not?

16

INEQUALITY, INCOME MOBILITY, AND THE BATTLE AGAINST POVERTY

We can compare two countries with relatively similar income distributions. If the first keeps most families in their economic place while the second allows much shifting of places, the second is surely more equal, even in strictly economic terms. But the international statistics all economists use from the UN or OECD—cannot report this simple, crucial economic fact.[1]

Mark Lilla

CHAPTER FOCUS

- How unequal are incomes in the United States? How does income inequality in the United States compare with that of other countries?

- How much income mobility is there in the United States—do the rich remain rich while the poor remain poor?

- What are the characteristics of the poor? Have they changed in recent decades?

- How is the poverty rate derived? Have income transfers reduced the poverty rate?

- Is social security an insurance program? Who is helped and who is hurt by social security?

In a market economy, the distribution of income is determined by the sale price of factor services, the resources of individuals, and the choices of individuals as to how their resources are to be employed. Because market income stems from the productive contribution of one's human and physical resources, owners have an incentive to employ their resources efficiently. When resources are allocated by market prices, there is no central distributing agency that carves up the economic pie and allocates slices to various individuals. The income of each person (or household) is determined by what they receive from others in exchange or as a gift. Since the basic abilities, opportunities, and preferences of individuals differ, income inequality will result.

Economics does not tell us that one distribution of income is better than another. It does help us better understand the process, however. It also sheds light on how policy alternatives designed to alter the distribution of income can be expected to work. This chapter focuses on these issues and related topics.

INCOME INEQUALITY IN THE UNITED STATES

Money income is only one component of economic well-being. Such factors as leisure, noncash transfer benefits, the nonpecuniary advantages and disadvantages of a job, and the expected stability of future income are also determinants of economic welfare. Nevertheless, since money income represents command over market goods and services, it is highly significant. Moreover, it is readily observable. It is the most widely used measure of economic well-being and degree of inequality.

Exhibit 1 indicates the share of before-tax annual money income received by quintile—that is, by each fifth of families ranked from the lowest to the highest. If there were total equality of annual income, each quintile (fifth) of the population would have received 20 percent of the aggregate income. Clearly that was not the case. In 1987, the bottom 20 percent of family income recipients received 4.6 percent of the total money income. At the other end of the spectrum, the 20 percent of families with the highest annual incomes received 43.7 percent of the total money income in 1987. The top quintile of income recipients thus received more than nine times as much money income as the bottom quintile of recipients.

As Exhibit 1 illustrates, there was a substantial reduction in income inequality between the mid-1930s and 1950. In 1950, the top five percent of recipients received 42.7 percent of the aggregate money income, down from 51.7 percent in the mid-1930s. Simultaneously, the income shares of the other quintile groupings increased during the 1935–1950 period. During the last four decades, however, there have been only minor changes in the distribution of pre-tax money income. During the 1950s and 1960s, there was a slight reduction in income inequality. This trend reversed during the 1970s and 1980s, leaving the income shares allocated to each quintile approximately the same in 1987 as they were in 1950.

Two points emerge from Exhibit 1. First, there is a great deal of inequality in annual income in the United States. Second, the degree of inequality in annual

---

[1]Mark Lilla, ''Why the 'Income Distribution' Is So Misleading,'' *The Public Interest, 77* (Fall 1984), pp. 63–76.

EXHIBIT 1   ■   Inequality in the Money Income of Families—Selected Years 1935–1987

	Percentage of Before-Tax Aggregate Money Income Received by:				
	Lowest 20 Percent of Recipients	Second Quintile	Third Quintile	Fourth Quintile	Top 20 Percent of Recipients
1935–1936	4.1	9.2	14.1	20.9	51.7
1950	4.5	12.0	17.4	23.4	42.7
1960	4.8	12.2	17.8	24.0	41.3
1970	5.4	12.2	17.6	23.8	40.9
1980	5.1	11.6	17.5	24.3	41.6
1984	4.7	11.0	17.0	24.4	42.9
1987	4.6	10.8	16.9	24.1	43.7

Source: Bureau of the Census, *Current Population Reports,* Series P-60, No. 159 (Table 12) and No. 161 (Table 4).

money income has changed by only a small amount during the last several decades.

IS ANNUAL INCOME A GOOD MEASURE OF ECONOMIC STATUS?

How meaningful are the data of Exhibit 1? If all families were similar except in the amount of income received, the use of annual income data as an index of inequality would be far more defensible. However, this is not the case. The aggregate data lump together (a) small and large families, (b) prime-age earners and elderly retirees, (c) multi-earner families and families without any current earners, and (d) husband-wife families and single-parent families. Even if individual incomes over a lifetime were exactly equal, these factors would result in substantial inequality in annual income data.

Consider just one factor, the impact of age, on the pattern of lifetime income. Typically, the annual income of young people is low, particularly if they are going to school or acquiring training. Many persons under 25 years of age studying to be lawyers, doctors, engineers, and economists will have a low annual income during this phase of their life. This does not mean they are poor, however, at least not in the usual sense. After completing their formal education and acquiring work experience, individuals move into their prime working years. During this phase of life, annual income is generally quite high, particularly for families in which both husband and wife work. It is, however, also a time period when families are purchasing houses and providing for children. All things considered, annual income during the prime working years tends to overstate the economic well-being of most households. Finally, there is the retirement phase, characterized by less work, more leisure, and smaller family size. Even families who are quite well off tend to experience income well below the average for the entire population during the retirement phase.

Exhibit 2 highlights major differences between high- and low-income families that underlie the distributional data of Exhibit 1. The typical high-income family (top 20 percent) was headed by a well-educated person in the prime working-age phase of life whose income was supplemented with the earnings of other family members, particularly working wives. In contrast, persons with little education, nonworking retirees, younger workers (ages 16–24), and single-parent families

EXHIBIT 2 ■	The Differing Characteristics of High- and Low-Income Families, 1986	
	Bottom 20 Percent of Income Recipients, 1986	Top 20 Percent of Income Recipients, 1986
Mean years of schooling (household head)	10.3	14.6
Age of household head (percent distribution)		
Under 35	37	15
35–64	39	77
65 and over	24	8
Family status (percent distribution)		
Married-couple family	55	95
Single-parent family	45	5
Persons per family	2.96	3.43
Earners per family	.85	2.31
Percent of married-couple families in which wife works	28	70
Percent of total earners supplied by group	10	28
Percent of total weeks worked supplied by group	7	31

Source: U.S. Department of Commerce, *Money Income of Households, Families, and Persons in the United States:* 1986, Washington, D.C.: U.S. Government Printing Office, 1988.

are substantially overrepresented among low-income families (bottom 20 percent of income recipients). The mean number of years of schooling for the household heads of high-income families was 14.6 years, compared with only 10.3 years for heads of families with low annual incomes. Seventy-seven percent of the high-income families had household heads in the prime working age category (age 35 to 64), compared with only 39 percent of the low-income families. Only one parent was present in 45 percent of the low-income families, whereas 95 percent of the high-income group were husband-wife families.

There was a striking difference in work time between low- and high-income families. This difference reflects factors such as family size, age, and incidence of working wives. The high-income families were larger—3.43 persons compared with 2.96 persons for low-income families. In the high-income families, the average number of workers per family was 2.31, compared with .85 for low-income families. Seventy percent of the high-income married couple families were characterized by a working wife, compared with only 28 percent for low-income married families. The top 20 percent of income recipients contributed 31 percent of the total number of weeks worked, while the low-income group contributed only 7 percent of the total work time.

Exhibit 2 sheds substantial light on the distributional data of Exhibit 1. The

EXHIBIT 3 ■ The Distribution of Income Among Three-person Households, 1976

Household heads in these data were 35 to 44 years old.

Income Grouping (1)	Market Income (in Billions) (2)	Percent Distribution of Market Income (3)	Cash and In-Kind Transfers minus Taxes (in Billions) (4)	Net Income (in Billions) (5)	Percent Distribution, Net Income (6)	Net Income per Hour (7)
Lowest fifth	2.29	5.3	+ 0.73	3.02	9.2	$5.78
Second fifth	5.42	12.6	− 0.86	4.56	13.8	5.77
Third fifth	7.76	18.1	− 1.84	5.92	17.9	5.68
Fourth fifth	9.90	23.0	− 2.34	7.56	22.9	6.66
Top fifth	17.60	41.0	− 5.61	11.99	36.3	9.82

Source: Edgar K. Browning and Jacquelene M. Browning, *Public Finance and the Price System* (New York: Macmillan, 1983), p. 244.

high-income recipients were better educated, more likely to be in their prime working years, and they worked approximately 4.5 times as many weeks as low-income families in 1986. Given these factors, it is not surprising that the top 20 percent of recipients earned a little more than 9 times the annual income of the bottom quintile.

FAMILY SIZE, AGE, AND THE INEQUALITY OF INCOME AFTER TAXES AND TRANSFERS

The income data of Exhibit 1 represent income *before taxes*. Noncash income transfers are excluded. Families of varying size and at various stages of their lifetime earnings are lumped together. Suppose these factors were taken into account—that income comparisons were made *after taxes and transfers* for families of the same size and age of household head. How much inequality would still be present?

A detailed study by Edgar Browning and William Johnson addresses this question. Browning and Johnson investigated the distribution of annual income in 1976 for three-person households headed by a 35- to 44-year-old.[2] Exhibit 3 presents their findings. As column 3 shows, the distribution of pre-tax market income was highly unequal, not unlike the distribution of income presented in Exhibit 1. The top fifth of the households surveyed, the high-income households, received 41.0 percent of the aggregate income, compared with only 5.3 percent for the lowest one fifth (column 3). However, the low-income families paid fewer taxes on their income and received more income transfers as supplements.

Once adjustment was made for cash and in-kind transfers, as well as for income tax, the distribution of net income was considerably more equal. As Exhibit 3 (column 6) shows, the top group of income recipients received 36.3 percent of the aggregate net income, compared with 9.2 percent for the bottom quintile. Thus, after taxes and transfers, the top quintile received approximately 4

---

[2]See Edgar K. Browning and William R. Johnson, *The Distribution of the Tax Burden* (Washington, D.C.: American Enterprise Institute, 1979).

times the annual income of the bottom 20 percent of recipients, compared with 8 times the amount of their income prior to taxes and transfers (column 3).

Perhaps even more surprising, Browning and Johnson found that most of the difference in the net income of three-person households headed by a 35- to 44-year-old reflects hours of work. The net income per hour of work for the top quintile was $9.82, compared to $5.78 for the bottom quintile (column 7). According to Browning and Johnson, the net income per hour worked of the top 20 percent of households was less than twice the net income of the bottom 20 percent of households. In fact, the net income per hour of work was almost identical for the bottom 60 percent of households. Just as Exhibit 2 implies, the findings of Browning and Johnson illustrate why it is important to consider the significance of family size, age, number of earners, hours worked, and taxes and transfers when interpreting data on income inequality.

INCOME INEQUALITY IN OTHER COUNTRIES

How does income inequality in the United States compare with that in other nations? Exhibit 4 presents a summary of household income data compiled by the World Bank. These data indicate that the distribution of income in the United States, Canada, and France is quite similar. The degree of income inequality in Japan, Sweden, and the United Kingdom is slightly less than in the United States. In light of the relatively homogenous populations—that is, uniformity with respect to race and ethnicity—of these three countries and the welfare state policies of Sweden and the United Kingdom, the lesser degree of inequality in these countries is not surprising.[3]

The share of income going to the wealthy is usually greater in less developed countries. According to the World Bank study, the top 20 percent of income recipients received 63.7 percent of the aggregate income in Brazil, 60.4 percent in Kenya, and 57.7 percent in Mexico. Although the degree of inequality was less pronounced in India, Indonesia, and Thailand, it was still substantially more unequal than for developed nations. Among the developing nations of Exhibit 4, only South Korea, Yugoslavia, Israel, and Hong Kong were marked by a degree of inequality similar to that of developed nations. A side effect of the greater inequality of most developing nations is the absence of a strong middle-income group. Note the middle three quintiles (Exhibit 4, middle column) generally received less income in developing than developed nations.

INCOME MOBILITY—DO THE POOR STAY POOR AND THE RICH STAY RICH?

The distribution of annual income is like a snapshot. It presents a picture at a moment in time. However, since the picture does not reveal the degree of movement across income groupings, it may be misleading. Consider two countries with

[3]See Gir S. Gupta and Ram D. Singh, ''Income Inequality Across Nations Over Time: How Much and Why,'' *Southern Economic Journal* 51 (July 1984), pp. 250–57 for an analysis of factors that influence income inequality among countries.

EXHIBIT 4   ■   Equality and Inequality Around the World

Country (Year)	Percentage Share of Household Income Received by:		
	Bottom 20 Percent	Middle Three Qunitiles	Top 20 Percent
Developing Nations			
India (1975–76)	7.0	43.6	49.4
Kenya (1976)	2.6	37.0	60.4
Indonesia (1976)	6.6	44.0	49.4
Thailand (1975–76)	5.6	44.6	49.8
Brazil (1982)	2.3	34.0	63.7
South Korea (1981)	8.0	52.4	39.6
Mexico (1977)	2.9	39.4	57.7
Yugoslavia (1978)	6.6	54.7	38.7
Israel (1979–80)	6.0	54.1	39.9
Hong Kong (1980)	5.4	47.6	47.0
Developed Nations			
United Kingdom (1982)	6.8	53.7	39.5
Japan (1979)	8.7	53.8	37.5
France (1975)	5.3	48.9	45.8
Australia (1978–79)	6.4	55.0	38.6
Canada (1981)	5.3	54.7	40.0
Sweden (1981)	7.4	50.9	41.7
United States (1980)	5.3	54.8	39.9

Source: The World Bank, *World Development Report*, 1988, Table 24, and The United Nations, *National Account Statistics: Compendium of Income Distribution Statistics*, 1985.

identical distributions of annual income.[4] In both cases, the annual income of the top quintile of income recipients is 8 times greater than the bottom quintile. Now, suppose that in the first country—we will refer to it as Static—the same people are at the top of the income distribution year after year. Similarly, the poor people of Static remain poor year after year. Static is characterized by an absence of **income mobility.** In contrast, earners in the second country, which we will call Dynamic, are constantly changing places. Indeed, every five years, each family spends one year in the upper-income quintile, one year in each of the three middle-income quintiles, and one year in the bottom-income quintile. In Dynamic, no one is rich for more than one year (out of each five) and no one is poor for more than a year. Obviously, the degree of economic inequality in Static and Dynamic is vastly different. You would not know it, though, by looking at their annual income distributions. In fact, the annual income distributions in the two countries are identical.

The contrast between Static and Dynamic indicates why it is important to consider income mobility when addressing the issue of economic inequality. Until recently, detailed data on income mobility were sparse. Fortunately, this situation is changing, primarily as the result of a group of researchers at the University of

Income Mobility: Movement of individuals and families either up or down income distribution rankings when comparisons are made at two different points in time. When substantial income mobility is present, one's current position will not be a very good indicator as to what one's position will be a few years in the future.

---

[4]The authors are indebted to Mark Lilla from whom this illustrative method was drawn.

EXHIBIT 5 ■ Income Mobility—Family Income Ranking in 1984 Compared with Ranking in 1980

Family Income Quintile, 1980	Family Income Quintile, 1984					
	Highest	Second	Third	Fourth	Lowest	Total
Highest	62.0	23.6	8.4	3.7	2.3	100%
Second	26.6	36.9	23.6	8.9	4.0	100%
Third	6.0	26.5	35.8	23.4	8.3	100%
Fourth	4.0	9.3	23.9	41.9	20.8	100%
Lowest	1.4	4.0	8.2	22.1	64.5	100%

Source: These data were supplied by the Institute for Social Research at the University of Michigan. An earlier version of this table was included in Greg J. Duncan et al., *Years of Poverty, Years of Plenty* (Ann Arbor: Institute of Social Research, 1984).

Michigan's Survey Research Center. Under the direction of James Morgan and Greg Duncan, the Center collects detailed socioeconomic data on a representative sample of the U.S. population and tracks the same individuals and their families each year. With these data, it is now possible to see how income and other indicators of economic status change with time.

Since 1968, the University of Michigan has published panel income data that allows us to follow the income of families from year to year.[5] Exhibit 5 summarizes the major findings of the study with regard to income mobility. After grouping families by their income in 1980, the table then looks at the relative income position of the families four years later. For example, the first row indicates the relative income position in 1984 of families who were in the top quintile of income recipients in 1980. Surprisingly, only 62 percent of the Americans who were best off (the top quintile) in 1980 were able to retain the same position just four years later. Nearly 15 percent fell to the bottom three quintiles of the 1984 income distribution. The bottom row of Exhibit 5 tracks the experience of families in the lowest-income quintile in 1980. A little less than two-thirds (64.5 percent) of the families in the bottom-income quintile in 1980 remained there in 1984. On the other hand, 13.6 percent of the families at the bottom in 1980 were able to move into one of the top three income quintiles by 1984.

The diagonal (color) numbers of Exhibit 5 provide a measure of income mobility. If there were little or no income mobility within the American system, each diagonal number would be close to 100 percent. For the three middle-income quintiles, the diagonal numbers are approximately 40 percent, indicating that roughly two-fifths of the persons in each of these quintiles remained in the same quintile. Nearly three-fifths moved either up or down the income ladder between 1980 and 1984.

The data of Exhibit 5 focus on changes in the income of families. What can we say about income mobility across generations? If your parents are poor (or wealthy), does it mean you will be poor (or wealthy)? The Michigan panel data are just now starting to yield information related to this issue. Nearly 1,500 young

[5]Greg J. Duncan et al., *Years of Poverty, Years of Plenty: The Changing Fortunes of American Workers and Families* (Ann Arbor: Institute for Social Research, University of Michigan, 1984). Also see Bradley R. Schiller, ''Relative Earnings Mobility in the United States,'' *American Economic Review,* vol. 67, no 5 (1977), pp. 926–939 for an earlier pioneer study of income mobility.

adults in the study have now left their parents and formed families of their own. Among those who came from families with incomes in the top quintile, 36 percent were able to attain this lofty ranking relative to the other newly formed families. In contrast, 41 percent of the offspring of families in the highest-income quintile fell to the bottom three income quintiles among the newly formed families. Among the offspring of poor families, less than half (44 percent) remained in the bottom quintile among the newly formed families. For middle-income families (the three middle quintiles), offspring were spread almost evenly among the five quintiles of the income distribution for newly formed families.

The data thus indicate that while high-income families are able to influence the economic status of their offspring, they are unable to pass along their lofty income position to most of their children. Similarly, the children of low-income families face disadvantages but they frequently attain income well above that of their parents. For the three middle-income quintiles, parents fail to exert a systematic impact on the success or failure of their children. Thus, the *intergenerational* distribution of income approaches perfect mobility among the middle-income groupings.

The findings of the Michigan panel data are highly consistent with the findings of Christopher Jencks, based on a less detailed, but much earlier study by the Center for Educational Policy Research at Harvard. Writing in 1972, Jencks stated:

> Among men born into the most affluent fifth of the population . . . we estimate that less than half will be part of the same elite when they grow up. Of course, it is also true that very few will be in the bottom fifth. Rich parents can at least guarantee their children that much. Yet, if we follow families over several generations, even this will not hold true. Affluent families often have at least one relatively indigent grandparent in the background, and poor families, unless they are black or relatively recent immigrants, have often had at least one prosperous grandparent.[6]

Our analysis indicates that drawing conclusions from *annual* income data must be done with care. The annual data camouflage the fact that many high-income earners had much lower incomes just a few years before. Similarly, many with low current incomes have attained significantly higher incomes previously (and they can be expected to do so again in the future). Panel income data indicate that the inequalities observed at a point in time are substantially reduced over time as individuals and families exchange relative economic positions. This income mobility is particularly important across generations. The ability of American parents to pass along their economic status to their children is quite limited.

POVERTY IN THE UNITED STATES

In an affluent society such as the United States, income inequality and poverty are related issues. Poverty could be defined in strictly relative terms—the bottom one fifth of all income recipients, for example. However, this definition would not be very helpful, since that would mean that poverty could never decline.

---

[6]Excerpt from Christopher Jencks et al., *Inequality: Reassessment of the Effect of Family and Schooling in America*, (New York: Basic Books, Inc. 1972), p. 216.

Poverty Threshold Income Level: The level of money income below which a family is considered to be poor. It differs according to family characteristics (for example, number of family members) and is adjusted when consumer prices change.

The official definition of poverty in the United States is based on the perceived minimum income necessary to provide food, clothing, shelter, and basic necessities economically for a family. This **poverty threshold income level** varies with family size and composition. The poverty threshold income is adjusted annually for changes in prices. For purposes of determining whether or not income is above the poverty threshold, the official poverty rate considers only money income. (See the Measures of Economic Activity box for additional details on how the poverty rate is measured.)

How many people are poor? According to the official definition of poverty, there were 33 million poor people and 7.1 million poor families in 1987. As Exhibit 6 indicates, 13.5 percent of the population and 10.8 percent of the families

MEASURES OF ECONOMIC ACTIVITY

Determining the Poverty Rate

Families and individuals are classified as poor or nonpoor based on the poverty threshold income level originally developed by the Social Security Administration (SSA) in 1964. Since consumption survey data indicated that low- and median-income families of three or more persons spent approximately one-third of their income on food, the SSA established the poverty threshold income level at three times the cost of an economical, nutritionally adequate, food plan. A slightly larger multiple was used for smaller families and individuals living alone. The poverty threshold income varies according to family size, because the food costs vary by family size and composition. The poverty threshold income level is adjusted annually to account for rising prices. The chart below illustrates how the poverty threshold for a family of four has increased as prices have risen:

Year	Poverty Threshold Income Level for a Family of Four
1959	$ 2,973
1970	3,968
1980	8,414
1987	11,605

Even though the poverty threshold income level is adjusted for prices, it is actually an *absolute* measure of economic status. As real income increases, the poverty threshold income will decline relative to the income of the general populace.

The official poverty rate is the *number of persons or families* living in households with a money income *below* the poverty income threshold *as a proportion of the total*. When determining a person's or family's income, the official poverty rate considers only money income. Income received in the form of *noncash* benefits such as food stamps, medical care, and housing subsidies, is completely ignored in the calculation of the official poverty rate.

Since noncash benefits targeted for low-income households have grown rapidly since the late 1960s, the failure of the official poverty rate to count this "income" reduces its accuracy as a measurement tool. To remedy this deficiency, Congress instructed the Bureau of Census to develop a poverty index that included noncash benefits as income. In addition to the official poverty rate, the Bureau now publishes annual data for three "adjusted" poverty rates based

on alternative methods of accounting for noncash benefits. Economists generally favor the use of the recipient value-adjusted poverty rate. This method values noncash benefits at the equivalent amount of cash income a recipient would be willing to exchange for the noncash benefits. It thus takes into account the possibility that recipients might rather have cash than the in-kind benefits.

When the value of noncash benefits is added to money income, the *adjusted* poverty rate for all age groups is reduced. For example, while the official poverty rate for families was 10.8 percent in 1987, the adjusted poverty rate based on the recipient value method of evaluating food, housing, and medical benefits was only 8.8 percent.

The poverty rate is calculated each year based on a current population survey of nearly 60,000 households designed to reflect the population of the United States. The most comprehensive source for detailed data on this topic is the Bureau of Census publication, "Characteristics of the Population Below the Poverty Level" (annual).

EXHIBIT 6 ■ The Poverty Rate of Persons and Families in the United States, 1947–1987		
	Poverty Rate (Percent)	
Year	Persons	Families
1947	n.a.	32.0
1960	22.2	18.1
1970	12.6	10.1
1980	13.0	10.3
1985	14.0	11.4
1987	13.5	10.8

Source: Bureau of the Census, *Money Income and Poverty Status of Families and Persons in the United States: 1987* (Table 16), and *Economic Report of the President 1964* (Table 7).

were officially classified as poor in 1987. During the 1950s and 1960s, the poverty rate declined substantially. By 1970, the official poverty rate for families had fallen to 10.1 percent, down from 18.1 percent in 1960 and 32.0 percent in 1947. During the 1970s, the overall poverty rate changed little. In fact, the official poverty rate was slightly higher in 1980 than it was in 1970. During the early 1980s, the poverty rate rose. Most commentators point to the stagnating economy during 1979–1982 and to cutbacks in transfer programs during the early years of the Reagan Administration as the source of the rising poverty rates in the 1980s. As we proceed, we will investigate the link between poverty and income transfers in more detail.

In recent years, the composition of the poverty population has changed substantially. As Exhibit 7 indicates, elderly persons and the working poor formed the core of the poverty population in 1959. Twenty-two percent of the poor families were headed by an elderly person in 1959. Most poor people (70 percent) worked at least some part of the year. By 1987, the picture had changed dramatically. In 1987, only 11 percent of the poor families were headed by an elderly person. In recent years, there has been a substantial growth in the proportion of female-headed families and an accompanying decline in the proportion of husband-wife families. Since the poverty rate of female-headed families is several times higher than the rate for husband-wife families (34.3 percent compared with 6.0 percent in 1987), an increase in family instability tends to push the poverty rate upward. In 1987, more than half (52 percent) of the poor families were headed by a female, up from 37 percent in 1970 and 23 percent in 1959. Many of these women were not in the work force. As a result, only 47 percent of the heads of poor households worked at all during 1987, compared with 70 percent who worked in 1959.

The poverty rate of blacks in 1987 was 29.9 percent compared to 8.2 percent for whites. Nonetheless, 70 percent of the poor people in the United States were white. Perhaps the most tragic consequence of poverty is its impact on children. During the last two decades, the poverty rate among children has increased substantially. Twenty percent of the children in the United States lived in poverty in 1987, up from 14.9 percent in 1970.

EXHIBIT 7 ■ The Changing Composition of the Poor and the Poverty Rate of Selected Groups: 1959, 1976, and 1987			
	1959	1976	1987
Number of Poor Families (in millions)	8.3	5.3	7.1
Percent of Poor Families Headed by:			
Female	23	37	52
Nonwhite	26	29	30
Elderly person (age 65 and over)	22	22	11
Prime working-age (25–64) person	57	66	77
Person who worked at least some during the year	70	55	47
Poverty Rate			
All families	18.5	10.1	10.8
Married-couple families	15.8	7.2	6.0
Female-headed families	42.6	32.5	34.3
Whites	16.5	8.1	8.2
Blacks	54.9	32.2	29.9
Children	26.9	14.9	20.0

Source: U.S. Department of Commerce, *Characteristics of the Population Below the Poverty Level: 1982* (Table 5), and *Money Income and Poverty Status in the United States: 1987* (Tables 15 and 19).

TRANSFER PAYMENTS AND THE POVERTY RATE

In the mid-1960s, it was widely believed that an increase in income transfers directed toward the poor would substantially reduce, if not eliminate, the incidence of poverty. The *1964 Economic Report of the President* (p. 77) presented the dominant view. The report stated:

> Conquest of poverty is well within our power. About $11 billion [approximately $40 billion measured in 1988 dollars] a year would bring all poor families up to the $3,000 income level we have taken to be the minimum for a decent life. The majority of the nation could simply tax themselves enough to provide the necessary income supplements to their less fortunate citizens. The burden—one fifth of the annual defense budget, less than 2 percent of GNP—would certainly not be intolerable.

The 1965–1975 period was characterized by a rapid growth in income transfer programs. Overall transfers, including those directed toward the elderly, approximately doubled *as a proportion of personal income* between 1965 and 1975. As the War on Poverty programs of the Johnson administration were put in place, income transfers directed toward the poor also grew rapidly. Measured in 1987 dollars, **means-tested income transfers** tripled, expanding from $28 billion in 1965 to $79.6 billion in 1975 (Exhibit 8). As a proportion of personal income, means-tested transfers jumped from 1.5 percent in 1965 to 3.0 percent in 1975.

Did the expansion in government income transfers reduce the poverty rate as the *1964 Economic Report of the President* anticipated? Exhibits 9 and 10 shed

Means-tested Income Transfers: Transfers that are limited to persons or families with an income below a certain cut-off point. Eligibility is thus dependent on low-income status.

EXHIBIT 8   ■   The Path of Government Income Transfers, 1965–1987[a]

| Year | Total Transfer Payments as a Percent of Personal Income | Means-Tested Transfer Payments | |
		Total (Billions of 1987 dollars)	As a Percent of Personal Income
1965	8.5	28.0	1.5
1975	17.4	79.6	3.0
1980	17.8	90.3	2.9
1987	18.4	99.3	2.7

[a]Includes noncash transfers such as food stamps, school lunch subsidies, public housing and other housing subsidies, Medicaid, and Medicare.

Source: *Economic Report of the President: 1989* (Table 25), and Department of Commerce, *Estimates of Poverty Including the Value of Noncash Benefits: 1987* (Table A), and *The Statistical Abstract at The United States: 1988* (Tables 557 and 575).

light on this question. Continuing the trend of the post-Second World War era, the official poverty rate fell throughout the 1960s. During the 1970s, however, the rate leveled off. By 1980, the official poverty rate was 10.3 percent, virtually unchanged from the 1968 rate.

After increasing during the sluggish economic conditions of the early 1980s, the official poverty rate for all families stood at 10.8 in 1987. Therefore, for nearly two decades, the poverty rate has stubbornly remained in the 10 to 11 percent range.

Aggregate poverty rate data as presented in Exhibit 9 conceal an important difference between the experience of the elderly and nonelderly that has largely gone unnoticed. Exhibit 10 highlights this point. The poverty rate for the elderly continued to decline throughout the 1970s. By 1987, the official poverty rate of the elderly had fallen to 7.2 percent, down from 17.0 percent in 1968 and 30.0

EXHIBIT 9

The Poverty Rate, 1947–1987

The official poverty rate of families declined sharply during the 1950s and 1960s, changed little during the 1970s, and rose during the early 1980s. The shaded area of the bars indicates the additional reduction in the poverty rate when noncash benefits are counted as income.

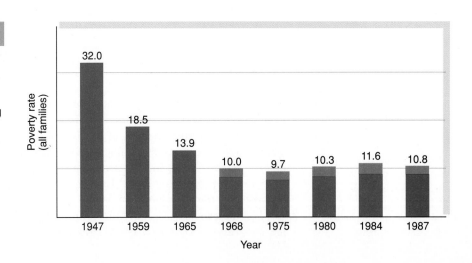

EXHIBIT 10

Changing Poverty Rates,
the Differing Experience of
the Elderly and
Nonelderly, 1959–1987

(a) The official poverty rate for elderly families has
declined sharply since 1959.

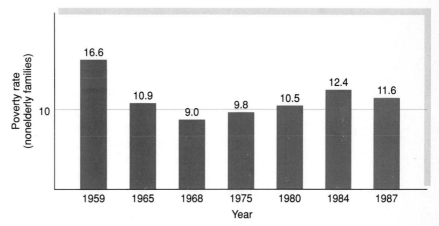

(b) In contrast, the official poverty rate for nonelderly
families has been rising since the late 1960s.

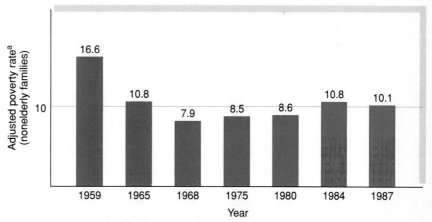

(c) Adjusting for noncash transfers reduces the poverty
rate of the nonelderly but it does not alter the basic
pattern.

[a]The recipient value method was used to adjust the poverty rate for noncash food, housing, and medical benefits.
The 1987 figure is an estimate of the authors.

Source: Derived from Department of Commerce, *Money Income and Poverty Status of Families and Persons in the
United States: 1984* and *1987* and *Estimates of Poverty Including the Value of Noncash Benefits: 1984.* See James
Gwartney and Thomas S. McCaleb, "Have Antipoverty Programs Increased Poverty?" *The Cato Journal* (Spring/
Summer, 1985).

percent in 1959 (Exhibit 10a). The experience of working-age Americans, however, was vastly different. After falling for several decades, the official poverty rate of nonelderly families bottomed in 1968 and rose throughout the 1970s and early 1980s (Exhibit 10b). In 1987, the official poverty rate of nonelderly families was 11.6 percent, compared with 9.0 percent in 1968 (and 10.9 percent in 1965, just prior to the injection of transfer programs accompanying the War on Poverty).

Why has so little progress been made against poverty—particularly poverty among the nonelderly—during the War on Poverty era? For a time, it was widely believed that the stagnating poverty rate of the 1970s reflected the failure of the official data to count noncash benefits derived from programs such as Medicare, Medicaid, food stamps, public housing, and school lunches. Since in-kind transfers have grown rapidly since 1970, this is a potential source of bias. Addressing this issue, the Department of Commerce now publishes adjusted poverty rates that count the in-kind benefits. Given the size of noncash transfers, it is now possible to reconstruct adjusted poverty rate data for earlier time periods.[7]

As Exhibit 9 illustrates, once noncash benefits are counted, the poverty rate is reduced. Adjusting the poverty rate for the value of noncash benefits to recipients reduces the poverty rate of families to 18.8 percent in 1987, compared with the official rate of 10.8 percent. However, as Exhibit 10c illustrates, adjustment for noncash benefits does not significantly alter the picture for working-age Americans. Even after accounting for noncash benefits, the poverty rate of working-age families has been rising since 1968.

Economic and social changes have retarded progress against poverty. While the employment rate has increased during the last 15 years, real wage rates have stagnated. The failure of real wage increases during the 1970–1985 period to match their growth during the 1960s has contributed to the poverty of *working* Americans. In addition, increases in the divorce rate, births to unwed mothers, and the incidence of female-headed households have contributed to the problem. Nonetheless, the results achieved from expanded expenditures (compared to the mid-1960s) on transfer programs have been disappointing. Whether one looks at the official or adjusted poverty rates, the picture is the same. Except for the elderly, the steady progress of the 1950s and 1960s came to a halt during the 1970s and 1980s.

FACTORS LIMITING THE EFFECTIVENESS OF TRANSFER PROGRAMS

How can one explain the relative ineffectiveness, at least compared to what was expected, of income transfer as a weapon against poverty? Analysis of the impact of transfers on the incentive structure confronting the poor enhances our understanding of this issue. While government transfers improved the living standards of many poor people, the programs also severely penalized self-improvement efforts of low-income Americans.

---

[7]See James Gwartney and Thomas S. McCaleb, "Have Antipoverty Programs Increased Poverty?" *The CATO Journal* (Spring/Summer, 1985), for additional details on this topic.

It is important to recognize that the poor are not a monolithic group. In fact, the poor consist of at least two rather distinct groups. There is a hardcore group characterized by individuals who are generally victims of debilitating disease, or physical, mental, or emotional disability. The hardcore poor remain poor during both the good times and the bad. There is also a second group, which might be called the marginal poor. The periods of poverty experienced by the marginal poor reflect factors such as loss of job, change in family status, premature termination of schooling (or training), or choice of a high-risk lifestyle. In contrast with the hardcore poor, the personal choices of the marginal poor exert an impact on the incidence and duration of their periods of poverty.

There are three major secondary effects that reduce the ability of transfer programs to uplift the living standards of the poor, particularly the marginally poor.

Marginal Tax Rate: The amount of one's additional (marginal) earnings that must be paid explicitly in taxes or implicitly in the form of a reduction in the level of one's income supplement. Since it establishes the fraction of an additional dollar earned that an individual is permitted to keep, it is an important determinant of the incentive to work.

1. *High implicit marginal tax rates reduce the incentive of the poor to earn. The net increase in income of the poor is thus much smaller than the transfer.* When the size of the transfer payments to the poor is linked to income, an increase in redistribution results in an increase in the implicit marginal tax rate of the poor. As the incomes of the poor rise, they qualify for fewer programs and the size of their income transfers is reduced. For the poor, higher earnings mean less transfer income. Under these circumstances, therefore, the link between additional earnings and additional net income is weakened for the income transfer recipient.

Transfer benefits derived from Aid for Families with Dependent Children (AFDC), food stamps, Medicaid, school lunch subsidies, rent supplements, and housing subsidies decline as income rises. The implicit marginal tax rate associated with individual programs appears to be quite reasonable. For example, food stamp benefits are reduced by $30 for each $100 of monthly earnings up to a monthly earnings of $800 for a family of four. The implicit marginal tax rate for AFDC is higher, usually in the 50 percent range. The real problem arises, though, when the potential benefits from several programs are considered. Exhibit 11 illustrates this point for a mother with two children residing in Pennsylvania. If she earned no income, she would be eligible for annual cash and in-kind benefits of $7,568 from AFDC, food stamps, Medicaid, and the Earned Income Tax Credit. If the family's earnings rose to $2,000, transfer benefits would be reduced and taxes increased, leaving the family with spendable income of $8,391. Additional earned income of $2,000 thus generates only $823 in additional spendable income, equivalent to a marginal tax rate of 58.8 percent. At higher levels of earned income, this implicit marginal tax rate is even greater. If earned income rose from $4,000 to $5,000, spendable income would *decrease* from $9,214 to $7,694, an implicit marginal tax rate of 252 percent. If income increased further to $6,000, the family would lose eligibility for AFDC, and its after-tax-and-transfer income would decrease again, this time by $246. In fact, a family earning $6,000 has less spendable income than a family with no earned income, and a family earning $10,000 each year (equivalent to a full-time year-round job paying $5 an hour) would have spendable income of $9,299, just $1,661 more than a family with no earned income at all. The loss in transfer benefits and the increased taxes when earnings rise from zero to $10,000 is equivalent to a tax rate of 83 percent on earned income.

EXHIBIT 11   ■   The Effect of Transfer Benefits and Taxes on the Incentive of a Pennsylvania Mother with Two Children to Earn Income (September 1983)

Annual Gross Wage	Transfer Benefits[a]	Income and Employment Taxes[b]	Spendable Income	Implicit Marginal Tax Rate
$ 0	$7,568	$ 0	$7,568	—
2,000	6,525	134	8,391	58.8
4,000	5,482	268	9,214	58.8
5,000	3,040	346	7,694	252.0
6,000	2,059	611	7,448	124.6
7,000	1,719	810	7,909	53.9
8,000	1,378	1,021	8,357	55.2
9,000	1,038	1,240	8,798	55.9
10,000	698	1,469	9,229	56.9

[a]The following benefits are included: AFDC, Earned Income Tax Credit, food stamps and Medicaid. The Medicaid benefits were valued at the 1978 national average adjusted for inflation between 1978 and 1982.

[b]Includes social security and federal and state income taxes.

Source: Data are derived from U.S. House of Representatives Committee on The Ways and Means, *Background Material on Poverty* (Washington, D.C.: Government Printing Office, 1983) Table 10, page 89.

Such extremely high marginal tax rates severely retard the incentive of persons with low income to earn. Many transfer recipients who would otherwise engage in market work decide to work fewer hours or not all all. (Note Exhibit 7 indicates that only 47 percent of the family heads of poor families worked at all during 1987 compared with 70 percent in 1959.) As a result, some portion of the transfer income is merely replacement income; it simply replaces income the recipient would have earned in the absence of the transfer. Thus, the net income of recipients increases by less than the amount of the transfer.

2. *The skills of the poor depreciate when they opt out of the labor force due to the high implicit marginal tax rates. Declining skills further limit their ability to escape poverty.* Individuals who do not use their skills for extended periods of time will find it difficult to compete with otherwise similar individuals with continuous labor force participation. The long-term consequences of an incentive structure that encourages nonwork is even more destructive than the short-term effects. As marginal poor people opt for nonwork, their work record deteriorates. With the passage of time, they become less and less able to support themselves. As the length of time out of the work force expands, marginally poor individuals move into the hardcore poor category.

3. *Some economists believe that transfer programs may encourage individuals to engage in behavior that can lead to poverty.* By insuring against adversity, these economists suggest, transfer programs reduce the opportunity costs of such activities as dropping out of school or drug and alcohol dependence. Furthermore, the detailed rules and guidelines intended to limit abuse of transfer programs tend to reduce the possibility of individually tailored solutions for recipients. Potential recipients may alter their behavior in order to meet program eligibility requirements, rather than take steps to reduce the likelihood of personal adversity and welfare dependence.

RECENT WELFARE REFORM

In an effort to minimize the perverse effects of welfare transfers, Congress passed the Family Support Act in 1988. This legislation provided for four major structural changes in transfer programs.

1. Child-support payments. The legislation requires states to establish a system of minimum child-support payments for absent parents that must be followed by judges (unless there is a written court finding explaining why the guidelines are inappropriate). All parents who are ordered to make child-support payments after January 1, 1994, will have the payments automatically deducted from their paychecks, just as payroll taxes are today. In the mid-1980s, only about half of the 4.4 million absent parents (mostly fathers) were making their court-mandated child-support payments. The new provision of the welfare reform legislation is designed to substantially increase that proportion, and thereby make absent parents more fully responsible for their children.

2. Extended Medicaid and child-care benefits. Under the new legislation, welfare recipients who go to work will be eligible for continued Medicaid and day-care benefits for an additional 12 months. This provision is intended to reduce the work disincentive of income transfers.

3. Two-parent families eligible for AFDC. By 1990, all states must extend AFDC payments to two-parent families where the principal wage earner is unemployed. Twenty-three states had already adopted this provision prior to the 1988 legislation.

4. Work and training requirements. States must enact a program requiring able-bodied welfare recipients to engage in some form of work, training, or job preparation, unless the recipient takes care of a child under age 3 (or under age 6 if day care is unavailable), or is under age 16, a full-time student, or at least 3 months pregnant. States are also required to provide child care, if such care is necessary, for the recipient's participation in work or training programs.

Will the new legislation reduce the poverty rate? Economic analysis indicates that it will generate conflicting effects. Holding absent fathers responsible for the support of their children will enhance the welfare of single-parent families, while reducing the incentive of fathers to abandon their families in order to escape support responsibilities. Additionally, child-support payments do not deter the work incentive of mothers the way welfare transfers do. Thus, the combination of more reliable child-support payments from fathers and additional earnings of working mothers should push a number of families above the poverty line.

The impact of the other provisions is more ambiguous. While the 12-month extension of Medicaid and day-care benefits to welfare recipients who take a job increases the work incentive of current recipients, it also makes spells of welfare more attractive to families not currently on welfare. In 1986, there were more than one million single-parent families with incomes below or only slightly above the poverty rate who were not on welfare. Under the new legislation, the extended Medicaid and child-care benefits increase the incentive of these families to move, at least temporarily, onto the welfare rolls.

Additionally, there is little reason for optimism that the work/training requirements will be very effective. More than 90 percent of the current welfare recipients are exempt (primarily because of the presence of small children in the home) from the work-training provision. The results of past training programs designed to move chronic recipients from welfare to work have been disappointing. Finally, most families in poverty will continue to confront high marginal tax rates when the effects of multi-programs are considered. In some respects, the new legislation does constitute a break from the past approach. However, most of the perverse disincentive effects remain. Thus, there is good reason for skepticism that the new legislation will significantly reduce the incidence of poverty and dependency.

THE MECHANICS OF A SIMPLE NEGATIVE INCOME TAX

Negative Income Tax: A system of transferring income to the poor, whereby a minimum level of income would be guaranteed by the provision of income supplements. The supplement would be reduced by some fraction (less than 1) of the additional income earned by the family. An increase in earnings would always cause the disposable income available to the family to rise.

Would it be possible to devise an income transfer system that would avoid the disincentive effects associated with the current system? Some economists, most notably Milton Friedman, believe that the cost of redistribution would be substantially reduced if a simple negative income tax were substituted for the current jungle of complex and sometimes conflicting welfare programs.

How would the negative income tax work? To begin with, a base income level would be established. This guaranteed income level would reflect family size, with larger families receiving greater income supplements. As income was earned, the base income supplement would be reduced by a fraction of the family's outside income. This fraction would be the *marginal tax rate*. A family would always face a marginal tax rate of substantially less than 100 percent. (Most plans suggest a 33 or 50 percent rate.) Recipients would always get to keep a significant amount of any additional earnings.

Exhibit 12 illustrates the mechanics of a negative income tax. Under this plan, a family of four would be guaranteed an income of $3,200 and a marginal tax rate of 33 percent. As outside income rises, the family's disposable income increases by two-thirds of the amount earned. For example, initial earnings of $1,200 would increase the family's disposable income by $800, from $3,200 to $4,000. The family would receive more in supplementary income than it would

EXHIBIT 12

The Mechanics of the Negative Income Tax

The graph illustrates how a negative income tax with a 33 percent marginal tax rate and a minimum income of $3,200 for a family of four would work. If the family had zero earnings during the year, it would receive a $3,200 annual subsidy. As earnings rose, the family's after-tax income would increase by 67 cents (and the subsidy would decline by 33 cents) for every dollar of income earned, until the break-even income level of $9,600 was attained.

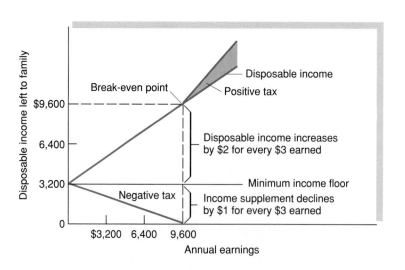

Break-Even Point: Under a negative income tax plan, the income level at which one neither pays taxes nor receives supplementary income transfers.

pay in taxes until income reached $9,600, the break-even point. At the break-even point, the family's tax bill would equal the income supplement; beyond the break-even point, the family would face a positive tax bill.

Would a negative income tax help the poor without generating major counterproductive side effects? During the 1968–1982 period, the United States government funded a number of negative income tax experiments in New Jersey, rural Iowa, Gary (Indiana), Seattle, and Denver. The data generated by these experiments have been extensively analyzed by economists. The results indicate that even a negative income tax transfer program would result in a significant reduction in work effort by the poor. Philip Robins, of the University of Miami, summarizes the findings in the following manner:

> The labor supply responses from the four NIT experiments are remarkably consistent. On average, husbands reduced labor supply by about the equivalent of two weeks of full-time employment. Wives and single female heads reduced labor supply by about the equivalent of three weeks of full-time employment. Youth reduced labor supply by about the equivalent of four weeks of full-time employment. Because women and youth work fewer hours per year than do husbands, their effects are correspondingly much larger in percentage terms. All of these responses may be viewed as those forthcoming from a fairly generous NIT program—one having a guarantee level equal to the poverty level and a tax rate equal to 50 percent.[8]

Once again, the NIT experiments indicate that in economics there are no solutions, only trade-offs.

ESTIMATING THE COSTS OF REDISTRIBUTION

Estimating the loss of output emanating from redistributive activities is a highly complex issue. Income transfers from the rich to the poor will increase the marginal tax rates (either explicit or implicit) of both. High marginal tax rates reduce the effectiveness of markets to allocate resources efficiently. They also tend to reduce labor supply. A recent study by Edgar Browning and William Johnson sought to measure the loss of output due to the reduction in the supply of labor associated with the rise in marginal tax rates accompanying income transfers.[9] Browning and Johnson estimated that it would cost $3.49 in terms of lost output to transfer an additional $1 from the top 60 percent to the bottom 40 percent of recipients under a negative income tax plan.

Transferring income from producers to nonproducers is an expensive undertaking. Perhaps a negative income tax might be able to reduce the loss of output compared to the current system. However, both the NIT experiments and the work of Browning and Johnson indicate that it is not a cure-all.

Are redistribution programs worth the cost? Economics cannot answer that question. It can only help identify and quantify the possibilities for redistributing income in relation to the total amount of income available to be distributed—the economic pie. Social security is the largest single income redistribution program. We will conclude this chapter by taking a closer look at this important income transfer program.

---

[8]Philip K. Robins, "A Comparison of the Labor Supply Findings from Four Negative Income Tax Experiments," *Journal of Human Resources* (Fall, 1985), p. 580.
[9]See Edgar K. Browning and William Johnson, "The Trade-off Between Equality and Efficiency," *Journal of Political Economy* (April, 1984).

APPLICATIONS IN ECONOMICS

Social Security and the Intergenerational Redistribution of Income

"Social security"—officially known as Old Age, Survivors, Disability and Health Insurance (OASDHI)—is the largest federal program providing for income redistribution. It offers protection against the loss of income that usually accompanies old age or death or dismemberment of a breadwinner. Its Medicare provisions are designed to offset the heavier health care expenses often incurred by the elderly and the disabled. In 1988, more than $300 billion was paid out to 40 million recipients under the various provisions of OASDHI.

The Financing of Social Security

Private pension and insurance programs set aside and invest funds in order to provide for future benefits. Social security does not follow this saving and investment model. Most of the tax revenues paid into the so-cial security system are distributed almost immediately to retirees and other beneficiaries of the program. In essence, the social security system is an intergenerational income transfer program. Taxes are collected from the present generation of workers and, for the most part, paid out to current beneficiaries.

The social security system is financed by a payroll tax, of which the employer and the employee each pay half. The tax is levied on the earnings of employees up to a maximum limit. In 1960, employees and their employers each paid a 3 percent tax on the first $4,800 of employee earnings. The maximum combined employee-employer tax was $288.

By 1988, both employee and employer were paying a 7.51 percent tax rate on a tax base of approximately $45,000. The maximum employee-employer tax in 1988 was $6,759. *Measured in real dollars,* the maximum social security tax in 1988 was almost six times the amount of 1960.

Despite the huge tax increases, the social security system has experienced financial problems in recent years. Two major factors have contributed to the financial troubles of the system. First, the number of beneficiaries has risen substantially relative to the number of workers. As with any new retirement program, only a few persons reached retirement age in the years just after social security was initiated (1935). As the social security system matured, however, more and more of the nation's retired workers became eligible for payments. As Exhibit 13 illustrates, in 1950, there were 16 taxpaying workers to finance the benefits of each social security recipient. By

The Declining Number of Workers per Social Security Recipient

In 1950, there were 16 workers for each Social Security beneficiary.

In 1970, there were 4 workers for each Social Security beneficiary.

In 1985, there were 3 workers for each Social Security beneficiary.

By 2025, there will be just 2 workers for each Social Security beneficiary.

Result: an increasing burden on each worker whose Social Security taxes support the program.

1970, there were only 4 workers per social security recipient. The ratio of workers per social security beneficiary has now fallen to 3.

Second, the level of social security retirement benefits has risen more rapidly than the earnings base that supports them. Between 1970 and 1986, the *real* average monthly benefits of social security recipients rose by 47 percent, far more rapidly than real earnings of the workers who support the system (Exhibit 14). Therefore, by 1986, the ratio of average retirement benefits to average gross earnings had risen to 37 percent, up from 23 percent in 1970. This combination of factors—an increase in the number of beneficiaries relative to workers and an increase in benefits relative to the tax base—provided the recipe for the financial troubles experienced by the system.

Winners and Losers Under Social Security

The primary beneficiaries of social security were persons close to retirement during periods when benefits were increased substantially. These workers paid lower tax rates (or higher rates for only brief periods of time). Yet, they received the higher benefits. Today's social security retirees are receiving real benefits of four or five times the amount they paid into the system. The return on the social security taxes they paid generally exceeds 25 percent, much better than they could have done had they invested the funds privately.

In contrast, studies indicate the workers paying for these large benefits will not do nearly as well. For example, those now at age 35 can expect to earn a real rate of return of only 2 or 3 percent on their social security tax dollars, less than what they could earn from personal invest-

ments. For two-earner couples just entering the labor force, the expected return from social security taxes is negative.

In summary, social security has been a good deal for current and past retirees. But, it is not a very good deal for younger workers. Workers now entering the labor force would probably be better off if they could invest their tax dollars elsewhere.

Fairness and Social Security

Fairness is not an economic concept. Nevertheless, economics does reveal information about benefits and costs that allow individuals to make more informed, subjective judgments. Three characteristics of the current social security system are important in this regard.

1. *The elderly are no longer the least well-off age group.* In the 1950s, the income status and poverty rate of the elderly indicated that they were significantly less well-off than the rest of the population. In

the 1980s, this is not the case. Adjusted for family size, the income of the elderly is now higher than for any other age grouping. The wealth holdings (ownership of houses, stocks, bonds, and so on) of the elderly are much higher than for the rest of the population. The official poverty rate of the elderly in 1987 was 7.2 percent, compared to 11.6 percent for nonelderly families and an even 20 percent rate for children (Exhibits 7 and 10). If the value of in-kind benefits were included, the adjusted poverty rate of the elderly would be even lower compared to the rest of the population. In contrast with the situation two decades ago, the social security system today transfers income from persons who are, on average, less well-off (current workers) to people who are better off (current retirees).

2. *The social security retirement system transfers income from blacks to whites.* This is not the intent of

EXHIBIT 14 ■ The Rising Social Security Benefits and the Earnings that Support Them

Year	Average Monthly Benefits per Retired Worker (1986 dollars)	Average Monthly Benefits as a Percent of Gross Average Monthly Earnings[a]
1950	199	19
1960	273	21
1970	332	23
1980	452	33
1986	488	37

[a]The gross average earnings are for production employees in the private sector.

Source: *Economic Report of the President: 1985* (Table 5–6) and *1988* (Table B–45) and *Statistical Abstract of The United States: 1988* (Table 565).

the program. Nevertheless, it is a result. Since blacks generally begin working earlier and have a lower life expectancy, their tax payments relative to retirement benefits will be substantially greater than for whites. Consider the case of two 25-year-old men, one white and the other black. Given his life expectancy, the average 25-year-old black male who works and pays social security taxes can expect to receive only five months of retirement benefits before his death. The white male of the same age can expect to draw benefits for 73 months, nearly 15 times longer than his black coworker. Similarly, a black female at age 25 can expect to draw social security retirements benefits for 8.3 years, compared to 13.0 years for her white counterpart.[10] Given the expected low or negative rate of return of youthful workers in general, the program clearly imposes a major net cost on blacks in general, and youthful workers in particular.

3. *The social security system taxes working wives while providing them little or no additional benefits.* The social security system was designed in the 1930s when few wives were in the labor force. Women are thus permitted to draw benefits based on either the earnings of their husband or their

personal earnings. Generally, the benefits based on the work history of the husband are greater. When this is the case, the working wife pays taxes into the system and receives no additional retirement benefits in return.

The Politics of Social Security

The early popularity of social security is easy to understand. Before the program "came of age"—while there were still 10 to 20 taxpayers for each recipient—pay-as-you-go financing enabled Congress to grant substantial benefits to retired and near-retired workers while increasing taxes by only very small amounts at the time of passage. Whenever coverage was expanded or benefits increased, future benefits were financed by writing future tax increases into the law. The added benefits were usually scheduled to begin accruing just before election time, and the tax increases were postponed until after the election. In addition, the growing numbers of workers entering the system added immediately to the pool of taxpayers but did not increase the drain on the trust funds until later. The political gains were enormous, since Congress could grant immediate benefits to a relatively concentrated group (composed primarily of older people, who are quite likely to vote in an election), while the cost of the program was widely dispersed

and would be incurred (or at least felt) primarily in the future.

Recent Reforms

The period of political profiteering, however, is over. Congress must now face up to the commitments made to future retirees. Demographic factors indicate that keeping these commitments is going to be even more difficult in the future. After a period of stability, the number of workers per beneficiary will decline to only two during the early 2020s—soon after the baby boom generation begins reaching retirement. This will place additional strain on the system. Recognizing this point, legislation passed in 1983 provides for a surplus of social security tax revenues relative to expenditures during the next two decades. In the early 1990s, a $25 billion to $50 billion surplus is expected each year. However, this pattern will be reversed around 2020. The system is expected to run huge deficits in the 2025 to 2050 period, during the retirement years of the post-Second World War baby boom generation.

The surpluses planned for the 1990–2015 period are intended to cushion the problems of financing the retirement benefits of the baby boom

[10]National Center for Policy Analysis, *Social Security and Race* (Dallas: National Center for Policy Analysis, 1987).

CHAPTER SUMMARY

1. The annual income data before taxes and transfers indicate that the bottom 20 percent of families receive approximately 5 percent of the aggregate income, while the top 20 percent receive slightly more than 40 percent. There has been little change in the distribution of annual money income during the past four decades. Adjustment for taxes and noncash transfer benefits reduces the differential between high and low earners.

2. A substantial percentage of the inequality in annual income distribution reflects differences in age, education, family status, number of earners in the family, and time worked. Young, inexperienced workers, students, and retirees are overrepresented

generation. However, there is a major problem with the strategy: currently the build-up of the social security trust fund is being used to finance budget deficits rather than capital formation. In effect, the government is giving the social security trust fund an IOU and using the funds to cover current operations and programs. No funds are being set aside or invested to cover future benefit payments to social security recipients. When the trust fund is used to finance budget deficits, it will not make it any easier to finance the future retirement benefits of the post-Second World War baby boomers. Rather, it merely *shifts* some of this burden from payroll taxes to other forms of taxation.

If the current real benefit levels are going to be maintained, staggering increases in taxes will be required. Fifty years from now, projections indicate that it will take 15 percent of national income just to finance this one program, up from 7 percent during the 1980s.

The Future of Social Security
Given current economic conditions, structural modifications of the social security system are a continuing topic of discussion. Three major changes have been widely discussed.[11]

1. *Raise the normal eligibility age with life expectancy and remove the full indexing of future benefits.* The retirement age is already scheduled to rise to age 67 after the turn of the century. Linking it to life expectancy would provide for additional increases in the eligibility age. Removal of full indexing of future benefits would gradually reduce *real* benefits. Proponents of this reform argue that the current level of benefits cannot be justified given the current economic status of the elderly.

2. *Gradually phase the system into an insurance program.* This idea, suggested by Michael Boskin, the current chairman of the President's Council of Economic Advisers, would require still higher taxes so that a trust fund could accumulate to finance earmarked future benefits for current taxpayers. Instead of taking a chance that future generations will levy higher taxes to pay for benefits, current taxpayers would be paying earmarked funds into a trust system to finance their own retirement benefits. If this plan were in place, no big leap in taxes would be necessary when the post-Second World War baby boom generation reaches retirement around 2010. The trust fund would add to the nation's savings, eliminating one of the defects of the current system.

3. *Allow people to substitute, at least partially, individual retirement accounts (IRAs) and/or the purchase of government bonds for social security taxes.* Essentially, this plan would permit individuals to use their social security tax dollars to acquire a property right to either a private investment fund or a government bond. Should the individual die prior to retirement, the property could be passed on to his or her heirs. As more people opt for this alternative plan over time, the provision of retirement benefits would shift away from social security and toward private investments and government bonds. This plan would also alleviate the adverse impact of the current system on blacks and working women. Interestingly, the United Kingdom has recently modified its social retirement system in this direction.

[11]See Michael Boskin, *Too Many Promises: The Uncertain Future of Social Security* (Homewood: Dow Jones-Irwin, 1986), A. Haeworth Robertson, *The Coming Revolution in Social Security* (McLean: Security Press, 1981) and National Center for Policy Analysis, *Social Security: Who Gains? Who Loses?* (Dallas: National Center for Policy Analysis, 1987) for additional details on how changing conditions are affecting the social security system.

among those with low incomes. Persons in their prime working years are overrepresented among high-income recipients. Persons with high incomes have substantially more years of schooling. Married-couple families with multi-earners are overrepresented among the high-income recipients, while single-parent families with few earners make up a large share of the low-income recipients. The number of weeks worked contributed by the top quintile of families was 4.5 times the number worked by the bottom 20 percent of income recipients.

3. Differences in the after-tax and transfer income per hour of work for persons of the same age are small. For example, the *net income per hour* of the top quintile of

earners was less than twice the *net income per hour* of the bottom quintile for three-person households headed by a 35- to 44-year-old.

4. In general, income is distributed more equally in the advanced industrial nations than in less developed nations. The degree of income equality is similar for the United States, Canada, Australia, and France. Compared with these nations, there is slightly less income inequality in welfare states, such as Sweden and the United Kingdom.

5. In interpreting the significance of the annual income distribution, it is important to recognize that the annual data camouflage the movement of persons up and down the distribution over time. Many persons with middle and high current income had substantially lower incomes just a few years ago. Similarly, many low-income recipients have attained significantly higher incomes in the past (and many will do so again in the future).

6. There is substantial intergenerational income mobility in the United States. Of the children born to parents who are in the top 20 percent of all income recipients, studies indicate that only 36 percent are able to attain this high-income status themselves. Similarly, more than half of the children of families in the bottom quintile of the income distribution attain a higher relative position when they form their own families.

7. According to the official data, approximately 11 percent of the families in the United States were poor in 1987. Those living in poverty were generally younger, less educated, less likely to be working, and more likely to be living in families headed by a female than those who were not poor.

8. During the 1965–1975 period, transfer payments—including means-tested transfers—increased quite rapidly in both real dollars and as a share of personal income. As income transfers expanded, the poverty rate of the elderly continued to decline. However, beginning in the late 1960s, the poverty rate for working-age Americans began to rise. Even after adjustment for in-kind food, housing, and medical benefits, the poverty rate of working-age Americans has been rising gradually since the late 1960s.

9. When considering the impact of current income transfer programs on the poverty status of working-age persons, it is important to recognize the following points:

   a. When the transfer benefits of low-income families decline with income, the incentive of the poor to earn personal income is reduced. Thus, means-tested transfers tend to increase the *net* income of the poor by less than the amount of the transfer.

   b. When high marginal tax rates accompanying transfers induce the poor to opt out of the labor force, their skills depreciate, further limiting their ability to escape poverty.

   c. The effectiveness of transfers may also be limited as the result of the tendency of programs designed to protect against adversity to encourage choices that actually increase the occurrence of the adversity.

10. Some economists believe that the cost of redistribution could be substantially lowered if the negative income tax were substituted for current social welfare programs. The major advantages of the negative income tax (relative to present programs) are (a) its simplicity and (b) its provision for the transfer of income to people because they are poor, rather than on the basis of other selective characteristics. However, the results of the negative income tax experiments indicate that it is no cure-all. Even transfers based on a negative income tax would reduce work effort and real output.

11. The social security program is primarily an intergenerational transfer program. At current levels of benefits and taxes, the program is expected to run a substantial surplus during the 1990–2015 period and a huge deficit during the 2025–2050 period, as the post-Second World War baby boom generation goes through their "prime working years" and then the "retirement phase" of their life cycle. Currently, the program surplus is being used to finance the budget deficit.

CRITICAL ANALYSIS QUESTIONS

1. Do you think the current distribution of income in the United States is too unequal? Why or why not? What criteria do you think should be used to judge the fairness of the distribution of income?

*2. Is annual money income a good measure of economic status? Is a family with a $50,000 annual income able to purchase twice as much goods and services as a family with $25,000 of annual income? Is the standard of living of the $50,000 family twice as high as the $25,000 family? Discuss.

3. What is income mobility? If there is substantial income mobility in a society, how does this influence the importance of income distribution data?

*4. Consider a table such as Exhibit 5 in which the family income of parents is grouped by quintiles down the rows and the family income of their offspring is grouped by quintiles across the columns. If there were no intergenerational mobility in this country, what pattern of numbers would be present in the table? If the nation had attained complete equality of opportunity, what pattern of numbers would emerge? Explain.

5. Do individuals have a property right to income they acquire from market transactions? Is it a proper function of government to tax some people in order to provide benefits to others? Why or why not? Should there by any constitutional limitations on the use of the political process to take income from some in order to provide benefits to others? Discuss.

*6. Since income transfers to the poor typically increase the marginal tax rate confronted by the poor, does a $1,000 additional transfer payment necessarily cause the income of poor recipients to rise by $1,000? Why or why not?

*7. Sue is a single parent with two children considering a job at $800 per month ($5 per hour). She is currently drawing monthly cash benefits of $300, plus food stamp benefits of $100, and Medicaid benefits valued at $80. If she accepts the job, she will be liable for employment taxes of $56 per month and lose all transfer benefits. What is Sue's implicit marginal tax rate for this job?

8. Between 1965 and 1975, there was a substantial increase in transfer payments, both in real dollars and as a share of total income. What impact did the government's expanded tax-transfer role have on the distribution of income and the poverty rate? Discuss.

9. Some argue that taxes exert little affect on people's incentive to earn income. In considering this issue, suppose you were required to pay a tax rate of 50 percent on all money income you earn while in school. Would this affect your employment? How might you minimize the personal effects of this tax?

*10. As Exhibit 8 indicates, transfer payments targeted to the poor make up only a small portion of the total government income transfers. Large income transfers are targeted toward the elderly, farmers, and the unemployed, regardless of their economic condition. Why do you think this is so? Does an expansion in the size of tax-transfer activities reduce income inequality?

11. "Welfare is a classic case of conflicting goals. Low welfare payments continue to leave people in poverty, but high welfare payments attract people to welfare roles, reduce work incentives, and cause higher rates of unemployment" (quoted from the *There Is No Free Lunch Newsletter*).
    a. Evaluate. (Hint: apply the opportunity cost concept.)
    b. Can you think of a plan to resolve the dilemma? Is the dilemma resolvable? Why or why not?

12. Suppose the government decides to increase taxes in order to provide a $2,000 per year real income supplement to persons age 65 year and over. Will the real income of

*Asterisk denotes questions for which answers are given in Appendix C, Selected Answers.

the elderly be $2,000 greater in the future than it would have been in the absence of this program? Why or why not?

13. "Means-tested transfer payments reduce the current poverty rate. However, they also create an incentive structure that discourages self-provision and self-improvement. Thus, they tend to increase the future poverty rate. Welfare programs essentially purchase a lower poverty rate today in exchange for a higher poverty rate in the future." Evaluate.

*14. Under legislation passed in 1983, after-tax social security benefits are reduced as income increases for recipients with incomes above $25,000. Recently, some have advocated that social security benefits be completely eliminated for elderly persons with high incomes. Do you think this is a good idea? Why or why not? If social security benefits are reduced (and perhaps eliminated in some cases) as income increases, how will this influence the incentive of the elderly to save and provide income support for their own retirement? How will the number of low-income elderly be affected?

*15. From the viewpoint of the entire economy, can the benefits of a "pay-as-you-go" social security system be called wealth? Might future retirees treat the benefits as wealth? If so, what will happen to the rate of private saving relative to the saving rate if there were no social security program? (Assume that people consume a fixed fraction of their wealth each year.)

16. Why do you think the social security system is operated by the government? Could a private insurance company establish the same type of plan? Why or why not?

17. "The social security system ensures a minimum income for the elderly, but the system also transfers income from the young to the old, from blacks to whites, and from the relatively poor to the relative well-to-do." Evaluate this statement.

17

ENERGY AND NATURAL RESOURCE ECONOMICS

Barren timber for building is of great value in a populous and well-cultivated country, and the land which produces it affords a considerable rent. But in many parts of North America the landlord would be much obliged to any body who would carry away the greater part of his large trees.[1]

Adam Smith

CHAPTER FOCUS

■ Can people "create" natural resources? What role does human knowledge, ingenuity, effort, and culture play in determining our stock of energy and other natural resources?

■ How important are substitutes in the case of natural resources?

■ What are proved reserves, and how can they expand over time?

■ What does the energy crisis of the 1970s tell us about natural resource markets? What was the role of the Organization of Petroleum Exporting Countries (OPEC) in the crisis? What was the role of U.S. energy policy?

■ Why do we periodically see "doomsday" projections about natural resources? How accurate have they been?

■ Why are property rights important for natural resource management?

The value of a resource depends very much on the situation in which it is found and on the people who have access to it. When Adam Smith wrote the sentences in the chapter-opening quote, and published them in 1776, large trees had great value in the British Isles, where the labor to use wood was cheap and trees were scarce. Large trees were a nuisance in America, though, where labor was scarce and trees were plentiful. It was costly even to remove the trees to make way for crops. In America today, workers armed with chain saws, lumber mills, and woodworking tools help make the big trees very valuable, and cleared farmland abounds. For these reasons, trees have increased in value over the years.

Natural resources, unlike manufactured items, are in one sense "gifts of nature." Crude oil, water, virgin forests, and native animal populations are examples of natural resources. They are not created by human hands. In most cases, though, their value (including even our esthetic appreciation of them) depends on human effort, technology, culture, and ingenuity. Wilderness, for example, was not appreciated by most people until recent decades. It was instead a problem to be overcome; now, wilderness is eagerly pursued by those in search of solitude and a pristine natural setting. Crude oil was simply bothersome—a sticky mess wherever it surfaced—until imagination and technology transformed it into "black gold."

In this chapter we will examine the production and use of energy and other natural resources. As we will see, the economic principles of earlier chapters are helpful in understanding people's choices and their decisions about natural resources. Economic principles apply here, just as they do in other decision-making situations.

The economic way of thinking can help us investigate and understand a great many issues and answer a great many questions. How responsive are petroleum supplies and demands when petroleum prices change? As demands for water increase, will we have enough? What can we say about the long-run availability of minerals, which are in finite supply on Earth? What pressures will population growth put on resource supplies? What roles can markets play in producing and allocating natural resources? What difficulties are there for such markets? What can economic thinking tell us about governmental policy toward natural resources? We will focus on these and related questions in this chapter.

IN NATURAL RESOURCE MARKETS, INCENTIVES MATTER

As in all markets, the quantity of a natural resource demanded will fall, and the quantity supplied will rise, when its price rises (other things constant). The higher price provides users with the incentive to conserve and to find substitutes for the newly expensive resource. The higher price also brings forth extra production, providing additional supplies. Lower prices have the opposite effect, reducing the quantity supplied of the resource, and increasing the quantity demanded.

---

[1]Adam Smith, *Wealth of Nations,* Edwin Cannan, ed. (New York: The Modern Library, 1937), p. 163.

EXHIBIT 1 ■ How Water "Requirements" Can Vary

When the use of water is expensive, people find ways to use less of it. These numbers, all from actual industrial plants, demonstrate the wide variations possible, even within specific industrial use. How much water is needed to generate a unit of electricity? That depends very much on how costly water is, as the table shows. The "need" can vary from 1.32 gallons to 170 gallons. With time, technology can further expand this range of options.

Product or User and Unit	Draft (in gallons)		
	Maximum	Typical	Minimum
Steam-electric power (kw-h.)	170	80	1.32
Petroleum refining (gallon of crude oil)	44.5	18.3	1.73
Steel (finished ton)	65,000	40,000	1,400
Soaps, edible oils (pound)	7.5	—	1.57
Carbon black (pound)	14	4	0.25
Natural rubber (pound)	6	—	2.54
Butadiene (pound)	305	160	13
Glass containers (ton)	667	—	118
Automobiles (per car)	16,000	—	12,000
Trucks, buses (per unit)	20,000	—	15,000

Source: H. E. Hudson and Janet Abu-Lughod, "Water Requirements," *Water for Industry*, Jack B. Graham and Meredith F. Burrill, eds. Publication no. 45 (Washington, D.C.: American Association for the Advancement of Science, 1956), pp. 19–21.

The use of water by industry, as illustrated in Exhibit 1, provides a good example of the importance of substitution. When automakers, steel producers, or oil refineries need water for their production processes, the amount they use will depend on the price they must pay to get the water. Some processes use much more water than others, and where water costs are high, producers use processes requiring less water. The same is true for any other industry and any other resource. Consumers will respond in the same way, reinforcing the effect of price changes.

As in most markets, time is an important factor in determining the responsiveness of producers and users to a price change—the price elasticities of supply and demand. The longer a very low or a very high price persists, the more its incentives cause stronger adjustments. A consideration of energy markets will help us illustrate these points.

RESOURCE DEMAND IS FAR MORE ELASTIC IN THE LONG RUN THAN IN THE SHORT RUN

The *immediate* response of consumers to higher energy prices is likely to be relatively weak. In the short run, individuals will find it costly to reduce their consumption of electricity, fuel oil, and gasoline by a large amount, even if the prices of these energy products rise sharply. Of course, some energy-saving measures can be adopted immediately. More care can be taken to turn off the lights in unoccupied rooms. Warmer clothing can be substituted for heating oil in the winter, and fans can replace air conditioning in the summer. Nonessential driving can be curtailed. These adjustments, though, will be small *compared to the potential reduction over a longer period of time*.

Consumption adjustments that would be very costly in the short run become easier with time. Old and new houses will be better insulated. Higher gasoline prices will induce new car buyers to exchange some power and size for more fuel economy, and auto makers will design more economical cars. Home appliances, farming, industrial processes, and vacation trips will become less energy intensive over time. Several years will pass, however, before old habits, old techniques, old buildings, and old machinery are completely replaced.

As Exhibit 2 illustrates, the demand for energy products can be highly inelastic in the short run. In the long run, though, energy-saving adjustments are more attractive. As our theory predicts, and as the boxed feature "Prices and Quantities: How Energy Buyers Respond" verifies, the demand for energy will be much more elastic in the long run than in the short run.

THE SHORT-RUN SUPPLY WILL BE INELASTIC DUE TO THE LENGTHY PRODUCTION CYCLE

New energy sources generally take years of development. Crude oil is a case in point. Oil companies will search more diligently for additional crude oil supplies when they believe the oil they find will be sold for a higher price. The search will take time, however. Promising areas must be tested, exploratory wells must be drilled, and production equipment must be put in place. These are time-consuming processes. It usually takes more than three years from the time the search begins until the refined product can be brought to market. Even though development and delivery can be somewhat accelerated (at a cost), higher product prices will have only a small effect on output in the short run.

EXHIBIT 2

Supply and Demand in the Energy Market

As frame 2a illustrates, both the supply of and demand for energy products tend to be highly inelastic during the short run. However, as frame 2b shows, both supply of and demand for energy products will be considerably more elastic in the long run.

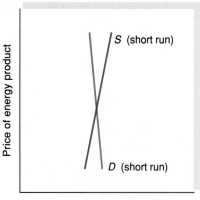

(a) Supply and demand in short run

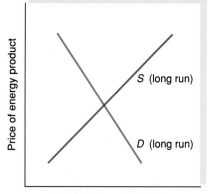

(b) Supply and demand in long run

APPLICATIONS IN ECONOMICS

Prices and Quantities: How Energy Buyers Respond

Economic theory tells us that the demand for a commodity depends on the price of the commodity, the income of buyers, and the price of substitutes. The theory is demonstrated clearly in energy markets.

Consumers determine how much electricity, gas, or other energy form is used. For example, in the case of electricity they choose whether or not to use electric heat and how high to set the thermostat. But they also decide how much aluminum (made with large quantities of electricity) to buy and which producers (those using more electricity per ton of aluminum, or less per ton) to buy from. Higher electricity prices raise aluminum prices relative to the prices of substitute metals and increase costs more significantly for producers using more electricity per ton. Producers using techniques and equipment that are rising less rapidly in price will enjoy a competitive advantage. Thus, even with very little knowledge of how or why electricity prices are rising throughout the economy, consumers make choices that move sales away from the energy form rising fastest in cost, and toward conservation, other energy sources, and other means of satisfying their wants.

How much less will be consumed when the price of an energy form rises? Exhibit 3, summarizing the results of several statistical studies, provides some answers in the form of estimated price elasticities. For residential electricity, a 10 percent rise in price would lead to a 2 percent short-run reduction in quantity demanded. The short run here means one year. When buyers have up to 10 years to respond, the long-run elasticity indicates that the same 10 percent price rise would cause a 7 percent decline in residential use of electricity, other factors held constant.

Price elasticities are useful in predicting fuel usage as fuel prices change. However, other factors, such as income and the price of substitutes, will also influence consumption. In addition, we cannot expect the same reaction to a price change from people in different situations. Once auto manufacturers have spent years in researching and developing techniques to save fuel, for example, even a return to the much lower gasoline prices of years past would not bring back the previous level of gas guzzling. Measured elasticities reflect history, but history can never be retraced exactly, even if the path of prices is somehow repeated. Estimated price elasticities are a rough but often useful guide to buyer behavior when prices of an important commodity like energy change.

EXHIBIT 3 ■ Price Responsiveness of Energy Forms: Estimated Price Elasticities

	Estimated Elasticity[a]	
Fuel	Short Run	Long Run
Residential electricity	0.2	0.7
Residential natural gas	0.1	0.5
Gasoline	0.2	0.7

[a]When income and other factors such as other fuel prices are held constant, the elasticities indicate the ratio of percent change in quantity to the percent change in price causing the quantity change. Each elasticity is actually a negative number, since price and quantity demanded move in opposite directions.

Source: Douglas R. Bohi, *Analyzing Demand Behavior* (Baltimore: Johns Hopkins University Press, 1981), p. 159.

As Exhibit 2b indicates, the supply response to an increase in price expands with time. Not only will more exploration and development of new wells occur, but additional extraction of oil from existing wells will be profitable at the higher price. On average, about two-thirds of a well's oil is left in an oil pool when the well is abandoned. Extracting the rest is too expensive. But, when oil prices rise, wells are not abandoned so quickly. The oil field can be flooded with water, or injected with steam or chemicals to increase total recovery. These measures take time and money, but higher production will result.

INFORMATION IS SCARCE AND COSTLY, SO INFORMATION IS IMPERFECT

What will be the long-run future availability of energy and other natural resources? This information is difficult to obtain. Natural resources are different from manufactured goods, whose long-run availability depends mainly on the size of the work force and the factories we choose to build and maintain. In the short run, manufactured inventories determine what can be supplied. For a natural resource such as a mineral, long-run availability depends not only on "factories" (mining equipment and refining capacity built and maintained) but also on reserves of the raw material, such as ore, or crude oil reserves in the ground, needed for production.

Mineral reserves are frequently misunderstood by observers outside the industry. They often confuse total reserves that *can become* available with the reserves we know about now. Known reserves are naturally much smaller in quantity.

Why do we not know more about reserves that might eventually be made available? To find oil or other mineral reserves not only takes time, it also requires the use of valuable equipment, skilled labor, and other factors of production. In other words, known, or "proved" reserves are expensive. **Proved reserves** are the discovered and verified quantity of resources that producers believe they can recover *at current prices and levels of technology*. To find and prove reserves too many years in advance would be wasteful, just as producing automobiles years before their use would be wasteful. Proved reserves, in fact, are similar to inventories in any other industry. To produce inventories too soon costs more than it is worth, and would reduce profits. Just as an auto dealer might hold a 2- to 3-month inventory of cars, oil and gas producers commonly hold a 10- to 15-year supply of oil and gas reserves. And, just as we do not worry about running out of cars in 2 to 3 months, both logic and the available evidence indicate that we need not fear running out of oil in 10 to 15 years.

Proved Reserves: The verified quantity of a resource that can be recovered at current prices and levels of technology.

RESOURCE DECISIONS ARE MADE AT THE MARGIN

In natural resource markets, as in all markets, decisions concern actions taken at the margin. In fact, two natural resources, diamonds and water, provide a classic way to explain the concept of marginal values. Writing before the discovery of the marginal principle, Adam Smith was puzzled by the fact that water, which is so valuable and necessary for life itself, is much cheaper than natural diamonds, which normally are "useless baubles." Modern economists know that price and market value are determined by the value of marginal units, rather than by the average value to buyers or sellers. Since the supply of water is very great compared to the supply of diamonds, the value of an *extra* unit of water is relatively small (at most times and in most places), even though the total value of the world's supply of water is far greater than the total value of it's diamond supply.

Crude oil wells provide another example. As we said earlier, each well is abandoned when the marginal cost of pumping becomes greater than the value of the oil extracted. This typically occurs when about two-thirds of the oil in the pool remains. But, when the price of oil is high, additional expenses to extract more of the oil are justified.

Various uses of water provide yet another useful application of the marginal principle. The willingness of a farmer or a municipality to pay for water reflects the *marginal* value of the water in farming or in the city. In the water-short American West, the marginal values can be high, and the differences quite large. Demand for water by residential, commercial, and industrial users in cities is growing, and roughly 90 percent of the water is used by farmers. Urban water prices are often at least ten times as great as agricultural prices, so there are large potential gains from trade. Despite some legal obstacles, some of these trades are proceeding, moving water from agriculture to the higher-valued municipal and industrial uses.[2] Does this mean that industry and the cities are likely to draw all of the water out of agriculture? If you are tempted to answer ''yes,'' remember that prices are determined at the margin. While nonagricultural users are willing to pay far more than the water is worth *at the margin* to farmers, each water trade reduces the value of additional water to the recipient, and increases the value of water to the seller. Suppose that cities and industries doubled their use of water, from 10 to 20 percent. Agriculture would still have about 80 percent of the total water in the West, and the marginal value of water to them would be higher, while the marginal value of water to others would be cut substantially by the doubling of their usage. Farmers will gain greatly from selling some of their water, but most of it will be retained. Trades tend to equalize the differing values of water at the margin, so agriculture is not likely to dry up and blow away.

In considering the problems and policy options for natural resources, it is essential to keep the marginal principle in mind. Prices and values are determined at the margin, and good decisions are made when the marginal effects of alternative choices are considered.

OPPORTUNITY COSTS ARE THE RELEVANT COSTS

Effective natural resource management requires the recognition of opportunity costs. This may seem obvious at this stage in your studies. But government resource policies that limit prices, prevent trading, or provide subsidies often make it difficult or unattractive for decision-makers to learn or to use opportunity costs in decision-making. Consider the case of federally owned hydropower—electricity generated by water falling through turbines in a dam built across a river. By law, such federally owned power must be sold ''at cost,'' meaning the out-of-pocket costs of generating and delivering the electricity, not its opportunity cost. This electric power is usually generated and sold at a price far below the cost of power from other generating plants selling electricity, including plants in the same power delivery system. Power that is available at such low prices is used even though it is more highly valued in another use. The opportunity cost of the power is ignored.

---

[2]See Zach Willey and Tom Graff, ''Federal Water Policy in the United States—An Agenda for Economic and Environmental Reform,'' *Columbia Journal of Environmental Law,* vol. 13, no. 2, 1988, for a description of these water markets.

Pacific Northwest electricity, generated mostly by dams on the Columbia River and sold by the federal Bonneville Power Administration (BPA), provides an example. It has been sold in recent years at prices far lower than other power in the region. Users pay only a fraction of the value of that power in other potential uses (a fraction of the opportunity cost). To see the inefficiency in the system, consider what would happen if users of electricity could sell their rights to the low-priced power. Suppose that each current user were given a certificate providing the right to continue purchasing power at the same price (adjusted periodically for utility cost increases, as always). But suppose also that the certificates could be sold, so that other electricity users, not now able to buy the cheap electricity, could buy the certificates from current users, thus obtaining the right to purchase the cheap power. If certificates were issued, and could be resold, some of the electric power would flow to users who valued it more highly than current users, who would find ways to conserve power and sell some of their certificates. With no increase at all in their power bills, users would notice the opportunity cost (offers made by others to get certificates) and have the appropriate incentive to conserve electricity. Both buyers and sellers would be better off, and the revenue to BPA would remain the same. Such efficient and mutually beneficial trades are not allowed, however. The profits to be made by the sale of certificates, allowing better use of electricity, are thought to be politically unacceptable, even though both buyers and sellers would gain. A side effect of the current policy is that with less conservation, growth in the region will require that additional nuclear or coal-fired power plants be built.

Water taken from the same river for irrigation provides another example. The federally financed Columbia River Project, designed to provide irrigation water for 1.1 million acres of farmland in the region, has been half completed. Completion of the remainder is proposed. The added construction would cost an estimated $5,000 per acre irrigated, in present value terms.[3] Of this, landowners receiving the water would pay an estimated $115 in present value. However, the water to be delivered would be drawn out of the river behind the Grand Coulee Dam, and thus would reduce the ability of that dam and the others below it on the Columbia to produce electric power. Additional coal or nuclear power plants would then be required to replace the power lost because of irrigation water withdrawals from the river, in addition to the electric power needed to pump the water up from the river's level to the farmland. The cost? Bonneville Power would have to charge its customers an estimated $110 million per year extra to pay the added power costs, which do not appear in the project's budget. That is an opportunity cost of about $4,050 per acre irrigated, in addition to the budgeted cost of delivering the proposed irrigation water budgeted. It would be spread over a great many power customers and taxpayers, few of whom are even aware of the proposed project. Once again, project decision-makers and those lobbying for project completion would not face the full opportunity costs of their actions.

National forests provide yet another example. What is the cost of managing a portion of a national forest for timber or for oil and gas production, rather than

---

[3]Data for this irrigation project are from a series of studies by Washington State University Professor of Agricultural Economics Norman K. Whittlesey and others. See Whittlesey, ''Should We Finish the Columbia Basin Project?'' a paper delivered to the Farm Forum in Spokane, Washington, in January 1984.

for wilderness? Environmentalists point out that when logging firms purchase the rights to cut timber on national forest lands, they frequently do not pay even the cost of preparing for the timber sale plus the cost of roads to serve the loggers, much less the cost of reduced wildlife habitat or the loss of roadless recreation. On the other hand, wilderness advocates (and users) generally pay nothing at all toward the cost of wilderness, even though official Wilderness designation precludes roads, logging, and, in effect, outlaws oil and gas extraction, which could be extremely valuable. Since the many would-be users do not pay the opportunity cost of what they get, agency decision-makers do not face the opportunity cost of the options they consider, and find it difficult even to estimate the size of those opportunity costs. Economists, however, are willing to try to provide estimates.

OPPORTUNITY COST AND BENEFIT-COST ANALYSIS

Benefit-cost Analysis (B-C): A process used to determine the efficiency of a project by estimating each benefit and each cost. A project is said to be efficient if it generates more benefits than costs.

When economists look at a project to judge whether or not it is an efficient use of resources, they analyze benefits and opportunity costs. Benefit-cost analysis (B-C) is a process to determine the efficiency of a project by estimating every benefit and every cost. The project is said to be efficient if benefits exceed costs. The benefit-cost ratio is often calculated by simply dividing total benefits by total costs. An efficient project has a benefit-cost ratio greater than one.

The purpose of using B-C is to separate efficient projects from inefficient ones, and to avoid the latter. Inefficient projects move resources from higher-valued uses to lower-valued ones. To do its job, B-C must correctly measure all of the benefits and all of the costs (present and future), implied by the choice being analyzed, and compare them properly. Then, the B-C must be used by decision-makers. There are thus three major reasons why even B-C may go astray:

1. *Measurement assigning a dollar amount to the costs and benefits can be very difficult.* Goods and services involved in natural resource projects often are unpriced. They frequently involve publicly provided goods and services, which are not marketed. Because of this, it is difficult to determine their value and their opportunity cost. Costs and values are subjective, so when preferences are not revealed by offers to buy and to sell, objective estimates may be almost impossible. In recent years, some especially difficult issues have arisen regarding the preservation of natural areas. (See the Applications in Economics box, "Tough Issues in Natural Resource Preservation.") But, economists and other policy analysts work hard to approximate willingness-to-pay or opportunity costs, since rational governmental decisions and policies may depend on the resulting estimates, even though they are imperfect.

2. *An inappropriate rate of interest may be used when calculating the benefits and costs.* The chapter on "Capital, Interest, and Profit," explained why comparing present and future dollar amounts requires the use of an interest rate and a discounting procedure. A dollar in benefits (or costs) today is worth more than a dollar next year. The choice of the appropriate interest rate can strongly influence estimated costs and benefits. That choice is not a simple one, however, and economists have long debated how the correct rate should be chosen. Projects involving natural resources have often been the stage for those debates.

3. *Policy-makers may fail to use the B-C analysis when making decisions on resource use.* Supporters of a project will usually lobby for it and opponents will lobby against it, regardless of the B-C results. Political considerations, rather than economics, may determine the outcome of the issue. Efficiency has no political constituency, and the success of political decision-makers depends more on pleasing politically effective interest groups than on making efficient decisions.

APPLICATIONS IN ECONOMICS

Tough Issues in Natural Resource Preservation

Some values claimed for natural resources are by their nature difficult to measure. An example of this is the existence value of a natural wonder, such as the Grand Canyon. Some people derive satisfaction just from knowing that the Grand Canyon exists in its unspoiled state. A few years ago, a dam for water storage and power generation to be built in the canyon was proposed. Some of the grandeur would be lost if the dam were built. The dam, like Hoover Dam farther west on the same river, would have a grandeur of its own,

Existence Value: The satisfaction people can derive simply from knowing that something—the Grand Canyon or Hoover Dam, for example—exists. It is extremely difficult to measure existence values.

Irreversibility: Once an action is taken, some physical effects may not be reversible—the prior physical conditions cannot be restored. Such a situation involves an irreversibility.

but it would certainly not be the same. Building the dam and harnessing the wild river would create existence value for some people and would destroy it for others. Since many of those who would appreciate the existence of either the unspoiled canyon or the dam would never visit the Grand Canyon, how can we take their evaluations into account? How can we estimate that component of the opportunity cost of building (or not building) the dam?

Voluntary organizations, such as those organized to preserve the Statue of Liberty or the Hawk Mountain Sanctuary, provide one way that existence values are expressed. People who never visit the sites contribute to their preservation. But, each of us who enjoys such value may choose to "free ride," leaving the cost of providing the existence value to others. In the end, existence values that individuals refuse to voluntarily support might have to be ignored. While existence values are everywhere, they are nearly impossible to estimate.

Another difficult issue in resource management is the problem of irreversible decisions. A dam built in the Grand Canyon would have some per-

manent physical effects. **Irreversibility** means that once the action is taken, some physical effects could not be reversed. Once the dam is built, even removing it would not restore the original beauty of the Grand Canyon, because the water behind the dam would permanently change the appearance of its walls. Opponents of such a project argue that irreversibility puts the project in a special category, so that postponing the project to preserve the option for the future is an especially attractive option. Unfortunately, the situation is not so easy to analyze.

Suppose the project were actually beneficial, producing $1 million of net benefits in electricity and water storage services per year. To delay the project 5 years would mean giving up $5 million in benefits, and giving them up forever. At an interest rate of 10 percent, $5 million is equivalent to $500,000 per year forever. What permanent conservation (or other) goals could be purchased with that permanent stream of income? While a delay can preserve an option, the delay itself may have irreversible effects.

In discussing the application of economic principles to natural resource issues, we have frequently used energy market examples. Bearing in mind these principles, we turn now to a description of energy markets and energy policy. Public policy always involves politics as well as economics. Nowhere has that been more important in the last 20 years than in energy markets.

POLITICS, POLICY, AND ENERGY

When world oil prices collapsed in the mid-1980s, the energy crisis of the 1970s became a dim memory for most of us. During the 1970s, however, worries about energy frequently dominated newspaper headlines and U.S. politicians enacted many laws designed to conserve oil and keep gasoline prices down. The history of the energy crisis, and its disappearance, tells us a lot about how markets, prices, and politics interact.

The most prominent development affecting the world petroleum market during the 1970s was the emergence of the Organization of Petroleum Exporting Countries (OPEC) as a strong producer cartel. Formed in 1960, OPEC tried to bring about the production controls needed to drive prices up. It did not succeed at first, but by 1970 the stage was set for some dramatic price increases. These price increases did not come about because of higher costs in producing oil, but resulted from forces developing over several decades.

Long before OPEC, governments in many oil-producing countries had begun seizing a larger role in production and pricing decisions. Most imposed higher taxes and forced the oil companies to change the agreements under which they developed petroleum resources. Some governments simply nationalized the oil companies in their countries. As oil companies saw their revenues being reduced increasingly by taxes, and their contracts for future oil development changed to give the governments more control, the oil companies began to pump oil rapidly. Between 1960 and 1970, world oil production more than doubled, even as world oil prices dropped. (See the Applications in Economics box, "Politics, Property Rights, and Pumping Rates.")

Falling world petroleum prices encouraged people to buy cars and build facilities that used a lot of oil. Because automobiles and capital equipment last a long time, these decisions locked in a high demand for oil for a number of years.

By 1970, however, excess capacity to produce oil for world markets had disappeared. Oil production in the United States, the world's largest producer, peaked that year. The world began to realize that falling oil prices could not continue, and that prices were likely to rise at some point in the future. That point arrived in 1973.

Arab oil producers responded to the Middle East war of 1973 by cutting back production and by placing an embargo on exports to the United States and certain other Western countries. Crude oil prices more than tripled to over $12 a barrel. OPEC lifted the embargo in 1974, but prices remained high.

Acting together, the 13 OPEC nations were in a position to exert an important influence on the world oil market. They produced about 40 percent of the world's oil and held over two-thirds of the proved reserves. Since demand was high, and since demand for energy is relatively inelastic in the short run, OPEC members were not forced to curtail output very much at first.

Expectations of future price increases spurred buyers to "stock up now, before prices go up," thus increasing current demand. Such expectations of future price increases also encouraged oil producers to raise their current prices. That meant they would produce less oil now and more in the future, when it would bring higher prices. Investors began to search for more oil and to develop techniques capable of increasing the production from existing wells. However, it would take several years for these investments to increase world oil supplies.

It appeared that the OPEC cartel had the world by the tail. This impression was even more vivid after the Iranian revolution occurred in 1978, virtually shutting down Iranian oil production for months. Oil prices more than doubled, reaching about $35 per barrel by the summer of 1980. Prices went up again at the end of 1980, after war broke out between Iran and Iraq. In early 1981, oil prices reached a peak of nearly $40 per barrel.

ENERGY POLICY AND THE ENERGY CRISIS IN THE UNITED STATES

Real Price: The cost of an item, corrected for inflation. For example, if the price of oil doubles while the prices of all other goods also double, the real price of oil is unchanged. Decisions are generally based on real prices, rather than the money (nominal) prices.

ENERGY SHORTAGES AND THE REGULATION OF NATURAL GAS PRICES

For Americans, the energy crisis of the 1970s resulted partly from world market conditions, and partly from the domestic policies of the 1950s and 1960s. Low and falling oil prices encouraged people to use large quantities of oil and to buy products—such as "gas-guzzling" cars and large, poorly insulated homes—that kept demand for energy high for years. Between 1950 and 1972, the **real price** of energy to the American consumer declined substantially. Gasoline prices fell 22 percent, residential electricity fell 54 percent, and residential natural gas fell 19 percent, all in real terms.

Against the backdrop of falling prices and rapid expansion in energy use, public policy in three important areas—price regulation, import restrictions, and tighter environmental regulation—added to the forces that culminated in the energy crisis.

Beginning in 1954, the Federal Power Commission (forerunner of today's Federal Energy Regulatory Commission) regulated the well-head price of natural gas. At first the commission allowed the real price of gas to rise, but in 1961, it began to use a pricing formula that substantially reduced the price. Throughout most of the 1960s and well into the 1970s, the FPC fixed the price of natural gas at about one-third the price of its energy equivalent in crude oil. This below-equilibrium price encouraged consumers to use more natural gas, and at the same time, it greatly reduced the incentive of producers to discover and produce more natural gas.

Needless to say, encouraging consumption while retarding production is the perfect formula for creating a shortage. By 1974, the ratio of proved reserves/

APPLICATIONS IN ECONOMICS

Politics, Property Rights, and Pumping Rates

In petroleum exporting countries, most of the exploration, development, and production of oil has been done by private oil companies. The companies signed contracts, called concession agreements, with the exporting nations, agreeing to explore for oil and produce it in exchange for royalty payments and the payment of taxes. Huge oil fields were discovered, and a great deal of oil flowed from them. Over the years the exporting countries changed the terms of the agreements by raising their tax rates, and occasionally by nationalizing the company properties, as Iran did in 1951. Competition increased worldwide, though, and oil prices fell from 1957 to 1970.

OPEC was formed in 1960 to try to seize some control over world markets. During the 1960s, OPEC members gradually increased tax rates, made modest attempts at reducing production growth, and took some steps toward nationalization of the concessions. In 1968, OPEC formally announced its intent to maximize tax revenues and, over time, to nationalize company operations. It became clear to the companies that even if they escaped nationalization, future production would mean much higher payments to the governments. Companies facing such probabilities increased their pumping rates in the 1960s, contributing to the 118 per-

cent increase in world crude oil production from 1960 to 1970.

One result was that each company in that situation faced a strong incentive to pump oil very rapidly, since oil left in the ground would probably not be theirs in the future anyway. There was little incentive for the companies to conserve for future production, since their rights to the oil under the existing contractual arrangements were coming to an end. The rapid production of oil during the 1960s was one result, and this helped push world oil prices down until 1970. When OPEC raised oil prices beginning in 1970, the starting point was an artificially low price.

consumption for natural gas had fallen to 10, from over 20 in 1961. The nation's inventory of known gas reserves had been cut in half, relative to annual consumption. Natural gas shortages put upward pressure on the demand for electricity and oil, raising costs and prices in those markets. The OPEC cartel could hardly ask for better cooperation.

IMPORT RESTRICTIONS, THE ORIGIN OF OPEC, AND DECLINING OIL RESERVES

After the Second World War, an increase in worldwide discovery and production of low cost crude oil turned the United States from a net exporter of oil to a net importer, and put downward pressure on oil prices. In 1959, a coalition of domestic oil companies lobbied successfully for mandatory import quotas, limiting the import of cheap foreign oil. This policy contributed to falling world oil prices at the time, and had the unplanned side effect of increasing the desire of oil exporting nations to form a cartel. In 1960, OPEC was formed. The "drain America first" policy of the United States government boosted production of increasingly expensive domestic crude, at the expense of consumers. This helped flood the world market with surplus oil, and world oil prices continued to decline through the 1960s. Domestic reserves declined, relative to consumption. American producers knew that as domestic oil became more expensive, there would be increasing pressure over time to import more foreign crude at very low prices. Once again, American policy was helping to set the stage for large OPEC price increases.

ENERGY MARKETS AND ENVIRONMENTAL REGULATIONS

Beginning in the late 1960s, the United States began to take steps to preserve air and water quality. Increasingly stringent emission standards for automobiles resulted in a substantial decline in the miles per gallon of fuel for the average auto. Together with rising incomes, a growing population, and expectations caused by falling real gasoline prices, this trend generated a strong increase in the demand for gasoline.

Simultaneously, the United States began to crack down on air and water pollution from oil refineries. New refineries had to meet tougher, more expensive standards. In many places, permission to build added refinery capacity was simply denied. Uncertainty about the future of import quotas—when and where might cheap foreign oil be allowed into the United States in the future—further reduced incentives to meet the growing demand for gasoline by adding refinery capacity.

THE ENERGY CRISIS AND OUR POLICY RESPONSE

In October 1973, when the Arab embargo began, the U.S. domestic consumption of energy was at a high level and could not be reduced easily. Simultaneously, the domestic supply of proved petroleum reserves had dwindled to a low level, due to energy price controls and other policies. Given the long production lags and the demand for energy by owners of cars, houses, and buildings designed for cheap energy, both the supply and the demand for crude oil were highly inelastic in the short run.

So, when OPEC raised the price of crude oil from $2.50 to over $10 in less than two years, strong conservation efforts were needed, along with vigorous efforts to call forth the most efficient additional energy supplies. A substantially higher price for petroleum and its products, which would naturally emerge in the market without price controls, would have brought both of these about. But price controls, both those existing on natural gas and those imposed in President Nixon's price freeze of 1971–1973, stifled these forces.

ENERGY CRISIS: THE MYTHICAL ENERGY GAP

In the national debate following the OPEC price increases of 1973–1974, many public leaders pointed out that while higher prices would provide the incentive for added petroleum production, they also would give "windfall gains" to those already holding proved reserves. Also, users of petroleum products could face hardships from the higher prices.

Many leaders also doubted that there would be large buyer and seller responses to changes in price. They simply ignored existing economic studies, which showed that, over time, price would exert a major impact on the production and allocation of energy. Most news reports referred to energy "needs" and "requirements" as if these grew in fixed proportion to population or to GNP, without regard to energy prices and responses to price changes. Exhibit 4 illustrates this mistaken view. Although the events since 1973 have clearly disproven this view, similar misconceptions are seen constantly in regard to other natural resources, such as water in the arid West. It is worthwhile to examine why such a way of thinking is misleading.

The "energy gap" notion overlooks the fact that energy is not desired for itself, but rather to produce other goods and services. Gasoline, for example, is used to produce transportation. The gasoline cannot be more indispensable than the transportation it helps make possible. Giving up the least important third of one's auto travel saves a third of one's gasoline use. Car pooling, shorter vacation trips, and Sunday excursions on bicycles instead of by car come quickly to mind.

The impact of price on energy supplies is also disregarded in the "gap" theory. Thus, data on *proved* reserves were mistakenly taken to indicate *absolute* reserves; Americans were warned that the supply of fossil fuels was sufficient to last only 10 to 15 years.

EXHIBIT 4

The Mythical Vertical Demand and Supply Curves for Energy

Leaders of popular opinion often assume that the demand and supply curves for energy resources resemble those presented here. Both economic reasoning and real-world data indicate that this view is incorrect.

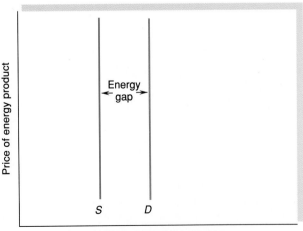

This grim view of our energy future was widely accepted. Fears that an uncontrolled market price would lead to extremely high prices without bringing forth much greater supplies led to the imposition of price controls. Low prices, however, meant that users had less incentive to conserve, and producers had less incentive to supply more oil. There was indeed an "energy gap"—caused by price controls!

PRICE CONTROLS— WINNERS AND LOSERS

Whenever a price is legally set below the market clearing level, shortages of course result. So it was with energy in the 1970s. As we have seen, natural gas consumers lucky enough to own natural gas hookups got a bargain. They could keep their houses warm and take long, hot showers cheaply, since the price was kept low by regulation. But, many who wanted to hook up their homes or apartments to natural gas lines were out of luck. For many utilities, not enough gas was available to serve additional customers.

There was another unwanted side effect of price controls: the demand for heating oil and electricity (much of it generated by oil-fired generators) increased. Consumers who could not get natural gas had to buy the much more expensive substitutes, which were often based on petroleum. In some neighborhoods, people in the newer houses had to pay much more for heating and cooling energy than did their luckier neighbors across the street, who happened to already have gas hookups. What about poor people? If they rented their housing, instead of owning it, they did not necessarily benefit from the low gas price. Owners of rental housing with gas hookups could now charge higher rents than their competitors who could not offer gas hookups in their rental units. Whenever price controls are effective, they keep prices below market-clearing levels. This means a shortage, and only those with access during the shortage can gain from the low price. Just as poor people lack access to goods via cash, they often lack nonmoney access. In this case, access meant ownership of a gas hookup. It was the owners of the hookups, not necessarily the ones paying the gas bill, who benefitted from the cheap natural gas.

One clear beneficiary of natural gas price controls was the OPEC cartel. The demand for their oil was increased by American price controls on natural gas, since additional fuel oil and electricity made with petroleum products had to be used due to the natural gas shortage brought on by price controls.

CRUDE OIL, THE ENTITLEMENT PROGRAM, AND SUBSEQUENT DECONTROL

Government price controls on domestic crude oil, which had come into effect when President Nixon controlled prices in 1971, caused numerous problems. Since price controls discouraged producers from exploring or drilling for oil, the government created exceptions, allowing some kinds of oil—such as newly discovered oil—to be sold at higher prices. The task of identifying and monitoring prices at the well was exceedingly complex and costly. The nation's top energy administrator testified that it cost $100 million a year to regulate crude oil prices.[4]

---

[4]Frank G. Zarb, quoted in *Federal Energy Administration Regulation,* Paul W. MacAvoy, ed. (Washington, D.C.: American Enterprise Institute, 1978), p. 54. Eventually, the Department of Energy was established to handle the regulatory problems. By fiscal year 1981, approximately 100,000 people were employed by the department, which had an annual budget of more than $10 billion.

Then there was the question of which refiners should be allowed to buy the controlled-price domestic crude and which should pay for the higher-priced foreign crude. So the government developed a system that was supposed to share crude oil supplies more equally among refiners. This "entitlement" program required refiners who had access to low-cost domestic crude oil, even if they had discovered and developed it, to pay monetary compensation to other refiners who were using high-cost foreign supplies.

The entitlement program meant that OPEC was subsidized by a tax on American oil producers. It also meant that American users of petroleum products failed to get the true price signal that conservation was really worth $36 per barrel of oil saved, rather than the subsidized $30 price paid by the refineries and passed on to consumers. Energy conservation was held back, and the demand for OPEC oil was further increased by the price control and entitlement programs. Price controls and the entitlement program, with their unintended side effects of reducing energy conservation and subsidizing the import of oil, strengthened the demand for imported oil.

In early 1981, the United States removed all price controls on petroleum products and abolished the entitlement program. By this time, world consumption and production of petroleum had responded to high prices. Consumers conserved energy and relied on more non-oil supplies, such as coal, gas, and nuclear power. U.S. oil consumption, which had peaked at almost 19 million barrels per day in 1978, fell to only 15 million barrels in 1982. Non-OPEC production increased, especially after the U.S. removal of price controls on domestic oil products. This provided oil refiners with an incentive to search for the cheapest oil, wherever it could be found. In 1981, the U.S. oil industry invested record amounts for exploration and development and new non-OPEC oil production came from British and Norwegian North Sea fields and Mexico.

The OPEC share of world production fell from about 40 percent in 1972 to less than 33 percent in 1985. To maintain the high price for its oil, the OPEC cartel began to cut production. Prices declined nevertheless. From an average of $37 per barrel during the peak year of 1981, the price of crude oil fell to $27 in 1985, and then collapsed to $11 per barrel in the summer of 1986. This collapse of world prices in the mid-1980s suggested that perhaps OPEC was not so powerful after all. It tended to confirm the point that economists have often made that a cartel arrangement is extremely difficult to administer and police, especially when there is no single governmental authority that controls all members.

THE ENERGY CRISIS— AN ALTERNATIVE VIEW

Not all economists agree on whether or not the OPEC cartel had a major influence on world oil prices. But if the price increases were not caused by the cartel's use of monopoly power, what did cause them?

A number of important factors, apart from monopoly power, can help explain the two big price hikes. We have touched on each of them:

1. The world's demand for oil had been increasing during the 1950s and 1960s due to rising incomes and a capital stock that reflected expectations of falling oil prices, which had been present during both decades.

2. The world was gradually coming to recognize, in the 1960s, that oil prices

would eventually rise, as demand continued to grow. Ordinarily, this would have caused a rising oil price, as some oil field owners cut back production to produce more later, at the expected higher price.

3. Production of oil in the 1950s and 1960s had been artificially stimulated by the anticipation of more governmental seizures of oil fields in many oil producing countries. This caused companies to pump very rapidly, to get what they could before their contracts in the oil fields ran out, or were simply taken away from them (as indeed happened in several cases). This rapid pumping had ended by 1973, as the oil companies had largely lost their properties in those countries where that danger existed.

4. By 1970, excess capacity had disappeared, and increased demand was pushing against short-run supply. Since it is marginal cost, not average cost, that sets a competitive market price, and since the artificially high pumping rates in some countries had just about stopped, the price increases of 1970–1973 are not hard to explain, even without a cartel. The far steeper increases of 1973–1974 and of 1979–1981 are another matter.

5. The two really steep price increases have followed political and military crises. The first was due, at least in part, to the 1973 war in the Middle East, and the ensuing Arab oil embargo applied to the United States and several other Western nations. The second followed the overthrow of the Shah in Iran and greatly reduced oil production there. This was accompanied by the outbreak of trouble in a number of Middle East locations, each signalling potential trouble for oil production.

But, were the price increases larger because the cartel helped enforce them? Clearly, most people *believed* that OPEC had monopoly power and was capable of using it to bring about higher future prices. Remember, a price increase that is expected to stick, rather than be reversed, will increase demand in the short run. The view of OPEC as a strong cartel certainly was widespread when the steepest price advances occurred. Undoubtedly, this view contributed to the rising prices.

WAS BIG OIL RIPPING OFF THE CONSUMER?

Surveys taken during the 1970s indicated a belief by the general public that more than 40 cents of every sales dollar in the petroleum industry was accounting profit. In reality, the figure was about 5 cents. The profit rates of firms in the petroleum industry differ little, on average, from those of other types of firms. During 1974–1981, the peak "energy crisis" years, the rate of return on stockholder equity was 18.0 percent, compared to 15.6 percent for all manufacturing. Only during 1974 and 1979–1981 were oil industry profits substantially greater than for other firms. Those added profits, of course, drew large investments into the industry, making possible an increased supply of petroleum products. In the years before 1974 and after 1981, the profits of large oil companies were slightly less than for manufacturing firms in general.

Since total profits were around 5 cents per sales dollar, the higher profits that did occur accounted for only a tiny part of petroleum product price increases. Profits had little to do with the energy crisis, aside from their normal and constructive role of encouraging investment where the additional investment would create the largest return for the economy.

THE FUTURE OF NATURAL RESOURCE MARKETS

Is the world running out of natural resources? (See the Myths of Economics box.) Can we forecast future supply and scarcity? What factors will determine the future of natural resource availability?

As we noted at the beginning of this chapter, the value of a resource depends on the knowledge and ingenuity possessed, and the circumstances faced by its potential users. In a very real sense, humankind creates resources, even though the physical resource is a gift of nature. The challenge, then, is to see that knowledge is created in a timely way, and ingeniously applied in a manner appropriate to the circumstances. Historically, the price system has provided information on approaching resource scarcity, and supplied inventors, innovators, and investors

MYTHS OF ECONOMICS

"We are running out of energy, minerals, timber and other non-renewable natural resources. Doomsday is just around the corner."

The first recorded doomsday forecast, says J. Clayburn LaForce,[5] was the fifteenth-century prediction that England would run out of wood. "At the time, wood was the main source of fuel, and terrible consequences were expected. What happened? The price of that resource gradually rose as forests around urban centers receded. In response to higher prices, people gradually began to substitute coal for charcoal [a wood derivative] in both personal and commercial uses. England entered its greatest period of economic growth and that 'sceptered isle' still has forests."

Doomsday forecasts have been made ever since, often by very responsible people. In 1865, the noted economist William Jevons argued that the industrial growth of that century could not be maintained far into the future because the world was running out of coal, the primary energy resource at the time.[6]

Governments have made some of

the worst forecasts. In 1905, Theodore Roosevelt predicted a timber famine if present rates of cutting continued. In 1914, the Bureau of Mines reported that the total U.S. supply of crude oil was approximately 6 million barrels. We now produce that much every 20 months.

A major energy crisis occurred in the United States in the early 1800s, when home lighting depended on lamps that burned whale oil, especially from the sperm whale. "As population rose," LaForce relates, "demand for this resource increased, and many predicted that soon there would be no more whales and that we would be faced with darkness during the winter nights."

The price of whale oil rose. Over some 30 to 40 years, the price of sperm whale oil rose from 43 cents per gallon to $2.55 a gallon, while the price of other whale oil rose from 23 cents to $1.42 a gallon. Higher prices motivated consumers and entrepreneurs to seek alternatives, LaForce explains, including distilled vegetable oils, lard oil, and coal gas. By the early 1850s, coal oil (kerosene) had won out. And very soon thereafter, a new substitute appeared:

petroleum replaced coal oil as the source of kerosene. A new industry was born.

As for whale oil, by 1896, its price had fallen to 40 cents per gallon, and even at that price few people used it. The whale oil crisis had passed.

"All this happened," says LaForce, "with no pretense of a national energy (or lighting) plan. There were no price controls. . . . Each change had been guided and coordinated by 'the invisible hand' of the market: the price mechanism."

Dire predictions about our natural resource future became a fad during the 1970s. The "year of exhaustion"

[5]Quoted from J. Clayburn LaForce, "The Energy Crisis: The Moral Equivalent of Bamboozle," International Institute for Economic Research, Original Paper 11 (Los Angeles, April 1978).
[6]In his book, *The Coal Question* (London: Macmillan, 1865), Jevons stated: "We cannot long maintain our present rate of increase of consumption; the cost of fuel must rise, perhaps within a lifetime, to a rate injurious of our commercial and manufacturing supremacy; and the conclusion is inevitable, that our present happy progressive condition is a thing of limited duration."

with the proper incentives to deal appropriately with the situation. For that to happen, however, prices must reflect the opinions of buyers and sellers, including speculators, on current and coming resource scarcities. Appropriate price signals, in turn, depend on the existence of well-defined, secure, and transferrable property rights.

PROPERTY RIGHTS AND NATURAL RESOURCE CONSERVATION

There is every reason to believe that resource markets will send both users and producers the proper signals, should proved reserves fall to dangerous levels. Owners of petroleum resources will make the decision to extract oil on the basis of the expected future price. If they believe petroleum is going to be worth 10 percent more next year, and if their best alternative investment yields less than 10 percent, they will hold their reserves. Of course, if property rights are not secure, as in the case of oil reserves in the 1960s that were about to be nationalized, then

of important natural resources, especially crude oil, was a popular news item. The arithmetic of the doomsday calculations was unassailable. One simply found the current annual consumption rate (averaged over, say, the last two decades) and divided that number into the quantity of proved reserves of the resource. That provided the years of the resource remaining. Add that number to the current date, and we have the "year of exhaustion."

Why then have the years to exhaustion projections proved to be so wrong? There are two major reasons for their inaccuracy. First, "proved reserves" of a mineral resource are an inventory. *Proved reserves are costly to find and verify, so we do not want to bear the cost of "proving" a mineral deposit too many years in advance*. We want to produce inventories, including proved reserves, only a few weeks, months, or years ahead of the time we need them. The size of currently proved reserves says nothing at all about the sufficiency for the future of absolute reserves.

Second, doomsday predictions have generally failed to consider the role of price changes and technology.

Both consumption rates and the expected recoverable supply are projected *assuming current technology and prices*. But when a resource becomes more scarce, its price rises. This provides additional incentive for innovators, engineers, and inventors to alter technology in a manner that will (a) conserve on direct use of the resource, (b) provide substitutes for the resource, and (c) develop new methods of discovering and recovering larger quantities of the resource. In resource economics, it is critical to remember that we want the services gained by using the resource, not the resource itself. There are very few services that we could not find substitutes for, if we really needed to. For all these reasons, the cost of most natural resources has remained constant or fallen for decades, and in most cases, for centuries.

The classic study of Harold Barnett and Chandler Morse illustrates this point. Using data from 1870 to 1963, Barnett and Morse found that resource costs declined during that long period.[7] Far from suggesting that doomsday was around the corner, the facts of natural resource availability tell a much more optimis-

tic story. Relative price data indicate that technology and the ever-increasing availability of substitutes have outrun our ability to use up scarce natural resources. When price changes are allowed to reflect changing scarcities, constructive human responses to specific scarcities are an understandable and predictable occurrence. Just as they have been wrong in the past, future doomsday forecasts that fail to incorporate human response to relative price changes will prove to be wrong in the future.

[7]See Harold Barnett and Chandler Morse, *Scarcity and Growth: The Economics of Natural Resource Availability,* (Baltimore: The Johns Hopkins University Press for Resources for the Future, 1963). An update and extension of the data, reaching similar conclusions, is in Manual H. Johnson, Fredrick W. Bell, and J. T. Bennett, "Natural Resource Scarcity: Empirical Evidence and Public Policy," *Journal of Environmental Economics and Management,* 7, (September 1980); pp. 258–269. Not all economists fully accept this view, however. See V. Kerry Smith, ed., *Scarcity and Growth Reconsidered* (Baltimore; The Johns Hopkins University Press for Resources for the Future, 1979).

markets will not convey the proper signal, and proper resource allocation may not take place. That oil was pumped too rapidly. Or, if rights to the resource are not transferrable (cannot be traded for profit), as in the case of some water rights, then once more, markets do not provide the proper incentives. The water may be used in low-valued uses, and in effect, be wasted. Only when property rights exist, can be easily protected, and can be traded, will markets provide owners of the resources with the information and incentive to see that the resources are properly cared for and used.

LOOKING AHEAD

We have seen that natural resource markets frequently can do far more than people realize, but only when property rights are appropriately defined, secure, and transferable. In the next chapter, we will return in more depth to our discussion from Chapter 4 on market failure. Natural resources for which property rights are not properly defined or are difficult to defend, such as water and air, are especially vulnerable to abuse, and play a prominent role in most discussions of market failure.

CHAPTER SUMMARY

1. Natural resources are "gifts of nature," but their value depends on human effort, knowledge, culture, and ingenuity, and on the circumstances in which people have access to the resources.
2. As with other markets, incentives matter in resource markets. Both the quantity demanded of a resource, and the quantity supplied, depend on the resource price. Substitutes can be found everywhere. Both the demand and the supply curves will be more elastic when buyers and sellers have more time in which to respond to a price change.
3. Information about the future availability of a natural resource is costly, and proved reserves of a mineral resource are equivalent to an inventory. Discovering and verifying an oil field or a mineral deposit far in advance of when it will be used may be more costly than it is worth.
4. Resource values are determined at the margin, rather than by the average usefulness or average cost of the resource. When a resource is worth more at the margin in one use than in another, gains from trade are possible.
5. The opportunity cost of a resource is its relevant cost. Nonmarketed resources, and projects involving those resources, are difficult to evaluate. Benefit-cost analysis is a process to conduct project evaluation.
6. The Organization of Petroleum Exporting Countries was formed in 1960, and appeared to have control of the world oil market in the 1970s. But, economists are now uncertain as to how much of the large price increases were brought about by the cartel's manipulations of supply and price, and how much was the result of normal market forces in the presence of wars and other disturbances in oil producing regions.
7. Perhaps inadvertently, the energy policy of the United States strengthened the OPEC cartel during rhe 1970s. Price controls on both domestically produced oil and natural gas reduced the supply of substitutes for OPEC oil. In effect, the entitlement program subsidized OPEC oil and increased the size of that subsidy when the price of OPEC oil rose. In addition, U.S. environmental regulations encouraged gasoline consumption and thereby increased the demand for OPEC oil. It is not a coincidence that the market power of OPEC declined dramatically as the entitlement program and price controls were eliminated in the early 1980s.
8. Neither economic analysis nor empirical evidence is supportive of the view that the world is about to run out of key natural resources. When private property rights are present, increased scarcity (relative to demand) of a natural resource will increase the price of the resource and thereby encourage conservation, the use of substitutes, and the development of new technologies capable of reducing our reliance on the resource.

The fact that the real prices of most natural resources have declined during the last century is inconsistent with the doomsday view of resource scarcity.

9. In a market setting, the existence of secure, transferable property rights is a key to proper conservation and wise use of natural resources, as with all other goods and services.

CRITICAL ANALYSIS QUESTIONS

*1. In what sense are crude oil and other natural resources "gifts of nature"? In what sense are they the result of human ingenuity?

2. Why is the price elasticity of demand for resources such as electricity and natural gas greater in the long run than the short run? What examples of responses to price changes can you think of that are more complete after one year than after one week?

*3. "Steel production typically requires 40,000 gallons of water per finished ton of steel. Steel is important to U.S. industry and our national defense. As water becomes more scarce in the nation, it is imperative that the required amounts of water be reserved for the steel industry." Evaluate.

4. "The federal government should do a complete survey of mineral availability in the nation. It is inexcusable that we do not know how much oil, for example, the country can ultimately produce." Evaluate.

*5. "If the federal government starts charging fees for outdoor recreation, only the rich will be able to participate. They will buy up all the opportunities, leaving none for the common citizen." Evaluate.

*6. Why will more oil *in total* be produced from an oil well, when the price of crude oil is higher?

*7. What is the difference between the total reserves of a mineral and its proved reserves? Why might both be important?

8. Will the world ever run out of any resource? Why are economists likely to answer in the negative? Does this imply that increasing resource scarcity will never be a problem?

*9. Does a resource that is not owned, and therefore is not priced, have a zero opportunity cost? Might it be treated as if it did?

10. Some of the oil now being produced in the world can be delivered to a Texas gulf-coast refinery for about $3 per barrel. Other oil now being produced costs more than $20 per barrel, delivered to the same refinery. What is the opportunity cost of selling the oil to the refinery, in each case?

11. "A successful natural resource cartel sows the seeds of its own destruction." Explain.

*12. Suppose that you were the owner of some land scheduled to be irrigated by water from a heavily subsidized dam project being proposed in Congress. If the project is built, you would receive increased net farming revenues from your land. The project's costs would occur over the next 2 years, but the benefits would start later and continue for the next 50 years. Would you want the federal benefit-cost analysts, whose report will be available to Congress, to use a high or a low interest rate in their analysis? Why?

13. When farmers who receive water from federal irrigation projects repay project costs, they do so over a long period, often 50 years, with no payments due during the first 10 years. They pay no interest, but of course the federal government does pay interest on the funds borrowed to build the project. Suppose that the relevant interest rate is 7 percent (a dollar doubles in value every 10 years at that rate), and the project built now costs $1 million. If the farmers simply give the federal government the full $1 million on a date 30 years after the project cost is paid, have they paid the full cost of the project? If not, how much is their subsidy?

*14. Did "Big Oil" interests cause the energy crises of the 1970s and early 1980s by increasing their profit margins?

*Asterisk denotes questions for which answers are given in Appendix C, Selected Answers.

FOUR

PUBLIC CHOICE

18 PROBLEM AREAS FOR THE MARKET

Thus, from the beginning, capitalism has been characterized by a tension between laissez-faire and intervention—laissez-faire representing the expression of its economic drive, intervention of its democratic political orientation. That tension continues today, a deeply imbedded part of the historic character of the capitalist system.[1]

Robert Heilbroner and Lester Thurow

CHAPTER FOCUS

■ Why do market decision-makers face inappropriate incentives when an externality is present?

■ What role do imperfect information and imperfect property rights play in causing externalities?

■ What can we learn from the theory of external effects about pollution problems and alternative solutions? Why are some solutions to pollution problems less effective than others?

■ What is the "free rider" problem? What kinds of goods are likely to be susceptible to this problem?

■ What can we say about buyers' and sellers' lack of knowledge in the market, and when is this problem likely to be most serious?

We have emphasized that a properly functioning market system uses prices to coordinate the decisions of buyers and sellers. Market prices give each decision-maker the information needed to make intelligent decisions, while weighing the relative desires of others. Equally important, prices provide the incentive to use that information. Even when they think only of themselves, decision-makers facing appropriate prices act as if they care about others. For example, to personally gain the largest return, resource owners have an incentive to move their resources to uses in which others value them most. Producers want to get the most highly valued production from the bundle of resources they use, and to minimize the cost (the value to others) of those resource inputs. Buyers have an incentive to economize on their consumption of goods and services to get as much satisfaction as possible from their limited budgets.

In short, the "invisible hand" of Adam Smith provides each decision-maker in the market economy with the information and incentive to act as if others matter. However, as we pointed out in Chapter 4, the invisible hand can slip. (At this point, the reader should review Chapter 4.) There are several potential causes of **market failure,** economic activity that results in allocative inefficiency relative to the hypothetical ideal of economists. The causes of market failure can be grouped into four general classes: (a) externalities, (b) public goods, (c) poorly informed buyers or sellers, and (d) monopoly.

In this chapter, we will delve more deeply into market failure and the possible responses to it, especially government responses. Since the impact of monopoly on the product and factor markets has already been investigated, this chapter will emphasize the other three categories of market failure.

Keep in mind that market failure is merely a failure to attain conditions of *ideal* efficiency. Alternative forms of economic organization will also have defects. Market failure creates an opportunity for government to improve the situation. In some circumstances, however, public-sector action will not be corrective. Sometimes there may even be good reason to expect it will be counterproductive. We will analyze market failure in this chapter and focus on the operation of the public sector in the next chapter.

EXTERNAL EFFECTS AND THE MARKET

The genius of a market exchange system lies in its ability to bring personal and social welfare into harmony. When two parties trade, and only they are affected, production and voluntary exchange also promote the *social* welfare. When externalities are present, though, production and exchange affect the welfare of nonconsenting secondary parties. The external effects may be either positive or negative.

If the welfare of nonconsenting secondary parties is adversely affected by actions not accounted for in market prices, the spillover effects are called **external costs.** A steel mill that belches smoke into the air imposes an external cost on surrounding residents who prefer clear air. A junkyard creates an eyesore, making an area less pleasant for passersby. Similarly, litterbugs, drunk drivers, muggers,

Market Failure: The failure of the market system to attain hypothetically *ideal* allocative efficiency. This means that potential gain exists that has not been captured. However, the cost of establishing a mechanism that could *potentially* capture the gain may exceed the benefits. Therefore, it is not always possible to improve the situation.

External Costs: Harmful effects of an individual's or a group's action on the welfare of nonconsenting secondary parties, not accounted for in market prices. Litterbugs, drunk drivers, and polluters, for example, create external costs.

[1]See Robert Heilbroner and Lester Thurow, *Economics Explained* (Englewood Cliffs: Prentice-Hall, 1982), p. 17.

"In other words, what you'll have us believe,
sir, is that all the fish in the river next to your
plant suddenly died of old age."

Reproduced by Special Permission of Playboy Magazine © 1980 by Playboy.

External Benefits: Beneficial effects of group or individual action on the welfare of non-paying secondary parties.

and robbers impose unwanted costs on others. If the spillover effects enhance the welfare of secondary parties, they are called **external benefits.** A beautiful rose garden provides external benefits for the neighbors of the gardener. A golf course generally provides spillover benefits if others own the surrounding property.

When external costs and external benefits are present, market prices will not send the proper signals to producers and consumers. This situation results in market failure.

Social Costs: The sum of (a) the private costs that are incurred by a decision-maker and (b) any external cost of the action that are imposed on nonconsenting secondary parties. If there are no external costs, private and social costs will be equal.

External Costs. From the viewpoint of economic efficiency, an action should be undertaken only if it generates benefits in excess of its social costs. **Social costs** include (a) the private cost borne by the consenting parties and (b) any external cost imposed on nonconsenting secondary parties.

When external costs are present, market prices understate the social cost generated by the use of resources or consumption of products. Decision-makers are not forced to fully bear the cost associated with their actions. Motivated by self-interest, they may undertake actions that generate a net loss to the community. The harm done to the secondary parties may exceed the net private gain. In such circumstances, private interest and economic efficiency are in conflict.

External Costs and Ideal Output. Externalities may result from the actions of either consumers or producers. When the actions of a producer impose external costs on others, the costs of the firm, reflecting only private costs, are not an accurate indicator of the total social costs of production.

Exhibit 1 illustrates the impact of external costs on the socially desirable price and output. Suppose there are a large number of copper-producing firms. They are able to discharge their waste products (mainly sulfur dioxide) into the air without charge, even though the pollution damages people and property downwind from the discharge. These air pollution costs are external to the copper producers. If allowed to operate freely, the producers have little incentive to adopt either cleaner production techniques or control devices that would limit the costs inflicted on others. These alternatives would only increase their private production cost.

Since pollutants can be freely discharged into the atmosphere, each copper producer expands output as long as marginal private costs (MC_p) are less than price. This leads to market supply curve S_1, the horizontal summation of the *private* marginal cost curves of the copper producers. Given the demand, the equilibrium market price for copper is P_1. Producers supply Q_1 units of copper. At output level Q_1, however, the *social* marginal cost of copper is MC_s, an amount substantially in excess of both the private cost and the consumer's valuation (as indicated

The supply curve, S_2, is the ideal, reflecting the social and private cost of producing copper, *and* incorporating production techniques that are chosen to minimize the *sum* of those costs. S_1, however, reflects purely the private costs, and production techniques chosen to minimize only the private costs. The latter production techniques result in S_3, the actual sum of private and social costs when social costs are being ignored by the producer. Thus, the ideal output is Q^* and the optimal cost (and price) is P^*. But, when the producer is not forced to be responsible for social costs, we can expect the larger output Q_1, and the much larger marginal cost MC_s, even though buyers only pay P_1 for copper output.

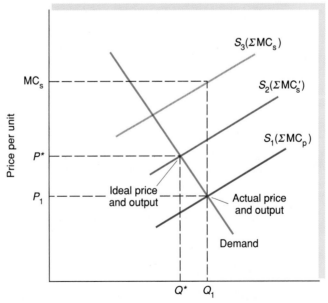

by the height of the demand curve at Q_1) of copper. As a result of the external costs, output is expanded beyond the ideal efficiency level. From the standpoint of efficiency, the market price, which fails to reflect the external cost, is too low. Additional units of copper are produced even though the value of the resources, as measured by the social marginal costs (and supply curve S_3) required to produce the units, exceeds the consumer's valuation of the units. A deterioration in air quality is a by-product.

If, on the other hand, copper producers are forced to pay for any downwind damages they caused, they probably would use different production techniques, including efficient pollution control methods. Supply curve S_2 (Exhibit 1) would result. Ideal output would be Q^* at price P^*. Customers would buy only the copper for which they are willing to pay all the costs, including the costs imposed on third parties. Since the consumer benefit derived from the marginal units of copper would be equal to the marginal cost to society of producing copper ($P^* = MC_s'$), production would be socially efficient.

When a producer's action imposes external costs on secondary parties, the producer's marginal costs will be understated. Therefore, the producer will choose to produce more of a good, charge less for it, and probably use different techniques to produce it, as compared to outcomes consistent with ideal economic efficiency.

External Costs and Property Rights. Clearly defined and enforced property rights are essential for the efficient operation of a market economy. The problems caused by externalities stem from a failure (or an inability) to clearly define and enforce property rights. Property rights help determine how resources will be used and who will be allowed to use them. **Private property rights** give owners the exclusive right to control and benefit from their resources as long as their actions do not harm others. It is important to recognize that private property rights do not include the right to use one's property in a manner that will injure others. For example, property rights do not grant the owners of rocks the right to throw them at automobiles.

> **Private Property Rights:** A set of usage and exchange rights held *exclusively* by the owner(s).

Property rights also provide individuals with legal protection against the actions of parties who might damage, abuse, or steal their property. While property rights are often associated with selfishness on the part of owners, they could more properly be viewed as a means by which owners (including corporate owners) are protected against the selfishness of others. If adequately compensated, though, property owners often allow others to use their assets, even though the value of the assets will become consequently lower. Rental car firms sell individuals the right to use their automobiles despite the reduction in the resale value of the car. Housing is often rented, even though normal use by the renter imposes a maintenance and upkeep cost on the homeowner. Since property rights are clearly defined and enforceable in these cases, the market exchange system induces people who use the property (including the owner, whose wealth is tied up in the value of the property) to fully consider the costs of their actions.

ENFORCEABLE PROPERTY RIGHTS AND INFORMATION

To legally enforce property rights, the owner must be able to show in court that those rights have in fact been violated. If John runs into Mary's car, the case is often fairly simple, and the parties may not even have to go to court. When John knows that Mary can prove him at fault and quantify the damages, he (or his insurance company) will simply compensate Mary for the damage done. (If John was insured, his rates will likely rise.) But, consider the case of Mr. Steel, the factory owner whose smoke fouls the air at Mary's home. Mary may have a right to clean air, which is violated by Mr. Steel's smoke. To receive compensation, however, she must be able to demonstrate in court: (a) the extent of the damage inflicted by the pollution, (b) that the pollutant in question actually caused the damage, and (c) that the pollutant came from Mr. Steel's plant. It is likely to be very costly, or even impossible, for her to do so. Her property rights, then, although defined, are probably not enforceable. They are useless, in effect, and external cost is the result.

The high cost (or the unavailability) of information can make property rights unenforceable, and bring about market failure. Unfortunately, the same lack of information may prevent governmental solutions from improving the situation. If we cannot estimate the consequences of certain actions, such as the emission of certain amounts of a pollutant at a specific time in a specific place, this lack of information will prevent any rational approach, private or public, to the problem.

COMMON PROPERTY RESOURCES AND EFFICIENCY

Common Property Resource: A resource for which rights are held in common by a group of individuals, none of whom has a transferable ownership interest. Access to the resource may be open (unrestricted), or may be controlled politically.

Open Access Resource: A resource to which access is unrestricted. No one has the right to exclude others from using the resource. Overuse and abuse of such a resource is typical.

Property rights are sometimes held in common. A **common property resource** is one for which rights are held in common by a group of individuals, none of whom has a transferable ownership interest. Access to a common property resource may be unrestricted, as in the case of air, or may be controlled politically, as wildlife is controlled by state governments in the United States.

If access to the resource is unrestricted, it is an **open access resource.** When there is more of it than people wish to use, then the open access resource is not scarce and there is no problem. However, trouble arises when such a resource becomes scarce. (See the Applications in Economics box, "The Importance of Common and Private Property Rights.") Without some form of political control to replace the ownership functions of controlling access and of caring for or maintaining the resource, external costs are almost guaranteed. For example, when water users are harmed by pollution, but cannot sue for damages, then external costs due to pollution are likely to occur. The polluter (who does not own the water) has no incentive to curtail his activities that cause pollution. Streams, like other resources, are much more likely to be abused when they are treated as open access resources. This, of course, is why we have environmental control agencies in government.

As we will see in more detail in the next chapter, political control of a common property resource, such as the air or a river, has its own problems. Typically, no one person or small, easily organized group has a large stake in seeing to it that decision-makers protect the resource and allocate its use efficiently. Would private ownership rights, then, be more efficient? Not necessarily. It is costly to establish and defend the property rights of certain resources.[2] Exclusive ownership can easily be defined and defended for such commodities as apples, cabbages, waterbeds, cars, and airline tickets, but how would one establish and defend property rights to salmon or whales, which travel thousands of miles each year? Sim-

[2]The problems entailed in defining and enforcing private, transferable property rights are discussed in Terry L. Anderson and P. J. Hill, "Privatizing the Commons: An Improvement?" *Southern Economic Journal,* vol. 50., no. 2 (October 1983).

ilarly, who owns an oil pool that is located on the property of hundreds of different landowners? In the absence of clearly assigned property rights, spillover costs and overutilization are inevitable. Certain whales have been on the verge of extinction because no single individual (or small group) has an incentive to reduce its own current catch so that the future catch will be larger. Each tries to catch as many whales as possible now; someone else will catch those whales, the argument goes, if the first person (or group) does not. The same principle applies to oil-pool rights when many well owners can draw from the pool and no single owner can control the rate of withdrawal. In the absence of regulation, each oil-well operator has an incentive to draw the oil *from a common pool* as rapidly as possible. When all operators do so, though, the commonly owned oil is drawn out too rapidly and the total amount that can be withdrawn falls.

EXTERNAL BENEFITS AND MISSED OPPORTUNITIES

Spillover effects are not always harmful. Sometimes the actions of an individual (or firm) generate external benefits; gains that accrue to nonparticipating (and nonpaying) secondary parties. When external benefits are present, the personal gains of the consenting parties understate the total social gain, including that of secondary parties. Activities with greater social benefits than costs may not be undertaken because no single decision-maker will be able to fully capture all the gains. Considering only personal net gains, decision-makers will allow potential social gains to go unrealized.

As in the case of external costs, external benefits occur when property rights are undefined or unenforceable. Because of this, it is costly—or impossible—to withhold these benefits from secondary parties and retain them for oneself at the same time. The producer of a motion picture has rights to the film and can collect a fee from anyone who sees or rents it. In contrast, a person who produces a beautifully landscaped lot that is visible from the street cannot collect a fee for the enjoyment that others derive from it. Some of the benefits of the landscaper's efforts accrue to secondary parties who probably will not help cover the cost.

Why should we be bothered if others benefit from our actions? Most of us are not, although it is quite possible, for example, that more people would better maintain their property if those who derived benefits from it helped pay for it. Generally, external benefits become important only when our inability to capture these potential gains forces us to *forgo* a socially beneficial activity. Exhibit 2 illustrates this point. Education adds to students' productivity, permitting them to attain higher future earnings. In addition, let us assume that those who receive at least a basic education may be better citizens, more competent voters, and may even commit fewer crimes. When some of the benefits of education accrue to the citizenry as a whole, not just to the students and their families, the private market demand curve understates the total social benefits of education. In the absence of government intervention, as shown in Exhibit 2, Q_1 units of education result from market forces. However, when external benefits MB are added to private benefits, the social gain from additional units of education exceeds the cost until output level Q_s is produced. The welfare of all in the community might thus be improved if output were expanded beyond Q_1 to Q_s, but since educational consumers cannot capture these external gains, they fail to purchase units beyond Q_1. The free market output is too small. A subsidy is required if the ideal output level Q_s is to be achieved.

When external benefits are present, the market demand curve understates the social gains of conducting the beneficial activity. Potential social gains go unreal-

APPLICATIONS IN ECONOMICS

The Importance of Common and Private Property Rights

What is common to many is taken least care of, for all men have greater regard for what is their own than for what they possess in common with others.[3]

Aristotle

The point made by Aristotle more than 2,000 years ago is as true now as it was then. It is as important in primitive cultures as it is in developed ones. When resources are held in common and access is unrestricted, the resource typically is abused and endangered. In contrast, when the rights are held by an individual (or family), conservation and wise utilization generally result. The following examples from sixteenth-century England, nineteenth-century American Indian culture, and ocean fisheries illustrate the point.

Cattle Grazing on the English Commons

Many English villages in the sixteenth century had commons, or commonly held pastures, which were available to any villagers who wanted to graze their animals. Since the benefits of grazing an additional animal accrued fully to the individual, whereas the cost of overgrazing was an external one, the pastures were grazed extensively. Since the pastures were communal property, there was little incentive for an *individual* to conserve grass in the present so that it would be more abundant in the future. When everyone used the pas-

ture extensively, there was not enough grass at the end of the grazing season to provide a good base for next year's growth. What was good for the individual was bad for the village as a whole. In order to preserve the grass, pastures were fenced in the enclosure movement. After the enclosure movement established private property rights, owners and managers saw to it that overgrazing no longer occurred.

The Property Rights of American Indians

Among American Indian tribes, common ownership of the hunting grounds was the general rule. Because the number of native Americans was small and their hunting technology was not highly developed, hunted animals seldom faced extinction. However, there were at least two exceptions.

One was the beaver hunted by the Montagnais Indians of the Labrador Peninsula. When the French fur traders came to the area in the early 1600s, the beaver increased in value and therefore became increasingly scarce. Recognizing the depletion of the beaver population and the animal's possible extinction, the Montagnais began to institute private property rights. Each beaver-trapping area on a stream was assigned to a family, and conservation practices were adopted. The last remaining pair of beavers was never trapped,

since the taker would only be hurting his own family the following year. For a time, the supply of beavers was no longer in jeopardy. However, when a new wave of European trappers invaded the area, the native Americans, because they were unable to enforce their property rights, abandoned conservation to take the pelts while they could.[4] Individual ownership was destroyed, and conservation disappeared with it.

The second animal that faced extinction was the communally owned buffalo. Once native Americans gained access to both the gun and the white man's market for hides, their incentive and ability to kill the buffalo increased. By 1840, Indians had emptied portions of the Great Plains of the area's large buffalo population.[5] In this case, the communal property problem could not be solved by the Indians. Unlike the beaver, the buffalo ranged widely over the Great Plains. Individual, family, and even

---

[3]Aristotle, as quoted by Will Durant in *The Life of Greece* (New York: Simon and Schuster, 1939), p. 536.

[4]For an economic analysis of the Montagnais management of the beaver, together with historical references, see Harold Demsetz, "Toward a Theory of Property Rights," *American Economic Review* (May 1967), pp. 347–359.

[5]This fascinating part of native American history has been recorded in Francis Haines, *The Buffalo* (New York: Crowell, 1970).

ized because no single decision-maker can fully appropriate or capture the gains; they are seen as "lost" when bestowed on nonpaying secondary parties. Decision-makers thus lack the incentive to carry an activity far enough to capture fully the potential social gains.

tribal rights were impossible to establish and enforce. Like oil in a common pool or the sperm whale on the high seas, buffalo were a "fugitive resource," the mobility of which made property rights (and therefore sound management) unattainable. Only the later fencing of the range solved the problem, after most buffalo herds had already been destroyed by both Indians and whites.

Property Rights and Ocean Fisheries

Once, the waters off the northeastern United States teemed with Atlantic Cod, haddock, flounder, and pollock—fish that many people love to eat, and many fishermen love to catch. But fish populations have fallen sharply in recent years due to overfishing, a problem for wild fisheries all over the world.[6] Wild fisheries of the oceans are open access resources. The only way to claim ownership of fish is to catch them. In addition, there is no individual incentive to leave some fish for next year's catch; other fisherman will probably catch them. Without an authority, such as an owner, in place to control access, the fish population faces possible extinction.

When demand for the fish is high, and new fishermen enter so that overfishing occurs, fishermen suffer losses. As the population of fish falls, costs rise because the sparser population of fish requires a more intensive effort to find them. The smaller catch may reduce supply enough to

raise the price of fish, but entry will occur until there is no profit, and if the population is falling, profit is likely to turn negative. Yet, in the short run, fishermen will continue to fish so long as they can cover their variable costs, keep the fishing pressure intense, and further reduce the number of fish and the available breeding stock.

Compare this open access fishery with one where the fish population or its territory is owned by a person or group who can control the rate of take, practicing conservation to protect next year's profits, which, after all, belong to the owner. We would expect that more conservation would be practiced, and overfishing would not occur, so that the income of fishermen would be higher. Richard J. Agnello and Lawrence P. Donnelley found just such results when they compared open access and private property oyster beds.[7] Using data from Maryland, Virginia, Louisiana, and Mississippi, they found that from 1945 to 1970 the ratio of harvest in the earlier part of the season to the later part was 1.35 for open access oyster beds and 1.01 for the private-property oyster bed. In the open access fishery, each fisherman tried to catch as many fish as quickly as possible, just as our logic predicts. Too much fishing effort was expended all season, relative to the more efficient allocation of fishing effort under the private property regime. Fishermen in the private-property state of Louisiana earned $3,207, while their

counterparts in the open access state of Mississippi earned $807. Such a finding supports the expectation of higher incomes and larger harvests over the years, under the private property regime. These and other findings of the study indicate that property rights, by solving the open access problem, help conserve a fishery resource and manage it more efficiently.

Could property rights be established for fisheries on the high seas? Such a scheme is not costless, and both federal and state governments have held that private rights violate antitrust laws. Informal unions of fishermen have tried to limit entry, but they have had limited success. Any agreement is difficult to maintain without an authority to enforce it.[8]

Don Leal, Research Associate, Political Economy Research Center Bozeman, Montana

[6]See Jennifer A. Kingston, "Northeast Fishermen Catch Everything, and That's a Problem," *The New York Times,* November 13, 1988.
[7]Richard J. Agnello and Lawrence P. Donnelley, "Prices and Property Rights in the Fisheries," *Southern Economic Journal,* XLII (October 1979), pp. 253–62.
[8]Ronald N. Johnson and Gary D. Libecap, "Contracting Problems and Regulation: The Case of the Fishery," *American Economic Review,* (December 1982), pp. 1,005–1,022.

EXHIBIT 2

Adding External Benefits

The demand curve D, indicating only private benefits, understates the social benefits of education. At output Q_1, the social benefit of an additional unit of education exceeds the cost. Ideally, output should be expanded to Q_s, where the social benefit of the marginal unit of education would be just equal to its cost. A public subsidy of AB, per unit of education, would lead to this output level.

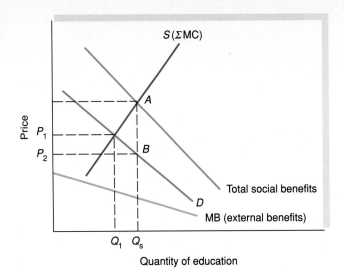

PUBLIC-SECTOR RESPONSES TO EXTERNALITIES

What can the government do to improve the efficiency of resource allocation when externalities are present? Sometimes private property rights can be more clearly defined and more strictly enforced. The granting of property rights to ranchers and homesteaders greatly improved the efficiency of land use in the Old West. More recently, the establishment of enforceable property rights to the oyster beds of the Chesapeake Bay improved the efficiency of oyster farming in the area. In many instances, however, it is difficult to delineate boundaries for a resource, determine who owns what portion, and enforce those rights. This is clearly the case with air and water rights. The clean-air rights of property owners often lack enforcement due to the high cost of information. In most states, water itself is not individually owned, although the right to use the water in certain ways may be privately held. Thus, the market process may fail to give good information and incentives to water users. External costs then result.

Why not simply prohibit activities that result in external cost? After all, why should we allow nonconsenting parties to be harmed? This approach has a certain appeal, but closer inspection indicates that it is often an unsatisfactory solution. Automobile exhaust imposes an external cost on bicyclists and, for that matter, on everyone who breathes. Dogs are notorious for using the neighbor's lawn for bone burying and relief purposes. Motorboats are noisy and frighten fish, much to the disgust of fishermen. Few people, though, would argue that we should do away with cars, dogs, and motorboats. From a social viewpoint, prohibition is often a less desirable alternative than tolerating the inconvenience of the external costs. The gains from the activity must be weighed against the costs imposed on those who are harmed, as well as against practical problems associated with controlling the activity.

When we cannot establish and enforce property rights, as in the case of our air resources, but we do not want simply to prohibit an activity, an alternative control strategy may be necessary. There are three general approaches that government might take. First, a government agency might act as a resource manager, charging the users of the resource a fee. Second, a regulatory agency might establish a maximum pollution emission standard and require that polluters attain at least that standard. Third, the agency might specify exactly what pollution control steps each polluter must take. We will consider each of these alternatives.

THE POLLUTION TAX APPROACH

Some economists favor a user's charge, which we will call a pollution tax. Exhibit 3 uses actual cost estimates from a copper smelter to illustrate the economics of this approach. The copper-producing firm has minimum costs of production when it spends nothing on pollution control. The marginal control cost curve reveals the cost savings (control costs avoided) that accrue to the firm when it pollutes. The marginal damage cost curve shows the cost ($32.50 per ton) imposed on parties downwind from the smelter. Without any tax or legal restraints, the smelter would emit 190,000 tons of sulfur dioxide into the air per year, causing $6.2 million in damage. A tax equal to the marginal damage cost of $32.50 per ton emitted would cause the firm to reduce its emissions to 17,100 tons per year and reduce pollution damage from $62 million to about $0.6 million per year. The control cost of reducing emissions to this level would be about $2.9 million per year. Total social costs each year would fall from $6.2 million (all borne by those suffering pollution damage) to $3.5 million (combined costs of pollution damage and control, paid entirely by the firm and its customers). The net social gain would be $2.7 million.

The tax approach would promote efficient resource allocation by altering several economic incentives in a highly desirable way. First, the pollution tax would increase the cost of producing pollution-intensive goods, causing the supply in these industries to decline. A properly set tax would approximate the ideal price and output conditions illustrated by Exhibit 1. The revenues generated by the tax

Taxing a Smelter's Emissions

The marginal control cost curve shows that the firm, if it pays no damage costs itself, will emit 190,000 tons per year while spending nothing on control costs. However, if taxed according to the marginal damages it imposes ($32.50 per ton), it will voluntarily cut back its emissions to 17,100 tons per year, which is the socially efficient level. Further control would cost more than its social benefit.

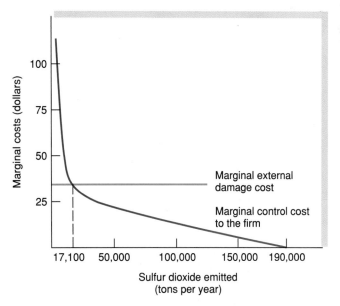

Source: Richard L. Stroup, "The Economics of Air Pollution Control" (Ph.D. diss., University of Washington, 1970).

could be used to compensate secondary parties harmed by the pollutants or to finance a wide range of projects, including applied research on alternative methods of improving air quality. Second, the pollution tax would give firms an economic incentive to use methods of production (and control technology) that would create less pollution. As long as it was cheaper for the firm to control harmful emissions than to pay the emission fee (tax), the firm would opt for control. Third, since firms would be able to lower their tax bills by controlling pollution, a market for innovative emission-control devices would exist. Entrepreneurs would be induced to develop low-cost control devices and market them to firms that would now have a strong incentive to reduce their levels of emissions.

The pollution tax is appealing, since it can, in theory, be efficient. But, it is seldom discussed seriously by policy-makers. There are three common objections: first, an efficient tax is one based on damage costs of the emissions. Without knowing what the damage costs are, an efficient tax cannot be stated or implemented. To determine the damage costs is difficult, yet any efficient control strategy an agency might choose will require a good estimate. This, then, is hardly a valid objection. A second objection is that an emission tax requires monitoring of the effluent. But, once again, any efficient strategy requires the agency to know what is being emitted, so this objection does not weaken the tax option relative to other strategies. A more telling objection is a political one: to switch from a situation in which the polluter does not pay any damages to one in which all (estimated) damages are paid to the tax collector by polluters would involve a huge wealth transfer. Whole industries would be shaken up, some of them dramatically. Some firms might be put out of business. Lobbyists for polluters have kept the tax strategy from being seriously considered by policy-makers.

Given the damage and control cost estimates of Exhibit 3, the pollution tax approach does not fully eliminate pollution emissions. Should it? Clearly, the answer is no. At pollution emission levels of less than 17,100 tons per year, the marginal costs of pollution control would exceed the marginal benefits of the control. In cases such as that illustrated by Exhibit 3, substantial improvement can be made at a modest cost. At some point, however, it will become extremely costly to make additional improvements.

The pollution tax approach recognizes that cleaning up the environment is like squeezing water from a wet towel. Initially, a great deal of water can be squeezed from the towel with very little effort, but it becomes increasingly difficult to squeeze out still more. So it is with the environment. At some point, the benefit of a cleaner environment simply becomes less than its cost.

People want clean air and water. However, since they want other things as well, those entrusted with the authority to control pollution should ask themselves two crucial questions: How many other goods and services are we willing to give up to fight each battle against pollution? And, how much would the public like us to spend, from its own pockets, to achieve additional freedom from pollution? Since we all want to obtain the maximum benefit from expenditures on pollution control, it is important that these questions be answered carefully, no matter which control strategy we adopt.

Maximum Emission Standard: The maximum amount of pollution that a polluter is permitted to emit, established by the government or a regulatory authority. Fines are generally imposed on those who are unwilling or unable to comply.

THE MAXIMUM EMISSION STANDARD APPROACH

Although economics suggests that the pollution tax approach would be much more efficient, a **maximum emission standard** is more often imposed. In this case, the regulatory agency forces all producers to reduce their emissions to a designated level. Producers who are unable to meet the standard are required to terminate production.

The problem with this approach is that the costs of eliminating pollution emissions generally vary widely among polluters. Some can control pollution much more cheaply than others, but the maximum emissions standard approach fails to use this fact to get more control per dollar of expenditure in control costs. It thus results in less efficient pollution control per dollar than, for example, the pollution tax strategy.

Exhibit 4 illustrates why the standard emissions approach is an inefficient method of reducing the pollution level. Estimated minimum costs of added control by three particulate pollution emitters are listed. Suppose the regulatory agency wants to reduce the total particulate emissions from the three firms by three tons. The emission standards approach might accomplish this simply by requiring each firm to reduce its particulate emissions by one ton. The cost of these equal reductions will differ substantially among the firms; it will cost the electric utility $80, the steel plant $990, and the petroleum refiner $573. If this method is adopted, it will cost society $1,643 in control cost to meet the new maximum pollution standard, which is three tons below the previous level of emissions.

Alternatively, the regulatory agency might levy a pollution tax and eliminate the same amount of pollution for much less. If we assume that a 3-ton reduction is small for each producer, so that each addition ton of pollution reduction raises

EXHIBIT 4

Controlling Pollution—
Cheaper For Some Than
for Others

Some polluters face much higher control costs than others. If the authorities' control strategy does not properly take this into account, control may be needlessly expensive and opposition to control needlessly strong. If each polluter were required to reduce particulate pollution by one ton, total control costs for that change would be $80 + $990 + $573 = $1,643. But, if a pollution tax of $82.50 were levied, the steel and petroleum plants would pay it, while the electric utility would find it cheaper to control some of its particulate pollution, and a reduction of 3 tons of emissions would cost roughly $240 instead of more than $1,640.

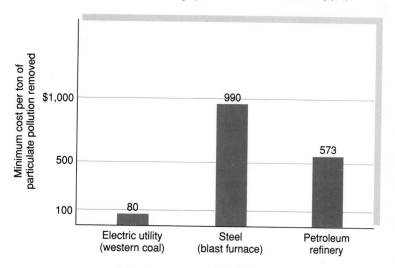

Source: EPA reports, summarized by Robert Crandall in *Controlling Industrial Pollution,* The Brookings Institution, Washington, D.C., 1983, (page 36).

control costs only by one dollar, then a tax of just $82.50 per ton would cause the electric utility to reduce particulate emissions by 3 tons, at a total cost of $243 ($80 + $81 + $82 = $243). That would allow the utility to escape 3 × $82.50 = $247.50 in added tax. The other polluters would not cut back emissions, but would choose to pay the tax, which is cheaper for them than the control costs. With the tax approach, which causes the cheapest control to take place, society buys the 3-ton reduction in pollution for $243, about one-seventh the cost incurred in the elimination of the same amount of pollution under the maximum emission control strategy.

TRANSFERABLE EMISSION RIGHTS

A much more efficient form of the maximum emission strategy is to require the same one-ton-per-firm reduction, but allow the remaining rights to pollute (their original pollution rate, minus one ton each) to be traded among the three. In this case, the electric utility would sell two tons of its rights-to-pollute, one to each of the other two firms. Why? It can profit by reducing its pollution by 3 tons for $243, then selling its "excess" pollution rights to the other two firms, saving the steel firm $990 and the refinery $573. The amount paid by the two firms to the utility for its service (added pollution control, beyond its own requirement) would be more than $80 per ton, but no higher than the $990 plus $573 saved by the other two. The net savings to society in getting the full 3-ton reduction in pollution is again the same as in the pollution tax case. The emission rights trading strategy also has an important political advantage: no large payments (or small ones either) would have to be made by the firms to the tax collector.

Since each polluter has a different control cost schedule, either the pollution tax strategy or the emission rights trading strategy would result in the most pollution control per control dollar spent, and reach any desired pollution level at the lowest possible price. Some people object to the emissions trading strategy because pollution emitted at one location may cause more damage or less damage than the same pollution at another place. This is true, but any efficient strategy would have to make adjustments to recognize this fact. The emissions trading strategy might allow polluters in densely populated areas to exchange their pollution rights with polluters in a sparsely populated area with a bonus. Two tons of pollution rights in Manhattan might trade for three tons on a sparsely populated part of the coast, where the winds usually blow the particulates out to sea with much less damage.

The emissions trading strategy is being seriously considered for adoption in many areas of the United States. One version of it, the "bubble concept," allows limited tradeoffs among pollution sources only within a plant or group of plants within a small area, for a single pollutant, holding total emissions constant within the plants. Rather than forcing each component of a single plant to meet the particulate emission standard, the bubble concept allows the plant manager to meet an overall emission standard within an imaginary bubble surrounding his or her plant. A highly restricted version of the bubble concept was instituted by the Environmental Protection Agency in 1979. In its 1984 annual report (released in February of 1986), the President's Council on Environmental Quality stated that by October of 1984, the EPA had approved 37 bubbles and proposed 9 others, for a total estimated saving of $200 million compared to the traditional control approach. Over half of the plants affected would reduce emissions by more than would be required under the traditional approach. Such sizable savings make this strategy seem worthy of further consideration!

**THE SPECIFIC
PRESCRIPTION
APPROACH**

We have shown how the emission standard approach (without emissions trading) is less efficient than the pollution tax. Even less efficient is the approach taken by Congress requiring the EPA to implement the Clean Air Act in the case of coal-burning electric power plants. Rather than set emission standards, Congress ordered the EPA to require that new plants use specific kinds of pollution control apparatus—giant ''scrubbers'' to clean exhaust gases from new coal-burning electric power plants. Even though cheaper and more reliable means are frequently available to produce electricity with the same or less pollution, especially the use of clean coal, the far more expensive scrubbers are required. This favors certain regions of the country over others, and delays the construction of newer, cleaner power plants, so that the air is dirtier than it would be with the cheaper control methods. As ironic and as well known as this situation is,[9] more efficient approaches have not proven to be politically feasible. For reasons that we will explore more fully in the next chapter, the government solution to market failure is often itself rather inefficient.

**SHOULD THE
GOVERNMENT ALWAYS
TRY TO CONTROL
EXTERNALITIES?**

When an externality is present, ideal efficiency of resource allocation may not be attained. It does not follow, though, that the government can always improve the situation and bring the economy closer to its ideal allocation level. In evaluating the case for a public-sector response to externalities, one should keep in mind the following three points.

1. *Sometimes the Economic Inefficiency Resulting from Externalities Is Small. Therefore, Given the Cost of Public-Sector Action, Net Gain from Intervention Is Unlikely.* The behavior of individuals often influences the welfare of others. The length of hair, choice of clothing, and personal hygiene of some individuals may affect the welfare of secondary parties. Should an agency in charge of personal appearance and hygiene be established to deal with externalities in these areas? Persons who value personal freedom would answer with a resounding no. From the standpoint of economic efficiency, their view is correct. The effects of externalities in these and similar areas are small. The costs of correcting externalities of this type would often be greater than the benefit.

Government intervention requires the use of scarce resources. Regulatory agencies must be established; suits and countersuits are typically filed. These actions require the use of scarce and costly legal resources. Most public-sector decision-makers lack the information necessary to determine which activities should be taxed and which should be subsidized. Administrative problems such as these greatly reduce the attractiveness of public-sector action. When the external effects are small, the cost of government intervention is likely to exceed the loss due to market inefficiency, *relative to the hypothetical ideal*. Under these circumstances, the best approach is usually to do nothing.

2. *The Market Often Finds a Reasonably Efficient Means of Dealing with Externalities.* The existence of externalities implies the presence of *potential* gain. If the external effects are significant, market participants have an incentive to organize economic activity in a manner that will enable them to capture the potential gain. If the number of parties affected by the externality is small, they may

---

[9]For fascinating accounts of the politics and economics of this situation, see Bruce A. Ackerman and William T. Hassler, *Clean Coal/Dirty Air* (New Haven: Yale University Press, 1981), and Robert Crandall, *Controlling Industrial Pollution: The Economics and Politics of Clean Air* (Washington, D.C.: The Brookings Institution, 1983).

be able to arrive at a multi-party bargain that will at least partially negate the inefficiency and loss resulting from the externality.

Some entrepreneurs have devised ingenious schemes to capture benefits that were previously external to private parties. Private developers of country clubs and golf courses can capture the benefits of these amenities by placing them on large tracts of land. The purchasers of lots and houses will benefit from trees, gardens, manicured lawns, and so on. If consumers are willing to pay for these amenities, as they often are, tract developers who provide such amenities will be able to benefit from their provision in the form of higher prices on the sale of surrounding lots.[10] The greater the potential gains, the greater the incentive to find answers to these kinds of problems. Thus, market participants will often devise efficient arrangements for dealing with external effects, when those effects become sufficiently large.

3. Government Action May Also Impose an External Cost on Secondary Parties. We have already mentioned that government intervention designed to correct the inefficiencies created by externalities is costly. Often, the costs of public-sector intervention exceed the benefits. Therefore, on efficiency grounds, intervention should be rejected. In addition, we should recognize that even democratic public-sector action results in the imposition of an externality—the majority imposes an external cost on the minority, which is opposed to the action. Just as an individual may carry an activity too far when some of the costs are borne by others, a majority may also carry an action beyond the point of ideal efficiency. The gains that accrue to the majority may be less than the costs imposed on the minority. So, even though the government can potentially take corrective measures, counterproductive economic action by the democratic majority may result if the external costs imposed on the minority are not fully considered. (Limits to the effectiveness of government action will be discussed more fully in the next chapter.)

MARKET FAILURE: PUBLIC GOODS

Public goods comprise the extreme case of commodities, the consumption of which results in spillover benefits to secondary parties. In the original formulation by Paul Samuelson, there are two distinctive characteristics of public goods. First, the availability of a public good to one person makes it equally available to all others. Public goods must therefore be consumed jointly by all. Second, because of this joint consumption, it may be impossible to exclude nonpayers from the

[10]The development of Walt Disney World in Florida is an interesting case in which entrepreneurial ingenuity made it possible to capture external benefits more fully. When Walt Disney developed Disneyland in California, the market value of land in the immediate area soared as a result of the increase in demand for services (food, lodging, gasoline, and so on). Since the land in the area was owned by others, the developers of Disneyland were unable to capture these external benefits. However, when Walt Disney World was developed near Orlando, Florida, the owners purchased an enormous plot of land, far more than was needed for the amusement park. As was the case with Disneyland in California, the operation of Walt Disney World caused land values in the immediate area to rise sharply. However, since the developers of Walt Disney World initially purchased a large amount of land near the attraction, they were able to capture the external benefits by selling prime property to hotels, restaurants, and other businesses desiring a nearby location.

APPLICATIONS IN ECONOMICS

Private Provision of Public Goods

An excellent example of a public good is the preservation of a locally or nationally significant form of wildlife. Hawks, sea lions, and wild geese belong to no one, but their survival keeps ecosystems in balance and intact. We all benefit when habitats are kept available to ensure that such species do not become extinct. Despite the fact that each of us can be a free rider if others make the effort and sacrifice needed to bring about such preservation, successful voluntary efforts in the private sector have done just that: thousands of organizations, each defying the free rider problem, have for many decades led the conservation movement, privately establishing successful conservation projects.

Some of these groups are very large. The Nature Conservancy owns and manages a national system of nearly 800 sanctuaries and has preserved some 2.4 million acres since 1951. The 1984 Annual Report of the President's Council of Environmental Quality reports that the National Audubon Society has a sanctuary system of over 63 units totalling over 250,000 acres. Others are small—a local garden club might own and manage two acres to preserve a particular wild flower.

Private groupings have often been leaders in educating the public, and have been well ahead of government in providing their particular public good. Two examples involve hawks and sea lions.

Example 1: The Hawk Mountain Sanctuary

In the 1930s, hawks were considered a nuisance or worse, since they killed certain other birds, including domestic chickens. There was often a bounty on them—the government would pay people who killed hawks. Conservationists, however, had begun to worry about the declining numbers of hawks, pointing out that among other things, hawks ate rodents, keeping down the grain losses experienced by farmers. The environmental movement was still very weak, however, and the slaughter of hawks continued.

In one area in particular, Hawk Mountain of eastern Pennsylvania, thousands of hawks were killed on certain days each year. So upset was Rosalie Edge, an early conservationist (and leading suffragist) that when reasoning with governmental authorities failed, she organized a small group of conservationists who simply bought Hawk Mountain for $3,500. They prevented further shooting from that critical spot, and established a nonprofit educational and conservation group—the Hawk Mountain Sanctuary Association. Seven thousand members from all over the nation, in addition to admission fees paid by 50,000 visitors per year, support a visitor and education center at the mountain where previously the hawks were slaughtered by the thousands each year.

Example 2: Sea Lion Caves, Inc.

Like hawks, sea lions on the Oregon coast were formerly hunted, and bounties were paid to those who killed them. Sea lions feed on fish, and during the 1920s the state of Oregon paid $5 per sea lion killed. Several bounty hunters made their living in this fashion. The intent was to reduce sea lion consumption of coastal salmon. Earlier, commercial fishing interests hired professional hunters to exterminate the sea lion. However, one important area of the sea lion's Oregon habitat was privately owned and used as a tourist attraction—Sea Lion Caves, where the animals could be viewed up close, in a natural setting. The owners of the caves had to spend a good deal of time driving off bounty hunters. By 1931, conservation legislation was passed to protect sea lions in most areas of the Oregon coast. Nevertheless, while the extermination pressure was on, the profit-seeking Sea Lion Cave operation had played an important part in the survival of the sea-going mammals. The sea lions themselves are not owned, and their survival is largely a public good. But, private ownership of the habitat had concentrated enough of the benefits in the hands of a tourist-based business to help guarantee the survival of the endangered animals at a critical time.

Can private clubs and businesses eliminate the public goods problem? Not necessarily, since there is no guarantee that the optimal amount of public goods will be provided. The problem continues to exist and to be an important source of market failure. However, these private-sector philanthropic and entrepreneurial solutions to certain public goods problems do remind us that whenever the will exists to solve such problems, government action is not the only possible way. The same sort of informed and determined efforts needed to convince government to do the right thing can frequently find private solutions more quickly and cheaply.

receipt of public goods. It is important to note that only goods with these two characteristics qualify as public goods in an economic sense. Goods provided by the public sector, ranging from food and medical services to education, are *not* necessarily public goods. Examples of *pure* public goods are rare. National defense is one. The defense system that protects you provides similar protection to all other citizens. The quality of the atmosphere might also be classified as a public good.

THE FREE RIDER PROBLEM

Free Rider: One who receives the benefit of a good without contributing to its costs. Public goods and commodities that generate external benefits offer people the opportunity to become free riders.

Since nonpaying consumers cannot be excluded (at a reasonable cost), a sufficient amount of public goods may not be provided by the market mechanism. If public goods were provided through the market, each of us would have an incentive to become a free rider, one who receives the benefits of a good without paying toward its costs. Why contribute to the cost of supplying a public good? Your actions will have a negligible impact on the supply of clean air, pure water, national defense, and legal justice. The sensible path will lead you to do nothing. As long as you travel that path alone, you will ride along, free and easy. If everyone else joins you, however, the aggregate lack of action will lead to an insufficient quantity of public goods.

Suppose national defense were provided entirely through the market. Would you voluntarily help to pay for it? Your contribution would have a negligible impact on the total supply of defense available to each of us, even if you made a *large personal* contribution. Many citizens, even though they might value defense highly, would become free riders, and few funds would be available to finance the necessary supply. If the military-industrial complex were dependent on market forces, it would be small indeed!

The harmony between private and social interests tends to break down for public goods. The amount of a public good available to an individual (and others) will be virtually unaltered by whether or not the individual pays for it. Each individual thus has an incentive to become a free rider. When numerous individuals become free riders, however, less than the ideal amount of the public good is likely to be produced.

NEAR PUBLIC GOODS

Few commodities are pure public goods, but a much larger set of goods are jointly consumed even though nonpaying customers can be excluded. For example, such goods as radio and television broadcasts, national parks, interstate highways, movies, and football games may be jointly consumed. Until congestion sets in, additional consumption of these "near public goods," *once they are produced,* is costless to society.

Should nonpaying customers be excluded when the marginal cost of providing the good to them is zero? Many economists argue that such near public goods as highways, national parks, and television programming should be provided free to consumers, at the expense of the taxpayer. Why exclude people from the consumption of these near public goods when their use of the goods does not add to the costs? The argument has a certain appeal.

We must be careful, however. Television programs, highways, parks, and other public goods are scarce. The consumption of other products must be sacrificed to produce such goods. If a zero price is charged, how does one determine whether or not consumers value additional units enough to cover their opportunity cost? How can an intensely concerned minority communicate its views as to the types of near public goods that should be produced? Taxes will be necessary to cover the costs of making near public goods freely available. Will such taxes lead to inefficiency? These factors reduce the attractiveness of public-sector provision of jointly consumed commodities when exclusion of nonpaying consumers is possible.

MARKET FAILURE: POOR INFORMATION

In the real world, market choices, like other decisions, are made with incomplete information. Consumers do not not have perfect knowledge about the quality of a product, the price of alternative products, or side effects that may result from a product. They may make incorrect decisions, decisions they will later regret, because they do not possess good information.

The reality of imperfect knowledge is not, of course, the fault of the market. In fact, the market provides consumers with a strong incentive to acquire information, and producers providing consumers with the best deal with an incentive to advertise that fact. Because consumers must bear the consequences of their mistakes, they certainly will seek to avoid the deliberate purchase of ''lemon'' products.

GETTING YOUR MONEY'S WORTH

Repeat-Purchase Item: An item purchased often by the same buyer.

The consumer's information problem is minimal if the item is purchased regularly. Consider the problem of purchasing a brand of soap. There is little cost associated with trying out brands. Since soap is a regularly purchased product, trial-and-error is an economical means of determining which brand is most suitable to one's needs. It is a **repeat-purchase item.** The consumer can use past experience to good advantage when buying repeat-purchase items such as soap, toothpaste, most food products, lawn service, and gasoline.

What incentive does the producer have to supply accurate information that will help the customer make a satisfying long-run choice? Is there a conflict between consumer and producer interests? The answers to these questions are critically affected by the seller's dependence on return customers.

If dissatisfaction on the part of *current* customers is expected to have a strong adverse effect on *future* sales, a business entrepreneur will attempt to provide accurate information to help customers make wise choices. The future success of business entrepreneurs who sell repeat-purchase products is highly dependent on the future purchases of currently satisfied customers. There is a harmony of interest because buyer and seller alike will be better off if the customer is satisfied with the product purchased.

LET THE BUYER BEWARE

Major problems of conflicting interests, inadequate information, and unhappy customers arise when goods either (a) are difficult to evaluate on inspection and are seldom repeatedly purchased from the same producer or (b) are potentially capable of serious and lasting harmful side effects that cannot be detected by a layperson. Under these conditions, human nature being what it is, we would expect some unscrupulous producers to sell low-quality, defective, and even harmful goods.

When customers are unable to distinguish between high-quality and low-quality goods, their ability to police quality and price is weakened. When this is the case, business entrepreneurs have a strong incentive to cut costs by reducing quality. Consumers get less for their dollars. Since sellers are not dependent on repeat customers, they may survive and even prosper in the marketplace. The probability of customer dissatisfaction is thus increased because of inadequate information and poor quality. Accordingly, the case for an unhampered market mechanism is weakened.

Consider the consumer's information problem when an automobile is purchased. Are most consumers capable of properly evaluating the safety equipment? Except for a handful of experts, most people are not. Some consumers might individually seek expert advice. It may be more efficient, though, to prevent market failure by having the government regulate automobile safety and require certain safety equipment.

As another example of the problem of inadequate consumer information, consider the case of a drug manufacturer's exaggerated claims for a new product. Until consumers have had experience with the drug or have listened to others' experiences, they might make wasteful purchases. Government regulation might benefit consumers by forcing the manufacturer to modify its claims.

ENTREPRENEURS AND INFORMATION

Consumers have the incentive to seek good information, but that can be very expensive. Entrepreneurial sellers, when they are in fact providing good value, have an incentive to bridge the information gap, and to let consumers know it. How? Expert evaluations are one way that consumers can learn about the special characteristics built into complex products. For car buyers and computer buyers, for example, publishers market dozens of specialized magazines containing expert analyses and opinions from almost any point of view. Laboratory test results are provided by consumer organizations on a wide variety of goods available nationwide.

Franchises are another way that entrepreneurs have responded to the consumer need for more information, as we pointed out in Chapter 2. The tourist traveling through an area for the first time—and very possibly the last—may find that eating at a franchised food outlet and sleeping at a franchised motel is the cheapest way to avoid annoying and costly mistakes. The franchiser sets the standards for all firms in the chain and establishes procedures, including continuous inspection, designed to maintain the standards. Franchisers have a strong incentive to maintain their reputation for quality, because if it declines, their ability to sell new franchises is hurt. Even though the tourist may visit a particular establishment only once, the franchise turns that visit into a "repeat purchase," since the reputation of the entire national franchise operation is at stake.

Similarly, the advertising of a brand name nationally develops a reputation that is at stake when purchases are made. How much would the Coca Cola Company pay to avoid a dangerous bottle of Coke being sold? Surely, it would be a large sum. The company's reputation is a hostage to quality control. Advertising investments act as a signal that the firm is serious about its future business, and has something important to lose if it cheats customers.

Johnson & Johnson's experience with Tylenol capsules is a concrete example of how far a company is willing to go to protect a brand name. In 1982, seven people died as a result of taking Tylenol capsules that had been laced with cyanide. Even though Johnson & Johnson, the producer of the capsules, was not at fault, the company spent at least $60 million to recall 31 million bottles of Tylenol, provide consumers and retailers with refunds, and introduce a new triplesealed bottle of Tylenol. Although Tylenol's share of the market dropped to below 7 percent immediately following the tragedy, by 1984, its share was almost as high as the 35 percent it had before the deaths occurred, according to *Business Week* magazine.

In early 1986, though, Johnson & Johnson faced a replay of the situation when a woman died from taking cyanide-laced capsules. This time the company decided to stop making Tylenol capsules, because it was unable to ensure their safety. It recalled existing bottles of Tylenol capsules and offered to replace them with more tamper-resistant Tylenol ''caplets.'' *The New York Times* estimated that this move to protect the reputation of Tylenol would cost Johnson & Johnson $100 million to $150 million.

As this example indicates, entrepreneurial measures such as assuring the quality of a franchiser or protecting a brand name can be expensive. They cannot, however, guarantee that customers will never be cheated or disappointed after a transaction. Despite the best efforts of entrepreneurs, the lack of consumer information will continue to assure that the market will remain imperfect relative to the economists' ideal, and that government will have a potential role to play in improving on the market's results.

ONE-SIDED INFORMATION

Asymmetric Information Problem: A problem arising when either buyers or sellers have important information about the product that is not possessed by the other side in potential transactions.

As useful and important as the published evaluations of experts, franchise operations, advertising and brand-name reputations are, they cannot solve a kind of information problem that has little to do with product design or manufacture. This is called the **asymmetric information problem,** and it can make markets themselves, for some products, difficult to operate effectively. The problem arises when either the potential buyer or potential seller has important information, but the other side does not have the same information.

Think for a moment about buyers trying to avoid ''lemons'' in the used car market. Sellers know which cars are above average quality and which are below average. Buyers on the other hand, cannot tell which is which simply by looking at and test-driving them. Thus buyers will be willing to pay no more than the average value of all cars they believe to be offered in the market. But if better-than-average cars cannot bring better-than-average prices, then fewer of them will be sold in the market, and if below-average cars bring average prices, then more of the below-average cars will be offered. Buyers understand this, so the average car they expect in such a market will be below the average of all existing cars of that age and type. Owners of better cars will be more reluctant to sell at the low market price. It will be hard to make a market for above-average quality cars, when buyers are not able to get good information about which cars are actually better.

Can anything be done to reduce this kind of asymmetric information problem? Even though the approaches listed above are aimed at large markets and have little value, we still can answer in the affirmative. Of course, sellers of the better used cars have an incentive to provide additional information in order to get a higher price for their superior goods. But how is this done? Who will believe their claims about their product being better? Car owners can support their claims in several ways. Some will keep their records of oil changes and lubrications, to show that these services, important to the long-run durability of a car, have actually been performed on schedule. Used car dealers whose mechanics inspect the cars before they are offered for sale, may offer money-back guarantees, or warranties that promise free repairs if needed within a specified time, on the most reliable cars they sell. The other cars they sell will be sold "as is" with no warranty. Sellers of products can even give price guarantees, as some stores do when they advertise that if the buyer finds a lower price for the same product within a specified period of time, the seller will refund the difference. By offering to bear such risks, sellers provide credibility to their claims about better products and prices. This gives information to buyers and provides some assurance that they will not later regard their purchase as a "lemon."

The problem of asymmetric information also arises when buyers know more than sellers. Consider the market for health insurance. If buyers know their own health problems better than insurance companies, then the one-price insurance offered will be most attractive to buyers with the greatest expected health problems. The buyers whose health history and life styles indicate greater potential health costs will pay the same, but later collect more from the insurance company. In contrast, the same insurance at the same price is less attractive to the healthiest people, and fewer of them will buy. When the company is unable to identify those with the greatest potential health costs and charge them more, it will have to charge their healthier customers a rate that exceeds their expected future insurance claims. But this would drive away even more of the healthier potential buyers, making the situation even worse. As in the case of used cars, asymmetric information reduces the effectiveness of the market. Just as the best used cars may be hard to sell, so, too, may the healthiest individuals be hard to insure when asymmetric information is present.

What can be done about asymmetric information when buyers have information, but sellers do not? Buyers, too, are willing to provide information to sellers, when it is to their advantage to do so. In the case of insurance buyers, those buyers with the best health record who are therefore least likely to have future insurance claims, can often get lower insurance rates by opening their private medical records to the insurance company. Sellers who otherwise have no right to see that information may find it gladly offered—at least by the healthiest buyers—when buyers with better records are offered lower insurance prices.

Another strategy sellers use to deal with the insurance problem is to offer "bundle purchases." Knowing that some employees in any sizeable firm are likely to have good health, and some bad health, insurance companies find it economical to offer a "group rate" policy, covering all the employees of the firm. By screening out only the easily identified bad risks, so that it can save the cost of carefully screening every employee's medical history, it can offer moderate rates.

We have discussed many ways in which market participants can reduce the problems they face due to the scarcity and cost of information. These are not totally effective, however, and poor information remains a problem that keeps markets from reaching their hypothetical ideal.

LOOKING AHEAD

In this chapter, we focused on the failures of the market. In the next chapter, we will use economic analysis to come to a better understanding of the workings of the public sector. We will also discuss some of the expected shortcomings of public-sector action. Awareness of both the strengths and weaknesses of alternative forms of economic organization will help us to make more intelligent choices in this important area.

CHAPTER SUMMARY

1. The sources of market failure can be grouped into four major categories: (a) externalities, (b) public goods, (c) poor information, and (d) monopoly.

2. When externalities are present, the market may fail to confront decision-makers with the proper incentives. Since decision-makers are not forced to consider external cost, they may find it personally advantageous to undertake an economic activity even though it generates a net loss to the community. In contrast, when external benefits are present, decision-makers may fail to undertake economic action that would generate a net social gain.

3. When external costs originate from the activities of a business firm, the firm's costs will understate the social cost of producing the good. If production of the good generates external costs, the price of the product under competitive conditions will be too low and the output too large to meet the *ideal requirements* of economic efficiency.

4. External costs result from the failure or inability of a society to establish private property rights. Clearly established private property rights enable owners to prohibit others from using or abusing their property. In contrast, common property rights with open access normally result in overutilization, since most of the cost of overutilization (and misuse) is imposed on others.

5. When external benefits are present, the market demand curve will understate the social gains of conducting the activity. The consumption and production of goods that generate external benefits will tend to be lower than the socially ideal levels.

6. The efficient use of air and water resources is particularly troublesome for the market because it is often impossible to apportion these resources and determine ownership rights. A system of emission charges or of transferable emission rights can induce individuals to make wiser use of these resources. Emission charges (a) increase the cost of producing pollution-intensive goods, (b) grant firms an incentive to use methods of production that create less pollution, and (c) provide producers with an incentive to adopt control devices when it is economical to do so.

7. When the marginal benefits (for example, cleaner air) derived from ending pollution are less than the social gains associated with a pollution-generating activity, prohibition of the activity that results in pollution (or other external cost) is not an ideal solution.

8. When the control costs of firms vary, the emission charge (pollution tax) approach will permit society to reduce pollution by a given amount at a lower cost than will the maximum emission standard method, which is currently widely used. The marginal cost of attaining a cleaner environment will rise as the pollution level is reduced. At some point, the economic benefits of a still cleaner environment will be less than the costs.

9. In evaluating the case for government intervention in situations involving externalities, one must consider the following factors: (a) the magnitude of the external effects relative to the cost of government action; (b) the ability of the market to devise means of dealing with the problem without intervention; and (c) the possibility that the political majority may carry the government intervention too far if the external costs imposed on the minority are not fully considered.

10. When it is costly or impossible to withhold a public good from persons who do not or will not help pay for it, the market system breaks down because everyone has an incentive to become a free rider. When everyone attempts to ride for free, production of the public good will be lower than the socially ideal level.

11. The market provides an incentive for buyers and sellers to acquire information. When a business is dependent on repeat customers, it has a strong incentive to promote customer satisfaction. However, when goods are either (a) difficult to evaluate on

inspection and seldom purchased repeatedly from the same producer or (b) have potentially serious and lasting harmful effects, consumer trial and error may be an unsatisfactory means of determining quality. Franchising and brand names often communicate reliable information on product quality to consumers and thereby reduce the likelihood that consumers will be cheated or misled, even in cases when the specific item is not purchased regularly. Asymmetric information provides an additional challenge to market participants.

CRITICAL ANALYSIS QUESTIONS

*1. When cattle grazed on the English commons—open access pastures—overgrazing took place. Eventually, many of the pastures became private property. What other option might have solved the open access problem?

2. Why might businesses operating currently, and causing pollution problems, prefer transferable emission rights to the pollution tax approach? When would they not have such a preference?

3. "Elementary education is obviously a public good. After all, it is provided by government." Evaluate.

*4. Why is it difficult to determine the proper output of a pure public good?

5. "Since free riders can enjoy public goods, there is no way that they will be provided privately." Evaluate.

*6. Are people more likely to take better care of an item they own jointly (communally) or one they own privately? Why? Does the presence of private property rights affect the behavior of persons in noncapitalist nations? Why or why not?

*7. **What's Wrong with This Way of Thinking?**
"Corporations are the major beneficiaries of our lax pollution control policy. Their costs are reduced because we permit them free use of valuable resources—clean water and air—in order to produce goods. These lower costs are simply added to the profits of the polluting firms."

8. **What's Wrong with This Way of Thinking?**
"Private property rights are a gamble. What if the owner doesn't take good care of what he owns? Communal property rights are better—there are more people to take care of what they own. Surely someone will exercise the needed care." (Hint: What was Aristotle's position on the issue?)

*9. Can you think of any public goods, or near public goods, that are supplied privately? Do such examples show that there is no such thing as a free rider problem?

*10. What factor limits the private supply of public goods?

*11. "Corporations in America are being persecuted unfairly by environmental legislation such as air pollution control laws. Corporate leadership is responsible and would work for cleaner air without all this legal hassle." Evaluate, using the economic way of thinking.

*12. In a small town located next to an interstate highway are two prospering family restaurants. Both are locally owned, but one is franchised, a part of a nationally advertised chain of such restaurants. The other does not advertise. Assuming that highway travelers and local residents have seen equal amounts of advertising from the chain, in which restaurant would you expect to find more highway travelers? Why?

13. Many consumers are willing to pay more for brand-name products (for example, Bayer aspirin or Minutemaid orange juice) than for generic versions of the same products. Is this irrational? Do consumers get anything for their additional expense? Explain.

---

*Asterisk denotes questions for which answers are given in Appendix C, Selected Answers.

19

PUBLIC CHOICE: UNDERSTANDING GOVERNMENT AND GOVERNMENT FAILURE

We no longer expect results from government. What was a torrid romance between the people and government for so long has now become a tired middle-aged liaison which we do not quite know how to break off.[1]

Peter Drucker

CHAPTER FOCUS

■ What are the major forces that determine outcomes under representative democracy?

■ Can government action be mutually advantageous to all citizens? Does it sometimes reduce the economic welfare of citizens?

■ Will government action sometimes be more efficient than market exchange? When is it likely to be less efficient?

■ Why does representative democracy often tax some people in order to provide benefits to others? What types of income transfers are attractive to politicians?

■ Can constitutional rules influence political outcomes? What types of constitutional rules and restraints make sense?

About two-fifths of U.S. national income is channeled through the various governmental departments and agencies. More than a third of the nation's land is owned by government, and the legal framework set by government establishes many of the "rules of the game" for the market sector. Government regulation of prices, of the use of land, water, and air, along with labor relations and business practices, exert a major impact on the operation of the economy. Given the size and influence of government, understanding how the political process works is a crucial issue.

During the last three decades, public choice economists have enhanced our knowledge of democratic politics. Public choice theory indicates that there are two general forces underlying political action: (a) the correction of market failure and (b) rent seeking—the pursuit of private gain at public expense. Citizens can reap gains from government action that reduces market inefficiency emanating from externalities, public goods, an absence of competition, and poor information. However, the political process is merely an alternative form of economic organization, not an automatic corrective device. It is not a pinch-hitter we can count on to supply a base hit whenever we fear the market might strike out.

As with markets, there are categories of activity that economic theory indicates even democratic governments will do poorly. As we discussed briefly in Chapter 4, there is government failure, as well as market failure. **Government failure** is present when the political process leads to economic inefficiency and the waste of scarce resources.

Public policy reflects the political decision-making rules and constitutional restraints of a society. Public choice theory enhances our knowledge of how alternative forms of political organization work and provides us with insight on how we might better design the rules of politics. As we proceed in this chapter, we will consider this issue. Most political decisions in Western countries are made legislatively. Therefore, we will focus our analysis on a democratic system of representative government. Let us see what the tools of economics reveal about the political process.

Government Failure: Failure of government action to meet the criteria of ideal economic efficiency.

REPRESENTATIVE DEMOCRACY

In modern democratic countries, voters elect representatives to direct the actions of governments. In turn, the representatives establish agencies and hire bureaucrats to conduct the day-to-day government affairs. Voters, politicians, and bureaucrats are the major players in the democratic political process. Under representative democracy, government action is the result of a complex set of interrelationships among the members of these three groups. Like consumers in the market, voters use their electoral support, money, and other political resources to express their demand for legislation. Like business entrepreneurs, politicians are suppliers: they design and shape legislation. Finally, just as managers and employers are assigned the details of the production process in the market, bureaucrats perform this task in the public sector.[2]

[1]Peter F. Drucker, "The Sickness of Government," *Public Interest* (Winter 1969), p. 5.
[2]For a more comprehensive view of public choice theory and the operation of democratic governments, see James Gwartney and Richard Wagner (ed.), *Public Choice and Constitutional Economics* (Greenwich: JAI Press, 1988). Our analysis borrows from this work.

Economists use the self-interest postulate to enhance our understanding of consumer behavior, business decision-making, and resource supply decisions. Likewise, public choice economists apply the self-interest postulate to political decision-making. They assume that, just as people are motivated by personal wealth, power, and prestige in the market sector, so, too, will these factors influence them when they make decisions in the political arena.

Closely related to self-interest as a motivator for politicians and bureaucrats are the concepts of survival and expansion. In the private sector, even if there are some managers not primarily seeking profits, it will be the profit-making firms which are most likely to survive, expand, and be imitated. Similarly in the public sector, politicians and the bureaucrats they hire must often act in the narrow self-interest of their constituents (and thus in their own career self-interests) if they hope to survive. Those who cooperate most closely with powerful constituency groups will tend to survive, to obtain more political clout, and to lead larger government agencies.

THE VOTER-CONSUMER

How do voters decide whom to support? No doubt, many factors influence their decisions. Which candidate is the most persuasive, and which presents the best television image? Who appears to be honest, sincere, and effective? However, the self-interest postulate indicates that voters, like market consumers will ask, "What can you do for me, and how much will it cost?" The greater the voter's perceived net personal gain from a particular candidate's platform, the more likely it is that the voter will favor that candidate. In contrast, the greater the perceived net economic cost imposed on the voter by the positions of a candidate, the less inclined the voter will be to support the candidate. Other things equal, voters will tend to support those candidates whom they believe will provide them the most political goods, services, and transfer benefits, net of personal costs.

As we discussed in Chapter 4, when decisions are made collectively, the direct link between the individual voter's choice and the outcome of the issue is broken. The choice of a single voter is seldom decisive when the decision-making group is large. Recognizing that the outcome will not depend on one vote, the individual voter has little incentive to seek information (which is costly) on issues and candidates in order to cast a more informed vote. Economists refer to this phenomenon as the "rational ignorance effect" (see Chapter 4, pp. 94–95).[3]

The rational ignorance effect explains why few voters are able to accurately identify their congressional representatives, much less identify and understand their position on issues such as minimum wage legislation, tariffs, and agricultural price supports. The fact that voters acquire scanty information merely indicates that they are responding rationally to economic incentives.

It is interesting to compare the incentive of both consumers and voters to choose wisely. The consumer who makes a poor choice—for example by purchasing a product that does not work well—must bear the consequences. Thus, each consumer has a strong incentive to acquire information, choose wisely, and search for quality goods that are attractively priced. In contrast, there is little incentive for voters to be concerned about the quality of their choices of candidates. Even if informed about the candidates, individual voters will exert little

---

[3]The concept of rational ignorance among voters was initially developed by Anthony Downs. See Downs, *An Economic Theory of Democracy* (New York: Harper & Row, 1957).

impact on the outcome of congressional elections. Whether mistaken or not, there is only a minuscule chance that an individual voter's decision will decide the election. Therefore, it makes no sense for the voter to "waste" time and effort making a careful choice. Given this incentive structure, there is reason to believe that the choices of consumers will be better informed and more carefully made than those of voters. (See Applications in Economics box, "Why General Motors Receives Better Signals Than Congress.")

The fact that one's vote is unlikely to be decisive explains more than lack of information on the part of voters. It also helps to explain why many citizens fail to vote. Even when there is a presidential election, only about half of all voting-age Americans take the time to register and vote. Given the low probability that one's vote will be decisive, this low voter turnout should not be surprising. The rationality of voters is further indicated by the fact that when voters perceive that the election is close, voter turnout is larger.[4] A vote in a close election has a greater chance of actually making a difference.

THE POLITICIAN-SUPPLIER

Public choice theory postulates that pursuit of votes is the primary stimulus shaping the behavior of political suppliers. In varying degrees, such factors as pursuit of the public interest, compassion for the poor, and the achievement of fame, wealth, and power may influence the behavior of politicians. But regardless of ultimate motivation, the ability of politicians to achieve their objectives is sorely dependent upon their ability to get elected and reelected. Just as profits are the lifeblood of the market entrepreneur, votes are the lifeblood of the politician.

Rationally uninformed voters often must be convinced to "want" a candidate. Voter perceptions may be based on realities, but it is always perceptions, not the realities themselves, that influence decisions. This is true regardless of whether the decisions are private or political. As a result, a candidate's positive attributes must be brought to the attention of the rationally ignorant voter, who may well be more interested in the local sports teams (which are probably more entertaining) than in seeking out detailed knowledge about the attributes of the various candidates. An expert staff, polls to ferret out which issues and which positions will be favored by voters, high quality advertising to present the candidate's image and favored positions, and other forms of political resources are of great value in politics. But they are also costly, as the following data from the 1988 elections indicate. A winning campaign for Congress in 1988 averaged over $300,000 in the House of Representatives and several million dollars in the Senate. In California, Senator Pete Wilson spent over $13 million in his successful bid for reelection. The total cost of nominating and electing a president, including primary campaigns and national conventions, totaled an estimated $500 million.[5] Thus money is a power source in politics.

Are we implying that politicians are selfish; that they consider only their own pocketbooks and ignore the public interest? The answer is no. When people act in the political sphere, they may genuinely want to help their fellow citizens. Factors

---

[4]This and other results consistent with the rational actions of voters can be found in Yoram Barzel and Eugene Silberberg, "Is the Act of Voting Rational?" *Public Choice,* vol. XVI (Fall 1973), pp. 51–58.

[5]Milton C. Cummings, Jr., and David Wise, *Democracy Under Pressure,* 6th edition (San Diego: Harcourt Brace Jovanovich, 1989), p. 332.

other than personal political gain, narrowly defined, influence the actions of many political suppliers. On certain issues, one may feel strongly that one's position is best for the nation, even though it may not be currently popular. The national interest as perceived by the political supplier may conflict with the position that would be most favorable to reelection prospects. Some politicians may opt for the national interest even when it means political defeat. None of this is inconsistent with an economic view of political choice.

However, the existence of political suicide does not change the fact that most politicians prefer political survival. There is a strong incentive for political suppliers to stake out positions that will increase their vote total in the next election. In fact, competition more or less forces politicians to make decisions in light of political considerations.

If a politician refuses to support policies that are vote-getters, perhaps because he or she thinks the policies are counterproductive or morally wrong, then he or she runs an increased risk of being replaced by a competitor who pays closer attention to the acquisition of votes. Just as neglect of economic profit is the route to market oblivion, neglect of potential votes is the route to political oblivion.

APPLICATIONS IN ECONOMICS

Why General Motors Receives Better Signals Than Congress

Most Americans are frustrated in their dealings with large, centralized organizations. The individual has very little impact on the decision-making of General Motors or Congress. One person's vote (or, in the case of a car purchase, even several thousand "dollar votes") will count very little. *Yet, taken together, the votes of millions of people do determine future policy choices and directions.* When we send a large corporation or Congress a message, how strong is the signal? How carefully are individual decisions made when dollar votes are cast by consumers or when political votes are cast by citizens?

There is good reason to believe that a giant corporation, such as General Motors, is voted for (or against) after a much more careful process of individual decision-making than goes into the choice of representatives for Congress. How can this be? After all, Congress controls a larger part of our earnings than General Motors. Why

spend more time and effort in choosing a car than in choosing a congressional candidate? Since time and effort are scarce, an individual spends them in a manner that will yield the greatest personal payoff. An extra hour of time will result in larger payoff if the individual spends it on an auto purchase decision. Why? There are two major reasons.

1. The individual's "dollar vote" is always decisive (one gets one's choice), but a political vote is seldom decisive. An individual must live with, and pay for, his or her own private choices, but one usually lives with, and pays for, the political choices of others, regardless of one's own vote.
2. Careful research by a voter on political issues may be largely fruitless at election time, since a vote must be cast for a single bundle of political stands (one candidate among two or three). When purchasing a car, the individual can

choose trunk size, upholstery, engine size, and passenger room from among many combinations *and get what she or he wants.* The time spent comparing each alternative yields a clear payoff.

With these factors in mind, we easily understand why the average person may know more about a car (or television set, golf clubs, or calculator) at purchase time than about congressional candidates at election time. In both cases, personal choices have minimal impact on society. However, the *personal* payoff derived from a careful purchase choice is very different. A person receives most of the benefit from a better market choice. A better political choice, however, is a public good. It is ironic that decisions determining which automobile executives prosper (or which lead their companies into financial trouble) are made more carefully than those that determine the makeup of Congress.

CORRECTING MARKET FAILURE AND THE DEMAND FOR GOVERNMENT

People participate in market activity because it is productive. Production and exchange is a positive-sum activity: it is mutually beneficial. It allows individuals to achieve a higher level of wealth than would be possible in the absence of trade.

People also "demand" certain types of government action because they are productive. When market failure (externalities, public goods, monopoly, or poor information) is present, corrective action can increase the size of the economic pie, generating personal net benefits for individual voters. Each form of market failure discussed in the previous chapter provides a potential opportunity for productive government action, action that generates benefits in excess of costs.

The protective actions of the state—government actions that protect the lives and property of individuals against intruders—are highly productive because they reduce the incidence of activities that impose external costs on others. Violence, theft, and fraud impose external costs on nonconsenting parties. We all gain when each of us is free from serious worry that a criminal can threaten, injure, rob, or defraud us. Therefore, government prohibitions against such activities that generate large external costs are highly productive. When external costs are less severe (than those that endanger our lives and substantially affect our wealth), regulation or taxation can still reduce the negative side effects emanating from the failure of markets to hold private decision-makers fully accountable for their actions. When there are external benefits of activities insufficiently provided by private means, regulation and tax policy again can intervene. For example, sidewalks can be required in residential neighborhoods, and owners can be compelled to keep them snow-free, in order to provide external benefits to pedestrians. Similarly, tax breaks can be provided for nonprofit organizations that fight diseases, preserve natural areas, art, or architecture, or do other charitable works generating benefits for individuals who do not pay for them.

The theory of public goods explains why certain activities cannot easily be provided through markets. Since it is difficult, if not impossible, to restrict their consumption to those who pay for the service, markets tend to undersupply public goods. For example, it would be quite difficult, if not downright impossible, for someone who builds a dam to control flooding to withhold flood protection from those who do not pay. This being the case, market exchange often fails to provide a sufficient amount of flood control protection.

On a larger scale, national defense is a classic public good. Whoever protects the nation against foreign threats or invasion provides a service to all including those who would try to be free-riders and let others pay for defense. Markets will supply an insufficient amount of national defense due to the public-good nature of the service. In contrast, government can tax everyone and use the revenue to provide protection against foreign intruders. Clearly, such action is potentially productive.

Poorly informed consumers can also be helped by government action. Government certification or licensure of accountants, doctors, and lawyers can protect uninformed consumers from those who would practice without the training and experience necessary to perform effectively. Building codes can protect people against unsafe building practices, and so on. When the cost of uninformed choices is high, and the cost of consumer protection is low, appropriate government action can create net benefits for individuals at large.

When monopoly power causes output to be lower, and prices to be higher than they would be in competitive markets, several government policies can potentially help the consumer and the economy as a whole. Anti-trust activities, regulation of monopoly prices, and governmental provisions in place of market provision all have some potential for providing net gains to society.

The theory of market failure highlights the potential for productive governmental action—action that generates benefits in excess of costs. Will representative government lead to constructive action? When the cost of a government project is spread among voters in the same proportion as the benefits received, all voters will gain from productive projects and lose if counterproductive projects (measures for which benefits are insufficient to cover costs) are undertaken. Correspondingly, their representatives have an incentive to support productive measures and oppose wasteful ones. The larger the net gain from a project, the greater the incentive of a representative to support the proposal.

Perhaps surprising to some, when a government project is productive, there is the potential for unanimity (100 percent approval) among voters and their representatives. *When voters pay in proportion to benefits received,* all voters would gain if the government action were productive (and all would lose if it were counterproductive).[6] When voters pay in proportion to benefits received, there is a harmony between good politics and sound economics.

THE DISTRIBUTION OF BENEFITS AND COSTS

With public-sector action, the link between receipt of and payment for a good can be broken—the beneficiaries of a proposal may not bear its cost. Public choice theory indicates that the pattern of benefits and costs among voters will influence the workings of the political process. The benefits derived from a government action may be either widespread among the general populace or concentrated among a small subgroup (for example, farmers, students, or residents of northern Vermont). Similarly, the costs may be either widespread or highly concentrated among voters. As Exhibit 1 illustrates, there are four possible patterns of voter benefits and costs: (1) widespread benefits and widespread costs, (2) concentrated benefits and widespread costs, (3) concentrated benefits and concentrated costs, and (4) widespread benefits and concentrated costs.

When both the benefits and costs are widespread among voters (type 1), essentially everyone benefits and everyone pays. While the costs of type 1 measures may not be precisely proportional to benefits, there will be a rough relationship. When type 1 measures are productive, almost everyone gains, there will be little opposition, and political representatives have a strong incentive to support such proposals. In contrast, when type 1 proposals generate costs in excess of benefits,

---

[6]The principle that productive projects generate the potential for political unanimity was initially articulated by Swedish economist Knut Wicksell in 1896. See Wicksell, "A New Principle of Just Taxation," in James Gwartney and Richard Wagner (ed.), *Public Choice and Constitutional Economics* (Greenwich: JAI Press, Inc., 1988). Nobel laureate James Buchanan has stated that Wicksell's work provided him with the insights that led to his development of modern public choice theory.

Distribution of Benefits Among Voters

	Widespread	Concentrated
Widespread	(1)	(2)
Concentrated	(4)	(3)

Distribution of Costs Among Voters

It is useful to visualize four possible combinations for the distribution of benefits and costs among voters and to consider how the alternative distributions affect the operation of representative government. When the distribution of benefits and costs are widespread among voters (1) or concentrated among voters (3), representative government will tend to undertake projects that are productive and reject those that are unproductive. In contrast, when the benefits are concentrated and the costs are widespread (2), representative government is biased toward adoption of counterproductive activity. Finally, when benefits are widespread but the costs concentrated (4), the political process may reject projects that are productive.

almost everyone loses and representatives will confront pressure to oppose such issues. Thus, for type 1 projects, political process is consistent with economic efficiency.

Interestingly, the provision of traditional public goods—like provision of national defense, a legal system for the protection of persons and property and enforcement of contracts, and a monetary system to oil the wheels of exchange—best fits category 1. Nearly everyone pays and nearly everyone benefits from public-sector action of this type.

Similarly, there is reason to believe that the political process will work pretty well for type 3 measures—those for which both benefits and costs are concentrated on a small subgroup. In some cases, the concentrated beneficiaries may pay for the government to provide services. This would be the case when user charges finance public services (for example, air safety or garbage collection) benefitting subgroups of the populace. Under these circumstances, voter support will provide politicians with an incentive to provide public services that generate value in excess of cost.

Of course, the subgroup of beneficiaries might differ from the subgroup footing the bill. But even in this case, if the benefits exceed the costs, the concentrated group of beneficiaries will have an incentive to expend more resources supportive of the measure than those harmed by it will expend opposing it. Thus, productive measures will tend to be adopted. Similarly, unproductive measures will tend to be rejected when both the benefits and costs are concentrated.

Problems are present, however, when the distribution of benefits differs substantially from the distribution of costs (categories 2 and 4 of Exhibit 1). In a democratic setting, representative government is biased toward adoption of type 2 proposals, even if they are counterproductive. Correspondingly, the democratic process may reject type 4 measures, even when they are productive. The following section will explain these biases and the accompanying economic problems.

RENT SEEKING, SPECIAL INTERESTS, AND GOVERNMENT FAILURE

Public-sector efforts to alleviate problems arising from market failure explain a substantial amount of government activity. However, another substantial portion of public sector activity reflects neither gains from improved efficiency nor a preference for less economic inequality. Rather, it is reflective of rent-seeking behavior, the political actions of individuals and groups seeking personal advantage at the expense of others.[7]

Rent-seeking activities are most likely to be successful when an issue generates substantial personal benefits for a small number of constituents, while imposing a small individual cost on a large number of other voters (type 2 of Exhibit 1). Economists refer to measures of this type as special interest issues.

It is easy to see how politicians can improve their election prospects by catering to the views of special interests. Since their personal stake is large, members of the interest group (and lobbyists representing their interests) have a strong incentive to inform themselves and their allies and to let legislators know how strongly they feel about an issue of special importance. Many of them will vote for or against candidates strictly on the basis of whether they support their interests. In addition, such interest groups are generally an attractive source of campaign resources, including financial contributions. In contrast, most other voters will care little about a special interest issue. For the non-special interest voter, the time and energy necessary to examine the issue will generally exceed any possible personal gain from a preferred resolution. Thus, most non-special interest voters will simply ignore such issues.

If you were a vote-seeking politician what would you do? Clearly, little gain would be derived from supporting the interest of the largely uninformed and disinterested majority. Predictably, politicians will be led as if by an invisible hand to serve well-organized, concentrated interests. Support of such special interests will generate vocal supporters, campaign workers, and most importantly, campaign contributors. One source of campaign money derives from political action committees (PACs). These are independent special interest groups, or, more often, political arms of corporations, unions, or interest groups. In 1984, PACs contributed $61.3 million to more than 1,500 congressional campaigns. PAC spending at the federal level in 1988 totaled more than $400 million.[8] In the age of media politics, there is strong pressure for politicians to support special inter-

---

[7]For an excellent survey of the literature on rent seeking, see Robert D. Tollison, "Rent Seeking: A Survey," *Kyklos, 35* (March 1982), pp. 575–602.
[8]Milton C. Cummings, Jr., and David Wise, *Democracy Under Pressure,* 6th edition (San Diego: Harcourt Brace Jovanovich, 1989), pp. 246, 338.

"It's good to be back where I can spend somebody else's money!"

Grin and Bear It by Fred Wagner © *by and Permission of News America Syndicate.*

ests, tap them for campaign funds, and use the contributions to project a positive candidate image on television.[9]

The rational ignorance effect strengthens the power of special interests. Since the cost imposed on individual voters is small, and since they are unable to avoid the cost even if they are informed, voters bearing the cost of special interest legislation tend to be uninformed. This will be particularly true if the complexity of the issue makes it difficult for voters to figure how an issue affects their personal welfare. Thus, politicians often make special interest legislation complex in order to hide the cost imposed on the typical voter.[10]

In addition, the interests of bureaucrats are often complementary with those of interest groups. The bureaucrats who staff an agency usually want to see their department's goals furthered, whether the goals are to protect more wilderness, build more roads, or provide additional subsidized irrigation projects. To accomplish these things requires larger budgets, which—not so incidently—are likely to provide the bureaucrats with expanded career opportunities while helping to satisfy their professional aspirations as well. Bureaus, therefore, are usually happy to work to expand their programs to deliver benefits to special interest groups, who, in turn, work with politicians to expand their bureau budgets and programs.

SPECIAL INTERESTS AND INEFFICIENT PUBLIC POLICY

The special interest bias of the political process helps to explain the presence of many programs that reduce the size of the economic pie. For example, consider the case of the roughly 33,000 rice farmers in the United States. In essence, the government guarantees rice growers an above market price for rice by paying them to grow less rice so the artificially high price can be maintained. The pro-

---

[9]For numerous examples of the link between special interest legislation and political contributions, see Brooks Jackson, *Honest Graft: Big Money and the American Political Process* (New York: Knopf, 1989).
[10]See Gordon Tullock, *Toward a Mathematics of Politics* (Ann Arbor: University of Michigan Press, 1966), pp. 103–106 for additional details on this topic.

gram reduces output, pushes up the price of rice, and results in higher taxes. As a nation we are worse off as the result of it.

Nonetheless, Congress continues to support the program. The 33,000 rice farmers gain more than $800 million in gross income, approximately $25,000 per farm. More than 60 percent of these subsidies go to rice farmers receiving payments of $50,000 or more.[11] The rice farmers are generally aware of the importance of the program to their well-being and they make their views known to members of Congress. In contrast, most Americans are unaware that they each pay approximately $4 in taxes and higher food prices more per year to help rice growers, most of which goes to wealthy farmers.

It is rational for rice farmers to inform themselves and become strong advocates of the rice price support program because it has such a large impact on their wealth. In contrast, it is irrational for taxpayers to spend time informing themselves on the nature and affects of the rice program (and the position of candidates on it) because for each taxpayer the cost of such an investigation would exceed the personal losses emanating from the program.

This special interest effect also helps to explain the presence of tariffs and quotas on steel, automobiles, textiles, and several other products. Regulations mandating that Alaskan oil be transported by the high cost American maritime industry reflect the industry's political clout, not its economic efficiency. Federally funded irrigation projects, subsidized grazing rights, subsidized loans, subsidies to airports—the list goes on and on. Policy in each of these areas is rooted in the special interest effect and not in sound economic doctrine. While each such program individually imposes only a small drag on our economy, in the aggregate they drain our resources, and impair our standard of living.

LOGROLLING AND PORK BARREL LEGISLATION

Logrolling: The exchange between politicians of political support on one issue for political support on another issue.

Pork-Barrel Legislation: A package of spending projects benefiting local areas at federal expense. The projects typically have costs that exceed benefits, but each is intensely desired by the residents of the district getting the benefits without having to pay much of the costs.

Logrolling within a legislative assembly also strengthens the political clout of special interest groups. **Logrolling** is the practice of trading votes by a representative (and his or her constituents) in order to pass intensely desired legislation. Representative A promises to vote for measures favored by other representatives in exchange for their support of a measure A strongly favors. With logrolling, legislative bodies often pass a bundle of proposals, each of which would be rejected if they were voted on separately.

Pork barrel legislation is a slight variant of logrolling. This type of legislation bundles together a set of projects to benefit regional interests (for example, water projects, dredging of harbors, or expenditures on military bases) at the expense of the general taxpayer. As in the case of logrolling, the bundle of pork barrel projects can often gain approval even if each is counterproductive and would individually be rejected by the legislative assembly.

Exhibit 2 provides a numeric illustration of the forces underlying logrolling and pork barrel legislation. Here we consider the operation of a five-member legislative assembly considering three projects: construction of a post office in district A, dredging of a harbor in B, and expenditures on a military base in C. In each case, the projects are inefficient—the net cost of the project exceeds the net benefits (by a 12 to 10 ratio). If the projects were voted on separately, and the representatives reflected the views of their constituents, each project would lose by a 4 to 1 vote. However, when the projects are bundled together through either log-

[11]*Economic Report of the President, 1987,* p. 157.

EXHIBIT 2 ■ Vote Trading and Passing Counterproductive Legislation

| Voters of District[a] | Net Benefits (+) or Costs (−) to Each Voter in District | | | |
	Construction of Post Office in A	Dredging Harbor in B	Construction of Military Base in C	Total
A	+$10	−$ 3	−$ 3	+$4
B	−$ 3	+$10	−$ 3	+$4
C	−$ 3	−$ 3	+$10	+$4
D	−$ 3	−$ 3	−$ 3	−$9
E	−$ 3	−$ 3	−$ 3	−$9
Total	−$ 2	−$ 2	−$ 2	−$6

[a]We assume the districts are of equal size.

---

rolling or pork-barrel legislation, representatives A, B, and C will vote yes. The legislative bundle will pass 3 to 2 even though it is counterproductive (on average, the projects, as a bundle, reduce the wealth of constituents by $6).[12]

Legislation providing subsidies to electricity consumers in California, Nevada, and Arizona illustrates the relevance of logrolling and pork-barrel legislation. Under legislation passed in 1937, electricity generated by Hoover Dam has been sold to residents in the three surrounding states at rates ranging between 10 percent and 25 percent of the market price. The law providing for the subsidized rates was scheduled to expire in 1987. However, before it did so, Congress extended the subsidies for another 30 years. The residents of many western states are the recipients of federally subsidized electricity. Every senator west of Missouri voted to continue the subsidized rates for electricity generated by Hoover Dam. In turn, they can expect senators and representatives from California, Arizona, and Nevada to support subsidized electricity rates in their states. In contrast, residents of other states will pay higher taxes so that many residents in western states can enjoy cheap electricity.

Why don't representatives oppose measures that force their constituents to pay for projects that benefit others? There is some incentive to do so, but the constituents of any one representative can capture only a small portion of the benefits of tax savings from improved efficiency, since they would be spread nationwide among all taxpayers. Just as we do not expect a corporation's president to devote the firm's resources to projects not primarily benefiting stockholders, we should not expect an elected representative to devote political resources to projects such as defeating pork-barrel programs, when the benefits of greater efficiency would not go primarily to that representative's constituents. Instead, each representative has a strong incentive to work for programs whose benefits are concentrated among his or her constituents—especially the organized interest groups who can help the representative be re-elected. Heeding such incentives is a survival characteristic. It will enhance the politician's re-election prospects.

---

[12]Logrolling and pork barrel policies can lead to the adoption of productive measures. However, if a project is productive, there would always be a pattern of finance that would lead to its adoption even if logrolling were absent. Thus, the tendency for logrolling and pork barrel policies to result in the adoption of inefficient projects is the more significant point.

GOVERNMENT FAILURE: THE SHORT-SIGHTEDNESS EFFECT

How does the political process handle benefits and costs across time periods? What happens *prior* to the next election is of crucial importance to incumbent politicians. Since issues of public policy are usually complex, it is often difficult for voters to anticipate *future* benefits and costs accurately. Moreover, principles of rational ignorance suggest there is little payoff from doing so in any case. Instead, voters tend to rely on current conditions. To the voter, the best indicator of how well the incumbent has done may be the state of affairs close to election day.

Policies that look good around election day will thus enhance the image of incumbents, even if those policies are likely to have substantial negative side effects after the election. On the other hand, policies that generate pre-election costs in order to provide long-term gains that emerge only after the next election reduce the re-election prospects of incumbents. As a result, the political process is biased toward the adoption of shortsighted policies and against the selection of sound long-range policies, when they involve observable costs prior to the next election.

SHORT-TERM COSTS AND GOVERNMENT INACTION.

It has been noted that public-sector action is "crisis-oriented." In recent years, we have experienced a welfare crisis, an inflation crisis, a poverty crisis, an energy crisis, and several environmental crises. One reason for this is that crises tend to loosen up budgetary purse strings; special interest groups, politicians, and agencies use a crisis to justify larger budget requests. Other crises, however, occur simply because important action was postponed. City governments, for example, often find it expedient to delay needed maintenance of roads, water systems, and sewers. Higher taxes would bring current political pain, but most of the benefit would lie in future decades. To postpone needed maintenance may be very costly, but most of the cost lies in the future. By the time the problem reaches crisis proportions, other politicians will be likely to have to deal with it. Rationally ignorant voters, after all, know more about the size of today's tax burden than about the problems that might result from delayed spending. Then, too, many of those affected in the future are not current voters.

How does this political tendency to put off needed expenditures compare with similar situations in the private sector? Wouldn't the owner of a hotel or a restaurant also be reluctant to bear the cost of shutting down the business temporarily and undertaking needed repairs? The owner also wants to avoid costs. But the distinction is that with private, transferable property rights, the value of the added future benefits is available immediately to the owner in the form of higher property values. The owner can immediately collect the *value* of the added future business revenue, either by borrowing against the increased value of the property, or simply by selling it. The salable property right makes the increased future benefits of investments available to the owner immediately. Of course the owner's wealth also falls immediately if the property deteriorates. Neither of these influences on the personal wealth of decision-makers is present in the public sector. In fact, one solution to the political problem of water supply, or public transportation investments, and so on, is to let private firms provide the capital facilities and supply the services.

Some cities take advantage of the private sector's willingness to invest by simply purchasing services or allowing customers to buy services, rather than by using government investments. For example, the subways in New York City were built by private companies, and the city took them over later only to keep subway fares well below costs—and still keep the wages of politically important subway workers high, at the expense of taxpayers. One result has been a deterioration of the subway system over time.

When competition among firms is too costly *within* the market, because one large firm can be more efficient than several small ones, then competition *for* the market is sometimes used to prevent problems of monopoly pricing.[13] (The boxed feature on "Private Versus Public-Sector Production of Fire Protection" describes one technique—the periodic contracting with private firms for services.) Regulation is another alternative, but the shortsightedness effect indicates that political pressures to keep current prices down at the expense of future costs may be brought to bear on the regulators, just as they are brought to bear on politicians when government owns the facilities. Private solutions cannot always be found, but, unfortunately, economic theory suggests the democratic decision-making, without transferable property rights, is often inconsistent with sensible long-range planning.

SHORT-TERM BENEFITS AND GOVERNMENT ACTION

While proposals with future benefits difficult to perceive are usually delayed, proposals with immediate benefits, at the expense of complex future costs—costs that will accrue after the next election—are very attractive to political entrepreneurs. Office-holders and candidates alike have a strong incentive to support such proposals and emphasize the immediate voter benefits.

Is there any evidence that the pursuit of short-term political gains has led to inappropriate public-sector action? Consider the issue of macroeconomic instability. In the 1960s and 1970s, inflationary expectations were relatively low, and slow to change. Expansionary monetary and fiscal policy could be used to "heat up" the economy and reduce the rate of unemployment in the short run. An overheated economy, though, leads to inflation. The shortsightedness effect predicts that the party in power would, in those circumstances, tend to follow an expansionary policy in the 12 to 24 months before an election, even if these policies would result in future inflation. The "stabilization" policies preceding the presidential elections of those two decades suggest the incumbent political suppliers made a substantial effort to give voters the impression that the economy was strong on election day. There is little doubt, however, that expansionary macropolicy overheated the economy in each case, causing the post-election increase in the rate of inflation. Once market participants began to recognize the inflationary effects of expansionary policy, the political profit from the policy fell. Expectations of inflation adjusted more quickly, and the expansionary portion of the cycle became more brief.

It is easy to think of other examples where positive short-term effects have increased the political attractiveness of policies that exert a long-term detrimental impact. Borrowing to finance short-term programs that benefit coveted voting

---

[13]See Steve H. Hanke (ed.), *Prospects for Privatization* (New York: Academy of Political Science, 1988) for a discussion of many such possibilities.

blocks is attractive even though the long-term results will be higher real interest rates, less capital formation, and higher future taxes. Rent controls tend to reduce rental housing prices in the short-term, even though housing shortages, black markets, and a deterioration in housing quality are the long-run result.

The shortsightedness effect can be a source of conflict between good politics and sound economics. Policies that are efficient from the standpoint of social benefits and costs are not necessarily the policies that will enhance a politician's election prospects. As a result, grossly inefficient projects may be undertaken and potentially beneficial projects may be ignored.

GOVERNMENT FAILURE: FEW INCENTIVES FOR INTERNAL EFFICIENCY

The day-to-day functions of government are performed by bureaus, which derive the major component of their revenues from the periodic appropriations of the legislature rather than from the direct sale of output to consumers. In effect, the legislative body supplies the bureau with a budget along with instructions for

APPLICATIONS IN ECONOMICS

Private- Versus Public-Sector Production of Fire Protection

Is private-sector production actually more efficient than public-sector production of the same service? A number of economic studies have been done that seem to confirm that it frequently is. One example is the case of the Scottsdale, Arizona, fire department. Scottsdale funds its fire protection publicly, through taxation, but purchases the protection from a private firm. It puts the contract out for bid, and the winning bidder provides the service.

Economist Roger Ahlbrandt did an extensive economic study of the Scottsdale fire service and its cost, comparing it with fire services in 49 other cities.[14] He concluded that governmental provision (rather than just government funding) of the service would cost Scottsdale 89 percent more than private provision. Was the private service effective? Did the cost reduction occur at the expense of effective fire control? Insurance rates are one indirect measure of the effec-

tiveness of the service. Insurance companies have strong incentives to adjust rates properly to fit the circumstances, since each insurance company needs low rates to be competitive, but rates set too low would not pay for fire damage claims. Scottsdale rates are the same as those in similar cities using governmental provisions of the services. The same level of services are apparently being provided, at a lower cost.

Why does the private, for-profit firm cut costs? To win the bidding, the firm must keep its price down. To make a profit, then, the service company has a strong incentive to be innovative and produce efficiently. The firm serving Scottsdale—Rural/Metro, Inc.—has pioneered several techniques to reduce costs without reducing service. Among its innovations have been robot firefighting equipment, high-visibility paint on fire trucks, and a high-capacity fire hose. It has also used creative staff-

ing patterns, including a mix of full-time and "reserve" firefighters to cut labor costs. The reservists are on call one week a month, are less intensively trained, and are used only on certain types of fires.

In the case of the Scottsdale fire service, as in many others, economic logic seems to be supported: When owners and managers are spurred on by the hope of profit and the fear of loss, and are guided by the price system, buyers gain. It is extremely difficult, and perhaps impossible to duplicate the information and incentives of the private sector in a governmental setting.

[14]This study and many others are summarized in E. S. Savas, *Privatizing the Public Sector* (Chatham: Chatham House, 1982) Ch. 6.

dealing with its assigned tasks. The function of the bureau is to transform the budget into public services.

What does economic analysis indicate about the cost-effectiveness of government-operated bureaus compared to private firms? In the private sector, there is a strong incentive to produce efficiently because lower costs will mean higher profits. Even though the stockholders of a private firm can seldom identify good and bad individual decisions, they can easily observe a "bottom line" index of efficiency—the firm's rate of profit. Current profits, together with stockholder judgments about the firm's investment strategy, determine stock prices. In the private sector, a low stock price relative to the firm's assets is an invitation for a restructuring or a takeover in which management is ousted. Together with bankruptcy, these possibilities are deterrents to economic inefficiency.

In contrast, public sector bureaus confront an incentive structure that is less conducive to operating efficiency. Direct competition, in the form of other firms trying to take an agency's customers, is rare in the public sector. And since there is no easily identified index of performance analogous to profit rates and stock prices, public-sector managers can often gloss over economic inefficiency. If a public-sector decision-maker spends money unwisely or uses resources primarily for personal benefit (such as excessive expenditures on plush offices or "business travel"), the burden of this inefficiency will fall on the taxpayer. The notorious and persistent cost overruns in the Pentagon are just one example of the difficulty inherent in cost control without a profit motive and without vigorously competing firms. The public sector is also not subject to the test of bankruptcy, which tends to eliminate inefficient operations in the private sector. Political finesse is far more important to success in the public sector than operational efficiency. At election time, political candidates and parties must offer something more impressive than efficiency in government if they expect to win.

Taxpayers would be the major beneficiaries of reduced costs and an improvement in public-sector efficiency. A public-sector manager seldom reaps personal reward by saving the taxpayers money. In fact, if an agency fails to spend this year's allocation, its case for a larger budget next year is weakened. Agencies typically go on a spending spree at the end of a budget period if they discover that they have failed to spend all of this year's appropriation.

It is important to note that the argument of internal inefficiency is not based on the assumption that employees of a bureaucratic government are necessarily lazy or incapable. Rather, the emphasis is on the structure of information and incentives under which managers and other workers toil. No individual or relatively small group of individuals has much incentive to ensure efficiency. Their performances cannot readily be judged, and without private ownership their personal wealth would not be significantly increased or reduced by changes in the level of efficiency. Since public officials and bureau managers spend other people's money, they are likely to be less conscious of cost than they would be with their own resources. Attempts to control waste and abuse are made through rules that try to anticipate problems, rather than by an owner's drive toward profit and away from loss. Without a need to compare sales revenues to costs, there is no test by which to define economic inefficiency clearly or measure it accurately, much less eliminate it. The perverse incentive structure of a bureaucracy is bound to have an impact on its internal efficiency.

Research by economists over the last several years has tended to verify this line of reasoning. When private firms are compared to government agencies providing the same goods or services, the private firms generally have been shown to provide them more economically. [15] The boxed feature on "Private- Versus Public-Sector Production of Fire Protection" reports on one such study.

THE PUBLIC SECTOR VERSUS THE MARKET: A SUMMARY

Throughout this text, we have argued that theory can explain why both market forces and public-sector action sometimes break down—that is, why they sometimes fail to meet the criteria for ideal efficiency. The deficiencies of one or the other sector will often be more or less decisive depending on the type of economic activity. Nobel laureate Paul Samuelson has stated, "There are not rules concerning the proper role of government that can be established by *a priori* reasoning."[16] This does not mean, however, that economics has nothing to say about the *strength* of the case for either the market or the public sector in terms of specific classes of activities. Nor does it mean that social scientists have nothing to say about institutional arrangements for conducting economic activity. It merely indicates that each issue and type of activity must be considered individually.

The case for government intervention is obviously stronger for some activities than for others. For example, if an activity involves substantial external effects, market arrangements often result in economic inefficiency, and public-sector action may allow for greater efficiency. Similarly, when competitive pressures are weak and when there is reason to expect consumers to be poorly informed, market failure may result, and again government action may be called for. (See the Thumbnail Sketch for a summary of factors that influence the case for market or for public-sector action.)

THUMBNAIL SKETCH

These factors weaken the case for market-sector allocation:

1. External costs and benefits
2. Public goods
3. Monopoly
4. Uninformed consumers

These factors weaken the case for public-sector intervention:

1. Voter ignorance, inability to recognize costs and benefits fully, and cost concealment
2. The power of special interests
3. The shortsightedness effect
4. Little incentive for operational efficiency

---

[15]For a summary of many such studies, along with a detailed explanation of why these results are to be expected, see Louis De Alessi, "The Economics of Property Rights: A Review of the Evidence," *Research in Law and Economics,* vol. 2 (Greenwich: JAI Press, Inc., 1980), pp. 1–47. Also see Anthony E. Boardman and Aidan R. Vining, "Ownership and Performance in Competitive Environments: A Comparison of The Performance of Private, Mixed, and State-owned Enterprises", *Journal of Law and Economics,* (April 1989), pp. 1–34.

[16]Paul A. Samuelson, "The Economic Role of Private Activity," in *The Collected Scientific Papers of Paul A. Samuelson,* J. E. Stiglitz (ed.), vol. 2, (Cambridge: MIT Press, 1966), p. 1423.

The identical analysis holds for the public sector. When there is a good reason to believe that special interest influence will be strong, the case for government action to correct market failures is weakened. Similarly, the lack of a means of identifying and weeding out public-sector inefficiency weakens the case for government action. More often than not, the choice of proper institutions may be a choice among evils. For example, we might expect private-sector monopoly if an activity is left to the market and perverse regulation due to the special interest effect if we turn to the public sector. Understanding the shortcomings of both the market and the public sectors is important if we are to improve our current economic institutions.

ECONOMICS, POLITICS, AND THE TRANSFER SOCIETY

As Exhibit 3 illustrates, direct income transfers through the public sector have increased sharply during the last six decades. In 1929, income transfers accounted for only 1.8 percent of national income; by 1988, the figure had risen to 14.7 percent.

As in other areas, both the market failure and rent-seeking models of government underly public-sector income transfers. As we discussed in Chapter 4, sometimes income transfers reflect the public good characteristics of antipoverty efforts. Since the number of poor people, like the strength of our national defense, is largely independent of one's personal contribution, individuals motivated by the desire to reduce poverty in general may simply become free-riders. When a large number of people become free-riders, though, less than the desired amount of anti-poverty effort will be voluntarily supplied. If everyone is required to contribute through the tax system, then the free-rider problem can be overcome. Under these circumstances, transfers directed to the poor are consistent with economic efficiency.

EXHIBIT 3

The Growth of Government Transfer Payments

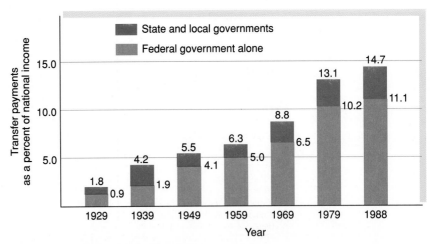

Source: *Economic Report of the President, 1988.*

However, means-tested transfers, those directed toward the poor, constitute only about one-sixth of all income transfers. No income test is applied to the other five-sixths and they are generally directed toward groups that are either well organized or easily identifiable. The recipients of these transfers often have incomes well above the average. This suggests that the rent-seeking model of government also plays an important role in the allocation of income transfers.

Within the framework of public choice analysis, the relatively small portion of income transfers directed toward the poor is not surprising. There is little reason to believe that transfers to the poor will be particularly attractive to vote-seeking politicians. After all, in the United States, the poor are less likely to vote than middle and upper income recipients. They are less likely than others to be well-informed on political issues and candidates. They are not united. Neither are they a significant source of financial resources that exert a powerful influence on the political process.

The incentive to engage in rent-seeking activities is directly proportional to the ease with which the political process can be used for personal (or interest group) gain at the expense of others. When the effective law of the land makes it difficult to take the property of others, or to force others to pay for projects favored by you and your interest group, rent seeking is unattractive. Under such circumstances, the benefits of rent seeking are relatively low and few resources flow into rent-seeking activities. On the other hand, as the government becomes more heavily involved in income transfers and other redistributive policies, the incentive to engage in rent-seeking activities increases.

As others have pointed out, rent seeking is similar to theft in terms of its impact on resource use.[17] Both rent seeking and theft are efforts to gain income by taking from others, rather than by helping others in exchange for income. Improved prospects for personal gain via either rent seeking or theft will expand the size of the redistributive sector and attract resources away from production. Just as an increase in the incidence of theft causes individuals to purchase more burglar alarms, safety deposit boxes, locks, guard dogs, and firearms, an increase in rent seeking will lead to more defensive actions designed to resist transfers. Both rent seeking and theft lead to negative-sum activity and the social waste of resources.

Nonetheless, public choice theory indicates that in the absence of restraints, income transfers based on rent seeking often will be politically attractive, even though they reduce the size of the economic pie. The special interest effect and rational ignorance effect combine to explain why transfers to easily identifiable concentrated interests (for example, farmers, union members, business interests, or the elderly) at the expense of widely dispersed, disorganized groups (for example, taxpayers, or consumers) are likely to generate political gain. The concentrated interests receiving the transfers will feel strongly about the issue. They offer a source of both votes and campaign funds. In contrast, when the costs are diffused, only a small personal cost will be imposed on the bulk of voters footing the bill for the transfers. Most of these people will be both uninformed and largely

---

[17]See Gordon Tullock, "The Welfare Cost of Tariffs, Monopolies, and Theft," *Economic Inquiry* (June 1967) and Terry L. Anderson and Peter J. Hill, *The Birth of the Transfer Society* (Stanford: Hoover Institution Press, 1980).

disinterested in the issue, since it exerts only a small impact on their personal welfare. Therefore, the political gain from the support of transfer recipients is likely to outweigh any loss of support from those paying the bill. Politicians who are adept at using transfers to help important constitutents (voting blocs) are likely to gain a competitive advantage relative to those who fail to gain campaign support in this manner.

Farm subsidies provide an excellent example of an income transfer program that reflects the rent-seeking model of government. In 1987 the federal government spent approximately $20 billion on various farm subsidy programs. These programs distort resource use and generate market surpluses of agriculture products. As Exhibit 4 illustrates, the primary recipients of these income transfers are high income farmers. Only 13.8 percent of the farms in the United States had annual sales of $100,000 or more in 1986. Yet, this small group of large farmers received 56.2 percent of the income transfers to farmers in 1986. More than four-fifths of the transfers went to farmers with annual sales in excess of $40,000. The complex array of income transfers to farmers cost the average taxpayer-consumer about $100 per year, while generating an average gain in gross income in the general vicinity of $5,000 per farmer. The persistence of these programs indicates that the prospect of a $5,000 gain for a small subgroup is vastly more effective at generating political support than the prospect of a $100 savings is in generating political opposition. This result is highly consistent with the rent-seeking, special-interest view.

Before leaving the topic of transfers, one final point should be stressed. Market adjustments and competition for the transfers will erode much of the long-run gain of the intended beneficiaries. This point follows from a standard proposition

---

EXHIBIT 4   ■   Distribution of Government Income Transfers to Farmers by Farm Size, 1986

Farm Size (Annual Sales in Dollars)	Percent of Farms	Direct Government Payments	
		Payments per Farm ($)	Percent of Payments Received
500,000 and over	1.3	36,000	9.0
250,000 to 500,000	3.0	26,400	14.7
100,000 to 250,000	9.5	18,300	32.5
40,000 to 100,000	13.3	10,390	25.9
20,000 to 40,000	10.1	5,570	10.5
10,000 to 20,000	10.7	2,000	4.0
5,000 to 10,000	12.0	810	1.8
Less than 5,000	40.1	220	1.6
All farms	100.0	5,340	100.0

Source: E. C. Pasour, Jr., *Price Support Payments for U.S. Farm Products: A Deregulation Opportunity* (Tallahassee: The James Madison Institute, 1988).

of economic theory: Competitors will be attracted to activities that yield abnormally high rates of return until the abnormally high profit is eroded. Application of this proposition to politics indicates that whenever the government establishes a criteria (as it must in a world of scarce resources) that must be met in order to qualify for transfers or other political favors, competition to meet the standard will erode the opportunity for profit. Unanticipated changes in public policy will impose temporary gains and losses on various groups. However, paradoxical as it may appear, it is extremely difficult to bestow favors upon a class of recipients in a manner that will *permanently* improve their well-being.

In order to understand why it is hard for the government to help people by giving them something, consider the following simple illustration. Suppose the government decided to give away $50 bills between 9 AM and 5 PM to persons willing to wait in line at the teller windows of the U.S. Treasury. Since long lines would emerge and discourage most people seeking the transfer, the program would have a finite cost (this is essential or otherwise it could not be financed). Persons with the lowest opportunity cost would be the primary beneficiaries. Many of them would perceive that the transfer benefits were worth the wait. However, much of the beneficiary's gain would be eroded as the result of competition (to meet the criteria) for the transfer. If a person's opportunity cost of waiting several hours was $30, his net gain from the $50 transfer would be $20. The opportunity cost of the wait for some would be $49.99. In that case, virtually the entire benefit of the transfer would be eroded by the cost incurred in its acquisition.

As people and markets adjust to the transfers, any abnormally high returns derived by recipients of government subsidies will dissipate. When one considers what one has to buy, or do, or be in order to qualify for transfers, it is clear that the net gain of the recipients is substantially less than the size of the transfers. In the case of the poor, high implicit marginal tax rates accompanying income-tested transfers severely retard the incentive of the poor to earn. Thus, the net increase in income of the poor is much less than the dollars transferred. To a large extent, the transfers merely replace income that would have been earned in their absence. The high implicit tax rates often induce the poor to drop out of the work force. When this happens the skills of the poor depreciate, further reducing their ability to support themselves and escape poverty. Government involvement in antipoverty transfers crowds out private charitable efforts by families, individuals, churches, and civic organizations. When taxes are levied to do more, predictably private individuals and groups will adjust and do less. When one considers these adjustments, it is not at all clear that the poor benefit from transfers, particularly in the long run.

If transfer programs fail to provide significant benefits to recipients beyond the windfall gains at the time the programs are instituted or unexpectedly expanded, what accounts for the continued political support for such programs? Gordon Tullock's work on the transitional gains trap provides the answer.[18] Elimination of the programs would be costly for recipients who have adjusted to or ''bought into'' the programs. Even though the programs do little to improve their

[18]Gordon Tullock, ''The Transitional Gains Trap,'' *Bell Journal of Economics,* 6 (Autumn 1975).

welfare, the current beneficiaries would be harmed by the elimination or unexpected reduction in the programs. Thus, they form a vocal lobby supportive of the programs.

CONSTITUTIONAL ORGANIZATION AND GETTING MORE FROM GOVERNMENT

Public choice theory indicates that political action can, and often does, reduce economic inefficiency emanating from market failure. However, it also indicates that unconstrained democratic governments will often enact programs that waste resources and impair the general standard of living of citizens. How can we reap the benefits available from government while minimizing its unwanted, counterproductive activities?

An efficient political organization does not emerge naturally. It must be shaped by the legal environment. The "founding fathers" of the United States recognized this point. They sought to establish a constitutional order that would limit the misuse of the ordinary political process, while allowing government to undertake activities important to the welfare of citizens. With time, many of the safeguards embodied in the U.S. Constitution have either eroded or been modified. Nonetheless, the general idea was a sound one.

What would a constitutional structure consistent with economic efficiency look like? Interestingly, public choice analysis indicates that it would incorporate a number of the ideas emanating from the Philadelphia convention, 200 years ago. First, it would seek to constrain rent-seeking activities—the use of the political process to take the rights and wealth from some in order to bestow them on others. The U.S. Constitution contains provisions designed to prevent such takings. The Fifth Amendment states, "nor shall private property be taken for public use without just compensation."[19] Article I, Section 10 mandates, "No state shall . . . pass any . . . law impairing the obligations of contracts." These provisions might be strengthened and supplemented with prohibitions against the use of government to fix prices and to bar entry into the production of otherwise legal goods, both of which restrain trade and are indirect forms of taking property without compensation. The federal government might also be barred from income transfer activities, other than those that are means-tested (directed toward the poor).

Second, the efficiency of the political process would be enhanced if the primary beneficiaries of government activities were required to foot the bill for their cost. Again, there is evidence that this is what the founding fathers had in mind. The U.S. Constitution, Article I, Section 8, states: "The Congress shall have power to lay and collect taxes, duties, imports and excises to . . . provide for the common defence and general welfare of the United States, but all duties, imports and excises shall be uniform throughout the United States." This constitutional provision indicates that it was the intent of the Founders that, at the federal level, uniformly levied taxes would be used only for the finance of expendi-

---

[19]For a detailed analysis of the importance of this clause from a law and economics viewpoint, see Richard A. Epstein, *Takings: Private Property and the Power of Eminent Domain* (Cambridge: Harvard University Press, 1985).

tures yielding general benefits—the common defense and general welfare (type 1 issues of Exhibit 1). In order to assure stricter adherence to this substantive provision, tax and spending proposals at the federal level could be required to secure the approval of a supra-majority (for example, three-fourths) of the legislative members. Such a provision would reduce the power of interest groups and the viability of pork-barrel spending projects.

Finally, if we want efficiency in government, the constitutional structure should strengthen independent state and local governments. In *The Federalist Papers,* James Madison argues that competition among state and local governments will help check abusive and counterproductive government action.[20] Public choice analysis indicates that Madison's perception was correct. How might the constitutional order promote competition among governments? One way would be to require more inclusive majorities the higher the level of government. For example, local legislative bodies (city commissions, county commissions, regional authorities, and so on) might continue to act with the approval of only a simple-majority, while a three-fifths majority might be required for legislative action at the state level, and a three-fourths majority at the federal level. The increasing majorities required for legislative action at higher levels of government would help remedy a deficiency of the current system—the tendency of federal and state governments to get involved with issues that are best dealt with at lower levels of governments. Decentralization in government would permit states and localities to adopt different governmental environments. Those that people like best—that supply public-sector goods that are highly valued relative to their tax cost—would grow and prosper relative to those people appreciate less. This structure would allow individuals and businesses to "vote with their feet," as well as with their ballots.

Of course, public choice theorists are continuing to investigate the operation of alternative forms of political organization. The challenge before us is to develop political institutions capable of bringing, to the fullest extent possible, the self-interest of politicians, bureaucrats, and voters into harmony with the general welfare of a society.

LOOKING AHEAD

Democratic governments are a creation of the interactions of human beings. Public choice analysis helps us better understand these interactions and think more clearly about constitutional rules capable of improving the results achieved from government. As we consider trade among nations, how economies develop, and alternative forms of economic organization, public choice analysis will enhance our understanding of important issues in these areas.

CHAPTER SUMMARY

1. It is fruitful to analyze the public sector in the same way in which we analyze the private sector. The public sector is an alternative to the market—it provides an alternative means of organizing production and/or distributing output.

---

[20]See Charles Tiebout, "A Pure Theory of Local Expenditures," *Journal of Political Economy* (October 1956); Vincent Ostrom, *The Political Theory of a Compound Republic* (Fairfax: Center for Study of Public Choice, George Mason University, 1971); and Robert Bish, "Federalism: A Market-Economics Perspective" in James Gwartney and Richard Wagner (ed.), *Public Choice and Constitutional Economics* (Greenwich: JAI Press, 1988) for additional information on the importance of competition among governmental units.

2. Voters cast ballots, make political contributions, lobby, and adopt other political strategies to demand public-sector action. Other things constant, voters have a strong incentive to support the candidate who offers them the greatest personal gain relative to personal costs. Obtaining information is costly. Since group decision-making breaks the link between the choice of the individual and the outcome of the issue, it is rational for voters to remain uninformed on many issues. Candidates are generally evaluated on the basis of a small subset of issues that are of the greatest personal importance to individual voters.

3. Under a democratic system, politicians have a strong incentive to follow a strategy that will enhance their chances of getting elected (and reelected). Political competition more or less forces politicians to focus on how their actions influence their support among voters.

4. Market failure presents government with an opportunity to undertake action that will result in additional benefits relative to costs. Other things constant, the greater the social loss resulting from the market failure, the stronger is the incentive for public-sector action. Ultimately, though, it is votes, not efficiency, which will determine political outcomes. The votes of citizens and their representatives will be influenced by the intensity as well as the direction of their preferences and interests. Logrolling and pork-barrel legislation are ways to make intensity more influential.

5. The distribution of the benefits and costs among voters influences how the political process works. When voters pay in proportion to the benefits they receive from a public sector project, democratic decision-making works quite well. Productive projects tend to be approved and counterproductive ones rejected. However, problems arise when the pattern of benefits among voters differs from the pattern of costs.

6. There is a strong incentive for political entrepreneurs to support special interest issues and to make the issues difficult for the unorganized, largely uninformed majority to understand. Special interest groups supply both financial and direct elective support to the politician. Constitutional rules are one way to limit the power of special interests to use the political process to achieve their interests at the expense of the group as a whole.

7. In government, where decision-makers normally do not hold private property rights to the resources they control, the shortsightedness effect is another potential source of conflict between good politics and sound economics. Both voters and politicians tend to support projects that promise substantial current benefits at the expense of difficult-to-identify future costs. There is a bias against legislation that involves immediate and easily identifiable costs but complex future benefits.

8. The economic incentive for operational efficiency is small for public-sector action. No individual or relatively small group of individuals can capture the gains derived from improved operational efficiency. There is no force analogous to the threat of bankruptcy in the private sector that will bring inefficient behavior to a halt. Since public-sector resources, including tax funds, are communally owned, their users are less likely than private resource owners to be cost conscious.

9. A growing portion of public-sector activity involves income redistribution. Economic analysis indicates two potential sources of pressure for income redistribution: (a) the public-good nature of antipoverty efforts and (b) rent seeking. From the viewpoint of a vote-maximizing politician, there is incentive to support redistribution from unorganized to well-organized groups. Considerable income redistribution in the United States is of this type.

10. Keeping government from engaging in counterproductive activities, while encouraging it to undertake things that it does well, is difficult. Properly designed constitutional rules and restraints can help us achieve that objective.

CRITICAL ANALYSIS QUESTIONS

*1. "Voters should simply ignore political candidates who play ball with special interest groups, and vote instead for candidates who will represent all the people when they are elected. Government will work far better when this happens." Evaluate.

*2. "Government can afford to take a long view when it needs to, while a private firm has a short-term outlook. Corporate officers, for example, typically care about the next 3 to 6 months, not the next 50 to 100 years. Government, not private firms, should own things like forests, where centuries, rather than the next few months, are at stake." Evaluate.

3. Suppose that you are part of a group of nature enthusiasts, and have discovered a bog that the group would like to preserve, although the site might soon be transferred to another use. Your group has some cash and can spend it several ways: it could buy the land and lease it, obtaining the right to manage it as it wishes. Alternatively, it could lobby the local authorities to regulate the land's use, forcing the current owner not to change the bog's condition or use. Using economic thinking, what analysis of the options could you provide to the group? The group wants to get the most for its money in the long run, and prefers cooperation to conflict.

4. Do you think that advertising exerts more influence on the type of car chosen by a consumer than on the type of politician chosen by the same person? Explain your answer.

5. Do you think that the political process works to the advantage of the poor? Explain. Are the poor well organized? Do they make substantial campaign contributions to candidates? Are they likely to be well informed? Is it surprising that only about one-sixth of the approximately $550 billion of cash income transfer payments in the United States is directed toward the poor? Explain.

6. Which of the following public-sector actions are designed primarily to correct "market failure": (a) laws against fraud, (b) truth-in-lending legislation, (c) rate regulation in the telephone industry, (d) legislation setting emission control standards, (e) subsidization of pure research, and (f) operation of the Post Office? Explain your answer.

*7. "When an economic function is turned over to the government, social cooperation replaces personal self-interest." Is this statement true? Why or why not?

*8. The liquor industry contributes a large share of the political funds to political contests on the state level. Yet its contributions to candidates for national office are minimal. Why do you think this is true? (*Hint:* Who regulates the liquor industry?)

9. One explanation for the shortsightedness effect in the public sector is that future voters cannot vote now to represent their future interests. Are the interests of future generations represented in market decisions? For example, if the price of chromium were expected to rise rapidly over the next 30 years due to increased scarcity, how could speculators grow rich while providing the next generation with more chromium at the expense of current consumers?

*10. **What's Wrong with This Way of Thinking?**
   "Public policy is necessary to protect the average citizen from the power of vested interest groups. In the absence of government intervention, regulated industries, such as airlines, railroads, and trucking, would charge excessive prices, products would be unsafe, and the rich would oppress the poor. Government curbs the power of special interest groups."

11. Are shoppers making decisions in the local supermarket likely to make better informed choices than voters making choices in political races? Why or why not?

12. Economics indicates that "principals" in both the private and public sector cannot be sure that their "agents" will act in their interests. Compare this principal-agent prob-

---

*Asterisk denotes questions for which answers are given in Appendix C, Selected Answers.

lem between a) stockholders and managers in the private sector and b) voters and politicians (and bureaucrats) in the public sector. Do you think inefficiencies arising from the principal-agent problem will be more or less severe in the public sector than in the private sector? Why?

13. Why might members of Congress who work for special interest and pork-barrel legislation under an unconstrained system of representative democracy nonetheless favor constitutional restraints limiting such spending?

FIVE

INTERNATIONAL ECONOMICS AND COMPARATIVE SYSTEMS

20 GAINING FROM INTERNATIONAL TRADE

If a foreign country can supply us with a commodity cheaper than we ourselves can make it, [we had] better buy it of them with some part of our own industry, employed in a way in which we have some advantage. The general industry of the country will not thereby be diminished, but only left to find out the way in which it can be employed with the greatest advantage.[1]

Adam Smith

CHAPTER FOCUS

■ How large is the international sector in the United States? What are the major import and export products of the United States? Which countries are the major trading partners of the United States?

■ Under what conditions can a nation gain from international trade?

■ How do trade restrictions affect the welfare of a nation?

■ Why do nations erect trade barriers? Are there valid economic arguments in support of trade restrictions?

■ Do trade restrictions create (or save) jobs?

■ Will free trade with low-wage countries cause wage rates in high-wage countries to decline?

We live in a shrinking world. Wheat raised on the flatlands of western Kansas may be processed into bread in a Russian factory. The breakfast of many Americans might include bananas from Honduras, coffee from Brazil, or hot chocolate made from Nigerian cocoa beans. The volume of international trade, enhanced by improved transportation and communications, has grown rapidly in recent years. Approximately 16 percent of the world's total output is now sold in a country other than that in which it was produced—nearly double the figure of two decades ago.

Although we speak of international trade, exchanges, for the most part take place between individuals (or business firms) that happen to be located in different countries. International trade, like other voluntary exchange, results because both the buyer and the seller gain from it. If both parties did not expect to gain, there would be no trade.

THE COMPOSITION OF THE INTERNATIONAL SECTOR

Exhibit 1 illustrates the growth in the size of the trade sector during the 1965–1986 period. The proportion of total output exported to a purchaser in another country has grown in all major industrial countries. The size of the trade sector varies substantially among nations. International trade comprises more than one-half of the GNP of the Netherlands and more than one quarter of the GNP in Sweden, West Germany, Canada, and the United Kingdom. The relative size of the trade sector is smaller for Australia, Japan, and the United States. Approximately 9 percent of the GNP in the United States results from trade.

However, the size of the international sector relative to GNP may actually understate the importance of trade. Many of the products we purchase from foreigners would be much more costly if we were dependent solely on our domestic production. We are dependent on foreign producers for several products, including almost all of our coffee and bananas, more than 90 percent of the bauxite we use to make aluminum, all of our chromium, diamonds, and tin, and most of our cobalt, nickel, manganese, and asbestos. The life-style of Americans (as well as that of our trading partners) would change dramatically if international trade were halted or even substantially reduced.

Exhibit 2 summarizes the leading products exported and imported by the United States. Motor vehicles, computers, aircraft, scientific equipment, and grain products are among the major export products of the United States. Petroleum, automobiles, clothing, footwear, coffee, and diamonds are among our major imports.

The structure of U.S. trade has changed in recent years. Agricultural products (wheat, corn, and soybeans) and high-technology manufacturing products (for example, aircraft, computers, telecommunication equipment, and machine tools) have comprised an increasing share of our total exports. On the other hand, foreign producers have supplied more and more import products to our domestic

---

[1]Adam Smith, *An Inquiry into the Nature and Causes of the Wealth of Nations* (1776; Cannan's ed., Chicago: University of Chicago Press, 1976), pp. 478–479.

EXHIBIT 1 ■ The Size of the Trade Sector for Selected Countries, 1965 and 1986

	Exports as a Percentage of Total Output	
Country	1965	1986
Netherlands	43	54
Sweden	22	33
West Germany	18	30
Canada	19	27
United Kingdom	19	26
France	13	22
Australia	15	16
Japan	11	12
United States	6	9

Source: The World Bank, *World Development Report: 1988* (Table 5) and *Economic Report of the President: 1988.*

markets in such established industries as steel, textiles, automobiles, electronic appliances, and crude petroleum.

International trade is far more important in some industries than in others. Exhibit 3 indicates both the major industries for which import penetration is highest and the industries for which export sales are greatest. Ninety-two percent of

EXHIBIT 2 ■ The Major Export and Import Products of the United States, 1986

Exports	Value (in billions)	Percentage of Total Exports	Imports	Value (in billions)	Percentage of Total Imports
Motor vehicles and parts	$ 17.7	8.6%	Automobiles	$ 66.3	17.9%
Computers	14.5	7.0	Petroleum	34.1	9.2
Aircraft	14.7	7.1	Clothing	17.3	4.7
Power generating machinery	9.2	4.4	Office machines	14.7	4.0
Scientific instruments	6.7	3.3	Iron and steel	8.2	2.2
Telecommunications equipment	4.4	2.1	Footwear	6.5	1.8
Soybeans	4.3	2.1	Fish	4.7	1.3
Coal	3.9	1.9	Coffee	4.3	1.2
Plastic materials	4.3	2.1	Paper	3.7	1.0
Wheat	3.7	1.6	Diamonds	3.5	0.9
Corn	2.7	1.3	Natural gas	2.9	0.8
Total	$206.4	—	Total	$370.0	—

Source: *Statistical Abstract of the United States, 1988,* pp. 775–778.

EXHIBIT 3 ■ Industries Most Affected by Imports and Exports

Industry	Imports as a Percent of U.S. Consumption, 1985	Industry	Exports as a Percent of U.S. Production, 1985
Footwear (shoes)	92	Oilfield machinery	65
Radios/TVs	64	Construction machinery	29
Children's coats	36	Phosphatic fertilizers	28
Office machines and typewriters	29	Computers	28
Crude petroleum	29	Aircraft	28
Men's shirts	29	Industrial machinery	23
Motor vehicles	28	Aircraft engines	21
Semiconductors	28	Internal combustion engines	21
Steel	18		

Source: *Statistical Abstract of the United States: 1988,* (Tables 1164, 1259, and 1261).

the shoes purchased by Americans and nearly two-thirds of our radio and television sets are produced abroad. Imports also supply a high percentage of children's coats, office machines, crude petroleum, men's shirts, and automobiles consumed in the United States. On the other hand, a large proportion of oilfield machinery, construction equipment, fertilizers, computers, and aircraft produced in the United States is exported to purchasers abroad.

With which countries does the U.S. trade the most? As Exhibit 4 illustrates, Japan and Canada head the list. In 1987, approximately one-third of U.S. exports were sold to purchasers in Canada and Japan. More than 40 percent of U.S. imports were produced in those two countries. Mexico, and the nations of the European Economic Community (particularly West Germany, the United Kingdom, France, and Italy) were also among the leading trading partners of the United States. During the 1970s, U.S. trade with petroleum-exporting countries such as Saudi Arabia and Venezuela grew rapidly. However, the volume of trade with these nations declined as the price of crude oil fell in the 1980s. South Korea, Hong Kong, and Brazil emerged as major trading partners of the United States during the 1980s.

GAINS FROM SPECIALIZATION AND TRADE

The law of comparative advantage, which we discussed in Chapter 2, explains why mutual gains arise from specialization and exchange. According to the law of comparative advantage, trading partners gain by specializing in the production of goods for which they are low opportunity cost producers and by trading for those goods for which they are high opportunity cost producers. Specialization in the area of one's comparative advantage minimizes the cost of production and leads to maximum joint output between trading partners.

International trading partners can gain if they specialize in those things they do best. We know that the resource base varies among nations. Countries with warm, moist climates such as Brazil and Colombia specialize in the production of

EXHIBIT 4

The Leading Trading Partners of the United States, 1987

Canada, Japan, Mexico, and Western European countries are the leading trading partners of the United States. In recent years, South Korea, Hong Kong, and Brazil have also emerged as important trading partners of the United States.

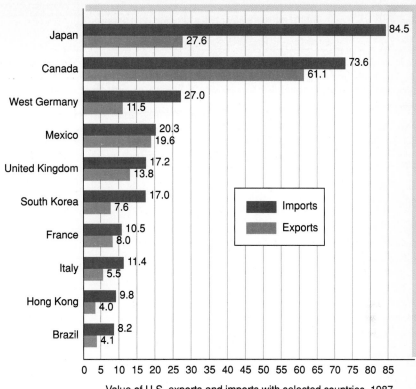

Value of U.S. exports and imports with selected countries, 1987
(billions of dollars)

Source: U.S. Department of Commerce, *Survey of Current Business,* June 1988, p. 48 (Table 3).

coffee. Land is abundant in sparsely populated nations such as Canada and Australia. These nations tend to specialize in land-intensive products, such as wheat, feed grains, and beef. In contrast, land is scarce in Japan, a nation with a highly skilled labor force. The Japanese therefore specialize in manufacturing, using their comparative advantage to produce cameras, automobiles, and electronic products for export.

It is easy to see why trade and specialization expand joint output and lead to mutual gain when the resource bases of regions differ substantially. However, even when resource differences among nations are less dramatic, mutual gain is possible. Since failure to comprehend the principle of mutual gains from trade is often a source of "fuzzy thinking," we will take the time to illustrate the principle in detail.

Suppose that the United States and Japan produce two products: food and clothing. Consider a case in which the output per worker of both food and clothing is higher for Japan than for the United States. Perhaps due to its previous experience or natural endowments, Japan has an absolute advantage in the production of both commodities. Using hypothetical data, Exhibit 5 illustrates this situation. Japanese workers can produce 3 units of food per day, compared to only 2 units per day for U.S. workers. Similarly, Japanese workers are able to produce 9 units of clothing per day, compared to only 1 unit of clothing per day for U.S. workers.

Absolute Advantage: A situation in which a nation, as the result of its previous experience and/or natural endowments, can produce a product with fewer resources than another nation.

EXHIBIT 5 ■ The Relative Cost and Production Possibilities of Food and Clothing in the United States and Japan—Hypothetical Data

Gains from exchange depend on comparative advantage, not absolute advantage. Here we illustrate a case in which U.S. workers are able to produce 2 units of food per day, compared to 3 units per day for Japanese workers. Similarly, U.S. workers are able to produce only 1 unit of clothing per day, compared to 9 units per day for Japanese workers. However, even though it is at an absolute disadvantage in the production of both goods, the U.S. has a *comparative* advantage in the production of food. The opportunity cost of producing a unit of food in the U.S. is one-half unit of clothing, compared to an opportunity cost of food in Japan of 3 units of clothing. Thus, the U.S. is the low opportunity cost producer of food. The table also illustrates various production possibilities for both the United States and Japan, given the size of their labor forces (200 million worker-days for the U.S. and 50 million worker-days for Japan) and their production efficiency. Exhibit 6 translates the data for each country into a pre-trade production possibilities curve.

	Units of Output per Worker-Day	Production Possibilities in Millions of Units (at full employment)				
		P_1	P_2	P_3	P_4	P_5
United States (200 million worker-days)						
Food	2	400	300	200	100	0
Clothing	1	0	50	100	150	200
Japan (50 million worker-days)						
Food	3	0	50	75	100	150
Clothing	9	450	300	225	150	0

Given that the Japanese workers are more efficient at producing *both* food and clothing than their American counterparts, are gains from trade possible? Perhaps surprising to some, the answer is yes. As long as *relative* production costs of the two goods differ between Japan and the United States, gains from trade are possible. Exhibits 6 and 7 illustrate this point.

Given the size of the labor force and the productivity of workers in each country, Exhibit 6 illustrates the pre-trade production and consumption possibilities for the United States and Japan. (For simplicity, we will assume that the relative cost of food and clothing in each country is independent of output. Relaxation of this assumption would not alter the basic analysis.) First, let us consider the pre-trade situation in the United States. The 200 million worker-days could be applied entirely to the production of food. In this instance, the U.S. could produce 400 million units of food (2 units per day) and zero units of clothing. Of course, clothing output could be expanded if labor were allocated from food to clothing production. However, the U.S. would have to sacrifice 2 units of food production for each unit of clothing produced. Thus, if clothing output in the U.S. is expanded from zero to 50 million, in the absence of trade, U.S. food output will have to be cut back by 100 million units—from 400M to 300M. (M refers to millions of units). Given the productivity of its workers in both food and clothing, Exhibit 5 outlines the various combinations of food and clothing that could be produced with the 200 million worker-days available in the United States.

Exhibits 5 and 6 also indicate the pre-trade production possibilities of Japan. If Japan uses all of its 50 million worker-days to produce clothing, 450 million units (9 per day times 50 million days) of clothing could be produced. It would

EXHIBIT 6

The Production
Possibilities of the United
States and Japan Before
Specialization and Trade

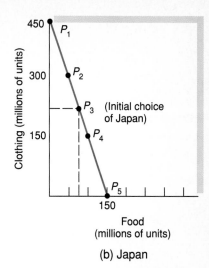

(a) United States (b) Japan

Based on the data of Exhibit 5, the production possibilities constraints of the U.S. and Japan prior to trade are illustrated here. The slope of the production possibilities constraint reflects the opportunity cost of food relative to clothing. Since Japan is the high opportunity cost producer of food, its production possibilities constraint is steeper than the constraint for the U.S. In the absence of trade, consumption in each country will be restricted by the country's production possibilities constraints. Prior to trade, the U.S. chooses combination P_4 (100M food, 150M clothing) and Japan chooses P_3 (75M food and 225M clothing).

thus be possible for Japan to produce the output combination of 450 million units of clothing and zero units of food. In the absence of trade, Japan must sacrifice 9 units of clothing for each 3 units of food it produces. A unit of food thus costs the Japanese 3 times as much as a unit of clothing. For example, if the Japanese want to produce 50 million units of food, they must be willing to sacrifice 150 million units of clothing, cutting clothing output from 450 million to 300 million. In the absence of trade, Exhibit 6b graphically illustrates the various combinations of food and clothing that the Japanese could produce with the employment of 50 million worker-days.

DIFFERENCES IN OPPORTUNITY COST— THE SOURCE OF GAINS FROM TRADE

As long as the opportunity cost of production of the two goods differs between Japan and the United States, trade will lead to mutual gain. Consider the opportunity cost of food in each of the two countries. If Japanese workers produce 1 additional unit of food, they sacrifice the production of 3 units of clothing. In Japan, the opportunity cost of 1 unit of food is 3 units of clothing. On the other hand, 1 unit of food can be produced in the U.S. at an opportunity cost of only ½ units of clothing. U.S. workers are therefore the low opportunity cost producers of food, even though they cannot produce as much food per day as the Japanese workers. Both countries can gain if the U.S. trades food to Japan for clothing at a trading ratio greater than 1 food = ½ clothing (the U.S. opportunity cost of food) but less than 1 food = 3 clothing (the Japanese opportunity cost of food). Any intermediate trading ratio between these two extremes would permit the U.S. to acquire clothing cheaper than it can be produced in the U.S. and simultaneously permit Japan to acquire food at a lesser sacrifice than it can be produced in Japan.

Suppose the two countries agree to a trading ratio (an "intermediate price") in which 1 unit of food exchanges for 1 unit of clothing. This would allow each country to specialize in the area of its comparative advantage—food for the U.S. and clothing for the Japanese—while trading for the commodity for which it is a high opportunity cost producer. As Exhibit 7 shows, specialization and trade benefits both countries. Rather than producing and consuming its initially preferred combination of 150M clothing and 100M food, the U.S. could produce 400M food and import 200M clothing from Japan in exchange for 200M food. This would permit the U.S. to consume the combination 200M units of food and 200M units of clothing. Following trade, the U.S. is able to consume a larger quantity of both food and clothing than the preferred bundle in the absence of trade.

Similarly, the Japanese benefit from specialization and exchange. Prior to trade, the preferred bundle in Japan was 225M clothing and 75M food. With trade, the Japanese could specialize in the production of clothing. If the Japanese produce 450M units of clothing and export 200M to the U.S. in exchange for

Prior to trade, the two countries produce and consume the combinations represented by US_1 (P_4 of Exhibit 6a) and J_1 (P_3 of Exhibit 6b). When trade takes place at an exchange ratio of one unit of food equals one unit of clothing, both countries gain by specializing in their area of comparative advantage. The U.S. specializes in the production of food, produces 400M units, and exports 200M units of food to Japan in exchange for 200M units of clothing. This permits the U.S. to consume the combination 200M food and 200M clothing (imported from Japan). Compared to the no-trade option chosen (150M clothing and 100M food), the U.S. is able to consume a larger quantity of both goods after trade.

Simultaneously, Japan can also increase its consumption of both goods. When Japan specializes in the production of clothing, it can produce 450M units, and export 200M units to the U.S. in exchange for 200M units of clothing. This permits Japan to consume 250M units of clothing and 200M units of food, compared to its initial preferred bundle of 225M clothing and 75M food. Specialization and trade thus expands the consumption possibilities of both countries.

(a) United States

(b) Japan

200M units of food, they would be left with the combination 200M units of food (imported from the U.S.) and 250M units of clothing. As was the case for the U.S., the exchange permits the Japanese to consume a larger quantity of both commodities relative to their preferred pre-trade output combination.

Specialization and exchange leads to an expansion in the joint output of the two countries. Prior to trade, the two countries produced 375M units of clothing (150M in the U.S. and 225M in Japan) and 175M units of food (100M in the U.S. and 75M in Japan). With specialization and trade, clothing production expands to 450M units, an increase of 75M. Similarly, food production jumps to 400M, an increase of 225M over the pre-trade output level.

Mutual gains accrue to trading partners when each nation specializes in the production of those products for which it is a low opportunity cost producer and trades them for those goods for which it is a high opportunity cost producer. Such specialization and exchange will permit nations to maximize their joint output. A country can gain from trade even when it is at an absolute disadvantage in the production of all goods. It is comparative advantage, not absolute advantage, that is the source of gains from trade.

Exhibits 4, 5, and 6 actually understate the potential of gains from trade across national boundaries. For simplicity, we can assume that each good was produced under conditions of constant cost. (This is why the production possibilities constraints of Exhibits 5 and 6 are straight lines.) Often, access to a larger market will lead to lower per unit costs, as the result of economies accompanying large scale production, marketing, and distribution. The aircraft industry illustrates this point. Approximately half of the jet planes of the major U.S. aircraft producers are sold abroad. Given the huge designing and tooling cost necessary for the production of a jumbo jet, the cost of airplanes to both domestic and foreign purchasers would be higher if it were not for international trade. Thus, economies accompanying an expansion in the size of the market will enlarge the gains from specialization and trade.

While our hypothetical example illustrates the case of complete specialization, a country need not specialize in the production of just a few products to realize gains from trade. The example of complete specialization was used for illustrative purposes only. Similarly, we ignored the potential importance of transportation costs. Of course, transportation costs reduce the potential gains from trade. Sometimes transportation costs, both real and artificially imposed, exceed the mutual gain. (See the Applications in Economics box, "Frédéric Bastiat on Obstacles to Gains from Trade.") When this is so, exchange does not occur. However, this does not negate the basic point: the potential realization of gains from specialization and exchange implied by the law of comparative advantage.

THE EXPORT-IMPORT LINK

Confusion about the merit of international trade often results because people do not consider all the consequences. Why are other nations willing to export their goods to the United States? So they can obtain dollars. Yes, but why do they want dollars? Would foreigners be willing to continue exporting oil, radios, watches, cameras, automobiles, and thousands of other valuable products to us in exchange for pieces of paper? If so, we could all be semiretired, spending only an occasional workday at the dollar printing press office! Of course, foreigners are not so naive. They trade goods for dollars so they can use the dollars to import goods and purchase ownership rights to U.S. assets.

Exports provide the buying power that makes it possible for a nation to import other goods. Nations export goods so that they will be able to import foreign products. If a nation does not import goods from foreigners, foreigners will not have the purchasing power to buy that nation's export products. Thus, the exports and imports of a nation are closely linked.

SUPPLY, DEMAND, AND INTERNATIONAL TRADE

How does international trade affect prices and output levels in domestic markets? Supply and demand analysis will help us answer this question. High transportation costs and the availability of cheaper alternatives elsewhere diminish the attractiveness to foreigners of some U.S. products. In some cases, U.S. producers will be unable to produce, transport, and market a product competitively. In other instances, however, U.S. producers will be able to sell profitably to foreigners even when transportation costs are considered.

APPLICATIONS IN ECONOMICS

Frédéric Bastiat on Obstacles to Gains from Trade

Since voluntary exchange is a positive-sum economic activity, obstacles to mutually advantageous exchange are costly. As Frédéric Bastiat notes in the following essay,[2] like bad roads and high transportation costs, tariffs limit the gains from voluntary exchange. Best known for his cutting satire, Bastiat chastises French legislators for spending tax funds to reduce the transport costs of goods and then turning around and erecting tariff barriers that, in effect, increase transportation costs. Even though it was written in 1845, the thrust of Bastiat's message remains valid today.

The illusions of inventors are proverbial, but I am positively certain that I have discovered an infallible means of bringing products from every part of the world to France, and vice versa, at a considerable reduction in cost.

It requires neither plans, estimates, preparatory study, engineers, mechan-

ics, contractors, capital, shareholders, or government aid.

Why does an article manufactured at Brussels, for example, cost dearer when it comes to Paris?

Between Paris and Brussels *obstacles* of many kinds exist. First of all, there is distance, which entails loss of time, and we must either submit to this ourselves or pay another to submit to it. Then comes [sic] rivers, marshes, accidents, bad roads, which are so many difficulties to be surmounted. We succeed in building bridges, in forming roads, and making them smoother by pavement, iron rails, etc. But all this is costly, and the commodity must be made to bear the cost.

Now, among these obstacles there is one which we have ourselves set up. . . . There are men who lie in ambush along the frontier, armed to the teeth, and whose business it is to throw difficulties into the way of transporting merchandise from the one country to another. They are called

customs officials, and they act in precisely the same way as ruts and bad roads. . . .

I often seriously ask myself how anything so whimsical could ever have entered into the human brain, as first of all to lay out many millions for the purpose of removing *natural obstacles* which lie between France and other countries, and then to lay out many more millions for the purpose of substituting *artificial obstacles* . . . so that the obstacle created and the obstacle removed neutralize each other.

[The] problem is resolved in three words: Reduce your tariff. You will then have done what is equivalent to constructing the Northern Railway without cost. . . [emphasis in the original].

---

[2]Frédéric Bastiat, *Economic Sophisms*, trans. Patrick James Stirling (London: Unwin, 1909), pp. 68–70. Reprinted with permission of T. Fisher Unwin, Ltd./Ernest Benn, Ltd., London.

Given our modern transportation and communication networks, the market for many commodities is worldwide. When a product can be transported long distances at a low cost (relative to its value), the price of the product is in effect determined by the forces of supply and demand in a worldwide market. If domestic producers have a comparative advantage in the production of the product, they will be able to compete effectively in the world market.

Using soybeans as an example, Exhibit 8 illustrates the relationship between the domestic and world markets for an internationally traded commodity. Worldwide market conditions determine the price of soybeans. In an open economy, domestic producers are free to sell and domestic consumers are free to buy the product at the world market price (P_w). At the world market price, U.S. producers will supply Q_p, while U.S. consumers will purchase Q_c. Reflecting their comparative advantage, U.S. soybean producers will export $Q_p - Q_c$ units at the world market price.

Let us compare the open economy outcome with the situation in the absence of trade. If U.S. producers were not allowed to export soybeans, the domestic price would be determined by the domestic supply (S_d) and demand (D_d) only. A lower ''no-trade'' price (P_n) would emerge. Who are the winners and losers as the result of free trade in soybeans? Clearly, soybean producers gain. Free trade allows domestic producers to sell a larger quantity (Q_p rather than Q_n). As a result, the *net* revenues of soybean producers will rise by $P_w bc P_n$. On the other hand, domestic consumers of soybeans will have to pay a higher price under free trade. Consumers will lose both (a) because they have to pay P_w rather than P_n for the Q_c units they purchase, and (b) because they lose the consumer surplus on the $Q_n - Q_c$ units now purchased at the higher price. Thus, free trade imposes a net cost of $P_w ac P_n$ on consumers. Nevertheless, free trade leads to a net welfare gain. The gains of producers outweigh the losses to consumers by the triangle *abc*.

When one focuses only on an export product, it appears that free trade benefits producers relative to consumers. As Exhibit 8 illustrates, that view is correct

(a) U.S. market for soybeans

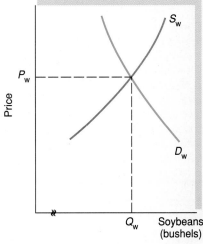

(b) World market for soybeans

as far as it goes. It is potentially misleading however, because it ignores the secondary effects. How will foreigners generate the dollars they will need to purchase soybeans and other export products of the United States? Remember, imports and exports are linked. If foreigners do not sell goods to us, they will not have the purchasing power necessary to purchase goods from us. U.S. imports—that is, the purchase of goods from low-cost foreign producers—provide foreigners with the dollar purchasing power necessary to buy U.S. exports. As the domestic supply of imported goods (used by foreigners to buy U.S. exports such as soybeans) expands, prices in import-competitive markets will decline. Of course, the lower prices in the import-competitive markets will benefit the U.S. consumers who appeared at first glance to be harmed by the higher prices (compared to the no-trade situation) in export markets.

Exhibit 9 illustrates the impact of imports, using shoes as an example. In the absence of trade, the price of shoes in the domestic market would be P_n, the intersection of the domestic supply and demand curves. However, the world price of shoes is P_w. In an open economy, many U.S. consumers would take advantage of the low shoe prices available from foreign producers. At the lower world price, U.S. consumers would purchase Q_c units of shoes, importing $Q_c - Q_p$ from foreign producers.

Compared to the no-trade situation, free trade in shoes results in lower prices and an expansion in domestic consumption. The lower prices lead to a net consumer gain of $P_n abP_w$. Domestic producers lose $P_n acP_w$ in the form of lower sales prices and reductions in output. However, the net gain of consumers exceeds the net loss of producers by abc.

For an open economy, international competition directs the resources of a nation toward the areas of their comparative advantage. When domestic producers have a comparative advantage in the production of a good, they will be able to compete effectively in the world market and profit from the export of goods to foreigners. In turn, the exports will generate the purchasing power necessary to

EXHIBIT 9

Consumer Benefits from Imports

In the absence of trade, the domestic price of shoes would be P_n. Since many foreign producers have a comparative advantage in the production of shoes, leads to lower prices. At the world price P_w, U.S. consumers will demand Q_c units, of which $Q_c - Q_p$ are imported. Compared to the no-trade situation, consumers gain $P_n abP_w$, while domestic producers lose $P_n acP_w$. A net gain of abc results.

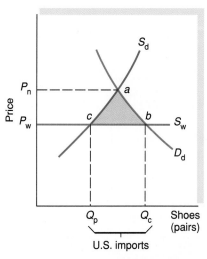

(a) U.S. market for shoes

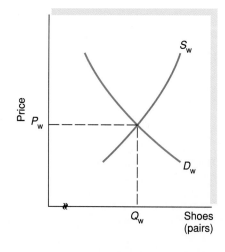

(b) World market for shoes

buy goods that foreigners can supply more economically than we can produce. Relative to the no-trade alternative, international trade and specialization result in lower prices (and higher consumption levels) for imported products and higher prices (and lower consumption levels) for exported products. More importantly, trade permits the producers of each nation to concentrate on the things they do best (produce at a low-cost), while trading for those things which they do least well. The result is an expansion in both output and consumption compared to what could be achieved in the absence of trade.

The pattern of U.S. exports and imports is consistent with this view. The United States is a nation with a technically skilled labor force, fertile farm land, and substantial capital formation. Thus, we export computers, aircraft, power generating equipment, scientific instruments, and land-intensive agricultural products—items we are able to produce at a comparatively low cost. Simultaneously, we import substantial amounts of petroleum, textile (clothing) products, shoes, coffee, and diamonds—goods for which it is costly to produce additional units domestically. Clearly, trade permits us to specialize in those areas in which our comparative advantage is greatest and trade for those products we are least suited to produce.

THE ECONOMICS OF TRADE RESTRICTIONS

Tariff: A tax levied on goods imported into a country.

Despite the potential benefits from free trade, almost all nations have erected trade barriers. What kinds of barriers are erected? Tariffs and quotas are the two most commonly used trade-restricting devices. A **tariff** is nothing more than a tax on foreign imports. As Exhibit 10 shows, tariff barriers in the United States have fluctuated. Until the 1940s, tariffs of between 30 and 50 percent of product value were often levied. In recent years, the average tariff rate has been approximately 5 percent of product value.

EXHIBIT 10

How High Are U.S. Tariffs?

Tariff rates in the United States fell sharply during the period from 1930 to 1950. Subsequently, after rising slightly during the 1950s, they have trended downward since 1960. They now represent approximately 5 percent of duty-eligible imports.

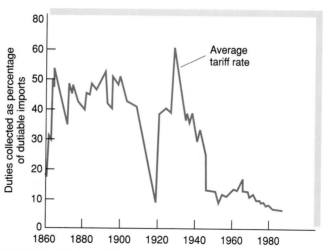

Source: U.S. Department of Commerce.

Exhibit 11 illustrates the impact of a tariff on automobiles. In the absence of a tariff, the world market price of P_w would prevail in the domestic market. At that price, U.S. consumers purchase Q_1 units. Domestic producers supply Q_{d_1}, while foreigners supply Q_1 minus Q_{d_1} units to the U.S. market. When the United States levies a tariff t on automobiles, Americans can no longer buy cars at the world price. U.S. consumers have to pay $P_w + t$ to purchase an automobile from foreigners. The market price thus rises to $P_w + t$. At that price, domestic consumers demand Q_2 units (Q_{d_2} supplied by domestic producers and $Q_2 - Q_{d_2}$ supplied by foreigners). The tariff results in a higher price and lower level of domestic consumption.

The tariff benefits domestic producers and the government at the expense of consumers. Since they do not pay the tariff, domestic producers will expand their output in response to the higher (protected) market price. In effect, the tariff acts as a subsidy to domestic producers. Domestic producers gain the area S (Exhibit 11) in the form of additional net revenues. The tariff raises revenues equal to the area T for the government. The areas U and V represent costs imposed on consumers that do not benefit either producers or the government. Simply put, U and V represent a deadweight loss (loss of efficiency) as the result of the tariff.

The story does not end here, however. Since foreigners are unable to sell goods for which they are low-cost producers in the U.S. market, they acquire fewer dollars. Foreign demand for U.S. exports, products for which we are low-

EXHIBIT 11

Impact of a Tariff

Here we illustrate the impact of a tariff on automobiles. In the absence of the tariff, the world price of automobiles is P_w: U.S. consumers purchase Q_1 units (Q_{d_1} from domestic producers plus $Q_1 - Q_{d_1}$ from foreign producers). The tariff makes it more costly for Americans to purchase automobiles from foreigners. Imports decline and the domestic price increases. Consumers lose the sum of the areas S + U + T + V in the form of higher prices and reduction in consumer surplus. Producers gain the area S and the tariff generates T tax revenues for the government. The areas U and V are deadweight losses due to a reduction in allocative efficiency.

cost producers, declines because our trade restrictions have diminished the ability of foreigners to acquire the dollars necessary to buy our goods. Because of this, we end up producing less in areas where we have a comparative advantage and more in areas where we are a high-cost producer. Potential gains from specialization and trade go unrealized.

Import Quota: A specific quantity (or value) of a good permitted to be imported into a country during a given year.

An **import quota,** like a tariff, is designed to restrict foreign goods and protect domestic industries. A quota places a ceiling on the amount of a product that can be imported during a given period (typically a year). Many products, ranging from steel to brooms, are subject to import quotas.

Since quotas reduce the foreign supply to the domestic market, the price of quota-protected products is higher than that which would result from free trade. In many ways, quotas are more harmful than tariffs. With a quota, additional foreign supply is prohibited regardless of how low the prices of foreign products are. With a tariff, products are at least supplied to the domestic market if the cost advantage of foreign producers is sufficient to overcome the tariff.

The United States maintains tariffs in excess of 15 percent on various products, including footwear, fruit juice, light trucks, wool fabrics, women's coats, ceramic tiles, and neckties. In addition, quotas restrict the sale of textiles, apparel, sugar, machine tools, steel products, peanuts, books, and dairy products, among other goods. How much do these trade restraints cost the American consumer? Estimates indicate that trade barriers increased the cost of goods and services to American consumers by $50 billion to $75 billion in the mid-1980s. This represents between $500 and $750 per household, or approximately 2 percent of our aggregate output.[3]

The higher prices emanating from trade restrictions exert an uneven impact across income groupings. Nearly half of the cost of trade restrictions comes in the form of higher prices for clothing and other textile products. Thus, it is not surprising that, on average, tariffs and quotas push up the prices of items that constitute a larger share of the family budget in low-income households than in high-income households. Exhibit 12 presents the results of a Federal Reserve study that indicates the size of an income tax surcharge that would be equivalent to the cost of the U.S. trade restrictions across income groupings.[4] For low-income families (income between $7,000 and $9,500), the costs of trade restrictions are the equivalent to a 66 percent increase in income taxes. In contrast, for high-income families (above $58,500) the same price increases impose a cost equivalent to only a 5 percent income tax surcharge. Clearly, the study indicates that a disproportionate share of the cost of trade restrictions in the United States is imposed on low-income households. In essence, the restrictions are equivalent to a highly regressive income tax used to subsidize selected industries.

---

[3]See Murray Weidenbaum and Michael C. Munger, "Protection at Any Price," *Regulation,* July/August 1983; Gary Clyde Hufbauer, Diane T. Berliner, and Kimberly Ann Elliot, *Trade Protection in the United States: 31 Case Studies* (Washington, D.C.: Institute for International Economics, 1986); and Michael C. Munger and Kathleen A. Rehbein, "The High Cost of Protectionism" *Europe,* May/June 1984.

[4]Susan Hickok, "The Consumer Cost of U.S. Trade Restraints," Federal Reserve Bank of New York, *Quarterly Review,* Summer 1985, pp. 10–11.

EXHIBIT 12 ■ Who Pays for Trade Restrictions?

Income Group	Income Tax Surcharge Equivalent to the Cost of the Trade Restrictions in 1984
7,000– 9,350	66%
9,350–11,700	47
11,700–14,050	39
14,050–16,400	33
16,400–18,700	28
18,700–23,400	24
23,400–28,050	20
28,050–35,100	17
35,100–46,800	13
46,800–58,500	10
58,500 and over	5

Source: Susan Hickok, ''The Consumer Cost of U.S. Trade Restraints'', Federal Reserve Bank of New York, *Quarterly Review* (Summer 1985), pp. 10–11.

WHY DO NATIONS ADOPT TRADE RESTRICTIONS?

If trade restrictions promote inefficiency and reduce the potential gains from specialization and trade, why do nations adopt them? Three factors contribute to the existence of trade barriers: partially valid arguments for the protection of specific industries under certain circumstances; economic illiteracy—ignorance as to who is helped and who is harmed by trade restrictions; and the special interest nature of trade restrictions. We now turn to a consideration of each of these factors.

PARTIALLY VALID ARGUMENTS FOR RESTRICTIONS

There are four major, at least partially valid, arguments for protecting certain domestic industries from foreign competitors.

1. *National Defense Argument.* Certain industries—aircraft, petroleum, and weapons, for example—are vital to national defense. A nation might want to protect such industries from foreign competitors so that a domestic supply of these materials would be available in case of an international conflict. Would we want to be entirely dependent on Arabian or Russian petroleum? Would complete dependence on French aircraft by wise? Most Americans would answer no, even if trade restrictions were required to preserve these domestic industries.

The national defense argument is sound; however, it is often abused. Relatively few industries are truly vital to our national defense. Partial reliance on foreign producers during peacetime may not weaken the capacity of certain domestic industries, particularly those that extract raw materials, to supply the nation's needs in case of war. When the merits of protecting a domestic industry are analyzed, the costs and benefits involved in the national defense argument must be weighed carefully.

2. *The Industrial Diversity Argument.* Economies that are largely dependent on the revenues from a few major export products or raw materials are character-

ized by instability. If a domestic economy specializes in the production of only one or two major goods, changes in world demand can exert a drastic influence on domestic economic conditions. Brazil's coffee-dominated economy is an example. Protection of domestic industries would encourage diversity. Clearly, this argument does not apply to the U.S. economy, which is already highly diversified.

3. *The Infant-Industry Argument.* The advocates of this view hold that new domestic industries should be protected from older, established foreign competitors. As the new industry matures, it will be able to stand on its own feet and

MYTHS OF ECONOMICS

"Free trade with low-wage countries such as China and India would cause the wages of U.S. workers to fall."

Many Americans believe that trade restrictions are necessary to protect U.S. workers from imported goods produced by cheap foreign labor. How can U.S. labor compete with Indian and Chinese workers receiving $1 per hour? The fallacy of this argument stems from a misunderstanding of both the source of high wages and the law of comparative advantage.

High hourly wages do not necessarily mean high per unit labor cost. Labor productivity must also be considered. For example, suppose a U.S. steel worker receives an hourly wage rate of $20. A steel worker in India receives only $2 per hour. Given the capital and production methods used in the two countries, however, the U.S. worker produces 20 times as many tons of steel per worker-hour as the Indian worker. Because of the higher productivity per worker-hour, *per unit* labor cost is actually lower in the United States than in India!

Labor in the United States possesses a high skill level and works with large amounts of capital equipment. These factors contribute to the high productivity and the high hourly wages of American workers. Similarly, low productivity per worker-

hour is the primary reason for low wages in such countries as India and China.

When analyzing the significance of wage and productivity differentials across countries, one must remember that gains from trade emanate from *comparative advantage,* not *absolute* advantage (see Exhibits 4, 5, and 6). The United States cannot produce everything cheaper than China or India merely because U.S. workers are more productive and work with more capital than workers in China and India. Neither can the Chinese and Indians produce everything cheaper merely because their wage rates are low compared to the U.S. When resources are directed by relative prices and the principle of comparative advantage, *both* high-wage and low-wage countries gain from the opportunity to specialize in those activities that, *relatively speaking,* they do best.

The comparative advantage of low-wage countries is likely to be in the production of labor-intensive goods such as wigs, rugs, toys, textiles, and assembled manufactured products. On the other hand, the comparative advantage of the United States, a country with a highly skilled labor force and an abundance of fertile farm land, lies in the production of high-technology manufacturing products (computers, aircraft, and scientific instruments, for example)

and land-intensive agricultural products (wheat, corn, and soybeans). The pattern of U.S. exports and imports confirms this point (see Exhibit 2).

Trade permits both high- and low-wage countries to reallocate their resources away from productive activities in which they are inefficient (relative to foreign producers) to activities in which they are highly efficient. The net result is an increase in output and consumption opportunities for both trading partners.

If foreigners, even low-wage foreigners, will sell us a product cheaper than we ourselves could produce it, we can gain by using our resources to produce other things. Perhaps an extreme example will illustrate the point. Suppose a foreign producer, perhaps a Santa Claus who pays workers little or nothing, were willing to supply us with free winter coats. Would it make sense to enact a tariff barrier to keep out the free coats? Of course not. Resources that were previously used to produce coats could now be freed to produce other goods. Output and the availability of goods would expand. The real wages of U.S. workers would rise. National defense aside, it makes no more sense to erect trade barriers to keep out cheap foreign goods than to keep out the free coats of a friendly, foreign Santa Claus.

compete effectively with foreign producers. The infant-industry argument has a long and somewhat notorious history. Alexander Hamilton used it to argue for the protection of early U.S. manufacturing. While it is clearly an argument for temporary protection, the protection, once granted, is often difficult to remove. Nearly a century ago, this argument was used to gain tariff protection for the young steel industry in the United States. Surely, today, steel is a very mature industry. Nevertheless, public policy has failed to remove the tariff.

Dumping: The sale of a good by a foreign supplier in another country at a price lower than the supplier sells it in its home market.

4. *Anti-dumping Argument.* **Dumping** is the sale of goods abroad at a price below their cost (and below their price in the domestic market of the exporting nation). In some cases, dumping merely reflects the exporter's desire to penetrate a foreign market. In other instances, dumping may emanate from export subsidies of foreign governments. At various times in the past, it has been alleged that Argentina has dumped textiles, Korea has dumped steel, and Canada has dumped radial tires into the U.S. market. Dumping is illegal. The Trade Agreements Act of 1979 provides for special anti-dumping duties (tariffs) when a good is sold in the United States at a price lower than that found in the domestic market of the exporting nation.

As in the case of imports, dumping generally benefits domestic consumers and imposes costs on domestic producers. The lower prices of the "dumped" goods permit consumers to obtain the goods more economically than they are available from domestic producers. Simultaneously, the lower prices make it more difficult for domestic producers to compete. Predictably, domestic producers (and their employees) are the major source of the charges that dumping is unfair.

Economists generally emphasize two points with regard to dumping. First, dumping can, in a few instances, be used as a weapon to gain monopoly power. For example, if the foreign firm temporarily cuts its price below cost, it might eliminate domestic competition and later raise its price to a higher level after the domestic competitors have been driven from the market. However, this is usually not a feasible strategy. After all, domestic producers may re-enter the market if price is raised in the future. In addition, alternative foreign suppliers limit the monopoly power of a producer attempting this strategy. Even though the charge that foreigners are attempting to monopolize the U.S. market is often made by producers, economists are generally skeptical. Before accepting this conclusion, economists believe that one would do well to consider whether the dumping charge might merely be a "red herring" reflecting the desire of domestic producers to reduce competition from abroad.

Second, the law of comparative advantage indicates that a country (as a whole) can gain from the purchase of foreign-produced goods when they are cheaper than domestic goods. This is true regardless of whether the low price of foreign goods reflects comparative advantage, subsidies by foreign governments, or poor business practices. Unless the foreign supplier is likely to monopolize the domestic market, there is little reason to believe that dumping harms the economy receiving the goods.

TRADE BARRIERS AND JOBS

Part of the popularity of trade restrictions stems from their ability to protect or create easily identifiable jobs. Whenever foreign competitors begin to make inroads into markets that have traditionally been supplied by domestic producers, the outcry for "protection to save jobs" is sure to be raised. Many politicians will recognize the potential political gain from a protectionist policy and respond accordingly.

The recent history of the automobile industry in the United States illustrates this point. During the 1970s, imported automobiles gained a larger and larger share of the U.S. market. There were several reasons for these gains. High wages in the U.S. auto industry, improved efficiency of foreign producers, excessive government regulation of the domestic auto industry, and failure of U.S. producers to offer high performance small cars when gasoline prices soared during the 1970s were all contributing factors. The increased competition from imports encouraged both management and labor to seek trade restrictions.

The Reagan administration, firmly on record as favoring free trade, was reluctant to request either tariffs or quotas. Nevertheless, the administration bargained with the Japanese government, which eventually agreed to restrict "voluntarily" the number of Japanese automobiles sold in the U.S. market to 1.6 million. As is the case with quotas, voluntary restrictions push up prices in the domestic market. Robert Crandall of the Brookings Institution estimates that, in 1987, the restraints increased the price of Japanese automobiles sold in the United States by approximately $2,500 and the price of American models by around $750. When foreign producers limit their sales to the U.S. market, they will be able to sell the restricted quantity at a higher *per unit* price. The voluntary restrictions of the Japanese illustrate this point. Prior to the restrictions, the price differential between a Toyota Corolla or a Nissan Sentra sold in Japan and the same automobiles sold in the U.S. was less than $500. After the restrictions, the Japanese-U.S. price differential for these automobiles jumped to approximately $3,000.[5] In a large measure, Japanese producers were the primary beneficiaries of voluntary restrictions.

The restrictions will also exert a secondary effect that usually goes unnoticed. Since the Japanese will be selling fewer automobiles in the U.S. market, they will earn fewer dollars with which to purchase grains, lumber, chemicals, and other U.S. export products. Workers in export industries will be hurt as the Japanese demand for their products declines. Jobs in these U.S. industries will be destroyed. Interestingly, the wage rates in most of these American export industries are approximately half the wage rates of the automobile workers helped by the restrictions.

In the long run, trade restrictions such as quotas, tariffs, and allegedly voluntary limitations can neither create nor destroy jobs. Jobs protected by import restrictions will be offset by jobs destroyed in export industries. The choice is not whether automobiles (or some other product) will be produced in the United States or Japan. The real question is (a) whether our resources will be used to produce automobiles and other products for which we are a high opportunity cost producer or (b) whether the resources will be used for agriculture, high-technology manufactured goods, and other products for which we are a low cost producer.

What about industries that are long-time recipients of protection? Of course, sudden and complete removal of trade barriers would harm producers and work-

---

[5]See Robert W. Crandall, "Detroit Rode Quotas to Prosperity," *The Wall Street Journal*, January 29, 1986.

ers. It would be costly to effect an immediate transfer of the protected resources to other areas and industries. Gradual removal of such barriers would minimize the cost of relocation and eliminate the shock effect. The government might also cushion the burden by subsidizing the retraining and relocation costs of displaced workers.

SPECIAL INTERESTS AND THE POLITICS OF TRADE RESTRICTIONS

Protectionism is a politician's delight because it delivers visible benefits to the protected parties while imposing the costs as a hidden tax on the public.

Murray L. Weidenbaum
(former Chairman of the Council of Economic Advisers)

Even when trade restrictions promote inefficiency and harm economic welfare, political entrepreneurs may be able to reap political gain from their enactment. Those harmed by a protectionist policy for industry X will individually bear a small and difficult-to-identify cost. Consumers who will pay higher prices for the products of a protected industry are an unorganized group. Most of them will not associate the higher product prices with the protectionist policy. Similarly, numerous export producers (and their employees) will individually be harmed only slightly. The rational ignorance effect implies that those harmed by trade restrictions are likely to be uninformed and unconcerned about our trade policy.

In contrast, special interest groups—specific industries, unions, and regions—will be very concerned with the protection of their industries. The benefits they derive will be quite visible. Thus, they will be ready to aid political entrepreneurs who support their views and penalize those who do not. Clearly, vote-seeking politicians will be sensitive to the special interest views.

Often, there will be a conflict between sound economics and good politics on trade restriction issues. Real-world public policy will, of course, reflect the politics of the situation.

EFFORTS TO LIMIT PROTECTIONISM

GATT AGREEMENTS

General Agreement on Tariffs and Trade (GATT): An organization composed of most non-Communist countries designed to set the rules for the conduct of international trade and reduce barriers to trade among nations.

After high tariffs restricted international trade during the early 1930s, Congress in 1934 adopted legislation authorizing the President to negotiate limited reductions in trade restrictions in exchange for similar concessions from our trading partners. Concern about the impact of trade restrictions on international economic health eventually led to the development of a multination organization called **General Agreement on Tariffs and Trade (GATT)** shortly after the Second World War. GATT has grown from 22 members to an international organization of 87 members representing nations that conduct approximately 80 percent of the world trade. GATT spells out the rules for international trade and oversees bargaining designed to reduce trade barriers among nations.

Modern U.S. trade policy conducted within the framework of GATT has substantially reduced tariffs. Under the Trade Expansion Act of 1962, Congress authorized the President to reduce tariffs by up to 50 percent and to completely eliminate duties of less than 5 percent. This led to the Kennedy Round of GATT negotiations that reduced tariffs on several industrial commodities. Legislation adopted in 1974 provided the President with similar authority and led to the Tokyo Round of tariff reductions which was completed in 1979. Authorizing the President to reduce tariffs within the framework of GATT without additional Congressional action limits the ability of special interests to erect and maintain overt trade barriers. Thus, tariffs have declined substantially during the post-Second World War period (see Exhibit 10).

Paradoxically, while tariffs have been reduced, various nations have established price controls and regulatory policies that also limit the freedom of international trade. An important feature of the Tokyo Round of GATT negotiations was an agreement to limit the growth of nontariff barriers. Whether this agreement will eventually lead to meaningful reductions in nontariff barriers is dependent on the bargaining processes within the framework of GATT.

THE CANADA–UNITED STATES FREE-TRADE AGREEMENT

As we previously discussed, Canada is the leading trading partner of the United States. Under an agreement ratified in 1988, Canada and the United States will (1) phase out all tariffs between the two countries during the next ten years, (2) reduce several nontariff trade barriers, (3) remove many of the restrictions on cross-border investment, and (4) create a U.S.–Canada Tribunal to settle trade disputes between the two countries. Approximately three-fourths of the trade between the two countries was tariff-free prior to the trade agreement. The pact phases out tariff barriers on seafood, forest products, textiles, petroleum products, and heavy equipment, either immediately or over time periods ranging from one to five years. The agreement is an important step toward the establishment of the world's largest (in terms of value of goods) free trade area.

Both Canada and the United States will reap substantial gains from the agreement. Domestic producers in both countries will now have free access to a larger market. Many products can be sold at a lower per-unit price if a larger volume of production can be planned and produced. When economies of scale are important, expansion in the size of the market generally leads to lower costs for producers and lower prices to consumers. Free access to the huge U.S. market will be particularly important to Canadian producers in markets where economies of scale are important. Elimination of trade barriers will also provide consumers with greater variety and an expanded choice among suppliers. Predictably, the domestic price of a product will fall when the nation's net imports of the good expand, and rise in response to the growth of net exports of the good. These price changes will direct resources into the areas where their comparative advantage is greatest. As a result, each country is able to specialize more fully in those products for which it is the low opportunity cost producer and to realize more fully the potential gains from economies of scale. The result will be a larger aggregate output and higher standard of living in both countries.

LOOKING AHEAD

There are many similarities between trade within national borders and trade across national boundaries. However, there is also a major difference. In addition to the exchange of goods for money, trade across national borders generally involves the exchange of national currencies. The next chapter deals with the financial arrangements under which international trade is conducted.

CHAPTER SUMMARY

1. The volume of international trade has grown rapidly in recent decades. In the mid-1980s, approximately 16 percent of the world's output was sold in a different country than that in which it was produced.

2. The trade sector comprises approximately 9 percent of the U.S. GNP. More than half of all U.S. trade is with Canada, Japan, and the developed nations of Western Europe.

3. Comparative advantage rather than absolute advantage is the source of gains from trade. As long as the *relative* production costs of goods differ between nations, the nations will be able to gain from trade.

4. Mutual gains from trade accrue when each nation specializes in the production of goods for which it is a low opportunity producer and trades for goods for which it is a high opportunity cost producer. This pattern of specialization and trade allows trading partners to maximize their joint output and expand their consumption possibilities.

5. Exports and imports are closely linked. The exports of a nation are the primary source of purchasing power used to import goods. When a nation restricts imports, it simultaneously limits the ability of foreigners to acquire the purchasing power necessary to buy the nation's exports.

6. International competition directs the resources of a nation toward their areas of comparative advantage. In an open economy, when domestic producers have a comparative advantage in the production of a good, they will be able to export their product and compete effectively in the world market. On the other hand, for commodities in which foreign producers have the comparative advantage, a nation could import the goods more economically (at a lower opportunity cost) than they can be produced domestically.

7. Relative to the no-trade alternative, international exchange and specialization result in lower prices for products that are imported and higher domestic prices for products that are exported. However, the net effect is an expansion in the aggregate output and consumption possibilities available to a nation.

8. The application of a tariff, quota, or other import restriction to a product reduces the amount of the product that foreigners supply to the domestic market. As a result of diminished supply, consumers face higher prices for the protected product. Essentially, import restrictions are subsidies to producers (and workers) in protected industries at the expense of (a) consumers and (b) producers (and workers) in export industries. Restrictions reduce the ability of domestic producers to specialize in those areas for which their comparative advantage is greatest.

9. Both high-wage and low-wage countries gain from the opportunity to specialize in the production of goods that they produce at a low opportunity cost. If a low-wage country can supply a good to the United States cheaper than the U.S. can produce it, the U.S. can gain by purchasing the good from the low-wage country and using the scarce resources of the United States to produce other goods for which it has a comparative advantage.

10. National defense, industrial diversity, and the infant-industry arguments can be used to justify trade restrictions for specific industries under certain conditions. It is clear, though, that the power of special interest groups and voter ignorance about the harmful effects of trade restrictions offer the major explanations for real-world protectionist public policy.

11. In the long-run, trade restrictions do not create jobs. A decline in our imports from other nations leads to a reduction in those nations' purchasing power and thus to a reduced demand for our export products. Jobs protected by import restrictions are offset by jobs destroyed in export industries. Since this result of restrictions often goes unnoticed, their political popularity is understandable. Nevertheless, the restrictions are inefficient, since they lead to the loss of potential gains from specialization and exchange.

12. Even though trade restrictions promote economic inefficiency, they are often attractive to politicians because they generate visible benefits to special interests—particularly business and labor interests in protected industries—while imposing costs on consumers and taxpayers that are *individually* small and largely invisible.

CRITICAL ANALYSIS QUESTIONS

*1. "Trade restrictions limiting the sale of cheap foreign goods in the United States are necessary to protect the prosperity of Americans." Evaluate this statement made by an American politician.

2. Suppose at the time of the Civil War the United States had been divided into two countries and that through the years no trade existed between the two. How would the standard of living in the "divided" United States have been affected? Explain.

*3. Can both (a) and (b) be true? Explain.

   a. "Tariffs and import quotas promote economic inefficiency and reduce the real income of a nation. Economic analysis suggests that nations can gain by eliminating trade restrictions."

   b. "Economic analysis suggests that there is good reason to expect trade restrictions to exist in the real world."

4. "Tariffs and quotas are necessary to protect the high wages of the American worker." Do you agree or disagree? Why?

*5. "An increased scarcity of a product benefits producers and harms consumers. In effect, tariffs and other trade restrictions increase the domestic scarcity of products by reducing the supply from abroad. Such policies benefit domestic producers of the restricted product at the expense of domestic consumers." Evaluate this statement.

*6. The United States uses an import quota to maintain the domestic price of sugar well above the world price. Analyze the impact of the quota. Use supply and demand analysis to illustrate your answer. To whom do the gains and losses of this policy accrue? How does the quota affect the efficiency of resource allocation in the United States? Why do you think Congress is supportive of this policy?

7. Suppose that it costs American textile manufacturers $20 to produce a shirt, while foreign producers can supply the same shirt for $15. (a) Would a tariff of $6 per shirt help American manufacturers compete with foreigners? (b) Would a subsidy of $6 per shirt to domestic manufacturers help them compete? (c) Is there any difference between the tariff and a direct subsidy to the domestic manufacturers?

*8. "Getting more Americans to realize that it pays to make things in the United States is the heart of the competitiveness issue." (quote from an American business magazine)

   a. Would Americans be better off if more of them paid higher prices in order to "buy American" rather than purchase from foreigners? Would U.S. employment be higher?

   b. Would Californians be better off if they only bought goods produced in California? Would the employment in California be higher?

   c. Do you think the above statement is true? Explain.

*9. It is often alleged that Japanese producers receive subsidies from their government that permit them to sell their products at a low price in the U.S. market. Do you think we should erect trade barriers to keep out cheap Japanese goods if the source of their low price is governmental subsidies? Why or why not?

10. How do tariffs and quotas differ? Can you think of any reason why foreign producers might prefer a quota rather than a tariff? Explain.

11. **What's Wrong with This Economic Experiment?**

A researcher hypothesizes that higher tariffs on imported automobiles will cause total employment in the United States to increase. Automobile tariffs are raised and the following year employment in the U.S. auto industry increases by 50,000. The researcher concludes that the higher tariffs on imported automobiles increased total domestic employment by creating approximately 50,000 jobs in the U.S. automobile industry.

---

*Asterisk denotes questions for which answers are given in Appendix C, Selected Answers.

*12. Does international trade cost Americans jobs? Does interstate trade cost your state jobs? What is the major affect of international and interstate trade?

13. ''The United States is suffering from a huge excess of imports. Cheap foreign products are driving American firms out of business and leaving our economy in shambles.'' Evaluate this statement from an American politician.

14. Do you think the United States would benefit if all trade barriers with Mexico were eliminated? Would Mexico benefit? Would wages in the United States fall to the level of wages in Mexico? Why or why not?

*15. Tariffs not only reduce the volume of imports, they also reduce the volume of exports. (True or false? Explain.)

*16. Suppose that as the result of traveling abroad, you are permitted to bring a limited quantity of goods into the United States duty-free. Will the presence of a tariff on a good affect the likelihood that you will find a bargain on the good while abroad?

21

INTERNATIONAL FINANCE AND THE FOREIGN EXCHANGE MARKET

Over the past 20 years, economic relationships among countries have been marked by an increasing degree of interdependence.[1]

Donald Kohn

CHAPTER FOCUS

■ What determines the exchange rate value of the dollar relative to other currencies?

■ How do monetary and fiscal policy influence the exchange rate?

■ What information is included in the balance of payments accounts of a nation? Why are these accounts important?

■ Is a trade deficit a sign of economic weakness? Is a trade surplus an indication of economic strength?

■ What are the advantages and disadvantages of the current international monetary system?

Since the Second World War, the volume of international exchange has grown rapidly. As we discussed in the last chapter, specialization and trade enable the countries of the world to expand their joint output, since the production of each good is undertaken by those producers who are most efficient. Like voluntary exchange within domestic markets, voluntary exchange between persons of different nations is mutually advantageous to the trading partners. Since international trade fosters a more efficient use of resources, the world has benefited substantially from its growth.

International trade is complicated by the fact that it generally involves two different currencies. Farmers in the United States want dollars, not some foreign currency, when they sell their wheat. Therefore, foreign purchasers must exchange their currency for dollars before they buy U.S. wheat. Similarly, French wine makers want to be paid in francs, not dollars. Therefore, U.S. importers must exchange dollars for francs when they purchase French wines (or French exporters must obtain francs before they pay the winemakers).

Since 1971, most Western nations have permitted the value of their monetary unit relative to other currencies to be determined largely by market forces. In this chapter, we analyze how international currencies are linked and how the rates for their exchange are determined.

THE FOREIGN EXCHANGE MARKET

Foreign Exchange Market: The market in which the currencies of different countries are bought and sold.

If a U.S. buyer wants to purchase a good or service from a seller in another country, the buyer can exchange dollars for the currency of the seller's country in the foreign exchange market. The foreign exchange market is a widely disperse, highly organized market in which the currencies of different countries are bought and sold. Commercial banks and currency brokers around the world are primary organizers of the market.

Suppose you own a shoe store in the United States and are preparing to place an order for sandals from a manufacturer. You can purchase the sandals from a domestic manufacturer and pay for them with dollars. Alternately, you can buy them from a British manufacturer, in which case they must be paid for in pounds because the employees of the British manufacturer must be paid with pounds. If you buy from the British firm, either you will have to change dollars into pounds at a bank and send them to the British producer, or the British manufacturer will have to go to a bank and change your dollar check into pounds. In either case, purchasing the British sandals will involve an exchange of dollars for pounds.

Exchange Rate: The domestic piece of one unit of foreign currency. For example, if it takes $1.50 to purchase one English pound, the dollar-pound exchange rate is 1.50.

The British producer sells sandals for 10 pounds per pair. How can you determine whether the price is high or low? To compare the price of the sandals produced by the British firm with the price of domestically produced sandals, you must know the exchange rate between the dollar and the pound. The exchange rate is simply the price of one national currency (the pound, for example) in terms of another national currency (such as the U.S. dollar). Exchange rates enable

---

[1]Donald Kohn, "Interdependence, Exchange Rates, Flexibility and National Economies," Federal Reserve Bank of Kansas City, *Monthly Review* (April 1975), p. 3.

consumers in one country to translate the prices of foreign goods into units of their own currency. When the exchange rate is expressed in terms of dollars per unit of the foreign currency, the dollar price is merely the foreign price multiplied by the exchange rate. For example, if it takes 1.50 dollars to obtain 1 pound, then the British sandals priced at 10 pounds would cost $15.00 (10 times the 1.50 dollar price of the pound).

Suppose the dollar pound exchange rate is $1.50 = 1 pound and that you decide to buy 200 pairs of sandals from the British manufacturer at 10 pounds ($15) per pair. You will need 2,000 pounds in order to pay the British manufacturer. If you contact an American bank that handles exchange rate transactions and write the bank a check for $3,000 (the 1.50 exchange rate multiplied by 2,000), it will supply the 2,000 pounds. The bank will typically charge a small fee for handling the transaction.

Where does the American bank get the pounds? The bank obtains the pounds from British importers who want dollars to buy things from Americans. Note that the U.S. demand for foreign currencies (such as the pound) comes from the demand of Americans for things purchased from foreigners. On the other hand, the U.S. supply of foreign exchange comes from the demand of foreigners for things bought from Americans.

Exhibit 1 presents data on the exchange rate between the dollar and selected foreign currencies during the 1973–1989 period, as well as an index of the exchange rate value of the dollar against ten major currencies. Under the current flexible system, the exchange rate between currencies changes from day to day and even from hour to hour. Thus, the annual exchange rate data given in Exhibit 1 are really averages for each year.

Between 1980 and 1985, the exchange rate value of the dollar appreciated against the major foreign currencies. An **appreciation** in the value of a nation's currency means that fewer units of the currency are now required to purchase one unit of a foreign currency. For example, in 1985, only 34 cents were required to purchase a German mark, down from 55 cents in 1980.[2] As the result of this appreciation in the value of the dollar relative to the mark, West German goods became less expensive to Americans. The direction of change in the prices that West Germans paid for American goods was just the opposite. An appreciation of the U.S. dollar in terms of the mark is the same thing as a depreciation in the mark relative to the dollar.

A **depreciation** makes foreign goods more expensive, since it decreases the number of units of the foreign currency that can be purchased with a unit of domestic currency. As Exhibit 1 shows, the number of cents required to purchase a French franc, German mark, Japanese yen, or British pound rose substantially during 1986–1987. The dollar thus depreciated against these currencies, increasing the price of goods purchased by Americans from producers in these countries during 1986–1987.

Appreciation: An increase in the value of a domestic currency relative to foreign currencies. An appreciation increases the purchasing power of the domestic currency over foreign goods.

Depreciation: A reduction in the value of a domestic currency relative to foreign currencies. A depreciation reduces the purchasing power of the domestic currency over foreign goods.

---

[2]Since an appreciation means a *lower* price of foreign currencies, some may think it looks like a depreciation. Just remember that a lower price of the foreign currency means that one's domestic currency will buy more units of the foreign currency and thus more goods and services from foreigners. For example, if the dollar price of the pound falls, this means that a dollar will buy more pounds and thus more goods and services from the British. Therefore, a lower dollar price of the pound means the dollar has appreciated relative to the pound.

EXHIBIT 1 ■ Foreign Exchange Rates, 1973–1989 (U.S. cents per unit of foreign currency)					
Year	French Franc	German Mark	Japanese Yen	British Pound	Canadian Dollar	Index of Exchange Rate Value of the Dollar (Ten Currencies)[a]
1973	22.5	37.8	0.369	245.10	99.9	99.1
1974	20.8	38.7	0.343	234.03	102.2	101.4
1975	23.4	40.7	0.337	222.16	98.3	98.5
1976	20.9	39.7	0.337	180.48	101.4	105.6
1977	20.3	43.1	0.373	174.49	94.1	103.3
1978	22.2	49.9	0.480	191.84	87.7	92.4
1979	23.5	54.6	0.458	212.24	85.3	88.1
1980	23.7	55.1	0.443	227.74	85.5	87.4
1981	18.4	44.4	0.45	202.43	83.4	102.9
1982	15.2	41.2	0.402	174.80	81.0	116.6
1983	13.1	39.2	0.421	151.59	81.1	125.3
1984	11.4	35.1	0.421	133.68	77.1	138.3
1985	11.1	34.0	0.419	129.74	73.2	143.2
1986	14.4	46.1	0.594	146.77	72.0	112.2
1987	16.6	55.6	0.691	163.98	75.4	96.9
1988	16.8	56.9	0.780	178.13	81.3	92.8
1989/May	14.7	49.6	0.699	1.568	82.8	100.2

[a]March 1973 = 100. In addition to the five currencies listed above, the index includes the Belgium franc, Italian lira, Netherlands guilder, Swedish krona, and Swiss franc.

Source: Council of Economic Advisers, *Economic Report of the President* (Washington, D.C.: U.S. Government Printing Office, 1989) and *The Wall Street Journal*, May 25, 1989.

The ten-currency index of the dollar's exchange rate value provides evidence on what is happening to the dollar's general exchange rate value.[3] An increase in the index implies an appreciation in the dollar, while a decline is indicative of a depreciation in the dollar. During the 1970s, the ten-currency index changed by only small amounts from year to year. However, between 1980 and 1985, the index indicates that the exchange rate value of the dollar increased sharply each year. The dollar appreciated by more than 60 percent during the five-year period. In contrast, it depreciated by almost as much during 1986–1987.

EXCHANGE RATES UNDER A FLEXIBLE EXCHANGE RATE SYSTEM

Flexible Exchange Rates: Exchange rates that are determined by the market forces of supply and demand. They are sometimes called "floating exchange rates."

What determines the exchange rate between two currencies? Under a system of floating or flexible exchange rates, the value of currencies in the exchange rate market is determined by market forces. Just as the forces of supply and demand

---

[3]In the construction of this index, the exchange rate of each currency relative to the dollar is weighted according to the proportion of U.S. trade with the country. For example, the index weights the dollar-Japanese yen exchange rate more heavily than the dollar-Swiss franc exchange rate because the volume of U.S. trade with Japan exceeds the volume of trade with Switzerland.

determine other prices, so too, they determine the exchange rate value of currencies in the absence of government intervention.

To simplify our explanation of how the exchange rate market works, let us assume that the United States and England are the only two countries in the world. Under these circumstances, the supply and demand for pounds is the supply and demand for foreign exchange.

In our two-country world, the demand for pounds in the exchange rate market originates from the demand of Americans for British goods, services, and assets (either real or financial). For example, when U.S. residents purchase men's suits from a British manufacturer, travel in the United Kingdom, or purchase the stocks, bonds, or physical assets of British business firms, they demand pounds from (and supply dollars to) the foreign exchange rate market to pay for these items. On the other hand, the supply of pounds (and demand for dollars) in the exchange rate market comes from the demand of the British for items supplied by Americans. When the British purchase goods, services, or assets from Americans, they supply pounds to (and demand dollars from) the exchange rate market.

Exhibit 2 illustrates the demand and supply curves of Americans for foreign exchange; British pounds in our two-country case. The demand for pounds is downward sloping because a lower dollar price of the pound—this means a dollar will buy more pounds—makes British goods cheaper for American importers and investors. The goods produced by one country are generally good substitutes for the goods of another country. This means that when foreign (British) goods become cheaper, Americans will increase their expenditures on imports (and there-

EXHIBIT 2

Equilibrium in the Foreign Exchange Market

The dollar price of the pound is measured on the vertical axis. The horizontal axis indicates the flow of pounds to the foreign exchange market. The equilibrium exchange rate is $1.50 = 1 pound. At the equilibrium price, the quantity demanded of pounds just equals the quantity supplied. A higher price of pounds such as $1.80 = 1 pound would lead to an excess supply of pounds, causing the dollar price of the pound to fall. On the other hand, a lower price, for example $1.20 = 1 pound, would result in an excess demand for pounds, causing the pound to appreciate.

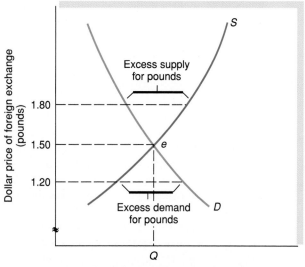

Quantity of foreign exchange (pounds)

fore the quantity of pounds demanded will increase). It will take time for Ameri-can consumers to respond fully to a change in the price of British goods. *Initially,* Americans may not increase their expenditures on British goods in response to the lower dollar price of the pound. However, with time, the American demand for British goods will be highly elastic. Thus, Americans will eventually increase their expenditures on the lower-priced (in dollars) British goods and therefore they will demand more pounds as the pound's dollar price declines.

The supply curve for pounds is dependent on the purchases of American goods by the British. An increase in the dollar price of the pound means that a pound will purchase more dollars and more goods priced in terms of dollars. The price (in terms of pounds) of American goods, services, and assets *to British consumers* declines as the dollar price of the pound increases. The British will purchase more from Americans and therefore supply more pounds to the exchange rate market as the dollar price of the pound rises. Because of this, the supply curve for pounds slopes upward to the right.

As Exhibit 2 shows, equilibrium is present at $1.50 = 1 pound—the dollar price of the pound that brings the quantity demanded and quantity supplied of pounds into balance. The market-clearing price of $1.50 per pound not only equates demand and supply in the exchange rate market; it also equates (a) the value of U.S. purchases on items supplied by the British with (b) the value of items sold by U.S. residents to the British. Demand and supply in the currency market are merely the mirror image of (a) and (b).

What would happen if the price of the pound was above equilibrium—$1.80 = 1 pound, for example. At the higher dollar price of the pound, British goods would be more expensive for Americans. Americans would cut back on their purchases of English shoes, glassware, textile products, financial assets, and other items supplied by the British. Reflecting this reduction, the quantity of pounds demanded by Americans would decline. Simultaneously, the higher dollar price of the pound would make U.S. exports cheaper for the British. For example, a $15,000 American automobile would cost British consumers 10,000 pounds when one pound trades for $1.50, but it would cost only 8,333 pounds when one pound exchanges for $1.80. If the price of the pound was $1.80, the British would supply more pounds to the exchange rate market to purchase the cheaper Ameri-can goods. Thus, at the $1.80 = 1 pound price, the quantity of pounds demanded by Americans falls and the quantity supplied by the British increases. An excess supply of pounds results, causing the dollar price of the pound to decline until equilibrium is restored at the $1.50 = 1 pound price.

At a below-equilibrium price such as $1.20 = 1 pound, an opposite set of forces would be present. The lower dollar price of the pound would make English goods cheaper for Americans and American goods more expensive for the British. The quantity demanded of British goods and pounds by Americans would in-crease. Simultaneously, the quantity of American goods demanded and pounds supplied by the British would decline. An excess demand for pounds would result at the $1.20 = 1 pound price. The excess demand would cause the dollar price of the pound to rise until equilibrium was restored at $1.50 = 1 pound.

CHANGING MARKET CONDITIONS AND EXCHANGE RATES

When exchange rates are free to fluctuate, the market value of a nation's currency will appreciate and depreciate in response to changing market conditions. Any change that alters the quantity of goods, services, or assets bought from foreigners relative to the quantity sold to foreigners will also alter the exchange rate. What types of changes will alter the exchange rate value of a currency?

Differential Growth Rates of Income. An increase in domestic income will encourage the nation's residents to spend a portion of their additional income on imports. Thus, when the income of a nation grows rapidly relative to its trading partners, the nation's imports tend to rise relative to exports. As Exhibit 3 illustrates, an increase in imports also increases the demand for foreign exchange, the pound in our two-country case. As the demand for pounds increases, the dollar price of the pound rises (from $1.50 to $1.80). The appreciation in the value of the pound (and depreciation in the value of the dollar) will reduce the incentive of Americans to import British goods, services and assets, while increasing the incentive of the British to purchase U.S. exports. These two forces will restore equilibrium in the exchange market at a new, higher dollar price of the pound.

Just the opposite happens when the income of a nation lags. A slow growth of domestic income coupled with rapid growth of income abroad will lead to a decline in imports relative to exports. The *relative* strength of the nation's exports will cause the demand for the currency of the slow-growth nation to rise. Paradoxical as it may seem, *other things constant,* sluggish growth of income relative to one's trading partners causes the slow-growth nation's currency to appreciate, since the nation's imports decline relative to exports.

Differential Rates of Inflation. Other things constant, domestic inflation will cause a nation's currency to depreciate on the exchange market, whereas deflation will result in appreciation. Suppose prices in the United States rise by 50 percent, while our trading partners are experiencing stable prices. The domestic inflation will cause U.S. consumers to increase their demand for imported goods (and foreign currency). In turn, the inflated domestic prices will cause foreigners to reduce

EXHIBIT 3

The Growth of Income and the Growth of Imports

Other things constant, if incomes grow more rapidly in the United States than in England, U.S. imports will grow relative to exports. The increase in the imports will increase the demand for pounds, causing the dollar price of the pound to rise (from $1.50 to $1.80).

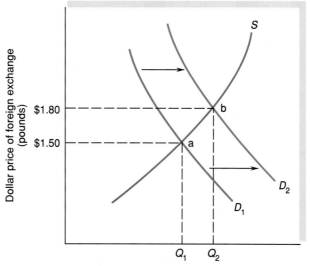

their purchases of U.S. goods, thereby reducing the supply of foreign currency to the exchange market. As Exhibit 4 illustrates, the exchange rate will adjust to this set of circumstances. The dollar will depreciate relative to the pound.

Exchange rate adjustments permit nations with even high rates of inflation to engage in trade with other countries experiencing relatively stable prices. A depreciation in a nation's currency in the exchange rate market compensates for the nation's inflation rate. For example, if inflation increases the price level in the United States by 50 percent and the value of the dollar in exchange for the pound depreciates 50 percent, then the prices of American goods measured in pounds is unchanged to British consumers. Thus, when the exchange rate value of the dollar changes from $1.50 = 1 pound to $2.25 = 1 pound, the depreciation in the dollar restores the original prices of U.S. goods to British consumers even though the price level in the U.S. has increased by 50 percent.

What if prices in both England and the United States are rising at an annual rate of 10 percent? The prices of imports (and exports) will remain unchanged relative to domestically produced goods. Equal rates of inflation in each of the countries will not cause the value of exports to change relative to imports. Identical rates of inflation will not disturb an equilibrium in the exchange market. Inflation contributes to the depreciation of a nation's currency only when a country's rate of inflation is more rapid than that of its trading partners.

Changes in Interest Rates. Short-term financial investments will be quite sensitive to changes in real interest rates—that is, interest rates adjusted for the expected rate of inflation. International loanable funds will tend to move toward areas where the expected real rate of return (after compensation for differences in risk) is highest. If real interest rates increase in the United States relative to Western Europe, borrowers in Britain, France, and West Germany will demand dollars

EXHIBIT 4

Inflation with Flexible Exchange Rates

If prices were stable in England while the price level increased 50 percent in the United States, the U.S. demand for British products (and pounds) would increase, whereas U.S. exports to Britain would decline, causing the supply of pounds to fall. The dollar would depreciate relative to the pound. When the dollar price of the pound has risen to $2.25 = 1 pound (rather than $1.50 = 1 pound), the original price of U.S. goods to British consumers is restored.

(and supply their currencies) in the exchange rate market to purchase the high yield American assets. The increase in demand for the dollar and supply of European currencies will cause the dollar to appreciate relative to the British pound, French franc, and German mark.

In contrast, when real interest rates in other countries are high relative to the United States, short-term financial investors will move to take advantage of the improved earnings opportunities abroad. As investment funds move from the United States to other countries, there will be an increase in the demand for foreign currencies and an increase in the supply of dollars. A depreciation in the dollar relative to the currencies of countries experiencing the high real interest rates will be the result.

MACROECONOMIC POLICY AND THE EXCHANGE RATE

The thumbnail sketch summarizes the major forces that cause a nation's currency to appreciate or depreciate when exchange rates are determined by market forces. Since monetary and fiscal policy exert an impact on income growth, inflation, and real interest rates, they also influence the exchange rate.

Monetary Policy and the Exchange Rate. Suppose the United States began to follow a more expansionary monetary policy. How would the more expansionary monetary policy influence the exchange rate market? When the effects are not fully anticipated, expansionary monetary policy will lead to more rapid economic growth, an acceleration in the inflation rate, and lower real interest rates.[4] As the thumbnail sketch shows, each of these factors will increase the supply of dollars (and the demand for foreign exchange), causing the dollar to depreciate. The rapid growth of income will stimulate imports. Similarly, the acceleration in the U.S. inflation rate (relative to our trading partners) will make U.S. goods less competitive abroad, causing a decline in exports. Simultaneously, the lower real interest rate will encourage the flow of capital abroad. The expected short-run effect of an

THUMBNAIL SKETCH

Currency Appreciation and Depreciation with Freely Fluctuating Exchange Rates

These factors will cause a nation's currency to appreciate:

1. A slow rate of growth in income that causes imports to lag behind exports.
2. A rate of inflation that is lower than one's trading partners.
3. Domestic real interest rates that are greater than real interest rates abroad.

These factors will cause a nation's currency to depreciate:

1. A rapid rate of growth in income that stimulates imports relative to exports.
2. A rate of inflation that is higher than one's trading partners.
3. Domestic real interest rates that are lower than real interest rates abroad.

[4]A complete analysis would show that neither growth nor the real interest rate will change if people fully anticipate the effects of the change in monetary policy on the price level. In this chapter, we assume for simplicity that the price level effects of monetary policy are unanticipated. This clearly is more relevant in the short run rather than in the long run.

unanticipated shift to a more expansionary monetary policy is a depreciation in the exchange rate value of the dollar.

The expected outcome of an unanticipated switch to a more restrictive monetary policy will be just the opposite. The restrictive monetary policy will retard economic growth, decelerate the inflation rate, and push real interest rates upward. Exports will grow relative to imports. Investment funds from abroad will be drawn by the high real interest rates in the United States. Foreigners will demand more dollars with which to purchase goods, services, and real assets in the United States. The strong demand for the dollar will cause it to appreciate.

Fiscal Policy and the Exchange Rate. Fiscal policy tends to generate conflicting influences on the exchange rate market. Suppose the United States unexpectedly shifts toward a more restrictive fiscal policy, planning a budget surplus or at least a smaller deficit. Just as with restrictive monetary policy, the restrictive fiscal policy may cause a reduction in aggregate demand, an economic slowdown, and a decline in the rate of inflation. These factors will discourage imports and stimulate exports, causing an appreciation in the exchange rate value of the dollar. However, restrictive fiscal policy will also mean less government borrowing, which will place downward pressure on real interest rates in the United States. The lower real interest rates will cause financial capital to flow from the United States. The supply of dollars to the exchange market will increase, placing downward pressure on the exchange rate value of the dollar. The final outcome is uncertain. If the impact of the reduction in imports dominates, the dollar will appreciate. On the other hand, if the impact of the low real interest rate dominates, the dollar will depreciate.

The analysis of expansionary fiscal policy is symmetrical. To the extent that an increase in the size of the deficit stimulates aggregate demand, income, and prices, it will stimulate imports relative to exports. This will cause the dollar to depreciate. However, to the extent it causes higher real interest rates in the United States, foreign investment will flow to the U.S., causing the dollar to appreciate. Thus, the net impact of expansionary fiscal policy on the value of a nation's currency in the foreign exchange market is indeterminate.

THE APPRECIATION AND DEPRECIATION OF THE DOLLAR, 1973–1988

During the late 1970s, the United States was in the midst of double-digit inflation. Compared to most of its major trading partners, the inflation rate was higher and real interest rates were lower in the United States. As our analysis indicates, a high inflation rate will discourage purchases by foreigners and low real interest rates will lead to an outflow of capital. Both of these forces will cause a nation's currency to depreciate in the exchange rate market. This is precisely what happened, as the dollar fell to new lows against most major currencies during 1977–1979.

These forces reversed sharply during the early 1980s, as the U.S. shifted toward a more restrictive monetary policy and expansionary fiscal policy. Beginning in 1981, the more restrictive monetary policy retarded the inflation rate. The

U.S. inflation rate plunged from the double-digit levels of 1979–1980 to 3.2 percent in 1983. Simultaneously, pushed along by both the restrictive monetary policy and huge budget deficits, real interest rates in the United States rose to historic highs. As Exhibit 5 illustrates, real interest rates in the United States were substantially higher than real rates in Europe and Japan during 1981–1984. Attracted by the high real return, financial capital flowed into the United States. This combination of forces—a low inflation rate and capital inflow attracted by high real interest rates—sharply increased the demand for the dollar. The dollar appreciated by approximately 60 percent against an index of ten major currencies during 1980–1984.

However, beginning in early 1985, the situation again changed abruptly. As the low rate of inflation persisted, real interest rates declined in the United States. The inflow of foreign capital slowed. Simultaneously, the U.S. economy rebounded strongly from the 1982 recession. Responding to both the rapid economic growth and the strong dollar, U.S. imports surged relative to exports during 1983–1985. During 1985–1986, the low U.S. interest rates relative to other countries (see Exhibit 5), and fears arising from the large excess of imports compared to exports, resulted in a sharp decline in the exchange rate value of the dollar.

EXHIBIT 5

Real Interest Rates and the Exchange Rate Value of the Dollar, 1974–1988

Our model indicates that a reduction in real U.S. interest rates compared with the rates in other countries will, other things constant, cause the dollar to depreciate. As shown above, this is precisely what happened in the late 1970s and again during 1985–1987. In contrast, when real interest rates are higher in the United States than in other countries, strong demand for dollars in order to make financial investments in the United States will cause the dollar to appreciate. The 1980–1984 period illustrates the potency of high real interest rates as a factor pushing the exchange rate value of the dollar upward.

Source: Charles P. Thomas, ''U.S. International Transactions in 1986,'' *Federal Reserve Bulletin* (May 1987); and Federal Reserve Bank of St. Louis, *International Economic Conditions* (monthly).

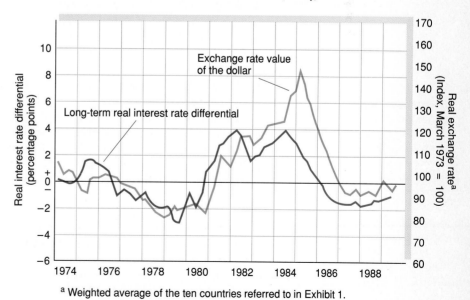

[a] Weighted average of the ten countries referred to in Exhibit 1.

THE OPERATION OF A FIXED EXCHANGE RATE SYSTEM

Fixed Exchange Rate System: An international monetary system in which each country's currency is set at a fixed rate relative to all other currencies and governmental policies are used to maintain the fixed rate.

Between 1944 and 1971, most of the world operated under a system of fixed exchange rates. Under a fixed exchange rate system, each nation "pegs" the price of its currency to another currency , such as the dollar (or gold), for long periods of time. Governments intervene in the foreign exchange market or alter their economic policies in an effort to maintain the fixed value of their currency.

Fixing the price of a currency in the exchange market, like fixing other prices, results in surpluses and shortages. As market conditions change, the exchange rate that equates the quantity supplied of each currency with the quantity demanded also changes. What happens when the fixed rate differs from the equilibrium rate? Building on the analysis of Exhibit 2, suppose the equilibrium exchange rate was $1.50 = 1 pound. If the price of the pound is fixed at $1.80 = 1 pound, an excess supply of pounds will result. At the $1.80 = 1 pound fixed rate, the pound is overvalued (and the dollar undervalued). At the $1.80 per pound exchange rate, the U.S. will persistently export more goods, services, and assets to the British than the British will import from the United States. The central bank in the United States will have to continually increase its holdings of pounds—that is, buy the excess supply of pounds, to maintain the above-equilibrium price of the pound. In essence, this situation leads to a surplus of exports over imports for the United States in its trade with England.

What would happen if the dollar price of the pound was set below equilibrium, such as $1.20 = 1 pound (Exhibit 2)? The below-equilibrium price of the pound would lead to an excess demand for pounds. Since the pound is undervalued (and the dollar overvalued) at the $1.20 per pound price, British imports are cheap to Americans (and U.S. exports expensive for the British). In its trade with the British, the U.S. would persistently buy (import) more than it sells (exports). To defend the $1.20 per pound fixed rate, the U.S. central bank would have to draw down its holdings of pounds, balances that were perhaps built up during periods when the dollar price of the pound was above equilibrium.

International Monetary Fund: An international banking organization, with more than 100 nation members, designed to oversee the operation of the international monetary system. Although it does not control the world supply of money, it does hold currency reserves for member nations and make currency loans to national central banks.

To make a fixed rate system work, each country must maintain a reserve balance of other currencies that will permit it to weather temporary periods of excess demand relative to supply. When the fixed rate system was put in place at the end of the Second World War, the International Monetary Fund (IMF) was established to perform this function. The IMF required each of its more than 100 member countries to deposit a specified amount of its currency into a reserve fund held by the IMF. Thus, it possessed substantial holdings of dollars, francs, pounds, marks, and other currencies of the participating nations. As the need arose, these reserves were loaned to nations experiencing difficulties with their balance of payments.

The premise of a fixed rate system is that a nation ordinarily pays for its imports with exports. Of course, countries may temporarily experience periods where imports exceed exports. During such periods, nations can draw down their reserve balance. However, chronic debtor nations—nations persistently importing more than they export—must take corrective action designed to bring exports and imports into balance. During the 1944–1971 period, the IMF provided discipline

Devaluation: An official act that changes the level of the "fixed" exchange rate in a downward direction. In essence, it is a one-step depreciation of a currency under a fixed exchange rate system.

to the system by encouraging and in some cases requiring member nations as a condition for the receipt of loans, to adopt policies that would bring their exports and imports into balance.

What steps can a nation experiencing an excess of imports over exports take to remedy this situation under a fixed rate system? Basically, there are three alternatives.

1. *A Nation Can Devalue Its Currency.* Devaluation is a one-step reduction in the value of a nation's currency under a fixed rate system. When a currency is overvalued, a devaluation can restore equilibrium between the demand and supply of the currency in the exchange market. For example, if there is an excess supply of dollars (excess demand for pounds) in the exchange market when the fixed exchange rate is $1.20 = 1 pound, a devaluation of the dollar (perhaps to $1.50 = 1 pound) could restore balance. A devaluation makes imports more expensive to domestic consumers, while encouraging exports. It thus tends to correct an excess of imports relative to exports.

2. *A Nation Can Heighten Trade Barriers, Adopting Tariffs and Quotas in an Effort to Reduce Imports and Bring the Value of Its Currency on the Foreign Exchange Market into Equilibrium.* This strategy is in conflict with economic efficiency and the promotion of the free flow of trade between nations. Nevertheless, it was often adopted during the period from 1944 to 1971. Once a nation's exchange rate was established, it tended to become sacred. Politicians during that period, including many in the United States, frequently argued that even though they did not like to impose trade restrictions, the barriers were necessary to avoid devaluation. The balance of payments issue was an excellent excuse to promote trade restrictions—which were advocated by special interests—against low-cost foreign goods.

3. *A Nation Can Follow Restrictive Macroeconomic Policy Designed to Promote Deflation (or at Least Retard Inflation) and High Interest Rates.* Policymakers might use restrictive monetary and fiscal policy to retard inflation and increase interest rates. A slower rate of inflation relative to one's trading partners would encourage exports and discourage imports. Higher domestic real interest rates would attract foreign investment and thereby increase the nation's supply of foreign exchange.

When a nation uses macroeconomic policy to restore balance in the exchange market, an important point emerges. This method of bringing about equilibrium in the exchange market attempts to manipulate the level of all other prices to maintain one price—the fixed exchange rate. In contrast, a flexible exchange rate system changes one price, the foreign exchange rate—to restore balance between what is bought from and what is sold to foreigners.

THE BALANCE OF PAYMENTS

Balance of Payments: A summary of all economic transactions between a country and all other countries for a specific time period—usually a year. The balance of payments account reflects all payments and liabilities to foreigners (debits) and all payments and obligations (credits) received from foreigners.

Just as countries calculate their gross national product so that they have a general idea of the domestic level of production, most countries also calculate their balance of international payments in order to keep track of their transactions with other nations. The balance of payments account is a periodic report that summarizes the flow of economic transactions with foreigners. It provides information on the nation's exports, imports, earnings of domestic residents on assets located abroad, earnings on domestic assets owned by foreigners, international capital movements, and official transactions by central banks and governments.

Balance of payments accounts are kept according to the principles of double-entry bookkeeping. Each entry on the debit (−) side of the ledger implies an identical entry on the credit side (+). Any transaction that supplies the nation's domestic currency (or creates a demand for foreign currency) in the foreign exchange market is recorded as a debit, or minus, item. Imports are an example of a debit item. Transactions that create a demand for the nation's currency (or a supply of foreign currency) on the foreign exchange market are recorded as a credit, or plus, item. Exports are an example of a credit item.

The balance of payments transactions can be grouped into three basic categories: current account, capital amount, and official reserve account. Let us take a look at each of these.

CURRENT ACCOUNT TRANSACTIONS

Current Account: The record of all transactions with foreign nations that involve the exchange of merchandise goods and services or unilateral gifts.

All payments (and gifts) that are related to the purchase or sale of goods and services during the designated period are included in the **current account.** In general, there are three major types of current account transactions: the exchange of merchandise goods, the exchange of services, and unilateral transfers.

Merchandise Trade Transactions. The export and import of merchandise goods comprise by far the largest portion of a nation's balance of payments account. As Exhibit 6 shows, in 1987, the United States imported $423.7 billion of merchandise goods and exported only $261.2 billion. When Americans import goods from abroad, they also supply dollars to the foreign exchange market. Imports are recorded as debits in the balance of payments accounts. In contrast, when U.S. producers export their products, foreigners demand dollars on the exchange market to pay for the U.S. exports. Exports are the credit item.

The difference between the value of a country's merchandise exports and the value of its merchandise imports is known as the **balance of merchandise trade.** If the value of a country's merchandise exports falls short of (exceeds) the value of its merchandise imports, it is said to have a balance of trade deficit (surplus). In 1987, the United States ran a balance of merchandise trade deficit of $162.5 billion.

Balance of Merchandise Trade: The difference between the value of merchandise exports and the value of merchandise imports for a nation. The balance of trade is only one component of a nation's total balance of payments.

Other things constant, a U.S. trade deficit implies that Americans are supplying more dollars to the exchange market than foreigners are demanding for purchase of American goods. If the trade deficit were the only factor influencing the value of the dollar on the exchange market, one could anticipate a decline in the foreign exchange value of the U.S. currency. However, several others factors also affect the supply of and demand for the dollar on the exchange market.

Service Exports and Imports. The export and import of "invisible services," as they are sometimes called, also exert an important influence on the foreign exchange market. The export of insurance, transportation, and banking services generates a demand for dollars by foreigners just as the export of merchandise does. A French business that is insured with an American company will demand dollars with which to pay its premiums. When foreigners travel in the United States or transport cargo on American ships, they will demand dollars with which to pay for these services. Similarly, income earned by U.S. investments abroad will

EXHIBIT 6 ■ U.S. Balance of Payments, 1987

Item		Amount (billions of dollars)
Current Account		
1. Exports of goods and services		+424.8
a. Merchandise exports (including military sales)	+261.2	
b. Services	+ 59.9	
c. Income from U.S. assets abroad	+103.7	
2. Imports of goods and services		−565.3
a. Merchandise imports (including military purchases)	−423.7	
b. Services	− 58.2	
c. Income from foreign assets in U.S.	− 83.4	
3. Net unilateral transfers abroad		− 13.4
a. U.S. government grants and pensions	− 12.2	
b. Private remittances	− 1.2	
Current Account Balance		−154.0
Capital Account		
4. Outflow of U.S. capital		− 85.2
a. U.S. direct investment abroad	− 44.5	
b. Loans to foreigners	− 40.7	
5. Inflow of foreign capital		+166.5
a. Foreign direct investments in U.S.	+ 42.2	
b. Loans from foreigners	+124.3	
6. Statistical discrepancy		+ 18.5
Capital Account Balance		+ 99.9
Official Reserve Account		
7. Increase (−) in U.S. official reserve assets		+ 9.1
8. Increase (+) in foreign official assets in U.S.		+ 45.0
Official Reserve Balance		+ 54.1
TOTAL	0.0	0.0

Source: U.S. Commerce Department, *Survey of Current Business*, June 1988.

cause dollars to flow from foreigners to Americans. These service exports are thus entered as credits on the current account.

On the other hand, the import of services from foreigners expands the supply of dollars to the exchange market. Therefore, service imports are entered on the balance of payments accounts as debit items. Travel abroad by U.S. citizens, the shipment of goods on foreign carriers, and income earned by foreigners on U.S. investments are all debit items, since they supply dollars to the exchange market.

These service transactions are substantial. As Exhibit 6 illustrates, in 1987 the U.S. service exports (including income from foreign investments) were $163.6 billion, compared with service imports of $141.6 billion.

Unilateral Transfers. Monetary gifts to foreigners, such as U.S. aid to a foreign government or private gifts from U.S. residents to their relatives abroad, supply dollars to the exchange market. These gifts are debit items in the balance of payments accounts. Monetary gifts to Americans from foreigners are credit items.

Gifts in kind are more complex. When products are given to foreigners, goods flow abroad, but there is no offsetting influx of foreign currency—that is, a demand for dollars. Balance of payments accountants handle such transactions as though the United States had supplied the dollars with which to purchase the direct grants made to foreigners. So, these items are also entered as debits. Because the U.S. government (and private U.S. citizens) made larger grants to foreigners than we received, net unilateral transfers of $13.4 billion were entered as a debit item on the current accounts for 1987.

Balance on Current Account. The difference between (a) the value of a country's exports of goods and services and (b) the value of its imports of goods and services plus net unilateral transfers is known as the balance on current account. This is a summary statistic for all current account transactions. As with the balance of trade, if the value of the exports is less than (exceeds) the value of the imports plus the unilateral transfers, the country is said to be experiencing a deficit (surplus) on current account transactions. In 1987, the United States ran a $154 billion deficit on current account transactions.

Balance on Current Account: The import-export balance of goods and services plus net private and government transfers. If a nation's export of goods and services exceeds (is less than) the nation's import of goods and services plus net unilateral transfers to foreigners, a current account surplus (deficit) is present.

CAPITAL ACCOUNT TRANSACTIONS

Capital account transactions are composed of (a) direct investments by Americans in real assets abroad (or by foreigners in the United States) and (b) loans to and from foreigners. If a U.S. investor purchases a shoe factory in Mexico, the Mexican seller will want to be paid in pesos. The U.S. investor will supply dollars (and demand pesos) on the foreign exchange market. U.S. investment abroad is thus entered on the balance of payments accounts as a debit item. On the other hand, foreign investment in the United States creates a demand for dollars on the exchange market. Therefore, it is entered as a credit.

Investment abroad can be thought of as the import of an asset. Importing ownership of a financial (or real) asset from abroad has the same effect on the balance of payments as importing goods from abroad. Therefore, both are recorded as debits. Similarly, in a sense, we are exporting the ownership of capital when foreigners invest in the United States. These transactions enter as a credit.

As for domestic markets, many international transactions are conducted on credit. When a U.S. banker loans $100,000 to a foreign entrepreneur for the purchase of U.S. exports, the banker is in effect importing a foreign bond. Since the transaction supplies dollars to the exchange market, it is recorded as a debit. On the other hand, when Americans borrow from abroad, they are exporting bonds. Since this transaction creates either a demand for dollars on the part of the foreign lender (in order to supply the loanable funds) or a supply of foreign currency, it is recorded as a credit in the U.S. balance of payments account.

In 1987, U.S. direct investments abroad were approximately the same size as foreign direct investments in the United States. However, U.S. borrowing abroad was substantially greater than the loans extended to foreigners. As a result, the United States ran a capital account surplus of $99.9 billion.

Special Drawing Rights: Supplementary reserves, in the form of accounting entries, established by the International Monetary Fund (also called "paper gold"). Like gold and foreign currency reserves, they can be used to make payments on international accounts.

THE OFFICIAL RESERVE ACCOUNT

Governments maintain official reserve balances in the form of foreign currencies, gold, and special drawing rights (SDRs) with the International Monetary Fund, a type of international central bank. Countries running a deficit on their current and capital account balance can draw on their reserves. Similarly, countries running a surplus can build up their reserves of foreign currencies and reserve balances with the IMF. Under the fixed exchange system present during 1944–1971, these reserve transactions were highly significant. Countries experiencing balance of payments difficulties were forced to draw on their reserves to maintain their fixed exchange rate. Countries that were selling more to foreigners than foreigners were buying from them accumulated the currencies of other nations.

Under the current (primarily) flexible rate system, nations usually permit a rise or fall in the foreign exchange value of their currency to bring about equilibrium in the exchange rate market. Thus, changes in the official reserve account are generally quite small. However, sometimes nations have their central banks buy and sell currencies in an attempt to reduce sharp swings in the exchange rate. For example, the Carter administration intervened with international reserves and loans from West Germany and Japan in order to moderate the fall of the dollar in 1978. Similarly, the Reagan administration arranged for foreign governments to buy dollars in an effort to stem the sharp depreciation in the dollar during 1986–1987. Therefore, the official reserve activities were unusually large in 1987, as foreigners increased their reserve holdings by $45 billion and the United States reduced its holdings by $9.1 billion.

BALANCING THE ACCOUNTS

Reflecting double-entry bookkeeping procedures, the aggregated balance of payments accounts must balance. The following balance of payments' identity must hold:

$$\frac{\text{current account}}{\text{balance}} + \frac{\text{capital account}}{\text{balance}} + \frac{\text{official reserve}}{\text{account balance}} = 0$$

However, the specific components of the accounts need not balance. For example, the debit and credit items of the current account need not be equal. Specific components may run either a surplus or a deficit. Nevertheless, since the balance of payments as a whole must balance, a deficit in one area implies a surplus in another.

If a nation is experiencing a deficit on its current account balance, it must experience an offsetting surplus on the sum of its capital account and official reserve account balances. Under a pure flexible exchange system, official reserve transactions are zero. Therefore, under a flexible rate system, a current account deficit implies a capital account surplus. Similarly, under a flexible rate system, a current account surplus would imply a capital account deficit.

A current account deficit means that, in aggregate, the citizens of a nation are buying more goods and services from foreigners than they are selling to foreigners. Under a pure flexible rate system, this excess of expenditures relative to receipts is paid for by borrowing from and selling assets to foreigners.

THE CURRENT ACCOUNT DEFICIT OF THE 1980s

Throughout the 1970s, the U.S. current account deficits and surpluses were quite small. As Exhibit 7 illustrates, this situation changed dramatically during the 1980s. The current account of the United States turned from a $6.9 billion surplus in 1981 to a $46 billion deficit in 1983 and continued upward, reaching a deficit of $154 billion in 1987. As we previously discussed, a strong demand for loanable

The Exchange Rate Value
of the Dollar and the
Current Account Deficit,
1973–1988

As the dollar appreciated
during the early 1980s, the
current account deficit of the
United States soared. The large
deficit continued during 1986–
1988, even after the dollar
depreciated sharply in the
exchange rate market.

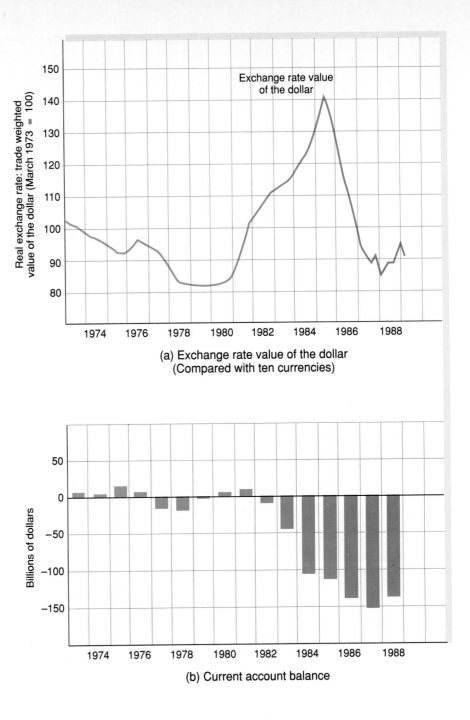

(a) Exchange rate value of the dollar
(Compared with ten currencies)

(b) Current account balance

funds to finance large budget deficits, coupled with a sharp deceleration in the
inflation rate, led to high real interest rates in the United States during the first
half of the 1980s (see Exhibit 5). In turn, the high real interest rates caused a
dramatic appreciation in the exchange rate value of the dollar as foreigners demanded dollars in order to undertake real and financial investments in the United
States. Of course, an appreciation in the dollar makes imports cheaper for Amer-

ican consumers and exports more expensive to foreigners. Given the magnitude of the dollar appreciation, a substantial increase in net imports and a large current account deficit is a predictable result.

However, the large current account deficits continued during 1986–1988, even though, by that time, the dollar had depreciated sharply. Why didn't the decline in the exchange rate value of the dollar reverse the current account deficit? It takes time for a depreciation in a nation's currency to turn around a current account deficit, and, initially, the depreciation generally enlarges rather than shrinks a trade deficit. The impact of a currency depreciation on a current account deficit can be broken down into a "price effect" and a "quantity effect." A 10 percent depreciation in the dollar means that import prices increase by 10 percent in terms of dollars. Of course, this increase in the dollar price of imports will discourage purchases. However, the 10 percent depreciation also means that *for a given quantity sold,* foreigners will earn 10 percent more dollars. Therefore, unless Americans reduce the *quantity* of their imports by more than 10 percent, their *expenditures* on imports will *increase* in response to a depreciation in the dollar. Similarly, the depreciation will make U.S. exports 10 percent cheaper to foreigners. Unless foreigners increase their *quantity* purchased by more than 10 percent, their demand for dollars in the exchange market will *decrease* as the result of the depreciation.

Since American and foreign-produced goods are excellent substitutes for one another, there is good reason to expect that both the U.S. demand for imports and foreign demand for U.S. exports will be highly elastic in the long run. However, this may not be true in the short run. When the dollar depreciates, it will take time for American consumers to substitute away from the more expensive imports and for foreign consumers to adjust their consumption, purchasing more of the now cheaper American exports. The new suppliers (or new customers) must be contacted. New agreements must be completed. In some cases, these developments must await the expiration of prior contracts. Therefore, initially, the decrease in the *quantity* of imports and increase in the *quantity* of exports may be less than the 10 percent reduction in price. If this is the case, for a time the depreciation will actually cause the current account deficit to worsen—the *dollar expenditures* on imports will rise while the *dollar sales* of exports will decline. Eventually, this situation will reverse. With the passage of time, the U.S. demand for imports and foreign demand for U.S. exports will become more elastic. The quantity effects will dominate and a depreciation will reduce the current account deficit.

J-Curve Effect: The tendency of a nation's current account deficit to widen initially before it shrinks in response to an exchange rate depreciation. This tendency results because the short-run demand for both imports and exports is often inelastic, even though the long-run demand is almost always elastic.

Economists refer to this time path of adjustment as the **J-curve effect.** According to this effect, a nation's current account deficit will initially widen (slide down the hook of the J) before it shrinks (moves up the stem of the J) as the result of a currency depreciation. This occurs because the *short-run* elasticity of domestic demand for imports and foreign demand for exports is inelastic. Thus, the depreciation initially increases import expenditures and export sales. However, in the long run, the demand for both imports and exports is elastic. Therefore, the depreciation of a nation's currency will eventually shrink the nation's current account deficit.[5]

---

[5]See Jeffery A. Rosensweig and Paul D. Koch, "The U.S. Dollar and the 'Delayed J-Curve,'" Federal Reserve Bank of Atlanta, *Economic Review,* (July/August 1988), pp. 2–15, for an interesting article on the J-curve effect as it applies to the trade imbalances of the United States during the 1980s.

Empirical studies indicate that it may take four or five years for trade flows to adjust fully to a change in exchange rates, although the major portion of the adjustment generally takes place in about two years. Viewed within this framework, the failure of the sharp depreciation in the dollar during 1986–1988 to quickly reverse the U.S. current account deficit is not surprising. However, the analysis does imply that, other things constant, a shrinking current account deficit can be expected during 1989–1990. It will be interesting to follow the results on this issue.

IS A CURRENT ACCOUNT DEFICIT A PROBLEM?

Should a nation be concerned when it is running a current account deficit? Under a flexible exchange rate system, a nation's current account position is an aggregate of the voluntary choices of businesses and individuals. In contrast with the government's budget deficit, there is no legal entity that is responsible for the current account deficit. As Herbert Stein, a former Chairman of the President's Council of Economic Advisers, states:

> The fact is that a certain (unknown) number of Americans bought more abroad than they sold abroad and a certain other (unknown) number of Americans sold more than they bought abroad. The trade deficit is the excess of the net foreign purchase of the first group over the net foreign sales of the second group. The trade deficit does not belong to any individual or institution. It is a pure statistical aggregate, like the number of eggs laid in the U.S. or the number of bald-headed men living here.[6]

The U.S. deficit or surplus on current accounts depends not only upon the choices of Americans, but also upon those of foreigners. When Americans purchase goods, services, and assets abroad, foreigners acquire dollars. If foreigners spend these dollars only on current goods and services (U.S. exports), then the U.S. will run a current account surplus. On the other hand, if foreigners find investment opportunities attractive in the United States, and therefore spend a large share of their acquired dollars on real and financial investments in the United States, then the U.S. will run a current account deficit (and a capital account surplus).

Whether a nation runs a current account deficit or surplus is dependent upon the investment opportunities in the country relative to the nation's saving rate. Under a flexible exchange system, countries with more attractive investment opportunities and a lower saving rate than their trading partners will run current account deficits. Correspondingly, countries with less attractive investment opportunities and a higher saving rate will run a current account surplus.

How long can a nation continue to run a current account deficit? Perhaps surprising to some, the answer is a long time. A current account deficit is not like business losses or an excess of household spending relative to income—conditions that eventually force decision-makers to alter their ways. The United States ran a current (trade) account deficit almost every year from 1800–1875. On the other

[6]Herbert Stein, "Leave the Trade Deficit Alone," *The Wall Street Journal*, March 11, 1987.

hand, the U.S. consistently ran current account surpluses during the 1946–1976 period. The trade accounts of other countries have followed similar lengthy periods of both deficits and surpluses.

Currently, the United States has a rapidly growing labor force (compared with Europe and Japan), a system of secure property rights, and political stability. This makes it an attractive country in which to invest. On the other hand, the saving rate of the United States, perhaps as the result of budget deficits, cultural factors, or less favorable tax treatment of saving, is low compared to our major trading partners. A continuation of this combination of factors—attractive investment opportunities and a low saving rate—will result in the long-term inflow of foreign capital and a corresponding current account deficit.

Of course, the U.S. current account deficit does mean that foreigners are investing in the United States and that Americans are borrowing abroad. But why is this a problem? Without the inflow of capital, real interest rates in the United States would be higher and domestic investment lower. Both the direct foreign investment in the United States and additional domestically financed investment resulting from the lower interest rates (lower than would be present in the absence of the capital inflow), increase the availability of tools and equipment to American workers and thereby increase their productivity and income. With regard to the funds borrowed abroad, their impact on the U.S. economy is no different than for other borrowed funds. If they are squandered on unwise and wasteful projects, they will reduce the wealth of the borrower. Alternatively, if they are used to finance profitable enterprises, the wealth of the borrower will grow. The impact of the funds on the U.S. economy is determined by how wisely the funds are used, not whether they are borrowed domestically or abroad.

The forces underpinning the U.S. current account deficit may change in the near future. The growth rate of the U.S. labor force may slow, reducing the return on investment and the inflow of capital. Or a period of slow growth in the income of Americans may motivate them to save a larger proportion of their income.[7] Correspondingly, as the income of foreigners increases, they may decide to consume more and save less. Perhaps the federal government will reduce the size of its deficit and thereby push U.S. interest rates lower. Changes of this type will close the current account deficit. But such changes need not take place. And if they do not, the current account deficit will continue, and there is little reason to believe that it is exerting a harmful impact on the U.S. economy.

THE CURRENT INTERNATIONAL MONETARY SYSTEM

The international monetary system in effect since 1973 might best be described as a managed flexible rate system. The system qualifies as a flexible rate system because all of the major industrial countries allow the exchange rate value of their currencies to float. Many small countries maintain fixed exchange rates against

---

[7]Some would argue that the net saving rate of the United States is low because of the large budget deficits. This may be true. But if it is, it is an argument for doing something about large budget deficits rather than for policies designed to directly reduce the current account deficit.

the dollar, the English pound, or some other major currency. Therefore, the exchange rate value of these currencies rises and falls with the major currency to which they are tied. The system is managed because the major industrial nations have from time to time altered their official reserve holdings in an effort to moderate major swings—say, swings of 20 percent or more within six months—in exchange rates.

Recent intervention has often involved coordinated efforts on the part of the major industrial nations. The macroeconomics policies and the purchases and sales of currency reserves of the Group of Seven (United States, Japan, France, United Kingdom, West Germany, Canada, and Italy) have been conducted with an eye for exchange rate stability in recent years.

ADVANTAGES OF THE CURRENT SYSTEM

The proponents of the current system stress three major advantages of the structure. We will discuss each of these in turn.

1. *The current system is flexible enough to adjust to major shocks that influence the value of currencies.* The system of floating exchange rates handled the

MEASURES IN ECONOMICS

Is the U.S. the World's Largest Debtor?

Large current account deficits have prompted concern that foreigners are buying up America and that the United States is becoming dangerously indebted to lenders from abroad. Clearly, foreign ownership of assets in the United States has been growing more rapidly than American-owned assets abroad. Exhibit 8 presents the Department of Commerce data on this topic. In 1979, U.S. assets abroad summed to $510.6 billion compared with $416.1 billion of foreign-owned assets in the United States. These numbers, which include both real and financial investments, indicate that U.S. citizens were net creditors to the tune of $94.5 billion in 1979. The U.S. net creditor position expanded to $141.1 billion in 1981. Since 1982, these

EXHIBIT 8 ■ U.S. Investments Abroad Compared to Foreign Investments in the United States— A Comparison of Assets and Income Flows, 1979–1987 (in billions of dollars)

	U.S. Assets Abroad (1)	Foreign Assets in U.S. (2)	Net Creditor (+) or Debtor (−) Position (3)	U.S. Income from Assets Abroad (4)	Income of Foreigners from U.S. Assets (5)	Net Income Inflow (+) or Outflow (−) (6)
1979	$ 510.6	$ 416.1	+ $ 94.5	$ 64.1	$33.0	+ $31.2
1980	607.1	500.8	+ 106.3	72.5	42.1	+ 30.4
1981	719.8	578.7	+ 141.1	86.4	52.3	+ 34.1
1982	824.9	688.0	+ 136.9	83.5	59.9	+ 28.7
1983	873.9	784.3	+ 89.4	77.5	52.4	+ 24.9
1984	896.1	892.5	+ 3.5	85.9	67.4	+ 18.5
1985	950.3	1061.0	− 110.7	88.8	62.9	+ 25.9
1986	1071.4	1340.6	− 269.2	90.1	67.0	+ 23.1
1987	1167.9	1536.1	− 368.2	103.8	83.4	+ 20.4

Source: *Economic Report of the President, 1989*, (Tables B-102 and B-106).

inflation and soaring oil prices of the 1970s and the unanticipated plunge in oil prices in the 1980s with a minimum of difficulty. The volume of international trade continued to rise even during periods of instability.

2. *The current system allows countries to pursue independent macroeconomic policies.* When inflation rates and growth rates vary across nations, a change in only one price—the exchange rate—will bring the flow of international transactions into balance. In contrast, countries often had to follow macropolicy designed to deflate or inflate their economies in order to solve trade imbalances under a fixed rate system. Clearly, it is less painful to alter one price rather than the level of all prices.

3. *The current structure solves trade imbalances without trade restrictions.* Under the fixed rate system, nations often raised tariffs and imposed quotas in an attempt to maintain the fixed exchange rate. Such policies retarded the potential gains from international exchange.

data imply that the situation has changed dramatically. By 1987, the foreign-owned assets in the U.S. exceeded U.S.-owned assets abroad by $368.2 billion, according to the Department of Commerce data. Observing these numbers, many commentators charge that the United States is now the world's largest debtor nation.

In evaluating this position, three points should be kept in mind. First, these numbers lump together equity assets, such as stocks, buildings, and land, with debt instruments, such as corporate bonds and direct loans. Since equity assets do not involve a contractual debt obligation, it is something of a misnomer to refer to them as debt. Second, the bulk of these assets represents private investments, either investments of U.S. citizens (or businesses) abroad or ownership of foreign private parties in the United States. Presumably, if either foreigners or Americans are worried about the ability of debtors to meet their obligations, they will curtail the holdings of such risky assets. Third,

the numbers in columns 1, 2, and 3 of Exhibit 8 represent the book value of the assets. In the case of investments that were made several years ago, book value may be a highly misleading indicator of the asset's value today.

An alternative way of viewing the net asset position of Americans would be to compare the income generated by U.S. assets abroad with the income of foreigners from assets held in the United States. After all, it is the expectation of income from an asset that determines its market value and motivates people to undertake the investment. The last three columns of Exhibit 8 provide this data. In 1979, the income flow of Americans from assets held abroad was $64.1 billion compared with $33 billion of income earned by foreigners on assets held in the United States. Thus, the inflow of income exceeded the outflow by $31.2 billion in 1979. In 1987, this *net* inflow of investment income exceeded $20 billion. This yardstick implies that the U.S. is still a creditor nation.

There is little doubt, however, that foreign investment in the U.S. has grown more rapidly than U.S. investment abroad in recent years. If this trend continues, the U.S. will become a debtor nation. Nonetheless, it is highly misleading to compare the U.S. position with that of developing countries, as many commentators have done. The U.S. debt is in its domestic currency (dollars), not the currency of another country. Much of the "debt" is in the form of equity capital, rather than bank loans and securities. And most significantly, the capital inflow largely reflects the views of private investors that their capital will be better employed in the United States than in other countries.

What proportion of American assets are now owned by foreigners? In 1987, the total value of physical assets in the United States was estimated to be between $20 trillion and $25 trillion. Thus, the $1.5 trillion foreign-investment total represents between 6 percent and 8 percent of the physical wealth of the United States.

APPLICATIONS IN ECONOMICS

The Gold Standard International Monetary System

Throughout history, gold has played an important role in monetary matters. The gold standard is an international monetary system under which the value of each nation's currency (for example, the dollar, pound, or mark) is defined in terms of gold. Most recently, the world economy operated on a gold standard during the period from the 1870s until the First World War.

When each currency is linked to gold, in essence, the precious metal becomes a world currency. Suppose the U.S. pledged it would buy and sell gold from both domestic citizens and foreigners at a price of $\frac{1}{20}$ of an ounce = $1. Simultaneously, suppose other countries set the value of their currencies in terms of gold. Perhaps the English would set the value of a pound equal to $\frac{1}{10}$ of an ounce of gold and the French would set the value of the franc at $\frac{1}{40}$ of an ounce of gold. Under these circumstances, when each country sets the value of its currency in terms of gold, the countries also establish a system of fixed exchange rates. For example, if a pound traded for twice as much gold ($\frac{1}{10}$ of an ounce rather than $\frac{1}{20}$ of an ounce) as the dollar, the fixed exchange rate value of the pound would be 1 pound = $2. No one would ever pay more for a pound than $2 because they could always buy $\frac{1}{10}$ of an ounce of gold for $2 and then use the gold to buy a pound. Similarly, the exchange rate between the French franc and the dollar would be $0.50 = 1 franc because the dollar exchanges for twice as much gold ($\frac{1}{20}$ versus $\frac{1}{40}$ of an ounce) as the franc. Since each currency is readily redeemable in gold, the currency of each nation is little more than a gold certificate under a gold standard system.

How did an economy adjust to the flow of international trade under a gold standard? Since domestic citizens could redeem gold for money, an inflow of gold, in effect, increased the nation's money supply. Under a gold standard system, the flow of gold among countries tended to bring imports and exports of nations into balance. If a nation's imports exceed its exports, the differential was paid in gold. Thus, "trade-deficit" nations exported gold to "trade-surplus" nations. These gold transfers caused the money supply of trade-deficit nations to fall and the money supply of trade-surplus countries to rise. Prices soon reflected these changes in the supply of money. Prices declined in the trade-deficit nations as a result of the shrinking supply of money. The price reductions made the goods of the trade-deficit nations cheaper on international markets, stimulated exports, and thereby restored the balance of trade. Similarly, prices in the trade-surplus nations rose as these countries acquired gold and expanded their money supply. The price inflation in the trade-surplus nations made their products less competitive. Exports declined, moving the trade balance of these countries toward equilibrium.

Despite the beauty of the system's simplicity, the gold standard had a number of drawbacks. First, real resources were tied up in the mining of gold so that it could be transferred between trading nations. Second, as the international sector grew in importance, the demand for exchange currency expanded. Since the supply of gold was virtually fixed, this expanding demand could not be satisfied. Third, with gold-backed currency used for both domestic and foreign transactions, the system placed a stranglehold on monetary planners. While this might be considered an advantage during periods of inflation, dissatisfaction arose when a reduction in a nation's gold stock (as a result of a trade deficit) not only placed downward pressure on prices but also caused a decline in employment and income. As the result of these disadvantages, the gold standard was abandoned in 1914.

While the gold standard is very much like a fixed exchange rate system, a fixed system can be maintained without linking currencies to gold. To make a fixed rate system work, countries must conduct their monetary policy *as if* they are on a gold standard. When a country runs a trade surplus, it should increase the growth rate of its money supply more rapidly. This will cause the domestic price level to rise, making its exports less competitive. Eventually, balance between what is sold to foreigners and what is bought from them will be restored. On the other hand, a country that is running a trade deficit should reduce its rate of monetary growth in order to reduce the domestic price level and make its goods and services more competitive in the world market. The more restrictive monetary policy will eventually restore balance in the trade sector.

Despite the similarities, there is one crucial difference between a pure gold standard and a fixed rate system such as was present during the 1944–1971 period. The gold standard does not allow policymakers a choice with regard to altering monetary policy. Under a pure gold standard, the money supply of nations experiencing a trade surplus increases automatically, while the money supply of trade deficit nations declines. The gold standard eliminates the discretion of the policymakers. Proponents of the gold standards usually find this to be one of its most attractive features.

DISADVANTAGES OF THE CURRENT SYSTEM

The current system is not without its critics. The critics of the system stress the following problems:

1. *The current system leads to volatile exchange rate changes which create uncertainty.* During 1980–1985, the dollar appreciated by 50 percent or more against major currencies such as the French franc, German mark, and British pound. In contrast, the dollar depreciated by a similar amount against several leading currencies during 1986–1988 (see Exhibit 1). Critics of the current system argue that fluctuations of this type make it difficult for exporters and importers to plan for the future.

When evaluating the merit of this charge, one should keep in mind that futures markets allow buyers and sellers to hedge against currency fluctuations when they engage in long-term contracts in another currency. For example, an American business contracting to purchase Japanese houseware products to be delivered in six months can arrange now *at a designated current price* for the delivery of the yen needed to complete the transaction. Thus, if international traders want to avoid the uncertainty implied by potential fluctuations in the exchange rate, futures markets in currencies permit them to do so at a moderate cost. This helps to explain the fact that, even during periods of rapidly changing exchange rates, the volume of international trade has continued to grow.

2. *Since the current system fails to impose macroeconomic policy discipline, we can expect more inflation than under a fixed rate system.* Under a fixed rate system, inflationary policies lead to balance of payments deficits. Since policymakers will not want to devalue the nation's currency, proponents of this view charge that fixed rates restrain policymakers more than a flexible rate system. In essence, this view stresses the cost of providing macroeconomic policymakers with greater independence—they are likely to abuse it.

3. *Changes in exchange rates alter trade balances slowly, only after the passage of time.* As we previously discussed, the demand for both imports and exports is often inelastic in the short run. When this is the case, a depreciation in a nation's currency will temporarily cause a current account deficit to worsen. Thus, changes in exchange rates are a crude and uncertain instrument with which to deal with trade imbalances, according to this view.

CONCLUDING REMARKS

The current international monetary system is the product of an evolutionary process. Future changes are likely. However, a return to a system of fixed exchange rates such as existed for nearly three decades following the Second World War seems unlikely. Nations are simply unwilling to subject their monetary and fiscal policies to the constraints that a system of fixed rates would require. Currently, there is widespread recognition that the economic health of nations is influenced by the flow of international trade. Perhaps this recognition will lead to a greater coordination of monetary and fiscal policies among Western nations. Recent events at the annual economic summits of Western nations appear to point in this direction.

CHAPTER SUMMARY

1. The foreign exchange market is a highly organized market in which currencies of different countries are bought and sold. The exchange rate is the price of one national currency in terms of another. The exchange rate permits consumers in one country to translate the prices of foreign goods into units of their own currency.
2. When international trade takes place, it is usually necessary for one country to convert

its currency to the currency of its trading partner. Imports of goods, services, and assets (both real and financial) by the United States generate a demand for foreign currency with which to pay for these items. On the other hand, exports of goods, services, and assets supply foreign currency to the exchange market because foreigners exchange their currency for the dollars needed to purchase the export items.

3. The value of a nation's currency on the exchange market is in equilibrium when the supply of the currency (generated by imports—the sale of goods, services, and assets to foreigners) is just equal to the demand for the currency (generated by exports—the purchasing of goods, services, and assets from foreigners).

4. Under a flexible rate system, if there is an excess supply of dollars (excess demand for foreign currencies) on the foreign exchange market, the value of the dollar will depreciate relative to other currencies. A depreciation will make foreign goods and assets more expensive to U.S. consumers and U.S. goods and assets cheaper to foreigners, reducing the value of our imports and increasing the value of our exports until equilibrium is restored. On the other hand, an excess demand for dollars (excess supply of foreign currencies) will cause the dollar to appreciate, stimulating imports and discouraging exports until equilibrium is restored.

5. With flexible exchange rates, a nation's currency tends to appreciate when (a) rapid economic growth *abroad* (and slow growth at home) stimulates exports relative to imports, (b) the rate of domestic inflation is below that of the nation's trading partners, and (c) domestic real interest rates increase relative to one's trading partners. The reverse of these conditions will cause a nation's currency to depreciate.

6. Unanticipated restrictive monetary policy will raise the real interest rate, reduce the rate of inflation, and, at least temporarily, reduce aggregate demand and the growth of income. These factors will in turn cause the nation's currency to appreciate on the foreign exchange market. In contrast, expansionary monetary policy will result in a currency depreciation.

7. Fiscal policy tends to generate conflicting influences on the exchange rate. To the extent that expansionary fiscal policy (larger budget deficits) stimulates income, it promotes imports relative to exports, causing a currency to depreciate. However, to the extent expansionary fiscal policy increases the real interest rate of a nation, it causes an appreciation of a nation's currency due to an inflow of foreign investment. The analysis is symmetrical for restrictive fiscal policy.

8. During the period from 1944 to 1971, most of the nations of the free world operated under a system of fixed exchange rates. Under this system, if the value of the goods, services, and capital assets exported to foreigners is less than the value of the items imported, there is an excess supply of the country's currency on the foreign exchange market. When this happens, the country must (a) devalue its currency, (b) take action to reduce imports (for example, heighten its trade barriers), or (c) pursue a restrictive macropolicy designed to increase interest rates and retard inflation. During the period when the fixed rates were in effect, corrective action taken to maintain the rates was often in conflict with free trade in international markets and the macropolicy objective of full employment.

9. Prior to the First World War, most countries set the value of their currency in terms of gold. When trade was conducted under the gold standard, the gold stock of a nation would fall if it imported more than it exported. The decline in the stock of gold would decrease the nation's money supply, causing prices to fall and making the nation's goods more competitive on the international market. In contrast, if a nation was a net exporter, its stock of gold would rise, causing inflation and making the nation's goods less competitive on the international market. However, alterations in the supply of gold often caused abrupt shifts in income and employment. The gold standard was abandoned in 1914.

10. The balance of payments accounts record the flow of payments between a country and

other countries. Transactions (for example, imports) that supply a nation's currency to the foreign exchange market are recorded as debit items. Transactions (for example, exports) that generate a demand for the nation's currency on the foreign exchange market are recorded as credit items.

11. In aggregate, the balance of payment accounts must balance since the accounts are kept according to the principles of double-entry bookkeeping. Thus, (a) the current account balance plus (b) the capital account balance plus (c) the official reserve account balance must equal zero. However, the individual components of the accounts need not balance. A deficit in one area implies an offsetting surplus in other areas.

12. Under a pure flexible rate system, there will not be any official reserve account transactions. Under these circumstances, a current account deficit implies a capital account surplus (and vice versa). Interestingly, an economy offering attractive investment opportunities to foreigners will tend to run a capital account surplus, which also implies a current account deficit under a flexible rate system.

13. Under a flexible exchange rate system, a nation's current account position is an aggregation of the voluntary choices of individuals and businesses. Some will have bought more abroad than they sold, while others will have sold more than they bought. The current account deficit simply indicates that the net foreign purchases (and unilateral gifts) of the first group exceed the net foreign sales of the latter group.

14. While flexible exchange rates bring the sum of the current and capital accounts into balance, they do not bring either component into balance. Thus, it is possible for a country to experience a *long-term* current account deficit or surplus. Whether a country runs a current account deficit or surplus is dependent upon the attractiveness of domestic investment opportunities relative to the nation's saving rate. Countries with more attractive investment opportunities and a low saving rate will tend to run capital account surpluses and current account deficits. On the other hand, countries with less attractive investment opportunities and a high saving rate will tend to experience capital outflow and current account surpluses under a flexible rate system.

15. Since 1973, most countries have operated under a managed flexible rate system. It is a managed system because the major industrial nations have used their official reserve balances in an effort to moderate swings in exchange rates. Nevertheless, market forces now play the major role in the determination of exchange rates among the major industrial nations. Given the severe shocks that international markets have suffered since it was instituted in 1973, the current system appears to be working reasonably well.

CRITICAL ANALYSIS QUESTIONS

1. During the early 1980s, the United States shifted toward a more restrictive monetary policy that sharply decelerated the domestic inflation rate. Simultaneously, the federal government was running a large budget deficit. Explain how this policy mix influences the value of the dollar in the exchange rate market.

2. How do flexible exchange rates bring about balance in the exchange rate market? Do flexible exchange rates lead to a balance between merchandise exports and imports? Do you think the United States should continue to follow a policy of flexible exchange rates? Why or why not?

3. "If a current account deficit means that we are getting more items from abroad than we are sending to foreigners, why is it considered a bad thing?" Comment.

*4. Suppose the exchange rate between the United States and Mexico freely fluctuated in the open market. Indicate which of the following would cause the dollar to appreciate (or depreciate) relative to the peso.

---

*Asterisk denotes questions for which answers are given in Appendix C, Selected Answers.

a. An increase in the quantity of drilling equipment purchased in the United States by Pemex, the Mexican oil company, as a result of a Mexican oil discovery.

b. An increase in the U.S. purchase of crude oil from Mexico as a result of the development of Mexican oil fields.

c. Higher real interest rates in Mexico, inducing U.S. citizens to move their financial investments from U.S. to Mexican banks.

d. Lower real interest rates in the United States, inducing Mexican investors to borrow dollars and then exchange them for pesos.

e. inflation in the United States and stable prices in Mexico.

f. Ten percent inflation in both the United States and Mexico.

g. An economic boom in Mexico, inducing Mexicans to buy more U.S.-made automobiles, trucks, electric appliances, and television sets.

h. Attractive investment opportunities, inducing U.S. investors to buy stock in Mexican firms.

*5. The chart below indicates the actual newspaper quotation of the 1989 exchange rate of various currencies:

	U.S. Dollar Equivalent	
	Feb. 1	Feb. 2
British pound	1.755	1.746
French franc	.1565	.1575

On Feb. 2, did the dollar appreciate or depreciate against the British pound? How did it fare against the French franc?

6. **What's Wrong with This Way of Thinking?**
"The government can change from fixed to flexible exchange rates, but we will continue to run a balance of payments deficit because foreign goods, produced with cheap labor, are simply cheaper than goods produced in the United States."

7. "A nation cannot continue to run a deficit on current account. A healthy growing economy will not persistently expand its indebtedness to foreigners. Eventually, the trade deficits will lead to national bankruptcy." Evaluate this view.

8. In recent years, a substantial share of the domestic capital formation in the United States has been financed by foreign investors. Is this inflow of capital from abroad indicative that the U.S. economy is in poor health? What does it indicate?

*9. Suppose that the United States were running a current account deficit. How would each of the following changes influence the size of the current account deficit?

a. a recession in the United States?

b. a decline in the attractiveness of investment opportunities in the United States?

c. an improvement in investment opportunities abroad?

10. "Foreigners are flooding our markets with goods and using the proceeds to buy up America. Unless we do something to protect ourselves, the Japanese, Europeans, and Arabs are going to own America." Evaluate this recent statement of an American political figure.

*11. If foreigners have confidence in the U.S. economy and therefore move to expand their investments in the United States, how will the U.S. current account balance be affected? How will the exchange rate value of the dollar be affected?

12. Is a trade surplus indicative of a strong, healthy economy? Why or why not?

*13. If the dollar depreciates relative to the German mark, how will your ability to purchase the BMW you have longed for be affected? How will this change influence the quantity of BMWs purchased by Americans? How will it affect the dollar expenditures of Americans on BMWs?

14. What is the J-curve effect? According to the J-curve effect, how will a depreciation in a nation's currency affect its current account balance?
15. Explain why a current account balance and a capital account balance must sum to zero under a pure flexible exchange rate system.
*16. Changes in exchange rates will automatically direct a country to a current account balance under a flexible exchange rate system. True or false?

22

ECONOMIC DEVELOPMENT AND THE GROWTH OF INCOME[1]

Development is not purely an economic phenomenon.
Ultimately it must encompass more than the material and
financial side of people's lives. Development should
therefore be perceived as a multidimensional process
involving the reorganization and reorientation of entire
economic and social systems.[2]

Michael P. Todaro

CHAPTER FOCUS

■ How do economists differentiate between developed and less developed countries?

■ How wide is the economic gap between rich and poor nations?

■ Are economic growth and development the same thing?

■ Why do some nations grow while others stagnate? What are the major obstacles that retard economic progress?

■ Is the economic gap between rich and poor nations narrowing or widening?

Throughout history, economic growth and income levels substantially greater than those required for survival have been rare. In the battle with Nature for survival, human beings have usually had to struggle and toil merely to eke out a minimal living. The wheels of progress have moved forward slowly. Economic growth and the rising standard of living taken for granted by much of the Western world did not exist for extended periods of recorded history and still do not exist for many non-Western countries. For example, Phelps Brown showed that the real income of English building trade workers was virtually unchanged between 1215 and 1798, a period of nearly six centuries. The living conditions of peasants in such countries as India and Pakistan are not much different from those of their ancestors 1,000 years ago.

Against this background of poverty and stagnation, the economic record of the Western world during the last 250 years is astounding. In 1750, people all over the world struggled 50, 60, and 70 hours per week to obtain the basic necessities of life—food, clothing, and shelter. Manual labor was the major source of energy. Animals provided the means of transportation. Tools and machines were primitive by today's standards.

In the last two centuries, petroleum, electricity, and nuclear power have replaced human and animal power as the major sources of energy. Automobiles, airplanes, and trains are now the major means of transportation. Subsistence levels of food, shelter, and clothing are taken for granted, and the typical Western family worries instead about financing summer vacations, obtaining video cassette recorders, and providing for the children's college educations. For the first time in history, economic growth is such that subsistence-level living standards have been far surpassed in many parts of the world.

DEVELOPED AND LESS DEVELOPED COUNTRIES

Less Developed Countries: Low income countries characterized by rapid population growth, an agriculture-household sector that dominates the economy, illiteracy, extreme poverty, and a high degree of inequality.

Like the rich nations, the poor countries of the world differ from each other in many respects. Some have grown rapidly in recent years; others have continued to stagnate. War and political upheaval have contributed to the poverty of some; cultural and tribal stability dominate others. There is no sharp division between developed and less developed countries. If per capita income were used to distinguish between the two, there would be no significant difference between the income level of the wealthiest less developed country and that of the poorest developed nation. In many respects, the division between the developed and less developed countries is arbitrary. However, there is a set of characteristics generally shared by the less developed countries.

1. *The Most Obvious Characteristic of Less Developed Nations Is Low Per Capita Income.* Extreme poverty, hunger, and filth are a way of life throughout much of India, Pakistan, most of Asia, Africa, and much of Central and South America. Exhibits 1 and 2 present the harsh statistics. In 1986, per capita *annual* income was $120 in Ethiopia, $160 in Bangladesh, and $290 in India. Approxi-

[1]The authors would like to thank James Cobbe for his helpful suggestions that contributed to the development of this chapter.
[2]Michael P. Todaro, *Economics for a Developing World* (London: Longman, 1977), p. 87.

EXHIBIT 1 ■ Annual Per Capita Output of Nations, 1986 (Derived by the Exchange Rate Conversion Method)

Poorest Countries (Annual Output Less than $450)		Poor Countries (Annual Output $450 to $1,800)		Middle-Income Countries (Annual Output $1,800 to $5,000)		High-Income Countries (Annual Output Greater than $5,000)	
Selected Countries	Per Capita GNP, 1986	Selected Countries	Per Capita GNP, 1986	Selected Countries	Per Capita GNP, 1986	Selected Countries	Per Capita GNP, 1986
Ethiopia	$120	Indonesia	$ 490	Brazil	$1,810	Hong Kong	$ 6,910
Bangladesh	160	Philippines	560	South Africa	1,850	United Kingdom	8,870
Zaire	160	Nigeria	640	Mexico	1,860	France	10,720
Uganda	230	Egypt	760	Poland	2,070	Australia	11,920
India	290	Thailand	810	Yugoslavia	2,300	West Germany	12,080
China	300	Peru	1,090	South Korea	2,370	Japan	12,840
Haiti	330	Turkey	1,110	Venezuela	2,920	Canada	14,120
Pakistan	350	Colombia	1,230	Greece	3,680	United States	17,480
Ghana	390	Chile	1,320	Spain	4,860	Switzerland	17,610

Source: The World Bank, *World Development Report, 1988* (Table 1).

mately 2.5 billion people—51.8 percent of the world's population—lived in the 39 poorest countries with a 1986 annual income per person of less than $450. Another 14.3 percent of the world's population lived in countries where the per capita GNP was between $450 and $1,800 in 1986. Even though these poor countries (the two poorest groups of Exhibits 1 and 2) contained two thirds of the

EXHIBIT 2 ■ World Population and Output in 1986 by Income Level of Countries

The 73 countries with per capita annual output of less than $1,800 accounted for 66.1 percent of the world's population but only 8.3 percent of the world GNP in 1986. In contrast, the 21.8 percent of the world's population living in countries with a per capita output of more than $5,000 produced 84.1 percent of the world GNP in 1986.

Category	Percent of World's Population	Percent of World GNP
39 Poorest Countries (Per capita output less than $450)	51.8	4.7
34 Poor Countries (Per capita output $450 to $1,800)	14.3	3.6
22 Middle-Income Countries (Per capita output $1,800 to $5,000)	12.1	7.6
28 High-Income Countries (Per capita output greater than $5,000)	21.8	84.1

Source: The World Bank, *World Development Report, 1988* (Table 1). The GNP figures were converted to U.S. dollars using the exchange rate method.

world's total population, they generated only 8.4 percent of the world's output. In contrast, 28 countries with a per capita GNP of $5,000 or more (the high-income countries) accounted for a little more than one fifth of the world's population in 1986, but they generated more than four fifths of the world's output. The low-income status of the poor countries of Exhibits 1 and 2 reflects the absence of economic development. By the same token, the standard of living of the wealthy nations is the fruit of past economic development.

2. *The Agriculture-Household Sector Dominates the Economy of Less Developed Nations.* Nearly two thirds of the labor force of the low-income countries of Asia, Africa, and South America is employed in agriculture. In contrast, 2 percent of the U.S. labor force is employed in this sector. The size of the household (nonmarket) sector in less developed countries is generally far greater than that in developed nations. Most households in less developed nations raise their own food, make much of their clothing, and construct the family shelter. The specialization and exchange that dominate developed economies are largely absent in less developed countries.

3. *Rapid Population Growth Generally Characterizes Less Developed Nations.* The population of the poor countries of Asia, Africa, and South America has been expanding at an average annual rate of approximately 2.5 percent. The population of these nations doubles every 25 or 30 years. In contrast, the population growth of the developed nations of Europe and North America is generally less than 1 percent each year.

4. *Income Is Usually More Unequally Distributed in Less Developed Countries.* Not only is the average income low in less developed countries, but most of the available income is allocated to the wealthy. The top 10 percent of all income recipients usually receives a larger proportion of the aggregate income in less developed countries than in developed nations. Often, this reflects the existence of a two-sector economy—a trade and financial sector linked to the developed world and an agriculture-household sector bound by tradition. The incomes of persons employed in the trade and financial sectors may be comparable to those of individuals in developed nations, but most of the population belong to the dominant agriculture-household sector and languish in poverty.

5. *Inadequate Health Care, Poor Educational Facilities, and Illiteracy Are Widespread in Less Developed Nations.* While nearly all school-age children attend primary school in North America and the European nations, less than half do so in many less developed countries. One third or less of the adult population is literate in such countries as Bangladesh, Ethiopia, Pakistan, and India. Physicians and hospitals are unavailable in many parts of the less developed world. Most of the resources of these nations are allocated to the provision of basic necessities—food and shelter. Health care and education are luxuries most people cannot afford.

HOW WIDE IS THE ECONOMIC GAP BETWEEN THE DEVELOPED AND LESS DEVELOPED NATIONS?

Most countries of the continents of Asia, Africa, and South America possess the characteristics of less developed nations. Per capita income is low. The agriculture-household sector dominates the economy. Rapid population growth, economic inequality, and poverty abound. On the other hand, these indicators of underdevelopment are generally absent from North America, Europe, Oceania, Japan, and the Soviet Union. Although there are a few exceptions, these areas by and large comprise the developed nations of the world.

Exchange Rate Conversion Method: Method that uses the foreign exchange rate value of a nation's currency to convert that nation's GNP to another monetary unit, such as the U.S. dollar.

How wide is the economic gap between the developed and less developed world? This is a difficult question to answer. The gross national product per capita is a measure of the goods and services available to individuals, but how can we draw meaningful comparisons when Mexico's GNP is measured in pesos, Brazil's GNP is measured in cruzeiros, France's GNP is measured in francs, and so on?

The simplest method used to deal with this problem is the exchange rate conversion method. This method uses the value of each nation's currency in the exchange rate market to convert the nation's GNP to a common currency, such as the U.S. dollar. For example, if the British pound is worth 1.5 times as much as the U.S. dollar *in the foreign exchange market,* then the GNP of the United Kingdom is converted to dollars by multiplying the British GNP *in pounds* by 1.5. Similarly, the exchange rate value of the currency of other nations is used to convert their GNP to dollars. Since the procedure is relatively simple, most international income comparisons are based on this technique.

Although the exchange rate conversion method is simple and straightforward, it may be a misleading indicator of differences in living standards among nations. The exchange rate of a currency reflects the relative purchasing power of the currency for goods traded in international markets. However, it may not be a reliable indicator of the relative purchasing power of the currency for goods and services not exchanged in international markets. For example, merely because a pound purchases 1.5 dollars in the foreign exchange market, it does not follow that it will purchase 1.5 times as much housing, education, recreation, child-care service, and similar items in the United Kingdom as a dollar will purchase in the United States. Since many items are not traded in international markets, the *domestic* purchasing power of a currency may be either more or less than its purchasing power in the exchange market.

The quality of comparative international income data would be greatly improved if the conversion ratio between currencies were expressed in terms of the ability of the currencies to purchase a typical bundle of goods and services in the country of their origin. The United Nations International Comparison Project study begun in 1968 by the United Nations Statistical Office, the University of Pennsylvania, and the World Bank, has devised such a purchasing power index for several currencies. The purchasing power parity method compares the costs of purchasing a typical bundle of goods and services in the domestic markets for various nations. Each category in the bundle is weighted according to its contribution to GNP. The cost of purchasing the typical bundle in each nation is then compared to the dollar cost of purchasing the same bundle in the United States. Once the purchasing power of each nation's currency (in terms of the typical bundle) is determined, this information can be used to convert the GNP of each country to a common monetary unit (for example, the U.S. dollar).

Purchasing Power Parity Method: Method for determining the relative purchasing power of different currencies by comparing the amount of each currency required to purchase a typical bundle of goods and services in domestic markets. This information is then used to convert the GNP of each nation to a common monetary unit.

Recently completed work by Robert Summers and Alan Heston of the University of Pennsylvania provides us with per capita output estimates for 130 countries derived by the purchasing power parity method.[3] Exhibit 3 presents these

[3]Robert Summers and Alan Heston, ''A New Set of International Comparisons of Real Product and Price Levels—Estimates for 130 Countries, 1950–1985,'' *The Review of Income and Wealth,* 34 (March 1988) pp. 1–25. For additional detail on the construction of the purchasing power parity estimates, see I. B. Kravis, Alan Heston, and Robert Summers, *World Product and Income: International Comparisons of Real Gross Product* (Baltimore: Johns Hopkins Press, 1982).

EXHIBIT 3 ■ A Comparison of the Per Capita GNP of Selected Countries—the Exchange Rate Conversion Method Versus the Purchasing Power Parity Method		
Country	1986 Per Capita GNP in 1986 Dollars (Exchange Rate Conversion Method)	1985 Per Capita GNP in 1980 Dollars (Purchasing Power Parity Method)
India	$ 290	$ 750
China	300	2,444
Thailand	810	1,900
Brazil	1,810	3,282
Mexico	1,860	3,985
Argentina	1,860	3,486
Hong Kong	6,910	9,093
United Kingdom	8,870	8,665
France	10,720	9,918
Australia	11,920	8,850
Canada	14,120	12,196
United States	17,480	12,532
Switzerland	17,680	10,640

Source: The exchange rate conversion estimates are from the World Bank, *World Development Report, 1988* (Table 1). The purchasing power parity estimates are from Robert Summers and Alan Heston, "A New Set of International Comparisons of Real Product and Price Levels—Estimates for 130 Countries, 1950–1985," *The Review of Income and Wealth,* 34 (March 1988).

newly constructed estimates for several countries as well as the more widely cited per capita GNP estimates based on the exchange rate conversion method. Even through the purchasing power parity estimates of Exhibit 3 are for 1985, they are in 1980 dollars, since they are based on the typical bundle consumed in 1980.

In general, the income comparisons derived by the purchasing power parity method indicate that the exchange rate conversion method overstates the income of developed nations relative to less developed countries. For example, the per capita GNP estimate for India derived by the purchasing power parity method is nearly 3 times the exchange rate conversion estimate. For China, the per capita GNP figure derived by the purchasing power parity method is more then 8 times ($2,444 compared to $300) the estimate based on exchange rate conversion! For most all less developed countries, including Thailand, Brazil, Mexico, and Argentina, the per capita GNP estimates based on the purchasing power parity method are substantially greater than the parallel estimates derived by exchange rate conversion. Just the opposite is the case for most developed countries. For France, Australia, Canada, United States, Switzerland, and most other industrial economies, the per capita GNP estimates based on the exchange rate conversion exceed the parallel estimates derived by the purchasing power parity method.

Exhibit 4 uses both the exchange rate conversion and purchasing power parity methods to estimate the size of the gap between the industrial nations and less developed countries. According to the exchange rate conversion method, the per capita GNP of the market economies of North America, Europe, Oceania, and Japan was $12,960 in 1986, compared with only $625 for the less developed

---

EXHIBIT 4   ■   Measuring the Economic Gap Between Developed and Less Developed Countries

If the per capita GNP of industrial, market-economy nations is estimated by the exchange rate conversion method, it is 20 times greater than that of less developed countries. However, if the more accurate purchasing power parity procedure is used, the gap narrows, indicating that the GNP per capita is approximately 6.5 times greater for industrial nations than for less developed countries.

	Per Capita GNP	
	Industrial Countries[a]	Less Developed Countries[b]
Exchange rate method		
1986 (in 1986 U.S. dollars)	$12,960	$625
1986 (industrial countries = 100)	100	5
Purchasing power parity method		
1985 (in 1980 U.S. dollars)	$9,660	$1,480
1985 (industrial countries = 100)	100	15

[a]North America, Europe, Japan, and Oceania. The Soviet Union and other centrally planned economies of Eastern Europe are not included in these data.
[b]Asia, Africa, South America, and Central America.

Source: The World Bank, *World Development Report, 1988* and Robert Summers and Alan Heston, ''Improved International Comparisons of Real Product and its Composition: 1950–1985,'' *Review of Income and Wealth,* 34 (March 1988), pp. 1–25.

---

countries of the world. This exchange rate conversion income comparison suggests that the per capita GNP of developed nations was approximately 20 times the comparable figure for less developed countries in 1986.

Using the purchasing power parity method, however, the estimated 1985 per capita GNP of industrial economies was $9,660, compared to $1,480 for the less developed nations (both figures are in 1980 dollars). This purchasing power parity comparison implies that in the mid-1980s the per capita GNP of the industrial economies was approximately 6.5 times the per capita GNP of less developed countries, a substantially smaller differential than the estimate based on exchange rate conversion.

Since they reflect the prices of a broader set of commodities rather than only items traded internationally, most economists believe that the purchasing power parity estimates are a more accurate indicator of international differences in per capita GNP than the more widely circulated estimates based on exchange rate conversions. Nevertheless, even the purchasing power parity method indicates the economic gap between developed and less developed countries is extremely large.

ARE GROWTH AND DEVELOPMENT THE SAME THING?

During the two decades following the Second World War, economists failed to draw a clear distinction between growth and development. Development was deemed present if a country was able to generate and sustain a significant rate of increase in GNP—for example, 5 percent or more. In recent years, it has become increasingly popular to define growth in strictly positive terms—the rate of change in GNP. Development is now widely perceived as a normative concept, encompassing not only growth but also distributional and structural changes that imply an improvement in the standard of living for most of the populace.

It is important to understand the distinction between two types of growth— extensive and intensive growth. **Extensive economic growth** is present when the output of a nation, as measured by real GNP, for example, is expanding. A nation may experience extensive growth even though the output per person is not rising. Since economists are interested primarily in the well-being of individuals, they generally focus on **intensive economic growth,** the expansion in the availability of goods and services per person. Per capita real output (or income) is a measure of intensive economic growth. If a society's production of goods and services is expanding more rapidly than is its population, per capita real income will rise. On average, the economic well-being of people will improve, reflecting the intensive economic growth. Conversely, if the population of the nation is expanding more rapidly than is production, per capita real income will decline. Economic regression, the opposite of intensive growth, will be the result.

Growth focuses on changes in output. The "new" view of economic development is concerned with the structure and division of the fruits of growth. In this normative view, development requires not only growth in output per person but also an improvement in the availability of consumption goods for a wide spectrum of the populace, including those people in the bottom half of the income distribution. Some economists adhere to the **trickle-down theory**—the view that intensive growth will, with time, lead to an improvement in the standard of living for all major segments of the society. They argue that the enlarged output and higher level of income will eventually "trickle down," bringing improvements in economic opportunity, education, and living standards to the masses.

The trickle-down theory is not without critics. Opponents of the theory argue that growth does not necessarily lead to an improvement in the status of those in the lower half of the economic spectrum. They refer to the experience of such countries as Brazil as evidence supporting their position. Since the mid-1960s, Brazil has achieved substantial economic growth. However, the distribution of income in Brazil is highly skewed. More than 60 percent of the aggregate income is allocated to the wealthiest 20 percent of the population. By way of comparison, the wealthiest one fifth of the population receives between 40 and 45 percent of the aggregate income in the developed countries of Europe and North America. Many development economists charge that the rapid growth of Brazil has failed to significantly alter the economic status of the overwhelming majority of its citizens. Perhaps this situation will change in the future, but the Brazilian experience has shaken the faith of many economists in the trickle-down theory.

Even though economic growth and development can be distinguished, it is obvious that growth is necessary for development. Without sustained economic growth, continuous improvement in the economic opportunities and status of a nation's populace, including those at the bottom of the economic spectrum, will be impossible.

Extensive Economic Growth: An expansion in the total output of goods and services, regardless of whether or not output per capita increases.

Intensive Economic Growth: An increase in output per person. When intensive economic growth is present, output is growing more rapidly than population.

Trickle-Down Theory: The theory that intensive economic growth will eventually lead to an improvement in the standard of living of the entire society, even for persons at the bottom of the economic spectrum.

SOURCES OF ECONOMIC GROWTH

Why do some countries grow rapidly while others stagnate? Lay persons often argue that natural resources are the key ingredient of economic growth. Of course, other things constant, countries with abundant natural resources do have an advantage. It is clear, though, that natural resources are neither a necessary nor sufficient condition for economic growth. Japan has few natural resources and imports almost all of its industrial energy supply. Similarly, Hong Kong has practically no raw materials, very little fertile soil, and no domestic sources of energy. Yet, the growth records of these two countries are envied throughout the world. In contrast, such resource-rich nations as Ghana, Kenya, and Bolivia are poor and experiencing only slow growth. Physical resources are not the key to economic progress.

If natural resources are not the key to growth, what is? Thus far, economists have been unable to construct a general theory of growth and development. Therefore, we cannot fully determine the essential ingredients necessary for the transition from stagnation to economic progress and development. Economics is nevertheless capable of pinpointing certain important determinants. Three factors stand out. Clearly, (a) investment in physical and human capital, (b) technological advances, and (c) improvement in economic organization play important roles in the growth process.

INVESTMENT IN PHYSICAL AND HUMAN CAPITAL

Machines can have a substantial impact on a person's ability to produce. Even Robinson Crusoe on an uninhabited island can catch far more fish with a net than he can with his hands. Farmers working with modern tractors and plows can cultivate many more acres than their great-grandfathers, who probably worked with hoes. Similarly, education and training that improve the knowledge and skills of workers can vastly improve their productivity. For example, a cabinet-maker, skilled by years of training and experience, can build cabinets far more rapidly and efficiently than can a lay person. Both physical capital (machines) and human capital (knowledge and skills) expand the productive capacity of a worker.

The acquisition of physical and human capital, though, involves an opportunity cost. When time and effort are expended on the production of machines or the development of skills, fewer resources are available for current production. There are no free lunches. The cost of additions to a nation's stock of physical and human capital is a reduction in current consumption, either domestically or abroad if the investment is financed by borrowing.

As we discussed in Chapter 2, nations that allocate a larger share of their resources to investment expand their productive base more rapidly. Stated another way, a nation's investment rate affects the growth rate of the nation's resource base and thereby affects its rate of economic growth. Other things constant, nations that invest more in human and physical capital tend to grow more rapidly.

Some economists argue that less developed countries are trapped in their poverty because they cannot generate a sufficient amount of savings for the finance of capital formation. According to this view, less developed nations are caught in

Vicious Circle of Underdevelopment: A pattern of low income and low economic growth, which tends to perpetuate itself. Since the current consumption demands of poor nations are large in proportion to available income, the savings and investment rates of these nations are low. In turn, the low investment rate retards future growth, causing poor nations to remain poor.

a **vicious circle of underdevelopment.**[4] Exhibit 5 depicts this view. Since living standards are barely above the subsistence level, less developed countries use most of their resources for the provision of current consumption goods such as food and clothing. Little is saved and invested for the future. But nations that save and invest only a small portion of their income will grow slowly, if at all. Thus, the poverty of less developed nations becomes self-perpetuating: poor societies are unable to save and invest, and lacking capital formation they are unable to escape their poverty.

This vicious circle of poverty theory has been severely criticized in recent years. The critics of the theory argue that the problem is not an absence of financing but rather low rates of return often due to uncertainties emanating from insecure property rights and perverse governmental policies.[5] If the returns on investments in less developed countries were attractive, the critics of the vicious circle of poverty theory argue, both domestic and foreign investors would be willing to supply the required financing.

TECHNOLOGICAL PROGRESS

Technological Advancement: The introduction of new techniques or methods of production that enable a greater output per unit of input.

Technological improvement makes it possible to generate additional output with the same amount of resources. Technological advancement—the adoption of new techniques or methods of production—enables workers to produce goods at a fraction of their former cost. Less human and physical capital per unit of output is required.

Technological advancement is brought about by capital formation and research investments. Modern technological breakthroughs are generally the result of systematic investments in research and development. Thus, advancements in science and technology, like other improvements requiring investment expenditures, necessitate the sacrifice of current consumption.

When analyzing the phenomenal growth of Western nations during the nineteenth century, economic historians often point to dramatic technological advancements as the major source of economic progress. This view certainly has some merit. From a technological viewpoint, a person living in 1750 would probably have felt more at home in the world at the time of Christ than in today's society. During the last 250 years, technology has radically altered our way of life. The substitution of power-driven machines for human labor, the development of new

---

[4]Ragnar Nurkse provides a clear statement of the vicious circle of underdevelopment:

In discussions of the problem of economic development, a phrase that crops up frequently is "the vicious circle of poverty."

A situation of this sort [the vicious circle of underdevelopment] relating to a country as a whole can be summed up in the trite proposition: "A country is poor because it is poor". . . . The supply of capital is governed by the ability and willingness to save; the demand for capital is governed by the incentives to invest.

On the supply side, there is the small capacity to save, resulting from the low level of real income. . . .

On the demand side, the inducement to invest may be low because of the small buying power of the people, which is due to their small real income, which again is due to low productivity.

See Ragnar Nurkse, *Problems of Capital Formation in Underdeveloped Countries* (New York: Oxford University Press, 1953), pp. 4–5.

[5]See Peter T. Bauer, *Equality, the Third World, and Economic Delusion* (Cambridge: Harvard University Press, 1981).

The Vicious Circle of Underdevelopment

Since incomes are low in underdeveloped nations, savings and investment rates are also low. Low rates of investment retard the future growth of income. Thus, underdevelopment is self-perpetuating. The circle is complicated by the population bomb, which often explodes when a country begins to break out of the pattern.

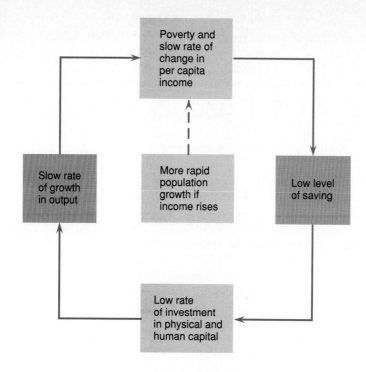

Invention: The discovery of a new product or process, often facilitated by the knowledge of engineering and scientific relationships.

Innovation: The successful introduction and adoption of a new product or process; the economic application of inventions.

sources of energy (for example, the steam engine, the internal combustion engine, hydroelectric power, and nuclear power), and developments in transportation and communications are the foundation of modern society. Without them, the growth and development of the last 250 years would have been impossible.

Obviously, technological progress encompasses **invention,** the discovery of new products or processes. But, it also includes **innovation,** the practical and effective adoption of new techniques. It is sometimes easy to overlook the significance of innovation, but it is crucial to economic development. Many innovators were not involved in the discovery of the products for which they are now famous. Henry Ford played a minor role in the discovery and development of the automobile. His contribution was an innovative one—the adoption of mass production techniques, which facilitated the low-cost production of reliable automobiles. J. C. Penney played an important role in American economic progress, not because he invented anything, but because he effectively introduced the department store. Inventions are important, but without innovators, inventions are merely ideas waiting to be exploited.

Although technological advancement has played an important role in the promotion of material progress, it is clearly not a sufficient condition for sustained economic growth. Modern technology is available to all, including the less developed nations. If technology were the only requirement for economic growth, the less developed nations would be growing rapidly.

Before modern technology can set growth in motion, the work force of a nation must be sufficiently knowledgeable to operate and maintain complex machines. Innovative entrepreneurs who are capable of adapting technology to the needs (and price structure) of a nation must be available and have access to resources. This means that capital investment and savings are required. Among less developed nations, these conditions are generally absent. Poverty and primitive methods of production thus survive in the modern world despite the availability of advanced technology.

EFFICIENT ECONOMIC ORGANIZATION

Allocative Inefficiency: The use of an uneconomical combination of resources to produce goods and services that are not intensely desired relative to their opportunity cost.

The efficiency with which the economic activity of a country is organized will influence the country's output and growth rate. If the economic organization of a nation encourages waste and fails to reward the creation of wealth, economic growth will be stunted. Regardless of the form of economic organization present, certain basic conditions must be met if waste and inefficiency are to be avoided. The incentive structure must encourage production of goods and services most desired by people. **Allocative inefficiency** results when a nation's resources are used to produce the wrong products. For example, waste results when a nation whose people intensely desire more food and better housing, uses valuable resources to produce unwanted national monuments and luxurious vacations for political leaders. In the same way, waste results when a nation ill-equipped to manufacture steel and automobiles insists on using resources that could be productive in other areas (for example, agriculture) to produce these prestige goods.

Efficient economic organization must also encourage producers to choose low opportunity cost methods of production. Regardless of whether an economy is centrally planned or market directed, efficient production requires that the marginal productive contribution of each resource reflect its opportunity cost. Waste results when producers are discouraged from the adoption of the least-cost resource combination. For example, if unfavorable tax treatment or interest rate controls discourage the use of capital, economic waste and higher production costs will result.

Infrastructure: The provision of a legal, monetary, educational, transportation, and communication structure necessary for the efficient operation of an exchange economy.

The supply of public goods and goods that generate substantial external benefits is also an important ingredient of efficient economic organization. Broadly speaking, this issue relates to the provision of an economic infrastructure. **Infrastructure** is a term used by economists to describe the economy's legal, monetary, educational, transportation, and communication structure. The provision of an adequate infrastructure involves several things, including a legal system that clearly defines property rights and a monetary system that encourages the wise use of resources across time periods (that is, something approximating price stability). It also involves the provision of an educational system that encourages children of all social classes to develop their skills and abilities.

Finally, an efficient economy requires the development of highways, telephones, and power sources necessary for the realization of gains from specialization, division of labor, and mass production methods—the "heart and soul" of a modern exchange system. These networks often are provided by government, but each has also been provided privately since users can be made to pay for the benefits they receive through tolls and user charges. However they are provided, a sound infrastructure is an integral part of efficient economic organization.

WHY POOR NATIONS REMAIN POOR: SOURCES OF ECONOMIC STAGNATION

During the last 250 years, sustained growth has taken place throughout most of Europe, North America, and Oceania. More recently, living standards have improved substantially in Japan, the Soviet Union, and several small countries in

Asia. At the same time, poverty, subsistence-level living standards, and malnutrition have persisted throughout much of Asia, Africa, South America, and Central America. In these places, most people continue to live and die in a world of poverty, malnutrition, and disease, just as they have done for thousands of years.

Why have industrialization and economic growth bypassed these people? There is no single, comprehensive answer to this question. However, we can point to several obstacles to economic growth.

Obstacle 1: The Population Bomb May Explode as Soon as Growth Improves Living Standards.

In 1798, Thomas Malthus argued that living standards would never climb much above subsistence level because an improvement in economic well-being would cause people to have more children. From this, any temporary improvement in economic welfare would cause the population to increase until per capita income returned to subsistence levels. Therefore, according to Malthus, economic growth would trigger a population explosion, which would eradicate the temporary gains associated with growth.

The experience of Europe and North America during the last 250 years is clearly inconsistent with the crude Malthusian theory. Recent historical data on income and population, however, have encouraged some development economists to reevaluate the relevance of Malthus's ideas. High rates of population growth do appear to retard economic growth in some countries. The rate of population growth in the poor countries of Asia, Africa, and South America is typically two or three times the rate in wealthy industrial nations. Poor countries would thus theoretically have to grow substantially more rapidly than industrial nations merely to maintain the same rate of growth of per capita income.

Rapid population growth in underdeveloped nations is also likely to increase the **dependency ratio,** the number of children and older persons in a society divided by the total population. Improvements in health associated with economic growth usually lead to a decline in the rate of infant mortality and an increase in the proportion of older people as a share of the total population. With more young children and elderly nonworkers, the burden imposed on the productive working-age population is compounded. The experiences of such countries as India, Bangladesh, Burma, and Egypt, all of which have a rapid rate of population expansion, suggest that the population bomb complicates the growth process.[6]

Dependency Ratio: The number of children (under a specific age—14, for example) and the number of the elderly (age 65 and over) living in a country, divided by the total population. An increasing ratio indicates that a larger burden is being placed on the productive-age work force.

---

[6]The dependency ratio for a typical group of less developed and developed countries is presented below.

Dependency Ratio, 1985
(Percentage of Population under the Age of 14 or over the Age of 64)

Less developed countries		Developed countries	
Bangladesh	47	United States	34
India	44	Canada	32
Burma	46	Japan	32
Egypt	45	United Kingdom	35
		West Germany	30

Although the productive contribution and consumption burden of children and the elderly differ among countries, it is clear that the prime-working-age population of the developed nations has fewer nonproducers to support than that of the less developed nations. See the World Bank, *World Development Report, 1988,* Table 31, for more extensive data.

Obstacle 2: Political Instability May Discourage Investment and Retard Growth.

Suppose in a certain country, a political revolution resulting in government expropriation of land holdings, buildings, and other business assets seemed imminent. Or, suppose you feared the rise of a new regime that would impose punitive taxes on interest income, profits, and/or capital assets. Would you want to invest your savings in such a country? Most people would not.

As a rule of thumb, the more securely present and future property rights are defined, the more capital formation there will be. In contrast, insecurely defined property rights and a potentially volatile political climate will repel capital investment and retard economic growth.

Unfortunately, the political climate of many underdeveloped nations is highly unstable. Prejudice and injustice, a highly unequal distribution of wealth, and a history of political favoritism to a ruling class make political upheaval a distinct possibility. Wise investors, both domestic and foreign, avoid investment in real assets under these conditions. Those who do undertake business ventures find it advantageous to seek favors (and assurances) from the military and ruling classes. This may aggravate the situation in the long run. Unquestionably, several Latin American countries have suffered because of their political instability. Nationalization and the threat of expropriation have discouraged both domestic and foreign investment. Continued poverty and economic stagnation have been the results.

Again, many underdeveloped nations are caught in a vicious cycle. The level of poverty is such that many are willing to support political revolution in the hope that it will better their lot. As the possibility of political upheaval increases, however, the investment necessary to improve the economic welfare of the citizenry comes to a standstill. In turn, the low rate of investment and accompanying economic stagnation make political revolution still more likely. Many underdeveloped nations will be unable to improve their economic conditions until they solve the problem of political instability.

Obstacle 3: Public Policy in Many Less Developed Countries Distorts Prices and Promotes Economic Inefficiency.

Prices direct resources. If resources are going to be allocated efficiently, the relative prices of products and factors must reflect their relative scarcity and true value. Inappropriate pricing signals are a potential source of inefficiency for market and centrally planned economies alike—and for developed and less developed countries.

Unfortunately, public policy in less developed countries has often distorted pricing signals and directed resources away from areas of high productivity. For example, several less developed nations (particularly African countries) have adopted price controls on agricultural commodities that have depressed agricultural prices below world market levels, made farming unprofitable, and driven investment from agriculture. While the intent was to help urban consumers, the result was a decline in agricultural output and widespread food shortages. Similarly, high marginal tax rates have often reduced the incentive to earn and have driven the most productive people away from less developed nations. (See the Applications in Economics box, "Do High Marginal Tax Rates Retard the Economic Growth of Less Developed Countries?") Strict business and occupational licensing, often administered for political purposes, has been a source of inefficiency, protected markets, and high costs in many less developed countries. Official exchange rates have often been set so high that they have eliminated the

APPLICATIONS ○ IN ECONOMICS

Do High Marginal Tax Rates Retard the Economic Growth of Less Developed Countries?[7]

Less developed countries of Asia, Africa, and South America have often levied high tax rates to raise revenue to finance government-directed projects. When high tax rates take a large share of the fruits generated by productive activities, the incentive of individuals to work and undertake business projects is reduced. High tax rates may also drive a nation's most productive citizens to other countries where taxes are lower. They also discourage foreigners from financing domestic investment projects. In short, economic theory indicates that high marginal tax rates will retard productive activity, capital formation, and economic growth.

To date, the most detailed study of the impact of high marginal tax rates on the economic growth of less developed countries has been conducted by Alvin Rabushka of Stanford University. Rabushka undertook the tedious task of reconstructing the 1960–1982 tax structure for 54 less developed countries for which data could be obtained. He found that some countries levied very high marginal tax rates, which took effect only at very high income thresholds.

Others levied high marginal rates on even modest levels of income. A few countries imposed only low or medium tax rates.

Rabushka used the tax structure data to classify each country as a low, medium, or high tax rate nation. Exhibit 6 presents Rabushka's data on tax rates and economic growth for both low and high tax countries among the 54 less developed nations. The data show that lower tax rates were generally associated with more rapid rates of growth. The lowest tax country among the 54 less developed countries was Hong Kong, which levied a flat tax rate of 15 percent on all income above a modest level ($6,410 in 1983). Only one of the 54 countries, Singapore, which was also a low tax nation, was able to exceed the 7.0 annual increase in per capita income achieved by Hong Kong during the 1960–1982 period.

The average growth rate of per capita income for the eight countries classified as low tax was 3.7 percent annually. In contrast, economic growth was much slower in the 10 countries that levied top marginal tax rates ranging from 50 to 70 percent

on incomes of less than $10,000. Among the 10 high tax countries, only two (Pakistan and Turkey) were able to attain an annual growth rate in excess of 1.3 percent during the 1960–1982 period. The average growth rate of the 10 high tax countries was 0.7 percent, less than one-fifth the average growth rate for the eight low tax countries.

Summarizing the findings of this study, Rabushka concluded:

> Good economic policy, including tax policy, fosters economic growth and rising prosperity. In particular, low marginal income tax rates, or high thresholds for medium- and high-rate tax schedules, appear consistent with higher growth rates. The key in any system of direct taxation is to maintain low tax rates or high (income) thresholds.[8]

---

[7]This feature is based on the work of Alvin Rabushka, "Taxation, Economic Growth, and Liberty," *Cato Journal* (Spring/Summer, 1987), pp. 121–148.

[8]Alvin Rabushka, "Taxation and Liberty in the Third World," paper presented to a conference on Taxation and Liberty held in Santa Fe, New Mexico, September 26–27, 1985.

---

competitiveness of a nation's export goods and necessitated the adoption of import restrictions. Interest rate controls have often discouraged savings and driven financial capital abroad.

Less developed nations do not, of course, have a monopoly on foolish economic practices. Developed nations do silly things, too. However, the effects of policies that distort prices, impede business activity, and discourage production are more pronounced in the less developed world. Here, the results are sometimes catastrophic.

Since price distortions emanate from a variety of sources, it is not easy to quantify their effects. Economists are just beginning to undertake research in this

EXHIBIT 6 ■ Marginal Tax Rates and Economic Growth

	Highest Marginal Tax Rate[a]	Income at Which the Top Rate Takes Effect[a]	Growth Rate of Per Capita Income, 1960–1982
Low Tax Rate Countries			
Hong Kong	15	6,410	7.0
Paraguay	30	31,250	3.7
Indonesia	34	50,000	4.2
Argentina	45	36,377	1.6
Ivory Coast	45	24,119	2.1
Solomon Islands	42	3,699	1.3
Singapore	45	355,450	7.4
Venezuela	45	804,020	1.9
Average Growth Rate			**3.7**
High Tax Rate Countries[b]			
Bangledesh	60	7,890	0.3
Chile	58	3,671	0.6
Ghana	60	450	−1.3
India	67.5	9,434	1.3
Jamaica	57.5	4,242	0.7
Pakistan	60	7,407	2.8
St. Vincent	55	5,555	0.6
Turkey	60	8,929	3.4
Uganda	70	4,277	−1.1
Zaire	50	1,986	−0.3
Average Growth Rate			**0.7**

[a]Marginal tax rates in effect in the early 1980s. However, a similar pattern of marginal tax rates was also present during the 1960s and 1970s. The income threshold of each country was converted to U.S. dollars at the exchange rate as of December 31, 1983.

[b]Developing countries with top marginal tax rates of less than 50 percent were classified as low tax rate countries. Countries with top marginal tax rates of 50 percent or more that apply to income levels of less than $10,000 were classified as high tax rate countries.

Source: Alvin Rabushka, "Taxation and Liberty in The Third World." Paper presented to a conference on Taxation and Liberty held in Santa Fe, New Mexico, September 26–27, 1985.

area. Exhibit 7 summarizes the findings of a World Bank research project that analyzed the impact of price distortions on the growth rate of less developed countries.[9] The World Bank study focused on price distortions arising from foreign exchange controls, trade restrictions, wage, price, and interest rate controls, and inflation. A price distortion index for 31 less developed countries was derived. In turn, the price distortion index was related to economic growth. The study found that the nine "low-distortion" countries were able to achieve an average annual growth rate of 6.8 percent during the 1970s. In contrast, the average growth rate

[9]The World Bank, *World Development Report: 1983,* Chapter 6.

APPLICATIONS IN ECONOMICS

Rich and Poor Nations—Are They Two Worlds Drifting Apart?

Since almost everyone was poor 250 years ago, people did not worry much about subsistence-level living standards and starvation in other countries. Of course, there were rich nations and poor nations, but the per capita income of the rich was seldom more than twice that of the poor.

During the eighteenth century, sustained economic growth took place throughout much of Europe and North America. By 1850, there was a virtual explosion of economic development, and it soon spread to Oceania, Russia, and Japan. Not only did industrial nations grow rapidly during this period, but the fruits of growth were also widely dispersed. The living standards of the well-off and those not so well-off increased substantially. Today, even poor people in North America, Europe, Oceania, and Japan are far better off than most citizens of an underdeveloped nation. The present level of affluence in the developed nations is unprecedented.

Economic growth over the last century has created an enormous gulf between developed and less developed countries. While the per capita income of wealthy nations in 1800 was approximately twice that of the poor countries, the average income of people in developed nations today is more than six times the figure for less developed countries (see Exhibit 4). Some observers have argued that the world is comprised of growing industrial nations on the one hand and stagnating, less developed countries on the other. According to this view, the widening gap between rich and poor nations threatens to plunge the world into crisis. Evidence indicates this view is an oversimplification. The less developed countries are not a monolithic block of humanity condemned forever to poverty and stag-

nation, but rather are nearly 100 nations with widely varying growth rates and records. Exhibit 8 highlights this diversity.

The less developed nations of the late-1980s can be broken down into several groups. (Even with this analysis, there will of course be some oversimplification.) First, there are densely populated nations that are losing the battle with economic growth. In fact, the per capita income of Ethiopia, Zaire, Uganda, Ghana, Bolivia, and Peru has actually declined since 1965. The twentieth century has passed by the people of these countries. Like their ancestors for centuries, these people spend their lives trying to eke out a bare subsistence living.

Most of these nations face all of the major obstacles to growth. Relentless poverty keeps their saving and investment rates very low. Political instability and insecure property rights discourage investment. High tax rates, trade restrictions, price controls, and government-imposed red tape limit exchange. As a result of the population explosion, there are more people for the productive members of the population to feed. The future of these nations is bleak.

Fortunately, there is a second group of less developed countries that *has* achieved a very impressive growth record. As Exhibit 8 illustrates, the growth of per capita income in China, Indonesia, Egypt, Cameroon, South Korea, Singapore, and Hong Kong has generally exceeded the growth rates of the wealthier developed countries. These countries are winning the race with scarcity.

The high growth, less developed countries are a diverse group. Some are large; others are small. Some (China and Indonesia) are rich with

minerals, but others (Hong Kong, Singapore, and Egypt) have few natural resources. But these high growth countries also have several things in common. First, they have an incentive structure that encourages farmers and business entrepreneurs to produce and earn income. Several of them (Hong Kong, Indonesia, and Singapore) are characterized by low marginal tax rates. Even in China, recent reforms have increased the ability of agricultural workers to capture the benefits of increases in production. Second, during recent decades, property rights have been relatively secure in each of the less developed countries experiencing rapid growth, and as a result, each has attracted substantial foreign investment. Interestingly, with the possible exception of Egypt, aid from foreign governments has played little part in the rapid growth of these nations. Finally, with the exception of Brazil, these countries have controlled inflation. While the price level in several of the countries has risen, inflation in the high growth countries has generally been much less rampant than in other less developed countries.

Compared to industrial nations, the population growth of poor nations—both those achieving economic growth as well as those stagnating—has been quite rapid. While the population of the United States, Japan, and the developed nations of Europe has been expanding less than 1 percent annually, the population growth rate of the less developed countries has generally exceeded 2.5 percent annually. (See Exhibit 8, column 3.)

For less developed countries, the rapid population growth is both a problem and an opportunity. It is a problem because population expansion is clearly running a tight race with economic growth. However, it also presents an opportunity. If less developed countries can reduce their birth rates, the initial impact on their growth rates is likely to be quite positive. A reduction in a nation's birth rate will result in a smaller number of dependents per working-age adult,

which would stimulate the growth in per capita income. The rising real income would in turn generate additional savings and the investment necessary to sustain a more rapid rate of economic growth. Nations currently experiencing rapid growth in aggregate GNP can expect a period of very rapid growth in *per capita* in-

come if they are able to reduce their birth rates. If this happens, less developed countries such as South Korea, Egypt, Thailand, Indonesia, Brazil, and perhaps China may well follow in the footsteps of Japan and by the turn of the century begin to move rapidly up the ladder of economic development.

EXHIBIT 8 ■ Wealth of Nations—Growth of Population and Income

Selected Countries	Per Capita GNP, 1987 (U.S. Dollars)[a] (1)	Percentage of World Population 1987 (2)	Population 1980–1987 (3)	Real Per Capita GNP 1965–1980 (4)	Real Per Capita GNP 1980–1987 (5)
Poor country (slow growth in per capita income)					
Ethiopia	120	0.8	2.4	0.0	−1.6
Zaire	160	0.6	3.1	−1.4	−2.8
Tanzania	220	0.4	3.5	0.4	−1.8
Uganda	260	0.3	3.1	−2.1	−2.4
Ghana	390	0.2	3.4	−0.8	−2.0
Bolivia	570	0.1	2.9	−2.0	−5.4
Chile	1,310	0.2	1.8	0.1	−1.8
Peru	1,430	0.4	2.6	−1.1	−1.0
Poor country (rapid growth in per capita income)					
China	300	19.2	1.2	4.2	9.1
Indonesia	500	3.0	2.2	5.6	1.9
Egypt	710	0.9	2.7	4.3	2.6
Thailand	840	1.0	2.0	4.7	2.6
Cameroon	910	0.2	1.0	2.4	4.2
Brazil	2,020	2.5	2.2	6.6	1.0
South Korea	2,690	0.8	1.4	7.6	7.3
Singapore	7,940	0.1	1.1	8.8	5.6
Hong Kong	8,260	0.1	1.2	6.4	5.5
Rich country					
United Kingdom	10,430	1.0	0.1	2.0	2.5
Australia	10,900	0.3	1.4	2.2	1.5
France	12,860	1.0	0.5	3.7	0.7
West Germany	14,460	1.1	−0.2	3.0	1.9
Canada	15,080	0.5	1.0	3.1	1.9
Sweden	15,690	0.2	0.1	2.3	1.8
Japan	15,770	2.2	0.6	5.1	3.1
United States	18,430	4.4	1.0	1.8	2.0

[a]Derived by the exchange rate conversion method.

Source: The World Bank, *World Development Report, 1988* and *The World Bank Atlas, 1988*

EXHIBIT 7   ■   Price Distortions and Economic Growth—The Result of the World Bank Study

	Annual Growth of Real GNP 1970—1979	
	Aggregate	Per Capita
Low-distortion countries[a]	6.8	4.5
Median-distortion countries[b]	5.7	2.9
High-distortion countries[c]	3.1	0.8

[a]The low-distortion countries were: Malawi, Thailand, Cameroon, South Korea, Malaysia, Philippines, Tunisia, Kenya, Yugoslavia, and Colombia.
[b]The median-distortion countries were: Ethiopia, Indonesia, India, Sri Lanka, Brazil, Mexico, Ivory Coast, Egypt, and Turkey.
[c]The high-distortion countries were: Senegal, Pakistan, Jamaica, Uruguay, Bolivia, Peru, Argentina, Chile, Tanzania, Bangladesh, Nigeria, and Ghana.

Source: The World Bank, *The World Development Report, 1983*, Table 6.1 and Table 19.

of the eleven ''high-distortion,'' less developed countries was only 3.1 percent. In terms of *per capita* GNP, the growth rate of the low-distortion countries was 4.5 percent, compared with only 0.8 percent for the high-distortion countries. Thus, the per capita real growth of the low-distortion countries was more than five times the comparable rate for high-distortion countries.

A recent study by Gerald Scully of the University of Texas-Dallas also sheds light on the link between political interference with market exchange and economic growth. Scully's study covered 115 countries during the 1960–1980 period. Scully found that economies that relied more extensively on market prices, private property, and the rule of law grew between two and three times more rapidly than economies characterized by political controls and interference with market forces.[10]

WHAT CAN GOVERNMENT DO TO PROMOTE PROSPERITY?

As we previously discussed, economists do not fully understand why some countries develop and others do not. Thus, we do not have a sure-fire recipe to promote growth and prosperity. However, both economic theory and historical experience do provide us with some knowledge of the conditions conducive to economic development. Foremost among these conditions are secure protection of private property, freedom of exchange, stable prices, and low marginal tax rates. As Adam Smith noted long ago, the wealth of nations is crucially dependent upon gains from (1) specialization and trade, (2) expansion in the size of the market, and (3) the discovery of better ways of doing things. Governments that respect property rights and freedom of exchange while following monetary (and fiscal) policies consistent with relatively stable prices establish the foundation for eco-

[10]Gerald W. Scully, ''The Institutional Framework and Economic Development,'' *Journal of Political Economy* 96 (June 1988), pp. 652–662.

nomic growth. All of the modern economic miracles, from the recovery of West Germany and Japan following the Second World War to the rapid growth of the "Asian tigers" (Hong Kong, South Korea, Indonesia, and Singapore) during the last two decades, followed this strategy.

In contrast with this approach, governments around the world have often used price controls, regulations, and taxes to restrain both domestic and international trade. They have often followed monetary policies that resulted in double- and even triple-digit inflation rates, which erode the value of property and increase the risk of time-dimension exchange. Similarly, governments have often levied high marginal tax rates on income, which, in turn, discourage production and drive both capital and productive citizens elsewhere. To varying degrees, these types of policies plague almost all poor countries. This is a strategy that doesn't work. And countries that follow this course will continue to experience poverty and economic stagnation.

LOOKING AHEAD

In the next chapter, we will use economic tools to analyze different economic systems. Our analysis indicates that the economic performance of nations varies considerably. Nations also differ with regard to the structure of economic institutions.

CHAPTER SUMMARY

1. For the first time in history, economic growth is such that per capita income far surpasses the subsistence level in most of Europe, North America, Oceania, Japan, and the Soviet Union. Living conditions have been transformed for the one-fifth of the world's population who reside in these regions.

2. The major characteristics of less developed countries are (a) low per capita income, (b) a large agriculture-household sector, (c) rapid population growth, (d) inequality of income distribution, and (e) widespread illiteracy coupled with poor educational and health facilities.

3. Although there is no sharp dividing line between developed and less developed countries, the nations of North America, Europe (including the Soviet Union) and Oceania, as well as Japan, can be classified as developed countries. In contrast, most of the countries of Asia, Africa, South America, and Latin America exhibit the characteristics of underdevelopment.

4. The exchange rate conversion method and the purchasing power parity method provide ways of comparing income among nations. Under the exchange rate conversion method, the exchange rate value of a nation's currency is used to convert the GNP of each nation into a common currency, usually the U.S. dollar. Alternatively, the purchasing power parity method uses data on the cost of purchasing a typical bundle of consumer goods and services to determine the relative purchasing power of each currency and to calculate the GNP of each nation in terms of a common currency. While the purchasing power parity method is likely to provide a more accurate measure of differences in living standards across countries, the data required to make the calculations are not readily available. As a result, most of the widely cited income comparisons are based on the exchange rate conversion method.

5. Income comparisons based on the exchange rate conversion method suggest that the per capita real GNP of industrial economies is approximately 20 times the figure for less developed nations. However, recent comparisons based on the purchasing power parity method indicate that the exchange rate conversion method overstates the relative income of the industrial nations. When measured by the purchasing power parity method, the per capita GNP of industrial countries is estimated to be 6.5 times that of less developed countries.

6. Economic growth is a positive concept. Extensive growth is present when the real GNP of a nation expands. Intensive growth requires an increase in output per person. Economic development is a normative concept, encompassing distributional and structural factors as well as higher per capita income. Economic development implies an advance in the standard of living for a broad cross-section of a nation's population, including those people in the bottom half of the income distribution.

7. The availability of domestic natural resources is not the major determinant of growth. Countries such as Japan and Hong Kong have impressive growth rates without such resources, while many resource-rich nations continue to stagnate.

8. While economists have been unable to develop a general theory of economic growth and development, several important determinants of economic progress have been pinpointed. The following factors have played an important role in the economic progress of developed nations: (a) investment in physical and human capital, (b) development and dissemination of technologically improved production methods and products, and (c) efficient economic organization.

9. The major obstacles to economic development among poor nations of the world are (a) rapid population growth; (b) political instability, which reduces the security of property rights and thereby retards investment; and (c) waste and inefficiency arising from public policy that distorts pricing signals and promotes economic inefficiency. Recent economic research indicates policies that depress agricultural prices, impose high marginal tax rates, limit international trade, and generate high rates of inflation retard the economic progress of less developed countries.

10. As Adam Smith noted more than 200 years ago, the wealth of nations is dependent upon gains from (a) specialization and trade, (b) expansion in the size of the market, and (c) the discovery of better (more productive) ways of doings things. Governments that respect property rights, protect the freedom of exchange, and follow monetary and fiscal policies consistent with a stable price level help provide the framework for the creation of wealth.

11. The economic growth record of less developed countries is mixed. A large portion of the world's inhabitants live in countries characterized by both extreme poverty and per capita real income that is either stagnating or falling. The rates of population growth in these countries are among the highest in the world. Their economic prospects are bleak. In contrast, the recent economic growth record in other less developed countries, including Egypt, Hong Kong, Indonesia, Singapore, South Korea, Thailand, Brazil, Cameroon, and more recently China, has been highly impressive. These countries may well duplicate the post-Second World War ''Japanese miracle'' of economic development and join the developed world in the near future, particularly if they are able to reduce their rates of population growth.

CRITICAL ANALYSIS QUESTIONS

1. Imagine you are an economic adviser to the president of Mexico. You have been asked to suggest policies to promote economic growth and a higher standard of living for the citizens of Mexico. Outline your suggestions and discuss why you believe they would be helpful.

*2. ''Without aid from the industrial nations, poor countries are caught in the poverty trap. Because they are poor, they are unable to save and invest; and lacking investment, they remain poor.'' Evaluate this view.

*3. It is often argued that the rich nations are getting richer and the poor are getting poorer. Is this view correct? Is it an oversimplification? Explain.

*4. As the people of a nation become wealthier, do you think they will save a larger percentage of their income? Why or why not? As a nation becomes wealthier, do you

*Asterisk denotes questions for which answers are given in Appendix C, Selected Answers.

think that length of the average workweek will decline? Why or why not? Does the experience of the United States support your answer? Explain.

5. The size of the population in some countries may partially reflect the desire of some people for additional security in the form of children to support them in their old age. Is this method of providing for one's retirement inferior to our system of compulsory social security? Why or why not?

6. Discuss the importance of the following as determinants of economic growth: (a) natural resources; (b) physical capital; (c) human capital; (d) technical knowledge; (e) attitudes of the work force; (f) size of the domestic market; and (g) economic policy.

7. What do the high growth countries among less developed nations have in common? How do they differ? What lessons of economic development can be drawn from the similarities and differences among these countries?

*8. Explain why the exchange rate conversion method may result in a misleading estimate for the per capita GNP of a country.

9. How do the exchange rate conversion and purchasing power parity methods differ as tools with which to compare relative incomes among countries? How do the estimated incomes of less developed countries compare with developed countries under the two methods?

*10. Do you think that the absence of international trade barriers will be more important for a small country like Costa Rica than for a larger country like Mexico? Explain.

23

COMPARATIVE ECONOMIC SYSTEMS

Since the activities of individuals in the use of the means of production are regulated, at any given time and place, through the institutions then and there prevailing, the precise manner in which society will use its means of production will depend upon and be determined by the character of its economic institutions.[1]

Howard R. Bowen

CHAPTER FOCUS

■ Are there basic economic principles that apply to all economies?

■ What are the distinguishing characteristics of capitalism and socialism?

■ How is the Soviet economy organized? How does the economic record of the Soviet Union compare with market-directed economies?

■ What are the distinguishing characteristics of the Yugoslavian economy? In what ways is the economy of Yugoslavia unique?

■ How has the economy of China changed in recent years? Have the changes affected economic performance?

■ How rapidly has the Japanese economy grown since 1950? How does the economic organization of Japan differ from that of other market economies?

The institutions and organizations of an economy influence economic outcomes. In previous chapters, we have focused our analysis on the operation of mixed capitalistic economies such as those that exist in the United States, Canada, Australia, Japan, and throughout most of Western Europe. Market forces play an important role in the allocation of resources in these countries. Government action is also important. Private industries are often regulated by government. Government ownership and operation of utilities, transportation, communication, and educational facilities are not uncommon, even in Western countries. In addition, taxes and government subsidies are sometimes used to alter market outcomes. Throughout this book, we have used economic tools to help us understand the incentives and expected results of governmental policy that redirects market forces.

Today, nearly one-third of the world's population lives in the Soviet Union, Eastern Europe, and China. The economies of these countries are organized along socialist lines. They are characterized by central planning and government ownership. Market-directed capitalism and centrally planned socialism are two systems of economic organization. There are, however, many variations of each. For example, the economic organization of Yugoslavia differs substantially from that of the Soviet Union. The Japanese economy differs somewhat from the capitalist organization of the United States and Western European countries. After examining the general institutional arrangements of socialist and capitalist systems, we will take a closer look at the economic organization and performance of four interesting economies—those of the Soviet Union, Yugoslavia, China, and Japan.

GENERAL APPLICATION OF BASIC ECONOMIC PRINCIPLES

All economic systems, despite their differences, face similar constraints. Scarcity of economic goods confronts individuals and nations alike with budgetary problems. No nation is able to produce as much as its citizenry would like to consume. Therefore, regardless of economic organization, choices must be made. The decision to satisfy one desire leaves many other desires unsatisfied. All economic systems are constrained by the bonds of scarcity.

Many of the economic concepts that have been discussed throughout this book apply to all economic systems. Let us reconsider and summarize four of these basic ideas.

1. *Opportunity Cost.* An economy can be organized so that various goods can be provided without charge to the consumer, but economic organization cannot eliminate the opportunity costs associated with the provision of goods. The provision of additional medical services, even if distributed free, necessitates the use of resources that could have been used to produce other things. Similarly, if there is an expansion of the national defense sector, there must be a contraction of other sectors. Whenever productive resources have alternative uses, as they almost always do, the production of goods is costly, regardless of the form of economic organization.

---

[1]Howard R. Bowen, *Toward Social Economy* (New York: Holt, 1946), p. 52.

2. *Diminishing Marginal Returns.* According to the law of diminishing marginal returns, increased application of a variable resource to a fixed factor of production, such as land or natural resources, will expand output by a smaller and smaller amount. Other things being equal, a nation cannot continue to expand output proportionally by simply using more labor with the current stock of physical capital. Neither can proportional increases in agricultural output be achieved by using more and more fertilizer with the current stock of land. The law of diminishing returns limits the ability of both the Soviet Union and the United States to expand output from a given resource base. It is applicable to all economies. With the passage of time, of course, capital formation (an expansion in the resource base) and improved technology will permit us to loosen the bonds of scarcity. Without capital formation and improvements in technical knowledge, growth of output in capitalist and socialist countries alike will be severely retarded.

3. *Comparative Advantage and Efficiency.* Total production is greatest when each good is generated by the low opportunity cost producer. The assignment of the productive task to a high opportunity cost producer is inefficient (that is, output will be below its potential level), regardless of whether the activity takes place in a capitalist or a socialist economy. No matter what the type of economic organization, the goal of efficient production can best be attained by heeding the principle of comparative advantage.

4. *The Law of Demand.* Reflecting the law of diminishing marginal utility, the law of demand states that the quantity demanded of a good will be inversely related to its price. The law of demand is just as relevant in socialist countries as it is in capitalist countries. High prices will discourage consumption in both. For example, if socialist planners set the price of color television sets quite high, few will be purchased. On the other hand, if planners set zero or extremely low prices for medical services or basic housing, the quantity demanded will be large—often greater than the supply. Waiting lines and other forms of nonprice rationing will result.

INCENTIVES MATTER

Changes in the structure of incentives alter human behavior in both capitalist and socialist countries. For example, at one time in the Soviet Union, the managers of glass plants were rewarded according to the tons of sheet glass produced. Not surprisingly, most plants produced sheet glass so thick that one could hardly see through it. The rules were changed so that the managers were rewarded according to the square meters of glass produced. The managers reacted in a predictable way. Under the new rules, Soviet firms produced very thin glass that easily broke. Incentives matter, even to the managers of Soviet firms.

In our analysis of alternative economic systems, we will focus on how economic organization affects people's motivations. Marxists often argue that communism will eventually alter basic human motivations. They believe that people will cease to respond in predictable, traditional ways to changes in personal costs and benefits. Perhaps this is so, but the experiences of the Soviet Union and other Communist countries have produced little evidence thus far to support this view. Therefore, until human nature does change radically, an analysis based on the postulate that incentives do affect human decisions is most relevant. This is not to say that only economic considerations matter. Religious, cultural, and political factors can and do influence economic behavior. The economic approach does not deny their importance.

CONTRASTING CAPITALISM AND SOCIALISM

Socialism: A system of economic organization in which (a) the ownership and control of the basic means of production rest with the state and (b) resource allocation is determined by centralized planning rather than by market forces.

Joseph Schumpeter, the renowned Harvard economist, defined socialism as:

> . . . an institutional pattern in which the control over means of production and over production itself is vested with a central authority—or, as we may say, in which, as a matter of principle, the economic affairs of society belong to the public and not the private sphere.[2]

As Schumpeter's definition implies, capitalist and socialist economic organizations differ in two important respects—ownership of physical capital and resource allocation.

OWNERSHIP OF PHYSICAL CAPITAL— PRIVATE OR GOVERNMENT

Every economic system has a legal framework within which the rights of resource owners are defined. Practically all economic systems guarantee the rights of individuals to sell their own human capital—their labor—to the highest bidder. Earnings are derived from the sale of labor services in capitalist and socialist societies alike. Under socialism, however, the rewards obtained from the use of physical capital (machines, buildings, and so on) in the production process accrue to the state. If the state actually owns the nonhuman productive resources, the earnings they generate go directly to the state. The state can also use taxation to gain at least partial control over earnings that would otherwise accrue to other owners of physical capital. In either case, under socialism, investment in physical capital reflects the views of those who control the state.

RESOURCE ALLOCATION—MARKETS OR CENTRAL PLANNING

Capitalism: An economic system based on private ownership of productive resources and allocation of goods according to the signals provided by free markets.

Every economy must have a mechanism that coordinates the economic activity of microunits—business firms, individual resource owners, and consumers. The mechanism must solve such problems as the use of resources, the selective production of goods, and the distribution of income.

Under market-directed capitalism, economic activity is coordinated by contractual agreements between private parties who possess property rights to products and resources. There is no central planning mechanism. Market prices direct the actions of decentralized decision-makers. The forces of supply and demand push prices up or down in response to the decisions of individual buyers and sellers.

Under a socialist economic organization, resources are used and allocated in accordance with the centrally determined and administered scheme. Economic decisions, such as what and how much will be produced, what the relative proportions of investment and consumption will be, how resources will be used in production, and to whom the product will be distributed, are made by a central authority. The central plan may also include decisions on quantities of raw materials and inputs, techniques of production, prices, wages, locations of firms and industries, and the employment of labor. Socialist economic objectives generally reflect the preferences and value judgments of central planners. These objectives may or may not reflect the views of consumers.

Exhibit 1 summarizes the distinctive characteristics of capitalist and socialist economic organization. Capitalist economies are characterized by private owner-

---

[2]Joseph A. Schumpeter, *Capitalism, Socialism, and Democracy,* 3rd ed. (New York: Harper, 1950), p. 167.

OUTSTANDING ECONOMIST

Karl Marx
(1818–1883)

Karl Marx was much more than an economist. He was a philosopher, a historian, a sociologist, a political scientist—and a revolutionary. More has been written about Marx than about any other economist. His most famous work, written with Friedrich Engels, is *The Communist Manifesto* (1848). The most complete statement of Marx's economic views is contained in his monumental *Das Kapital* (1867). Like other socialists, Marx advocated collective ownership and control of factories and other capital assets. But, unlike most socialist theoreticians, Marx advocated a mass working-class movement to overthrow capitalism and usher in a new socialist world order.

While studying at the University of Berlin, Marx developed an interest in the philosophy of Hegel that was to influence his own work considerably. Marxian theory applies Hegel's dialectical method of logic (thesis-antithesis-synthesis) to the observable, concrete phenomena of nature and society. To Marx, history was perceived as a dynamic, dialectical process characterized by the struggle between social classes. Each ruling class becomes outmoded with time, reactivating the struggle with other classes, causing political and economic crises, and eventually leading to the overthrow of the existing social structure and the creation of a new structure. Marx used the decline and fall of feudalism and the rise of capitalism and the bourgeoisie in Europe as an illustration of his theory. He stressed that the transition periods are sometimes violent, as in the case of the Enclosure Movement (in which English peasants were driven from the land) and the 1789 French Revolution.

Marx predicted that the capitalist ruling class, having fulfilled its economic functions, would eventually fall. He believed that capitalist growth would depress the rate of profit, causing severe economic crises (recessions and depressions) and forcing capitalists to oppress the working class further in order to maintain their own standard of living. This would not only encourage the workers to take power but would allow them to do so, because the capitalist class would grow weaker and weaker. Although Marx believed the final victory of the industrial proletariat over the bourgeoisie was inevitable, he advocated revolutionary activity to accelerate the process and prepare the working class for its future role. Once the revolution became a reality, the ruling proletariat would "centralize all instruments of production in the hands of the state," which Marx believed would lead to a rapid increase in production and efficiency. But, Marx emphasized that workers must directly control not only the means of production but also the political process.

Marx argued that a workers' government would dismantle the existing state institutions and set up a new, fundamentally more democratic system, even if violence were required to do so. The successful revolution would thoroughly eliminate the bourgeoisie and culminate in a classless society, to which all individuals would voluntarily contribute "according to their abilities" and by which they would be awarded "according to their needs."

Marx believed that proletarian revolutions would take place first in the most developed countries. Thus, he surely would have been surprised to find that the major socialist revolutions have occurred in Russia and China—countries that at the time of their revolutions were underdeveloped and largely agricultural, with only a small industrial working class.

The postrevolutionary stage is a troublesome area for modern followers of Marx. Contrary to Marx's views, there is little evidence that the state will eventually wither away after capitalism is abolished. In fact, the all-powerful bureaucratic state is most imposing in the Soviet Union, the most highly developed of the existing communist societies.

EXHIBIT 1 ■ Contrasting Capitalism and Socialism

	Capitalism	Socialism
Property rights	Nonhuman resources are owned by private parties (that is, individuals or corporations)	Nonhuman resources are owned by the government
Allocation of goods and resources	Determined by market forces	Determined by centralized planning
Employment	Workers are self-employed or employed by private firms	Workers are employed by the government or government-controlled cooperatives
Investment	Undertaken by private parties seeking profits and higher future incomes	Undertaken by the government in accordance with the objectives of the planners
Income distribution	Determined by market forces that reward productivity and ownership of economic resources	Determined by central planners who may seek to promote equality or any other desired pattern of income distribution

ship of physical assets and the use of market forces to coordinate the actions of buyers and sellers and thereby determine the allocation of goods and resources. Markets also coordinate employment and investment decisions and determine the distribution of income under capitalism. In contrast, government ownership (or control) of physical assets and the allocation of resources by central planning are the distinctive characteristics of socialist economic organization. Under socialism, the central planners also determine the patterns of employment and investment as well as the distribution of income.

CLASSIFYING REAL-WORLD ECONOMIES

In reality, all modern economies use some combination of capitalist and socialist economic organization. Exhibit 2 classifies several economies according to their reliance on (a) private ownership or public ownership of assets and (b) market allocation compared to central planning. Economies characterized by both private ownership and market allocation best fit pure capitalism. Hong Kong, Japan, the United States, and Canada fall at the capitalism end of the spectrum (the southwest corner of Exhibit 2). On the other hand, economies characterized by government ownership of assets and central planning approximate pure socialism (the northeast corner of Exhibit 2). The Soviet Union, China, and most of the centrally planned economies of Eastern Europe fall into this category.

Yugoslavia and Sweden are interesting exceptions to the pure capitalism or pure socialism classifications. In Yugoslavia, most of the means of production are owned by the government. Market prices, though, are widely used to allocate goods and resources. Thus, the Yugoslavian economy is something of a hybrid. In Sweden, most physical assets are owned by private individuals and corporations. Nevertheless, the government uses taxes, subsidies, and regulatory powers to shape the allocation of resources. More than half of the national income of Sweden is channelled through government, a significantly larger proportion than for France, West Germany, or the United Kingdom, for example. The Swedish economy, too, is something of a cross between capitalism and socialism.

EXHIBIT 2

The Classification of Economies

The Soviet Union and China most closely approximate pure socialism, while Hong Kong, and the United States come closest to pure capitalism. The Yugoslavian economy is characterized by government ownership coupled with substantial reliance on markets. Thus, it lies in the southeast corner of the diagram. On the other hand, Sweden has only modest government ownership, but government planning plays a major role in the allocation of resources. Therefore, it lies toward the northwest corner.

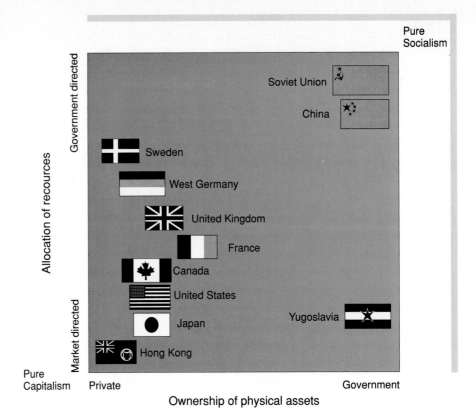

THE SOVIET ECONOMY

The Soviet Union is the largest socialist economy in the world. Since Soviet planning relies heavily on central directives, the economy is also sometimes referred to as a command economy. A **command economy** is characterized by detailed directives—detailed instructions to productive agents concerning what they are to do and how they are to do it.

The Soviet government owns and operates almost all of the business-industrial sector, including manufacturing firms, the wholesale and retail network, and the banking, finance, transportation, communications, and agricultural sectors. Organizationally, the state-operated Soviet economy is a giant vertically and horizontally integrated corporation, with Communist party members acting as stockholders. The party establishes the economic policy objectives, strives to ensure their execution and oversees the bureaucracy necessary to carry out the details of the planning directives. Much like individual factories (or other subunits) of a large U.S. corporation, Soviet business firms (''enterprises'') are supposed to implement the directives of the central planning authorities.

The **Gosplan,** the government's central planning agency, is directly responsible to Communist party officials. The Gosplan drafts the basic plan for the entire

Command Economy: An authoritarian socialist economy characterized by centralized planning and detailed directives to productive units. Individual enterprises have little discretionary decision-making power.

Gosplan: The central planning agency in the Soviet Union.

economy, which takes on the force of law when it is approved by the Soviet government. At present, both a five-year plan (which focuses on long-range objectives) and a one-year plan are constructed by the Gosplan. The central planning agency supplies each of the more than 200,000 Soviet enterprises with a thick document outlining their available resources and production targets. This planning document tells each enterprise what commodities are to be produced, the amounts of labor and raw materials it is allocated, new machinery that should be installed, the timing of available credit, and other operational details. The problem of the enterprise is to transform its allotted inputs into the target output. The operational targets of the annual plan are used as criteria in evaluating the performance of a firm at the end of the planning period and in rewarding it accordingly.

COORDINATION UNDER CENTRAL PLANNING

Material Balance Method: A method of central planning employed in the Soviet Union and other Eastern European countries whereby the planning agency keeps track of the physical units of resources and allocates them among state enterprises in a manner that will permit each enterprise to achieve its targeted output and thereby lead to the fulfillment of the economy's central plan.

Under Soviet planning, commodities and raw materials are centrally rationed in physical terms. The central planners decide how much of each good will be produced and the quantity of resources, including intermediate goods, that will be used to produce the final output. How do Soviet planners accomplish this task? Essentially, they use the **material balance method** to reconcile the supply and demand for resources. Under this method, the central planning agency prepares a balance sheet of all available resource supplies and sources of resource demand. Beginning with the total supply of all productive resources—labor, raw materials, minerals, imports, and so on—the planning agency allocates these resources to individual enterprises in the quantities it believes will be necessary to produce the enterprise's targeted output. Simultaneously, the central planners assign each enterprise output targets that, when fulfilled, will produce the quantity of each good called for by the central plan. Of course, the Gosplan must ensure that the total quantity of each input allocated to the enterprises (the total demand for the input) balances with the total supply of the input.

Under the material balancing system, the output of one enterprise (steel, for example) is generally the input of another enterprise (a tractor-producing firm, for example). The failure of one firm to meet its production quota sets off a domino effect. Firms that are not supplied with adequate inputs fail to meet their production quotas unless they make adjustments.

Consider the problem that arises if the target output for, say, trucks is increased by 20 percent. The planners must take additional steps to ensure that the truck-producing enterprises receive the right amount of labor, capital equipment, component parts manufactured by other enterprises, and raw materials such as steel, aluminum, glass, and copper. If other suppliers fail to meet their quotas to truck-manufacturing enterprises, the truck manufacturers will also fail to meet their quotas.

The Soviet planners confront an enormous coordination problem in ensuring that each enterprise receives just the right amount of labor and materials at just the right time to keep things moving smoothly. Literally billions of interrelated planning decisions must be made.

Of course, with mathematical techniques and computer technology, it is theoretically possible to arrive at a solution that will provide the right amount of each input to each enterprise so that quotas can be met. What happens, though, when there is an unexpected change—perhaps adverse weather conditions or equipment failure? Bottlenecks will develop. Confronted with an input shortage, enterprise managers often cut corners to meet their production quotas. For example, they may use less than the specified amount of the input in short supply.[3] Alternatively, they may attempt to make a deal with other enterprise managers to supply the input in exchange for a similar future or past favor. An informal system of connections exists among successful enterprise managers in the Soviet Union.

It is interesting to compare the response of a market system and a material balance planned system to an imbalance between supply and demand in the resource market. Under market allocation, if there is an excess supply of steel and excess demand for lumber, steel prices will fall and lumber prices will rise until the imbalances are corrected. Changes in relative prices will motivate literally millions of producers and users of steel and lumber to take the steps needed to restore balance between supply and demand in the two markets. Under material balance planning, an imbalance will trigger administrative action. In response to an excess demand for lumber, the planners could either increase their output target for enterprises producing lumber or reduce the allocation of lumber to enterprises using lumber. If the lumber output targets are increased, then inputs will have to be reallocated from other industries, such as steel, to lumber producers. On the other hand, if the allocation of lumber to users is reduced, planners will have to reduce the output targets of enterprises using lumber. In either case, the plans of numerous enterprises will have to be altered. Each revision will require administrative action at several different levels. Clearly, the correction of even a simple supply and demand imbalance is a formidable task, one unlikely to be accomplished quickly.

MOTIVATING SOVIET MANAGERS

Although the central plan is composed by the planners, it is the responsibility of the enterprise managers to carry out the plan. An incentive structure combining the "carrot" and the "stick" is used to motivate enterprise managers. Both pecuniary and nonpecuniary factors play a role. Managers who meet their production quotas are rewarded with bonuses, promotions, and medals. When the output of an enterprise is falling short of the production quota, it is up to the manager to exhort the employees to work longer and harder, to obtain additional labor and material inputs, or to persuade the higher authorities that the production quota should be lowered. If these efforts are insufficient and the enterprise fails to meet its production target, the manager can expect demotion.

How do the planning authorities know how much an enterprise is capable of producing? Just as a government bureau in the United States has an incentive to confront legislative authorities with the image of an over-worked agency squeezing the maximum output from an unrealistically small budget, so too, do Soviet enterprise managers have an incentive to project this image to the central planners. From the viewpoint of an enterprise manager, the ideal plan is one that provides a quantity of resources such that the firm's output target can be easily achieved.

---

[3]Technically, an enterprise can sue a supplier that fails to deliver inputs according to the specifications of the plan. However, since the procedures are cumbersome and unlikely to bring satisfactory results quickly, most enterprise managers find it easier to make an exchange with other managers, use less than the specified amount of ingredients to stretch out supplies, and/or follow other, more direct procedures in order to meet their production targets. See Hedrick Smith, *The Russians* (New York: Quadrangle/The New York Times Book Co., Inc., 1976), for several interesting accounts of how Soviet plant managers react to material shortages.

Managers thus have an incentive to provide the central planners with misleading and even false information with regard to the actual productive capability of the firm. Since high-level central planners have limited knowledge of the real output that an efficiently operated firm can achieve in its particular circumstances, they are in a weak position to control the actions of the enterprise managers.

Even if an enterprise manager is able to persuade the planners to provide sufficient resources for the easy achievement of the plan, they are unlikely to exceed the targeted output by much. After all, a large output relative to the target will reveal the true potential of the enterprise and lead to a substantially larger output target next year. Shrewd enterprise managers will prefer to stockpile resources or trade them to other enterprises for future favors, while exceeding this year's target by only a modest margin.

Of course, Soviet leaders are not unaware of these problems. Stiff penalties are applied to persons who fail to carry out their assigned responsibilities. Procedures designed to provide more accurate information and limit collusion have been established. Both economic and noneconomic incentives are used by the Soviet government to motivate managers and workers to meet the targets of the central plan. However, the system itself makes it difficult to detect misrepresentation and collusive behavior (the Russians call it "familyness") among enterprise managers and low-level planners.

Perhaps even more significant, the Soviet enterprise manager has little incentive to innovate, improve product quality, or experiment with alternative production techniques. The potential gains associated with the discovery of a better way of doing things are small, while the risks are great if an innovative method proves to be a failure. In addition, resource combinations supplied by the central planning authority often limit the adoption of innovative production methods. Since quantifying the gains from quality improvements and innovative achievements is difficult, the Soviet reward system emphasizes *quantity rather than quality* of output.[4] Predictably, innovative behavior and product quality suffer as a result of this incentive structure.

PRIORITIES UNDER SOVIET PLANNING

With central planning, the allocation of resources is in accordance with the preferences of the planners. In the past, Soviet planners have consistently emphasized two priorities. First, heavy industries such as steel, mining, and military hardware have been favored over light industries such as textiles and household goods. Second, investment goods have been emphasized relative to consumption goods.

---

[4]Under the recent openness of the Gorbachev era, the problem of shoddy product quality has been well publicized. The Soviet magazine *Ogonek* reports that exploding TV sets caused 18,000 fires, 512 serious injuries, and 929 deaths between 1980 and 1986. The Soviet Union recently established independent quality inspector groups at 2,300 plants manufacturing consumer goods and machine tools. According to the Soviet press, up to 30 percent of the output in these plants was initially rejected. Seventy percent of the shoes at a factory in Volgograd were rejected and 40 percent of all products from plants in the Ukraine were rejected. As the result of the failure to meet the tighter quality control standards, many plant managers and workers lost bonuses. It remains to be seen whether the new firmness will exert any long-term impact on product quality. In addition to the problem of product quality, many household appliances, including automatic dishwashers and toasters, are simply unavailable in the Soviet Union. Hair dryers are allegedly produced, but no one knows where one could be bought. See Peter Galuszka and Bill Jovetski, "Reforming the Soviet Economy," *Business Week* (December 7, 1987) and Barry Newman, "Russians Want Stuff to Spend Money On," *The Wall Street Journal* (June 17, 1988).

EXHIBIT 3   ■   The Functional Use of GNP in the United States and the Soviet Union

The Soviet economy, responding to the views of the planners, allocates a much larger share of GNP to investment and defense.

	Percent Share of Total GNP	
	United States	Soviet Union
Consumption	72	54–58
Defense	7	12–16
Investment	19	25–29
Government administration	3	3

Source: *Economic Report of the President: 1989*; Josef C. Brada and Ronald L. Graves, ''The Slowdown in Soviet Defense Expenditures,'' *Southern Economic Journal*, 54 (April 1988); and Svetozor Pejovich, *A Report Card on Socialism—Life in the Soviet Union* (Dallas: The Fisher Institute, 1979), pp. 65 and 98.

As Exhibit 3 shows, the Soviet Union allocates a much larger share of its GNP to investment and military defense and a much smaller share to consumption than does the United States. In fact, the investment rate of the Soviet Union is among the highest in the world. Centralized economic organization enables the planners to emphasize industrialization and capital accumulation, even though this may not reflect the views of the citizens. Current consumption, of course, is sacrificed as a result.

PRICES AND THE ALLOCATION OF SOVIET GOODS

The Soviet Union does use prices to ration goods among consumers. However, the central planners determine both the aggregate quantity of each consumer good and its price. When the supply of a product is exhausted, there is no pricing system that will induce producers to supply a larger amount. Thus, as Exhibit 4 illustrates, the supply curve for each good is independent of its price. However, the demand curve for consumer goods does obey the law of demand. Like their counterparts in other countries, Soviet consumers will want to buy more at lower prices.

The central planners set the prices of more than 200,000 products and resources. Sometimes the planners attempt to set the price of a good at the level that will bring the quantity demanded into line with the available supply (for example, P_e of Exhibit 4). However, this is not always true. In some cases, the price of a good is deliberately set below the market equilibrium for reasons of income distribution. When this happens, shortages develop and waiting lines form. The price of housing provides an example. Of course, almost all housing is owned by the state and is rented to households at very low prices. But the availability of housing is substantially less than the quantity demanded. Thus, families wait for years before an apartment is available.[5] On the other hand, the price of

---

[5]While the consumption of housing is highly subsidized, recent evidence indicates that the housing shortage in the Soviet Union is more severe than was previously thought. On average, Soviet families have 100 square feet of housing space *per person*. This implies that a typical family of four lives in a twenty foot by twenty foot apartment. In order to apply for a housing upgrade, a family's current per person housing space must be less than 36 square feet (for a family of four, this would imply a space approximately equal to an average-size American bedroom). Nonetheless, the Soviet press recently reported that nearly one-fifth of all Soviet families are wait-listed for a housing upgrade.

EXHIBIT 4

Prices, Shortages, and Surpluses in the Soviet Union

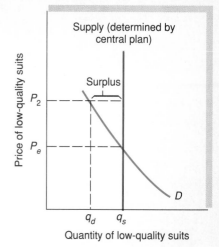

(a) Low prices and shortages

(b) High prices and surpluses

The supply of each good is determined in accordance with the priorities of the central plan. Thus, the supply curve is perfectly inelastic (vertical). However, the demand curve for goods like housing and clothing will obey the law of demand. Soviet central planners also set the price of goods. Sometimes they will attempt to establish a price (such as P_e) that will equate amount demanded with the available supply. In other cases, the price of a good will be set either below or above equilibrium. When price is set below equilibrium, such as illustrated for the housing market (frame a), shortages and waiting lines will result. In contrast, when the price of a product, such as low-quality suits, is set above equilibrium (frame b), a surplus of unsold goods will develop.

some goods will exceed the equilibrium level. As Exhibit 4b illustrates, above equilibrium prices lead to surpluses (unsold goods). Low quality, poorly designed goods that are out of line with the preferences of consumers often linger on the shelves of Soviet stores.

The price of products in the Soviet Union seldom changes. The last update of prices was in 1982 and before that it was 1967. Prices are not adjusted in light of changing demand conditions, technology, and production costs. Therefore, even if the price of a good approximates an equilibrium price when it is initially established, changing market conditions often lead to either a shortage or a surplus of the good with the passage of time.

The results of Soviet price-setting policies are easily observable. Western tourists are nearly always struck by the simultaneous occurrence of (a) lengthy waiting lines, as consumers seek to purchase goods in short supply and (b) state-operated stores overflowing with unpurchased goods, particularly items that are less desired because of their poor quality relative to their price. This combination—shortages of some goods and unsold quantities of others—is precisely what one would expect given the Soviet system of price-fixing.

Hedrick Smith paints a vivid picture of the plight of the Soviet consumer:

> I had heard about consumer shortages before going to Moscow but at first it seemed to me that the stores were pretty well stocked. Only as we began to shop in earnest as a family did the Russian consumer's predicament really come through to me. First, we needed textbooks for our children (who went

to Russian schools) and found that the sixth-grade textbooks had run out. A bit later, we tried to find ballet shoes for our 11-year-old daughter, Laurie, only to discover that in this land of ballerinas, ballet shoes size 8 were unavailable in Moscow. . . . Goods are produced to fill the Plan, not to sell. Sometimes the anomalies are baffling. Leningrad can be overstocked with cross-country skis and yet go several months without soap for washing dishes. In the Armenian capital of Yenevan, I found an ample supply of accordians but local people complained they had gone weeks without ordinary kitchen spoons or tea samovars. In Rostov, on a sweltering mid-90s day in June, the ice cream stands were all closed by 2 p.m. and a tourist guide told me that it was because the whole area had run out of ice cream, a daily occurrence.[6]

These results are a natural outgrowth of a *centrally imposed* pricing structure.

THE PRIVATE SECTOR IN THE SOVIET UNION

Soviet law prohibits (a) a private person from acting as a trade middleman and (b) the hiring of an employee for the purpose of making a profit. However, there are two major areas where some private enterprise is permitted: personal services and a portion of agriculture. Soviet professionals (for example, physicians and teachers) and craft laborers (for example, painters and shoe repairers) are free to sell their services to consumers. These "self-employed" workers are generally moonlighters. They work regular hours for a state enterprise but also provide their services to private consumers during nonworking hours. Under recent economic reforms in the Soviet Union, the number of job categories where private enterprise is permitted has been expanded.

The agricultural sector has consistently been a problem for the Soviet economy. Initially, there was substantial opposition to collectivization. Crop failures and low productivity (in comparison with that of other advanced economies) have been commonplace for years. Peasants on the collective farms are permitted to grow products on a small assigned plot—usually one acre in size. Products raised on the private plots may be consumed or sold in the market for prices determined by the fluctuations of supply and demand. In total, these private plots constitute slightly more than 1 percent of the total agricultural land under cultivation. Nevertheless, as Exhibit 5 illustrates, they account for approximately 25 percent of the total Soviet agricultural output. A major share of the total output of such products as eggs, potatoes, vegetables, fruits, meat, and dairy products is derived from these private plots.[7] Despite their less than optimal size, these private plots are an important source of agricultural production.

THE LABOR MARKET AND INCOME INEQUALITY IN THE SOVIET UNION

Soviet workers are not only guaranteed the "right" to work, they have an obligation to do so. Article 60 of the Soviet Constitution states, "the evasion of socially useful labor is incompatible with the principles of socialist society." Furthermore, Soviet law specifies that any able-bodied individual who is unemployed

---

[6]Ibid., p. 60. Reprinted by permission of Times Books, a division of Quadrangle/The New York Times Book Co., Inc., New York.

[7]The fact that more land-intensive agricultural products—grains and cotton, for example—are grown on the collective farms partially accounts for the fact that the productivity of these farms (measured in terms of value per acre) is lower than that of the private plots. However, the large disparity strongly suggests that incentives matter. Apparently, Soviet farmers cultivate the private plots, which generate personal gain, much more intensively than the collective farms, where most of the gains from efficiency accrue to others.

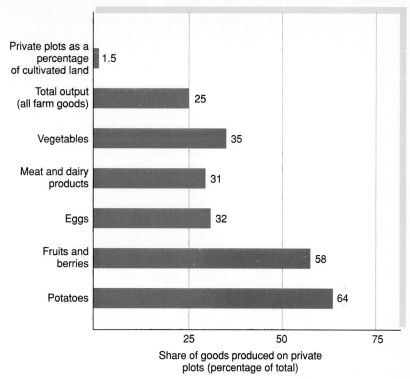

EXHIBIT 5

Agriculture Production on Private Plots in the Soviet Union

Although the private agriculture plots constituted only 1.5 percent of the land under cultivation, output on these plots accounts for approximately 25 percent of the total value of agriculture production. Each year a large share of the aggregate output of several products is produced on these private plots.

Private plots as a percentage of cultivated land — 1.5

Total output (all farm goods) — 25

Vegetables — 35

Meat and dairy products — 31

Eggs — 32

Fruits and berries — 58

Potatoes — 64

Share of goods produced on private plots (percentage of total)

Source: *U.S. News and World Report,* November 9, 1981, p. 41. Also see A. Yemelyanov, "The Agrarian Policy of the Party and Structural Advances in Agriculture," *Problems of Economics* (March 1975), pp. 22–34.

for more than four months a year may be liable for two years of imprisonment. Given these inducements, it is not surprising that labor-force participation rates in the Soviet Union are higher than for other industrial countries. For men between the ages of sixteen and sixty, the labor-force participation rate is 87 percent. For women age fifteen to fifty-four, the labor-force participation rate is 80 percent. Wages are the major source of income in the Soviet Union. Despite the ideal communist distributional ethic put forth by Karl Marx ("From each according to his ability, to each according to his need"), substantial occupational wage differentials exist in the Soviet Union. The earnings of skilled craft workers are generally two to four times those of unskilled laborers. The earnings of scientists, engineers, journalists, athletes, and high-level central planners are several times greater than the national average.

How does income inequality in the Soviet Union compare with that in Western nations? Comparable data are difficult to obtain. Exhibit 6 presents data on income shares of low- and high-income households for several countries. These data imply that the degree of income inequality in the Soviet Union is somewhat less than for the United States. After taxes, the bottom 20 percent of households received 8.7 percent of the aggregate personal income in the Soviet Union (1972–1974), compared to only 6.2 percent in the United States (1976). Correspondingly, the top quintile of households received a smaller share of the aggregate income in the Soviet Union than in the United States. However, the distribution of income in the Soviet Union is apparently not much different than several West-

> **EXHIBIT 6   ■   The Distribution of Income Shares in the Soviet Union Compared to Selected Market Economies**
>
> | | Percentage of Aggregate Income Received | | |
> | --- | --- | --- | --- |
> | Country and Year | Bottom 20% of Households | Top 20% of Households | Top 10% of Households |
> | *(After Taxes)* | | | |
> | Soviet Union, 1972–1974[a] | 8.7 | 38.5 | 24.1 |
> | United States, 1976 | 6.2 | 42.0 | — |
> | Sweden, 1972 | 9.3 | 35.2 | 20.5 |
> | *(Before Taxes)* | | | |
> | United States, 1980 | 5.3 | 39.9 | 23.3 |
> | Canada, 1981 | 5.3 | 40.0 | 23.8 |
> | Japan, 1979 | 8.7 | 37.5 | 22.4 |
> | United Kingdom, 1979 | 7.0 | 39.7 | 23.4 |
>
> [a]For urban households only.
>
> Source: The after-tax data for the Soviet Union (1972–1974) and Sweden (1972) are from Abram Bergson, "Income Inequality Under Soviet Socialism," *Journal of Economic Literature, 22* (September 1984). The after-tax data for the United States (1976) are from Edgar K. Browning and Jacquelene M. Browning, *Public Finance and the Price System* (New York: MacMillan Publishing Co., 1983) (Table 8–7). The before-tax data are from *The World Development Report: 1985* (Table 28).

ern market economies. Perhaps surprising to some, the degree of income inequality in Sweden appears to be somewhat less than for the Soviet Union. The distribution of income in Japan and the United Kingdom is quite similar to the Soviet Union.

Income inequality data in the Soviet Union, though, should be interpreted with caution. The prices of many products purchased intensively by the poor (medical service, clothing, and food) are, relatively speaking, cheaper in the Soviet Union than they are in most Western economies. In contrast, most luxury goods, such as automobiles and air travel, are relatively more expensive in the Soviet Union. As the result of these structural factors, data on income inequality may overstate differences in economic status between the rich and the poor in the Soviet Union. Opposite biases, however, are also present. Soviet elites are often presented with special privileges that do not show up in the income statistics. Automobiles can usually be easily obtained by upper-level bureaucrats and Communist party members. Soviet officials and members of favored groups, such as scientists, writers, actors, ballet stars, and economic managers, are granted the right to shop in special stores that offer goods at cut-rate prices and that stock many items unavailable to other citizens. Such products as choice meats, fine wines, fresh fruits and vegetables, French perfumes, Japanese electronic equipment, American cigarettes, and imported clothing are sold in these stores.[8] Since income data do not incorporate privileges of this types, they understate economic inequality in the Soviet Union.

---

[8]See Hedrick Smith, *The Russians,* pp. 26–30,

INCOME AND GROWTH IN THE SOVIET UNION

It is interesting to compare the size and growth record of the Soviet economy with Western market economies, particularly the United States. In terms of development, the Soviet's economy lags well behind the Western industrial nations. Nearly one-quarter of the Soviet labor force is still involved with agriculture, compared to only 3 percent in the United States. As Exhibit 7 illustrates, the *per capita* GNP of the Soviet Union is less than one-half that of the United States and only about two-thirds the *per capita* GNP of Western Europe and Japan. Of course, both the land area and population of the Soviet Union exceed the United States. Thus, the *aggregate* GNP of the Soviet Union is approximately 54 percent as large as for the United States. While the total size of the Soviet economy is larger than Japan, it is substantially smaller than the combined size of the economies of the European Economic Community (Exhibit 7).

For nearly 25 years following the Second World War, the growth record of the Soviet economy was quite impressive. Spurred on by a high rate of capital formation, the Soviet economy grew at an annual rate of approximately 7 percent during the 1950s and 5 percent during the 1960s, according to most analysts. During 1950–1970, the economic growth rate in the Soviet Union exceeded the rate for the United States and it compared quite favorably with the growth rate of Western European countries. Among Western industrial nations, only Japan was able to chalk up a more impressive growth record.

As Exhibit 8 illustrates, economic growth in the Soviet Union has slowed substantially since the mid-1970s. During 1976–1988 the average annual growth rate of the Soviet economy was only 2 percent, down from 4 percent during 1966–1975. Since the mid-1970s, the major Western industrial economies have consistently out-performed the Soviet Union. In recent years (1983–1988), real GNP in

EXHIBIT 7

The Gross National Product of the Major Economic Powers

The per capita GNP of the Soviet Union lags well behind that of the United States, the EEC countries, and Japan. In aggregate, output in the Soviet Union is a little more than one-half as great as that of the United States and approximately two-thirds that of the EEC countries. The countries of the European Economic Community (EEC) are Belgium, France, West Germany, Italy, Greece, the Netherlands, Denmark, Ireland, and the United Kingdom.

Source: *The World Bank Atlas, 1988* ("Table 1) and Karen Elliot House "The Superpower Contenders Compared," *The Wall Street Journal*, January 23, 1989. The data for other countries were converted to U.S. dollars at purchasing power equivalents.

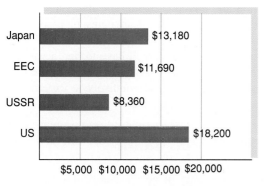

Per capita GNP, 1987

Japan $13,180
EEC $11,690
USSR $8,360
US $18,200

$5,000 $10,000 $15,000 $20,000

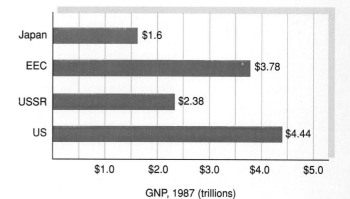

GNP, 1987 (trillions)

Japan $1.6
EEC $3.78
USSR $2.38
US $4.44

$1.0 $2.0 $3.0 $4.0 $5.0

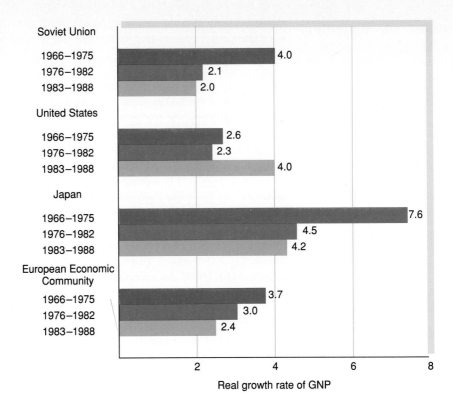

EXHIBIT 8

The Average Annual Growth Rate in Gross National Product of the Major Economic Powers

The average annual growth rate of real GNP for the Soviet Union, United States, Japan, and the European Economic Community for selected periods during the 1966–1988 period are presented.

both Japan and the United States has grown at an annual rate of 4 percent, twice the growth rate of the Soviet economy. The market economies of Western Europe have also grown more rapidly than the Soviet Union. Therefore, not only is the per capita income higher for the Western market economies, but the economic gap between these economies and the Soviet Union is widening.

The decline in the growth of the Soviet economy is not surprising. During the 1950s and 1960s, the Soviet growth rate was enhanced by the borrowing of more advanced technology from the West. As the technological gap between Western economies and the Soviet Union narrows, economic growth emanating from this factor dissipates. Innovation and entrepreneurship are important ingredients of growth for modern economies. These are not strengths of a socialist planned economy. If the Soviet economy is going to duplicate its impressive growth rate of the 1950–1970 period, Soviet planners will have to find a way of building more incentives for innovative behavior into the system. If they are unable to overcome this deficiency, the Soviet economy is unlikely to exceed the growth of the more advanced Western industrial economies.

RECENT REFORMS IN THE SOVIET UNION

Prodded by slow economic growth, poor quality of goods, and continued shortages in many areas, Soviet leaders have adopted several economic reforms in recent years. The common thread running through most of the reforms is decentralization: less reliance on bureaucratic commands and greater freedom of action at the firm level. Let us consider a number of the more significant recent changes in the Soviet economy.

1. *An Expansion in the Freedom to Operate Small Private Businesses.* In 1987, the Soviet Union increased the number of categories where private individuals could legally offer their services to consumers. Under this reform, self-employed individuals are now legally allowed to operate taxicabs; tailor clothing; sand floors; and repair appliances, watches, and even automobiles. In all, 40 new categories of services were opened up to private enterprise. In order to operate legally in these areas, individuals need a license from the state, and they are also required to hold a full-time job working for the state. Family members are permitted to assist, but the business is not allowed to hire other workers. To a degree, the law merely recognizes activities that were already quite widespread. Nonetheless, it may prove to be quite significant. According to current estimates, several hundred thousand Soviet citizens are now engaged in these private business activities. The permissibility of such activities will generate pressure to expand the list of categories, where private enterprise is, in fact, acceptable.

2. *An Expansion in Business Cooperatives.* Recent reforms also permit private cooperative businesses to operate restaurants, retail stores, and in some cases, small farms. The cooperative businesses are joint ventures undertaken by up to 25 people. The businesses are permitted to pay premiums in order to get top-quality resources and sell their products at unregulated prices. In Moscow alone, there were nearly 100 cooperative restaurants in 1988.

In the agricultural sector, the private cooperatives are called "contract brigades." Under this arrangement, a small number of workers—the contract brigade—is assigned some of the land from the collective farm. The "brigade" contracts with the collective farm for both productive resources (machinery and fertilizer, for example) and the sale of its output. In turn, the members of the brigade are permitted to keep a share of the profits. By way of comparison with the large collective farms, this arrangement provides the members of the brigade with a greater incentive to work hard and achieve a larger output from the available resources.

3. *Enterprises are given more discretion.* The administration of President Gorbachev moved to expand the discretionary decision-making powers of plant managers and to relax the control of the central planners. Enterprises are now allowed to keep a portion of their net income, rather than return 100 percent of it to the government treasury. These funds may be used to either reward workers for high productivity or expand productive capacity in ways other than those specified by the central plan. As the net income of enterprises provides a larger share of their investment funds, firms will be better able to produce goods that can be profitably sold, even if their production is not part of the central plan. Historically, the Soviet government has subsidized enterprises that fail to earn sufficient revenues to cover their costs. Under the Gorbachev reforms, this practice is supposed to be halted. The sales revenue of enterprises will be expected to cover not only operating costs, but also the firm's capital costs. Firms making profits are supposed to be granted broad discretion with regard to use of the funds. In contrast, firms losing money will be allowed to go out of business.

Will these reforms really make a difference? At this point, it is too early to tell. Clearly, there are major obstacles. The central planning bureaucracy of the

Soviet Union is highly entrenched. It will not be easy to reduce the size of the planning bureaucracy, as called for by the Gorbachev reforms. Neither will price reform come easily. Currently, there is often little relationship between price and scarcity (or opportunity cost). In areas where prices are currently below equilibrium, decontrol will lead to sharply higher prices. When price is above equilibrium, decontrol will result in lower prices. Movements toward decontrol of some prices, but not others, will lead to inequities and bottlenecks. Finally, the experience of Soviet managers is that of bureaucrats, not entrepreneurs. Direct experience with a market system has been absent in the Soviet Union far more than 60 years. Thus, it may be difficult to reconstruct risk-taking and entrepreneurial attributes among the populace.

YUGOSLAVIA—SOCIALISM OR THE MARKET

After stagnating under a socialist system of detailed central planning, Yugoslavia moved toward a decentralized economy that permitted market forces to play a significant role in the allocative process.

Today, the Yugoslavian economy is a hybrid economy, characterized by both government ownership of the major physical assets and considerable reliance on market prices. The bulk of economic activity—estimates range from 80 to 90 percent—is conducted by worker-managed, socially owned business firms. However, the enterprise managers in Yugoslavia are given substantial decision-making discretion. The enterprise managers are chosen by the employees of the firm and they are expected to pursue profits. In Yugoslavia, citizens are permitted to own and operate small-scale enterprises, employing a maximum of five workers. In agriculture, peasants can privately own up to 25 acres. In addition, certain business firms, such as law firms, hotels, restaurants, and craft shops, are operated by private entrepreneurs, much as they are in Western countries. In many respects, the Yugoslavian system appears to have much in common with the form of organization the Soviets expect to evolve from the Gorbachev reforms.

THE YUGOSLAVIAN BUSINESS FIRM

Even though the government maintains ownership of the firm's assets, the management of individual enterprises in Yugoslavia is turned over to the employees. The employees of each firm elect a workers' council, which manages the firm. Each employee has one vote, and the workers' council is elected by secret ballot. The council, like a manager of a Western firm, purchases raw materials and determines the quantity and quality of goods produced, the level of employment, the method of production, and even the price charged for finished products. When the firms' revenues exceed costs, the firm's net profits go, with no strings attached, to the employees (including managers) of the firm.

As in the capitalist West, Yugoslavian business firms that satisfy consumers— that provide them with goods highly valued relative to their costs—will earn profits. The "employee owners" divide the firm's profit among themselves in a manner prescribed by the workers' council. When a worker retires, leaves his or her job, or is fired (by a vote of all employees), the worker's rights to any profits from the firm expire.

What impact does this form of economic organization have on economic incentives and production methods? Since the income of employees is directly affected by the firm's profit level, they have an incentive to elect managers who will operate the firm efficiently. In a sense, the position of the employees of the firm is parallel to that of stockholders in the West. The employees, like stockholders, seek efficient operation and a high level of profits because they are residual income recipients (in addition to wage recipients). However, unlike stockholders, individual workers in Yugoslavia can neither hold on to these rights when no longer attached to the firm nor sell them. Only current workers, collectively, are allowed to own factors of production.

There are several important ramifications of the Yugoslavian form of economic organization.

1. *Since the employees of the firm are also, at least indirectly, involved in the management of the firm, no separation between ''labor'' and ''management'' is present.* According to the Yugoslav view, capitalist relations in production and distribution are characterized not only by private ownership but also by separation of labor and management. Since capitalist workers do not participate in the firm's decision-making, they become disillusioned with the production process and dissatisfied with the income distribution. This is unlikely to happen under the Yugoslavian system. After all, the workers are management. Since employees have a direct stake in the profits of the firm, they will support management that pursues profits and seeks to avoid waste and other activities that increase the firms' costs.

2. *The Yugoslavian form of economic organization encourages workers to push for an immediate distribution of profits among themselves rather than for the allocation of profits to investment or future fringe benefits (for example, fancier offices or a company recreation center).* This is perfectly rational behavior because present capitalization of future profit-sharing rights cannot be realized through the private sale of ownership rights. Unlike stockholders in the West, Yugoslav workers can ill afford not to declare dividends every year. Postponed dividends may be lost forever for those with the likelihood of departing from the firm. In contrast, Western stockholders can always sell their shares whenever they are dissatisfied with the dividend policy of the management.

3. *Predictably, Yugoslavian enterprises will be constantly plagued by shortages of funds for both working capital and fixed investment.* The workers' tendency to allocate larger shares of the enterprise profits for purposes of wage and salary augmentation puts a continual strain on the firm's liquidity. Consequently, many enterprises have to resort to heavy borrowing and are thus forced to operate under perpetual indebtedness.

4. *Yugoslav firms have a strong tendency to substitute capital goods for labor.* The workers' profit-sharing right increases the cost, as seen by current employees, of hiring additional units of labor (that is, additional profit-sharing partners). Other things constant, increasing the size of the firm's work force will reduce the size of the profit share granted to each current employee. The employee's share of the firm's profit will be smaller as one of 1,100 workers than as one of 1,000 workers. Consequently, Yugoslav enterprises tend to use highly capital-intensive techniques of production. As a result, many laborers, both skilled and unskilled, have been forced to emigrate to other countries to find work.

5. *Yugoslav enterprises have little or no pecuniary incentive to invest their funds in the establishment of new enterprises.* Even though money invested in new ventures can draw interest, investors have no claim to management rights or dividends. These are reserved exclusively for the workers of the new enterprise.

Consequently, the financing of new enterprises comes primarily from governmental authorities, either through direct investment or by guaranteeing bank loans. Here, the gains of the public authority are basically twofold. First, it secures a dominating influence over the firm's management and its policies. Second, it obtains a certain return on its investment through taxation. Taxes levied on the enterprise profits generate a major portion of state revenues in Yugoslavia.

THE YUGOSLAVIAN ECONOMIC RECORD

Under a system of market socialism, Yugoslavia moved from a predominately agricultural economy to a manufacturing and service economy. Today, only 25 percent of the Yugoslav labor force is in agriculture, compared with 75 percent following the Second World War. Prior to 1980, the growth record of Yugoslavia was quite impressive. Between 1952 and 1960, real GNP in Yugoslavia grew at an annual rate of nearly 10 percent. During the 1965–1980 period, the annual growth of industrial production averaged 6 percent. However, since 1980, the growth rate of real GNP has been less than 1 percent; per capita GNP has come to a complete standstill.

Inflation has played a central role in the stagnation of the Yugoslav economy in the 1980s. In recent years, Yugoslavia has financed much of its capital formation by borrowing from its central bank. This has resulted in a rapid growth in the money supply and an average annual inflation rate in excess of 50 percent during the 1980s. An inflation rate of this magnitude creates uncertainty and undermines an exchange economy.

In recent years, the Yugoslavian economy has also experienced relatively high rates of unemployment. Throughout most of the 1980s, the unemployment rate in Yugoslavia exceeded 10 percent. Semi-skilled and skilled workers are often unable to find employment because the incentive structure of the Yugoslav system encourages firms to use capital-intensive production methods. As a result, employment in Yugoslavia has grown slowly. Consequently, approximately one million Yugoslavs, 5 percent of the total population, are employed as "guest workers" in neighboring Western European countries.

THE CHINESE ECONOMY IN TRANSITION

Following the Second World War, China adopted a system of detailed central planning patterned after the Soviet Union. Prior to 1979, the Chinese economy encompassed the basic features of the Soviet model: state ownership, collectivization of agriculture, government-determined prices, and state directives to enterprises. Except for private agricultural plots, which comprised approximately 7 percent of the Chinese farm land, private enterprise was virtually exterminated from mainland China during the 1950–1978 period.

Following the death of Mao Zedong, the Chinese began to move away from detailed central planning in the late 1970s.[9] The initial reforms focused on agriculture, a sector of the economy that encompasses nearly three-fourths of the

[9]For additional detail on recent economic developments in China, see Dwight Heald Perkins, "Reforming China's Economic System," *Journal of Economic Literature,* 26 (June 1988), pp. 601–645; Luc DeWulf, "Economic Reform in China," *Finance and Development* (March 1985), pp. 8–11; and Alvin Rabushka, *The New China* (San Francisco: Pacific Institute for Public Policy, 1987).

Chinese work force. Meeting in December 1978, the Third Plenum of the Eleventh Central Committee of the Communist Party stressed the importance of increasing the material rewards of farmers and expanding agricultural output. Shortly thereafter, reforms were adopted that led to the dismantling of the Chinese system of collective farms.

The Chinese established what they refer to as a "contract responsibility system" in agriculture. Under this system, individual families are permitted to lease land for up to 15 years in exchange for supplying the state with a fixed amount of production at a designated price (which is generally below the market price). Amounts produced over and above the required quota belong to the individual farmer. The output in excess of the production quota may either be consumed or sold at a free market price. In effect, this system of long-term land leases provides farmers with something akin to a private property right. **Legal ownership remains with the state, but individual farmers are permitted to lease the land for long periods of time at a predetermined price. The farmer pays a 100 percent tax—the fixed amount of production owed the state for the land—on the first part of the produce, but no tax at all on what is grown beyond the quota. Thus, the farmer's marginal tax rate is zero.** Clearly, this system provides farmers with a strong incentive to produce.

Other reforms were adopted that enhanced the development of markets in agricultural products. Restrictions on individual stock breeding, household sideline occupations, transport of agricultural goods, and trade fairs (marketplaces) were removed. Farmers were permitted to own tractors and trucks, and even hire laborers to work in their "leased" fields. By the late 1980s, less than 15 percent of the grain (rice, wheat, and barley) produced in China was turned over to the state. The rest was marketed privately.

Production in agriculture expanded at an impressive rate as market forces replaced bureaucratic commands. Real output in agriculture expanded at an annual rate of 8 percent during 1980–1986, compared to 3 percent during 1965–1980.[10] Grain production increased by a third. The output of cash products, including cotton, sugar cane, fruits, and meats, increased even more rapidly—approximately doubling during the 1980–1986 period. Suddenly, China had evolved from an importer to an exporter of agricultural products.

The success in agriculture encouraged reforms in other sectors. Restrictions on the operation of small-scale service and retail businesses were relaxed. Private restaurants, stores, and repair shops sprang up and began to compete with state-operated enterprises. By the mid-1980s, Chinese cities were teeming with sidewalk vendors, restaurants, small retail businesses, and hundreds of thousands of individuals providing personal services. After losing their monopoly position, state enterprises began to stay open longer and pay more attention to serving their customers.[11]

Finally, China began to take steps toward greater reliance on markets in the production and distribution of industrial products. Measures incorporated into the Seventh Five-Year Plan (1986–1990) call for prices—whether state-controlled or not—that reflect production costs. The plan recognizes that this will mean in-

---

[10]The World Bank, *World Development Report, 1988* (Table 2).
[11]Dwight Heald Perkins, "Reforming China's Economic System," *Journal of Economic Literature* (June 1988), p. 619.

creased prices for some commodities that are currently subsidized. In other cases, prices of commodities that are now taxed heavily will decline. Currently, China has a dual allocative system in the industrial sector. More than half of all industrial inputs and outputs continued to be produced and distributed at state administered prices. Many of these state enterprises continue to receive state subsidies and derive investment funds from the government budget (rather than internal financing). Often there is little relationship between the state-mandated prices and opportunity cost. As a result, some firms producing goods in short supply cannot expand because the sale price of their product is set below market equilibrium. Simultaneously, other firms do quite well turning out products with high state-mandated prices that go unsold in the state-operated stores. Moves that reform the industrial pricing system and rely more extensively on market forces have slowed in the industrial sector.

THE CHINESE ECONOMY: TODAY AND TOMORROW

Despite the continued problems with resource allocation in the industrial sector, the recent growth rate of China has been quite impressive. During 1980–1987, real GNP in China increased at an annual rate of 9.1 percent, compared with 4.5 percent during the 1953–1980 period. The growth of output in the agricultural and service sectors—the two sectors that dominate the economy—was particularly striking. Nonetheless, China is still a very poor country by Western standards. In 1985, the per capita income of China was an estimated $2,444, compared with $12,532 for the United States.[12]

The Chinese economy is now going through a very sensitive period. After years of virtually stable prices (controlled by the state), consumer prices rose at an annual rate of 7.3 percent in 1987. A double-digit inflation rate occurred in 1988. Most economists, including those in China, attribute this inflation to a highly expansive monetary policy. Enterprises seeking funds to cover losses and undertake investments typically go to local banks for loans. An expansion in these loans leads to an increase in the money supply. According to International Monetary Fund data, the money supply in China increased at an annual rate of 35 percent during 1984–1986. Clearly, such rapid expansion in the money supply will generate inflationary pressures.

Even though the inflation emanates from monetary expansion, many people associate it with a general relaxation of government control over the economy. Thus, the inflation tends to weaken the political position of reformers favoring greater reliance on markets. There is already evidence for this. In 1988, the Communist Party Central Committee deferred for at least two years any further action toward the decontrol of prices and decreed that price decontrol would be carried out over a period of 20 years.

What does the future hold for the Chinese economy? If the monetary system is reformed and the recent inflation is brought under control, most observers believe the Chinese economy will evolve into a system of market socialism similar to that of Yugoslavia. However, there are strong forces that stand to lose from a

[12]These figures are from Robert Summers and Alan Heston, "A New Set of International Comparisons of Real Product and Price Levels: Estimates for 130 Countries, 1950–1985," *The Review of Income and Wealth,* 34 (March 1988). They were derived by the purchasing power parity method. Estimates derived by the exchange rate conversion method imply that this per capita income in China is substantially less than the above figures, but most economists believe that this method understates income in China.

continuation of the movement away from detailed central planning. The state bureaucracy that has dominated economic decision-making for several decades cannot be expected to relinquish its power without a struggle. Many leaders in the Communist party, perhaps with good reason, fear the loss of political control should China move toward greater reliance on markets. The party changes accompanying the political unrest during the summer of 1989 strengthened these forces, at least temporarily. As a result, the trend toward markets in China may well come to a standstill, or even be reversed, during the 1990s.

On the other hand, there are strong forces continuing to push China toward the increased use of markets. China is surrounded by some of the most successful market economies in the world—including Japan, South Korea, Singapore, Taiwan, and Hong Kong. In 1997, the latter will become part of China. In contrast with the Soviet Union, many current-day Chinese have had prior experience with markets and private businesses. This enhances the likelihood of success where markets are adopted. The Chinese have been highly successful as entrepreneurs, developers, and traders throughout the world. In fact, they have succeeded economically just about everywhere *except* mainland China. In a world where the experience of other countries is increasingly visible, the success both of market economies and of people of Chinese descent in other areas strengthens the reform movement and reduces the likelihood of a reversal in the recent moves toward decentralization and development of markets.

THE JAPANESE "MIRACLE"

By American and European standards, the Japanese people in 1950 were poor and their methods of production primitive. Forty-two percent of the Japanese labor force was employed in agriculture, compared with 12 percent in the United States.[13] The per capita GNP of Japan was one-eighth that of the United States.

The transformation of the Japanese economy during the last three decades is the success story of the postwar era. Today, the Japanese economy is the third largest in the world, ranking after the U.S. and Soviet economies. Adjusted for inflation, the GNP of Japan grew approximately 9.5 percent annually between 1950 and 1980. During that period, the income of the typical Japanese family, measured in dollars of constant purchasing power, doubled every eight years!

The data of Exhibit 9 illustrate the phenomenal economic growth of Japan. Measured in inflation-adjusted 1982 U.S. dollars, the Japanese per capita GNP in 1950 was $1,004, compared to $7,950 for the U.S. During the 1950–1987 period, the real per capita GNP of Japan increased thirteenfold. By 1987, it was 85 percent that of the U.S., compared with only 12.7 percent in 1950.

The land area of Japan is 10 percent smaller than that of California. Its population is approximately one-half as great as that of the United States. It lacks natural resources; almost all of Japan's petroleum is imported. On the surface, it would appear to be an overpopulated nation, lacking energy and natural resources. How can we explain the economic performance of Japan?

[13]By 1981, the percentage of the Japanese work force employed in agriculture had declined to 12 percent. Since labor productivity is generally higher in manufacturing than in agriculture, this shift from agriculture contributed to the rapid growth of Japan.

EXHIBIT 9   ■   The Japanese "Miracle"

	United States (1982 dollars)	Japan[a] (1982 dollars)	Japan as a Percentage of United States
Gross National Product			
(in billions)			
1950	1,204	82	6.8
1960	1,665	191	11.5
1970	2,416	529	21.9
1980	3,187	1,029	32.3
1987	3,847	1,636	42.5
Gross National Product			
per capita			
1950	7,905	1,004	12.7
1960	9,215	2,046	22.2
1970	11,782	5,007	42.5
1980	13,995	8,803	62.9
1987	15,770	13,400	85.0

[a]The Japanese data were converted to U.S. dollars by the exchange rate conversion method.

Source: U.S. Department of Commerce and *The World Bank Atlas, 1988.*

Several factors underlie the Japanese "miracle." Japan's economy is primarily a capitalist market economy. Nevertheless, it differs in several important respects from the market economies of Western Europe and North America. Let us consider some of the unique features of the Japanese economy.

THE JAPANESE LABOR MARKET

Lifetime Employment Commitment: An arrangement offered by most large firms in Japan whereby employees are guaranteed employment until the age 55 unless guilty of misconduct.

In contrast with laborers in most market economies, Japanese workers are intensely loyal to the firms in which they are employed. Two factors appear to explain this loyalty. First, the large Japanese firms make a **lifetime employment commitment** to their employees. After a probationary period, which is usually less than one year, employees acquire tenure. Henceforth, they cannot be discharged except for misconduct (for example, excessive absenteeism, commission of a crime, or fighting on the job). Since seniority largely determines the wage scales of blue- and white-collar workers, the lifetime employment commitment system provides workers with economic security. As long as the firm is able to meet its economic obligations, the employee need not worry about layoffs, unemployment, or loss of income. Of course, the employee may resign, but this is unusual. The tenure of the employee is maintained until he or she reaches the age of 55, when retirement is compulsory.

Second, employee unions in Japan are almost exclusively company unions, and they represent both white- and blue-collar workers rather than particular types of jobs, as in the United States. For this reason, national federations of unions in Japan have little to do with the establishment of compensation and working conditions; these matters are dealt with by labor and management at the company, not the national, level. Approximately one-third of the Japanese labor force is unionized, compared to one-sixth in the United States. In contrast to U.S. labor-management relations, however, the union-management relationship in Japan is characterized by cooperation rather than conflict. Japanese unions often support wage reductions as a means of avoiding employment cutbacks during periods of weak demand for the product of their firm. Thus, unemployment in Japan is substantially lower than it is the United States.[14] In contrast to the United States and Western European economies, the proportion of managers who are experienced union leaders is high in Japan. Consultation between management and employee representatives is an integral part of Japanese industrial relations. Each has certain areas of control: Unions play an important role in the establishment of wage differentials among jobs; management is given a great deal of flexibiity in the assignment of employees, and the movement of employees among positions in the firm is seldom resisted by the union. Areas of joint labor-management consultation include future production plans, projected technological changes, and the transfer of personnel to new plants. Since the long-run economic prospects of employees, including provisions for retirement, are closely tied to the success of the firm, it is not unusual for management and the union to work out a temporary reduction in wages during an economic slowdown or in order to enable the firm to expand into a new market.

Ichiro Nakayama, a senior Japanese labor economist, summed up the labor-management relationship as follows:

> One of the facts that is frequently referred to as the most marked characteristic of labor-management relations in Japan is the relative absence of conflict between employer and worker in all phases of industrial relations. . . . This manifests in various features of the trade union organization known as the enterprise-wide union—for example, the lack of a strong feeling of confrontation at the collective bargaining table, the ambiguous distinction between union membership and employee's status . . . and the importance attached to the system of life-long employment. When compared with those in Western countries, labor-management relations in Japan are conspicuous, in the last analysis, by the common characteristic of a close human relationship between employers and employees.[15]

SAVINGS AND INVESTMENT

The savings and investment rates of Japan are much higher than those of other market economies. Urban workers in Japan save approximately 20 percent of their disposable income. Not surprisingly, the major share of corporate profits is rechanneled into investment. During the 1960s and 1970s, nearly one third of the GNP of Japan was allocated to investment, substantially more than the share allocated to investment in other industrial market economies. No democratic market economy has ever chosen to allocate such a large share of its output to capital formation during peacetime.

The Japanese tax structure is at least partially responsible for these high rates of saving and investment. Capital gains derived from the sale of securities are not taxed in Japan. Businesses and land capital gains are taxed at much lower rates than they are in Western countries. Interest and dividends are taxed at a maximum rate of 25 percent, compared to marginal tax rates of 50 percent and more for

[14]For example, the Japanese unemployment rate in 1987 was 2.9 percent compared with 6.2 percent in the United States.
[15]As quoted in Hugh Patrick and Henry Rosovsky (eds.), *Asia's New Giant* (Washington, D.C.: Brookings Institution, 1976), p. 639.

income derived from interest and dividends in most Western nations. A system of tax credits encourages various forms of saving.

TAXES IN JAPAN

Although the Japanese tax structure is progressive, there are so many exemptions that high marginal rates can generally be avoided, particularly if one is willing to save. Until recent years, taxes were substantially lower in Japan than in the United States, Canada, and Western Europe. During the past decade, the size of the public sector has grown substantially in Japan. Thus, the "tax gap" between other industrial nations and Japan has narrowed. As Exhibit 10 illustrates, however, taxes still consume a smaller share of GNP in Japan than in other market-directed economies. In 1985, tax revenues accounted for 28 percent of GNP in Japan, compared to 29.2 percent in the United States, 38.1 percent in the United Kingdom, and 50.5 percent in Sweden. Many believe that low tax rates, particularly during the 1950–1976 period, have contributed to the impressive growth record of Japan.

THE ECONOMIC FUTURE OF JAPAN

In recent years, the phenomenal growth rate of Japan has slowed. The Japanese real GNP expanded at an annual rate of 4.3 percent during 1976–1988, compared with 7.6 percent during 1966–1975. Nevertheless, Japan is still growing more rapidly than any other major industrial nation (see Exhibit 9).

The slowdown of the Japanese economy from the lofty growth records of 1950–1975 period was expected. During the 1950s and 1960s, Japan, like the Soviet Union, was able to profit by drawing on the technology and methods of production of more advanced countries.[16] Since Japanese manufacturing is now as modern as that of other industrial economies, this potential source of growth is no longer present. There is reason to question whether the Japanese growth rate will return to the levels of the 1960s. As real incomes of Japanese workers continue to expand, they are likely to opt for a shorter work week and longer vacations in the future. An increase in environmental pollution has accompanied Japan's rapid growth. The Japanese will probably allocate more resources to pollution control as their standard of living rises. These factors will most likely cause the growth rate of the Japanese GNP to fall below the rate of the 1950–1975 period.

SOCIALISM AND CAPITALISM

Isolating the importance of economic organization is a complex task. The availability of natural resources, cultural characteristics, locational assets and liabilities, and historical experiences differ from country to country. These differences make it more difficult to isolate the significance of economic organization as a source of prosperity.

However, there are a few cases where similar people have opted for alternative forms of economic organization in recent decades. Exhibit 11 summarizes the results of these "experiments" in economic organization. This exhibit presents

---

[16]A study by the Brookings Institution found that the major determinants of the growth rate differential between Japan and other major market economies were (a) rapid capital formation, (b) advances in knowledge and technology, and (c) economies of scale. See Edward F. Denison and William K. Chung, "Economic Growth and Its Source," in Patrick and Rosovsky, *Asia's New Giant*.

EXHIBIT 10 ■ Taxes in Selected Western Countries, 1985

Country	Tax Revenues as a Percentage of GNP, 1985
Sweden	50.5
France	45.6
United Kingdom	38.1
West Germany	37.8
United States	29.2
Japan	28.0

Source: *Facts and Figures on Government Finance,* 1988–1989 (Washington, D.C.: Tax Foundation, 1988), Table A33.

---

data on real GNP and key indicators of economic development for centrally planned socialist economies compared to similar primarily market economies. The socialist and market economies of Europe are compared. The per capita GNP of the socialist European economies is only about two-thirds as great as the real GNP of the European market (primarily) economies. Similarly, the life expectancy at birth is greater and the share of the labor force in agriculture is smaller for the market economies. Data are also presented for two European economies—East

---

EXHIBIT 11 ■ The Per Capita Real GNP and Other Indicators of Economic Development—A Comparison of Similar Market and Socialist Countries

Country or Area (Socialist economies are in italics)	Per Capita Real GNP, 1985[a]	Life Expectancy at Birth, 1986	Percent of Labor Force in Agriculture, 1980
Eastern European-Socialist Countries[b]	$ 5,670	71	24
European Market Economies[c]	$ 8,370	76	10
East Germany	$ 8,740	72	11
West Germany	$10,708	75	6
China	$ 2,444	69	74
Hong Kong	$ 9,093	76	2
Taiwan	$ 3,581	n/a	n/a
North Korea	$ 1,670	68	43
South Korea	$ 3,056	69	36

[a] In 1980 U.S. dollars.

[b] The countries included in this group are: Bulgaria, Czechoslovakia, East Germany, Hungary, Poland, Romania, and Yugoslavia.

[c] The countries included in this group are: Austria, Belgium, Denmark, Finland, France, West Germany, Greece, Ireland, Italy, Netherlands, Norway, Portugal, Spain, Sweden, Switzerland, and the United Kingdom.

n/a Not available.

Source: Except for North Korea, the per capita real GNP figures are from Robert Summers and Alan Heston, "A New Set of International Comparisons of Real Product and Price Levels: Estimates for 130 Countries, 1950–1985," *The Review of Income and Wealth,* 34 (March 1988). They were derived by the purchasing power parity method. The per capita GNP data for North Korea are derived from the U.S. Arms Control and Disarmament Agency, *World Military Expenditures and Arms Transfers, 1987* (Washington, D.C.: U.S. Government Printing Office, 1988). The life expectancy and labor force data are from *The World Development Report: 1988.*

Germany and West Germany—that were quite similar until different forms of economic organization were adopted following the Second World War. Once again, the per capita income, life expectancy, and share of labor force in agriculture indicate a higher level of development for the market economy (West Germany) than the centrally planned economy (East Germany). Comparisons between socialist China and market-directed Hong Kong and Taiwan and between North Korea and South Korea paint a similar picture.

Comparisons like those in Exhibit 11 have caused many socialists to question whether detailed central planning can deliver rapid economic growth, quality products, and sustained prosperity. No socialist country has been able to provide the abundance and diversity of goods and services available to consumers in the high-tech industrial, market economies of North America, Western Europe, and Japan. Neither has any less-developed socialist economy been able to match the impressive growth rates of the market-directed economies of Hong Kong, Singapore, South Korea, Taiwan, and Indonesia during the 1975–1988 period, to say nothing of the post-1950 record of Japan.

Of course, a comparison of economic systems involves more than material goods and economic data. One's view of human nature, personal freedom, and equality are also important considerations. However, recent events in socialist countries highlight the importance of economic performance. Clearly, disappointment in the economic record of socialism has been a driving force for economic change in China, Eastern Europe, and the Soviet Union. It is not obvious where these changes will lead. But one thing is certain: analysis of these changes will be an integral and exciting part of economics in the 1990s.

CHAPTER SUMMARY

1. Basic economic concepts, such as opportunity cost, diminishing marginal returns, comparative advantage, and the law of demand apply to socialist and capitalist economies alike. Different forms of economic organization can change the incentives faced by decision-makers (for example, managers and workers), but basic economic principles do not differ from one type of economy to another.

2. Capitalist economies are characterized by private ownership of productive assets and the use of markets to allocate goods and resources. The distinguishing characteristics of socialist economies are government ownership of physical capital and resource allocation by central planning.

3. Central planning is the dominant characteristic of the Soviet economy. The Gosplan, a central planning agency, presents state enterprises with an allocation of inputs and target levels for output. Key commodities and raw materials are centrally rationed in physical terms. The rewards of managers and workers are affected by their success at meeting the targets of the central planning authority. Pecuniary as well as nonpecuniary incentives are used to motivate managers and workers to carry out the directives of the central planners.

4. The supply of goods in the Soviet Union is determined by the priorities of the central planners. Just as for market economies, however, the quantity demanded by Soviet consumers is inversely related to price. Soviet central planners set the price of more than 200,000 products and resources. Sometimes the planners will attempt to set the price of a good at a level that will bring the quantity demanded into balance with the available supply. However, this is not always the case. Shortages and surpluses occur when the planners set the prices of various goods either below or above the market-clearing price.

5. Even though small, private plots constitute slightly more than 1 percent of the land under cultivation in the Soviet Union, they have accounted for approximately one fourth of the total value of Soviet agricultural production in recent years.

6. The distribution of income in the Soviet Union is probably less unequal than for the United States. The distribution of income shares in Japan, the United Kingdom, and Sweden, however, appears to be quite similar to that of the Soviet Union. Comparisons of income inequality of market-directed economies with the Soviet Union may be misleading. The prices of many items purchased intensively by the poor, including medical service, basic food products, and housing, are low in the Soviet Union. This, of course, is beneficial to low-income families. On the other hand, the state provides privileges—such as the use of automobiles and the right to shop at stores where high-quality goods are sold at low prices—only to government officials and other members of the Soviet elite. Such benefits are an important source of economic inequality in the Soviet Union.

7. The per capita GNP of the Soviet Union is substantially less than that of Japan, the United States, and the countries of the European Economic Community. Nevertheless, the economic growth record of the Soviet economy was quite impressive during the 1950s and 1960s, but it has declined substantially since the mid-1970s. During the 1976–1988 period, the annual growth of the Soviet economy fell to 2 percent, well below the growth rate of both Japan and the United States.

8. Slow economic growth, poor quality of goods, and shortages of many products provided the foundation for recent economic reforms in the Soviet Union. Under the leadership of President Gorbachev, the Soviets have expanded the number of categories where small-scale private businesses are permitted, encouraged the development of private cooperative businesses, and expanded the discretionary decision-making powers of plant managers.

9. The Yugoslavian economy combines socialist and capitalist economic organization. Central planning directs the economy and channels capital investment into designated areas. However, business firms have a great deal of discretionary decision-making authority. Employees of each firm elect a workers' council, which manages the firm. The firm is usually free to decide what products it will produce, the production techniques to be used, the employment level, and even product prices. As in market economies, business firms in Yugoslavia pursue profits that are then distributed to employees according to their wishes.

10. For three decades following the Second World War, the Chinese economy was characterized by Soviet-style detailed central planning. Beginning in the late 1970s, China began to move away from collectivism and toward market allocation. A system of long-term land leases to family farmers replaced collectivization in agriculture. Restrictions limiting the operation of small-scale service and retail businesses were relaxed. Some industrial prices were deregulated. Rapid growth of GNP, particularly in the agricultural and service sectors, accompanied the recent reforms of the Chinese economy. However, rapid monetary expansion and a soaring inflation rate has slowed the move toward market incentives in the late 1980s.

11. The growth record of Japan has been the most impressive of the major industrial nations during the postwar period. The following factors have contributed to this rapid growth: (a) institutional arrangements that have encouraged harmonious labor-management relations, (b) very high rates of saving and capital formation, and (c) low tax rates.

CRITICAL ANALYSIS QUESTIONS

1. Compare and contrast the role of business managers of firms in the United States, the Soviet Union, and Yugoslavia. In which country would managers have the greatest incentive to operate the firm efficiently?

2. What do you think are the major advantages of a centrally planned economy? What are the major disadvantages? Do you believe that market allocation is superior or inferior to centralized planning? Explain your answer.

3. How does Yugoslav socialism differ from socialism as practiced in the Soviet Union? Which system do you think is better? Why?

4. "Socialism means production for use, not for profit. Workers contribute according to their qualifications, and they are rewarded according to egalitarian principles. Socialism takes power from the business elite and grants it to the workers, who, after all, produce the goods." Analyze this point of view.

*5. What major factors have contributed to the rapid economic growth of Japan? Do you think the Japanese economy will grow as rapidly in the future as it has in the past? Why or why not?

6. Do you think the United States should encourage firms to adopt the lifetime employment commitment offered by the major firms in Japan? Why or why not? What are the advantages and disadvantages of this system?

*7. **What's Wrong with This Way of Thinking?**

"Central planning makes it possible for an economy to invest more and to expand at a more rapid rate. Consumer incomes, stimulated by the high rates of capital formation, also increase rapidly. Thus, the consumer is the major beneficiary of central planning, which stresses a rapid rate of capital formation."

*8. "Capitalism is better at producing wealth; socialism is better at distributing it fairly." Evaluate.

9. What major economic reforms have recently taken place in China? What have been the effects of these reforms?

*10. Socalists often claim that under capitalism resources are wasted producing luxury goods for the rich. Evaluate the charge.

*Asterisk denotes questions for which answers are given in Appendix C, Selected Answers.

PRODUCTION THEORY AND ISOQUANT ANALYSIS

When analyzing production theory and input utilization, economists often rely on isoquant analysis. Since the technique is widely used at the intermediate level, some instructors explain the concept in their introductory course.

WHAT ARE ISOQUANTS?

Generally, several alternative input combinations can be used to produce a good. For example, 100 bushels of wheat might be produced with 2 acres of land, 5 bushels of seed, and 100 pounds of fertilizer. Alternatively, the wheat could be produced with more land and less fertilizer, or more seed and less land, or more fertilizer and less seed. Many input combinations could be used to produce 100 bushels of wheat.

Isoquant: A curve representing the technically efficient combinations of two inputs that can be used to produce a given level of output.

The word "isoquant" means "equal quantity." An **isoquant** is a curve that indicates the various combinations of two inputs that could be used to produce an equal quantity of output. Exhibit 1 provides an illustration. The isoquant labeled "100 units of cloth" shows the various combinations of capital and labor that a technically efficient producer could use to produce 100 units of cloth. Every point on a isoquant is technically efficient. By that we mean that it would not be possible, given the current level of technology, to produce a larger output with the input combination. If a producer wanted to produce a larger output, 140 units of cloth, for example, it would be necessary to use more of at least one of the resources. Since larger output levels require additional resources, isoquants representing larger levels of output always lie to the northeast of an isoquant diagram.

CHARACTERISTICS OF ISOQUANTS

Isoquant analysis must be consistent with the laws of production. What do the laws of production imply about the characteristics of isoquants?

1. *Isoquants Slope Downward to the Right.* Within the relevant range of utilization, an increase in the usage level of an input makes it possible to expand output. If, for example, the use of the labor input is expanded, it is possible to produce the same output level (stay on the same isoquant) with a smaller quantity of capital. Since both labor and capital can be used to increase production, they can be substituted for each other. Constant output can be maintained either by (a) using more labor and less capital or (b) by using more capital and less labor. Thus, every isoquant runs from the northwest to the southeast, as illustrated by Exhibit 1.

2. *Isoquants Are Convex When Viewed from the Origin.* The convexity of isoquants stems from the fact that as one continues to substitute labor for capital, larger and larger amounts of labor are required to maintain output at a constant level. As labor is used more intensively, it becomes increasingly difficult to substitute labor for each additional unit of capital. Since larger and larger amounts of labor are required to compensate for the loss of each additional unit of capital (and thus maintain the constant level of output), the isoquant becomes flatter as labor is used more intensively (see Exhibit 2, point B).

On the other hand, when capital is used more and more intensively, larger and larger amounts of capital are required to compensate for the loss of a unit of

The Isoquant

An isoquant represents all input combinations that, if used efficiently, will generate a specific level of output. As illustrated here, 100 units of cloth could be produced with the input combinations L_1K_1 or L_2K_2 or any other combination of labor and capital that lies on the isoquant representing 100 units of cloth.

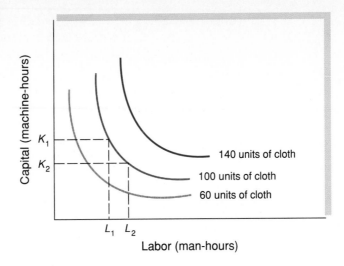

labor. Thus, an isoquant becomes steeper as capital (the y factor) is used more intensively (see Exhibit 2, point A). It is convex when viewed from the origin.

3. *The Slope of the Isoquant Is the Marginal Product of Labor Divided by the Marginal Product of Capital.* The slope of the isoquant is determined by the amount of labor that must be added to maintain a constant level of output when one uses one less unit of capital. This slope is dependent on the marginal productivity of labor relative to capital. When labor is used intensively relative to capital, its marginal product is low, relative to capital. Under these circumstances, as Exhibit 2 (point B) illustrates, the slope of the isoquant is small (the isoquant is flat). In contrast, when capital is used intensively (Exhibit 2, point A), the marginal product of labor is high, relative to capital. The steepness of the isoquant reflects this fact. At any point on the isoquant, the slope of the isoquant is equal to MP_L / MP_K.

Convexity and the Slope of the Isoquant

When labor is used intensively relative to capital (point B), the shape of the isoquant is much flatter than it is when capital is used more intensively (point A). The slope of an isoquant is the ratio of the marginal products of the two factors (MP_L divided by MP_K). When labor is used intensively relative to capital, its marginal product falls (and that of capital increases). Since the marginal product of labor is low (and the marginal product of capital is high) when labor is used intensively (as at point B), the isoquant is relatively flat.

THE ISOCOST LINE

Isocost Line: A line representing the various combinations of two factors that can be purchased with a given money budget (cost).

A set of isoquants outlines the technically efficient input combinations that could be used to produce alternative levels of output. Before we can determine the economically efficient input combination for producing a level of output, we must also incorporate information about cost and resource prices.

Firms generally can purchase inputs at a fixed price per unit. The **isocost line** shows the alternative combinations of inputs that can be purchased with a given outlay of funds. As the term implies, the cost of purchasing an input combination on the isocost line is equal to the cost of purchasing any other input combination on the same line. To construct an isocost line, two pieces of information are required: (a) the prices of the resources and (b) the specific outlay of funds. Exhibit 3 illustrates the construction of three different isocost lines, assuming that the price of labor is $5 per unit and that the price of capital is $10 per unit. Consider the $500 isocost line. If all funds were spent on labor, 100 units of labor could be purchased. Alternatively, if the entire $500 were expended on capital, 50 units of capital could be purchased. It would be possible to purchase any input combination between these two extremes—for example, 80 units of labor and 10 units of capital—with the $500. The input combinations are represented by a line connecting the two extreme points, 100 units of labor on the x-axis and 50 units of capital on the y-axis. Note that the slope of the isocost line is merely the price of labor divided by the price of capital (P_L/P_K).

If the outlay of funds were to increase, it would be possible to purchase more of both labor and capital. Thus, as Exhibit 3 illustrates, the isocost lines move in a northeast direction as the size of the outlay of funds increases.

MINIMIZING THE COST OF PRODUCTION

A profit-seeking firm will want to choose the minimum-cost method of production. We can combine isoquant analysis and the isocost line to derive the minimum-cost input combination for producing a given output level. As Exhibit 4

EXHIBIT 3
The Isocost Line

The isocost line indicates the alternative combinations of the resources that can be purchased with a given outlay of funds. When the price of a unit of labor is $5 and that of a unit of capital is $10, the three isocost lines shown here represent the alternative combinations of labor and capital that could be purchased at costs of $500, $1000, and $1500. The slope of the isocost line is equal to P_L/P_k ($5/$10 = ½ in this case).

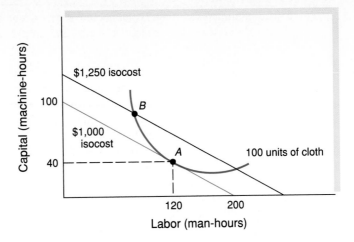

EXHIBIT 4

The Cost-Minimization Resource Combination

When the cost of producing an output level (for example, 100 units of cloth) is minimized, the isoquant is tangent to the isocost line. At that point (A), $MP_L / MP_K = P_L / P_K$.

illustrates, the minimum-cost input combination for producing 100 units of cloth is represented by the point at which the lowest isocost line just touches (is tangent to) the isoquant for 100 units of cloth. At that point (A of Exhibit 4), the producer will be able to combine 120 units of labor purchased at a cost of $600 ($5 per unit) with 40 units of capital purchased at a cost of $400 ($10 per unit) to produce 100 units of cloth. The total cost of the 100 units is $1,000 ($10 per unit).

Of course, other input combinations could be used to produce the 100 units of cloth. However, they would be more costly, given the current prices of labor and capital. For example, if the input combination B were used to produce the 100 units, the total cost would be $1,250 ($12.50 per unit).

When costs are at a minimum, the isoquant is tangent to the isocost line. The slopes of the two are equal at that point. In other words, when the cost of producing a specific output is at a minimum, the MP_L/MP_K (the slope of the isoquant) will be equal to P_L/P_K (the slope of the isocost line). Since:

$$\frac{MP_L}{MP_K} = \frac{P_L}{P_K}$$

then:

$$\frac{MP_L}{P_L} = \frac{MP_K}{P_K}$$

The latter equation represents precisely the condition that our earlier analysis, in the chapter devoted to supply of and demand for productive resources, indicated would be present if the cost of production were at a minimum.

The isoquant analysis indicates that when a firm chooses the minimum-cost method of production, the ratio of the price of labor to the price of capital will equal the ratio of the marginal productivities of the factors. This makes good economic sense. It implies, for example, that if capital is twice as expensive per unit as labor, the firm will want to substitute the cheaper labor for capital until the marginal product of capital is twice that of labor.

COST MINIMIZATION AND CHANGES IN RESOURCE PRICES

The minimum-cost input combination is dependent on both (a) the technical relationship between the productive inputs and output, as illustrated by the isoquant, and (b) the price of the factors, represented by the isocost line. If the ratio of the price of labor to the price of capital changes, the minimum-cost input combination will be altered.

Exhibit 5 illustrates this point. Exhibit 4 shows that if the price of labor were $5 and the price of capital were $10, the minimum-cost input combination to produce 100 units of cloth would be 120 units of labor and 40 units of capital. The total cost of the 100 units would be $1,000. Exhibit 5 indicates what would happen if the price of labor increased from $5 to $10. At the higher price of labor, a $1,000 outlay of funds would now purchase only 100 units of labor (rather than 200). As a result of the increase in the price of labor, the isocost line would become steeper, as indicated by the change in isocost lines from *MN* to *OP*. The lowest isocost line that is tangent to the isoquant for 100 units would now be *OP*. The new minimum-cost input combination would be 90 units of labor and 60 units of capital. Cost-minimizing producers would substitute capital for labor. The cost of producing the 100 units would rise (from $1,000 to $1,500).

THE SIGNIFICANCE OF ISOQUANT-ISOCOST ANALYSIS

Isoquant-isocost analysis is most applicable in the long run, when all factors are variable and the possibilities for substitution are greatest. It is a conceptual tool, more suitable for illustrating principles than for solving management problems. Few firms would try to design their production activities by drawing isoquants, although some managers might make mental use of the model to design numerical techniques for minimizing costs. In any case, firms that do maximize profits behave as though they were using the analysis.

Isoquant-isocost analysis helps clarify the production conditions that must be met if a firm is to minimize its production cost and get the largest possible output from a specific outlay of funds.

EXHIBIT 5

The Impact of an Increase in the Price of a Resource

The slope of the isocost line increases as the price of a unit of labor rises from $5 to $10. As a result of the increase in the price of labor, (a) cost-minimizing producers substitute capital for the more expensive labor, and (b) the minimum cost of producing 100 units of cloth rises.

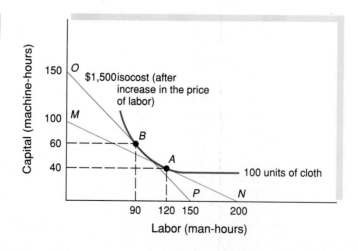

B

ANSWERS TO
SELECTED
QUESTIONS

CHAPTER 1

2. Production of scarce goods always involves a cost; there are no free lunches. When the government provides goods without charge to consumers, other citizens (taxpayers) will bear the cost of their provision. Thus, provision by the government affects *how* the costs will be covered, not whether they are incurred.

6. For most taxpayers, the change will reduce the *after-tax* cost of raising children. Other things constant, one would predict an increase in the birth rate.

7. False. The key to sound policy is not the intentions of the advocate, but rather the ability of the policy to bring individual self-interest and the general welfare into harmony. People are not like pieces on a chess board. They have self will and personal interests. As Adam Smith pointed out in *The Theory of Moral Sentiments* (1759), "In the great chess board of human society, every single piece [individual] has a principle of motion of its own, altogether different from that which the legislature might choose to impress on it. If the two coincide [the self-interest of individuals and the objectives of a policy], the game of human society will go on easily and harmoniously, and is very likely to be happy and successful. If they are opposite or different, the game will go on miserably, and the society must be at all times in the highest degree of disorder."

9. Raising the price of new cars by requiring safety devices, which customers would not have purchased if given the choice, slows the rate of sales for new cars. Thus the older, less safe cars are driven longer, partially offsetting the safety advantage provided by the newer, safer cars. Also, drivers act a bit differently when they are told that the new cars have the safety devices. They count on them for help in the event of an unexpected accident. In fact, economist Gordon Tullock says that the greatest safety device of all might be a dagger built into the center of the steering wheel, pointed directly at the driver's chest!

10. Money has nothing to do with whether an individual is economizing. Any time a person chooses, in an attempt to acheive a goal, he or she is economizing.

CHAPTER 2

2. Even though the productivity of painters has changed only slightly, rising productivity in *other areas* has led to higher wages in *other occupations,* thereby increasing the opportunity cost of being a house painter. Since people would not supply house painting services unless they were able to meet their opportunity costs, higher wages are necessary to attract house painters from competitive (alternative) lines of work.

6. The statement reflects the "exchange is a zero sum game" view. This view is false. No private business can force customers to buy. Neither can a customer force a business to sell. Unless both buyer and seller believe the exchange is in their interest, they will not enter into the exchange. Mutual gain provides the foundation for voluntary exchange.

9. Yes. The market value of the land will increase in anticipation of the future harvest, as the trees grow and the expected day of harvest moves closer. Thus, with transferable private property, the tree farmer will be able to capture the value added by his planting and holding the trees for a few years even if the actual harvest does not take place until well after his death.

10. In general, it sanctions all forms of competition except for the use of violence (or the threat of violence), theft, or fraud.

12. When used to generate *personal* services for the owner, *private property rights* permit owners to satisfy their own preferences while ignoring the wishes of others, if they so choose. However, when property is used for investment purposes or put up for sale, owners must cater to the preferences of others, if they want to maximize the return on sale value of the property. Finally, private property rights do provide legal protection against selfish persons who would use violence or theft to take the property of another.

14. If the food from land, now and in the future, is worth more than the housing services from the same land, then developers will not be able to bid the land away from farmers. However, since it is comparative advantage that determines the efficient use of a resource, even the best farm land, if situated in the right location, may be far more valuable for buildings. Other, poorer land can always be made more productive by the use of different (and more costly) farming techniques, irrigation, fertilizer, and so on. Physical characteristics alone do not determine the value or the most valuable use of a resource.

CHAPTER 3

1. a. and **b.** would increase the demand for beef; **c.** and **d.** would affect primarily the supply of beef, rather than the demand; **e.** leads to a change in quantity demanded, not a change in demand.

4. a. Reductions in the supply of feed grains and hay led to sharply higher prices. **b.** The higher feed grain and hay prices increased the cost of *maintaining* a cattle herd and thereby caused many producers to sell (an increase in *current* supply), depressing cattle prices in 1988. **c.** The reduction in the size of cattle herds led to a smaller future supply and higher cattle prices in 1989.

6. Agreement of both buyer and seller is required for an exchange. Price ceilings push price below equilibrium and thereby reduce the quantity sellers are willing to offer. Price floors push prices above equilibrium and thereby reduce the quantity consumers wish to buy. Both decrease the actual quantity traded in the market.

8. True, "somebody" must decide who will be the business winners and losers. Neither markets nor the political process leave the determination of winners and losers to chance. Under market organization, business winners and losers are determined by the decentralized choices of millions of consumers who use their dollar votes to reward firms that provide preferred goods at a low cost and penalize others who fail to do so. Under political decision-making, the winners and losers are determined by political figures and planning boards who use taxes, subsidies, regulations, and mandates to favor some businesses and penalize others.

10. a. Profitable production increases the value of resources owned by people and leads to mutual gain to resource suppliers, consumers, and entrepreneurs. **b.** Losses reduce the value of resources which reduces the well-being of at least some people. **c.** No.

12. In the absence of trade restrictions, modest price increases in France will attract wheat from other regions, minimizing the effects in the drought region and resulting in slightly higher prices worldwide.

14. Rationing by price encourages future output; waiting in a line does not. Like a higher price, a longer wait in line rations the *current* supply by increasing the consumer's opportunity cost. However, the consumer's cost of waiting in line is wasted. It generates nothing for suppliers. In contrast, while a higher price also increases the consumer's opportunity cost, this cost transfers resources to suppliers, increases their returns, and thereby encourages them to expand the future availability of the good.

CHAPTER 4

2. When payment is not demanded for services, potential customers have a strong incentive to attempt a "free ride." However, when the number of nonpaying customers becomes such that the sales revenues of sellers are diminished (and in some cases eliminated), the sellers' incentive to supply the good is thereby reduced (or eliminated).

5. Disagree. As long as changes in personal costs and benefits influence choices predictably, theories for both market and public-sector action can be developed and tested against real-world events. Theory building and testing are the essential ingredients of a positive science.

6. The antimissile system is a public good for the residents of Washington, D.C. Strictly speaking, none of the other items are public goods since each could be provided to some consumers (paying customers, for example) without being provided to others.

9. In both markets and government, mutual consent is the only conclusive test of whether an action is productive. If all parties affected by an activity agree to it, then it is productive. Projects favored by a majority are not necessarily productive because the cost imposed on the nonconsenting minority may exceed the net gain to the majority.

11. The invisible hand principle is present only when the self-interest of individuals is consistent with the general welfare. Both the special interest effect and the shortsightedness effect indicate that this will not always be the case, even when political choices are made democratically.

12. True. Since individual computer customers both decide the issue (what computer, if any, will be purchased) and bear the consequences of a mistaken choice, they have a strong incentive to acquire information that will help them make a wise choice. In contrast, voters recognize that their choice, even if mistaken, will not decide the congressional election. Thus, they have little incentive to search for information that will help them make a better choice.

CHAPTER 5

2. Local and state governments operate in a more competitive setting than does the federal government. The competition reduces their ability to exploit taxpayers. Taxpayers who feel they are paying high taxes and getting little in return can vote with their feet; they can move to another local (or state) governmental unit that offers them more value for their tax dollar.

3. User charges differ from general taxation in that they impose the cost of a government activity on users in proportion to their consumption of the good. If you do not use the good, you do not have to pay for it. Taxes earmarked to finance specific activities may approximate user charges, but general taxation does not. The use of general taxes to finance a government activity breaks the link between consumption and payment and thereby forces nonusers to pay for things enjoyed by others. Like market prices, user charges provide valuable information about value relative to cost. If the revenue from user charges is sufficient to cover opportunity cost, this is strong evidence that consumers value the good more than the alternatives foregone. Conversely, if user charges are insufficient to cover cost, this is evidence that consumers place a higher value on other things that might be produced.

6. True. In addition to the outlay cost of the project, the collection cost of the taxes and the deadweight losses emanating from the taxes implied by the project must also be covered if the project is going to enhance economic welfare.

7. High marginal tax rates make tax-deductible expenditures (for example, business entertainment, elegant office, or luxury automobile for business use) cheap *to the purchaser* (but not to society). A reduction in marginal tax rates will increase the purchaser's cost of deductible expenditures, since the lower rates reduce the tax savings accompanying deductible expenditures. Thus, lower marginal rates will tend to reduce expenditures on deductible items and other forms of tax avoidance.

10. False. Just as businesses do not pay taxes, neither dó inanimate objects such as trucks. Only people pay taxes. In this case, the increased costs accompanying the tax translates into higher freight rates. These costs will be paid by consumers of the products transported (in the form of higher prices), by truck owners (in the form of lower profits), and by trucking employees (in the form of lower earnings).

CHAPTER 6

1. a. increase demand; **b.** decrease demand; **c.** decrease incentive to develop nongasoline powered car; **d.** leave *demand* unchanged, *quantity demanded* declined; **e.** increase demand.

3. a. 0.21; 1.2. **b.** substitutes; higher fuel oil prices lead to an increase in demand (and consumption) for insulation.

8. Water is usually cheaper than oil because its *marginal utility* at current consumption levels is less than that of oil. Since water is so abundant relative to oil, the benefit derived from an *additional* quart of water is less than the benefit from an *additional* quart of oil, even though the *total utility* from all units of water is far greater than the *total utility* from all units of oil. However, the price of a product will reflect marginal utility, not total utility.

9. Both income and time constrain our ability to consume. Since, in a wealthier society, time becomes more binding and income less binding, time-saving actions will be more common in a wealthier society. As we engage in time-saving actions (fast-food, automatic appliances, air travel, and so on) in order to shift the time restraint outward, our lives become more hectic.

12. All three statements are true.

13. a. No; even for things we like, we will experience diminishing returns. Eventually, the cost of additional units of pizza will exceed their benefits. **b.** Perfection in any activity is generally not worth the cost. For example, reading every page of this text 3, 4, or 5 times may improve your grade, but it may not be worth it. One function of a text is to structure the material (highlighted points, layout of graphs, and so on) so that the reader will be able to learn quickly (at a lower cost).

14. Carole.

15. False. Since the demand for agricultural products is generally inelastic, farm incomes may well increase. But the total utility of farm output reflects not only the sales revenues but also the consumer surplus. *For the units produced,* the utility is unchanged as the loss of consumer surplus by consumers is exactly offset by higher payments to farmers. However, both the payments to farmers and consumer surplus are lost *for those units not produced*. Therefore, the decline in production will reduce the total utility of farm output and the nation will be worse off as a result.

18. Deceit and dishonesty will be encouraged by methods of organization that increase the returns to such behavior. The returns to deceitful and dishonest claims will be inversely related to the ease with which they can be countered by rivals. Other things constant, the presence of rivals will tend to reduce deceitful behavior. Is a politician more or less likely to tell the truth when he regularly confronts rivals? Is the news media more or less likely to be balanced and trustworthy when it faces rivals in the news business? Is a court witness more or less likely to tell the truth when there are other witnesses and cross-examination can be expected? Is a firm selling automobiles, cough drops, or hamburgers more or less likely to be honest when it faces competitors? Answers to such questions are obvious.

19. The deadweight loss is the loss of the potential gains of buyers and sellers emanating from trades that are squeezed out by the tax. It is an excess burden because even though the exchanges that are squeezed out by the tax impose a cost on buyers and sellers, they do not generate tax revenue (since the trades do not take place).

CHAPTER 7

1. The economic profit of a firm is its total revenues minus the opportunity cost of all resources used in the production process. Accounting profit often excludes the opportunity cost of certain resources—particularly the equity capital of the firm and any labor services provided by an owner-manager. Zero economic profit means that the resources owned by the firm are earning their opportunity cost—that is, the rate of return is as high as the highest valued alternative forgone. Thus, the firm would not gain by pursuing other lines of business.

2. a. sunk costs are irrelevant; **b.** there is an opportunity cost of one's house; **c.** sunk costs should not affect one's current decision; **d.** there is an opportunity cost of public education even if it is provided free to the consumer.

9. Since owners receive profits, clearly profit maximization is in their interest. Managers, if they are not owners, have no property right to profit and therefore no *direct* interest in profit maximization. Since a solid record of profitability tends to increase the market value (salary) of corporate managers, they do have an indirect incentive to pursue profits. However, corporate managers may also be interested in power, nice offices, hiring friends, expansion of sales and other activities, which may conflict with profitability. Thus, the potential for conflict between the interests of owners and managers is present.

10. a. The interest payments **b.** the interest income forgone. The tax structure encourages debt rather than equity financing since the firm's tax liability is *inversely* related to its debt/equity ratio.

11. True. If it could produce the output at a lower cost, its profit would be greater.

13. Did your marginal cost curve cross the ATC and AVC curves at their low points? Does the vertical distance between the ATC and AVC curves get smaller and smaller as output increases? If not, redraw the three curves correctly. See Exhibit 6b.

17. $2,500; the $2,000 decline in market value during the year plus $500 of potential interest on funds that could be obtained if the machine were sold new. Costs associated with the decline in the value of the machine last year are sunk costs.

18. Because they believe they will be able to restructure the firm and provide better management so that the firm will have positive net earnings in the future. If the firm is purchased at a low enough price, this will allow the new owners to cover the opportunity cost of their investment and still earn an economic profit. Alternatively, they may expect to sell off the firm's assets, receiving more net revenue than the cost of purchasing the firm.

CHAPTER 8

1. In a highly competitive industry such as agriculture, lower resource prices might improve the rate of profit in the short run, but in the long run, competition will drive prices down until economic profit is eliminated. Thus, lower resource prices will do little to improve the long-run profitability in such industries.

2. New firms will enter the industry and the existing firms will expand output; market supply will expand, causing the market price to fall until the economic profit is eliminated.

6. The statement is nonsense. If a reduction in demand leads to losses and exits from the industry, this reduction in supply will lead to a higher price and the restoration of normal returns.

8. a. increase **b.** increase **c.** increase, firms will earn economic profit **d.** rise (compared with its initial level) for an increasing cost industry, but return to initial price for a constant cost industry **e.** increase even more

than it did in the short run **f.** economic profit will return to zero.

9. a. decline **b.** increase **c.** decline **d.** decline.

11. The firms are unable to earn long-term economic profit because the barriers to entry into a competitive industry are low. Thus, profit attracts rival firms who "spoil the market." Even though competitive firms earn only normal returns in the long run, profits and losses direct entrepreneurs into the production of those goods that are in short supply *relative to their cost* in the short run. This is a vitally important function.

14. a. room prices (including the tax) will increase **b.** decline in the short run. In the long run, supply will fall and profit will return to normal **c.** increase when the demand for rooms in the city is inelastic, but decline when demand is elastic.

16. True. Sellers undercut other sellers in order to gain business. Buyers outbid other buyers in order to obtain a good.

17. b. Six or seven tons; $250 profit **c.** seven or eight tons; $600 profit **d.** five or six tons; $50 loss; Since the firm can cover its variable cost, it should stay in business if it believes that the low ($450) price is temporary.

CHAPTER 9

1. Profits cannot exist in the long run without barriers to entry because without them new entrants seeking the profits would increase supply, drive down price, and eliminate the profits. But as the chapter shows, barriers to entry are no guarantee of profits. Sufficient demand is also a necessary condition.

3. No; no; no

7. With a single tuition for all, it can nevertheless price-discriminate by giving financial aid to effectively lower the cost for students from lower-income families. These students presumably are more sensitive to higher tuition, so that their elasticity of demand for the university's services is greater.

9. Once an item has been invented and patented, short-run efficiency is indeed reduced by the monopoly given by the patent. The market will probably be understocked, with a price set higher than marginal cost. Patents are inefficient in this sense. Over time, however, consumers benefit by the efforts of innovators, and the investors who support them. These efforts would be smaller if there were no patents to provide some monopoly power to successful innovators.

12. No. The firm's new profit-maximizing output rate will be 10 percent larger, but the profit-maximizing price will be unchanged. Construct a graph that illustrates this point.

13. Yes; **b.** implies that in the observed price range, the demand for petroleum products was inelastic. But a monopolist would never set price in this range—the inelastic portion of the demand curve—because a higher price would both increase revenues and reduce cost (since fewer units are produced and sold).

15. Reductions in the cost of transportation generally increase competition because they force firms to compete with distant rivals and permit consumers to choose among a wider-range of suppliers. As a result, the U.S. economy today is generally more competitive, in the rivalry sense, than it was 100 years ago.

CHAPTER 10

2. Building the new resort is more risky (and less attractive) because if the market analysis is incorrect, and demand is insufficient, it probably will be difficult to find other uses for the newly built resort. If the airline proves unprofitable, however, the capital (airplanes) should be extremely mobile. However, the resort would have one offsetting advantage: If demand were stronger than expected, and profits larger, it would take competitors longer to enter the market (build a new resort), and they would be more reluctant to make the more permanent investment.

5. The stock price, when the uncle bought the stock, no doubt reflected the well-known profits of Mammoth. The previous owners of the stock surely would not have sold it at a low price that failed to reflect the future dividends. In the language of the text, the uncle was not an "early bird." It is unlikely that he will profit, in the economic sense, from the purchase.

6. Product variation provides each firm in the oligopoly a chance to "cheat" by raising the quality of its product in order to entice customers from rivals. This raises cost and helps to defeat the purpose, for the oligopolistic group, of controlling price. But if collusion has raised price much above marginal cost, there will be a powerful incentive for each firm to compete in a hidden way to get more customers.

9. The concentration ratio of an industry depends very much on how the industry is defined by the analyst calculating the ratio. It can overstate or understate the market power of the firms in question. Even potential entrants may influence price decisions by market producers. But sellers in local markets may have much more market power than the concentration ratio indicates. And finally, even a monopoly does not guarantee the ability to cover costs, much less a large profit. The firm's costs, as compared to willingness of consumers to pay, and number of such consumers, also must be considered.

12. The amount of variety is determined by the willingness of consumers to pay for variety relative to the cost of providing it. If consumers value variety highly and the added costs of producing different styles, designs, and sizes is low, there will be a lot of variety. Alternatively, if consumers desire similiar products or if variation can be produced only at a high cost, little variety will be present. Apparently, consumers place a substantial value (relative to cost) on variety in napkins, but not in toothpicks.

13. The tax would increase the price of lower quality (and lower priced) automobiles by a larger percentage than higher quality automobiles. Consumers would substitute away from the lower quality autos since their relative price has increased. This substitution would increase the average quality of automobiles sold. Since the funds from the tax are rebated back to citizens through the lottery, one would expect this substitution effect to dominate any possible income effect.

CHAPTER 11

1. Employment in manufacturing is declining, but output is not. Manufacturing productivity is rising, and the sector is holding its own as a share of the economy. The trend for more than a century (see Boxed Feature), has been away from blue-collar occupations and toward information-related service occupations, including managers, professional and technical workers, and sales personnel. Noninformation service jobs have risen only a little. Incomes per worker have been rising—not an indication of a second-rate economy.

4. Reduced competition is a potential danger for consumers. But if a merger makes a firm more efficient and better able to undercut the prices of other competitors, it may in effect increase the degree of competition, even as the firm increases its share of the market.

6. Making cars more safe is good, but if the cost has previously kept consumers from demanding the safety measures, it is possible that they are not worth the cost to many consumers. Some very expensive cars, such as Mercedes-Benz, had air bags when there was no requirement, but Volkswagen did not. Should only the more costly cars be sold? If so, then some people, probably the less affluent, will drive older, even less safe cars. This is not a clearcut issue.

8. Profitability may be adversely affected in the short run, but in the long run prices will rise enough for the firms to cover their opportunity cost of production. Consumers bear the cost of such legislation and get the associated benefits, large or small.

9. Since this would increase competition from foreign

sources, the effect should be to reduce the fears of market power being held by domestic firms. The need for antitrust action should decline.

12. Existing airlines could be expected to define "necessary" in such a way that no new service would be allowed. Service by existing firms would always, in their view, be sufficient. Customers would be expected to favor (and thus define as necessary) any new service that would reduce prices and/or increase service with a sufficiently small price increase. Since the airlines are far fewer in number and better organized politically than customers, we would expect the airline view of "necessary" to prevail, as it did until the regulatory system grew so that it stifled competition, and prices became so demonstrably high, that deregulation occurred and the CAB was abolished.

15. The statement is essentially true. In the short run, capital may be invested in an industry such that it cannot easily be moved elsewhere. If customer demand is elastic, the industry may bear a large part of the cost burden in the short run. In the long run, however, capital is mobile. Factories don't have to be replaced, for example. If costs in the industry are high, relative to the revenues, then capital will migrate over time to other industries, and supply in the regulated industry will fall until the price buyers will pay is again high enough to provide the market rate of return to capital.

17. Experts often do know far more about the technical options than do consumers, although consumers can and do read the advice of experts. Suppliers of safer products also make it a point to advertise data and expert opinion indicating their products are indeed safer. Nevertheless, experts usually do understand the technologies better. On the other hand, experts cannot know about how products will be used. A consumer may prefer to pay for a high degree of safety for the family car, which will carry the whole family at high speeds over long distances, while preferring a much cheaper, less reliable car for running errands near home. Such choices are hard to allow if all vehicles are strictly regulated for safety. Decision-maker knowledge (and incentives) is, in some cases, better with consumer choice than with thorough and strict regulation.

CHAPTER 12

3. a. five **b.** $350 **c.** four The firm will operate in the short run but it will go out of business in the long run unless the market price rises.

4. Yes. General increases in the productivity of the labor force will cause a general increase in wages. The higher general wage rates will increase the opportunity cost of barbering and cause the supply of barbers to decline. The reduction in the supply of barbers will place upward pressure on the wages of barbers, even if technological change and worker productivity have changed little in barbering.

8. No. The dressmaker needs to employ more capital and less labor because the marginal dollar expenditures on the former are currently increasing output by a larger amount than the latter.

10. Other things constant, a lengthy training requirement to perform in an occupation reduces supply and places upward pressure on the earnings level. However, resource prices, including those for labor services, are determined by *both* demand and supply. When demand is weak, earnings will be low even though a considerable amount of education may be necessary to perform in the occupation. For example, the earnings of people with degrees in English literature and world history are generally low, even though most people in these fields have a great deal of education.

12. b. 4 **c.** Employment would decline to 3.

CHAPTER 13

2. U.S. workers are more productive. By investing in human capital, the laborers are somewhat responsible, but the superior tools and physical capital that are available to U.S. workers also contribute to their higher wages.

6. While this statement often made by politicians sounds true, in fact, it is false. Output of goods and services valued by consumers, not jobs, is the key to economic progress and a high standard of living. Real income cannot be high unless real output is high. If job creation was the key to economic progress it would be easy to create millions of new jobs. For example, we could prohibit the use of farm machinery. Such a prohibition would create millions of jobs in agriculture. However, it would also reduce output and our standard of living.

8. The opportunity cost of leisure (nonwork) for higher wage workers is greater than for lower wage workers.

9. a. decreases **b.** increases **c.** decreases **d.** increases

10. False. Several additional factors including differences in preferences (which would influence time worked, the trade-off between money wage and working conditions, and evaluation of alternative jobs), differences in jobs, and imperfect labor mobility would result in variations in earnings.

12. a., b., e., and **f.** will generally increase hourly earnings; **c.** and **d.** will generally reduce hourly earnings.

13. a. They increase the cost of employment. Yes. **b.** Sure, if the higher wages are sufficient to compensate for the absence of the fringe benefits. **c.** No. Employees pay for them in the form of lower money wages that could be earned on comparable jobs that do not provide the fringe benefits.

15. a. The cost of employing part-time workers would rise and their employment level would fall. **b.** The *money* wages of part-time workers would fall; the higher fringe benefits would increase the supply of workers willing to work at a given *money* wage, and thereby reduce the wage.

17. Hourly wages will be highest in B because the higher wages will be necessary to compensate workers in B for the uncertainty and loss of income during layoffs. Annual earnings will be higher in A in order to compensate workers in A for the additional hours they will work during the year.

18. The employment level of low-skill workers with large families would decline. Some would attempt to conceal the presence of their large family in order to get a job.

20. Not necessarily. Compared with married men, single men tend to be younger, have fewer dependents, are more likely to drop out of the labor force, and less likely to receive earnings-enhancing assistance from another person. All of these factors will reduce their earnings relative to married men.

CHAPTER 14

2. All of the changes would increase interest rates in the United States.

6. The project is profitable at 8 percent but not at 12 percent. Use Exhibit 3 to calculate the present value of $400 received at the end of each of the next three years at the two interest rates.

8. a. approximately $1.277 million **b.** yes. **c.** The lottery earnings are less liquid. Since there is not a well-organized market transforming lottery earnings into present income, the transaction costs of finding a ''buyer'' (at a price equal to the present value of the earnings) for the lottery earnings ''rights'' may be higher than for the bond, if one wants to sell in the future.

9. No. The *average* outstanding balance during the year is only about half of $1,000. Therefore, the $200 interest charge translates to almost a 40 percent annual rate of interest.

12. No. At an 8 percent discount rate, the present value of her earnings is equal to approximately $10.6 million (assuming the first $200,000 is paid now). At a 12 percent discount rate, the present value of the earnings is approximately $8.366 million. In addition, she will confront a tax liability on the earnings.

13. a. and **b.** The ''we will all starve'' argument is irrelevant and illustrates a lack of understanding about how markets work. If a decline in agriculture output accompa-

nied the abolition of farm subsidies (a highly questionable assumption), agricultural prices would rise, providing farmers with additional incentive to produce a larger output. The same process also applies to automobiles, shoes, and other goods.

15. To the extent that the price supports increase farm revenues, the larger income stream drives up the price of land with allotments. Therefore, at the higher level of land prices, farming is no more profitable with the supports than it would be in their absence. Thus, today's farmers are not helped by the program. However, since repeal would reduce the current value of their land, the reluctance of farmers to support the repeal of the programs is understandable.

CHAPTER 15

2. If the union is able to raise the wages of the farm workers: (a) The cost of Florida oranges will rise, causing supply to decline and their price to rise in the long run; (b) profits of the Florida orange growers will decline in the short run, but in the long run they will return to the normal rate; (c) mechanization will be encouraged; and (d) the employment of fruit pickers will decline—particularly in the long run.

3. The higher wages in the South would increase the costs of the southern firms and thereby make them less competitive with their northern rivals.

7. If only part of an industry is unionized, the costs of nonunion firms in the industry will be lower than the costs of unionized firms, if the unionized firms have higher wage rates. If the union wages are much higher than nonunion wages, then the unionized firms will be unable to compete successfully.

9. False. Investors do not have to supply capital to an industry. If the expected profit rate of a highly unionized industry is low, then investment funds will flow elsewhere. An *unanticipated* increase in union wages might reduce profitability in the short run, but it will not be able to do so in the long run. The primary effects of the higher wages will be higher prices. Consumers, rather than investors, will bear the primary cost of high union wages.

10. False. Competition constrains both employers and employees. Employers must compete with *other employers* for labor services. In order to gain the labor services of an employee, an employer must offer a compensation package superior to what the employee can get elsewhere. If the employer does not offer a superior package, then the employee will work for a rival employer or choose self-employment.

Similarly, employees must compete with *other employees*. Therefore, their ability to demand whatever wage they would like is also restrained. Thus, competition prevents both the payment of low (below market) wages by employers and the imposition of high (above market) wages by employees.

12. Remember, union members compete with *other workers,* including less skilled workers. An increase in the minimum wage makes unskilled, low-wage workers more expensive. A higher minimum wage increases the demand for high-skill employers who are good substitutes for the low-skill workers. Union members are over-represented among the high-skill group helped by an increase in the minimum wage. Therefore, while union leaders will generally pitch their support for a higher minimum wage in terms of a desire that all workers be paid a "decent wage," the impact of the legislation on union members indicates that self-interest rather than altruism underlies their support for the legislation.

13. The union and the manufacturer would be most likely to favor the tariff because it would make foreign-produced automobiles more expensive and thereby increase the demand for American-made automobiles and the labor with which they are made. In contrast, the higher gasoline tax makes driving more expensive. In response, the demand for higher-gasoline-consumption automobiles will fall, which will adversely affect both American automobile manufacturers and workers.

15. Not necessarily. Adjustment must be made for differences in (a) the productivity characteristics of the union and nonunion workers and (b) the types of jobs they occupy (for example, work environment, job security, likelihood of layoff, and so on). Adjustment for these factors may either increase or reduce the $1.50 differential.

CHAPTER 16

2. Differences in family size, age of potential workers, nonmoney "income," taxes, and cost-of-living among areas reduce the effectiveness of annual money income as a measure of economic status. In general, high-income families are larger, more likely to be headed by a prime-age worker, have less nonmoney income (including leisure), pay more taxes, and reside in higher cost-of-living areas (particularly large cities). Thus, money income comparison between high- and low-income groups often overstates the economic status of the former relative to the latter.

4. If there were no intergenerational mobility, the diagonal numbers would all be 100 percent. If there were complete equality of opportunity, the numbers in each column and row would be 20 percent.

6. No. The increase in marginal tax rates will reduce the incentive of the poor to *earn* income. Therefore, their income will rise by $1,000 minus the reduction in their personal earnings due to the disincentive effects of the higher marginal tax rates.

7. 67 percent.

10. Here, as in other areas, it is important to remember that government is merely an alternative form of social organization, rather than a corrective device. The structure of income transfers reflects political clout. The elderly, farmers, and business and labor interests are easily identifiable, politically potent interest groups. In contrast, the poor have a low voter participation rate and offer little in the way of financial support to politicians. Given these factors, it is not surprising that most income transfers go to the nonpoor.

14. Adjustment of individuals to redistributive programs often leads to unintended side effects. If a higher income from private saving means a lower level of social security benefits, people will save less for retirement. Other things constant, the number of low-income (and therefore high-benefit) elderly will grow. Stated another way, programs that subsidize low-income status (and penalize high-income status) during retirement will expand the number of people in the former category and reduce the number in the latter category with the passage of time.

15. Under a pay-as-you-go system, social security benefits do not constitute societal wealth because the benefits imply a liability of equal size. However, *individuals* may treat the expected future benefits as wealth and reduce their saving accordingly. If they do, a society with a pay-as-you-go social security system will have a lower rate of saving and capital formation than a society without such a program.

CHAPTER 17

1. Crude oil, for example, is a gift of nature in the sense that it was put in place without the help of human beings. But as a resource, it is not simply a gift of nature, because human ingenuity and effort are required to make the naturally occuring substance valuable.

3. The "requirement" of water for the steel industry depends on the value placed on water, as well as on the value placed on steel. The same amount of steel can be produced with vastly differing amounts of water, as illustrated in Exhibit 1 of this chapter. Also, steel itself is not indispensible in all its uses, including national defense uses. There are many substitutes, not only for water in the making of steel, but also for steel in the making of tanks, and for tanks in providing national defense. So a given amount of water for steel is not really a requirement.

5. Remember, the marginal principle. There are a limited number of rich people, and they have a limited amount of time to spend on recreation. It is unlikely that the rich will be willing or able to "buy up all the recreation opportunities.'' Remember also that if the price of the best fly fishing access, for example, rises because rich people like it, then more such areas will be provided by profit-seeking entrepreneurs who can improve existing streams and create additional habitat, when it is profitable to do so.

6. Wells are abandoned by producers when the cost of extracting and delivering additional oil exceeds its value. When the value of crude oil rises, additional oil can be produced since water flooding, steam and chemical measures—all of which are costly—can be paid for by the higher prices gained from the extra oil.

7. Total reserves of a mineral include all the resources that are in place, and which might become available in the future, given sufficiently high prices or technological advances. Proved reserves are the resources which producers believe they can produce with current technology, at today's prices. Proved reserves are what count in the short-term, but if we are concerned with the long-run prospect of much greater scarcity, with higher prices and incentives for technological advances in mineral exploration and production, then total reserves might also become important.

9. The use of an unowned, unpriced resource might have a high opportunity cost. Yet if there is no owner to protect it, or to allocate it to its highest-valued use, then it might indeed be treated as if it had no opportunity cost. If it is valuable, however, then it might pay an entrepreneur to find a way to establish ownership. That, in fact, is the history of many natural resources in the United States. Ownership of land, for example, was often not established until it became economically attractive enough to reward the initial claimants who established ownership.

12. A lower interest rate would increase the present value of benefits, which occur farther in the future, relative to a high interest rate. (See our earlier chapter on Capital, Interest, and Profits, if this is confusing to you.) Since the project's costs occur sooner, the interest rate chosen has less impact on the present value of costs than on the present value of benefits. As a result, a lower interest rate would make this project look more attractive. A person trying to get the project approved by Congress would want a low interest rate used in the benefit-cost analysis.

14. The rises in oil prices in the early 1970s and again in 1979–1981 were very large relative to oil company profits, even when those profits were at their highest. Other factors caused the price increases, including rising world oil demand, military crises, and changing policies in both oil producing and oil consuming countries.

CHAPTER 18

1. The commons could have been managed politically, without any private ownership. The open access prob-

lem is the absence of *both* private property and of political control of access to the resource.

4. By definition, a public good cannot be marketed, because free riders (nonpayers) can consume it. There is little incentive for the consumer to state his or her true preference, even if asked. So a producer, including government, has a difficult time knowing how much an extra unit of the public good is worth.

6. We expect that private ownership, which concentrates both the costs and the benefits of stewardship on the owner(s), will result in better care than will joint ownership, at least if the joint owners are many. In the latter case, the benefits are spread among the joint owners, while the costs of care fall on the person doing the care—unless, of course, the group arranges to assign and enforce duties, or to jointly pay for care.

7. Permitting all firms to use air and water resources for ''free garbage removal'' services would reduce the producer's costs of supplying pollution-intensive goods. However, as long as free entry is present, the lower cost would lead to lower prices not higher profits. Except for unanticipated changes in pollution control policy, competition will drive the profit rate of all firms, including those in industries that pollute, toward the normal rate of return.

9. Many goods with public-good aspects are provided privately. Free museum admission, free concerts, wildlife preservation, and so on defy the free-rider problem. But the public good problem is still with us, and we cannot know whether the right amounts are produced when goods have public goods aspect.

10. An inability to exclude nonpaying consumers. Since consumers cannot be prevented (at least not at a low cost) from consuming a public good if they fail to pay, each has an incentive to ''free ride,'' which undermines the private supplier's ability to cover the cost of production.

11. Economics doesn't say what is fair, but corporations—like all firms—want to minimize their costs in order to maximize profits. If they can reduce costs by emitting more pollution into the air and by avoiding costly abatement measures, then they are likely to do so. And those who do will gain a competitive advantage over those who do not, so long as the legal system does not hold polluters responsible for downwind damages. Without effective court procedures or bureaucratic action on behalf of those harmed by the pollution it would be folly to expect even public-spirited corporate executives to sacrifice profits to gain a public good—air quality, if their competitors were allowed to pollute.

12. Knowing that the firm's national reputation is at stake at every franchise, travelers would probably find the nationally advertised restaurant more appealing. Also, if they had seen the advertising, they would have a better idea of what sort of food is available. Their relative lack of knowledge about the unadvertised place probably deters their using it. In contrast, the local people would know more than the travelers about the local restaurant, as the result of personal experience or by talking with friends who had tried it.

CHAPTER 19

1. It is difficult for the voter to know what a candidate will do once elected, and the rationally ignorant voter is usually not willing to spend the time and effort required to understand issues, since his or her vote will not be the decisive one anyway. Special interest voters, on the other hand, will know which candidate has promised them the most on their issue. Also, the candidate who is both competent and prepared to ignore special interests will have a hard time getting these facts to voters without financial support from special interest groups. Each voter has an incentive to be a "free rider" on the "good government" issue. Controlling government on behalf of society as a whole is a public good, requiring much private activity. Like other public goods, it tends to be underproduced.

2. Corporate officers, while they surely care about the next few months and the profits during that time, care also about the value of the firm and its stock price. If the stock price rises sufficiently in the next few months—as it will if investors believe that current investments in future-oriented projects (planting new trees, for example) are sound—then the officers will find their jobs secure even if current profits do not look good. Rights to the profits from those (future) trees are saleable now in the form of the corporation's stock. There is no such mechanism to make the distant fruits of today's investments available to the political entrepreneurs who might otherwise fight for the future-oriented project. Only if the project appeals to today's voters, and they are willing to pay today for tomorrow's benefits, will the program be a political success. In any case, the wealth of the political entrepreneur is not directly enhanced by his or her successful fight for the project.

7. No. The government is merely an alternative form of organization. Government organization does not permit us to escape either scarcity or competition. It merely affects the nature of the competition. Political competition (voting, lobbying, political contributions, taxes, and politically determined budgets) replaces market competition. Neither is there any reason to believe that government organization modifies the importance of personal self-interest.

8. The regulatory and taxation policy toward the liquor industry is usually conducted at the state, rather than at the federal level. Thus, liquor industry interests will be more likely to use lobbying and campaign contributions to influence the action of state-level politicians.

10. When the welfare of a special interest group conflicts with that of a widely dispersed, unorganized majority, the legislative political process can reasonably be expected to work to the benefit of the special interest.

CHAPTER 20

1. Availability of goods and services, not jobs, is the source of economic prosperity. When a good can be purchased cheaper abroad than it can be produced at home, a nation can expand the quantity of goods and services available for consumption by specializing in the production of those goods for which it is a low-cost producer and trading them for the cheap (relative to domestic costs) foreign goods. Trade restrictions limiting the ability of Americans to purchase low-cost goods from foreigners stifles this process and thereby *reduces* the living standard of Americans.

3. Answers **a.** and **b.** are not in conflict. Since trade restrictions are typically a special interest issue, political entrepreneurs can often gain by supporting them even when they promote economic inefficiency.

5. True. The primary effect of trade restrictions is an increase in domestic scarcity. This has distributional consequences, but it is clear that as a whole, a nation will be harmed by the increased domestic scarcity accompanying the trade restraints.

6. The quota reduces the supply of sugar to the domestic market and drives up the domestic price of sugar. Domestic producers benefit from the higher prices at the expense of domestic consumers (See Exhibit 11). Studies indicate that the quota expanded the gross income of the 11,000 domestic sugar farmers by approximately $130,000 per farm in the mid-1980s, at an expense (in the form of higher prices of sugar and sugar products) of approximately $6 per year to the average domestic consumer. Since the program channels resources away from products for which the U.S. has a comparative advantage, it reduces the productive capacity of the United States. Both the special interest nature of the issue and rent-seeking theory explain the political attractiveness of the program.

8. a. No. Americans would be poorer if we used more of our resources to produce things for which we are a high opportunity-cost producer and less of our resources to produce things for which we are a low opportunity-cost producer. Employment might either increase or decrease, but the key point is that it is the value of goods produced, not employment, which generates income and provides for the wealth of a nation. The answer to **b.** is the same as **a.**

9. In thinking about this issue, consider the following points. Suppose the Japanese were willing to give products such as automobiles, electronic goods, and clothing to us free of charge. Would we be worse off if we accepted the gifts? Should we try to keep the free goods out? What is the source of real income—jobs or goods and services? If the gifts make us better off, doesn't it follow that partial gifts would also make us better off?

12. While trade reduces employment in import-competing industries, it expands employment in export industries. On balance, there is no reason to believe that trade either promotes or destroys jobs. The major affect of trade is to permit individuals, states, regions, and nations to generate a larger output by specializing in the things they do well and trading for those things that they would produce only at a high cost. A higher real income is the result.

15. True. If country A imposes a tariff, other countries will sell less to A and therefore acquire less purchasing power in terms of A's currency. Thus, they will have to reduce their purchases of A's export goods.

16. Yes. The price equalization theorem indicates that goods will tend to sell for similar prices in all markets except for differences due to taxes and transport costs. Therefore, except in cases where there is a high tariff (or some other U.S. tax) on a good, it is unlikely that the good will be much cheaper abroad than it is in the United States.

CHAPTER 21

4. Answers **a.** and **g.** would cause the dollar to appreciate; **b.**, **c.**, **d.**, **e.**, and **h.** would cause the dollar to depreciate, **f.** would leave the exchange rate unchanged.

5. On February 2, the dollar appreciated against the pound and depreciated against the franc.

9. Each of the changes would reduce the size of the current account deficit.

11. The current account balance will move toward a larger deficit (or smaller surplus) and the dollar will appreciate.

13. The depreciation will make the dollar price of BMWs more expensive which will reduce the *quantity purchased* by Americans. If the American demand for BMWs is inelastic (elastic), then the dollar expenditures on BMWs will rise (fall).

16. False. Flexible exchange rates bring the *sum* of the current and capital accounts into balance, but they do not necessarily lead to balance in either component.

CHAPTER 22

2. Many economists believe that this view is essentially true. However, there are reasons for doubt. Foreign aid has not played a significant role in the progress of most of the high growth, less developed countries. Often, financial aid disrupts markets and retards the incentive of producers in less developed countries. Finally, attractive invest-

ment alternatives will draw investment from abroad even if domestic saving is inadequate. Thus, the efficacy of aid as a tool to promote economic growth is highly questionable.

3. There is considerable diversity among the poor nations. The real GNP of several poor countries has declined during the last two decades (see Exhibit 8). Others have stagnated or experienced only slow growth. Still others have experienced rapid growth. On the encouraging side, the average growth rates of per capita GNP in China and India (the two most populous less developed countries) were 5.1 percent and 1.8 percent during the 1965–1986 period. These rates—particularly the rate for China—compare quite favorably with the growth rates of industrial developed economies. If these two giants are able to follow the path of Japan, and more recently Hong Kong, South Korea, Singapore, and Indonesia, perhaps two-thirds of the world's population will have incomes well above subsistence levels early in the next century.

4. The evidence indicates that as nations become wealthier their saving rate increases only slightly, if at all, while the length of the work week declines. The U.S. experience is consistent with this general pattern. The length of the average work week in the United States has steadily declined for at least 100 years, while the saving/GNP rate has changed little.

8. In order to make income comparisons among countries, we must estimate the purchasing power of each nation's currency in terms of a common currency (such as the U.S. dollar). The exchange rate value of a nation's currency may be a misleading indicator of its domestic purchasing power over a broad range of goods typically purchased by households. Only a small portion of the typical bundle of goods consumed by households is traded in international markets. In addition, exchange rates are influenced by factors such as interest rate differentials and capital movements among countries. Thus, the relative exchange rate value of a nation's currency may fail to accurately reflect the currency's purchasing power over a broad bundle of consumer goods. When this is the case, the exchange rate conversion method will yield a misleading estimate of the nation's income in terms of the common currency.

10. Yes. Trade barriers limit the ability of both businesses and consumers to benefit from economies associated with an expansion in the size of the market. This limitation will be more restrictive for small countries than for large countries because the latter will often have sizable domestic markets.

CHAPTER 23

5. The taxes on productive effort in Japan are low compared with taxes in the United States and other Western nations. Similarly, the rates of saving and investment are high in Japan compared with those of other countries. Think about how these factors affect the rate of growth in Japan. Consider also the role played by the ability (and willingness) of the Japanese to import innovative technologies developed elsewhere during the 1950s and 1960s when their technology generally lagged behind other industrial nations. However, this is no longer the case. Since the application of technology to production is now up-to-date in Japan, they can no longer borrow previously developed technologies from more advanced economies. This restraint is likely to slow the growth rate of Japan compared with the growth rate achieved during the 1950s, and 1960s.

7. This view ignores the fact that additional current investment necessitates a reduction in current consumption. Thus, while *future* consumers may gain from a high level of capital formation, *current* consumers clearly must sacrifice consumption, when a large share of resources is allocated to investment.

8. Points to consider in your answer: What kinds of wealth do the two systems produce? Is there more personal security under socialism? If wealth is acquired from production and exchange that does not involve the use of theft, violence, or fraud, is it fair for the wealth to be taken and given to someone else?

10. Under capitalism, mass production and market penetration lead to wealth. But you cannot have large scale production without pricing the product so that it will be affordable to the mass consumer market. Thus, a market system rewards producers who figure out how to make products affordable to lots of consumers rather than just the rich. The careers of Henry Ford and Sir Henry Royce illustrate this point. Ford became a multimillionaire by bringing a low-cost automobile within the budget of mass consumers. In contrast, Royce died a man of modest wealth. He engineered the Rolls Royce, a car far superior to the Ford, but he designed it for the rich. The market rewarded him accordingly.

GLOSSARY

A

Ability-to-Pay Principle: The equity concept that people with larger incomes (or more consumption or more wealth) should be taxed at a higher rate because their ability to pay is presumably greater. The concept is subjective and fails to reveal how much higher the rate of taxation should be as income increases.

Absolute Advantage: A situation in which a nation, as the result of its previous experience and/or natural endowments, can produce a product with fewer resources than another nation.

Accounting Profits: The sales revenues minus the expenses of a firm over a designated time period, usually one year. Accounting profits typically make allowances for changes in the firm's inventories and depreciation of its assets. No allowance is made, however, for the opportunity cost of the equity capital of the firm's owners, or other implicit costs.

Acreage Restriction Program: A program designed to raise the price of an agricultural product by limiting the acreage planted with the product.

Active Budget Deficits: Deficits that reflect planned increases in government spending or reductions in taxes designed to generate a budget deficit.

Activist Strategy: The view that deliberate changes in monetary and fiscal policy can be used to inject demand stimulus during a recession and apply restraint during an inflationary boom and thereby minimize economic instability.

Adaptive Expectations Hypothesis: The hypothesis that economic decision-makers base their future expectations on actual outcomes observed during recent periods. For example, according to this view, the rate of inflation actually experienced during the last two or three years would be the major determinant of the expected rate of inflation for next year.

Administrative Lag: The time period between when the need for a policy change is recognized and when the policy is actually administered.

Aggregate Demand Curve: A downward sloping curve indicating an inverse relationship between the price level and the quantity of goods and services that households, business firms, governments and foreigners (net exports) are willing to purchase during a period.

Aggregate Supply Curve: A curve indicating the relationship between the price level and quantity of goods supplied by producers. In the short run, it is probably an upward sloping curve, but in the long run most economists believe the aggregate supply curve is vertical (or nearly so).

Allocative Efficiency: The allocation of resources to the production of goods and services most desired by consumers. The allocation is ''balanced'' in such a way that reallocation of resources could not benefit anyone without hurting someone else.

Allocative Inefficiency: The use of an uneconomical combination of resources to produce goods and services that are not intensely desired relative to their opportunity cost.

Anticipated Change: A change that is foreseen by decision-makers, in time for them to adjust.

Anticipated Inflation: An increase in the general level of prices that is expected by economic decision-makers. Past experience and current conditions are the major determinants of an individual's expectations with regard to future price changes.

Appreciation: An increase in the value of a domestic currency relative to foreign currencies. An appreciation increases the purchasing power of the domestic currency over foreign goods.

Asymmetric Information Problem: A problem arising when either buyers or sellers have important information about the product that is not possessed by the other side in potential transactions.

Automatic Stabilizers: Built-in features that tend automatically to promote a budget deficit during a recession and a budget surplus during an inflationary boom, even without a change in policy.

Automation: A production technique that reduces the amount of labor required to produce a good or service. It is beneficial to adopt the new labor-saving technology only if it reduces the cost of production.

Autonomous Expenditures: Expenditures that do not vary with the level of income. They are determined by factors (such as business expectations and economic policy) that are outside the basic income-expenditure model.

Average Fixed Costs: Fixed cost divided by the number of units produced. It always declines as output increases.

Average Product: The total product (output) divided by the number of units of the variable input required to produce that output level.

Average Tax Rate: One's tax liability divided by one's taxable income.

Average Total Cost: Total cost divided by the number of units produced. It is sometimes called per unit cost.

Average Variable Cost: The total variable cost divided by the number of units produced.

B

Balance of Merchandise Trade: The difference between the value of merchandise exports and the value of merchandise imports for a nation. The balance of trade is only one component of a nation's total balance of payments.

Balance of Payments: A summary of all economic transactions between a country and all other countries for a specific time period—usually a year. The balance of payments account reflects all payments and liabilities to foreigners (debits) and all payment and obligations (credits) received from foreigners.

Balance on Current Account: The import-export balance of goods and services plus net private and government transfers. If a nation's export of goods and services exceeds (is less than) the nation's import of goods and services plus net unilateral transfers to foreigners, a current account surplus (deficit) is present.

Balanced Budget: A situation in which current government revenue from taxes, fees, and other sources is just equal to current expenditures.

Barriers to Entry: Obstacles that limit the freedom of potential rivals to enter an industry.

Benefit-cost Analysis (B-C): A process used to determine the efficiency of a project by estimating each benefit and each cost. A project is said to be efficient if it generates more benefits than costs.

Break-Even Point: Under a negative income tax plan, the income level at which one neither pays taxes nor receives supplementary income transfers.

Budget Constraint: The constraint that separates the bundles of goods that the consumer can purchase from those that cannot be purchased, given a limited income and the prices of products.

Budget Deficit: A situation in which total government spending exceeds total government revenue during a specific time period, usually one year.

Budget Surplus: A situation in which total government spending is less than total government revenue during a time period, usually a year.

Business Cycle: Fluctuations in the general level of economic activity as measured by such variables as the rate of unemployment and changes in real GNP.

C

Capital Formation: The production of buildings, machinery, tools, and other equipment that will enhance the ability of future economic participants to produce. The term can also be applied to efforts to upgrade the knowledge and skill of workers and thereby increase their ability to produce in the future.

Capitalism: An economic system based on private ownership of productive resources and allocation of goods according to the signals provided by free markets.

Cartel: An organization of sellers designed to coordinate supply decisions so that the joint profits of the members will be maximized. A cartel will seek to create a monopoly in the market.

Choice: The act of selecting among alternatives.

Classical Economists: Economists from Adam Smith to the time of Keynes who focused their analyses on economic efficiency and production. With regard to business instability, they thought market prices would adjust quickly in a manner that would guide an economy out of a recession back to full employment.

Collective Bargaining Contract: A detailed contract between (a) a group of employees (a labor union) and (b) an employer. It covers wage rates and conditions of employment.

Collective Decision-making: The method of organization that relies on public-sector decision-making (voting, political bargaining, lobbying, and so on). It can be used to resolve the basic economic problems of an economy.

Collusion: Agreement among firms to avoid various competitive practices, particularly price reductions. It may involve either formal agreements or merely tacit recognition that competitive practices will be self-defeating in the long run. Tacit collusion is difficult to detect. The Sherman Act prohibits collusion and conspiracies to restrain interstate trade.

Command Economy: An authoritarian socialist economy characterized by centralized planning and detailed directives to productive units. Individual enterprises have little discretionary decision-making power.

Commercial Banks: Financial institutions that offer a wide range of services (for example, checking accounts, savings accounts, and extension of loans) to their customers. Commercial banks are owned by stockholders and seek to operate at a profit.

Common Property Resource: A resource for which rights are held in common by a group of individuals, none of whom has a transferable ownership interest. Access to the resource may be open (unrestricted), or may be controlled politically.

Competition as a Dynamic Process: A term that denotes rivalry or competitiveness between or among parties (for example, producers or input suppliers), each of which seeks to deliver a better deal to buyers when quality, price, and product information are all considered. Competing implies a lack of collision among sellers.

Complements: Products that are usually consumed jointly (for example, lamps and light bulbs). An increase in the price of one will cause the demand for the other to fall.

Concentration Ratio: The total sales of the four (or sometimes eight) largest firms in an industry as a percentage of the total sales of the industry. The higher the ratio, the greater is the market dominance of a small number of firms. The ratio can be seen as a measure of oligopolistic power.

Conglomerate Merger: The combining under one ownership of two or more firms that produce *unrelated products*.

Constant Cost Industry: An industry for which factor prices and costs of production remain constant as market output is expanded. Thus, the long-run market supply curve is horizontal.

Constant Returns to Scale: Unit costs are constant as the scale of the firm is altered. Neither economies nor diseconomies of scale are present.

Consumer Price Index: An indicator of the general level of prices. It attempts to compare the cost of purchasing the market basket bought by a typical consumer during a specific period with the cost of purchasing the same market basket during an earlier period.

Consumer Surplus: The difference between the maximum amount a consumer would be willing to pay for a unit of a good and the payment that is actually made.

Consumption: Household spending on consumer goods and services during the current period. Consumption is a flow concept.

Consumption Function: A fundamental relationship between disposable income and consumption. As disposable income increases, current consumption expenditures will rise, but by a smaller amount than the increase in income.

Consumption Opportunity Constraint: The constraint that separates the consumption bundles that are attainable from those that are unattainable. In a money income economy, it is usually called a budget constraint.

Countercyclical Policy: A policy that tends to move the economy in an opposite direction from the forces of the business cycle. Such a policy would stimulate demand during the contraction phase of the business cycle and restrain demand during the expansionary phase.

Credit Unions: Financial cooperative organizations of individuals with a common affiliation (such as an employer or labor union). They accept deposits, including checkable deposits, pay interest (or dividends) on them out of earnings, and channel funds primarily into loans to members.

Crowding-Out Effects: A reduction in private spending as a result of high interest rates generated by budget deficits that are financed by borrowing in the private loanable funds market.

Current Account: The record of all transactions with foreign nations that involve the exchange of merchandise goods and services or unilateral gifts.

Cyclical Unemployment: Unemployment due to recessionary business conditions and inadequate aggregate demand for labor.

D

Dead-End Jobs: Jobs that offer the employee little opportunity for advancement or on-the-job training.

Deadweight Loss: A net loss associated with the forgoing of an economic action. The loss does not lead to an offsetting gain for other participants. It thus reflects economic inefficiency.

Decreasing Cost Industries: Industries for which costs of production decline as the industry expands. The market supply is therefore inversely related to price. Such industries are atypical.

Deflationary Gap: The situation present when the short-run equilibrium output is less than full employment potential. Weak demand conditions place downward pressure on prices.

Demand Deposits: Noninterest-earning deposits in a bank that either can be withdrawn or made payable on demand to a third party via check. In essence, they are ''checkbook money'' because they permit transactions to be paid for by check rather than by currency.

Demand for Money: At any given interest rate, the amount of wealth that people desire to hold in the form of money balances; that is, cash and checking account deposits. The quantity demanded is inversely related to the interest rate.

Dependency Ratio: The number of children (under a specific age—14, for example) and the number of the elderly (age 65 and over) living in a country, divided by the total population. An increasing ratio indicates that a larger burden is being placed on the productive-age work force.

Deposit Expansion Multiplier: The multiple by which an increase (decrease) in reserves will increase (decrease) the money supply. It is inversely related to the required reserve ratio.

Depreciation: A reduction in the value of a domestic currency relative to foreign currencies. A depreciation reduces the purchasing power of the domestic currency over foreign goods.

Depression: A prolonged and very severe recession.

Derived Demand: Demand for an item based on the demand for products the item helps to produce. The demand for resources is a derived demand.

Devaluation: An official act that changes the level of the ''fixed'' exchange rate in a downward direction. In essence, it is a one-step depreciation of a currency under a fixed exchange rate system.

Differentiated Products: Products distinguished from similar products by such characteristics as quality, design, location, and method of promotion.

Discount Rate: The interest rate the Federal Reserve charges banking institutions for borrowing funds.

Discounting: The procedure used to calculate the present value of future income. The present value of future income is inversely related to both the interest rate and the amount of time that passes before the funds are received.

Discouraged Workers: Persons who have given up searching for employment because they believe additional job search would be fruitless. Since they are not currently searching for work, they are not counted among the unemployed.

Discretionary Fiscal Policy: A change in laws or appropriation levels that alters government revenues and/or expenditures.

Discretionary Monetary Policy: Changes in monetary policy instituted at the discretion of policy-makers. The policy is not predetermined by rules or formulas.

Disposable Income: The income available to individuals after personal taxes. It can either be spent on consumption or saved.

Division of Labor: A method that breaks down the production of a commodity into a series of specific tasks, each performed by a different worker.

Dumping: The sale of a good by a foreign supplier in another country at a price lower than the supplier sells it in its home market.

E

Economic Efficiency: Economizing behavior. When applied to a community, it implies that (a) an activity should be undertaken if the sum of the benefits to the individuals exceeds the sum of their costs and (b) no activity should be undertaken if the costs borne by the individuals exceed the benefits.

Economic Good: A good that is scarce. The desire for economic goods exceeds the amount that is freely available from Nature.

Economic Profit: A return to investors that exceeds the opportunity cost of financial capital.

Economic Regulation: Regulation of product price or industrial structure, usually imposed on a specific industry. By and large, the production processes used by the regulated firms are unaffected by this type of regulation.

Economic Theory: A set of definitions, postulates, and principles assembled in a manner that makes clear the "cause-and-effect" relationships of economic data.

Economies of Scale: Reductions in the firm's per unit costs that are associated with the use of large plants to produce a large volume of output.

Economizing Behavior: Choosing the objective of gaining a specific benefit at the least possible cost. A corollary of economizing behavior implies that when choosing among items of equal cost, individuals will choose the option that yields the greatest benefit.

Elasticity of Supply: The percentage change in quantity supplied, divided by the percentage change in the price that causes that change in quantity supplied.

Employment Discrimination: Unequal treatment of persons on the basis of their race, sex, or religion, which restricts their employment and earnings opportunities compared with others of similar productivity.

Employment discrimination may stem from the prejudices of employers, consumers and/or fellow employees.

Entrepreneur: A profit-seeking decision-maker who decides which projects to undertake and how they should be undertaken. A successful entrepreneur's actions will increase the value of resources.

Equation of Exchange: $MV = PQ$, where M is the money supply, V is the velocity of money, P is the price level, and Q is the quantity of goods and services produced.

Equilibrium: A balance of forces permitting the simultaneous fulfillment of plans for buyers and sellers.

Escalator Clause: A contractual agreement that periodically and automatically adjusts the wage rates of a collective-bargaining agreement upward by an amount determined by the rate of inflation.

Eurodollar Deposits: Deposits denominated in U.S. dollars at banks and other financial institutions outside the United States. Although this name originated because of the large amounts of such deposits held at banks in Western Europe, similar deposits in other parts of the world are also called Eurodollars.

Excess Burden of Taxation: A burden of taxation over and above the burden associated with the transfer of revenues to the government. An excess burden usually reflects losses that occur when beneficial activities are forgone because they are taxed.

Excess Reserves: Actual reserves that exceed the legal requirement.

Excess Supply of Money: Situation in which the actual

money balances of individuals and business firms are in excess of their desired level. Thus, decision-makers will increase their spending on other assets and goods until they reduce their actual balances to the desired level.

Exchange Rate: The domestic piece of one unit of foreign currency. For example, if it takes $1.50 to purchase one English pound, the dollar-pound exchange rate is 1.50.

Exchange Rate Conversion Method: Method that uses the foreign exchange rate value of a nation's currency to convert that nation's GNP to another monetary unit, such as the U.S. dollar.

Exclusive Contract: An agreement between manufacturer and retailer that prohibits the retailer from carrying the product lines of firms that are rivals of the manufacturer. Such contracts are illegal under the Clayton Act when they "lessen competition."

Existence Value: The satisfaction people can derive simply from knowing that something—the Grand Canyon or Hoover Dam, for example—exists. It is extremely difficult to measure existence values.

Expansionary Fiscal Policy: An increase in government expenditures and/or a reduction in tax rates such that the expected size of the budget deficit expands.

Expansionary Monetary Policy: An acceleration in the growth rate of the money supply.

Explicit Costs: Money paid by a firm to purchase the services of productive resources.

Exports: Goods and services produced domestically but sold to foreigners.

Extensive Economic Growth: An expansion in the total output of goods and services, regardless of whether or not output per capita increases.

External Benefits: Beneficial effects of group or individual action on the welfare of nonpaying secondary parties.

External Costs: Harmful effects of an individual's or a group's action on the welfare of nonconsenting secondary parties, not accounted for in market prices. Litterbugs, drunk drivers, and polluters, for example, create external costs.

External Debt: That portion of the national debt owed to foreign investors.

Externalities: The side effects of an action that influence the well-being of nonconsenting parties. The nonconsenting parties may be either helped (by external benefits) or harmed (by external costs).

F

Fallacy of Composition: Erroneous view that what is true for the individual (or the part) will also be true for the group (or the whole).

Federal Funds Market: A loanable funds market in which banks seeking additional reserves borrow short-term (generally for seven days or less) funds from banks with excess reserves. The interest rate in this market is called the federal funds rate.

Federal Reserve System: The central bank of the United States; it carries out banking regulatory policies and is responsible for the conduct of monetary policy.

Fiat Money: Money that has little intrinsic value; it is neither backed by nor convertible to a commodity of value.

Final Goods and Services: Goods and services purchased by their ultimate users.

Fiscal Policy: The use of government taxation and expenditure policies for the purpose of achieving macroeconomic goals.

Fixed Costs: Cost that does not vary with output. However, fixed cost will be incurred as long as a firm continues in business and the assets have alternative uses.

Fixed Exchange Rate System: An international monetary system in which each country's currency is set at a fixed rate relative to all other currencies and governmental policies are used to maintain the fixed rate.

Flexible Exchange Rates: Exchange rates that are determined by the market forces of supply and demand. They are sometimes called "floating exchange rates."

Foreign Exchange Market: The market in which the currencies of different countries are bought and sold.

Fractional Reserve Banking: A system that enables banks to keep less than 100 percent reserves against their deposits. Required reserves are a fraction of deposits.

Free Rider: One who receives the benefit of a good without contributing to its costs. Public goods and commodities that generate external benefits offer people the opportunity to become free riders.

Frictional Unemployment: Unemployment due to constant changes in the economy that prevent *qualified* unemployed workers from being immediately matched up with existing job openings. It results from lack of complete information on the part of both job seekers and employers and from the amount of unemployed time spent by job seekers in job searches (pursuit of costly information).

Fringe Benefits: Benefits other than normal money wages that are supplied to employees in exchange for their labor services.

Full Employment: The level of employment that results from the efficient use of the civilian labor force after allowance is made for the normal (natural) rate of unemployment due to dynamic changes and the structural conditions of the economy. For the United States, full employment is thought to exist when between 94 and 95 percent of the labor force is employed.

G

General Agreement on Tariffs and Trade (GATT): An organization composed of most non-Communist countries designed to set the rules for the conduct of international trade and reduce barriers to trade among nations.

GNP Deflator: A price index that reveals the cost of purchasing the items included in GNP during the period relative to the cost of purchasing these same items during a base year (currently, 1982). Since the base year is assigned a value of 100, as the GNP deflator takes on values greater than 100, it indicates that prices have risen.

Going Out of Business: The sale of a firm's assets, and its permanent exit from the market. By going out of business, a firm is able to avoid fixed cost, which would continue during a shutdown.

Goods and Services Market: A highly aggregate market encompassing all final user goods and services during a period. The market counts all items that enter into GNP. Thus, real output in this market is equal to real GNP.

Gosplan: The central planning agency in the Soviet Union.

Government Failure: Failure of government action to meet the criteria of ideal economic efficiency.

Government Purchases: Current expenditures on goods and services provided by federal, state, and local government; They exclude transfer payments.

Gross National Product: The total market value of all "final product" goods and services produced during a specific period, usually a year.

H

Head Tax: A lump-sum tax levied on all individuals, regardless of their income, consumption, wealth, or other indicators of economic well-being.

Herfindahl Index: A measure of industry concentration, calculated by squaring the percentage share of each firm in the industry, then summing the squares. The index can range from zero to 10,000. It is a more sophisticated measure of concentration than the traditional concentration ratio, and is used by the Justice Department in antitrust policy.

Homogeneous Product: A product of one firm that is identical to the product of every other firm in the industry. Consumers see no difference in units of the product offered by alternative sellers.

Horizontal Merger: The combining of the assets of two or more firms engaged in the production of *similar products into a single firm.*

Human Resources: The abilities, skills, and health of human beings that can contribute to the production of both current and future output. Investment in training and education can increase the supply of human resources.

I

Impact Lag: The time period between when a policy change is implemented and when the change begins to exert its primary effects.

Implicit Costs: The opportunity costs associated with a firm's use of resources that it owns. These costs do *not* involve a direct money payment. Examples include wage income and interest forgone by the owner of a firm who also provides labor services and equity capital to the firm.

Import Quota: A specific quantity (or value) of a good permitted to be imported into a country during a given year.

Imports: Goods and services produced by foreigners but purchased by domestic consumers, investors, and governments.

Income Effect: That part of an increase (decrease) in amount consumed that is the result of the consumer's real income (the consumption possibilities available to the consumer) being expanded (contracted) by a reduction (increase) in the price of a good.

Income Elasticity: The percent change in the quantity of a product demanded divided by the percent change in consumer income. It measures the responsiveness of the demand for a good to a change in income.

Income Mobility: Movement of individuals and families either up or down income distribution rankings when comparisons are made at two different points in time. When substantial income mobility is present, one's current position will not be a very good indicator as to what one's position will be a few years in the future.

Increasing Cost Industries: Industries for which costs of production rise as the industry output is expanded. Thus, the long-run market supply is directly related to price.

Index of Leading Indicators: An index of economic variables that historically has tended to turn down prior to the beginning of a recession and turn up prior to the beginning of a business expansion.

Indexing: The automatic increasing of money values as the general level of prices increases. Economic variables that are often indexed include wage rates and tax brackets.

Indifference Curve: A curve, convex from below, that separates the consumption bundles that are more preferred by an individual from those that are less preferred. The points *on* the curve represent combinations of goods that are equally preferred by the individual.

Industrial Capacity Utilization Rate: An index designed to measure the extent to which the economy's existing plant and equipment capacity is being used.

Inferior Goods: Goods for which the income elasticity is negative. Thus, an increase in consumer income causes the demand for such a good to decline.

Inflation: A continuing rise in the general level of prices of goods and services. The purchasing power of the monetary unit, such as the dollar, declines when inflation is present.

Inflationary Gap: The situation present when the short-run equilibrium output exceeds full employment potential GNP. The strong demand places upward pressure on prices.

Inflationary Premium: A component of the money interest rate that reflects compensation to the lender for the expected decrease, due to inflation, in the purchasing power of the principal and interest during the course of the loan. It is equal to the expected rate of future inflation.

Infrastructure: The provision of a legal, monetary, educational, transportation, and communication structure necessary for the efficient operation of an exchange economy.

Innovation: The successful introduction and adoption of a new product or process; the economic application of inventions.

Intensive Economic Growth: An increase in output per person. When intensive economic growth is present, output is growing more rapidly than population.

Intermediate Goods: Goods purchased for resale or for use in producing another good or service.

International Monetary Fund: An international banking organization, with more than 100 nation members, designed to oversee the operation of the international monetary system. Although it does not control the world supply of money, it does hold currency reserves for member nations and make currency loans to national central banks.

Invention: The discovery of a new product or process, often facilitated by the knowledge of engineering and scientific relationships.

Inventory Investment: Changes in the stock of unsold goods and raw materials held during a period.

Investment: The flow of expenditures on durable assets (fixed investment) plus the addition to inventories (inventory investment) during a period. These expenditures enhance our ability to provide consumer benefits in the future.

Investment in Human Capital: Expenditures on training, education, and skill development designed to increase the productivity of an individual.

Invisible Hand Principle: The tendency of market prices to direct individuals pursuing their own interests into productive activities that also promote the economic well being of the society.

Irreversibility: Once an action is taken, some physical effects may not be reversible—the prior physical conditions cannot be restored. Such a situation involves an irreversibility.

J

J-Curve Effect: The tendency of a nation's current account deficit to widen initially before it shrinks in response to an exchange rate depreciation. This tendency results because the short-run demand for both imports and exports is often inelastic, even though the long-run demand is almost always elastic.

K

Kinked Demand Curve: A demand curve that is highly elastic for a price *increase* but inelastic for a price *reduction*. These differing elasticities are based on the assumption that rival firms will match a price reduction but not a price increase.

L

Labor Force: The portion of the population 16 years of age and over who are either employed or unemployed.

Labor Union: A collective organization of employees who bargain as a unit with employers.

Laffer Curve: A curve illustrating the relationship between tax rates and tax revenues. The curve reflects the fact that tax revenues are low for both very high and very low tax rates.

Law of Comparative Advantage: A principle that states that individuals, firms, regions, or nations can gain by specializing in the production of goods that they produce cheaply (that is, at a low opportunity cost) and exchanging those goods for other desired goods for which they are high opportunity cost producers.

Law of Demand: A principle that states that there is an inverse relationship between the price of a good and the amount of it buyers are willing to purchase.

Law of Diminishing Marginal Utility: A basic economic principle that states that as the consumption of a commodity increases, the marginal utility derived from consuming more of the commodity (per unit of time) will eventually decline. Marginal utility may decline even though total utility continues to increase, albeit at a reduced rate.

Law of Diminishing Returns: The postulate that as more and more units of a variable resource are combined with a fixed amount of other resources, employment of *additional* units of the variable resource will eventually increase output only at a decreasing rate. Once diminishing returns are reached, it will take successively larger amounts of the variable factor to expand output by one unit.

Law of Supply: A principle that states that there will be a direct relationship between the price of a good and the amount of it offered for sale.

Less Developed Countries: Low income countries characterized by rapid population growth, an agriculture-household sector that dominates the economy, illiteracy, extreme poverty, and a high degree of inequality.

Lifetime Employment Commitment: An arrangement offered by most large firms in Japan whereby employees are guaranteed employment until age 55 unless guilty of misconduct.

Liquid Asset: An asset that can be easily and quickly converted to purchasing power without loss of value.

Loanable Funds Market: A general term used to describe the market arrangements that coordinate the borrowing and lending decisions of business firms and households. Commercial banks, savings and loan associations, the stock and bond markets, and insurance companies are important financial institutions in this market.

Logrolling: The exchange between politicians of political support on one issue for political support on another issue.

Long Run: A time period of sufficient length to enable decision-makers to adjust fully to a market change. For example, in the long-run, producers will have time to alter their utilization of all productive factors, including the heavy equipment and physical structure of their plants.

Long Run (in Production): A time period long enough to allow the firm to vary all factors of production.

Loss: Deficit of sales revenue relative to the cost of production, once all the resources used have received their opportunity cost. Losses are a penalty imposed on those who use resources in lower rather than higher valued uses, as judged by buyers in the market.

M

Macroeconomics: The branch of economics that focuses on how human behavior affects outcomes in highly aggregated markets, such as the markets for labor or consumer products.

Mandated Benefits: Government mandated fringe benefits that must be included in the total compensation package of employees.

Marginal: Term used to describe the effects of a change, given the current situation. For example, the marginal cost is the cost of producing an additional unit of a product, given the producer's current facility and production rate.

Marginal Cost: The change in total cost required to produce an additional unit of output.

Marginal Factor Cost: The cost of employing an additional unit of a resource. When the employer is small relative to the total market, the marginal factor cost is simply the price of the resource. In contrast, under monopsony, marginal factor cost will exceed the price of the resource, since the monopsonist faces an upward-sloping supply curve for the resource.

Marginal Product: The increase in the total product resulting from a unit increase in the employment of a variable input. Mathematically, it is the ratio of (a) change in total product to the (b) change in the quantity of the variable input.

Marginal Propensity to Consume: Additional current consumption divided by additional current disposable income.

Marginal Rate of Substitution: The change in the consumption level of one good that is just sufficient to offset a unit change in the consumption of another good without causing a shift to another indifference curve. At any point on an indifference curve, it will be equal to the slope of the curve at that point.

Marginal Revenue: The incremental change in total revenue derived from the sale of one additional unit of a product.

Marginal Revenue Product: The change in the total revenue of a firm that results from the employment of one additional unit of a factor of production. The marginal revenue product of an input is equal to its marginal product multiplied by the marginal revenue (price) of the good or service produced.

Marginal Tax Rate: Additional tax liability divided by additional income. Thus, if $100 of additional earnings increases one's tax liability by $30, the marginal tax rate would be 30 percent.

Marginal Utility: The additional utility received by a person from the consumption of an

additional unit of a good within a given time period.

Market: An abstract concept that encompasses the trading arrangements of buyers and sellers that underlie the forces of supply and demand.

Market Failure: The failure of the market system to attain hypothetically *ideal* allocative efficiency. This means that potential gain exists that has not been captured. However, the cost of establishing a mechanism that could *potentially* capture the gain may exceed the benefits. Therefore, it is not always possible to improve the situation.

Market Mechanism: A method of organization that allows unregulated prices and the decentralized decisions of private property owners to resolve the basic economic problems of consumption, production, and distribution.

Market Power: The ability of a firm that is not a pure monopolist to earn unusually large profits, indicating that it has some monopoly power. Because the firm has a few (or weak) competitors, it has a degree of freedom from the discipline of vigorous competition.

Material Balance Method: A method of central planning employed in the Soviet Union and other Eastern European countries whereby the planning agency keeps track of the physical units of resources and allocates them among state enterprises in a manner that will permit each enterprise to achieve its targeted output and thereby lead to the fulfillment of the economy's central plan.

Maximum Emission Standard: The maximum amount of pollution that a polluter is permitted to emit, established by the government or a regulatory authority. Fines are generally imposed on those who are unwilling or unable to comply.

Means-tested Income Transfers: Transfers that are limited to persons or families with an income below a certain cut-off point. Eligibility is thus dependent on low-income status.

Measure of Economic Welfare: A new measure of economic well-being that focuses on the consumption of goods and services during a period. It differs from GNP in that (a) the estimated cost of various economic "bads" are deducted, (b) expenditures on "regrettable necessities" are excluded, and (c) the estimated benefits of leisure and various nonmarket productive activities are included.

Microeconomics: The branch of economics that focuses on how human behavior affects the conduct of affairs within narrowly defined units, such as individual households or business firms.

Middleman: A person who buys and sells, or who arranges trades. A middleman reduces transaction costs, usually for a fee or a markup in price.

Minimum Wage Legislation: Legislation requiring that all workers in specified industries be paid at least the stated minimum hourly rate of pay.

Monetarists: A group of economists who believe that (a) monetary instability is the major cause of fluctuations in real GNP and (b) rapid growth of the money supply is the major cause of inflation.

Monetary Base: The sum of currency in circulation plus bank reserves (vault cash and reserves with the Fed). It reflects the stock of U.S. securities held by the Fed.

Monetary Policy: The deliberate control of the money supply and, in some cases, credit conditions for the purpose of achieving macroeconomic goals.

Money Interest Rate: The interest rate measured in dollars. It overstates the real cost of borrowing during an inflationary period. When inflation is anticipated, an inflationary premium will be incorporated into the nominal value of this rate.

Money Rate of Interest: The rate of interest in monetary terms that borrowers pay for borrowed funds. During periods when borrowers and lenders expect inflation, the money rate of interest exceeds the real rate of interest.

Money Supply: The supply of currency, checking account funds, and traveler's checks. These items are counted as money since they are used as the means of payment for purchases.

Money Supply (M1): The sum of (a) currency in circulation (including coins), (b) demand deposits, (c) other checkable deposits of depository institutions, and (d) traveler's checks.

Money Supply (M2): Equal to M1, plus (a) savings and time deposits (accounts of less than $100,000) of all depository institutions, (b) money market mutual fund shares, (c) money market deposit accounts, (d) overnight loans from customers to commercial banks, and (e) overnight Eurodollar deposits held by U.S. residents.

Money Supply (M3): Equal to M2, plus (a) time deposits

(accounts of more than $100,000) at all depository institutions and (b) longer-term (more than overnight) loans of customers to commercial banks and savings and loan associations.

Monopolistic Competition: A situation in which there are a large number of independent sellers, each producing a differentiated product in a market with low barriers to entry. Construction, retail sales, and service stations are good examples of monopolistically competitive industries.

Monopoly: A market structure characterized by a single seller of a well-defined product for which there are no good substitutes and by high barriers to the entry of any other firms into the market for that product.

Monopsony: A market in which there is only one buyer. The monopsonist confronts the market supply curve for the resource (or product) bought.

Multiplier: The ratio of the change in equilibrium output to the independent change in investment, consumption, or government spending that brings about that change. Numerically, the multiplier is equal to 1/(1-MPC) when the price level is constant.

Multiplier Principle: The concept that an induced increase in consumption, investment, or government expenditures leads to additional income and consumption spending by secondary parties and therefore expands total spending by a larger amount than the initial increase in expenditures.

Mutual Savings Banks: Financial institutions that accept deposits in exchange for interest payments. Historically, home mortgages have constituted their

primary interest-earning assets. Under recent banking legislation, these banks, too, are authorized to offer interest-bearing checkable accounts.

N

National Debt: The sum of the indebtedness of the federal government in the form of outstanding interest-earning bonds. It reflects the cumulative impact of budget deficits and surpluses.

National Income: The total income payments to owners of human (labor) and physical capital during a period. It is also equal to NNP minus indirect businesses taxes.

Natural Monopoly: A market situation in which the average costs of production continually decline with increased output. Therefore, average costs of production will be lowest when a single large firm produces the entire output demanded.

Natural Rate of Unemployment: The long-run average of unemployment due to frictional and structural conditions of labor markets. This rate is affected both by dynamic change and by public policy. It is sustainable in the future.

Negative Income Tax: A system of transferring income to the poor, whereby a minimum level of income would be guaranteed by the provision of income supplements. The supplement would be reduced by some fraction (less than 1) of the additional income earned by the family. An increase in earnings would always cause the disposable income available to the family to rise.

Net Federal Debt: The portion of the national debt owed to

domestic and foreign investors. It does *not* include bonds held by agencies of the federal government or the Federal Reserve.

Net National Product: Gross national product minus a depreciation allowance for the wearing out of machines and buildings during the period.

Net Present Value: The current worth of future income after it is discounted to reflect the fact that revenues in the future are valued less highly than revenues now.

Neutral Tax: A tax that does not (a) distort consumer buying patterns or producer production methods or (b) induce individuals to engage in tax avoidance activities. There will be no excess burden if a tax is neutral.

New Classical Economists: Modern economists who believe there are strong forces pushing a market economy toward full employment equilibrium and that macroeconomic policy is an ineffective tool with which to reduce economic instability.

Nominal GNP: GNP expressed at current prices. It is often called money GNP.

Nominal Values: The value of economic variables such as GNP and personal consumption expressed in current prices. A general increase in prices will cause nominal values to rise even when there is no real change in the variable (quantity produced or consumed).

Nonactivist Strategy: The maintenance of the same monetary and fiscal policy—that is, no change in money growth, tax rates, or expenditures—during all phases of the business cycle.

Nonhuman Resources: The durable, nonhuman inputs that can be used to produce both current and future output. Machines, buildings, land, and raw materials are examples. Investment can increase the supply of nonhuman resources. Economists often use the term "physical capital" when referring to nonhuman resources.

Nonpecuniary Job Characteristics: Working conditions, prestige, variety, location, employee freedom and responsibilities, and other nonwage characteristics of a job that influence how employees evaluate the job.

Nonpersonal Time Deposits: Time deposits owned by businesses or corporations.

Normative Economics: Judgments about "what ought to be" in economic matters. Normative economic views cannot be proved false, because they are based on value judgments.

O

Oligopoly: A market situation in which a small number of sellers comprise the entire industry. It is competition among the few.

Open Access Resource: A resource to which access is unrestricted. No one has the right to exclude others from using the resource. Overuse and abuse of such a resource is typical.

Open Market Operations: The buying and selling of U.S. government securities (national debt) by the Federal Reserve.

Opportunity Cost: The highest valued benefit that must be sacrificed (forgone) as the result of choosing an alternative.

Opportunity Cost of Capital: The implicit rate of return that must be paid to investors to induce them to continuously

supply the funds necessary to maintain a firm's capital assets.

P

Passive Budget Deficits: Deficits that merely reflect the decline in economic activity during a recession.

Patent: The grant of an exclusive right to use a specific process or produce a specific product for a period of time (17 years in the United States).

Permanent Income Hypothesis: The hypothesis that consumption depends on some measure of long-run expected (permanent) income rather than on current income.

Personal Income: The total income received by individuals that is available for consumption, saving, and payment of personal taxes.

Phillips Curve: A curve that illustrates the relationship between the rate of change in prices (or money wages) and the rate of unemployment.

Policy Ineffectiveness Theorem: The proposition that any systematic policy will be rendered ineffective once decision-makers figure out the policy pattern and adjust their decision-making in light of its expected effects. The theorem is a corollary of the theory of rational expectations.

Political Good: Any good (or policy) supplied by the political process.

Pork-Barrel Legislation: A package of spending projects benefiting local areas at federal expense. The projects typically have costs that exceed benefits, but each is intensely desired by the residents of the district getting the benefits without having to pay much of the costs.

Positive Economics: The

scientific study of "what is" among economic relationships.

Positive Rate of Time Preference: The desire of consumers for goods now rather than in the future.

Potential Output: The level of output that can be achieved and sustained into the future, given the size of the labor force, expected productivity of labor, and natural rate of unemployment consistent with the efficient operation of the labor market. For periods of time, the actual output may differ from the economy's potential.

Poverty Threshold Income Level: The level of money income below which a family is considered to be poor. It differs according to family characteristics (for example, number of family members) and is adjusted when consumer prices change.

Predatory Pricing: The practice by which a dominant firm in an industry temporarily reduces price to damage or eliminate weaker rivals, so that prices can be raised above the level of costs at a later time.

Price Ceiling: A legally established maximum price that sellers may charge.

Price Discrimination: A practice whereby a seller charges different consumers different prices for the same product or service.

Price Elasticity of Demand: The percent change in the quantity of a product demanded divided by the percent change in the price causing the change in quantity. Price elasticity of demand indicates the degree of consumer response to variation in price.

Price Equalization Principle: The tendency for markets, when trade restrictions are absent, to establish a uniform price for each good throughout the world (except for price differences due to transport costs and differential tax treatment of the good).

Price Floor: A legally established minimum price that buyers must pay for a good or resource.

Price Searcher: A seller with imperfect information, facing a downward sloping demand curve, who tries to find the price that maximizes profit.

Price Support Programs: Legislative action establishing a minimum price for an agricultural product. The government pledges to purchase any surplus of the product that cannot be sold to consumers at the support price.

Price Takers: Sellers who must take the market price in order to sell their product. Because each price taker's output is small relative to the total market, price takers can sell all of their output at the market price, but are unable to sell any of their output at a price higher than the market price. Thus, they face a horizontal demand curve.

Principal-Agent Problem: The incentive problem arising when the purchaser of services (the principal) lacks full information about the circumstances faced by the seller (the agent) and thus cannot know how well the agent performs the assigned activity. The agent may to some extent work toward objectives other than those sought by the principal paying for the service.

Private Property Rights: Property rights that are held exclusively by an owner, and that can be transferred to others at the owner's discretion.

Production Possibilities Curve: A curve that outlines all possible combinations of total output that could be produced, assuming (a) the utilization of a fixed amount of productive resources, (b) full and efficient use of those resources, and (c) a specific state of technical knowledge. The slope of the curve indicates the rate at which one product can be traded off to produce more of the other.

Productivity: The average output produced per worker during a specific time period. It is usually measured in terms of output per hour worked.

Profit: An excess of sales revenue relative to the cost of production. The cost component includes the opportunity cost of all resources, including those owned by the firm. Therefore, profit accrues only when the value of the good produced is greater than the sum of the values of the individual resources utilized.

Progressive Tax: A tax that requires those with higher taxable incomes to pay a larger percentage of their incomes to the government than those with lower taxable incomes.

Property Rights: The right to use, control, and obtain the benefits from a good or service.

Proportional Tax: A tax for which individuals pay the same percentage of their income (or other tax base) in taxes, regardless of income level.

Proved Reserves: The verified quantity of a resource that can be recovered at current prices and levels of technology.

Public Choice Analysis: The study of decision-making as it affects the formation and operation of collective organizations, such as governments. The discipline bridges the gap between economics and political science. In general, the principles and methodology of economics are applied to political science topics.

Pure Competition: A model of industrial structure characterized by a large number of small firms producing a homogeneous product in an industry (market area) that permits complete freedom of entry and exit.

Public Goods: Jointly consumed goods. When consumed by one person, they are also made available to others. National defense, poetry, and scientific theories are all public goods.

Purchasing Power Parity Method: Method for determining the relative purchasing power of different currencies by comparing the amount of each currency required to purchase a typical bundle of goods and services in domestic markets. This information is then used to convert the GNP of each nation to a common monetary unit.

Q

Quantity Theory of Money: A theory that hypothesizes that a change in the money supply will cause a proportional change in the price level because velocity and real output are unaffected by the quantity of money.

R

Rate of Employment: The number of persons 16 years of age and over who are employed as a percentage of the total noninstitutional population 16 years of age and over. One can calculate either (a) a civilian rate of employment, in which only civilian employees are included in the numerator, or

(b) a total rate of employment, in which both civilian and military employees are included in the numerator.

Rate of Labor Force Participation: The number of persons 16 years of age or over who are either employed or actively seeking employment as a percentage of the total noninstitutional population 16 years of age and over.

Rate-of-Return Equalization Principle: The tendency for capital investment in each market to move toward a uniform or normal rate of return. An abnormally high return in a market will attract additional investment which will drive returns down. Conversely, an abnormally low return will result in investment flight from the market which will eventually lead to the restoration of normal returns.

Rate of Unemployment: The percent of persons in the civilian labor force who are not employed. Mathematically, it is equal to:

$$\frac{\text{Number of persons unemployed}}{\text{Number in civilian labor force}} \times 100$$

Rational Expectations Hypothesis: This viewpoint expects individuals to weigh all available evidence, including information concerning the probable effects of current and future economic policy, when they formulate their expectations about future economic events (such as the probable future inflation rate).

Rational Ignorance Effect: Voter ignorance that is present because people perceive their individual votes as unlikely to be decisive. Voters rationally have little incentive to inform themselves so as to cast an informed vote.

Rationing: An allocation of a limited supply of a good or resource to users who would like to have more of it. Various criteria, including charging a price, can be utilized to allocate the limited supply. When price performs the rationing function, the good or resource is allocated to those willing to give up the most ''other things'' in order to obtain ownership rights.

Real Balance Effect: The increase in wealth emanating from an increase in the purchasing power of a constant money supply as the price level declines. This wealth effect leads to a negative relationship between price (level) and quantity demanded in the goods and services market.

Real GNP: GNP in current dollars deflated for changes in the prices of the items included in GNP. Mathematically, real GNP_2 is equal to nominal GNP_2 multiplied by (GNP Deflator$_1$/ GNP Deflator$_2$). Thus, if prices have risen between periods 1 and 2, the ratio of the GNP deflator in period 1 to the deflator in period 2 will be less than 1. This ratio will therefore deflate the nominal GNP for the rising prices.

Real Interest Rate: The interest rate adjusted for expected inflation; it indicates the real cost to the borrower (and yield to the lender) in terms of goods and services.

Real Price: The cost of an item, corrected for inflation. For example, if the price of oil doubles while the prices of all other goods also double, the real price of oil is unchanged. Decisions are generally based on real prices, rather than the money (nomimal) prices.

Real Rate of Interest: The money rate of interest minus the expected rate of inflation. The

real rate of interest indicates the interest premium, in terms of real goods and services, that one must pay for earlier availability.

Real Values: The measurement of a variable after it has been adjusted for changes in the general level of prices.

Recession: A downturn in economic activity characterized by declining real GNP and rising unemployment. In an effort to be more precise, many economists define a recession as two consecutive quarters in which there is a decline in real GNP.

Reciprocal Agreement: An agreement between firms whereby the buyer of a product requires the seller to purchase another product as a condition of sale. The practice is illegal under the Clayton Act when it substantially reduces competition.

Recognition Lag: The time period between when a policy change is needed from a stabilization standpoint and when the need is recognized by policy-makers.

Regressive Tax: A tax that takes a smaller percentage of one's income as one's income level increases. Thus, the proportion of income allocated to the tax would be greater for the poor than for the rich.

Rent Seeking: Actions by individuals and interest groups designed to restructure public policy in a manner that will either directly or indirectly redistribute more income to themselves.

Repeat-Purchase Item: An item purchased often by the same buyer.

Required Reserve Ratio: A percentage of a specified liability category (for example, transaction accounts) that banking institutions are required to hold as reserves against that type of liability.

Required Reserves: The minimum amount of reserves that a bank is required by law to keep on hand to back up its deposits. Thus, if reserve requirements were 15 percent, banks would be required to keep $150,000 in reserves against each $1 million of deposits.

Reserves: Vault cash plus deposits of the bank with Federal Reserve Banks.

Residual Claimant: Individual in a firm who receives the excess of revenues over costs. A residual claimant gains if the firm's costs are reduced and if revenues are increased.

Resource: An input used to produce economic goods. Land, labor, skills, natural resources, and capital are examples.

Resource Market: A highly aggregate market encompassing all resources (labor, physical capital, land, and entrepreneurship) that contribute to the production of current output. The labor market forms the largest component of this market.

Resource Markets: Markets in which business firms demand factors of production (for example, labor, capital, and natural resources) from household suppliers. The resources are then used to produce goods and services. These markets are sometimes called factor markets.

Resource Mobility: A term that refers to the ease with which factors of production are able to move among alternative uses. Resources that can easily be transferred to a different use or location are said to be highly mobile. In contrast, when a resource has few alternative uses, it is immobile. For

example, the skills of a trained rodeo rider would be highly immobile, since they cannot be easily transferred to other lines of work.

Restrictive Fiscal Policy: A reduction in government expenditures and/or an increase in tax rates such that the expected size of the budget deficit declines (or the budget surplus increases).

Restrictive Monetary Policy: A deceleration in the growth rate of the money supply.

Right-to-Work Laws: Laws that prohibit the union shop—the requirement that employees must join a union (after 30 days) as a condition of employment. Each state has the option to adopt (or reject) right-to-work legislation.

Roundabout Method of Production: The use of productive effort to make tools and other capital assets, which are then used to produce the desired consumer good.

S

Saving: Disposable income that is not spent on consumption. Saving is a "flow" concept. Thus, it is generally measured in terms of an annual rate.

Savings and Loan Associations: Financial institutions that accept deposits in exchange for shares that pay dividends. Historically, these funds have been channeled into residential mortgage loans. Under recent banking legislation, S & Ls are now permitted to offer checkable deposits (NOW accounts) and extend a broad range of services similar to those of commercial banks.

Say's Law: The view that production creates its own demand. Thus, there cannot be a general over-supply because

the total value of goods and services produced (income) will always to available for purchasing them.

Scarcity: Fundamental concept of economics which indicates that less of a good is freely available than consumers would like.

Scientific Thinking: Development of theory from basic postulates and the testing of the implications of that theory as to their consistency with events in the real world. Good theories are consistent with and help explain real-world events. Theories that are inconsistent with the real world are invalid and must be rejected.

Secondary Effects: Economic consequences of an initial economic change, even though they are not immediately identifiable. Secondary effects will be felt only with the passage of time.

Shirking: Working at less than a normal rate of productivity, thus reducing output. Shirking is more likely when workers are not monitored, so that the cost of lower output falls on others.

Shortage: A condition in which the amount of a good offered by sellers is less than the amount demanded by buyers at the existing price. An increase in price would eliminate the shortage.

Short Run: A time period of insufficient length to permit decision-makers to adjust fully to a change in market conditions. For example, in the short run, producers will have time to increase output by using more labor and raw materials, but they will not have time to expand the size of their plants or to install additional heavy equipment.

Short Run (in Production): A time period so short that a firm is unable to vary some of its factors of production. The firm's plant size typically cannot be altered in the short run.

Shortsightedness Effect: Misallocation of resources that results because public-sector action is biased (a) in favor of proposals yielding clearly defined current benefits in exchange for difficult-to-identify future costs and (b) against proposals with clearly identifiable current costs yielding less concrete and less obvious future benefits.

Shutdown: A temporary halt in the operation of a business. The firm does *not* sell its assets. Its variable cost will be eliminated, but the firm's fixed costs will continue. The shut-down firm anticipates a return to operation in the future.

Social Costs: The sum of (a) the private costs that are incurred by a decision-maker and (b) any external cost of the action that are imposed on nonconsenting secondary parties. If there are no external costs, private and social costs will be equal.

Socialism: A system of economic organization in which (a) the ownership and control of the basic means of production rest with the state and (b) resource allocation is determined by centralized planning rather than by market forces.

Special Drawing Rights: Supplementary reserves, in the form of accounting entries, established by the International Monetary Fund (also called "paper gold"). Like gold and foreign currency reserves, they can be used to make payments on international accounts.

Special Interest Issue: An issue that generates substantial individual benefits to a small minority while imposing a small individual cost on many other voters. In total, the net cost to the majority might either exceed or fall short of the net benefits to the special interest group.

Stagflation: A period during which an economy is experiencing both substantial inflation and a slow growth in output.

Strike: An action of unionized employees in which they (a) discontinue working for the employer and (b) take steps to prevent other potential workers from offering their services to the employer.

Structural Unemployment: Unemployment due to structural changes in the economy that eliminate some jobs while generating job openings for which the unemployed workers are *not* well qualified.

Substitutes: Products that are related such that an increase in the price of one will cause an increase in demand for the other (for example, butter and margarine, Chevrolets and Fords).

Substitution Effect: That part of an increase (decrease) in amount consumed that is the result of a good being cheaper (more costly) in relation to other goods because of a reduction (increase) in price.

Sunk Costs: Costs that have already been incurred as a result of past decisions. They are sometimes referred to as historical costs.

Supply Shock: An unexpected event that temporarily either increases or decreases aggregate supply.

Supply-Side Economists: Modern economists who believe that changes in marginal tax rates exert important effects on aggregate supply.

Surplus: A condition in which the amount of a good that sellers are willing to offer is greater than the amount that buyers will purchase at the existing price. A decline in price could eliminate the surplus.

T

Tariff: A tax levied on goods imported into a country.

Tax Base: The level of the activity that is taxed. For example, if an excise tax is levied on each gallon of gasoline, the tax base is the number of gallons of gasoline sold. Since higher tax rates generally make the taxed activity less attractive, the size of the tax base is inversely related to the rate at which the activity is taxed.

Tax Incidence: The manner in which the burden of the tax is distributed among economic units (consumers, employees, employers, and so on). The tax burden does not always fall on those who pay the tax.

Tax Rate: The per-unit or percentage rate at which an economic activity is taxed.

Tax Shelter Industry: Business enterprises that specialize in offering investment opportunities designed to create a short-term accounting or "paper" loss, which can then be deducted from one's taxable income; at the same time, future "capital gain" income is generated, which is sometimes taxable at a lower rate.

Technological Advancement: The introduction of new techniques or methods of production that enable a greater output per unit of input.

Technology: The body of skills and technological knowledge available at any given time. The level of technology establishes the relationship between inputs and the maximum output they can generate.

Thrift Institutions: Traditional savings institutions, such as savings and loan associations, mutual savings banks, and credit unions.

Total Cost: The costs, both explicit and implicit, of all the resources used by the firm. Total cost includes an imputed normal rate of return for the firm's equity capital.

Total Product: The total output of a good that is associated with alternative utilization rates of a variable input.

Transaction Accounts: Accounts including demand deposits, NOW accounts, and other checkable deposits against which the account holder is permitted to transfer funds for the purpose of making payment to a third party.

Transaction Costs: The time, effort, and other resources needed to search out, negotiate, and consummate an exchange.

Transfer Payments: Payments to individuals or institutions that are not linked to the current supply of a good or service by the recipient.

Trickle-Down Theory: The theory that intensive economic growth will eventually lead to an improvement in the standard of living of the entire society, even for persons at the bottom of the economic spectrum.

U

Unanticipated Change: A change that decision-makers could not reasonably foresee. Thus, choices made prior to the event did not take the event into account.

Unanticipated Inflation: An increase in the general level of prices that was not expected by most decision-makers. Thus, it catches them by surprise.

Underground Economy: Unreported barter and cash transactions that take place outside recorded market channels. Some are otherwise legal activities undertaken to evade taxes. Others involve illegal activities such as trafficking in drugs, prostitution, extortion, and similar crimes.

Unemployed: The term used to describe a person, not currently employed, who is either (a) actively seeking employment or (b) waiting to begin or return to a job.

Union Shop: The requirement that all employees join the recognized union and pay dues to it within a specified length of time (usually 30 days) after their employment with the firm begins.

Utility: The benefit or satisfaction expected from a choice or course of action.

V

Value Marginal Product: The marginal product of a resource multiplied by the selling price of the product it helps to produce. Under perfect competition, a firm's marginal revenue product will be equal to the value marginal product.

Variable Costs: Costs that vary with the rate of output. Examples include wages paid to workers and payments for raw materials.

Velocity of Money: The average number of times a dollar is used to purchase final goods and services during a year. It is equal to GNP divided by the stock of money.

Vertical Merger: The creation of a single firm from two firms, one of which was a supplier or customer of the other—for example, a merger of a lumber company with a furniture manufacturer.

Vicious Circle of Underdevelopment: A pattern of low income and low economic growth that tends to perpetuate itself. Since the current consumption demands of poor nations are large in proportion to available income, the savings and investment rates of these nations are low. In turn, the low investment rate retards future growth, causing poor nations to remain poor.

W

Work-Leisure Substitution Effect: The substitution of leisure time for work time when higher tax rates reduce after-tax personal earnings. In effect, the reduction in the take-home (after-tax) portion of earnings reduces the opportunity cost of leisure, and thereby induces individuals to work less (and less intensively). Of course, lower tax rates would exert the opposite effect.

Y

Youth Work Scholarship: A proposed scholarship providing subsidies to younger workers who maintain jobs. Some scholarships would limit the subsidies to employment that offered on-the-job training.

INDEX

logrolling, 471
  monopoly regulation and, 234
  pork barrel legislation, 471–72
  socialized firms, 235
  special interest issue, meaning of, 95–96
Specialization
  comparative advantage, 42–43
  mutual dependence and, 44
  production and, 40
  trading partners, 492–95
  wage differentials and, 318–19
  worker alienation and, 44–45
Spillover effects, externalities, 85–87
Standard Oil, 274, 277
Stein, Herbert, 532
Stigler, George, 260n, 261
Strike
  cost of, 366–67
  meaning of, 365
  worker-hours lost and, 367–68
Stroup, Richard, 336n
Substitutes
  in consumption, 301
  demand elasticity and, 145–46
  good substitutes, 217
  marginal rate of substitution, 158
  in production, 301
  substitution effects, indifference curve and, 162
Summers, Robert, 546, 546n, 547n, 548n, 586n, 591n
Sunk costs, 186–87
Supply
  elasticity of supply, 152–53
  law of
    definition of, 58
    graphic representations, 58
  natural disasters and, 67
  political disruptions and, 67–68
  price of resources and, 65–66
  shifts in, 65–68
  technological changes and, 66
Supply curve, 58, 65
Supply and demand
  international trade and, 498–501
  for loanable funds, 344–45
  long run and, 61–62
  market consideration of, 58
  price legislation and, 70–71
  resources and, 311–13
  short run, 59
Surplus
  consumer surplus, 137–38
  meaning of, 71
Swartz, Caroline, 321, 321n

Taft-Hartley Act, 365, 366
Tariffs, 501–3
  impact of, 502
  meaning of, 501
Taxation
  ability to pay principle, 110
  average tax rate, 107

burden of taxation, distribution of, 122–23
  corporate income tax, 109
  deadweight loss, 111
  economic efficiency and, 111–12
  equity concept and, 110
  excess burden of taxation, 111–12
  excise tax, 108–9
  firm costs and, 184
  head tax, 111
  as illustration of elasticity, 149–53
  Laffer curve, 116, 117, 118, 119
  marginal tax rate, 108, 113
  neutral tax, 111
  payroll taxes, 108–9
  personal income tax, 107–8
  progressive tax, 107, 113
  property taxes, 109
  proportional tax, 108
  regressive tax, 108
  sales tax, 108–9
  tax base, 116
  tax incidence, 112
  tax rate, 116–17
  underground economy and, 114
  work efforts issue, 113–17
Tax base, 116
Tax incidence, 112
Tax rate, 116–17
  See also Marginal tax rate
Tax reform
  indexing, 117, 120
  international view, 121
  marginal tax rate changes, 113, 117, 118
Tax Reform Act of 1986, modifications of, 117, 120–21
Taylor, Lester D., 146n, 149n
Technology
  economic growth and, 551–53
  firm costs and, 184
  innovation, 39, 552–53
  invention, 39, 552
  production and, 39–40
  resources and, 302–3
  supply shifts and, 66
  technological progress, meaning of, 551
  unemployment and, 326–27
Teenage employment, minimum wage and, 333, 337
Thomas, Charles P., 523n
Thurow, Lester, 438n
Tiebout, Charles, 483n
Time cost, consumer choice and, 136
Todaro, Michael P., 543n
Tollison, Robert D., 90n, 94n, 469n
Total costs, 170
Total product, 175–76
Trade Agreements Act of 1979, 506
Trade Expansion Act of 1962, 508
Trade restrictions
  import quota, 503
  jobs and, 505, 506–8
  limitations on
    Canada-U.S. free trade agreement, 509

General Agreement on Tariffs and Trade (GATT), 508–9
  rationale for
    anti-dumping argument, 506
    industrial diversity argument, 504–5
    infant-industry argument, 505–6
    national defense argument, 504
  special interests and, 508
  tariffs, 501–3
Trade transactions
  current account, 526
  productive aspects, 44
Training, to reduce unemployment, 403
Transaction costs, meaning of, 32
Transferable emission rights, 450
Transfer payments
  alternatives to, negative income tax, 404–5
  failure of, 481
    detrimental secondary effects, 401–2
  Family Support Act changes, 403–4
  historical view, 397–98
  political support for programs, 481–82
  poverty rate calculation and, 400
  rent-seeking and, 479–81
Tregarthen, Timothy, 328n
Trickle-down theory, economic growth, 549
Trucking industry, deregulation, 283–86
Tullock, Gordon, 90n, 94n, 228, 470n, 479n, 481
Turner, Donald J., 268n
Two-dimensional graph, 23–24

Ujifusa, Grant, 89n
Uncertainty, profit and, 352
Underground economy
  components of, 114
  international view, 114
  taxation and, 114
Unemployment, automation and, 326–27
Unilateral transfers, current account, 527–28
Unions
  collective bargaining, 364–68
  contribution of, 381–82
  functions of, 363
  inflation and, 378–80
  international view, 380
  Japan, 588–89
  membership decline, 363–64
  monopoly and, 372–73
  strength of, influencing factors, 373–74
  union shop contract, 365
  wage increase strategies
    bargaining power, 368
    demand increases, 368–70
    supply restrictions, 368
    wages and union/nonunion workers, 376–79
Unitary elasticity, demand curve, 143, 144
United States economy
  big business activity and, 272–73
  changes in structure of, 268–69